Virtual Ea

Reflecting: (inserts left to right):

Physics (atom), Genetics (DNA), Dragon, Ubaid Statue of
Anunnaki, UFO (TR3B), and *Castillo* at Mayan Chichen Itzá.

Center: Earth with Soul Graduate

Background: Electromagnetic Dark Energy Matrix

Categories: Metatags: Anunnaki, Nephilim, Djinn, interdimensionals, ET, UFO, Moon, Mars, UFO propulsion, Nazis, Breakaway Civilization, TR3B, Apollo, Mankind, origins, Genetic engineering, Greys, abductions, hybrids, DNA, Epigenetics, Quantum Physics, Einstein, Subquantum Kinetics, Archeology, Maya, Egyptian, extraterrestrial influences, Morphic resonance, Mouravieff, soulless, sociopaths, auras, OPs, NPCs, creation, evolution, Darwin, reptile, Sumeria, Serpent Wisdom, Catholic Church, Martin Luther, religion, Koran, Bible, Apollonius, Jesus, Fortean phenomena, Jacques Vallee, John Keel, David Jacobs, Stuart Wilde, Bishop John Shelby Spong, Anatoly Fomenko, Robert Monroe, OBE, Control System, Virtual Reality, Simulation, holograms, Holodeck, Angels, Beings of Light, demons, Gnostics, shapeshifting, souls, Scripts, Karma, Reincarnation, recycling, Déjà vu, homosexuality, Interlife, chi, biophotons, bionet, Earth Graduate.

Cover design:
(source: multiple images from Yahoo Image Library:
     Atom , DNA, dragon, Ubaid statue, TR3B, Mayan pyramid;
     Earth and graduating soul)
https://images.search.yahoo.com/search/images

(background source: Holographic Waves: www.Flickr.com)

Book text in Garamond 11 font.

Author may be reached at **TJ_cspub14@yahoo.com**

ISBN – 13: 978-1494951627

Other Books by the Author

The Transformation of Man	TOM
The Earth Warrior	TEW
Quantum Earth Simulation	QES
The Science in Metaphysics	TSiM
Anunnaki Legacy	AL
The Great Earth Puzzle	GEP

Genesis of the Book

It is expected that some people will find this book upsetting, disturbing and confusing and will react with disbelief and even anger. There will be attempts to make the book wrong and maybe throw it out. The information on UFOs, ETs, Earth History and Religion that I had collected in hand-written journals over the 50+ years suggested certain conclusions that I **also** found hard to accept, and so my first idea was to do a book exposing what appeared to be the errors and false information. I was going to "expose" Zechariah Sitchin and his Anunnaki fraud… among others.

However, before you discard the book or any of its concepts, it may be helpful to know the following about how the book came to be. It is unique and so was its genesis (explained in more detail in the <u>Great Earth Puzzle</u>, Ch. 1).

Background

It all began in 1958 with an interest in UFOs – what are they, where do they come from, and how does a possible ET presence affect us? I was a follower of George **Adamski** and had all the materials, I had read his books and seen the pictures, and was impressed at the age of 15 with the Cosmic Consciousness and brotherly message of hope and peace contained therein. It all inspired me to consider being a New Thought minister and I began studying the major religions of the world, looking for common truths and information on what God, the world, Man and the universe really were.

I read a lot of books on UFOs, as they became available, but I was never interested in science fiction novels… I wanted what might turn out to be the real thing. I also read books on Physics, Genetics, Anthropology, Astronomy, Geology, Chemistry and Biochemistry, Metaphysics, Quantum Mechanics, and other cultures, especially those with mysterious structures – the Mayans, Egypt and the Great Pyramids, England and Stonehenge, and India and the Vimanas… China and her pyramids.

Later becoming a Christian, I read the Bible several times and led Bible-study classes at church, and because I read so many pages of the Bible at one time, I became aware of numerous inconsistencies (some of which are now in Chapters 1 and 11) and in discussing these with our pastor, I was invited to leave the church. I still really wanted to know, so I broadened my search into the Aramaic texts and the Gnostic teachings… finally to wind up checking out the New Age. I attended many services in assorted New Thought churches to get a feel for what truths they might have. I was into so many different things that people thought I was weird. I was just a true seeker and I read and joined an Edgar Cayce study group, later to very briefly join a Course in Miracles group. I also did Silva, *Est*, NLP, Zen, Yoga and Qigong and pranic/*chi* healing.

I spent many years in Unity and Religious Science (now CSL) churches and learned much about metaphysics, dropping conventional religion in favor of Truth. Along that path I had some interesting teachers.

All of that to say that I examined many different ism's and ologies, and read widely, still determined to discover what Earth, Man and the Multiverse really were.

Discoveries

The search into and out of everything occupied about 50+ years and initially I made notes, copied pages from books and magazines, kept letters of correspondence, and inserted any insights I had. Later about 1996 I copied the information into topical folders on my PC. Then I explored the Internet capturing more documents and pictures, still researching the basic areas of UFOs, Anunnaki, holograms, metaphysics, physics and genetics, to name a few. There were also obvious froo-froo websites and I discarded their information.

It initially dawned on me about 1997 that I might have **enough data to do an exposé of the lies and disinformation**, and my bad experience with the former pastor led me to consider Religion as the first target. I wasn't thinking of writing a book but of doing an article for *Nexus* magazine. I never got around to it because I discovered that other scholars with credentials had already done that. At that time, my computer occupation (MIS Director) continued to occupy a lot of my time and I just continued to randomly discover certain issues in unique books and websites, and I noted whatever insights I had in the PC journals.

All the while, in the background, there was developing a sense that the History, Religion and Physics I had read up on was not all holding water… it was at first just a nagging sense that some of it didn't make sense, like Einstein's $E = MC^2$ (examined in Chapter 8). Later when I discovered they had rewritten the history of the Alamo in a 2004 movie (my ancestor was there and wrote letters home which I read in 1965), I became really suspicious of generally-accepted History, and started digging. When I discovered that the Sumerian civilization had just appeared overnight, with no precedent, no gradual layers of tribe to town to city, I became really suspicious that we weren't being told everything – in fact, even in college, in required history courses, I had never heard of Sumeria, or another interesting civilization, Khazaria, – they had been kept out of the history books. Now, I wanted to know why. Then I discovered Zechariah Sitchin and the race to understand Man and History was on. Much more came out of that deeper research.

By 2004, I had discovered enough to write more than a magazine exposé and thus the first idea for a book was born. All I wanted to do was **expose the lies and errors**. So I set about with the very first chapter of this book, enumerating and analyzing the major religious teachings I had found in my wanderings – to prove them wrong. What I found as I dug far, wide and deep, was very upsetting. Yes, there were the obvious frauds and BS of some authors and websites, but through it all came a clear picture that Man was more than we were being told, Others had been here who were responsible for Man and his civilization, and we even had what appeared to be some off-planet technology. There was a core of responsible, serious, credentialed authors whose message **consistently held water over the years** but was not in synch with what we had always been told by parents, teachers, or pastors. The experts were just repeating what they had been told, so they were not a source I could trust.

The Interlife

At this point, it needs to be pointed out that there had been a recurrent theme in my life that so irritated me that it not only got my full attention, but drove me in 1991 at the age of 48 to seek a licensed therapist to do a hypnotic **Regression** to get some answers. Namely: I either could not get what I wanted in life, or if I did, it was taken from me by forces/circumstances beyond my control. We discovered in the Regression that that was karmic payback for what I had done, and was "meeting myself." I had denied others and so was myself denied. But the most interesting thing that occurred was the insight that due to the violent murder I underwent last lifetime, I had begged the Masters on the Other Side (the Interlife) to let me come back and atone for my errors and do something really proactive for Man. I saw that They agreed and said that I would finish my Karma first and by age 54 I might be visited and set on a new, second path in my life… it was all set up over there, but there was no mention of a book.

As luck would have it, in December 1997 I was diagnosed with severe **Addison's Disease** and given 3 years to live. That was upsetting, because I remembered asking to serve in the Regression, but I accepted it, I was nobody, had never gotten married (how could I bring a woman into that mess called my life?), and I quit my high-paying job, withdrew all my savings and retirement to travel and visit the places I wanted to see before I died. And in June 1998 while on a beautiful hike in Sedona, I was overcome with sadness that I was on the way out and would not be able to do anything to make a positive statement with my life after all.

I knelt down in a glade and prayed a very intense request, reminding the gods of what I was told in the Regression, to do something proactive during whatever time I had left – to make my life count for something. Silence. That was it. There was no answer, no insight, no voice, no hand-thru-the-clouds with a 3x5 card telling me what to do… I was not healed, either. I guessed I wasn't heard and due to Karma was not good enough to serve… I continued to travel and explore new areas.

I decided to move to Arizona and in **October 1998** was on my way, staying the night in a motel. That's when **Their Visit** took place. 3am. I had a very vivid dream and was allowed to remember it and the strange experience of being out of my body, surrounded by a swirling green energy cloud, and then I was put back in my body. That was it. I was not told anything, and was just allowed to remember the experience… or dream… I was not healed. But the next 3 days were fantastic: I just knew things, and anything I wondered about while driving around through the Southwest was just there – like I already knew it. So I'd stop and write it all down. It had not been a dream – I was somehow different.

By 2001 I was still alive and went to a Holistic Seminar where a woman in white called me out of the crowd, laid hands on me and long story short, I was healed. Two trips to the doctor in the next two months confirmed that. Somebody has a sense of humor: now I was healed and had run out of money! Now I had to go back to work…. And because I had years of computer programming, I went back to work in data processing… except that whatever They did that night during the Visit had removed my ability to program. But I had a new way of knowing… and that is where a lot of the information in this book came from.

And there was more to come…

Further discoveries

About 2004 I began to research the issues in this book again, and I just seemed to be led to certain books, magazines, and websites… and not others. I continued making notes in the journals on my PC. Insights to several of the key topics in this book happened in a very interesting way. Let me share 3 of them.

Sitchin and the Anunnaki : my research showed that there were hundreds of thousands of clay tablets, cylinders and stones that related the story of the Sumerians and the Anunnaki – their gods. Not only were the tablets hidden and discovered by accident when a new highway was being excavated in Iraq, meaning they were not meant to be found, but their very large number meant that the subject matter was very important to the Sumerians. Even Professor Kramer (an expert on Sumeria) acknowledges their existence but claims it is all a myth – one that the Sumerians recorded in great detail showing their sky gods to be very mortal and petulant, violent, lying and yet the source of Sumerian civilization. Is this the way one records a myth that does not beatify the gods – but records their ugly appearance, their pettiness, and low morality? I could not prove Sitchin wrong, and so finally suggested he was basically correct (Chapter 3) and the Anunnaki were real visitors who jump-started Man's civilization. I add some things he didn't tell us.

Soulless Humans on Earth: This is another controversial issue among moderns – although, as recorded in Chapter 5 – the ancients knew all about them: the **Greeks** would not let them teach their young, nor hold public office, the **Mayans** called them "figures of wood" in their *Popul Vuh*, and even Valentinism and other **Gnostics** knew about them… A modern-day researcher, **Dr. Mouravieff**, wrote several books about them, and I still had trouble accepting it – haven't we all been told that we are all alike? The gods who agreed to help me (Interlife episode during my Regression) helped me out: the *coup de grace* to convince me, was to **let me see auras for about 3 years**. About 60% of the people on any day, wherever I was, did not have auras, which means no soul… and no conscience. **OPs** also are called Organic Portals. **Dolores Cannon** called them Backdrop People. (Whatever They did was causing me eye problems and I made several trips to the eye doctor who found nothing wrong, but after I had seen enough and made studies – counts and recorded characteristics of those I saw – They removed the ability and my eyes pretty much went back to normal.) They convinced me, and I learned that the soulless (OPs) exist and have a purpose. (More on this in Appendix D in ASOM.)

Quantum Physics and Simulation: This is perhaps the hardest revelation to accept, yet my studies into holograms, vision, quantum mechanics, and simulation/virtual reality were borne out by three things:
  (1) a place where I have lived for 20+ years all of a sudden was lacking trees and buildings that I had always seen whenever I drove down a certain street. Suspecting urban renewal at work, I got out of the truck and closely examined

the ground where a large building had stood… and a man came over and asked me what I was doing on his property. I asked what happened to the building that was there. He thought I was nuts – he said that was his property and there had never been a building there. Yes, there was! And now there was no trace of it. Nothing. Maybe a different Timeline? (See Ch 2 in TOM.)

(2) Even the physicists are questioning our reality and saying that we most likely are in a Simulation because the "physical constants" are changing, **anomalons** show up when you expect them to, and aspects of subatomic reality border on the holographic – see Chapters 9, 12, and 13. There were so many physicists speaking <u>for</u> the subject I had to document them in Chapter 13. (Also see QES book.)

(3) A third insight I got was late in coming to me because I don't play video games. There are players in a video game that we don't control but are part of the game's Drama – they are called NPC's (Non Playable Characters). It was a **1-second drop** that showed me that the **NPCs are the OPs** in our world, again lending credence that this is a very sophisticated Simulation, and the OPs help drive the Earth Drama and souls' Scripts.

Interlife Help

True to Their word, the Masters had agreed to help me – as I saw in my 1991 Regression. They said They would be there to guide me in what They apparently knew I would be doing (writing a book) but that was kept from me until 2008. For example, at 3am one morning in January 2008 (when the book was started) I was awakened with the Table of Contents clearly in mind and I went to the PC and entered it – it is the same one I use today. During the typing of the book, I'd get stuck and wonder how some of the years of information I had could be connected, or did it connect? And in **only 7 instances**, They did a **1-second drop** – the information comes up from within – as if I had always known it, and it sometimes takes 10-15 minutes to review it all… They are the source of those Insights.
The Jesus revelation in this Appendix D was the last one They gave me. They connected the dots for me and I just facilitated the writing of the book.

Reservations

Lastly, I had reservations about the book being too confrontational and causing massive **cognitive dissonance** among the readers… and I didn't want to even appear to be trying to destroy others' faith when it came to Religion, which was a significant part of the book – and for 20 years a part of my life. So I adapted, added my apologetics to the beginning of Chapter 11, and I removed 4 'sensitive' parts from the overall book which are **not** now part of it, but the book's dots are still complete and still connect.

My primary concern was to be **not guilty of disseminating disinformation** via the book as that would count against me again in the Interlife (Chapter 14). I already had enough to answer for from the previous lifetime, which cost me **karmic payback** the first 54 years of my life this time, and I wanted to do something proactive for mankind before I died. Obviously I needed Their support to put this book together. I recognize that They are the

Source for the 1-second drops that were critical in composing the book. So in 2008 I was given a 'green light' for this book – not one to just expose errors. 2003-2007 was a kind of 'training' (see Chapter 5) and 2008 was the book's writing… it was written in 7 months and I could not have done that without Their help.

However, because I was concerned that I might still have false information, I sat on the book for another 5 years – trying to prove key ideas wrong. Researching a number of issues, when I found substantial or credible evidence, I added the reference to what I had already written – as a footnote. That is to say that the references were not the source for the original information… they just corroborated what I had been given.

Then, five years later in December 2013, I was relaxing in my Study when a strong, loving presence entered the room. I turned off the TV…. And it was **Baldy** (my guardian angel), who had visited me in person during the Summer of 2003. Always smiling, never condemning, he asked me if I had an agreement to do a book? I said yes, and I have come up with two showstoppers – things I can't answer. He said he knew, and would I like the answers? Of course I said Yes, and I received an immediate 1-second drop. I was stunned, and now a lot more dots connected. I added the info to Chapter 4 and created an Appendix D to show what had been given me on Jesus, the Shroud, and the Crusades. The original version of this book was released thru Amazon in March 2014.

The focus of the book was no longer to expose the errors and make people wrong, but to show where we have come from, where we are in Truth, and where we souls must go – back to the Realm where we really belong as an **Earth Graduate**. Thus I felt urged to release a more spiritual book (with the latest addition of Chapter 16) that more people can assimilate and opt into a choice of where they go when they die. And that is how and why this book exists. The book contains a lot of Light and I hope it will be a blessing to those that read it.

Note: throughout the book, it is more convenient to abbreviate my other books' titles – please refer to the bottom of the Copyright page. Thus: *Transformation of Man* is TOM.

Table of Contents

Part IV   Problem & Solution

Introduction

Why was this book written and why should you read it? First, as explained in the preceding 'Genesis' section, I was asked to, and secondly because there is strong evidence that:

o   This is not our planet and Man is not alone.
o   You are not living on the planet you think you are.
o   That **many things** we think we know about Physical Science, Earth
      History and Religion are wrong – seemingly by design.
o   Man has a divine potential that he is to develop – to serve in other Realms…
      when his DNA is reconnected he is an awesome creation.
o   The Elite seek to help Man but the human PTB will not let go of their
      agenda to be Lords ruling over ignorant Slaves.

There is no attempt to be weird, or scary. This book deals with **facts** that are all around us but have been ignored or suppressed. When the dots in this book are connected, they paint a picture of Man and Earth that is enlightening, intriguing and will **'set you free.'**

If the points above resonate with you, then I invite you to read the book and become an Earth Graduate. If you think those ideas are weird, perhaps you would enjoy the book as fiction – I guarantee it is exciting and different! But it is the result of 50+ years of research and it is really a non-fiction documentary. And if you want to learn something new, how about the following?:

Did you know –

o	… that Man has very special DNA and that it is flexible?	(Ch 9)
o	… that the speed of light is not a maximum limit?	(Ch 8)
o	… that Noah took cryogenic DNA on board his small 'Ark?'	(Ch 1)
o	… that the Egyptians did not build the Great Pyramid?	(Ch 4)
o	… that oil/coal can be formed without centuries of pressure?	(Ch 10)
o	… that there is no 'junk DNA' – it was deliberately deactivated?	(Ch 7)
o	… that the Russians created a 'Chuck' – part chicken, part duck?	(Ch 9)
o	… that world history backwards of AD 900 is largely unknown?	(Ch 10)
o	… that physicists suspect that Earth is a Simulation?	(Ch 12-13)
o	… that many UFOs are IFOs and are not ET craft?	(Ch 4)
o	… that Man DID go to the Moon, but not the way you think?	(Apx A)

…and can you handle blunt facts about UFOs, the Apollo Moon Missions, and what is unique about Mars?

All of these points <u>and more</u> are explored in this book. Its purpose is to expose mis-information in many areas, examine the truth about Man and his world, leading to a final suggestion that s/he become an **Earth Graduate**.

This is not a religious book.

There are those who love being Lords and they seek to keep Man as a dumbed down Serf because the Lords love power, control and ruling – if Man wakes up, and leaves, they lose their naïve audience. While this book is not about any conspiracy, it does point out that the PTB are heavily invested in controlling Man, largely through the Media and Education (or lack of it), and Man's task is to wake up, forget trying to fix anything here on Earth – just get out – with 51% Light (or true Knowledge).

Above all, the book is not a rehash of other author's ideas – it is unique in that it takes the new information I was given (see 'Genesis of the Book' section), plus some supporting authors' relevant ideas, and **connects all the dots** thus giving the new paradigm contained herein… **for that 10% of the public who are looking for this information.**

> **Above all, the book is catalyst, something to think about, like "brain candy" and should not be blindly believed.**

Chapter Overviews

Throughout the book's chapters there are references (in parentheses) from one chapter to another. This is *in lieu* of an Index, for the reader's convenience, thus selected major topics are easier to track throughout the book. This version does not have an Index because the book is best read sequentially through the chapters, from Chapter 1 to 16.

Part I: deals with the Creation and how Man got here. **Chapter 1** examines some cherished notions which contain errors and inconsistencies that have been blindly and traditionally promoted, to Man's detriment. "Origin of Man" theories were added from other sources, to round out the overview, since the Gnostics had promoted ideas similar to what I was given. It began to look like the Gnostics in **Chapter 2** were in fact mythologizing the same information that is presented in **Chapter 3** where the ET aspect is examined according to extensive Sumerian records on the Anunnaki.

> **Note: This book is not Anunnaki 101; it assumes the reader has read some other books on them.**

Chapter 4 is an overview of corroborative thinking and discoveries by contemporary authors who share in what this place is, and for the first time in this book, the Control System governing Earth is introduced. Types of UFOs, their operation, Abductions and Grey interference are also examined along with the possibility of a Breakaway Civilization and where it is today.

This first part is a kind of summary and reminder of what we think is true, so that subsequent chapters can examine what is really going on.

Part II: deals with Man and the Others. A review of who is here with Man and why, and what Man really is. The Others include the ubiquitous Organic Portals (OPs) in **Chapter 5**, the soulless humans, the Neggs, discarnates, and thoughtforms in **Chapter 6**, and a few accounts of the Others I have personally encountered. **Chapter 7** is an examination of what Man is, the Multiverse he is in and <u>why</u> he is special. This is given so that Man can be more aware of why he is observed and that he can be influenced by beings (+ and -) that he is not normally aware of.

Part III: covers the three areas of Physical Science, Religion and Earth History and besides exposing some pretty common (but often unknown) Science errors in **Chapter 8**, **Chapter 9** includes new Science information designed to support a more optimistic view of Man and the world. **Chapter 10** includes an incredible examination of the manipulation of Western Chronology, the manipulation of Western Religions, and the young appearance of our supposedly old planet. **Chapter 11** examines the way Religion has been manipulated, and why, over the centuries – **and the need for a more Spirit-driven theology to meet Man's need to connect with his Source…** But again this book is not a religious book, nor is it anti-Christian.

Whereas the first three Parts deal a lot with "the way it was" type of information, the last Part IV of the book deals with connecting the preceding chapters' data into a coherent description of where we are <u>now</u> with an eye to the challenges facing Man, what is likely to happen, and what one can do about it.

Part IV: **Chapter 12** is the first summarization that examines what Earth really is today, and why Man is here. There is a summary to tie preceding chapter concepts together. **Chapter 13** explores virtual reality and Simulation in more detail since Chapter 12 shows Earth is a <u>very</u> sophisticated type of Holographic Simulation. (Appendix B explores more of this.) Then **Chapter 14** explains why being here is a problem – including some information that is largely unknown or ignored by most people. **Chapter 15** summarizes the book's main points, reinforces the Earth "Stage & Script" concept, freewill and control issues, and emphasizes the **Earth Graduate** concept begun in Chapter 7. Lastly **Chapter 16** explores how to get out of here – what the ensouled human can do to 'graduate' from Earth School.

Encyclo-Glossary: included to clarify terms and concepts as used in this book, some of which may be new to the reader.

Appendix A : designed to review salient aspects of the Moon and Mars enigmas, with pictures. Evaluates how we could have gone to the Moon and what signs of intelligence are on Mars. Evaluates the Apollo Program. See also GEP (Book 7).
Appendices B and C: designed to give more information on topics that were partially covered in Chapters 12 and 13: Vision & Holograms, and UFOs & the Control System, respectively. The book's chapters include references to this related material.
Appendix D: gives a deeper explanation of God, Jesus, and the Christ issues initially examined in Chapters 1 and 11. The latter part of the Jesus section includes Dr. Fomenko's scientific, plausible speculation on Jesus' birth and death dates.
Appendix E: gives a deeper examination of Serpent Wisdom, from Chapter 10.
Appendix F: gives a global review of Serpent art with an eye to eerie similarities.

Bibliography: many relevant books plus many references to related Internet sources of information for the reader to explore. Also a list of interesting videos to consider.

Micro Index – lists significant data and issues that are not listed *per se* in the Table of Contents.

Annotation

It needs to be said with the inclusion of controversial information in this update of the book (v. 17.1) that this information was also given to me in 2008 and I withheld it until I saw in 2014 that the information is leaking out onto the Internet and the TV programs on the Science, NatGeo and H2 channels. It is also in many books I have read. I was urged to update my book and include it at this time, and point out the errors, inconsistencies, and disinformation. They do want it "out there" now for that small percentage of the population that is seeking and wants to know what is going on.

Since the book is basically about waking up, getting one's spiritual/soul act together, and becoming an Earth Graduate, and exploring disinformation and errors in Religion, History and Science supports the awakening process, why include information on the Moon, Mars and UFOs?

First, it completes the 'package': it rounds out our understanding of where we are and helps us realize what is true about our reality. Remember:

Knowledge protects, Ignorance enslaves.

Second, it is impetus to realize that Earth is not our home, and we're not going to the Moon or Mars (because we're not wanted there) and escape the planet that way. We must focus on being a better person, gaining more Light (Knowledge) to get out of here.

Third, gaining the Light, or 'escape velocity,' to leave Earth as an Earth Graduate requires that we <u>not</u> be compromised with all the false beliefs and disinformation that surround us.

This is better explained throughout the book, but we need to realize that when we die, just being a loving person is <u>not</u> enough. Being a person who loves everything and everybody just the way they are, permits anything/everything, doesn't discipline their children, or rationalizes injustice, and doesn't speak up for what is right, has **missed the lesson** and will be recycled back to Earth. (Sorry, the Beatles were wrong: "All You Need Is Love"). You need true Knowledge and must have a set of values/ethics and live by them. Then Love, respect, forgiveness and humility complete the package.

> **You cannot be of service on the Other Side if you are full of lies, errors, false beliefs and/or disinformation. Every soul has a unique role to fill in the Multiverse and should graduate from Earth School. Those that don't graduate are recycled. Those that are recycled too many times are 'disassembled' (Chapter 7). That is why this book was written.**
>
> **Also please see Index for Earth Graduate: Areas of Service.**

Chapter 1: In the Beginning... God

Are we really living on the planet we think we are?

We are told that Man is the pinnacle of creation, our science has never been greater than it is right now, and we have been told that our history has been a struggle from living in caves, beating off wild animals with sticks and stones, to finally landing on the Moon. We have also been led to believe that religion adequately describes the God of the Universe, Man's creation and Man's relationship with the Almighty. What if a lot of that is false?

If it is false, even part of it, might we not be living on the kind of planet that we have been told we are? Could Earth be something else that the early scientists and clergy assumed was true, but like the Flat Earth Theory, they got it wrong? Is it possible that Man was not created by the God of the Universe on Earth?

What if almost all that we have taken as truth about Science, History and Religion was an assumption that was later modified to suit someone else's agenda and most of it is questionable at best? We used to believe the Earth was flat. We used to believe the Sun revolved around the Earth – because it does look like it – but appearances and assumptions can be wrong. Even by scientists and the clergy.

Could it be that our ideas about Science, Religion and History are so outmoded that without an update to them, we have also had an erroneous idea of what Earth really is? Recent developments in Quantum Physics, Genetics and Anthropology, as shown in this book, can easily lead one to question the world we live in, and that is healthy if we see issues as **catalyst** and are not too quick to form cast-in-concrete dictums.

For years Man thought the Earth was flat and yet someone questioned why a ship sailing out to sea disappears from view as if it were sailing downhill... suggesting the unthinkable (for that time): the Earth might be curved. In the same way, Man's astronomy is discovering many Earth-like planets in our Galaxy and if any of those are inhabited, there could be advanced ET lifeforms visiting us who were capable of modifying DNA and taking an extant hominid and making it a more viable 'worker' to help mine the resources of Earth. And if ancient Man didn't have a frame of reference to understand what the Visitors were doing, would he not create myths about gods and flying dragons (i.e., rocket ships spitting flame and noise), beings that flew through the air (pictured with wings and calling them Angels which just means 'messengers')? Would he record a version of the Genesis of Man by these advanced beings ("angels?") from the skies ("Heaven?") who flew and had super powers, so that today's mankind would assume ancient Man was describing the creation of Man by the God of the Universe?

The current developmental stage of Earth is almost capable of space travel and genetic manipulation. We have ships that go to the Moon, Rovers that go to Mars, we have cloned sheep and discovered genetic codes to diagnose and improve newborns' ability to survive... Man is almost doing what ETs are alleged to have been doing here for some time... If we are almost there, why is it so hard to see that the Visitors may already have done it in coming here? Could Earth at one point have been a planet of slaves? Or could Earth have been an Experiment in genetics? Are we really in 3D?

If Man traveled to a distant planet, landed and began displaying his advanced technology among the primitive hominids there, would he not appear to be a god? That very scenario happened in New Guinea, post WW II, where a team of men in flight suits and goggles took a helicopter into the jungle, landed, photographed objects and ruins, shot game for food, and set up antennae and watched monitors that communicated with California and Hawaii – they were taken as gods among the local primitive, stone-age-like people there. After all, they did descend from the sky with power…

And then, after the 'gods' left, the natives built wooden replicas of the flying machine and some of the equipment and emulated what they saw the gods do --- in hopes that such actions would encourage the gods to return, or drop more goods and supplies by parachute. This event was later called the **Cargo Plane Cult.**

This book suggests that Man and his horizons have broadened considerably, his capabilities are now such that it would be profitable to re-examine time-worn stories of Man's creation, his place in the Universe, religious ideologies, historical irregularities, and just what Man really is and can do with divine potentials that we are just now beginning to discover.

This book is about finding out what Man is, what the Earth is, why Man is here , and what can be done about it. So this chapter and the next few deal with the origins of Man and review what we think we know about the subject, only to have Chapters 8-11 update the three issues (Science, History and Religion) with new discoveries. In addition, the real nature of Earth emerges in Chapters 12 – 13 and the final chapters suggest a proactive course of action based on the revelation(s).

Please note that Judaism, Islam and Christianity are given equal weight in this book, in various chapters.

Biblical Creation

"In the beginning, God created the heavens and the earth." (Gen. 1:1.) The word God here is *Elohim* – **plural** for gods. *El* is the singular for God.

And on the beginning of the **Sixth** day of creation "…God said, let **us** make man in **our** image, after **our** likeness…" (Gen. 1:26). The word "God" again is *Elohim* – <u>more</u> than one god. Who is "us"? What is "our" likeness? It has been argued for years that the Supreme God was speaking to His heavenly court, but they were not gods, nor did they look like Him. So, why didn't the writer use the word *El Shaddai*, God Almighty? Or *Adonai*, My Lord? Or even *El* as the singular of *Elohim*?

So Man was created in the image of God.

Genesis is very specific about this, for it states "then God said 'I will make Man in my image, after my likeness.'" Adam was thus created in both the image, or *selem,* and likeness, or *dmut,* of his creator. The use of both terms in the Biblical text was meant to leave no doubt that man was similar to the gods in appearance. It is this likeness, or lack of it as we shall see, that is at the root of the **admonitions** of the Bible and the Sumerian literature. [1] [emphasis added]

What admonitions? To not make any images of God (or the gods). To be told that means automatically that Man <u>was able to</u> see God and thus he <u>could</u> make "graven images" of God. So God must have had a reason for telling Man to not make images of Him...so this God must have been physical. And He told Man to not make any images of Him because He didn't want it known what He looked like... and images in stone, whether statues or carved in walls, tend to last for years... thus it means that He didn't want images for later generations of Man to find and be able deduce something ... His image was to be a secret... which will be examined in Chapter 3.

So, in Gen. 1:27 we're told that not only was man created in God's image, but "... male and female He created them." What does The God look like? Remember that He would not let Moses on Mount Sinai see His face, and yet He let Moses feel His powerful presence. (Ex. 33:18-23)   In Ex. 24:17 it says His glory was like a 'devouring fire' – no one could look upon the Lord God and live. Since we don't know what God looked like, it cannot be substantiated that the Man as created by God looked like Him – and if He is an intelligent, powerful Consciousness at the center of Creation, He would not have a physical form anyway.

Two Creations

Now we have a contradiction: the God of Eden is physical (He was walking in the Garden) and the God of the Universe is a powerful consciousness, or Great Spirit as the Amerindians said. Remember that God rested on the **Seventh** day, and He said that everything was "very good" (Gen. 1:31). Then we learn just 7 verses later, in Gen. 2:7, that God again creates man from the dust of the earth, and breathed life ('*ruach*') or living spirit into his nostrils thus giving Adam a soul... on the **Seventh** day.

What happened to the man and woman of the Sixth day (in Genesis 1)?
What happened to God resting on the Seventh day?

So on the 7th day, man is alone (Gen. 2:7) and God says this is not good, so He (the gods?) takes one of Adam's ribs and creates a woman in Gen 2:22 complementary to him – meaning she also had the breath of life, or **a soul**. But we were told in Gen. 1:27 that He created man and woman, with no time gap between them as we see in Genesis 2.

There were 2 creations? (Yes) Multiple men and women were created? (Yes) The high-level Bible account raises more questions than it answers.

Not to be outdone by the facts, the Church declared (via the invention of **Apologetics**) that Genesis 2 was a restatement of Genesis 1, and they forgot to explain how God rested on the Seventh (Gen. 2:2) but somehow recreated man on that same day (Gen. 2:7).... If you asked the above questions 500 years ago, the Inquisition paid you a terminal visit.

Obviously, something is amiss – something other than what we were taught was going on because the writer of Genesis was not dumb, nor could he have forgotten so soon what he said just 26 verses earlier. And the reason for taking these Genesis verses literally is that they **do** generally reflect what actually happened… as some Bible scholars contend, there <u>were</u> two creations, and that will be examined in Chapter 3.

The Inter-creation Gap

Bible scholars and other students of Man's history have noted the Genesis 1 creation issue, and examined just how big the time gap between the first and second creations might have been. And to better understand the reasons for there to be two creations, one must dig into the Sumerian, Egyptian, and Hebrew texts -- the *Edfu* texts from Egypt, the *Enuma Elish*, the *Epic of Gilgamesh*, and the *Atra Hasis* from Sumeria, and the Old Testament and the *Haggadah*, a source of Jewish oral tradition.

While there is no way of knowing what the time element was between the first creation and the subsequent one, what has to be considered is that there must have been a gap if after Cain slew Abel, Cain was expelled from Adam's family and went and took his wife from the people in the Land of Nod. That means there were other people on the Earth – again support for multiple creations. (See later Chart 1a.)

Since Adam and Eve were supposedly the first and only ones and they produced only Abel, Cain and later Seth… **where would the other people in Nod have come from**? There had to have been an <u>earlier</u> creation preceding that of Adam and Eve because Cain took a <u>wife</u>, not a little girl, nor a baby, from Nod which was a larger population. There was another earlier civilization. Thus there was an earlier creation.

> *And by the way, if Adam and Eve had three **boys**, Abel, Cain and Seth, how did their lineage propagate itself with no girls? Even if there had been a girl or two in the offspring of Adam and Eve, why is the writer of Genesis unaware of it? Let's not suggest that the future generations were conceived through incest…*

Obviously, there had to be more people that were created, or there were originally <u>at least</u> two creations, and Seth and Cain (of the second creation) may have taken their wives from the first creation in Nod… The problem is the Bible is too vague, too general, and does not give an acceptably coherent account of things.

For simplicity's sake, let us identify the first creation in Genesis as the **pre-Adamic** race. Then something happened to cause a second creation involving Adam and Eve, herein referred to as the **Adamic** race – maybe the first did not work out, maybe they were defective, or maybe they weren't quite what was wanted in some way. That also suggests that The God of the universe did not do the first creation (pre-Adamic) as it implies that for some reason the creation had to be done again (Adamic) – Does the God of the universe create errors?

Apparently years did go by after the first creation and there was at least a second creation. This one specifically says that the spirit of life, *ruach*, was breathed into Adam, and Eve: a 'soul' was imparted to Adamic Man as the Gnostics later also tell us (Chapter 2). One might infer that the first Pre-Adamic creation had 'something missing', and that was probably **a soul** since we are not told that God breathed the spirit into them as He did with the second creation. That means that Cain took a grown woman for his wife who did not have a soul since she was from the first creation (pre-Adamic). See Chart 1A.

We will return to this issue again and again as it is very important. It will be seen that there <u>were</u> two creations and only the second creation (Adamic) received a soul. Thus Adam was the first soul man.

Two Seeds

Genesis 3 deals with the Serpent supposedly deceiving Eve, and the Man and Woman discover they're naked and hide. God comes looking for them and doesn't know where they are – is this cute or what? The all-knowing and all-powerful Biblical God, "walking in the Garden", not knowing where they were, and then His getting angry when they tell Him they hid because they were naked… this is a God with very human aspects. This God was upset because until they ate of the fruit, Adam and Eve did not know they were naked. So He turns to the Serpent (who walked upright) and removes his legs, and declares the Serpent will henceforth crawl… and then He makes a very interesting pronouncement in Genesis 3:15:

> "…I will put enmity between thee and the woman, and **between thy seed and her seed**; and it [he] shall bruise thy head, and thou shalt bruise his heel." (Gen. 3:15) [emphasis added]

God is talking to the Serpent. And over in the Koran, Islam expresses the same idea:

> 'Adam,' we said, 'Satan is an enemy to you and your wife. Let him not turn you both out of Paradise and plunge you into affliction…. [Satan shows Adam the Tree of Knowledge and they both eat…and then God discovers their sin, but relents and admonishes Adam and Eve <u>and</u> the serpent:] 'Get you down hence, both,' He said, 'and **may your offspring be enemies** to each other….' Surah 20:119 [emphasis added]

Two different religions but from the same part of the world, with one common teaching in this case – that says they both have **a common source** (Abraham) who turns out to be more than a myth. [2]

In addition, the Bible repeats the different 'seed' message over in Daniel 2:43:

> And whereas thou sawest iron mixed with miry clay, they shall **mingle themselves with the seed of men: but they shall not cleave to one another** even as iron is not mixed with clay. [emphasis added]

That verse really does not fit in the context of Daniel explaining the king's dream – what has the "seed of men" got to do with explaining the "great image" or statue comprised of

21

5 elements: gold, silver, brass, iron, and a mixture of iron and clay? The different elements represent different kingdoms that come and go, not versions or species of Man…. or do they? It is almost as if verse 2:43 is part of a longer insert that is missing, or it was added for those who have "ears to hear."

Apparently the Two Seeds ("they") will not unite or 'cleave to one another' [as in marriage] and that is suggested in the Genesis 3:15 passage as well. Chapter 5 also warns about this.

There will be basically Two Seeds on the earth – the (human) woman's and something else related to the Serpent. Follow this closely: If Adam and Eve have souls, their offspring Cain and Abel also have souls; Adam and Eve were thus the **second** creation ("2nd Seed") where God specifically breathed the *pneuma* or 'spirit of life' into them. And because Adam and Eve are one of the 2 seeds, for Gen. 3:15 to be true, the man-like Serpent's seed is the other seed -- but the Serpent was <u>not</u> made in the **first** creation of Gen. 1:26. The first creation of Genesis was the pre-Adamic (soulless) Man ("1st Seed") whose lineage has survived to this day.

> In Chapters 5 – 6 it is noted that the Two Seeds do in fact n<u>ot</u> have the same potential, and the soulless seed often obstructs the second ensouled seed. There **is** enmity between the two seeds, coming from the resentment of the 1st seed of the 2nd seed.

The Serpent was present at the 2nd creation, and at the 1st one as well, thus can we infer that the Serpent being was part of (involved in) the Creation. Gen. 1:27 said: "So [the gods] created man in [their] own image… male and female created [they] them." This was the **first** creation; we assumed that those initially created looked just like us, or maybe just the second creation did…

Appearances

Consider for a moment that the Serpent in the Garden was supposed to be one of the Watchers known as **Gadrel** (according to Enoch), but more likely it was the Anunnaki Science Officer, **Enki** [3] That means that God walking in the Garden was Enlil, Head of the Earth Command, Enki's superior officer. This is getting ahead of Chapter 3, but is mentioned here because it is important to realize that (1) the Serpent was already in the Garden, before Adam and Eve, (2) the Bible does not specify his creation in Genesis, and (3) it is important to realize who/what the Serpent was.

And remember the Serpent was a reptile that walked upright – It spoke, so it had a mouth, and it saw her so it had eyes, and it heard her responses so it had ears (real snakes don't have ears)…**Humanoid in appearance**. Intelligent because it knew what the Tree was good for and what effect it would have. And because its seed would be the enemy of the woman's, we know that it procreated…. very interesting.

Left: Gul Dukat, displaying the gray skin and scale patterns typical of *Star Trek* Cardassians, humanoid reptilians. Credit: http://en.wikipedia.org/wiki/Star_Trek/Cardassians

Therefore, Adam was semi-human and the Serpent was reptilian in appearance and genetics… perhaps like the **Cardassians** [above] on the TV show *Star Trek Deep Space Nine?* The series ran from 1993-1999.

According to Genesis and other documents, and long before humans ever existed, the Serpent lived in the Garden of Eden and did the necessary work to maintain it.

This Biblical serpent was not just a lowly snake; it could converse with Eve, and knew the truth about the Tree of Knowledge. It was of such a stature that it unhesitatingly questioned the deity. Genesis concedes this point when it asserts that "the serpent was the **shrewdest** of all the world beasts that God had made."

Ancient Jewish legends describe the serpent of Eden as **manlike** – he looked like a man, and talked like a man. The part of the *Haggadah* which deals with the Creation depicts the serpent who inhabited the Garden as an **upright creature that stood on two feet and who was equal in height to the "camel"** [i.e., 8-9' tall.]. He was said to be the lord over all the beasts of Eden… In the Jewish *Haggadah* there seems to be little doubt that he was legged and walked like a man. The tempter of Eve was **not** actually a [snake]. [4] [emphasis added]

(Credit: Bing Images)

One of the truer pieces of art based on the Biblical story. However, this is a good place to spike the myth that a sadist somewhere said that Adam wore a **fig leaf**. While it is a big leaf, it is very prickly and if you are sensitive to oxalic acid in the white latex sap, you have signed up for a bad itchy/scratchy time! [5]

And there was **no apple**: the Tree was representative of Reproduction (see later section, 'Serpent Truth'.) Adam and Eve were its 'fruit.' Apples were not native to the Middle East.

To repeat: it was said that Man and the Serpent-like creature (and its offspring or progeny) would be enemies (Gen. 3:15). This in fact, does become the case, and the exact form it takes is not Man hating snakes, but, as will be seen shortly in Chapters 3 and 5, the two types of Man on the planet, the "2 Seeds," do not really get along, and that is by design.

Garden of Eden

Before going forward with the general thrust of this chapter, it is interesting to consider that the Garden of Eden has been located. An archeologist, **Juris Zarins**, began with the Biblical account in Genesis, which said there were 4 rivers associated with the Garden: Tigris, Euphrates, Gihon and Pison. He easily located the Tigris and Euphrates rivers since they still flow to this day, but the other two were more of a challenge, especially where the writer of Genesis incorrectly said the Gihon "compassed the whole land of Ethiopia" – but Africa is not close to the other three, so that has been judged to be an error.

To solve the puzzle, Zarins resorted to LANDSAT space images of the area around the Persian Gulf, and discovered two "fossil rivers" – dried up today, but which did come together and met **at the north end of today's Persian Gulf**...actually, they now meet under water. The Pison [Wadi Batin in Kuwait] and Gihon [Karun in Iran] had been found and as a result, it meant that **Eden is today under the waters of the Persian Gulf** – due to the water level raising due to (1) the Flood, and (2) the Flandrian Transgression, when about 4000 BC the Gulf reached its current level and put Eden under 500 feet of water: [6]

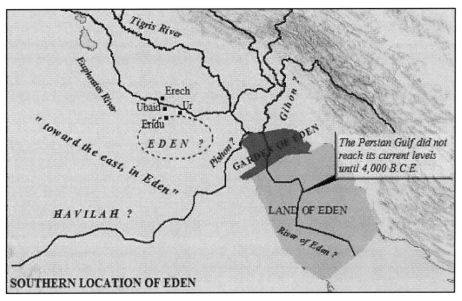

Zarin's Location of Eden (note: Ur and Ubaid)
(Credit: Bing Images)

Much like what is theorized to have happened to the **Black Sea area** several thousand years ago, a similar break in the land allowing the Mediterranean ocean to pour in and flood fertile, inhabited valleys is also thought to have happened to create the Persian Gulf. Called the

Flandrian Transgression, it was a worldwide phenomenon due to the oceans rising 400-500' as the Ice Age came to a close and the ice masses melted. The rising waters overflowed earthen dikes and low-lying land-bridges to inundate whatever lay beyond.

Native to the area were the **Ubaidians** [proto-Sumerians] who built cities, wrote on tablets, and farmed the land about 5000 BC, and as the story of Man progresses, it will be seen that they also created some unique and interesting **sculptures shown in Chapter 3** reflecting their association with serpent-like beings who were also found in the Garden of Eden. Could these be the images Man was told to not make…? ("Thou shalt make no graven image of thy God…" Ex. 20:4.) Does Man always do as he's told?

Serpent Deception

Note that according to Gen. 3:1 - 5 it is clear that the God of Genesis had intended for Man to be like dumb sheep – not knowing good from evil, just existing…as if the Garden of Eden was a living zoo existing at the pleasure of God. The Serpent asks Eve to think about it: "…you shall surely not die…" and she chooses to know more, to deal with good/evil, right/wrong …soul growth… and so she eats of the fruit of the Tree of Knowing. What kind of a God keeps his creation in ignorance?

> *Note that later in the Bible, Jesus advises his followers to "…be ye therefore **wise as serpents** , and harmless as doves." Matt. 10:16. A very interesting thing for Jesus to say, considering that the serpent was later said by the Church to be a negative role-model!*

It begins to appear that the Serpent was setting them free from the Garden of Ignorance and its very petulant god who represents himself as a very human god throughout the Old Testament: **jealous, angry, and vengeful.** When God tells Saul (I Sam. 15: 3) to go smite the Amalekites – were they not part of God's creation? And then when God sees that Saul didn't do what He ("the Lord of the Hosts": I Sam 15:8-9) wanted, He repents (I Sam 15:11)… What kind of All-knowing God set Saul up and then sees He made a mistake and **repents**?

And this is a god who notices gold and says so right in the beginning of Genesis. Of course, He made it all, but He appears to be proud of it:

> And a river went out of Eden to water the Garden; and from thence it
> was parted, and became into four heads. The name of the first is Pison
> [Wadi Batin today]: that is it which compasseth the whole land of Havilah,
> where there is gold; and the gold of that land is good… (Gen. 2:10-12)

The God of the Universe would not be **impressed by gold** nor would He tell you where to find it. He can create as much gold as He wants, so it must be the writer of Genesis who was impressed with gold. And for a good reason – gold was actually mined in the Garden of Eden area [i.e., Southern Iraq] as late as the 1950's. [7]

And He demands **sacrifice** -- Ex 25:2: "Speak unto the children of Israel that they bring me an offering…" and if one has sinned, killing an animal to pay for one's sin – is this a godly precept? Or more like a pagan sacrifice?

> Ex 29:14: "But the flesh of the bullock, and his skin, **and his dung**, shalt thou burn with fire without [outside] the camp: it is a sin offering."

Good thing they burned it <u>outside</u> the camp; hot dung must have made their enemies think twice about taking the Israelites into captivity…

But sacrifice is exactly what Noah does after the Ark lands, and supposedly he has 2 of every creature and is supposed to restart animal life on Earth with all the animals he rescued via his Ark. So what brilliant thing does Noah do? He builds an altar and takes "… of every clean beast, and of every clean fowl, and **offered burnt offerings** on the altar." (Gen. 8:20) Talk about "cabin fever" driving one nuts…. the next verse is even more amazing:

> And the Lord smelled a sweet savor …. and said in His heart… neither will I again smite any more living thing, as I have done!! (Gen. 8:21)
>
> *Note that He <u>did</u> later smite the Amalekites later in the Bible (I Sam. 15: 3) .*
> *He had Saul do it for Him. So this god does not tell the truth, nor keep His word.*

And, the **smell of frying meat** in Noah's sacrifice really turned Yahweh on. No one noticed that those sacrificed animals won't be procreating soon. This was a god who could be reached by barbecue. Next time you want something from this god, light up the grill, and invite him over!

> *Seriously, it is to be suspected that this story of the sacrifice of the only and unique animals on the Ark must be a fabrication, since not only would killing and sacrificing the animals be idiotic (Noah was to **save** them), but as will be seen in Chapter 3, the Ark and the <u>seed</u> to restart life after The Flood was done with very few <u>live</u> animals.[8] (Think: cryogenics.)*

The First Commandment

I suggest that this is **not** the loving God of the Universe, the one that Jesus called Abba, Father, but the god called YHWH or Yahweh, aka Jehovah. He has very human traits and egotistically seeks to be worshipped:

> Ex. 34:14 "For thou shalt worship no other god; for the Lord, whose name is Jealous, is a **jealous** god."

The word jealous can also be translated zealous, but these are human traits, or those of a lesser god. Would the God of the Universe be so insecure as to fear mankind worshipping another god instead of Him? This YHWH must be a 'local' god of some sort… and reappears in Chapter 2 with a different name.

The Bible states that God gave Moses Ten Commandments and the first said: "Thou shalt have no other god before Me." In the Jewish Torah, it states "You shall have no other god beside Me." This implies other gods exist in a pantheon, otherwise why didn't God just say: "You will have no other god" or "I am THE God" -- and leave off the "before/beside Me?"

> If the phrase was meant to be "you shall have no other gods," why not just stop right there and not add the phrase "before me." If anything, the Commandments are the spirit of conciseness and certainly would not contain any unnecessary verbiage. Therefore, the sentence can only mean that "you will have no other gods 'above' or 'over' me." In other words, **Yahweh is declaring that he is the superior god of a pantheon.** [9] [emphasis added]

And this will be seen to be true in Chapter 3 where this god is revealed, along with the 300 others who actually and historically came with him to Earth.

Additionally, since this god apparently created Man in his image, perhaps his DNA with his traits would be promoted throughout subsequent generations of Man on the Earth. Is it any wonder we see so much violence, greed, ego and pettiness coming from the offspring of this jealous god's creation?

Petty, vindictive and jealous behavior can result in a reputation as a viper.

Vipers

Furthermore, isn't this viper issue what got Jesus into trouble with some of the Pharisees when He said to them that they were "vipers" (reptiles) in Matt. 23:33? And "Ye are of your father, the devil and the lusts of your father will ye do. He was a murderer from the beginning…. he is a liar and the father of it." (John 8:44), and "…in vain do they worship Me… teaching the commandments of men" (Matt 15:9). In John 8:47: "He that is of God [has a soul] hears God's words, ye therefore hear them not, because ye [soulless] are not of God."

This does sound like Jesus is saying that Mankind had 2 fathers – thus:

there are Two Seeds on the Earth. (At least.)

In John 8: 23-26, Jesus tells the Pharisees:

> "Ye are from beneath, I am from above; ye are of this world, I am not of this world…. I have many things to say and to judge of you."

Yes, Jesus was supposedly conceived by the Spirit, thus making Him "from above," but the phrase can also be read to imply that the Pharisees have corrupt earthly DNA and Jesus represents more of a pure stock (see Chart 1A) without their corruption.

Jesus and the Vipers

In addition, when Jesus called the Pharisees vipers, He was not saying that the Pharisees looked like serpents, nor that all Pharisees were vipers, but as will be seen shortly, that **some of them** (the ones He was speaking to), were descended from the other 'seed' line – that they had a reptilian/Nephilim blood-line (i.e., genetics). Chapter 3 will clarify this important point as human hybrids (not of the 2nd Creation) carry the 1st Seed genetics – to this day. They look human but their genetics are slightly different.

Metaphorically speaking, one could say that the Pharisees just followed or served the Father of Lies, and were not descended from the devil, but some Pharisees were in fact genetically related to the same line as the Serpent in the Garden. And, there is an ancillary, deeper issue running through this whole matter which will be brought to bear in Chapter 5. There is a very strong reason for taking the Two Seeds information literally.

Serpent Truth

Jesus lays it on the line: the Pharisees are not of the same God as Jesus or His 2nd Creation, nor do they teach the real God's precepts. They serve the 'father of lies'… and notice that the Serpent in the Garden did not lie – he told Eve the truth. So the Serpent did not serve the father of lies, either; it is as if he was setting Adam and Eve free. Free from the petulant god who set up the Garden and didn't want His creation to "be as gods, knowing good and evil." (Gen. 3:5) In fact, God told them that if they ate of the fruit, they'd die. And that was a lie; the fruit would not cause their death. So the Serpent told the truth and YHWH misled them… but then, the god in the Garden was **not** the God of the Universe, as we'll see.

> **It is very important to note that the Jewish YHWH is the God of the Universe, but the god walking in the Garden of Eden was not YHWH. The reasons why will shortly be seen.**

What is interesting is that Adam and Eve were told by God that they could eat of any tree they wanted in the Garden, except the Tree in the Middle of the Garden, the Tree of Knowledge. (Gen. 3:1-3) There were two special trees: the Tree of Knowledge (reproduction), and the Tree of Life (longevity). Adam and Eve might have eaten of the Tree of Life (immortality), but when they ate of the Tree of Knowledge (i.e., sexual reproduction; Biblical 'knowing' was intercourse with another, and this means Adam and Eve were immortal but could not reproduce before being expelled from Eden), they acquired the ability to procreate, but **lost their immortality**. So, ultimately, they will die normal deaths from a normal (and now shortened) lifespan. But the Serpent told the truth: just eating the fruit will not kill you.

> They were free to partake of the "tree of life," that is the tree of immortality [as long as they lived in the Garden and did not eat of the Tree of Knowledge]. In other words, Adam and Eve were immortal while they lived in the Garden of Eden. Only the fruit of the tree of knowledge was forbidden… The knowing [procreation] that was withheld from Man … was something good for Man, but something which the creators did not want him to have. As long as Adam and

Eve lacked it, they lived in the Garden of Eden without offspring. [10]

So if the Serpent told the truth and was acting as a mentor, why did God say that the Serpent's seed would be the enemy of the woman's seed? When it is understood who this God is, and who/what the Serpent (*nachash*) was, the statement will become clear.

There <u>are</u> Two Seeds: the Serpent is the progenitor of one line and Adamic Man is of the other line. **Reptilian versus Mammalian**. Genetics is the issue, as will be seen. We know that Adam and Eve have the 'breath of life' (soul), so it would appear that the **first** creation (before Adam and Eve) was the pre-Adamic race, and is the soulless creation -- the "1st Seed." That is a major difference right there and accounts for much of the enmity between the two seeds. The rest is due to genetics which is why tracing ancestry to prove one's lineage was so important.

Remember: the Serpent is <u>not</u> from the first creation because he was <u>already</u> in the Garden and was part of the group of gods who said "…let's make Man in our image." (Trust this for now – Chapter 3 makes this much clearer.)

There are three main players on Earth <u>at this point</u>: the gods/Serpent group, Adam and Eve (ensouled) from the 2nd creation, and the other pre-Adamic humans (soulless) from the 1st creation (i.e., Nod). (See Chart 1A later in this chapter.) This situation is one of the major issues in this book and will be developed as the book proceeds.

Uraeus and Caduceus

For now, just consider that the Garden of Eden Serpent (*nachash,* or *"one who knows secrets"*) was not actually a snake. "Serpent" was also a reference to wisdom and healing – hence today's use of the twin serpents on the *caduceus* (medical symbol), it was also used by Moses when he told the people to look upon the bronze snake on the pole.

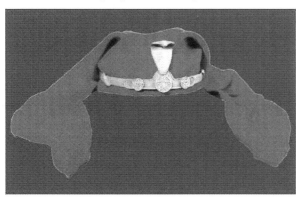

It was a symbol of wisdom as a poised-to-strike cobra, on the headpieces of the Pharaohs in Egypt, called a *uraeus*.

The Uraeus

(Credit: Bing Images)

In addition, Tutankhamun's Death Mask displays a Vulture on the left, and a Cobra on the right. The Vulture was a symbol of the cult of the dead, and the Cobra is the *uraeus* and symbolizes a pharaoh whose "3rd eye" (or 6th chakra in the forehead) is open or functional – in other words, the pharaoh was enlightened. In the average person, the 6th chakra (connected to the pineal gland) is not developed and requires the snake-like *kundalini* to move up the spinal column, awakening the individual by opening his charkas.

Yahweh

At this point, let's see who this god in the Garden was. He was alleged to be the creator of Man, and was the same one walking in the Garden, and the one who declared that there would be enmity between the woman's seed and the seed of whoever/whatever was also standing there, allegedly tempting Eve.

> **Note that when referring to the God of the Universe, YHWH, the word God is capitalized. When referring to the as yet unknown god in the Garden of Eden, the word god is not capitalized. In short, reading Professor Bloom below, keep in mind that Yahweh is the god in the Garden, and YHWH is The God of the Universe.**

The God of the Old Testament was known as YHWH, the unspeakable tetragrammaton, and so epithets were used in the Pentateuch such as Lord, and Yahweh, or (later) Jehovah. It was not permitted to speak the real name of The God, nor to make images of him. Yet, in Eden this appears to be a god who demanded blood sacrifice and kicks his creation out to fend for themselves. The local god (the Jews assumed it was the God of the Universe) would permit only one specially prepared and cleansed priest to visit him in the Holy of Holies area of the Jewish Temple. So terrible and unforgiving could this god be that the Temple priest had a rope tied around one of his ankles to retrieve his body should he make a worship mistake and the local god killed him on the spot!

This is the same god who would not let Moses see His face on Mt. Sinai when he received the Ten Commandments, and the same god who later allegedly let Job suffer tremendously just to prove that he, Job, would not doubt this god's grace and curse or renounce him. Actually, this sounds a bit like an allegory designed to teach faith more than a real event – and the same with Abraham slaying his only son.

Again, this does not appear to be The loving God of the Multiverse, but one who puts his creation occasionally through Hell to administer discipline and reward/punishment. In the same way, this god denies Moses passing into the Promised Land because he disobeyed and struck the rock (while in the desert to obtain water) instead of speaking to it as he was told to do. Moses and Job were human in their weaknesses, and this all-too-human god doesn't always care or forgive, or make any allowances for that – they are punished anyway. It looks like a 'power trip' on this god's part.

Professor Harold Bloom

Significantly, a renowned Jewish scholar, Professor Harold Bloom of Yale University, has this to say about Yahweh:

> "….Jesus Christ and his putative father, Yahweh, do not seem to be
> two persons of one substance, but of very different substances
> indeed. Yahweh…. is sublimely stubborn, and cannot be divested
> of his human, **all too human traits** of personality and character."

and

> "Historicism…. seems incapable of confronting the total incompatibility of Yahweh and Jesus Christ."

and

> "My sole purpose [in <u>Jesus and Yahweh</u>] is to suggest that Jesus, Jesus Christ and Yahweh are three totally <u>incompatible</u> personages, …. Of the three beings….Yahweh troubles me the most …. A capricious god." [11]

and

> Yahweh has an uncanny turbulence "….who cuts covenants with his people yet is perfectly free to break out against them…. Yahweh shows awareness of his own King Lear-like temperament, much given to sudden furies." [12] [emphasis added]

This does not sound like The loving God of the Universe. Professor Bloom's Yahweh quoted above is actually referring to the lesser god (erroneously) assumed to be YHWH but is in fact the irascible, all-too-human god in the Garden. Prof. Bloom also makes an interesting note that **Yahweh is different from Christianity's God** and Islam's Allah:

> "I am inclined to argue that Jesus Christ, Allah and Yahweh are antithetical to one another." [13]

Professor Bloom has written over 27 books, including scholarly works on the issue of Jesus and Christianity, and he easily exposes religious fallacies that escape the average person due to his much deeper research. He is repeating the idea that Jesus' father was not Yahweh of the Garden, but that he <u>does</u> appear to be the father of some Pharisees, as Jesus suggested earlier. What he very clearly sees is <u>three</u> personages: Yeshua of Nazareth (a human being), Jesus <u>the Christ</u> (aka the Son of God), and "….a human, all-too-human God, Yahweh." Later he says "Yahweh cannot be divested of his human, all-too-human traits of personality and character." [14]

As Professor Bloom opines, Yahweh in the Garden is very much closer to a personage in a Shakespearean play and out of character as The God of the world we live in:

> … theology fails when confronted by the J writer's [a biblical source] Yahweh, whose closest literary descendant is Shakespeare's King Lear, at once father, monarch, and irascible divinity.

and

> Historicizing Yahweh seems to me even more useless than historicizing Shakespeare… [because] no one is more beyond our apprehension as is Yahweh.

and

> Mischievous, inquisitive, jealous, and turbulent, Yahweh is fully as personal as a god can be… [even] Allah's dignity does not permit such descents into human vagaries. [15]

In short, Professor Bloom shows Yahweh to be all too human and unbelievable as The God of the Universe. Yahweh begins to sound a lot like a minor god of this world as we will see, and he is fully believable as **a more local god**, and Chapter 3 will make clear who that was.

Two Seeds

Let's do some summarizing and clarifying, so that Chapter 3 will make more sense.

Gen. 3:15 spoke of enmity between 2 seeds – between that of the woman (later descending allegedly through the generations to Jesus himself), and that of the Serpent (or the Serpent's offspring/progeny). Interesting that there was a lot of enmity between Jesus and the Pharisees and no wonder He referred to some of the Pharisees and some of His fellow Jews as 'vipers', sons of the Father of Lies. Jesus is of one lineage (the woman's), and some of the Pharisees are implied to be of the other lineage (the Serpent's). And it isn't just the priestly sect that Jesus is attacking – Jesus has to be referring to the lineage from the Serpent of Eden through several tribes, including the Levite (priestly) tribe, and consummating in that current group of Jews – some of whom still bear the DNA genetics of their lineage.

> *It will be clarified in subsequent chapters that the Two Seeds are a basic distinction between soulless and ensouled and that <u>all</u> races of Man today (and 2000 years ago), contain a mix of both types. The soulless 'vipers' are more closely examined in Chapter 5, and in* **in no way** *should it be construed that the Jews are a race of vipers or are soulless. Far from it. Note that the paragraph above specifically says "some" people were vipers – reflecting a mix within every race.*

Note that lineage was very important in that day because people knew that there had been the mixing of DNA with the advent of the Nephilim (the 3rd Seed) and their offspring (Gen. 6:2-5). This is why the Bible traces Jesus' lineage so specifically – to show that He was of **the pure lineage** (the 2nd Seed) dating from Noah's day. Just as DNA was mixed, so was iron and clay and there is more to the analogy in verse 2:43 in Daniel than meets the eye.

The second point is that even Jesus is referring to Two Seeds on the earth, just as Genesis 3 did.

And the third point is that Yahweh is too human to be considered a God of the Universe; he is a lesser god-like being that was involved in the creation of Man, he has been obliquely referred to as a god, or Enlil, as we will see shortly in Chapter 3.

Seeds and Enmity

Remember these distinctions:

> The 1st Seed = the pre-Adamics who are soulless.
> > There were two types here: *Lulus* and *Adamas* according
> > to Sitchin. One of these two could have been the ill-fated Neanderthal.

> The 2nd Seed = the Adamics who have souls.
> > Enki sexually upgrades this version to *Adapa*, more like Cro-Magnon.

The 3rd Seed = the Nephilim (offspring of the Watchers and Earth women, sometimes Anakim, or giants). Most perished in The Flood. The ones that didn't perish were removed by Enlil's orders.

The Word says in Gen. 3:15 that there will be enmity between the woman's seed, and that of the Serpent. This is jumping ahead a bit, but the Biblical text needs clarification. Try this for an explanation of the Garden of Eden scenario including the Creation:

Yahweh walking in the Garden was actually Enlil, head of the Earth Command. Because he is 3D, "flesh and blood", he could not find Adam and Eve because he was not omniscient. Hence, his upset at them telling him they were naked – which meant that they had awakened to the truth of their condition by interaction with the Tree of Knowledge.

The **Serpent in the Garden** was Enki, Chief Science Officer, serving Enlil, and a master of genetic science. Adam and Eve are his creation (genetically) and he wants to see them grow and be fully functioning… hence he adds gene #23 for reproduction (from the Tree of Knowledge) as "knowing" was a Biblical way of referring to reproduction, or sex between a man and a woman. Enki had given his progeny the 'gift' of reproduction. (That is why Enlil was angry.)

This reproductive ability had to have also been done (sooner or later) to the humans who populated Nod, even as pre-Adamics who had no souls, as they were a populous group of Humans, pre-existing outside of Eden.

Enki told them the truth, but now they were no longer able to eat of the Tree of Life and live forever (as Enlil's pets). Enlil would cast them out of the Garden. Enki is now constrained to see that his progeny survive and he must improve their genetics – which he does by having sex with an Earth woman himself (bypassing genetic trial and error) and the offspring become a superior version of Man, called *Adapa* (or Cro-Magnon).

The enmity in Gen. 3:15 thus takes on two aspects, because of what Enlil (Yahweh) did:

First, since Enki had created both pre-Adamic and Adamic humans, the "1st Seed" without souls would come to resent the ensouled "2nd Seed" and even become sociopaths, trying to kill 2nd Seed humans. (Chapter 5) Thus when Enlil tells the Serpent (Enki) that there will be enmity between the seeds, that is what he is referring to – Enlil IS actually wise and knows that the humans have deficits, and he doesn't want them to procreate and spread what he knows to be their questionable genetics. They are just worker slaves.

Second, Enlil is disgusted with Enki, but they are brothers, so Enlil chooses not to kill Enki for disobedience, and he does need him on Earth. However, as Enki spreads humans around the planet (multiple Edens), he tries to educate the humans and improve them, creating the **Brotherhood of the Serpent**, or Serpent Wisdom group (See Appendix E), with esoteric knowledge and tools to raise Man to a higher consciousness. This does not work because Enlil defames Enki, denounces him and his Brotherhood to the humans, and

33

the humans (later under the tutelage of the Church) come to despise the Serpent … and it is thus today in many parts of the world. This was also a form of enmity between the Serpent offspring and the humans.

This is somewhat represented in the following simplified Chart 1A.

Chart of Creation

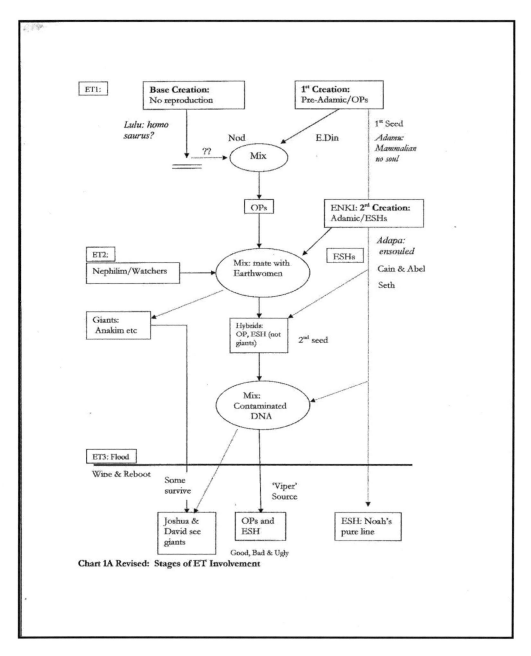

Chart 1A Revised: Stages of ET Involvement

The other half of this 2-part chart is at the end of Chapter 3.

While this initial chart is far from complete, it is a starting point to understand the different types of humans that were created – narrowing it down to the three main types:

Lulu = the first Man or Pre-adamic [soulless],
Adamu = the 2nd Man, or Adamic [ensouled],
Adapa = Enki's unique upgrade of Adamu,
and the offspring aka Nephilim: giants, or Anakim, Gibborim, and Rephaim.

The Lulu, Adama and Adapa are pictured at the end of Chapter 4.

Not pictured: **Eve** – Adamu's helpmate.
Lilith – Adamu's first woman helpmate (according to Jewish folklore).

According to Wikipedia:

In Jewish folklore, from the 8th–10th century *Alphabet of Ben Sira* onwards, **Lilith** becomes Adam's first wife, who was created at the same time and from the same earth as Adam. This contrasts with Eve who was created from one of Adam's ribs. The legend was greatly developed during the Middle Ages, in the tradition of the **Zohar**, and Jewish mysticism. In the 13th century writings of Rabbi Isaac ben Jacob ha-Cohen, for example, Lilith left Adam after she refused to become subservient to him and then would not return to the Garden of Eden after she mated with archangel Samael. Lilith was then demonized.

The Chart which follows is a graphic attempt to identify who was interbreeding with whom, and how the **Land of Nod**, Cain, and the giants (Anakim, etc) fit in.

"ET1" refers to information coming from Chapter 1.
"ET2" refers to information coming from Chapter 2.
"ET3" refers to information coming from Chapter 3.

"OP" refers to Organic Portals (soulless humans) examined in Chapter 5 …these are the pre-Adamic or "1st Seed" of Genesis 1

"ESH" refers to EnSouled Humans examined in Chapters 5-7 …these are the "2nd Seed" Adamic creation of Genesis 2.

"Base Creation" is the first creation of the gods – creating a worker who could not reproduce, the "Lulu"… This was very impractical as cloning additional workers was very time-consuming. This is not the 1st Creation of the Bible, but precedes it.

"Wipe & Reboot" refers to The Flood when Mankind was cleared away and restarted with Noah. (See Glossary.)

"Vipers" are the lineage that Jesus referred to earlier in this chapter. They are not giants, but 'contaminated' human stock whose DNA is corrupt. Maybe 1st or 2nd Seed.

"**Noah's Pure Lineage**" were the ensouled humans who were not contaminated. These would be the lineage of Adam, Eve, Seth, and Cain until Man polluted his genetics with those people from Nod.

E.Din means "home (E) of the righteous (Din)."

The **Land of Nod** had to be created before Cain was expelled from the Garden because he took his wife from those people. It is assumed to be "East of Eden."

The **Mark of Cain** was to be beardless, and when he was banished, he was relocated far West of Eden… probably to the New World where the Spaniards later met a lot of natives without facial hair.

Remaining Biblical Issues

There are two remaining and interesting aspects of the Bible Old Testament stories which are worth looking at, and clarifying.

Aspect I: Serpent in God's Garden

The first point: What was a Serpent doing in the Garden of Eden – God's perfect environment – unless he had a place there as one of God's servants, which might mean either that the god of the Garden was himself a reptile, or that the translation of *nachash* for 'serpent' is incorrect? According to Zecharia Sitchin, who spoke Hebrew, *nachash* can also mean 'a Diviner' and 'He who unveils secrets'. [16] So the Serpent being was wise and confronted Eve with a choice – to gain knowledge or stay ignorant, each with its own consequence. Or maybe the whole account is so mythologized that what really happened is now totally lost in antiquity… Let's take a closer look at this issue…

Serpent Wisdom

This is a good a place to point out, before the book goes too far, that many earlier cultures used the **serpent as a symbol of wisdom** – only Christians denigrated it. (Appendix E.)

The ancients, including the Gnostics and Hindus, knew about DNA and its importance in the human body. They knew that it had a double helix shape, resembling a snake, or serpent. The Hindus referred to the rising of base chakra energy/Light through the spinal column to the higher, crown (head) charka, as *kundalini*. This was seen as a good force. If the *kundalini* rises to the top chakra (without killing you!) you will be enlightened. If however, it hits an energy blockage, the build-up of pressure and heat may cause neural damage to the person rather than enlightenment. Instead of a sage, one might wind up an idiot. Such was the power of the force moving through the spinal cord (channel).

As a symbol, DNA was represented as a serpent, and still is today in the **caduceus**, or the symbol of two serpents entwined around a pole used in the medical community. It was also the symbol of Enki (also called Ea), a benefactor of mankind in Sumer centuries ago (covered in Chapter 3) who had extensive medical and genetic knowledge. For this reason,

Enki and his race (the Anunnaki) were associated with the Serpent Wisdom (reflecting: microbiology, DNA, chemistry, medicine and the like Arts). Note its sphere, the wings and the 2 serpents. The sphere and wings were a symbol of the Anunnaki.

source: Wikipedia

Anunnaki Symbol

In reality the above symbol bears a lot of resemblance to the Anunnaki symbolic representation of their flying craft [17] – which was **later borrowed by the Egyptians** to represent RA (aka Marduk), their Sun god.

Winged Sun
(Source: upload.wikimedia.org/wikipedia/commons/e/e0/N...)

Note again the sphere, the wings and this time the central sphere has 'tail feathers' (symbolizing rocket exhaust). Many versions had the symbol for the Anunnaki home planet Nibiru **inside the sphere** – the 4-pointed cross, or X, meaning that it was the "Planet of the Crossing." [18]

These two illustrations are both related to the Anunnaki, and variations on the theme are shown in several of Zechariah Sitchin's books. [19] The point is that the Anunnaki were associated with Serpent wisdom, the Sun, and flight, as will be seen in Chapter 3.

Serpents as Evil

It seems that the Christians are obsessed with the idea of the Serpent as a symbol of evil, but it wasn't that way with Moses in the desert, lifting up the **bronze serpent** so that people could be healed (Appendix E picture), nor was it that way in the beginning of Christianity.

> Interestingly, the Gnostic Christians held a different view of the serpent. The Gnostics believed in a direct contact with the divine without need for an intercessor (thus they were not particularly popular with the Church of

Rome). To the Gnostics, the serpent was a hero, not a villain. By persuading Eve to partake of the fruit of knowledge, the serpent led mankind to the path of spiritual autonomy. This requires Man to leave paradise where all his or her needs are met at the cost of subservience and unconsciousness. The quest for understanding that the serpent of Eden symbolically represents is attained by leaving the "blessed ignorance" of un-consciousness for the "hard won" fruit of increased awareness. [20]

In a nutshell, because it is relevant here (and as will be seen in Chapter 3):

> …the ABs (Advanced Beings), led by one named **Sin** (of the family of Enki), who wanted to provide more technical assistance to humans, were overruled by the senior ABs, led by Enlil (who became known as Yahweh). The ABs who won that vote, punished those who had given some science to humans, by casting them out of certain positions… and labeling them as "Sinners."

> The winners wanted to limit human access to science and the truth …They "demonized" the ABs favoring human development, such as **Enki whose symbol was the caduceus** (two intertwined serpents). That's why the AB desiring to give knowledge to Eve in the Bible is associated with a serpent…

> To complicate the story, it seems that the "good" guys, those who bring knowledge to mankind are related to the **snake** (the role of the good snake against the [bad] Archons in the Gnostic texts), a reptilian symbolism … In most traditions, the **reptile totem** has had very positive meanings (as in the Chinese and Celtic cultures). In fact **the Christian culture is the most prominent to use the reptile image in a negative manner**. It should be obvious that this was done by the priesthood to scare believers away from the true story of Enlil/Yahweh's desire to control us. [21] [emphasis added]

While the foregoing appears to jump ahead of the current topic, it is necessary to explain the Serpent and Gnostic aspect here such that Chapters 2 and 3 will make more sense. The Gnostics revered Serpent Wisdom and understood the 'hero' symbology of the Serpent in the Garden of Eden, and that is another reason for stating this information here.

Serpent wisdom will be more fully covered in Chapter 10 and Appendix E.

Garden of Eden Symbology

Note that the **Tree of Knowledge** and the **Tree of Life** were both in the "middle of the Garden" (Gen. 3:3) --- there were no guards protecting either of the two Trees. <u>After</u> Man and Woman eat of the Tree of Knowledge, and they are removed from the Garden, <u>then</u> the god stations cherubim and a flaming sword to keep <u>others</u> away from the Tree of Life (immortality) … What others? Adam and Eve were supposedly the only ones at that point, and they were kicked out.

Yet, the author of Genesis' repeated use of the word *"Elohim"* for gods (plural) bears noting. Recall that he could have said *"El"* or *"El Shaddai"* or YHWH (Yahweh), but he didn't.

So the putative god/Yahweh now says, again: "…the man is become as one of **us**, to know good and evil…" (Gen. 3:22) – there's that "us" again. We can assume The God wasn't schizophrenic, and the Supreme Creator does not consist of multiple beings (no Pantheism), so to whom is He talking? And why doesn't He want man to live a long life (via fruit of the Tree of Life)? It is noted that everyone from Adam down thru Enoch, Methuselah, Melchizedek, Abraham and Moses lived progressively shorter lives but started out around 1000 years as a life span. Scientists today tell us that the human body is still currently designed to last 120 years (Gen. 6:3 confirms this), but due to stress, diet and pollution we don't get there.

> Note: today's genetics has discovered that if our chromosomes were not capped with telomeres, we would have longer lifespans:
> The **telomere-shortening** mechanism normally limits cells to a fixed number of divisions, and animal studies suggest that this is responsible for aging on the cellular level and sets a limit on lifespans.[22] [emphasis added]

Aspect II: Sins of the Fathers

Second point: How are the fathers' sins passed on to subsequent generations? This is an important aspect related to Man's origin and procreation.

> The Bible says: Ex: 20:5 "…. for I the Lord am a jealous god, visiting the iniquity [sin] of the fathers upon the children unto the third and fourth generation…"

Note that any "sins" of the father/mother are passed on to the next 4 generations (we now know it's via DNA and **Epigenetics**) to the offspring, as in Deut. 5:9 -- and now the meaning of those Biblical phrases is clear.

So to be "born in sin" can also mean that one is born with corrupted DNA – the result of someone else's error(s) carried forward in the DNA --- more on this in Chapter 9, dealing with DNA and Epigenetics. It can also refer to the prior quote about "Sinners" under the heading 'Serpents as Evil' above. Later, this problem would be circumvented by the 'virgin birth' concept – emphasizing that the original human design could work if one had a perfect body and didn't have any corrupt DNA to overcome.

The Earth Experiment

For a final point of view, and one that this author was asked to include, the higher entity RA has been channeled by a reputable group known as **L/L Research Group** with Carla Rueckert.[23] Their efforts to carefully channel, study and print RA's words led to a series of books called The Law of One. (Later Chapter 12 quotes RA from this series.)

In the course of the question and answer activity with RA, it was learned that, not only is the human design fairly common in this part of the Galaxy, there is a 4D **Confederation of Planets** in this neck of the Galaxy and they are responsible for "…managing the transfer and evolution of souls from one planet to another." [24]

The Confederation tries to keep soul groups together on the same planet, interacting and evolving with each other, but at the time of the last Harvest when souls should have been ready to move on together to a new experience, there weren't enough 'graduates' from other planets, including Earth, and so there were several leftover groups on scattered planets and none was large enough to justify terra-forming the planet, just for them.

Note that "not enough graduates" means that many souls had made no progress in their lifetimes – they were still rebellious, maybe dysfunctional, or defective. (See Chapter 14, 'Life is a Film' section.) The scenario below could easily apply to the time after the Flood on Earth – when Mankind was reset on the planet.

> Therefore, Earth was chosen as a unique experiment, wherein **"cycle repeaters"** from many different planetary populations would be combined together under one roof. **It is uncommon for a planet to have as much racial diversity as we do on Earth**; for example, just within the Caucasian races there are broad differences in appearance that can be seen among Slavic, Mediterranean, and Western European peoples. The same is true in the Asian races with Chinese, Filipinos, and Japanese as three of the clearest examples.
>
> The reason for all this genetic diversity is that these souls have come here from different planets; the Chinese people for example are said … to have come from a planetary system surrounding the star Deneb. Thus their souls originated from stars and planets that had slightly different "personalities" [vibrations] in terms of how the DNA was structured to form the appearance of the human being. These basic differences cannot and should not be erased… since they are all aspects of the inner character and harmony of the soul.
>
> RA explains that **this great "experiment" went awry**, in the sense that not a single entity graduated after the end of the first major cycle some 50,000 years ago. Normally it is expected that perhaps 10 to 20% of the people make it after the first cycle. At the end of our second major cycle some 25,000 years ago, only 120 entities were ready for graduation, and they chose to stay behind to help out the others.
>
> By the end of the second major cycle on Earth, it became alarmingly clear that the "experiment" of combining all the **cycle repeaters** was not working. Great spiritual suffering was occurring, and a dramatic form of assistance was required in order to try to turn things around. As a result, massive numbers of entities from the fourth, fifth and especially the sixth density – including those from the RA group itself – volunteered to take on human incarnations in order to help. RA refers to these souls as **"Wanderers,"** and if you feel an intuitive connection with this idea, then you might be one of the nearly 100 million "wanderer souls" who now walk the face of the Earth.

Wanderers are not necessarily expected to "do" anything or to "save the world" by their own efforts, but by simply remaining in a physical body and preferably by maintaining a joyful state of mind, they have a tremendously beneficial energetic effect as they just **"anchor the Light."** This, in turn, can dramatically increase the number of souls who will qualify for graduation from third density to fourth. [25] [emphasis added]

RA considers all Wanderers to be potential liberators of the world, since they are higher dimensional souls who have volunteered to be human so as to raise the planetary vibrations. [26]

What this suggests is that the Higher Beings did a "fifth column" maneuver to sort of stack the deck with the odds of winning in their favor – forcing the "100th Monkey" phenomenon, so to speak. And all they do at minimum is anchor the Light wherever they are. Another way to see this is as if there are 100 tuning forks on a table (their bases in a slot so they stand up), and among them are 30-40 <u>higher</u> vibrating tuning forks – who maintain their higher pitch – pretty soon all the tuning forks, even the low-pitch ones, will all be vibrating at a higher rate due to the effects of **entraining resonance**.

We have never been alone on Earth, as will be seen, and even if we are an 'experiment' which is now defective, we are still loved and watched over. Our goal is to become an Earth Graduate (Chapter 15) and participate in the Harvest. Chapter 13 will explain in detail what has been done to offset the poor graduation statistics.

So, in a nutshell, that is a credible explanation of how Earth got to be the giant "tossed salad" that it appears to be. And of course, the time frame being 50,000 to 75,000 years back, puts it during the waning Anunnaki years on planet Earth, and more will be said about that in Chapter 3.

The basic sequence of events appears to be: there was the initial creation of souls, then the <u>initial</u> God-based placement of hominids and other lifeforms throughout the Universe, Earth is visited and goes through at least two creations [genetic manipulations], the Nephilim interference happens, and the 'experiment' <u>all</u> helped to create Earth's present scenario and problems. Chapters 12-15 will elaborate more on this.

Summary

It is becoming evident that the Creation may not have been exactly what we have assumed it to be, nor is it what we have been traditionally taught it was. The simplistic and sketchy version of Creation given in Genesis really appears to be at such a high level as to be almost useless... and then some young souls take it literally.

There appear to have been at least two recorded creations: the 'Basic Creation' encountered genetic failures, but eventually created **soulless workers** but who could not reproduce. Then followed the 1st Creation (the 1st Seed) , and the 2nd Seed was assisted (from Enki's sex foray in Chapter 3) to finally birth *Adapa* ensouled humans. The 2nd creation was also the source of the 2nd Seed, and the Nephilim hybrid offspring were the source of the 3rd Seed. (Chart 1A) The giants in Mesopotamia and the Middle East appear to have come down from the Nephilim, although others around the world are said to be the result of later genetic tinkering in Atlantis.

We also are questioning who this God of Genesis and the Old Testament really was -- keeping in mind that Yahweh was an all too human lesser god, and certainly was not The God of the Universe, or Abba Father that Jesus spoke of. In other words, the Christian explanation for the difference in behavior of God in the Old Testament and that of God in the New Testament is based on a false assumption: that they are the same God, before and after 'Redemption'. Wrong. The OT Yahweh and the NT Abba are not the same. The God, or YHWH, is Abba because the NT god is a God of Love, and is "never changing."

> *Apologetics has said that after Jesus paid for Man's sins, God in the NT could be loving and forgiving, but this is a statement reflecting the erroneous assumption just identified. There **is** a God of the Universe and He is Love and Knowledge (Light). And then there is the god of the Old Testament (Genesis) who has nothing to do with the Father of Light.*

And the issue of Man's **"sin nature"** begins to resolve itself in an examination of the sources of Man's corrupt DNA…which is inherited, frail and subject to untoward changes depending on what we eat, drink, smoke, breathe …

Note, however, that it is also part of this book to focus on a much bigger issue than historicity: also important to the remainder of this book is the unseen **Astral interference** that has prevailed for centuries. One needs to be aware of the unseen spiritual influences IF one is going to 'overcome' and become an Earth Graduate with the Truth setting them free. It will be seen that this interference is due to: (1) the influence of the first creation's soulless humans, now called OPs (Chapter 5), and (2) the Astral entities (Neggs and discarnates) to be examined in Chapter 6.

At this point in the discussion of Man's origins, we can turn to a brief look at what the Gnostics taught about our world, to gain a better understanding of where certain ideas and myths come from. Remember that the Gnostics knew what the truth was and had to mythologize it into a story that could be passed from generation to generation. The story they and Enoch tell in Chapter 2 will be clarified in Chapter 3.

Chapter 2: -- Spiritual Origins

Alternate Religious Views on Creation

If Man had a purely spiritual genesis, or creation by some non-3D gods, he would also have had continued interaction of some sort with the spiritual beings responsible – even if only interference from some (like the incarcerated Watchers) who may have deserted their assigned duties, as will later be seen. Whether it was The God, or the Gnostics' Archons, or some ethereal Higher Beings, the purpose for creation must have logically included some purpose for interacting with Them – even if only down the road…. And if so, being that Man can be dense intellectually, it would have been expedient to tell Man plainly what is expected of him -- no doubt by sending messengers or teachers to him.

It would have been nice if the original Man had come with an instruction manual, and not just 2 stone tablets. Of course, over the centuries, Man developed his own precepts, and there have been plenty of philosophers and theologians who have argued for centuries about who and what Man is and what the end goal is – so obviously, there has been no one, definitive, written-in-stone Guide to Man that everyone agrees on.

Of course, some will argue that Deuteronomy and Leviticus in the Bible were such "operation manuals" and they did prescribe a lot of dietary and behavioral Do's and Don'ts. However, these instructions were not given to mankind as a whole – they were intended for God's 'chosen people.' (Think: Mosaic Law) Had they been intended for all of mankind, there would have been copies made in the Heavenly Kinko's and distributed by UPS (United Preaching Service) to the Chinese, Arabs and Hindus, to name a few.

Of course, teachers appeared in most major civilizations, such as Buddha in India and China, Lao-Tzu in China, Jesus in Palestine, Quetzalcoatl, Kukulkan and Viracocha in the Americas, Krishna in India, and a messenger to Mohammed and Joseph Smith. Obviously, these teachers' messages interfered with unruly humans' freewill to have fun and so were largely ineffective. We all know we're here to have fun…

Realm Relevance

And further, it seems logical that because the 3D world is so limiting, that Man would <u>not</u> have been created by a Higher Being in His image to permanently dwell in 3D physicality – otherwise why give Man a soul, with a god-like potential, and then tell him that he was born in sin and he'd better subdue the world in which he is trapped? Subduing the world is a sure way to become attached to it, and is not something that an advanced, benevolent Being would advocate that Man do.

Think about it. What possible payoff was there for a God to create spiritual beings, or souls, and then confine them to a 3D physicality where they cannot develop their God-given abilities as they can in 4D realms and above? There was a reason for this constraint, as will be seen (Chapters 7 and 13-16).

Of what use would it be to get bogged down in physical attachments, addictions, habits… and later quarrels engendering further karmic debt? If souls were created perfect, at least according to God's purposes, would He not have had a use for Man, the souls, sparks from His Likeness, in some part of His Creation without 'burying' them in 3D dense physicality? On the other hand, if the souls were created as incomplete (unfinished) souls, what does that tell us about the purpose of Earth? (Think: School.)

If the souls were created complete and purposeful, they would be of more use to God in the 4D realm and above, run by the Higher Beings – who have never incarnated. Do we as parents, give birth to 3D children and then insist that they go down into the 2D realm (animal and plant) to live and learn? Or do we send them to school… to learn? Why create them as 3D then? As anyone who has gone OOBE, or had a Near Death Experience, or seen auras can tell you, **the soul is what we are**, and it not only survives death, it has extended abilities (Chapter 9) beyond what we can use in the 3D physical. So Man is at least 4D in the real nature of his soul.

So what is Man doing on this 3D Earth? What is Earth?

The answer to that is one of the great revelations of this book. But to better appreciate and understand what that is, it is necessary to expose some common fallacies that Man thinks are valid. And to that end, we have begun the quest for truth with the Bible and ancillary spiritual/religious documents – to see what truth may or may not be there.

> **Note: as the reader goes through this chapter, the significance of the different, ancient teachings will enlighten him/her to what religion is all about, and where it came from. The reader will then be better able to evaluate religious teachings and better understand future chapters. This is done at the layman level.**

Ancient Views

Book of Enoch

The Book of Enoch was written by a man who is said to have walked very closely with The God. So closely that he knew what God was up to and had knowledge of what was going on in the heavenly (Astral) realm that was affecting Earth. If someone didn't want Man to have a clue about what other beings might also be on the Earth, or who may be afflicting Man, they would suppress this book and keep it out of the Bible.

While The Book of Enoch is basically a lament over the sinful condition of Mankind, and a call to repent with blessings for those who are righteous, it also expands on Genesis 6 which says that angelic host descended and created giants and havoc in the Earth.

The Book of Enoch dates to about the 2nd and 1st centuries B.C., and was held in great reverence by many of the early Church Fathers. However, due to efforts of the emerging Christian church, by the 4th century A.D. it was looked on as heretical, and later condemned.[1] Thank you, Constantine.

Watchers and Angels

The story of Enoch concerns how God set 300 Watchers over the earthly Creation and how some 200 came down and immersed themselves in 3D, teaching forbidden knowledge and procreating with Earth women (Gen. 6), thus defiling themselves. [2] Their offspring were giants who, when they died, became nasty spirits which were bound to the Earth. [3] Enoch attempts to intercede for the Watchers but fails and is shown that their spirits are to remain **earthbound** until the Final Judgment. [4]

According to Enoch, the Watchers were led by 2 main 'fallen' entities – **Samayaza** and **Azazyel**, who in turn led other Watchers by the names of Gadrel, Yekun, Kesabel and Kayyade. The rest of the Watchers remained true to their orbital post and are apparently still there today. Some of the good Watcher names are familiar to readers of the Bible: Uriel, Raguel, **Michael**, Saraqael, **Gabriel**, Phanuel, and Suriel.

It will be appreciated that the terms 'Angels' and 'Watchers' are used interchangeably by Enoch and they both occupied a realm just above the Earth. Angels have been traditionally seen as the way God communicates and interacts with His Creation, and hence they come from above the Earth – assumed to be Heaven, but it will be seen in the next chapter that it was just **from Earth orbit**. It will be seen that confusing these two terms is an error; Angels are 4D Beings of Light, but Watchers are actually 3D entities.

"Angel" (*malakh*) means 'messenger' or 'one who is sent' and does not have to be a winged, transcendental Being of Light. It is important to note that these Watchers were physical beings who normally had a function above the Earth, and descended to have sex with Earth women. It is thus easier to believe that the Watchers were 3D beings in this case rather than some amorphous 4D Beings of Light. **Angels are not Watchers**.

Power Differential

Said one critical author:

> The whole concept of angels has always troubled me… Why in heaven would the 'all-powerful,' omnipotent GOD need a bunch of lower spiritual forms in a physical form, to run His errands? To convey messages, to deliver warnings and threats, and to actually do the destruction on His behalf? Why would GOD need this kind of menial support? Surely the all-powerful GOD can facilitate all the interactions with humans in the blink of an eye, instead of long-winded tedious instructions, **threats and the monitoring of humans** who have apparently been behaving sinfully while conspiring against Him! It simply does not wash.[5] [emphasis added]

This is a very simplistic view of God and erroneously suggests thet God can directly communicate with Man. Not so. To a large extent, I agree that God could communicate directly with Man, but chooses not to – for the same reason that Man cannot live if he touches a million volt high power line. It's an issue of **power differential**. Angels are a necessary intermediary with lower power. Yet the use of Angels has been overdone –

used where it is not appropriate, as in this case. The naïve sheep have bought the 'Angel' explanation instead of being told about other beings out there who do "threaten and monitor" – they are in Chapter 3 and 6.   The question is: Why intermediaries?

As will be seen at the end of this chapter (section on 'Central Sun'), there have to be intermediaries between God and Man since God cannot directly interact with Man – Angels are a kind of **stepping down of His Power** which would otherwise "fry" us were He to directly visit us. Angels are like transformers – were you to plug your TV set direstly into a 220V line, it would blow the set up.

> *And as I transcribed this book, I was occasionally connected with a higher energy that was giving me the information, connecting data, and the guidance ("1-sec drops" in the Glossary). My body was not used to that higher level of energy. I appreciate it that my Source only did it 7 times in 8 months.*

In addition, real Angels from 4D and above cannot have intercourse with 3D humans, despite Biblical suggestions to the contrary (e.g., "virgin births" are really 3D artificial inseminations by genetically-savvy ETs), so the most logical explanation for the 'fallen angels' of Enoch is that they were in reality 3D beings whose genetics were slightly different and the mixing of their genetics with Earth women initially produced the giant **Nephilim** (aka Anakim).

Anakim Warrior   **Goliath Was a Nephilim Descendant**
(Credit: Bing Images)

Nazorean, Gnostic, Johannite, Ebionite, Pauline teachings or otherwise, there is a belief in 'fallen angels' on planet earth – mistakenly called the **Nephilim**. The Nephilim were the offspring of the Watchers + Earth women. The concept is that of a humanoid being, a Watcher, descending to Earth in a form a little different from, for instance, one's next door neighbor, yet distinguished by a distinct psychology and genetics. Enoch said the Watchers **shapshifted** (in a later section, 'Appearances Important') and that is how they deceived the Earth women.

> *Shapeshifting is not physically changing the molecular structure of one's body; rather it is controlling what others see. And that can also be done by an electronic device.*

Other than the Gnostics, and the Bible, the only other major source for the account of the fallen ones is in The Book of Enoch, which is briefly referred to in Chapter 6 of Genesis. BUT the Bible does not specifically say that the offspring were giants, it just says they were "…in the earth in those days" and the original Bible word was not "giant" it was "Nephilim" which they say means "great men, men of renown." This is another error in the Bible (see Chapter 11). It is The Book of Enoch which says that the offspring were physical giants. While their exact origin may be in question, yet terrible **giants called Anakim, Geborim and Rephaim** were created who finally turned on man and began to literally devour him.

Giants

There is evidence for the giants all over the Earth in skeletons that have been unearthed.

> In 1833, soldiers digging at Lompock Rancho, California, discovered a male skeleton 12 feet tall… [it] had double rows of upper and lower teeth…In Ohio in 1872 an earthen mound was discovered to contain three skeletons that … stood at least eight feet tall. Each also had double teeth…[6]

And the **Celts** and their cousins across the English Channel in Germany were also quite tall and fierce warriors, and that is why the Roman Empire had such a hard time conquering them. They finally did subdue the Celts and Germanic tribes, but at quite an expense.

> Indeed at the famous **Battle of the Teutobergerwald**, the Germans would so utterly decimate **four Roman armies** in the brutal fighting that Rome would maintain a more or less **defensive** posture with respect to the Germans until the Western [Roman] Empire's final collapse….
> Eventually, however, some of these Germans were captured by the Romans, and one of them, a particularly troublesome King by the name of **Teutobokh** was paraded in Rome in the customary triumph. The Roman historian Floras reports that this king was so tall that…Teutobokh could be 'seen above all the trophies or spoils of the enemies, which were carried upon the tops of spears.' …Teutobokh was easily nine feet tall… perhaps considerably taller.[7]

Yes, skeleton frauds have been exposed, but not all of the pictures of giants are faked. There is a museum in Ecuador that has a 25' human skeleton on display. It was found in Loja, Ecuador in October 2012. Also, there is a picture of a 12' Irish giant in an open coffin leaning against a railroad car in London from the 1800's. [8] This was also supposedly the same height of the Philistine, Goliath, who was at least 9' tall.

Giants Today

The genetics that produce giants have not disappeared.

The man on the left (8' tall) is in modern-day Iraq,

and the man below (7.5' tall) is in modern-day Russia.

(Credit: Bing Images)

Giant Skeletons

Steven Quayle created a chart of reported giant's heights – next page. It is a comparative *Chart of Known, Excavated Giant Skeletons* showing the different sizes of giants found in different places on the Earth. He also records that

> "Near Mezarino in Sicily in 1516 there was found the skeleton of a giant whose height was at least 30 feet… and in 1548 and 1550 there were others found of the height of 30 feet. The Athenians found near their city skeletons measuring 34 and 36 feet in height. In Bohemia [Germany] it is recorded that there was found a human skeleton 26 feet tall, and the leg-bones are still kept in a medieval castle in that country. [9]

Thus it is clear that **there actually were giants in the Earth,** in different places, in not-so-ancient days. Note that Goliath was between 9-12 feet tall, so in OT days (and perhaps near the end of the Roman Empire as recorded above), the average height had come down to 9-12 feet tall from the much larger Nephilim.

Note (below in Chart) that Man **A** is 6 feet tall, today's human. **D/E** is Goliath, and **E** is King Og spoken of later in this chapter. The others represent sizes of actual skeletons found around the world. Skeletons found in the Middle East are B, D, E, and I. Skeletons found in France are F, G, and H in Ecuador, and D in Georgia (Russia).

French Chart Showing Comparisons of Giants based on Physical Remains (or in the case of Goliath, biblical testimony).

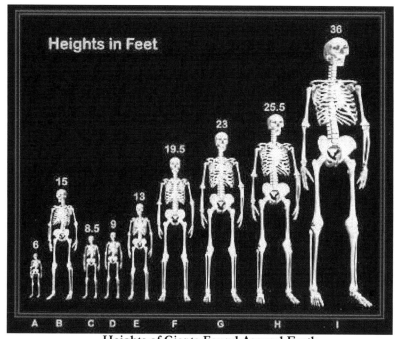

Heights of Giants Found Around Earth
(source: http://www.bibliotecapleyedes.net/gigantes)
(Credit: Steven Quayle)

Problems for Man

Mankind cried out to God to protect them from the Nephilim and their offspring and several 'Angels' were sent to bind the Nephilim, and then God allegedly sent The Flood to do a "Wipe and Reboot" of planet Earth. The Anakim, Rephaim and Giborim were allegedly wiped out in The Flood <u>and</u> not permitted to reincarnate; their spirits were henceforth earthbound. [10]

Enoch was chosen to judge them and they were bound to the Earth's Astral realm, **unable to re-incarnate**. They certainly did and probably still do hate mankind, but their incarceration has kept them from harassing Man from the Astral. But it will be seen that some 'giant' DNA did carry forward <u>after The Flood</u> as Joshua later discovered giants in the Promised Land, and David fought a giant Philistine, Goliath.

> The existence of this evil race, known by various names, pervades the New Testament as well as the Old Testament. They are also called "children of the wicked one", **vipers**, workers of iniquity, heathens and evildoers. According to Enochian prophecy, however, the [good] Watchers will hold power over man until the fallen angels are finally judged…. What is most significant about the text is its insistence on the presence of "evil spirits <u>on earth</u> in physical bodies [who were] moving among mankind." [11] [emphasis added]

Chapters 5-6 will examine who these entities might be.
And again, there is reference to the viper and reptilian issue:

> Even the **serpent** who seduced Eve was not a mere snake, but one of the fallen Watchers whose name was Gadrel. Yekun, whose name means 'rebel', likewise seduced all the sons of the 'holy angels' and caused them to descend to earth, thus leading astray the offspring of men. Kesabel, another Watcher, induced the holy angels to "corrupt their bodies by generating mankind" [12] [emphasis added]

It sounds like the Watchers were **physical** reptilian-humanoids, but in Man's basic physical image -- else how could ethereal Angels mate with Earth women? But then again, how many Earth women would find a reptilian humanoid attractive… unless they had no choice and were taken against their will…? Shapeshifting to fool the women is not suggested because most 3D beings can't shapeshift… The Watchers mating with the Earth women is given as simply happening, and is rather vague in every source examined, so that suggests that the whole story has not been told since it does not all fit together; it is hard to reconcile the concept of human women and angelic Watchers (as Reptiles), and so that is a major issue to be cleared up in the next few chapters.

Testament of Amram

It is particularly frustrating to find that Enoch and other Bible authors give no description of the Watchers; in fact, they appear to be deliberately avoiding the issue (or the descriptions were removed). Except for one little description by a known biblical character, Amram, who was the father of Moses.

Robert Eisenman and Michael Wise in 1992 co-authored a book describing some 50 unknown biblical documents in <u>The Dead Sea Scrolls Uncovered</u>. Amram wrote a text called the *Testament [witness] of Amram* that describes an experience he had in which he saw an Angel and a demon and there is some insight into what the Watchers looked like [some words are partially obliterated in the damaged original text]:

> "[I saw **Watchers**] in my vision, the dream vision. Two [men] were fighting over me. I asked them, 'who are you that you are thus

empowered over me?' They answered me, 'We [have been em]powered and rule over all mankind.' They said to me, 'Which of us do yo[u] choose to rule you?'

I raised my eyes and looked. [One] of them was terrifying in his appearance, [like a **s]erpent**, [his] c[loak] many colored, yet very dark… [And I looked again] and … in his appearance, his **visage like a viper**… [I replied to him,] 'This Wa[tcher], who is he?' He answered me, 'This Wa[tcher]… [and his three names are Belial, and Price of Darkness] and King of Evil… He is empowered over all Darkness, while I [am empowered over all Light]… and over all that is of God. I rule over [every] man.'

I asked him, ['What are your names…?'] He said to me, '[My] three names are [Michael and Prince of Light and King of Righteousness']. [13] [emphasis added]

Interesting that the viper is described, but Michael isn't. The viper is serpent-like and frightening, yet Michael did not look like the evil Watcher. This will be clarified more in Chapter 6 where the 'evil' Astral beings will be recognized as the Neggs – an Astral negative entity – who works with the Beings of Light (BoL or Angels). Angels can assume any form they want.

This is another 'vote' for the existence of the serpent-like beings that Man used to see. (See Appendix F.) Why can't we just ignore this document, this *Testament*, as the product of an over-active imagination? Why is it being given importance? For several reasons: back in the days of Moses, and his father Amram, (1) not a lot of people could write, and (2) the vellum or parchment and ink were not something that anyone had, nor could they afford to waste time, money and parchment on a made-up story. In short, the fact that this got written down means that Amram convinced someone that it was a true event, worthy of documenting for posterity. Naturally, the main people who would see and read the account were the educated, the priests and other scribes… which is why it wasn't generally available information just as the Dead Sea Scrolls were also 'hidden' for centuries.

Later in Chapter 3 there will be another explanation of the term Watcher and instead of an Astral entity, they were real, 3D entities who descended to the Earth, mated with women and produced the Nephilim (or giants).

Appearances Important

Enoch is finally led to where the Watchers are being held and he sees that they are now in spirit form – no longer 3D, but now in their etheric (4D) bodies, and are now able to shapeshift and assume various appearances. According to Enoch:

And they [the angels] took me to a place where those who were there were like burning fire, and, when they wished, **they appeared as men**. [14] [emphasis added] and again...

> And Uriel said to me: 'Here stand the angels who have connected themselves
> with women, and their spirits, **assuming many different forms**... [15]
> [emphasis added]

It appears that the fallen but now incarcerated Nephilim **spirits** could still appear as whatever they pleased. Enoch is not directly saying that the 3D Watchers could shapeshift. And it will be later seen that the 4D Neggs (in Chapter 6) **do** have the same ability. It may be safely repeated that most 4D+ entities can shapeshift, but not normal 3D entities.

According to Enoch**,** Gadrel (a 3D Watcher) appeared to Eve in the Garden, and that was a reptilian form.

> And the third was named Gadrel: he it is who showed the children of men
> all the blows of death [i.e, ways to kill others], and he led astray Eve... [16]

Thus, whatever we can determine Gadrel's normal form to be, is what the Watchers also looked like. And now we hear that he led Eve stray...sounds like a Serpent-being. Be clear that there is nothing saying that they were winged angels to start with – except Man calling them that because they came from above, and they could 'fly'. And that is important, despite the tendency of Enoch's book to have us believe that the Watchers were somehow fallen 'Angels', the enochian Watchers were merely fallen/descended 3D entities (Igigi), as we will see in Chapter 3.

We will also see that Gadrel was not really the name of the 'fallen angel' who tempted Eve... remember the Watchers were busy about their duties around and above the Earth. But be aware that Enki was an Anunnaki, the Watchers were Anunnaki (Igigi) , thus it matters little whether Gadrel or Enki did the tempting of Eve in the Garden – unless Gadrel worked with Enki...It makes more sense for the god walking in the Garden to be upset with Enki than it does a Watcher called Gadrel since Enki was the genetic creator of humans.

The Nephilim

In his book, The Nephilim and the Pyramid of the Apocalypse, Mr. Heron gives quite a bit of information about the Watchers, Nephilim, and Bible history, all to make the point, in synch with the Gnostics of old, that we have been oppressed by the spirits of the deceased Nephilim and their offspring who, according to the Book of Enoch, were mostly killed by The Flood and were 'imprisoned' spirits around the Earth.

The actions of the Watchers mating with the Earth women also relates to Genesis 3:15 again – the conflict between Two Seeds. While Enoch does not say specifically that the Watchers were reptilian, it can be logically inferred from Enoch's later statement that Gadrel (Enki) tempted Eve in the Garden, [17] and the Bible (and the Jewish *Haggadah*) says that that was a Serpent-like being (Gen. 3:1-5) – see picture earlier in this chapter. Thus, Watchers were not angelic because true Angels are not reptilian.

Watchers are often equated with angels and Beings of Light; they are usually proactive beings helping Man. Note that Watchers <u>then</u> and Watchers <u>now</u> are not the same beings. Watchers then were the Igigi (Chapter 3), and the Watcher function now is performed by the Beings of Light AND the Neggs, and to a lesser 'contracted' extent, Greys. Through it all, the traditional Angel, or Being of Light, has always been here and is still called a Watcher. Watchers have also been called Custodians.

It all fits an emerging picture that the enochian Watchers were 3D reptilian hominids… reptilian human-like beings. In <u>The Book of Enoch,</u> it is now clear that the Serpent who beguiled Eve was one of the 'heavenly host' who were serpentine in appearance. [18] It is also known (from the *Haggadah*) that the entity in the Garden who led Eve to eat of the fruit is also a reptilian hominid. A Serpent-like (reptilian) being. This will all have more significance and be examined further in Chapter 3.

The Nephilim offspring (giants) were a very evil group, and they were doing such a good job of abusing Man that the gods had to intervene with The Flood… but the giants didn't all die, and this bears repeating: at least their DNA <u>did</u> carry on into the land across the Jordan where Joshua and his men saw giants, and later David fought another giant called Goliath [13' tall] who had 3 brothers… all <u>after</u> The Flood.

Polluting Mankind

Suffice it to say that the Nephilim hated Man as much when they walked the Earth as when they were bound by the Higher Beings as spirits to the Earth. Their leaders, **Azazyel** and/or **Samayaza,** and the 200 were locked up and removed by the Anunnaki, even though Enoch (or a later scribe) colorfully suggests they were incarcerated in an Astral realm.

The Biblical Adam had the DNA to support a soul, because God breathed the life or spirit into him in Genesis 2. This meant that Man could over time develop his spiritual component and reconnect with his 'godhood' -- if he could overcome his corrupt, inherited DNA, that is. Man's overcoming had to be prevented by the Nephilim and their offspring if they were to **block Man's development so that enlightened Man could not rule over them**. Man was created to be eventually higher than the angels, but is still lower and this is a problem for Man.

Thus it was necessary to **pollute the genetics of Man** (as Patrick Heron suggested) and from that mating of the Watchers with Earth woman came the Anakim, Giborim, and Rephaim – who due to their size and appetite, went thru the food and then started on Man, and almost wiped out Mankind. As Heron said:

> So [Darkness] has some of his own band procreate with women and produce children. But these are no ordinary children. They are the **offspring** of superhuman … beings, half-human, [half-reptile], whose only intent is evil…. the evil was **in their genes**. [19] [emphasis added]

Remember that their purpose was to corrupt the human genetics.

> Things must have been extremely bad when we are told that "every inclination of the thoughts of man's heart was only evil all the time," and that the whole world was full of violence…. millions of people… had become totally evil and morally bankrupt as a result of the activities of the Nephilim. [20]

So the Nephilim were monsters of iniquity, and Heron adds:

> ….we have a most bloodthirsty lot. For throughout the legends concerning these people, we have debauchery, infanticide, matricide, patricide, rape, murder, adultery, incest, treachery and even **cannibalism**. You name it, they did it. This fits in exactly with the Genesis record, which tells us that the entire world was filled with violence…. **Human sacrifice** was a significant feature of these times….[21] [emphasis added]

Note that the issue of **sacrifice** comes up again; sacrifice was also demanded by Yahweh, later Baal, Molech, Ishtar, throughout history. It was also encouraged among the Aztecs and the Maya by Huitzilopochtli – by the Remnant later descended from the Anunnaki hybrids of Chapter 3 – was there a link between the Nephilim/Watchers and Yahweh? (Yes, and Chapter 3 explores it.)

Nephilim Legacy

However, Man was not alone on the Earth, and Others including the one called Yahweh, would have seen what was happening to Man, and sensing a certain responsibility and a fear no doubt that the Nephilim and their offspring could also turn on <u>them</u>, they let a Flood cleanse the Earth to get rid of Man and the evil-doers. Note again that this evil did not require any supernatural entity's manipulation to create the chaos and evil that was rampant -- largely due to the DNA being defective. And it needs to be emphasized that genetics must have been responsible for the size of the Anakim, Giborim and Rephaim, or "giants," as well as the baser predisposition to sex and violence.

Since this is in Man's genetics as well, is it any wonder Earth is a constant battlefield with war after war throughout history? And we encourage more pettiness, violence and lust through the sex and violence on TV and in video games. Such is the legacy of that corrupted DNA through many generations. (Epigenetics is covered in Chapter 9.)

After The Flood, the humans started all over again, without the technology, but with the supplied knowledge of how to farm, irrigate, medicate, stargaze, etc. Watchers are still present, by the way, but it's a different group. And because The Flood was not totally world-wide, but more local to the known 'world' of Africa and the Middle East, the humans and the "2nd Seed" genetics are still present as well.

And there is something else in that mix... as will be seen by Chapter 5.

Two Seeds Revisited

Again, we visit the concept of Two Seeds on the Earth. As has been seen, **the issue is corrupt DNA in the 2nd Seed,** and thus some of mankind, and there is the issue of the former reptilian Watchers interfering in Man's world.

When Jesus attacks the Pharisees and calls them "offspring of vipers" (Matt 23:33) and "serpents," note that "viper" could also be another term for the fallen Angels' genetic offspring – both then and today. According to Mr. Macchio, perhaps the Earth-bound spirits of the Nephilim, if they exist, try to return to Earth lives via discarnate possession… an ugly thought [22] but this will be better addressed in Chapter 6.

Stop and think: What kind of a loving God would permit His creation to be almost wiped out by reprobate ('fallen') entities? He wouldn't, but **the battle is for souls** and early Man was aware of the battle and came up with his own explanations for it… which tend to mirror what really happened.

Before addressing this issue, let's segue to the issue of evil as seen by Man. Man thinks in terms of duality – good and bad, light and dark, etc and so there had to be (invented) a Satan to explain Man's problems … because Man could not accept that (1) the Anunnaki creator 'gods' were still here trying to control Man, and (2) Man himself was responsible for some problems that led to the Anunnaki doing what they did… so myths were developed to explain Man and his world.

What evolved over time was a Gnostic view of the world wherein the Anunnaki were represented by Archons and spirits, and Man (soulless and ensouled) was at effect with them. This even included a myth dealing with Man's creation… just different names for the players in the Drama.

Gnostic Overview

Ialdabaoth

> There are Christian and pre-Christian Gnostic texts that describe the usurper deity, **Ialdabaoth** and his Archons (minions), who create Man by the light they have stolen from above. Christian-Gnostic Theologians in the 2nd century wrote of "*hylics*" (Greek: material) who possessed **no soul** and who were doomed to extinction…" [23]   [emphasis added]

This is an alternate explanation for the origin of the soulless ones i.e., related to the "1st Seed" pre-Adamic creation mentioned earlier. Archons creating the soulless humans is an allegory for the Anunnaki having created them – the parallel is examined in Chapter 3. This issue was well-known and debated before the 4th century and eventually gave rise to the **Doctrine of Embodied Evil** which the orthodox Church promoted to categorically reject the issue. It was not solved, just brushed aside by an edict. "It suggested that some men on Earth may actually be the offspring of the Devil (Nephilim) and that, in turn, presupposed reincarnation which the church was [also] adamantly against." [24] Thus was Church doctrine evolving…

Current-day author Joseph Macchio points out that if the soulless 1st Seed are still <u>on earth</u> as the ancient texts say, both the canonical and the apocryphal, "would they not seek to suppress evidence that they, in fact, exist?" [25] Is this why we have so many errors, omissions and disinformation dealing with earth history and religion?

As a revolt against the suppression by the orthodox Church of information that was felt to be esoteric and not for the masses, but important enough to keep alive until Man could some day handle the truth, many groups of men and women became initiates of secret orders to protect and preserve ancient teachings – long since rejected by orthodoxy.

The Gnostics were one such group protecting the truth, thinking outside the box, which is why they were severely attacked by orthodox religion. But who/what were the Gnostics and what was their Creation myth that reflects the real event?

First let's look at who the Gnostics were and what they believed, as it mirrors the actual Creation story, and second we'll take a look at the unique Gnostic Creation story itself. All in preparation to see that the ancients DID know how Man got here and who was here with him, which is one of the major points of this book.

Gnostic Teachings

The Gnostics were an esoteric group of followers of the truth, like the Essenes and the Naassenes, who dutifully copied their earliest teachings and quietly spread the word that **Man could achieve enlightenment and release from this earthly prison by acquiring true knowledge**. The Bible restated it as "…and the Truth will set you free…" but the Bible forgot to tell people what they would be set free from – and it wasn't just ignorance.

The Gnostic Seeker
(source: www.crystallinks.com)

Gnosis means 'insight.' There were degrees of initiation and levels of esoteric knowledge, all based on knowing God through an <u>experience</u> of Him. They taught that Man did not need any intermediary to approach and know God – another idea that the fledgling Catholic Church had to suppress.

> *The source of the Gnostic teachings will be seen in Chapters 3 and 11 to have been the product of Enki, one of the benefactors of Man. Enki was discredited, his teachings reversed, and his Brotherhood of the Serpent was vilified such that the later Catholic Church wound up promoting the opposite of what Man needed to know to be an Earth Graduate.*

Dr. Elaine Pagels

One of the major authorities on Gnosticism is Dr. Elaine Pagels, a PhD from Harvard, who has extensively studied the Gnostics and their teachings which have lately emerged in the Nag Hammadi scrolls. These ancient writings date back to just after the time of Jesus, about AD 400 when they were buried, and were as sensational a discovery in Egypt in 1945 as were the Dead Sea Scrolls in Israel in 1947. Because the Nag Hammadi library was not in textual agreement with the teachings of the Dead Sea Scrolls, the Gnostic library remained unknown for another 30 years, kept in locked Catholic archives in Jerusalem. [26] Further, Pagels indicates that some of the scrolls such as the *Testimony of Truth*

> ….tell the origins of the human race in terms very different from the usual reading in Genesis: the *Testimony of Truth*, for example, tells the story of the Garden of Eden **from the viewpoint of the serpent**! Here the serpent, long known to appear in gnostic [sic] literature as the principle of divine wisdom, convinces Adam and Eve to partake of knowledge while "the Lord" threatens them with death, trying jealously to prevent them from attaining knowledge, and expelling them from Paradise when they attain it. [27] [emphasis added]

> *That echoes what we just saw in Chapter 1, and will be expanded again in Chapter 3. A jealous god seeking to control his creation. And a modern-day researcher, Zechariah Sitchin in Chapter 3, will echo and explain that information with a new significance.*

Pagel's definition of Gnosticism is found in a key phrase in her book: "…. the Gnostic is convinced that whoever receives the spirit communicates directly with the divine…. at first people believe because of the testimony of others…. but then they come to believe from the truth itself." [28]   For example, Valentinus claimed to have received his gnosis from Paul of the New Testament who allegedly possessed a secret teaching. Upon receipt of the secret teaching, he is said to have had a vision which became the source of his own gnosis. [29] Such people were considered to be spiritually alive, or as will be seen shortly, they were called *pneumatics* – filled with the Spirit.

Just as Paul did not teach the inner secret to everyone and anyone, so Valentinus kept his revelation and gnosis to initiate only "those who are mature" [30] as not everyone would be able to comprehend it and he was not into throwing pearls before swine. The teaching was later revealed as follows:

> What this secret tradition reveals is that the one whom most Christians naively worship as creator, God, and Father is, in reality, only the image of the true God. According to Valentinus, what Clement and Ignatius mistakenly ascribe to God actually applies only to the *creator*. Valentinus, following Plato, uses the Greek term for 'creator' (*demiurgos*), suggesting that he is **a lesser divine being** [Satan as Ialdabaoth] who serves as the instrument of the higher powers. It is not God, he explains, but **the demiurge who reigns as king and lord**, who acts as a military commander, who gives the law and judges those who violate it -- **in short, he is the "God of Israel."** [31] [emphasis added]

Could Ialdabaoth be equated with Yahweh? In a revealing Gnostic passage:

> Epiphanius… reported that the [Gnostic] Ophites venerate the Serpent because God has made it the cause of Gnosis for mankind. **Ialdabaoth [Gnostic name for Jehovah, the false creator god]** did not wish humankind to have any recollection of the Generators (Aeons), the Cosmic Mothers and Fathers on high. It was the serpent, who by tempting them, brought Gnosis to our parents; who taught the first people of our kind the complete knowledge of the Mysteries from on high. [32] [emphasis added]

There will be more to say on this aspect of Yahweh/Jehovah in Chapter 3, but the above bracketed note indicates that the author of the passage sees Yahweh as synonymous with the demiurge, or pseudo-creator – **a local god**.

Self-discovery

Gnosis requires self-discovery and one is encouraged to "light the lamp within you." [33] Such is the meaning of the Gnostic Book of Thomas, verse 70:

> Jesus said, "If you bring forth what is within you, what you have [brought forth] will save you. If you do not have [bring forth] that within you, what you do not have within you [not bring forth] will kill you." [34]

Essentially: **Use it or lose it.** Salvation is achieved by bringing forth (applying) what spiritual strength and development one already has; those who do not have enough, will perish. Like the theme of this book: gather Knowledge and let its Light raise your PFV so that you can get out of here (i.e., save yourself), and become an Earth Graduate.

This enlightened saying will be made clear when the end chapters reveal how and why to get out of here. It is very interesting that man 2000 years ago knew some very profound truths, and then with the advent of the structured, patriarchal and controlling mother Church, most of it was lost. Control, not truth, was the issue.

While there were a number of Gnostic mainstream groups, with some eventually replacing others, the following versions called Valentinian and Manichean are noteworthy as relates to Man's origins. It is also valuable information for potential **Earth Graduates.**

Valentinian Gnosticism

We first come to Valentinian Christianity (Gnosticism around AD 140) which addressed the basic nature of Mankind, attempting to classify Man according to one of 3 aspects: [35]

> **The Elect**: the '**pneumatic**' or spirit-filled who were searching for a deeper Christian message because they lived through gnosis/insight;

> **The Called**: the '**psychic**' or mental man who was happy with what he knew (knowledge) and he walked by faith;

> **The Material man**: the '**hylic**' who was incapable of understanding any spiritual message, and did not have the soul-awareness of the other two types.

What is significant about this schema is that in the early centuries AD, man was aware that **all men were not 'created equal'**, and that some men had souls and some didn't. **Hylics didn't have a soul**. [36] (These 3 types are examined again in Chapter 5.)

Somehow, perhaps deliberately in an attempt to 'level the playing field,' that information has been lost to the modern world. And by simple inspection, we can see that this 3-tiered system could have bred a spiritual elite in the 'pneumatics' which appears to be a simple "better-than-you" philosophy... enough to create division in any church. (And it did among those calling themselves the Illuminati.) And this is probably what led to the whole teaching being hidden or rejected, and everybody was deemed (inaccurately) to be the same as everybody else. Needless to say, Valentinus' teachings were denied and refuted by the young and growing Church; he was later denounced as a heretic. So much for truth.

Three Types of Humanity

To get around objections to this doctrine, it was quickly explained that "these were three types of humanity [ensouled] at different stages of unfoldment." That meant that the pneumatics had the most developed souls and the hylics none, or they had a very weak, pre-soul. Later it will be seen that these hylics have also been called pre-Adamic and Organic Portals (OPs) by more recent researchers who still note a soul or aura difference in Man.

This information is valuable in that the hylic was known to exist over 2000 years ago, and the definition and presence of same matches today's descriptions of the OP or pre-Adamic Man. While the exact origins of the OP/hylic can be questioned, the fact remains that these people **do** exist, and they can be a nuisance, and as will be seen in Chapter 5, they have either a weak or no aura. Lack of an aura means lack of a soul, as the soul is what 'radiates' as an aura. (The hylics were also called **Somatics**.)

While the hylics cannot be redeemed, the Gnostics taught that if a Christian (pneumatic or psychic) falls in sin, s/he is able to reverse the downward slide into Darkness by virtue of the divine seed ('conscience') within – or today we say that the ensouled person can go within and connect with the 'god force' and be redeemed. This can also be represented today by receiving the Baptism of the Holy Spirit.

The 'unfoldment' teaching sounds elitist, but there is a basic truth of soul development hiding in it. For now, it is important to say that we do <u>not</u> all have the spark of divinity within us. And the assumption that we do leads to a number of errors, including marrying the wrong person, working for the wrong boss, or trusting the wrong person. This will be further examined in Chapter 5.

2nd Seed Prejudice

So again, we have been dealing with <u>at least</u> **two seeds** on the Earth. Also note that even the Greeks who recognized these hylics would not let them hold public office nor teach their young, such was the justified prejudice against them. They were considered to be 'sons of the devil by nature' and therefore could not be saved and it was taught that the wicked seed, the giant Nephilim, propagated itself throughout humanity even <u>after</u> The Flood.

Joshua reported:

> **Num. 13:32-33:**
> And they brought up an evil report of the land which they had searched saying…. all the people that we saw in it are men of a great stature… And there we saw the giants, the sons of Anak [Anakim], which come of the giants, and we were in our own sight as grasshoppers… (NKJV, 252)

> **and Josh. 13:12:**
> All the kingdom of Og in Bashan….who remained of the remnant of the giants… for these [Rephaim] did Moses smite, and cast them out.

Note that Moses lived <u>after</u> The Flood, so there were giants, offspring of the Nephilim, <u>after</u> the Flood, too. And by the way, King Og's bed was 9 cubits by 4 cubits in size, or 18 feet long by 8 feet wide. [37]

This brings to mind the bas-reliefs of Sumeria and Egypt which show normal-size humans in the same scene with what are clearly giants. (Last picture in Chapter 3.) This is usually explained away as the 'giant' human symbolically representing the importance that person (sometimes a king) had in that time and the greater authority he had over his subjects. What they forget to point out was that the person in authority always had the symbols of authority in his hands, or stated in the hieroglyphs, so why was it necessary to also picture him physically larger, as if he were a giant? Unless of course he was…. this will be seen to be a recurring theme.

Bible Not Literal

Giants existing <u>after</u> The Flood means that we cannot totally trust the Bible as a literal account of The Flood because the Bible says:

Gen. 6:17:
And behold I, even I, do bring a flood of waters upon the earth …
to destroy **all** flesh…. and **everything** that is in the earth shall die.

and Gen 7:21:
And **all** flesh died that moved upon the earth…

and Gen. 7:23:
And **every** living substance was destroyed… both man and cattle…
creeping things, and fowl of the heaven … and Noah **only** remained
alive and they that were with him in the arc. [emphases added]

Oh really? The facts indicate that The Flood wasn't a complete wipeout … the giants still existed, or was there a mis-translation…? Chapter 11 explores that issue.

Manichaeanism

The prophet **Mani** was born in 216 AD in what is now called Iraq. At the age of 12 he received a complete 'download' (a 1-sec drop?) of divine information that was to be his basis for teaching spirituality in the years to come. He received complete info on the nature of existence and the purpose of the universe from a being he came to identify with as the Holy Spirit. He wrote many books, letters and personal insights – none of which have survived, but his dream of **a universal religion** was later called Manichaeanism. He always signed himself, "Mani, Apostle of Christ." He was a true apostle of the Light.

Mani taught that there is a war between the Light and Darkness; a battle between Good and Evil. He taught that the real man is the soul, and his **true home is the Land of Light**, not Earth. He taught that there is a realm of darkness ruled by a Satan-like being and his minions and they afflict man on this planet for their own ends. As a result of his teachings, he was "the most persecuted, reviled and hated of all religious leaders…" [38]   and his message was the most threatening to Evil itself, "acting through the powers that be [PTB] in this world who perhaps wished to keep certain 'secrets' regarding the nature of evil from the masses." No surprise.

This information is very close to what this book also teaches. And Chapter 11 also supports a universal religion to come. It is nothing new, but it has been suppressed.

Mani taught "the counterfeit creation of man by evil powers" – in essence saying that there were human beings **who had no soul**, and were the product of Darkness. Further, he said that the Archons [demonic Astral powers] attempted to "bind man permanently to a genetically and otherwise manipulated physical **matrix**, an envelope of matter and consciousness tainted with rebellion and the lust of the Archons." [39] Again, corrupt DNA.

Archons are said to be those 'powers and principalities' referred to in Ephesians 6:12 – negative, self-serving and demonic powers in heavenly places. The putative Satan, then, would be their leader… or maybe, **Azazyel** … or Ialdabaoth (aka Yaldabaoth).

A Conspiracy of Darkness was thought to enslave man and part of it is summarized below. While it is long, it is extremely insightful, relevant, and worthy of consideration – a relevant message from 1800 years ago:

> … the fallen [angelic] hierarchies sought to imitate the spiritual Creation by capturing the spiritual beings [souls] in dense bodies which they **fabricated** by various means, not excluding **genetic engineering**. Thus in order to sustain themselves, the rebellious powers needed the "light" or energy of the heavenly realms of which the souls created by God were composed. The souls then became the 'food' of the Archons, without which they would perish. This interference and manipulation of humanity's spiritual evolution as one of the causes of duality and mortality in men was clearly taught by the ancient Christian initiates of various schools and communities and was apparently known by Jesus. **The creation of physical, material man by the Archons**, and what might be considered subsequent 'nth derivative' creations of 'homo sapiens' by the [Anunnaki] and the propagation of an ungodly race by the Watchers, thus rendered man subject to not only the laws of mortality but to inbred emotions of rebellion and lust and animal-like behavior that could only be eradicated by 'spiritual surgery' as it were, by man's submission to the path of initiation whereby he is restored to his original, inner Divine Nature. The initial means to this restoration or redemption was provided by the Avatars, such as Jesus… [40] [emphasis added]

Mani also stated that Man being born of flesh and blood, relates to the

> …genetic material in the bodies worn by humanity for aeons, which originated not from a Divine Source but from the evil or **lesser creators**, whether we consider them to be advanced scientists ("gods") or self-proclaimed rulers (Archons) who sought to make or remake the race of mankind in their own image. [41] [emphasis added]

This echoes Chapter 1 and sounds like evidence for Chapter 3.

It gets better:

> We ask again the question, were mankind, or at least the bodies of mankind created by God or the fallen powers? If we closely examine the teachings of ancient Christianity, the answer seems to be that the bodies of humanity were created or formed by both: by God (Elohim) as vehicles of self-expression in the material cosmos and by the fallen powers **in imitation of God's creation**. And what of the soulless beings created by genetic engineering or other means? This was simply answered by the understanding that all beings, whatever their origin, have the potential to receive the divine spark, and thus become spiritual beings. [42] [emphasis added]

It is clear why Mani was attacked so vehemently and the Church particularly said he was worse than a heretic – and yet he was teaching the authentic roots of Christianity that the Church seemed to have forgotten. Or wanted to distance itself from as it created the new Christianity. Gnosticism and particularly Manichaeanism were soundly denounced by the Church in favor of a more tame, 'straight vanilla' version of man's origins… yet the Church did allow the possibility of Man being created by fallen Angels by maintaining that he was a 'fallen creature' and 'born in sin'… which concepts are now taking on a new meaning.

Apochryphon of John

At the risk of belaboring the issue, there is one final important Gnostic explanation for our world, and it is also a key treatise. The following is a summarization of the longer, original text, and it is significant as it (1) was the original Christian-Gnostic teaching that the Catholic Church sought to stamp out when it persecuted Gnosticism in general, and (2) being from the era 30 AD – 120 AD, it presents a coherent teaching that is very compatible with the further development of the Two Seed theme, and (3) it gives an alternate explanation as to who did which of the two creations in Genesis. [43]

Ialdabaoth Again

It was very early taught that there was another deity besides the Supreme God, and he was considered a usurper, "…even mimicking the Creation …. by producing physical beings without souls." The character of **Ialdabaoth [also spelled Yaldabaoth]** approximates that of Satan in the Bible and in other apocalyptic texts as well, as well as other fallen angels…. such as Sammael, Beliar, or Belial." (Yaldabaoth is also called Sammael elsewhere.) His name means 'begetter of armies'. "Ialdabaoth is considered … an enslaver of humanity." [44]

He is also considered to be the Demiurge and runs a despotic world aimed at enslaving Man. His main agenda is to destroy the divine spark placed within Man that enables Man to overcome, connect with the God force, and eventually rule over Ialdabaoth. This is the ancient basis of Satan's/Ildabaoth's/Azazyel's hatred and oppression of mankind.

The Demiurge is often pictured (left) as semi-reptilian, and a secret message is contained in that (revealed in Chapter 3).

(Credit: Bing Images)

From the <u>Apocryphon of John</u> we learn that the goddess of wisdom, **Sophia**, fell spiritually and entangled herself in the 3D creation.

She had not consented with the Holy Spirit before she created a creature that had the form of a lion-faced **serpent**. She hides it in a cloud and calls it Yaldabaoth. And he grew in arrogance and power being the child of a god. So he calls himself God, but he is really a false, counterfeit, inferior creation who considers himself a Lucifer, or 'light-bearer.' All evil is considered to have resulted from the activities of this usurper, or demiurge.

The Goddess of Wisdom, Sophia

(Credit: Bing Images)

Yaldabaoth does have the power to create, but he cannot create a soul – that is the Father of Light's prerogative. This is significant as souls are from God, and **the soulless beings would then be a counterfeit creation**. Significant is the fact that early Man knew there were humans without souls – interesting that they had to devise a myth to account for them. Chapters 3 & 5 will give a more realistic origin of the soulless among us.

Counterfeit Creation

The text at this point says Yaldabaoth spoke to his minions:

> I am a jealous God and there is no other God beside me.
> But by announcing this, he indicated to the angels who
> attended him that there exists another God…[45]

Sophia sees this and repents, so the true Father creates Archtypal Man [a Jesus], a Divine Being with power greater than the **Archons** and their chief. An immortal man of Light. Sophia warns Yaldabaoth that he is about to be judged and thrown into the abyss…

Meanwhile, Yaldabaoth creates a world in 6 days, and says "Come **let us create a man according to the image of God and according to our likeness**, that his image may become a light for us." Sophia wanted to retrieve some of the power with which she had imbued her creation and so she petitioned Father God who then speaks to Yaldabaoth and advises him to "blow into the face of Adam… something of your **spirit** and his [Adam's] body will arise. Yaldabaoth then blew into Adam the power of Sophia [*ruach*], not knowing that he was endowing his creation with the divine spark." Since he could not create a soul, nor empower one, what he blew into Adam was an energizing spirit-force [*ruach*] which then permitted the entry of an existing soul.

It was soon discovered that Adam was more intelligent than Yaldabaoth and he had a **soul**: the same transformed body that Jesus later displayed to His disciples during the Transfiguration on the Mount. In his rage, Yaldabaoth hurls Adam into the lower levels, presumably to Earth that was just created. Enraged, his minions mix earth, fire and water and create a new physical body for Adam, they then encase him in it, but Adam still has the hidden divine spark.

As the story continues, Adam is placed in a paradise [Eden] and they suggest he eat of the trees of "….godlessness, hate, deception and desire." The **Tree of Knowledge**, also in Paradise, was hidden from him, lest he eat and discover his divine heritage. Next the minions put Adam to sleep and try to locate the divine spark in him and take it from him. Failing this, they create "another creature in the form of a woman [Eve]." Adam awakens and Sophia comes and illumines Adam, who now knows good from evil, and **Yaldabaoth in his anger, kicks the two out of Paradise.**

Yaldabaoth sees how fair Eve is and has intercourse with her, creating two sons – Cain and Abel. This means Cain and Abel had souls because Eve had one. Later Cain will choose a wife from [soulless] Nod yet their son Enoch is also ensouled. [46] But Adam begets Seth with Eve, and he is also heir to the divine spark [soul]. From this point forward, Yaldabaoth's plan is to "…. people the earth with their godless reproduction of bodies without the divine spark, injected with lust and their counterfeit spirit."[47] The summary goes on to relate the corruption of the race of Man through the Watchers (or Sons of God) and shifts into The Book of Enoch (examined earlier).

> *It will be seen in Chapter 3 that the actions of Yaldabaoth (in bold text above) are identical to an **alternate version of the Creation**. Interesting that Cain's wife has no soul, and this is a Gnostic explanation of where the soulless humans on Earth came from. While this account was just a version of what actually happened back in antiquity, it bears a lot of similarity to the version in the next chapter. (Hence it being presented here. The truth was mythologized.)*

Soulless Beings

Note that the Gnostics ignored the Land of Nod and the 1st Creation, yet they do identify the soulless beings and the fact that they also propagate.

What is interesting is that even back 2000 years ago, the story of Two Seeds on the Earth was widely known and shared. In addition, man was aware that some men had souls and some didn't. So the Greeks were aware of the soulless *hylics* and somewhere for Western civilization, the teaching was not too surprisingly suppressed along with Gnosticism.

Then 1800 years later, in today's world, investigators like the Russian Boris Mouravieff would call these beings **'pre-Adamics,'** and the ensouled humans would be called **'Adamics.'** (Chapter 5.) G. I. Gurdjieff would rediscover the Gnostic teaching, renaming the phenomenon: **Organic Portals (OPs),** and so teach it to Boris Mouravieff. Thus, the concept of Two Seeds still lives, it just now means that the corrupt DNA from the older "1st Seed" and Nephilim interference has permeated the ensouled and the soulless humans, and so the '2 Seed' concept now applies to (and lives on in) the DNA of Man. (See Chart 1A in Chapter 1.)

Refocus

Hence, the Two Seed concept now has been reduced to, and henceforth refers to, the ensouled humans (ESH) vs soulless humans (OPs) on Earth. And this evolved meaning of Two Seeds is now used throughout this book, especially as Boris Mouravieff's material (Chapters 5 and 14) uses it that way, too.

Contemporary Views

Dr. Shakuntala Modi, M.D.

Before leaving this section dealing with Man's spiritual origins, it is valuable to have a look at something that comes to us again from an enlightened M.D. who is engaged in hypnotherapy and dealing with her patients' problems. A more complete overview of her work and the attendant information will be given in Chapter 6. The following review is presented to round out the overview of Man's origins from a spiritual viewpoint, but it is important to remember that her patients may have colored what they said based on their religious beliefs.

Creation of Souls

In Dr. Modi's book, there is a passage wherein several people recalled, under hypnosis, the creation of their souls. Because this is basically correct, it is repeated here:

> They describe the process of creation of their individual soul similar to birth. They describe it as being something intense going on around them, being shaken and squeezed. Finally the intensity becomes great and all of a sudden they find themselves being thrust out as a separate soul from the core of God (the mother), but still connected to God with a silver cord (like a cosmic umbilical cord).
>
> My hypnotized patients report that God is surrounded by the Godheads. Each soul emerges from the core of God and after a time, when ready, it enters one of the Godheads. For a time after its separation from God, each soul waits in the Godhead. Feelings of nervousness, anticipation and abandonment surround the soul as it waits…. [and] nervous confusion. Patients describe this waiting in the Godhead like waiting in a cosmic womb. After a time, however, the soul adjusts to being part of the Godhead, only to be cast out again at the point of incarnation.

Under hypnosis, some of my patients have even recalled when God first created human life and several souls were infused into adolescent human bodies and placed in strategic places throughout the universe to generate human life. These **original couples** can be identified as the "Adam and Eve" concept. That is, they were the first humans ... placed there to create more like themselves. [48] [emphasis added]

*Note: It is probably no coincidence that the patient revelation of the Adam and Eve concept corroborates the long-promoted teaching by the Church. Such revelations under hypnosis do not give instant credibility to what is being said, as there are also 'false memories' and **'filtering' of archetypal thoughtforms** to agree with what the patient believes. Yet, it is presented as relevant material, also to be considered in a search for the Truth as Dr. Modi was non-suggesting in her questioning.*

And then, upon being ejected (or 'birthed') from the Godhead, the soul experiences alienation and separation as never before. Then it heads for the womb, where it is again comfortable, until it is again ejected into the cool air and harsh light of the hospital room. This is a cold, foreign place. And worst of all, the soul cannot communicate with anybody and it feels really abandoned and frightened. At this point, the soul loses all its memories of its true 'home' due to the dense vibration of 3D Earth. (See Chart 3a in Chapter 7.)

Miscellaneous Support

Another source of a very interesting insight into creation is given by a quiet, unknown man from Bridgeport, Connecticut, whose claim to fame was to have researched the UFO issue, run a huge bureau for the investigation of the phenomena, and then was contacted by otherworld entities and given some very interesting information. Whereas this information would normally be subject to ridicule as just speculation, it was given to the public in 1962 and has since been corroborated by Robert Monroe, Kenneth Ring, and others who have ventured out of body in recent years.

Central Sun

The most interesting part of the information **Al Bender** shares is the nature of God and our universe, as given him by the ET entities:

Space or the great void has no end as far as we have been able to explore. As we explained previously, there is a large main body from which all the planets and their suns are formed by means of being cast off into this vast void we call space. This main body seems to grow in size and never diminishes, despite the fact that it discards new bodies constantly. It is so hot a mass you could not go near it, even in terms of billions of your light years. All the bodies cast off are hot burning balls of fire, and as they reach the cooler parts of space they explode and form smaller bodies that circle them. These smaller bodies become planets as they cool off, but the cooling-off period consumes many, many years. We have sent out spacecraft to explore the regions beyond the circling bodies where there is an area that is deep black and in which you are unable to see anything. This vast black area is waiting for bodies to fill it. We have lost many of our exploring craft that went too far into the deep black and never returned. [49]

The Great Central Sun, The One
(Credit: Bing Images)

Despite the problems Bender had (examined in Chapter 4), and his occult naiveté, the above account rings true and it is echoed by two other credible sources.

First there is the corroboration by **Near Death Experiencers** who while out of the body, ventured to the Great Central Sun, or God. [50] (Their accounts followed that of Bender by 40 years and his book is out of print.)

> Then, off in the distance, I saw a vast area of illumination that looked like a galaxy. In the center, there was an enormously bright concentration. Outside the center, countless millions of spheres of light were flying about, entering and leaving what was a great Beingness at the center…. As we approached the great luminous center I was permeated with palpable radiation… [it was like] being exposed to complete knowledge… I was in touch with everything, but subsequently, I couldn't recall the knowledge. [51]

The second source is **Robert Monroe** who, while out of body in his **OOBE** voyages, asked his guide [*Inspec*] to show him God. His guide takes him as close to the presence of God as he can stand, and has to put himself between God (the Central Sun) and Monroe to shield him – the effect is too great and Monroe is not ready for it.

> …the radiation was so strong that it was nearly unbearable… I was melting… but it wasn't heat… then the radiation eased… There was a form between me and the radiation, shielding me … the wondrous and brilliant joy, awe, reverence, melded into one… I knew if I responded to this degree from just

the reflection … the full force of the radiation would have shattered me, I was *not* ready for it…

there in the long view, was **a radiant living form** of incredible size… a shining globe, edges indistinct … [from which came] numberless beams or rays… so close that I felt I could reach out and touch one…

[he is invited to do so]…

I stretched a part of me out, cautiously, and touched the smallest ray near me… in an instant the shock spread throughout all what I thought I was…and I knew and in knowing, knew that I would forget if I tried to remember, because what **I was could not yet handle the reality of it**… yet I never again would be the same even without remembering… the echoes would reverberate in me throughout eternity …[52] [emphasis added]

It was said earlier that God uses a hierarchy of intermediaries between Himself and Man due to the great energy/power difference.

A similar effect on two souls who did not compare notes beforehand. Somewhere in the center of our universe (and Galaxy?) is this radiant Sphere, or living, shining Globe, often referred to as a Central Sun, or The One. THE God. The Father of Light.

Bender asked his ETs whether they worship anything..?

We do not worship anything, but we all know that **the great central body** created all of us, and cast us off into space to form a life or remain a barren piece of matter floating about. [53] [emphasis added]

There are not that many different main versions of God and creation; ultimately the non-Christian ones begin to sound a lot alike. If you have a soul, you know there is Something greater than you are, of which you are a part. If you have no soul, you could care less, and you sometimes try to convince others that they shouldn't care either. And a godless society is a dangerous one. Fortunately, they don't last long.

Summary

All this Gnostic origin of Man sounds related to the standard information we have in the Bible: in Genesis, the rebellion in heaven, Satan tricking angels and people, and the establishment of the human race on Earth. There are even some corollaries with the Gnostic information where the gods are upset with the 'usurper' (Yaldabaoth aka Satan aka Azazyel) and see to it that Man has a divine spark that Darkness can't touch.

From the religious standpoint, Man's biblical creation was repeated and elaborated on by the Gnostics, and we can see that the version in Genesis is a highly abbreviated account of what the esoteric groups taught. But that is not the end of the story. What if the Gnostic teaching, as well as Enoch's story, is but a veiled account of something that occurred on a much more physical, 3D level – involving ETs?

69

It isn't hard to accept that a powerful God could create a gazillion souls and send them throughout the Universe, incarnating in a myriad of different forms. And eventually some of those mature, develop the technology, and visit Earth. What is so hard about that? And what if the ETs that visited us also were masters of genetics and upgraded a hairy Earth hominid (Homo *habilis* or *erectus*) to turn it into a worker for them? And we may do that ourselves someday on a distant planet…

Then at some point, we encounter the issue of ETs 'out there' and we come right back to the question of who created <u>them</u>? And that <u>would have to be</u> the case with the very first creation, somewhere, of the human form, Man and Woman. What about ETs that allegedly created other ETs… or Man? At some point there had to be a **first creation**; not that ETs could not manipulate DNA and create a humanoid, but the traditional, limited Bible teaching is not really that easy to accept in light of the latest findings in genetics, anthropology and archeology.

It **is** necessary that the souls were created by <u>The</u> God of the Universe, but it is <u>not</u> necessary that Man's physical form was created and put here by <u>The</u> God of the Universe.

What is fascinating is that not only did the 'Counterfeit Creation' story of Yaldabaoth by the Gnostics above have some similarity to the Genesis Creation (Yahweh) story, Yaldaboath's activities also have an incredible amount of similarity to what is disclosed in Chapter 3 where Enlil is credited with Man's creation. Somebody way back when knew what was going on and it looks like the Yaldabaoth story was <u>a deliberate allegory of Man's real origins.</u>

Gnostic Yaldabaoth aka Judaic Yahweh aka Sumerian Enlil?

In the next chapter, the ET creation story promoted by Zecharia Sitchin, for example, is so alluring, so interesting, somehow so …plausible that it deserves a lot of analysis and reflection. Just because ETs may have created Man on Earth does not mean there is no God – just that the God of the Universe did not have to create <u>physical</u> Man on Earth. Yet Man as a **soul** was created by God, and the distinction needs to be worked into people's consciousness, or we will never be able to meet and relate with other beings in the Galaxy because we will be seen as so backward, quaint, parochial…. as many are now.

It would be very helpful in Man's growth to give a thought every now and then to what he looks like to others coming here from across the Galaxy. Does he want to be seen as petty, violent, rebellious, fantasy-prone, greedy, crude, stupid, control-freak, etc…. Or does he want to be seen as a true seeker, intelligent, respectful of others and the planet, patient, compassionate, tolerant of differences, and cooperative? Until he makes the right choice, he will not be let off the planet – and **that is a major point in this book**.

New Religion Needed

Bishop John Shelby Spong has been saying something similar for years: Man needs to re-examine his religious beliefs (Chapter 11). It could be a healthy re-alignment with the truth of Man's origins, especially IF the ETs have an understanding and a respect for the life force, its Source, and IF that all engenders a respect and compassion for life forms everywhere... If they didn't, we'd be in trouble because they have been here for centuries, and could have removed us any time they wanted to...

The Gnostic texts quoted earlier are merely presented to round out the contemporary picture – to consider the major lines of thought that have been repeated for centuries, and which to this day affect our religious thinking. They need to be reexamined and re-considered in the light of modern day knowledge, keeping the relevant parts, clarifying the speculative issues, and discarding the errors to synthesize a workable, modern view of Man and the Universe – which is a second major point of this book.

Man's real goal is to be an Earth Graduate. He doesn't belong here; this is not his planet and he is not here alone. Let's see why...

"Ye shall know the truth and it will set you free [from Earth]." John 8:32.

Chapter 3: In the Beginning... ETs

Man Is Not Alone

As man has grown intellectually and technologically, so too has his awareness of the possibility of life on other planets – even the possibility of such life visiting Earth. It is not out of the realm of possibility that Man can today reach Mars and start a colony there, so why not a more advanced civilization coming to Earth from another solar system?

And if Man traveled to another habitable planet, what would he do there? Look for resources that he could use, food to eat, and probably set up an outpost there – later developing it into a small colony, and then a small city, and then another populated world would have been created. That's the key word: **created**. Man can create a world after his own image, and in the likeness of his cities and world on Earth.

It is also within the realm of possibility that Man will soon master the science of Genetics and be able to modify sentient, hominid life on a future planet he finds. Has he not already cloned a sheep named Dolly (1996)? More to the point, could he capture an ape-like animal and modify its genome to make it more intelligent, but not too smart, so that it can be controlled as a slave worker? To what end? To **serve**: in working the mines, sowing and reaping the fields, fighting as a soldier, and constructing his buildings.

Just 100 years ago, Man traveling to another planet would have been pure science fiction. Unbelievable and impossible with the non-technology of the primitive pre-Industrial Age. And yet, Man is smart, and learns fast, so fast that most of what we know today has been developed within the last 50 years, and technological know-how has grown to where knowledge builds exponentially upon each previous year's knowledge… Will Man very soon reach the technology level of Zecharia Sitchin's Anunnaki ? It is suggested that he has.

There have been many books written about the Anunnaki but we owe our understanding of these alleged progenitors of Man to an incredible latter-day scholar in Middle Eastern history and language named Zecharia Sitchin. He has presented us with a translation of Sumerian tablets in his 1978 landmark book, The 12th Planet, that main-stream historians simply ignore because they are victims of **'cognitive dissonance'** – what he has said disagrees with what they think they already know, so they discount it. Yet his work is credible, the evidence exists and is gaining in acceptance, so we need to begin a review of alternative, non-religious origins of Man with the late Mr. Sitchin and his work.

While the Anunnaki (ANU.NA.KI or "a god [ANU] comes to [NA] Earth [KI]") were not the only ETs visiting Earth, setting up camp, building structures that we still see today, and interacting with the flora and fauna, they are the best documented account that we have and as such will be used to examine Man's probable and alternate genesis.

Alternative Creation Scenarios

Zecharia Sitchin: The Anunnaki

The previous chapters were not meant so much as a detraction of the Bible, as much as it was to point out that something else appears to be happening in the origins of Man that the Bible only loosely relates. Man's origins have been revisited and made the subject of recent speculation since the discoveries and translations that have come from Zechariah Sitchin, and several others. He has produced a dozen books showing that the Bible is a very high-level allegory whose stories in Genesis are mirrored in the Sumerian accounts that he has translated from the clay tablets and cylinders found buried in old Sumerian territory – now present-day Iraq, Iran and Pakistan. And what he relates, regarding Man's origins, removes a lot of the ambiguity which has generated the superstition of the Biblical tradition.

If Sitchin is correct, what standard science has accepted as the origins of Man, including related fossil evidence from Africa, has been largely sanitized and rearranged for public consumption – to agree with the Bible's Book of Genesis, which was someone else's sanitized version of Man's creation.

According to Sitchin, Man's genesis began with the (alternate spelling:) AN.UNNAK.KI or Anunnaki ("Those who from Heaven to Earth came") who are also called "the Sons of God" (*bene elohim*) in Genesis 6, and who have been variously called Watchers equated with the IGI.GI or Igigi ("Those who observe and see", or "Watchers"). The Sumerian cuneiform clay tablets and cylinders mostly use the term Anunnaki for a group of about 600 who came to Earth looking for gold to use back on Ne.Bi.Ru, their home planet, which is allegedly in a very tilted orbit about our Sun and crosses between the orbits of Mars and Jupiter on its way back out into space.

> *Where the Anunnaki actually came from is open to speculation since it is today being recognized that their "planet of the crossing" was also a mistaken notion of earlier eras, and in reality the object that comes through every 3600 years appears to be a failed sun, a Brown Dwarf.* [54] *Nibiru is not returning.*

The Bible in Gen. 6:4 formerly used the word Nephilim for 'the fallen', but should translate it to mean 'giants' (which would be Anakim, Rephaim, or Giborim), so the biblical translation is not accurate. [55] There is some variation and confusion in terms depending on whom you read. And at times even Sitchin refers to the Anunnaki (Igigi) as the Nephilim. [56]

Terminology Clarified

Be clear : Watchers (Igigi) + Earth women => Nephilim (giants).

The Anunnaki called themselves **Anunna**, ("Sons of An") where An or Anu was the king on **Nibiru** ("the planet of the crossing") allegedly their home planet. Their abode on Earth was called E.DIN, or "Abode of the righteous ones." [57] Their name for Sumer was KI.EN.GIR ("Earth Lord of the Rockets"). Their full title was DIN.GIR ("The Righteous [Ones] of the Rocketships [*shem or GIR*]").

The **Watchers**, or Igigi are the 200-300 Anunnaki who were stationed above the Earth in ships and normally did not come down to Earth – they handled the transfer of goods between Earth ships and those bound for Mars and Nibiru. Mars was another outpost in the solar system and had more air and water – later to disappear in a number of catastrophes. [58]

The story goes that the Watchers were lonely up on the ships orbiting Earth and desired female companionship, and once the *Adapa* women were created, as the superior offspring of Enki, they were very beautiful and perhaps because they were already used to seeing reptilian hominids, the Earth women were not totally freaked out by the lusty advances of the Watchers… Perhaps that is why the genetics of the taller Watchers (8-9 feet tall) and the mammalian Earth women 'misfired' and produced giants, as well as creating some Annunaki-Human hybrids… and perhaps there are more particulars given in the Sumerian tablets that we haven't yet found (or weren't released).

According to another source, the Watchers also had a serpentine appearance.[59]

> *It is important to note that the term Watchers by Sitchin and others with respect to the Igigi has led to confusion when we come to the account by Enoch where he identifies the fallen angels as the ones guilty of mating with Earth women… For this reason, this chapter makes no distinction between ancient Watchers and Igigi. Those who fell were the Anunnaki Igigi (whose progeny were the Nephilim).*

Epic Sources

It can be noted that the ***Epic of Gigamesh*** from Sumeria correlates well with the Genesis account of the Flood (recall that the Gilgamesh version is <u>much older</u> than the Bible), and the ***Enuma Elish*** (Epic of Creation) also from the Sumerian region, correlates well with the Genesis story of Creation – and is longer and is also at least a thousand years older. There is also a Sumerian ***Atrahasis Epic*** account of mankind in Sumeria which details more of Noah and the Anunnaki activities.

The Sumerians wrote their epics in clay with much more detail than the Bible contains, and yet the two accounts are remarkably similar and tell a coherent story of creation, involving gods, that is largely unknown in Western civilization.. The main eye-opener (to be established in this chapter) is that the gods of the Sumerian tablets who created Man "in their own image and likeness" were extraterrestrials. And reptilian in appearance.

Anunnaki Discovered

Before looking at the salient points of the Anunnaki creation, it is important to briefly establish the credibility of the thousands of Sumerian tablets. One of the reasons Sitchin's account is credible is that it mirrors and explains events in the Bible. The other reason is more one of common sense: The way that the clay tablets and cylinders were found was (1) by accident while a new highway was being cut thru northern Iraq, and (2) they were hidden – not meant to be found, and (3) there are simply too many of them to have been the product of someone's imagination who had nothing else to do but create an epic myth in clay, and (4) the Sumerian creation account precedes the Bible's Genesis version by several thousand years – is that a coincidence, or did the writer of Genesis repeat the Sumerian account?

There were 25,000 clay tablets in cuneiform script which related to the Anunnaki epic, [60] and they predate the Bible by as much as 3,000 years. [61] Another 500,000 clay tablets have been found in Sumeria (today's Iraq) dealing with many general aspects of the lost civilization which was established <u>fully developed</u>. The tablets tell how the civilization was set up about 9,000 BC (following The Flood) <u>fully functioning</u>, complete with agriculture, science, math, plumbing, incredibly accurate astronomy, and writing (to name just a few aspects) and thus there was no progressive development of nomadic tribes into Sumerian civilization. There were no older layers of city built upon city built upon city as is found with most ancient civilizations in other parts of the world. [62] **Sumeria sprang up fully developed.**

> **Note: there are too many tablets, cylinders and related accounts (e.g., Enuma Elish, Epic of Gilgamesh, and the Atrahasis) for a people to have been leisurely creating a myth in their spare time. Just the time, expense, and effort of keeping it all coherent over years of effort says otherwise.**

By the way, it is interesting that the meaning of Sumer or Sumeria derives etymologically from the Sumerian: KI.EN.GIR ("Earth. Lord. Righteousness"). The implication being that the visitors brought Light to the human inhabitants, teaching them civilization skills. The Anunnaki provided Man with knowledge from their computerized disks, or perhaps crystalline stones, called *MEs* [63] which stored data/programs like flash-drives.

Academic Sumeria

While most anthropologists and historians of the ancient world tend to write off the Sumerian gods as pure myth, it is difficult to do so because the accounts are so literal and specific – not exactly the stuff of generalized myths. **Professor S.N. Kramer**, a renowned but traditionalist scholar, says:

> The Sumerian gods, as illustrated graphically by the Sumerian myths, were entirely anthropomorphic; even the most powerful and most knowing among them [Enlil, Enki…] were **conceived as human in form, thought, and deed.** Like Man, they plan and act, eat and drink, marry and raise families, support large households, and are addicted to human passions and weaknesses… Although the gods were believed to be immortal, they nevertheless had to have their sustenance; they could become sick to the point of death; they fought, wounded and killed and presumably could themselves be wounded and killed. [64] [emphasis added]

A traditional, scholarly interpretation of the Sumerian gods as myth is to be expected from Academia – and yet, to describe gods in human terms is to denigrate them – <u>they are not really gods, then.</u> Gods don't get sick. Professor Kramer says they were "human in form… and deed" and that tends to say that they looked humanoid and did human-type things –

but even the Greek gods who looked human, did <u>more</u> than human deeds and that is the mark of a real god.

As Sitchin suggests in his analysis of the Sumerian god issue, these gods were beings all too like us (in thought and deed) who just happened to come from the heavens <u>with advanced technology</u> and that latter part earned them the title of 'gods' just like the current day scientists to New Guinea mentioned earlier.

Major Anunnaki Aspects

In brief, what Mr. Sitchin has told us is: [65]

1. Mankind was developed by extraterrestrials as **a slave race** – to work in the mines in southern Africa and work the agricultural fields in Sumeria. The Anunnaki discovered earth 400,000 + years ago and grew tired of working the mines and fields, more preferring a life of leisure and to be waited on. So they created Man as **Blacks in Africa** (about 250,000 years ago) as a physically superior specimen to work the mines for gold.

2. The original species of Man could not procreate (only 22 chromosomes) and every time more workers were needed, the Anunnaki had to clone them (*in vitro*) – in their image: humanoid, fully adult, like Adam was. The emphasis was on brawn not brains in the *Lulu* ("One who serves") as the **first** created worker was called.

Note this quote from the Sumerian text *Enki and Ninmah: The Creation of Mankind*:

> The newborns' fate, thou shalt pronounce;
> Ninki would fix upon it **the image of the gods**. [66]

Ninki ("Lady of Earth") was the spouse of Lord Enki; his name means "Lord of Earth." [67] Enki had a brother Enlil ("Lord of the Command") who was in charge of the Earth expedition; Enki was more of a science officer. And it is significant that these two had disagreements about how to run the expedition and how to manage the *Lulus* (or 'Man', the term also implies 'mixed' as in hybrid). [68]

3. Against Enlil's wishes, scientist Enki later included the ability to procreate among the workers. This was a **second** genetic bit of engineering, and resulted in a human [*Adamu*] that could reason and better serve the later aims of the Anunnaki, which was to set up rulers and run the cities for them.

4. It was a 'train wreck' from that point forward: the *Lulu* and *Adamu* were noisy, crude and smelly, and occasionally their numbers had to be cut back – lest they rise up and overcome their masters. They had been given a major dose of Anunnaki genes and were becoming a violent, petty species in their own right. Enlil wanted to get rid of the humans.

5. Lastly, mankind as created in the Sumerian region was more Middle Eastern in appearance, and apparently the women were quite beautiful, leading the young Anunnaki men to have sex with them. The usual mating byproduct often resulted in hybrid **demigods**, not giants, who went on to be called Noah, Gilgamesh, Sargon, Moses, Alexander the Great… [69]

6. As time went on, Man was getting out of control; **Sodom & Gomorrah** had to be destroyed because the genetics were 'devolving' and Man was turning to all sorts of unexpected behavior, and the Rephaim (10-12' tall) who were not being 'served' by Man, began to abuse, then kill and eat Man to satisfy their huge appetites. This led to the destruction of Man and most of creation on the Earth via The Flood. Of course, Noah (Utnapishtim in the Sumerian Epic, and Ziusudra in Sitchin's translations) was warned and a genetic copy of all valuable DNA on earth was put in **cryogenic storage** under Noah's care – to restart life after the Flood. [70], [71]

7. The Anunnaki could not always stay around on earth, as the Sun's rays caused them to age prematurely, [72] so they would spend a lot of time up on their ships in orbit, or on the Moon, or even on their world which orbited thru our solar system every 3600 years. Or underground, as will be seen. The main group left Earth between 610 BC and 650 BC [73] while some stayed behind: Enki, Inanna and Nannar (Enlil's son) are probably still here. [74]

However, they dared not leave Man unattended – so a skeleton Anunnaki crew was set up (living underground), and another human race was created and chosen to infiltrate and make sure that Man never got it together and became his own master, thus supporting Anunnaki control. This **alternate human race's** job was to create enough subterfuge, chaos and deception that Man would always be kept off-guard and suspicious of other men. This 'controller' race was headquartered in an area that later became known as Khazaria.

While this is not Sitchin's teaching, it is noted that God in Genesis 2 created Man with a soul and the 2nd beings (*Adamu*) later created by the Anunnaki had a soul – so the Anunnaki may also have had souls, but this is not a 'given' … merely that *Adamu's* mental and body attributes were such that souls <u>could</u> inhabit those bodies, whereas the *Lulus* were seen as too primitive. The *Lulus*, or first Anunnaki creation, did not need a soul and their DNA being incomplete (just enough to activate the body), they could not sustain a connection to the God force, nor pursue spiritual goals. When intelligence was needed, the DNA could be changed to give the *Lulus* higher centers and a larger frontal lobe area in the brain, thus encouraging souls to enter these bodies, and these were called *Adamu*. And because the Watchers found the later Earth women (*Adapa*) very desirable, and lusted after them, some DNA improving the looks of early Man and Woman must also have been added.

Now we have a choice: the soulless humans that were allegedly created by Yaltabaoth, according to the Gnostics, were probably the same as *Lulu* as created by the Anunnaki in one of their initial attempts to create a worker human. The Gnostics seem to have been obliquely relating the Anunnaki story and disguised it, calling Enlil Yaltabaoth…?

Somehow it is easier to accept the 3D Anunnaki hypothesis versus the interdimensional account of the Gnostics… and it will later be seen that the Gnostics <u>were</u> probably referring to the same group.

Creation Of Man

There were **several 'creations' of Man** – from the first *Lulu* then *Adamu* to the later more refined, intelligent and self-sustaining *Adapa* ('model man'). Some scholars have seen the *Adamu* of Genesis 2 and the *Adapa* of the Sumerian epic as a similar being. [75] What is interesting is that the Anunnaki mixed their own genetics with that of a pre-existing bipedal hominid on the Earth. And even more interesting is that the *Atrahasis Epic* from Sumeria gives a rather grizzly account of how the Anunnaki genetics were obtained:

> On the first, seventh and fifteenth of the month,
> He made a purification by washing,
> Ilawela who had intelligence,
> They slaughtered in their assembly.
> Nintu mixed clay with his flesh and blood. [76]

The Anunnaki morality was such that they were not above sacrificing one of their own to obtain the genetic material. And that is a little weird since they could have gotten his DNA without killing him – unless they were after his body parts, too, but that is not said.

According to Boulay:

> Since the previous experiment in the laboratories of the spaceship did not turn out successfully, it was decided to commission Enki, working with the Chief Nurse Ninhursag, to produce a primitive being. This creation, called a *Lulu* by the Anunna, was to be the first primitive man.

> Enki and Ninhursag conducted a number of experiments in the Abzu [Africa], and Enki's floating laboratory near Eridu [southern Sumeria]… **There were many attempts which ended in failure** for one reason or another…. Finally a successful method was found… [but] the process had one main drawback… the creatures were **clones** [*Lulus*] and could not reproduce themselves.

> In this manner, the first primitive man or Adam was created, looking like its creator(s)… the gods' essence is mixed with the malleable clay of the earth [Earth-based genetics]. In the Sumerian tablets, the clay is mixed with the essence of the gods and upon this creation they "impressed upon it the image of the gods."

> The Adam of the Bible was not the Homo *sapiens* of today. He was what one might call Homo-*saurus*, a hybrid mammal-reptile creature that was to become our ancestor and the first step in the creation of modern man. [See pictures, next section.]

> Since the Adam of Genesis [1] and the *Lulu* of the Sumerians were created in

the image of the serpent-gods, shouldn't traces of this fact be found in some of the ancient scriptures?... Indeed, it is... One tract describes Eve's reaction in the Garden of Eden:

> She looked at the tree. And she saw that it was beautiful and magnificent, and she desired it. She took some of its fruit and ate and she gave to her husband also, and he ate, too. Then their minds opened. For when they ate, the light of knowledge shone for them. When they put on shame, they knew they were naked with regard to knowledge. When they sobered up, they saw that they were naked, and they became enamored of one another. *When they saw their makers,* **they loathed them** *since they were beastly forms.* [77] [emphasis added]

The human hybrid that was created probably looked semi-reptilian since he was created "in the image of God." [78]

Dinosauroids

On a related note, paleontologist **Dale Russell**, curator of vertebrate fossils at the National Museum of Canada in Ottawa, has speculated what the smarter species of dinosaur, the Raptors, could have evolved into had they undergone an evolution of their own, and he theorizes that they could have looked like what this book calls a Homo *saurus*, or to use his term, a "dinosauroid:"

Homo *saurus?*
(Source: http://en.wikipedia.org/wiki/Reptilian_humanoid)

Could this be close to what the Anunnaki looked like and in whose image Man was created?

It looks similar to the next statue image…which is what the **Ubaid** people made as an image of their gods. The viper/serpent issue rises again in the ancient proto-Sumerian stone statue (below) from **UR** in Mid Iraq that pictures a serpent-type being created back in 3500 BC: (See map of Eden in Chapter 1 for location of Ur and Ubaid.)

Sumerian Serpent Goddess Statue
(Source: http://www.bibliotecapleyades.net/sumer_anunnaki/reptiles/reptiles40.htm)

Reptilian Image

Is this why God (Yahweh) would not let Moses see his face on Mount Sinai? It was also an injunction to Man to not have any "graven images" of God around – therefore His appearance had to be withheld from Man, and the ziggurats served to distance the Anunnaki from Man.[79] And yet, there <u>are</u> some small reptilian statues pictured (Ubaid statue shown above) in some of David Icke's books, and Icke's African shaman friend, Credo Mutwa, wears an ancient 'creation story' necklace containing the figure of a reptile, an Earth woman and a UFO. (Appendix F has more serpent images from around the world.)

Berossus, a Babylonian priest writing about the appearance of the gods, said that Man's ancestry traced back to the **Oannes**, an amphibious creature which came to teach civilization to Man.

Berossus called them ***Annedoti*** which means "the repulsive ones" in Greek.

81

He also refers to them as *musarus* or an "abomination." It is in this way that Babylonian tradition credits the founding of civilization to a creature which they considered to be a "repulsive abomination." [80]

According to another source, the reason 'Annedoti' looks like 'Anunnaki' is because the **Oannes were another name for the Anunnaki**. [81], [82]

One would think that if the gods were so superior and grand as indicated in ancient texts that they would be flattered to have Man make images of them, and display their greatness. But, after Man was created, the gods forbade Man to make images of them and they tended to stay atop their Mesopotamian ziggurats and Mayan pyramids to be waited on by certain servants who knew the truth, but did not speak of the gods with the worker population below, or in the city and fields, that had been created to serve the Annuna. So their physical **repulsiveness** must be true, otherwise Man would have flattered and praised their god's appearance. And again, the reptilian nature of the Anunnaki is explicit in the Sumerian accounts:

> **The reptiles verily descend**,
> The Earth is resplendent as a well-watered garden,
> At that time Enki and Eridu [his city] had not appeared,
> Daylight did not shine,
> **Moonlight had not emerged**. [83] [emphasis added]

> *Note: the absence of Moonlight is also addressed at the end of Appendix A.*

The above refers to the fact that the watery firmament was still in place above the Earth (disappearing later during The Flood?). In addition, the Sumerians referred to the Anunnaki as USHUMGAL – "great fiery flying serpents" – referring to them in their rocketships. From thence came the stories of **Dragons**, since rocketships spit fire and flew through the air. [84]

And while Man got the Anunnaki DNA characteristics, which should have been an uplifting, improvement to the Homo *erectus* base genetics, the mix resulted in a human population that later drove Enlil crazy – the constant noise and activity, even violence, among the worker groups was too much, as discussed later.

And things haven't changed that much even today. The average human cannot sit still without having to have something to listen to, eat, do or watch. Today's youngsters cannot stay with a TV program that doesn't have a lot of action, noise and color … or their attention wanders. And some of the older teens and people in their twenties have not outgrown this tendency: How many young people have to have MP3 going while they work or, God forbid, text while they are driving? And they have to have repetitive Rap or Heavy Metal or Country Music going – they cannot sit and enjoy peace and quiet. ADD and ADHD may be rooted in some very primitive genes. (Chapter 9 explains this.)

Reptilian to Mammalian

So if Man was created as a semi-reptilian hominid (the original *Lulu*), in his god's image and likeness, how is it he is today, a <u>mammalian</u> hominid?

An ancient source in the *Haggadah* said that **Man in the beginning was semi-reptilian**:

> Before their bodies had been *overlaid with a horny skin, and enveloped with the cloud of glory*. No sooner had they violated the command given them [to not eat of the Tree] that *the cloud of glory and* **the horny skin** *dropped from them*, and they stood there in their nakedness, and ashamed (emphasis ours).

> Describing man before the Fall, it was said that "his skin was as bright as daylight and covered his body like a luminous garment." This luminous and bright skin or hide was their "cloud of glory." [85]

That sounds like a **very fine coat of scales** that glistened in the sunlight. But Man had to have clothing for protection as he had (above symbolically) gone thru another of Enki's genetic updates that gave Man the ability to procreate, and as this was a mammalian trait (giving live birth), so Man, or *Lulu*, picked up more (dominant) mammalian DNA in the process, and Man was then called *Adamu*.

> Now that Man required clothing… an apparent sympathetic deity "made shirts of skins for the Man and his wife, and clothed them." This generous deity, however, probably had other reasons in mind, for as the *Haggadah* reveals, the clothes were made of **skins sloughed off by the serpents**. Was this done to remind Man of his serpent origins? It was an ironic way of impressing on Man's memory that he originated as a saurian and that **he existed at the tolerance of the gods**. [86] [emphasis added]

If Man had retained his reptilian form, and the longevity that went with it, he would have been like a mule, a limited Homo *saurus* – unable to procreate. By gaining the ability to procreate, he saved the Annuna a lot of work because up until Man could reproduce himself, the Anunnaki had to make more workers by cloning them, and that was very time-consuming, and error-prone. And in the process of gaining reproductive ability, Man had to be given <u>mammalian</u> DNA to support live birth, since most reptiles give birth to eggs which have to be hatched.

> The sad story is that Man could not have the best of two possible worlds, mammal form and long life. It explains why **Man's lifespan shortened steadily** as each generation diluted the saurian gene more and more… The gods were unhappy with the ensuing changes… To them the reptile form was "divine" and the further Man evolved from his saurian origins, the less he remembered his saurian origins. [87] [emphasis added]

It is significant that the Anunnaki genetics still passed to the hybrid offspring, often creating demigods, "men of renown" as the Bible says. And yet the humanized, mammalian off-spring still had some recessive reptilian features that every now and then showed themselves – babies might have tails, patches of scaly skin (like Noah), vestiges of cranial horns (like Moses), and of course Man has had the reptilian brain stem as part of his 3-part brain for centuries (examined in 'Horns and Crowns' section).

Apparently, the mammalian genetics had morphed enough to where the Anunnaki DNA merging with it resulted in the dominance of the mammalian genetics. (See Epigenetics topic in Chapter 9.)

The "divine" race was becoming diluted and the mammalian genes appeared to **dominate the reptilian strain** which became recessive. [88] [emphasis added]

Inanna and Marduk

Statues of Inanna and Marduk, offspring of the original reptilian Anunnaki, are shown as human, and **Inanna was said to be quite beautiful**. Obviously Enki had a hand in this since he was the genetics expert and especially favored his human creation. In fact, Enki had relations with two *Adamu* women and the result was a much-improved hybrid, very much human, called *Adapa*. Is it but a short step to inseminate Anunnaki women, such as Ninti, Enki's wife, with hybrid seed and she then gives birth to Marduk in a **hybrid** human (mammalian) form?

Inanna, for example, was said to be quite pretty, like Anna the Queen on **V**, the TV Series. Inanna was also known as Ishtar, Astarte, and Athena and was born of Anunnaki parents on Earth. [89]

Inanna, Queen of the Indus Valley
(credit: Bing Images)

The statue on the left is more flattering, but the one on the right is an older image which reflects her Anunnaki "roots" (her feet), and the wings indicating her way of flying around the Sumerian area in her **hovercraft.** In both pictures, she has her regal crown of horns on her head (indicating rank). Her rank was 15, so 1 horn is a more correct image. When she ruled the Indus Valley, she may have had herself pictured with 3 horns – more than she was entitled to. Owls symbolize wisdom and she holds rods of power – from which the Egyptian ankh was derived and stylized.

Horns and Crowns

Related to the issue of Anunnaki appearance was the comment by Sitchin that the Anunnaki king, Anu, had a rank of 60, Enlil had a rank of 50, and Enki had a rank of 40, Inanna had a rank of 15 (women had odd-numbered ranks), and all their ranks were indicated by horns. [90], [91]   In most drawings of the main Anunnaki leaders, they have hats signifying rank. Enki has a hat with 4 horns on it. [92]   Each horn was worth 10 points.

Horns represented rank, power and ultimately, kingship. Since there was an injunction to not depict the Anunnaki as they really were, could it be that the drawings of men wearing hats with horns was the only way the artists could depict the Anunnaki and live to tell about it?   (See Sitchin's drawing of Enki next page.)

As they were reptilian, many of the Internet pictures of reptilian entities
(seen by people around the world) show them with the horns actually coming
out of their heads… [like the Sith in *Star Wars*?] perhaps that is the way the horns looked? Refer to the pictures of Moses and Alexander the Great which follow—they are pictured with vestigial horns coming from their skulls.

The Sith of Star Wars

(credit: http://en.wikipedia.org/wiki/File:Star_Wars_Episode_1)

The following is a drawing of **Enki** from Sitchin's The 12th Planet, p.130. Note the 4 horns, and the life-giving symbology of the water. Enki was always associated with water. He was also called E.A – which means "place [E] on the water [A]" and Enki's house was located at the edge of the watered plain. He was also later called **Poseidon**, and had another home in ancient Atlantis.

(Source: The Twelfth Planet, Z. Sitchin, p. 130)

It is also said that since kings were established by the Anunnaki to rule in their stead (by 'divine right'), the human hybrids did not have horns indicating rank, and so they wore crowns, **which is why Kings' crowns all had points on them**, and those points also originally indicated power, or rank.

Most kings' crowns had 7-8 points on them, and later, symbolic of submission to a Divine authority in the Church, the points would converge inward connecting to a single orb surmounted with a cross.

Hybrids and Horns

And an examination of Sitchin's books will reveal that there were hybrid gods in the years before the Anunnaki left Earth, leaving such outstanding examples as Alexander the Great, Gilgamesh, Sargon, Nimrod, Odin and Noah – part Man, part Annuna (i.e., hybrid). And as the mammalian genes continued to dominate, Man was left with the core reptilian brain, and the useless coccyx, and a decline in abilities that had been natural to the Anunnaki.

Even today, there are people born into our world with horns on their head, a recessive vestige of the Anunnaki genetic inheritance. [93] In fact, that is nothing new… **Alexander the Great** was depicted with small horns on his forehead on some of his coins, **Moses** was said to have two small horns on his head (see pictures below).

 The Russian monk **Rasputin** was said to have a bump on his forehead (over which he combed his hair to hide it)... his daughter Maria described it as "…an odd little bump, reminiscent of a budding horn." [94], [95] And Rasputin was probably the proud possessor of some hybrid Anunnaki genes since he was clairvoyant and could heal people.

Statue of Moses
(source: http://en.wikipedia.org/wiki/File:Moses_San_Pietro_in_Vincoli.jpg)

The following is a coin commemorating **Alexander the Great**… with horns.

Credit: kingofmacedon.net via Yahoo [96]

If the great men of yore were Anunnaki hybrids, they could still have had reptilian vestiges, such as horns. It's interesting that they were portrayed that way, so it must have been a compliment… otherwise it would have been banned.

If the Anunnaki were just like Man, i.e., non-reptilian (according to Sitchin), then where did the reptilian recessive genes come from in Man's genetics? And why did some of the ancients make such a fuss about their gods being 'repulsive'?

Interesting Similarity

It has been said that we get our system of rank on soldiers' sleeves from the Anunnaki system of horns denoting rank. The horns have been replaced by chevrons…

Here is an Anunnaki rank (of 40 = 4 horns) and the US military ranking:

Enki's Rank of 40   US army Sergeant   US Air Force E5 SSGT

Coincidence?

Horns Still Afflict People

Because the Anunnaki were originally reptilian, and some reptiles do have horns, when they merged their DNA with that of an earth-bound hominid, to create the *Adamu*, the reptilian genetics not only gave Man his reptile stem (lowest part of the brain), it also passed some DNA for horns (and sometimes tails).

(credit: Bing Images)

Apparently the gene which grows a horn on a human was not completely eradicated … and we later hear of Rasputin sporting a budding horn just covered by his hair.

DNA Flawed

This is significant as it is a major point in this book that the genetic material that Man inherited was flawed, or corrupted. Man's traits, both good and bad, can be the product of Anunnaki DNA (or Anunnaki DNA that was later modified by other visiting ETs). In addition, Enlil is pretty cold-hearted when he permits the coming Flood to wipe out not only Enki's creation, Man, but the offspring of the Nephilim. [97] And Enki himself was pretty busy keeping the genetics flowing, kind of like a former-day **Rasputin** himself – small wonder where Rasputin got his (genetic) sex drive.

In all seriousness, to say Enki was "horny" was not a joke. Perhaps this is where the expression comes from, since the Anunnaki were known to have strong sexual appetites[98] and horns.

For another example, it was accepted practice among the Anunnaki for a brother to marry his sister or cousin, just as the Egyptian dynastic lines did.[99] The Anunnaki gods Enki and Enlil shared their sister Ninhursag; Enki fathering Marduk, and Enlil fathering Ninurta. This kept the bloodline pure and marriage between Anunnaki and *Adapa* was originally forbidden, then frowned on, and then ignored. Egypt had the same practice among the Pharaohs.

In fact, this ability to marry, or just have sex with whomever, produced three interesting results – about the time the *Adapa* was created:

1. Enki procreated with Nergal and created **Lilith** – a "pure" Anunnaki line;
2. Enki also had sex with (Adam's) Eve and created a hybrid, or an ultra-hybridized Anunnaki-human line, called ***Adapa;***
   …remember that one of the Gnostic stories had Yaldabaoth having relations with Eve, yielding Cain… was the Sumerian Anunnaki account the source?
3. And then there was the original, prior Adam and Eve line (*Adamu* and *Tiamat*), a "pure" human line. [100] See Chart 1A.

Later, indiscriminate intercourse with the **third** Enki creation, the *Adapa (2ⁿᵈ Adam)* and *Titi (2ⁿᵈ Eve)*, created **hybrids** and problems -- eventually raising Enlil's wrath as he wanted to keep the lineage pure and have his people take pride in the Anunnaki genetic heritage. Besides the humans' constant racket, this was another reason Enlil wanted to destroy the humans.

Enlil was also upset about the hybrid humans as they posed a threat to the Anunnaki – no longer was it the submissive and not-too-bright *Adamus* – now it was the *Adapas* who were almost as smart as the Anunnaki. [101] This would be remedied.

ENKI, Lord [En] of Earth [Ki]

The hybrids have been described as 'chimerical' – "an organism containing a mixture of genetically different tissues," and "a DNA molecule with sequences derived from 2 or more different organisms, formed by laboratory manipulation." [102] And that describes not only the first *Lulu*, and the later *Adapa*, but it also describes Enki:

> ....there is an odd corroboration of the tradition of chimerical offspring of such unions from yet another source, and this is the traditional depiction of Enki, who is sometimes "shown with the legs of a goat complete with cloven hooves, whilst his upper body is clothed in the scales of a fish." He is a "goatfish", a Capricorn. Enki himself, in other words, is a chimerical being, who in turn, as a 'son of God' in the Biblical perspective, sires similar chimerical offspring [*Adapa*]. [103]

This would explain his heart for his chimerical offspring, Adam and Eve, and why he protects them in the Garden from Enlil's wrath, and later from Enlil's decision to let a Flood to cleanse the Earth.

But more than that, it is reported that Enki was at least one-half amphibian:

> [Carl] Sagan goes on to discuss some fascinating creatures credited with founding the Sumerian civilization (which sprang up out of nowhere, as many Sumerian archaeologists will unhappily admit). They are described in a classical account by Alexander Polyhistor as **amphibious**. He says they were happier if they could go back to the sea at night and return to dry land in the daytime.... It is these Sumerians to whom Sagan has just referred, with their legend of an amphibious creature [Oannes] who founded their civilization. [104]

Why is that important? Without going into all the detail, it can be noted that

> ...the amphibious creature **Oannes**, who brought civilization to the Sumerians, is sometimes equated with the god Enki (Ea) who ruled the star Canopus of the *Argo*. Enki is a god who sleeps at the bottom of a watery abyss, reminiscent of Oannes who retired to the sea at night. [105]

And Sitchin himself has said as much:

> Though the Nephilim in time established a spaceport on dry land, some evidence suggests that at least initially they landed by splashing down into the sea in a hermetically sealed capsule.... In ancient texts and pictures, the craft of the Nephilim were initially termed **"celestial boats."** The landing of such "maritime" astronauts... might have been described in ancient epic tales as the appearance of some kind of submarine from the heavens in the sea from which **"fish-men"** emerged and came ashore.
>
> The texts do, in fact, mention that some of the AB.GAL who navigated the spaceships were dressed as fish. One text...[speaks of a chief navigator] who had gone away "in a sunken boat." [106] [emphasis added]

The "sunken boat" is elsewhere called *elippu tebiti* – "sunken ship," for a craft that can go underwater like a submarine. [107] Today's USOs?

The Sumerian account tells us that Enki has two names: EN.KI ("Lord of the Earth") and E.A ("[whose] house/place is water"). [108] Eridu, which was Enki's city on dry land, was built on ground artificially raised above the marshland water – **reminiscent of the Aztec city of Tenochtitlán** (Chapter 10), no doubt. Enki himself says:

> When I approached Earth, there was much flooding…
> I built my house in a pure place…
> My house – its shade stretches over the Snake Marsh…[109]

Reptibians

And the house was appropriately named E.ABZU ("House of the Deep"). It was built on serpent-infested swampland. All of this to establish that Enki was an amphibian-looking humanoid. Or maybe he was more reptilian, like a serpent, or both: **a 'Reptibian.'** But in any case, he later came to be associated with serpents and adopted the symbol which we now use in our *caduceus.* He was also called a *Nachash*, or 'one who knows secrets.' Ea or Enki was like a medical officer among the Anunnaki and in ancient Babylonian times, wisdom was symbolized by the Serpent. [110] **Moses** also lifted up a bronze serpent on a stick while in the wilderness to get his people healed (Appendix E).

In addition, it adds credibility to the Sumerians' account of the Anunnaki that "…the amphibians to whom they owed everything were disgusting, horrible and loathsome to look upon." [111] Again, a more normal approach would have been to glorify the gods who founded the civilization, but "… instead we find specific descriptions of 'animals endowed with reason' (Alexander Polyhistor's account) who make their awed and thankful beneficiaries want to be sick with revulsion. And what is more, tradition admits this freely!" [112]

Were they really completely amphibians, then how did they walk on land? Polyhistor recounts Berossus (an ancient Babylonian priest of the era 290 BC) as saying:

The whole body of the animal [**Oannes**] was like that of a fish; and had under a fish's head another head, and also feet below, similar to those of a man, subjoined to the fish's tail. His voice, too, and language, was articulate and human; and a representation of him is preserved even to this day. [113] (See picture, left)

The gods admonished Man to not make (accurate) pictures of them, so any image on a temple wall is suspect. And the image looks like a man wearing a "fish cape" and obviously a humanoid wearing a fish-like 'cape' and what appear to be bracelets. As they were technologically advanced, those 'bracelets' may be watches or communication devices.

(Credit: Bing Images)

Another possibility is that Enki was part amphibian, part reptile, sort of an amphibious reptile – a **Reptibian**. And could the descriptions of him as part amphibious be due to his donning scuba-like gear for underwater work? Whatever it was, as we have seen, the reports said that the original Anunnaki were "repulsive."

> *Earlier it was seen that the Anunnaki offspring born on Earth, such as Inanna, were more human because the goddess Inanna was the result of further genetic modifications so that the Anunnaki could interface with the humans. (See 'Revelation' section this chapter.)*

Alternate View

In another work of research, the author suggests that Enki was known as the **Dragon** (in the same way that some esoteric societies have a Grand Dragon as headmaster), and in his city of Eridu there were **People of the Serpent**, whose sacred rituals were designed to promote and facilitate the awakening of kundalini in the initiates. In addition, the veneration of the Serpent in Mesopotamia is an oblique reference to the Celestial Serpent, the Pleiades.

So that's a possible answer to the appearance of Enki/Oannes, and an interesting link to the Pleiades which may be a home of some the Anunnaki…

ENLIL, Lord [En] of the Command [Lil]

Enlil and Enki were brothers, but Enlil's rank was that of 50 and Enki's was 40. **ANU**, the Anunnaki king (reigning over their own planet of Nibiru) held a rank of 60. Enlil was also Anu's eldest son, and was made the ruler of Earth, presiding over meetings of the Anunnaki Elders on Earth. Enlil was all-powerful, and "… the gods of Sumer [50 Elder Anunnaki from Nibiru] considered Enlil to be Supreme." [114] Enlil took one wife and was faithful to her, unlike Enki who had intercourse with his half-sister, then Eve (of the *Adamu* line), and later Lilith and Inanna of the pure Anunnaki line, among others. [115]

In the Mesopotamian texts, it is Enlil who is unhappy with the way Mankind turns out, it is Enlil who decides to let a Flood wipe out Mankind[116], and it is Enlil who created and runs E.DIN ("home of the righteous ones"). Reminiscent of Yahweh…

Enlil and the Humans

As it is relevant to Enlil's treatment of the *Adapa*, it bears mentioning <u>why</u> he would seek to wipe mankind out after letting Enki create and train them.

For starters there was an Anunnaki law that forbade creating <u>new</u> beings wherever they went, and Enki got around that by (1) claiming that all he had done was 'upgrade' an existing hominid, and (2) the Council accepted that because of the dire need for workers to mine the gold which was sorely needed back on Nibiru to allegedly provide an atmospheric shield. (See 'Sitchin Expose' section, following.)

Secondly, Man was a hybrid of the gods and contained some Anunnaki genetics, and maybe body parts, too. Perhaps Enlil expected too much of Man – to somehow live up to the proud Anunnaki heritage. At any rate, the Sumerian *Atrahasis Epic* account of mankind in Sumeria has this to say about *Adapa*:

> And the country became too wide, **the people too numerous**.
> The country was as **noisy** as a bellowing bull.
> The God [Enlil] grew restless at their **racket**,
> Enlil had to listen to their noise.
> He addressed the great [50 Anunnaki] gods,
> > "The noise of mankind has become too much,
> > I am losing sleep over their racket.
> > Cut off food supplies to the people!" [117]

In addition to famine, Enlil used ***suruppu* and *asakku* diseases**[118] to thin their numbers, and then Atrahasis [aka Noah] beseeches Enki to step in and stop Enlil from killing mankind outright. [119] What actually happened, as Sitchin reveals, is that the **Antarctic icecap** was unstable and Enlil knew that Nibiru's flyby unseating it would create a Deluge – and it inundated Africa northward to Sumeria (a 'localized' flood). [120] The Sumerian *Epic of Gilgamesh* says that the flood came from the south. [121]

After The Flood, mankind had survived, and Enlil was furious. He would later, much like Yahweh, use the humans to fight his battles for him; humans were then trained in war techniques and weapons and ordered to fight whomever the gods declared was the enemy of the day – even other gods and hybrid kings. This was how the gods acquired territory from each other and allegedly settled disputes.[122] In fact Sodom & Gomorrah were nuked by Enlil to stop Marduk from gaining control over the Sinai Spaceport; the gods had awesome technological weapons and freely used them. [123] (See Appendix A: Mars' scar.)

Lastly, Enlil did not like other Anunnaki procreating with humans, creating hybrids, and since the Anunnaki were aging too fast on Earth, there were plans in the works to leave, and the plan included wiping out all the humans and the hybrids.

Suruppu Disease

The Sumerian *Atrahasis Epic* is quite clear that Enlil at a point after The Flood DID afflict Mankind with ***Suruppu* disease** and a great part of the population died as a result. Man was just too hard to control and besides starvation, disease was another way to make the point that the gods were tired of the noise, the overpopulation, and lack of control.

> **Note:** *Atrahasis was the name of Noah who lived in Shurrupak,[124] hence the name of the disease reflects the city and locale. He was also Utnapishtim and Ziusudra depending on country and epic source.*

Post Flood, before 6-4000 BC, the disease was released upon Man and according to the Epic:

> The gods send the disease and the humans suffer with many loss of lives [sic].
> However there was one among the population Atrahasis [Noah] who had the

ear of his creator and friend to human-kind Enki. Atrahasis asks his master how long will the gods make them suffer, will they suffer the illness forever. Wise Enki then gives Atrahasis instruction on how to have the illness removed. Atrahasis does as Enki instructed and the illness is removed from the human population.[125]

Is it possible that the viral disease that we today call HIV/AIDS was the original *Suruppu* disease of centuries ago? Or The Plague? Or Ebola? The Anunnaki were master geneticists and it would not have been beyond their ability to create HIV/*Suruppu* and later implement the CCR5 gene with the *delta*32 mutation (32 base pairs deleted) to suppress the disease… and as Man survived, over the centuries the genetic advantage was passed down through succeeding generations. An interesting possibility…

> The most recent genetic studies… have shown that **CCR5delta32** actually arose much earlier in human history than previously thought— around 5,000 years ago—and that it was just as common in Europeans 3,000 years ago as it is now. [126] Was this the Anunnaki 'cure?'

Their dating is pretty accurate, if The Flood occurred about 10,500 BC as some scholars have insisted, and Enlil suffered 5000 years before releasing *Suruppu* disease on the over-populating humans… it would take time for the post-flood human population to reach a significant number to cause a major racket. Nonetheless, the Anunnaki 'fix' left its mark and according to the same quoted source, about 2% of mankind (largely in Northern Europe) is immune to HIV. [127]

Disease Control

Bramley in his book <u>The Gods of Eden</u> also makes an interesting connection between disease and the ETs. He substantially cites documents from AD 1347 – 1849 in which the inhabitants of Europe and Asia reported 'comets' and glowing spheres in their skies followed by mists on the ground which events were then followed by disease, including the Black Plague. Sometimes the 'lethal mists' affected plants and trees.

> The link between unusual aerial phenomena and the Black Death was established immediately during the first outbreaks of the Plague in Asia. As one historian tells us:
>> The first reports [of the Plague] came out of the East… of comets and meteors trailing noxious gases that killed trees and destroyed the fertility of the land.
>
> The above passage indicates that strange flying objects were doing more than just spreading disease… [128]

And again he adds

> Sightings of unusual aerial phenomena usually occurred from several minutes to a year before an outbreak of Plague. Where there was a gap between such a sighting and the arrival of the Plague, a second phenol-

menon was sometimes reported: the appearance of frightening humanlike figures dressed in black. [129]

He goes on to say that these figures were seen [in AD 1559] in the town's agricultural fields, apparently using scythes to cut the oats, but it was apparently a sort of spraying equipment and the Plague would follow very soon after. The townspeople understood these events as a sign from God that they were being punished – and indeed it was the 'gods' doing it to them.

This slight addendum to the *Suruppu* information above is to emphasize that disease has been used since the time of the Anunnaki to control Man's numbers. While the Black Plague was not necessarily the *Suruppu* or *Asakku* diseases, some hybrids (Remnants) are still here and intend to limit Man's numbers – (**Georgia Guidestones** Chapter 11).

Enlil and Yahweh

With the Biblical Yahweh using a Flood to wipe out wicked Mankind, and Yahweh as the Lord who ran Eden, is it really hard to see that Enlil was Yahweh? Enlil was the Lord of Eden, and he wanted to wipe out obnoxious mankind. [130] Sitchin evaluates several Anunnaki gods or leaders for the role of Yahweh, but none fits so well as that of Enlil (and later, Marduk [Enki's son]).

In addition, **Enlil's attributes match those of Yahweh**. Enlil was a strict law-giver and had a host of attendants to do his bidding. Enlil could be harsh and punishment was swift, or he could be very rewarding to those who carried out their assigned tasks. Enlil was known to the Sumerians as Father Enlil, the all-beneficent. Enlil was also the one who had to approve the local kingship list – local hybrid humans who had been setup by **'divine right'** to rule over the rest of the *Adapa*, just as Yahweh gave the right to rule to his loyal subjects in the Bible.

Says Sitchin:

> These two characteristics of Enlil – strictness and punishment for transgressions, benevolence and protection when merited – are similar to how Yahweh has been pictured in the Bible. Yahweh can bless and Yahweh can accurse, the Book of Deuteronomy explicitly states… In all that, **Yahweh and Enlil emulated each other**. [131] [emphasis added]

In a move to unify humans and show their loyalty to him, Enlil required that if humans were going to be "his people," they **circumcise** each other AND follow his commandments that he gave to Moses. (It is all in the Sumerian tablets.) [132]

Rewind: Anunnaki Appearance

The issue of Anunnaki appearance is relatively important, so it is re-examined here. Nowhere does Sitchin say what the Anunnaki looked like, and yet we have allusions to amphibians, talk of Serpents, and David Icke, Boulay, Tellinger, and earlier Berossus and the *Haggadah* who say they were reptilian:

> Enlil was the leader of the Anunnaki on Earth, according to the Sumerian tablets, and they refer to him as the "**splendid serpent** of the shining eyes."[133]

> A Sumerian tablet dating back to around 3500 BC leaves us in no doubt as it describes the arrival of the Anunnaki: **"The reptiles verily descend."** [ref: **The Book of Dzyan**] In Hebrew myth, the Biblical "Nephilim," the "sons of the gods," are called *awwim*, which means devastators or... serpents. Even [an academic like] Dr. Arthur David Horn.... has concluded that humanity was seeded by an extraterrestrial race and that the Anunnaki were reptilian. [134] [emphasis added]

> *Note: the word 'Dzyan' is pronounced as Zion.* [135]

Height Issue

Another aspect that has been ignored is that of height. Since the Nephilim were Anunnaki, and their offspring were sometimes giants, it is not inappropriate to suggest that the Anunnaki were taller than humans --- 8-9' tall. This is also suggested by some of the drawings by the Sumerians where the Anunnaki god is larger than the humans pictured in the same scene. [136], [137] When the pictured scene is all Anunnaki gods, they are all the same height (except for those seated). [138]

> *Chapter 10 will examine the structure of the Mayan pyramids with regard to the builders' height and the spacing of the steps leading up the pyramids.*

In the picture below, the seated Anunnaki god is larger than the human subjects, not because of his importance, but because he actually was taller... 8-9' on average. The humans had been created about 5' tall.

The god pictured (left) was obviously 9-10' tall and as Chapter 2 examined, there were giants among Man in ancient days. The disk on the wall is the symbol of Nibiru.

Note Seated god (Shamash) and 4-Horned Headdress.
(source: http://www.blinkbits.com/blinks/anunnaki)

The tablet above is from about 900 BC in the Temple of Shamash at Sippar. He was worshipped as the Sun god who traversed the sky every day. He also commanded the **astronauts at Baalbek** and was also called **the god Sin** – who later ruled the Moon. He was also Inanna's twin and Enlil's grandson. Shamash ruled in Lebanon, notably Baalbek – see picture in Chapter 4. He was said to measure the Earth… he is holding a ruler's rod.

> **Note: it was possible for a human to be born in Sin (i.e., the Moon) as Enki moved his genetics lab to the Moon and created some humans there.**

Revelation

Hang on to your hats. There is an answer to what the Anunnaki looked like in their later years on Earth. And it makes perfect sense, considering Enki's wizardry with genetics. In the beginning as many quotes have shown, the Anunnaki descended as **Reptibians,** created Man, and found themselves rejected – repulsive – to their creation. So they build ziggurats and stay apart, so the masses can't see them, and they rule through human priest intermediaries.

Then Enki creates a human **mammalian** upgrade, the *Adapa*, and has sex with it, creating the very comely *Adapa* women – which turn on the Watchers. It is not hard to see that future Anunnaki born on the planet, Marduk, Inanna, Dumuzi, Nergal etc were Anunnaki **hybrids** – human-looking with the best of Anunnaki genetics in their DNA. These were the 3rd or 4th major generation of Anunnaki born on Earth, [139] and it was said that Inanna was extremely beautiful – obviously she was no longer Homo *saurus*, but had to be a human-like Anunnaki (Elite) hybrid. [140]

The original Anunnaki, Enlil, Enki, Ninharsag, Ninmah, etc from the original landing party, stayed Reptibian – proud of their heritage, and they stayed up in their ziggurats, or ships – hidden from human view – and prohibited Man from making idols or drawings of them.

Such 'evolutionary' change in Anunnaki appearance would explain the differences in Anunnaki description and appearance by the researchers that is so common when one digs deeper into the issue.

The ultimate issue is what were the ET beings' traits and what DNA legacy did they pass on to us? The record shows that the Anunnaki could be petty, violent, back-biting, power-crazy, lusty and rebellious, but they could also be kind and patient. Enlil had hoped to wipe out Mankind with The Flood, and afterward when he discovered that Man had survived The Flood, Enki was able to convince him to relent and see the humans as useful… and have some of Noah's barbecue. And yet, in some ways their personal morals could be those of 'vipers' as Jesus later called their offspring. Man inherited some of the Anunnaki DNA and traits.

Rewind: Anunnaki Appearance

Sitchin's works also inform us that the word *Nachash* in the Garden (normally translated as 'Serpent') could also be translated as "a Diviner" and "he who unveils secrets". [141] These were all "epithets applied to Enki, who in a subsequent genetic manipulation of *Adamu* gave Adam and Eve **'knowing' – the biblical term for the ability to procreate.**"[142] So the entity in the Garden that tempted Eve could have been Enki, and was not a literal snake.

According to Boulay, in this chapter's earlier section 'Reptilian to Mammalian', since Adam and Eve were also said to be something akin to Homo *saurus*, even according to the *Haggadah*, that suggests that the Anunnaki, as the 'gods' who created Man in their image, must also have been reptilian. And that supports the emphasis on the traditional idea of the Serpent being wise and knowing secrets. It begins to come together. While Sitchin does not corroborate this idea, it **is** a possibility as **Sitchin does not tell us what the Anunnaki looked like**, but several other researchers, already quoted, do state the reptilian nature of the Anunnaki. Thus, Man would still have been created "in their image," whether they were humanoid amphibian or humanoid reptilian in appearance. It is clear, however, that since they were said to be "repulsive" that **the <u>original</u> Anunnaki were not fully human-looking**.

Sitchin Exposé

Having said all that, the late Zechariah Sitchin was a rascal and didn't tell us four key things about the Anunnaki.

Appearance:	they were initially reptilian, later created genetic mammalian version, as for Inanna and Marduk, and then for hybrids like Noah, Moses, Sargon, Alexander the Great…;
Gold:	they mined gold but not for their planet's atmosphere; it was ingested as monoatomic gold to sustain their longevity;
Nibiru:	was a planet similar to the *Star War's* Death Star -- a virtual travelling Battlestar that won't be coming back – it was destroyed near Jupiter in April 2003 as it was returning;
Remnant:	most Anunnaki left Earth in 650-600 BC; a portion stayed on due to Galactic Law governing Creator Races (see **Prime Directive**, Chapter 12 and Glossary).

Serpent Wisdom

As far as reptiles and snakes go, both Enki and his father, Anu the king, both used the serpent as a symbol of wisdom, and this symbol was later adopted by the Brotherhood of the Serpent, which later was called the **White Brotherhood**. [143] Today's medical people use the *caduceus* (2 serpents wrapped around a pole) to symbolize medical knowledge (including being symbolic of DNA), so the issue of a serpent being evil, or a symbol of evil, is a connotation deriving from a false understanding of the Biblical Garden of Eden story. The Serpent in the Garden may also be seen as a benefactor liberating Eve and Adam, and was so seen by the Gnostics. [144] (See Chapter 11 section on Serpent Worship.)

Accompanying the wisdom of the Anunnaki, which was not to be shared with the humans, were two Trees – what they were exactly is not known, but they were symbolized as 'trees.' They might have been feeding machines, dispensing *manna*, among other things.

Tree of Knowing: Reproduction

In the Garden of Eden, or E.DIN ("house of the righteous"), as written by the Sumerians, there were two trees – a Tree of Knowledge, and a Tree of Life. By calling the first tree, the Tree of Knowledge, instead of Knowing as the Sumerian texts do, the meaning was skewed to look like the Tree furnished the knowledge of good and evil. In reality, the **Tree of Knowing refers to the ability to reproduce.** The early *Lulus* could not sexually reproduce, and Enki's solution was to add that genetic capability to his creation, thus creating the *Adamu*, so that the increasing needs for making more workers could be met by letting the 'mankind' population reproduce itself.

As Sitchin says:

> Adam and Eve discovered their sexuality, having acquired "knowing" – a Biblical term that connoted sex for the purpose of procreation ("And Adam *knew* Eve his wife and she conceived and gave birth to Cain.")….
> With that, "The Adam," Elohim said, "has become as one of us." He was granted "Knowing." [145]

The Anunnaki gods in general did not want the created *Lulu* or *Adama* to be like them, intelligent, able to reproduce, and live long lives. Their leader, Enlil, was furious that Enki had done the prohibited genetic upgrade to be able to reproduce. In fact, since Enki's rape of two *Adamu* females produced beautiful Earth women called the *Adapa*, Enlil was already upset that the Anunnaki males were now mating with these new Earth women and 'defiling' themselves (polluting the pure Anunnaki genetics).

This irascible side to Enlil is reminiscent of Yahweh… and it <u>was</u> reasonably Enlil that was walking in the Garden, looking for Adam and Eve, and when he discovers them, and learns that they are aware that they are naked, he turns to **Enki** (as the Serpent in one version) and says that his seed (offspring) will be the enemy of the woman's seed.

Gen. 3:15 continues to make a lot more sense in this light.

So, if the Anunnaki were amphibian, yet had 2 legs, 2 arms, a torso and a head with 2 eyes, 2 ears, a nose and a mouth, **Man would indeed be "created in their image."** Man looked more like a hominid than an octopus. Not exactly looking like them, but "of a similar image," in their likeness. Man and Anunnaki were both bipedal hominids.

> According to the Gnostic version of Eden, after Adam and Eve ate of the forbidden fruit, "they saw their makers (the Elohim) and loathed after them since they were beastly (reptilian) forms. They understood very much." [146]

And lastly, since Anacondas are amphibious, yet reptilian, it begs the question as to whether the Anunnaki were more like the Anaconda in facial appearance – amphibious or aquatic, true, but also serpentine…. very possibly a **'Reptibian.'**

Tree of Life: Longevity

The other Tree in the Garden granted something that the Anunnaki did not want the worker *Lulus* to have: eternal life. The Anunnaki lived for thousands of years, aided by some sort of elixir and the Great Pyramid (Ch. 4). Enki, as much as he cared for his creation, was very careful to not include this gift in his creation, and yet, the Bible says that the original humans, Adam, Seth, Enoch, Methusaleh, etc., all lived nearly a thousand years as a result of the initial Anunnaki genetics. The Anunnaki themselves had to be careful to not stay too long on Earth as the Sun's rays shortened their lifespans, too. This may be why they eventually went home.

Adam lived to be 930 years old, Seth was 912 when he died, and Enosh lived to be 905. Over the centuries, Man lived shorter and shorter lives until we come to Terah (Abraham's father) who lived 205 years, Abraham who lived 175 years, Isaac died at 180 years old, and Jacob's son died at 110. [147] Man currently is said to be capable of living 120 years, but due to stress, toxins, and DNA degradation, it rarely happens.

It has lately been determined that stress and **excititoxins** *acting as free radicals in the body affect the DNA replication process and the 'endcaps' to the chromosomes called* **telomeres** *are worn down thus shortening a human's lifespan (see Book 2).*

Sitchin and the Vatican

One might well ask what the Church response is to Sitchin's scholarly translations, and subsequent interpretation of the Bible? The Catholic Church's response is particularly proactive and revealing.

In Sitchin's book <u>Journeys to the Mythical Past</u> he relates how he traveled to the Vatican in March of 2000 while in Rome to give a presentation on "The Mystery of Human Existence" -- including a discussion of ETs. One of the other presenters was Msgr. Corrado Balducci, a respected theologian and high authority in the Vatican. Naturally, Mr. Sitchin was anxious to meet and personally discuss his Sumerian findings with such an eminent Vatican authority. It turned out that Msgr. Balducci was "…actually designated by the Vatican to speak out on the UFO/ET subjects." [148]

Mr. Sitchin gave his presentation with translator and slides to over 1000 people and later that day met with Msgr. Balducci at a restaurant where they mutually agreed on the following:

1. ETs can and do exist on other planets.
2. They can be more advanced than us.
3. Materially, Man could have been fashioned from a pre-existing sentient being. [149]

Incredible and encouraging. During Msgr. Balducci's talk the next day at the same Conference, Sitchin listened very closely as this jewel was presented to the attendees:

> ….Angels are beings who are purely spiritual, devoid of bodies, while we are made up of spirit and matter and [are] still at a low level. It is entirely credible that in the enormous distance between Angels and humans, there could be found some middle stage, that is beings with a body like ours but more elevated spiritually. If such intelligent beings really exist on other planets, only science will be able to prove. In spite of what some people think, we would be in a position to reconcile their existence with the Redemption that Christ brought us.[150]

Sitchin's key question of <u>Anunnaki</u> creation of Man being acceptable to the Church went unaddressed. So he questioned Msgr. Balducci specifically on this issue and the Msgr. replied that it was "a difference of matter versus spirit" and the proof remained to be seen in some physical evidence. When pressed further, the Msgr replied:

> …. I can bring up the view of the great Professor Father Marakoff who is still alive and greatly respected in the Church. He formulated the hypothesis that when God created Man and put the soul in him, perhaps what is meant is not that Man was created from mud or lime, but *from something preexisting, even from a sentient being capable of feeling and perception*. **So the idea of taking a pre-Man or hominid and creating a someone who is aware of himself is something that Christianity is coming around to.** The key is the distinction between the material body and the soul granted by God. [151] [emphasis in original]

Even if the Anunnaki premise had been accepted by the Msgr., Mr. Sitchin admits there still remains the question of <u>who created the Anunnaki</u>? At some point, when one goes all the way back, tracing Man's ultimate origins, one is faced with the inevitable First Creation of a man-like being: we must have "divine roots" somewhere, sometime.

Sitchin himself goes on to add:

> God imparting a soul to Man is a most profound understanding of the tale in Genesis of Creation of Man by the *Elohim* – a term usually translated 'God' but which is most definitely **plural** – who decided to fashion the *Adamu* [earth man] "in our image and after our likeness" (as Gen. 1:26 states). Amazingly it is an understanding of the biblical tale that is in accord with the Sumerian creation texts about the genetic engineering by the Anunnaki that advanced man from a preexisting hominid to the intelligent *Homo sapiens [Adapa]*. [152] [emphasis added]

He further elucidates that it was "… in those texts [that] the general feat was attained by Enki, assisted by the goddess Ninharsag and his son Ningishzidda whose Sumerian name literally meant 'lord/god of the Tree of Life'." [153] So the Tree of Life and the Tree of Knowledge were somehow connected with the <u>technological</u> superiority of the Anunnaki.

Rewind: Vatican & ETs

Of course the Msgr. Balducci did not endorse Sitchin's ideas directly, but the Vatican **is** entertaining the idea of extraterrestrials interacting with us. In the year 1993 the Vatican built a very technologically advanced telescope on Mt. Graham near Tucson, Arizona, and they are very quiet to this day about just what they may be looking for – Mr. Sitchin asked but was told only that certain Jesuits in the Vatican are very interested in celestial mechanics. Coincidentally, the Anunnaki were expected to return to Earth in the near future according to Mr. Sitchin. [154] Is the Vatican looking for them?

In May-June 2000, the Vatican held another Conference with discussions ranging over a wide topic base: the "Big Bang to Extraterrestrial Civilizations". At the same time, a Fr. Jose Funes released a story to a local Rome newspaper with the headline: "Extraterrestrials Exist and They are Our Brothers." [155]

Lastly, Sitchin says it all: The Vatican "….**knows more than it divulges about what was and what will be; that it even knows about 'my' Anunnaki and their planet Nibiru**." [156] [emphasis in original]

> *From the creation of Christianity to the acknowledgement of ETs, the Church is more aware of and involved with Man's growth than we have given it credit for.*

ET Intervention

There was a Chart 1A in Chapter 1 that showed the general elements in a Chart of Creation. This is the other half:

Chart 1B Notes & Explanation

Note1: Since the Watchers/Nephilim were Anunnaki Igigi, it fell to the Anunnaki to clean up the mess in genetics – after the Flood. All giants were relocated or exterminated, and remaining Nephilim DNA in humans had to be located, identified and neutralized.

Note2: There were other ETs in the mix: notably the Sirians (Oannes/Nommo), and others – remember the section "The Earth Experiment" from Chapter 1.

Note3: There are beneficent (+) and antagonistic (-) Anunnaki Remnants, as indicated by the Chart. In later chapters, they are referred to as Insiders and Dissidents, respectively. The beneficent (STO) are like Enki and seek to help mankind; the antagonistic ones are STS and work to assist the Draconians (from Orion) to subvert Man's progress.

The **Draconians** are not evil – they just want what they want and believe that their repressive, hierarchical, societal structure works best. They are STS like "space pirates." They do not have a soul, nor do they have higher centers, and so Man is a potential threat – if he is allowed to develop his divine potential and connect with his 'godhood.' (Hence Man was removed from their direct access – see Chapter 12 Quarantine.)

As will be seen later, in Chapter 12, there isn't too much to worry about and the upcoming 'harvest' (Chapters 15-16) will separate the sheep from the goats and Man will move forward. Despite the best efforts of the Draconians and Dissidents, they will not prevail.

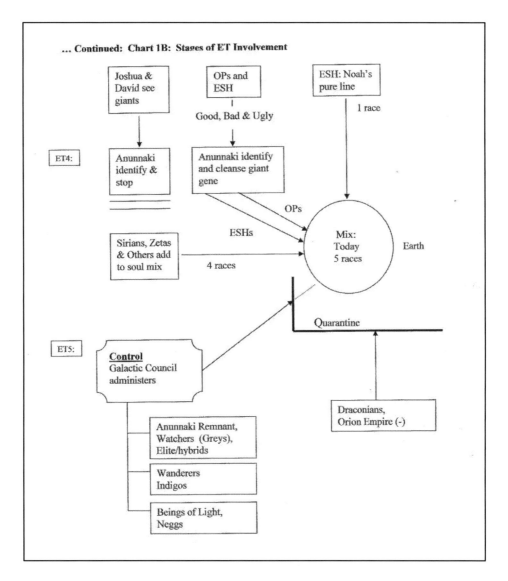

... Continued: Chart 1B: Stages of ET Involvement

Summary

It was shown that Zechariah Sitchin has done a major scholarly work of translating and communicating about Man's early history – even though created by ETs as a slave race in Africa (archeologists confirm that **Man originated in Africa**). It was shown that the Anunnaki had rocket ships ('shem') that spit fire as they flew through the air (origin of Dragons?), and they had a superior knowledge of genetics – both of which Man today has. Man seems to have reached the level today that the Anunnaki were at 200,000 years ago... including nuclear power as the Anunnaki bombed Sodom & Gomorrah, Harappa and Mohenjo-Daro, and the Sinai Peninsula. And able to modify hominids...

Mankind's Heritage

One thing is for sure: the successive forms of Man on the planet are mute witness to the fact that Man <u>was</u> changed – from **Homo *erectus*** to Neanderthal to Cro-Magnon to Homo *sapiens*, and lately to Homo *noeticus* (Indigo children).

See Chapter 7: 'Extra 223 Genes in Man' section.

The Anunnaki could have modified Homo *erectus* when they created *Lulu,* or their sterile worker human (the 1st creation). The improvement, by Enki, into *Adamu* could have been closer to the Cro-Magnon man (the 2nd creation). Enki would later 'personally upgrade' *Adamu* to *Adapa* -- much like Homo *sapiens*. And the Greys are behind the latest genetic change to Homo *noeticus* (the Indigos). Neanderthal was one of many experiments that didn't work out and was replaced by Cro-Magnon. In a similar way, The Change as discovered by Dr. Jacobs portends a **replacement of Homo *sapiens* with Homo noeticus**. With a gradual phase-in, Dr. Greer's Disclosure will not be necessary. And there appears to be another reason that full Disclosure will not happen…

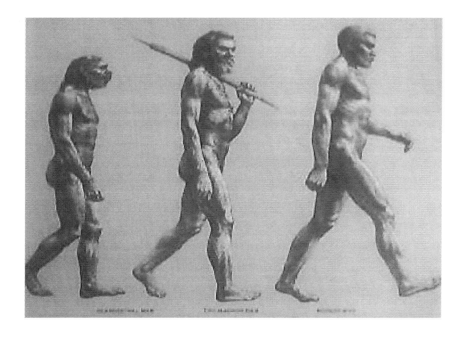

Man: Neanderthal, Cro-Magnon, & Homo Sapiens
Or: The *Lulu, Adamu,* and *Adapa*.
(source: http://www.wilderdom.com/evolution/HumanEvolutionSequencePictures.htm)

Chapter 4: -- Physical Origins

This book began with a review of traditional thinking on Man's origins according to Biblical, Gnostic, Sumerian, and ancient spiritual and esoteric sources. Interestingly, there turned out to be high correlation between them which leads one to speculate: Can they all be generally correct, somehow telling the same story from different aspects? On the other hand, are only parts of them right and thus some of the ancient scribes practiced disinformation in their day, too?

It certainly seems that the writers of Genesis and The Book of Enoch were being rather vague in their story-telling and that's due to long-standing oral transmission of events before Man could write. Once something is written down, it preserves it better. And Genesis does not explain how a snake in the Garden could walk and speak, nor what Adam & Eve looked like, much less Noah – Noah was semi-described by Enoch in terms that would raise many eyebrows, and gives some hint as to why Ham covered his naked father as he did – Noah was not completely human. [157] And how was Man's one language split into many different ones at the Tower of Babel – and what was the Tower of Babel?

Further, the story of Noah is very glossed over in the Bible, but the complete story has much more detail in the *Epic of Gilgamesh* and the story of *Atra Hasis*.

First, Man has been told that he is alone on Earth, then that the Earth was flat, then that the Sun revolved around the Earth, and then that he was created by a loving anthropomorphic God, who looks just like him. Then he was told that Man has never been more advanced on the planet than he is now. All misinformation.

Either Man has been setup for a nasty surprise and stroke (if he ever meets his true creators), or the conspiracists are correct: Man is not soon going to be permitted to leave the planet. If you planned to keep Man like cattle, in the corral forever, you would not need to broaden his horizons… you would make sure that death, disease and dis-information kept Man ignorant, confused, and trapped. Which has to mean that Anunnaki influence is still here, and this chapter will explore the significant aspects of that.

New Considerations

Certainly, if one could remove the ET Creation component, then there would remain just a spiritual or God-based Creation – which is what a lot of people already believe. But if one removed the God/spiritual aspect to Man's creation, then we'd have a very physical, 3D version of Creation. Both views are incomplete without each other. What if God created the **souls** first, then placed Man and Other lifeforms throughout the Universe, and then the Others came here to Earth and created **physical** Man? Not implausible. And the Sumerian tablets DO share that information, and most of the complete story is there, which is unusual if ancient writers were hiding something.

ET lifeforms other than the Anunnaki were involved in the later stages of tinkering with Man's genetics, but the Anunnaki were the first and the most enduring progenitors. Says

Dr. Joe Lewels:

> Whatever they choose to call the beings, those who lean towards what I call "the God Hypothesis" believe that they have been around much longer than a mere 100 years. They have come to the conclusion that **they have always been here**, that they were involved in the creation of the human race, that they are involved in the process of human evolution and that they have been responsible for most, if not all, of the world's religions. [158] [emphasis added]

Exactly. It is interesting that some educated ministers do not find the ET hypothesis an impossible consideration. **Dr. Barry Downing** is a Presbyterian minister who holds degrees in divinity and physics, and as a devoted Christian, he takes a bold stand:

> It is my assumption that the alien/angelic reality was involved in the development of both the Old and New Testaments, as well as perhaps providing stimulation to other religious leaders like Mohammed, or the development of the Hindu Vedic tradition… They also were responsible for the experience at Fatima and the experience of Joseph Smith, founder of the Mormon Church… **UFO alien reality and what the Bible calls the angelic divine reality, are the same reality**.

> My theory does put the Christian view of God at risk. And here is how. I am convinced that **modern UFOs are fully capable of having brought about the biblical religion**. That is, whatever the UFO reality is, it has the power to **control** our minds and our physical reality so totally, that it could have performed <u>every</u> miracle the Bible lists. If UFOs carry the angels of God, then this is fine. They are acting for God, and the traditional Judaeo-Christian view of God is **validated by UFOs**, not contradicted by them. [159] [emphasis added]

And this is like the more progressive viewpoint that Dr. Jacques Vallée has promoted (see Appendix C) in his **Control System**. Man is coming face to face, more and more, with **a controlled reality** in today's world which will surely have the effect of changing religion to more reflect that reality. As technology progresses and Man understands more about his world, the scientific findings are bound to impact his religion and understanding of himself and God. This issue of Science and Religion is dealt with more fully in Chapters 8-11.

The fact that, in today's world, there appears to be considerable UFO activity and reported abductions by little Greys does not necessarily prove that the ET Creation hypothesis is correct. It also doesn't disprove it. It <u>is</u> important to remember that the current UFO activity and abductions have a little to do with the Anunnaki themselves – the Greys are a creation of the Anunnaki to continue Enki's genetic work on humans, not all Greys are a separate race from another planet. Greys are trying to fix the human genome.

There is something going on which the average person is not able to figure out due to the large amount of disinformation spread by those who don't want Man to know who and what he is... the question is: Why? And that has already been partially answered , but it will be more fully addressed in coming chapters. The sometimes bizarre but intriguing picture will unfold. As the book progresses, the veil of disinformation and confusion will lift enough so that the reader can fairly accurately discover what is happening for himself.

Misinterpreting the Evidence

But first, just to remind the reader of how Man can make assumptions that bear no fruit, or false fruit, it would be instructive to consider a few examples of physical evidence on the planet and how Man has misinterpreted it. Keep in mind that the Great Pyramid, Sphinx, Stonehenge, Nazca Lines, Statues on Easter Island, Baalbek Trilithons and the Aztec Calendar were all creations of the Anunnaki but have no use in today's world.

Throughout Man's history on the planet, there have been anomalous events and strange edifices that have amazed him and often led to his formulation of anything but accurate explanations for what was observed. For example, **Stonehenge was built by the Anunnaki**.[160] Man does not know to this day what the stone megalith arrangement was really used for, but it has been said to be a temple for Druid sacrifice, a celestial calendar for tracking the seasons and solstices, or a temple to Apollo before the Celts.

Another puzzling structure, in Lebanon, is the temple the Romans dedicated to their gods at **Baalbek** (which the Anunnaki previously built as a spaceport). [161] What is so unique are the huge blocks of stone, called the Trilithons, 65' long, 20' x 20' width and height, and each one weighs 800+ tons each, so heavy in fact that modern Man cannot lift them with any machinery at his disposal. [162] Sitchin says this was a Landing Place for Anunnaki spaceships (also see *Epic of Gilgamesh*).

One of the Huge Baalbek Trilithons
(source: http://www.world-mysteries.com/mpl_5.htm)

In fact, there are similar huge stones under the **Temple Mount** in Jerusalem upon which the Dome of the Rock stands today. [163] The Rock has several levels below it, and was used as an Anunnaki Command and Control Center according to Sitchin in The Earth Chronicles Expeditions.

We're led to believe that Baalbek was just a Roman temple and that the huge stones were moved and placed through clever use of block and tackle. If you believe that, I have some ocean-front property for sale in Montana...

In very ancient days, around the time of Neanderthal, Man surmised that the lightening and thunder were displays of the gods' anger. Later, among the **Maya and Aztec** cultures, human sacrifice was practiced to appease the god of the Sun so that he would return the next day. Rituals and sacrifices were done by primitive Man misinterpreting the elements.

A current-day bit of offbeat deduction involves the **Nazca Lines** – supposedly they were 'runways' guiding the takeoff and landing of ET airships. It has been pointed out many times that the top soil is dark while the underlying earth is lighter in color, and one can drag a stick across the ground and make all the designs one wants. The top surface is very easy to disturb. So, if there were rocket ships running up and down these 'runways', wouldn't the topsoil have been blown away in many places by the exhaust – especially at the ends of the Lines? That is not observed anywhere among the designs, so their original purpose appears to be to orient someone in the air to something.

With regard to the Nazca Lines, it is obvious the designs were intended to be seen from the sky. So others have proposed that the drawings were made as signs by the local people of the time to their gods. It is amusing to consider that the ETs might have had extra time on their hands and began to doodle in the dirt with a laser on their ships perched 2000' above the plateau, saying to themselves, "Let the future generations try to figure this one out!"

Chapter 10 offers a more plausible explanation for the Nazca Lines.

Thirty some years ago, in 1977, a Japanese fishing trawler pulled in its nets to discover a large, strange-looking marine creature in it. It was partly decomposed, as other denizens of the deep had been feeding off its flesh, but from the series of pictures, one can see that it had a long neck, and several large flippers as if it were some form of **Plesiosaur.** [164]

PHOTO BY YANO MICHIHIKO/ WWW.GENNET.ORG

Of course, no official announcement was made to that effect – to do so would let the cat out of the bag: namely that despite a Flood 8,000+ years ago, swimming dinosaurs did not disappear – some survived The Flood, like **Pterodactyls** which are seen in Indonesia to this day. But the politically correct teaching is that all dinosaurs disappeared millions of years ago – including many **Coelacanths** which were discovered alive and well off the coast of Madagascar in 1938. [165] Recently, **Megalodon** has been filmed off the South African coast.

Is This The Remains of A Plesiosaur ?

Great Pyramid of Egypt

A special case in point is the Great Pyramid of Giza. Man even today cannot replicate the Great Pyramid as its 52° sides are too steep – and the one classic attempt by Man to copy it resulted in what is called the **Bent Pyramid**: It starts out with a 52° slope to its sides, but the builders discovered the angle was too steep and had trouble keeping the stone blocks in place. So about half way up, the pyramid's sides change to a lesser angle and they finished the pyramid that way. And yet, the Egyptians proudly claim that the Pyramid of Giza is something their ancestors built thousands of years ago with simple tools and manual labor. The Anunnaki are still laughing… or whatever lizards do…

In defense of the Egyptians, or their forerunners, and their cleverness, it has recently come to light that the Great Pyramid was easier to build than previously thought. It always seemed a harebrained idea to drag heavy stone blocks across the desert <u>sand</u> (in the absence of trees which would have served as 'rollers'). Finally Michael Barsoum decided to investigate the earlier work done by a French scientist, **Joseph Davidovits** who had an alternate, brilliant theory for how the pyramids were built.

The Large Blocks of Stone Comprising the Great Pyramid.
(source: http://www.sacredsites.com/shop/images/africa/egypt/building-blocks-great-pyramid-750.jpg

In short, the builders were very clever and, in the quarry, pounded the limestone into small bits and dust, and carried that in sacks across the Nile to where the Great Pyramid was being built. They then used molds or casings made of papyrus, mixed the powdered limestone with water (and clay and lime) and **poured it into the mold** – that is why a lot (but not all – see the picture above) of the outer huge stone blocks fit so closely together.

So Barsoum and his staff gathered some rock samples from the base of the Great Pyramid, to test Davidovits' theory: they would either show standard limestone geologic formation, meaning the blocks had been quarried and dragged, or they would show evidence of having been assembled in a manner like concrete.

> … after extensive scanning electron microscope (SEM) observations and other testing, Barsoum and his research group finally began to draw some conclusions about the pyramids. They found that the tiniest structures within the inner and outer casing stones were indeed consistent with a **reconstituted** limestone… The stones also had a **high water content** – unusual for the normally dry, natural limestone found on the Giza plateau – and the cementing phases… were **amorphous**… Sedimentary rocks such as limestone are seldom, if ever, amorphous… Therefore… **it's very improbable that the … stones that we examined were chiseled from a natural limestone block**.
>
> More startlingly, Barsoum … recently discovered the presence of silicon dioxide **nanoscale spheres** in one of the samples. This discovery further confirms that these blocks [of the Great Pyramid of Giza] are not natural limestone. [166] [emphasis added]

Incredible. The ancients were not as primitive and dense as we prefer to think. Even the Anunnaki could have built the Great Pyramid this way, if they didn't use laser-like devices to cut the rock (as was done at Baalbek) and teleported them into position via their craft. Since they used Baalbek as a landing platform, it is likely that they cut and lifted those huge stones into place, too. [167] The outer blocks were done by pouring them in place. The shiny limestone facings (most now missing) were cut and placed manually. **The Great Pyramid was never a tomb**. The **Subterranean Chamber** (under the pyramid) was for Anunnaki regeneration.

While the outer blocks of the Great Pyramid were likely formed by 'pouring' them in place, the area directly above the King's Chamber, called the Relieving Chambers, consisting of 'chevrons of **granite**', reveal technique and skill beyond the ability of the Egyptians and were probably placed by the original builders using their advanced technology. The same thing applies to the construction of the Grand Gallery with its huge stone blocks forming a corbelled arch. Granite (quartz) resonates with energy, focusing it downward and like most pyramids, things in it are regenerated… especially if an Anunnaki ship sent energy via the (now missing) capstone.

> *The **Sphinx** was also cut by the same builders, around 10,000 BCE from the Plateau itself, and represented Ningishzidda (the pyramids' designer, aka Thoth) who was Enki's son and in charge of Egypt – until Marduk took over Egypt.* [168]

And so it goes. Man devises explanations based on his past experience and to some degree on what education and conditioning he has had. Yet, in many cases, his experience and what science or archaeology he has studied do not provide answers, and then he either ignores the evidence, or goes into denial and insists on some mundane explanation for what is obviously amazing. (See Unscientific Method chart, beginning of Chapter 8).

The strange and inexplicable surrounds us, almost as if it exists to say, "Look at this, Earthling!" And several men in the last 150 years have done just that. In fact, they had the courage to really explore the unusual and unknown, and then document it for others. And their documented works collectively make a strong argument for how unusual this planet really is… and that is, as will be seen later, part of Dr. Valleé's Control System.

Charles Fort

William Bramley in his book, <u>The Gods of Eden,</u> makes a point that a much-esteemed researcher, Charles Fort, investigated the paranormal and wrote several books cataloging unusual events all over the USA and England, and later in different parts of the world – such things as worms, snails, fish, rocks, mud, toads and ice falling from the sky on a clear day, as well as unusual noises when nobody is around.

Mr. Fort wrote <u>The Book of the Damned</u> in 1919 as a result of his investigations that led to only one conclusion: that 'Earth skies were hosting an array of extraterrestrial craft which he called "**super-constructions**."' [169] It was surmised that the objects falling from the sky were the doings of the entities piloting the super-constructions. Absolutely amazing that he figured that out in 1919 <u>before</u> any UFO information was commonly available, but Fort was very sharp.

In his book he wrote:

> **I think we're property**. I should say we belong to something. That once upon a time, this Earth was No-Man's Land, that other worlds explored and colonized here, and fought among themselves for possession, but that now it's owned by something: That something owns this Earth – all others warned off. [170] [emphasis added]

Very close to the truth. Fort also concluded, like Tellinger, that the human race is not highly regarded among the extraterrestrial beings. In response to why such beings don't come and chat with us:

> Would we, if we could, educate and sophisticate pigs, geese, cattle? Would it be wise to establish diplomatic relation with the hen that now functions…?

In addition to comparing earth people to smug livestock, Fort also thought that the owners exerted a distinct influence over human affairs:

> I suspect that after all, we're useful – that among contesting claimants adjustment has occurred, or that **something now has a legal right to us, by force** …. that all of this has been known perhaps for ages to certain ones upon this earth, a cult or order, members of which function like bellweathers to the rest of us, or as superior **slaves** or overseers, directing us in accordance with instructions received – from Somewhere else – in our mysterious usefulness. [171] [emphasis added]

What that usefulness might be, Fort didn't say, yet the Anunnaki so treated Man as slaves when they were here. And it may be assumed that some form of slavery was our usefulness… and this reflects Mr. Tellinger's first book's title: *Slave Species of god [sic]*, and it makes one think again about the abductions people have reported by the little Greys – more on this later in this chapter (and Book 2).

ETs, Man and Cattle

Suffice it to say that a potentially ugly ET picture may be coming together regarding (1) our origins and (2) our place on this planet today. And Fort's ideas don't help us feel any better about what may be our lot on this strange planet… given that the best minds throughout history have occupied themselves with where we came from, who we are, what we're doing here, and where we're going. As will be seen later, such things are not obvious, by design, and some people got it wrong, including Darwin and Einstein (Chapter 8).

Given that Man thinks he's here all alone and that this is his planet, it might come as a serious shock to discover that he no more owns the planet (yet) than the cattle own the range upon which they graze.

Equally intriguing about Fort's conclusion is the fact that UFOs and ETs were not in people's awareness back in the early 1900's. Zechariah Sitchin's Sumerian tablets and translations had not yet been found. And Fort did **not** theorize that the objects came from another dimension (as did John Keel), nor that they were the work of the Devil. So it is very interesting that following his years of research and reflection that he suggested ETs as the source who interfere with us, including causing people to disappear.

To clear up the strange objects falling from the sky, a later researcher **Morris K. Jessup** postulated that such objects were the result of

> …alien scientists studying such lifeforms on UFOs. He speculated that the *falls* of lower lifeforms could have originated with dumps from hydroponic tanks in UFOs such as the fish that Betty [Andreasson] witnessed being emptied from a tank on an alien craft. [172]

Jessup suggested that these primitive lifeforms have high reproductive rates, simple living habits, and require a minimum of attention to oversee. Who knows to what end their genetics (like cattle) may have been put…?

So William Bramley, writing about Charles Fort, apparently came to similar conclusions and summarizes what he feels to be the key points:

> Human beings appear to be **a slave race languishing on an isolated planet** in a small galaxy. As such, the human race was once a source of labor for an extraterrestrial civilization <u>and still remains a possession today</u>. To keep control over its possession and to maintain **Earth as something of a <u>prison</u>**, that other civilization has bred never-ending conflict between human beings has promoted human spiritual decay, and has erected on Earth conditions of unremitting physical hardship. This situation has existed for thousands of years and it <u>continues today</u>.[173]   [emphasis added]

If that doesn't make your day, nothing will. Yet it is the point of this book that such **WAS** the case until about AD 800-900, when things changed slightly (as examined in Chapters 12-13) in Man's favor, even though current day aspects still reflect centuries of abuse.

What is clear, when one does the research, is that something wants us to remain ignorant, docile, go along with the program (whatever it is), and keep quiet. In a word, sheep -- or cattle as Fort would suggest. And that is <u>one</u> of the still-ongoing aspects.

Not So Modern Man

At this point, it is appropriate to point out that most older civilizations were not always backward and ignorant. There is a tendency to believe the lie that is promoted in today's world that we, modern Man, are the pinnacle of creation, the smartest, the most technologically advanced, and that we know more than any past civilization – this is (falsely) based on the notion that man has been in a slow, upward evolution for millions of years. Not so. For the specifics, please refer to Dr. Fomenko in Chapter 10.

Modern Man is in some ways 'dumber' than those of just 1,000 years ago – at least our ancestors knew about pre-Adamics, OPs or *hylics* (covered in Chapter 5), how to build a 52° angle pyramid (8,000 years ago), or how to lift 1000+ ton granite blocks…. modern man doesn't. What kind of 'advancement' is that?

The point is that something has been going on that does not fit nicely into the 'history box' that has been prepared for us by archaeological, anthropological, religious and sociology 'experts.' What we seem to have is a 'sanitized' view of our planet from the 40,000' level where the details and their significance have purposely been lost.

At this point, having basically covered the historical origins of Man, it is necessary to now take a look at what current-day manipulations have been reported to see what <u>aspects of Anunnaki control are still with us</u>. Then we can examine all the evidence and begin to consider who we are, who is also here, and how the info in Chapters 1 thru 3 can be synthesized into a coherent picture so that we can know what we're up against – even though some people will want to deny that we're up against anything.

Dr. David Jacobs

Associate Professor of History at Temple University, in Philadelphia, PA, Dr. Jacobs has undertaken to solve the abduction phenomenon. He is also the Director of the International Center for Abduction Research (ICAR). He has produced several books on the subject, recounting the experiences of UFO abductees who agreed to submit to **hypnotic regression**. Many accounts take the form of a transcript, repeating exactly what was said by Dr. Jacobs and the abductee. It is obvious from the questions posed that they are very non-directive, not encouraging 'expected' answers, yet some of what the abductees say is quite unexpected.

In his 1998 book, *The Threat,* Dr. Jacobs recounts how many people had experiences with **human-looking hybrids** created by the Greys' genetic work, occasional discovery of implants and removal of same (tracking devices), and the Greys show the abductees something like a video of what will happen to the Earth if Man doesn't take better care of the planet. Others are taken on board and 'programmed' to be of use later – at which time their programming will be activated. (More on this in Book 2: they are not the enemy.)

Hybrid Humans

Some female human abductees were even encouraged to have 'relations' with the hybrid male humans, or to hold what they were told were their (hybrid) children that had been removed from their womb after a few months' gestation. In all cases the hybrids were telepathic and much more intelligent than the Homo *sapiens* version. Such information has led to the speculation that **a new race is being prepared** -- perhaps for Earth. [174]

By the way, the Greys always refer to our human bodies as 'containers' since they seem to hold our souls – but they don't usually abduct people without souls, unless it supports their Genetics Program overall.

One of the interesting byproducts of the alien-human interface:

> Abductees and aliens have 'melded' together in some way and in a sense **abductees and aliens are the same.** Abductees live their present lives with a 'dual reference,' human and alien. [175]   [emphasis added]

Again:

> ...[early] abductees say that the phenomenon has had a devastating effect on their personal lives. Many have phobias, scars, bruises, and psychological problems, especially gynecological and urological dysfunction. [176]

And again:

> Abductees also feel that the aliens have effected some sort of **neural manipulation** that makes them different ["rewired' is a common term – ed.]   For example it is common for abductees to feel increased "psychic" abilities – they 'know' what people are thinking. [177] [emphasis added]

So Dr. Jacobs naturally is concerned and after countless years of exploration in the 90's he is confident that the picture presented by the abductees is NOT a positive one. This is largely due to the message relayed from the aliens through the abductees that something is coming this way, and that after **The Change**, they and humans will be on the planet together – and if you don't see auras, you will not be able to tell them from normal human beings. (Book 2 examines this issue in much more detail; it is not negative.)

The key words are **'hybrid'** and **'interspecies.'** [178] The Greys are reportedly here trying to undo the negative Anunnaki genetic legacy; that is why all the genetic samples and tests. The Greys are evaluating the effects of the fallout from atom bomb testing in the 1950s, the effects of air and water pollution on the human body, and in some cases they are trying to use viral vectors to reprogram human DNA.

Alien Hybrid Agenda

Of particular note is what several of Dr. Jacob's patients related under hypnosis about the Alien Agenda referred to as The Change. Many abductees were shown scenes of people picnicking in a park and they were asked to examine the scene closely to see if they could spot any differences in the people. Specifically, the aliens were proud to show the results of their genetic handiwork: each scene shown had normal humans, aliens and hybrids together outdoors in the future and they all looked like normal humans. Dr. Jacobs asked several abductees to describe what they saw: [179]

> Abductee: He's showing me some real wonderful pictures. I think this is the way things are supposed to be with us together.
>
> Dr. Jacobs: With you and the big [Grey], or aliens and humans?
>
> A: It's a mixture of aliens and humans. It's all different types of aliens though, all different colors of humans…. There are no little grays, there's only the hierarchy [taller] grays… they're intermingled in there and they are fostering this and everybody's happy with this.

And with another abductee, regressed to a similar picnic scene: [180]

> DJ: What kind of an image are you looking at?
>
> A: It varies. There's flowers, there's gardens, there's families, there's families interacting. I don't know. I can't tell. I can't tell.
>
> DJ: Can't tell what?
>
> A: They want us to see this and tell them the "thems" from the "us's" and you can't tell…. I can't tell if there's a family of "thems" or if there's "thems" intertwined within the established families. If they're the same, I cannot, I cannot [tell the difference].
>
> DJ: Is this the point of it? That you can't tell?
>
> ….
>
> A: There are **hybrids** there, there are people – I can't even call them hybrids anymore – there are **people** there that were not brought about thru a normal human evolution and here we are. They were brought about in the process of many years of **experimentation**. "Find where they are. You can't tell the difference." *I* can't tell the difference… [emphasis added]

It gets better… [181]

> DJ: …Do they give you any clues or hints as to who's who or what's what?
>
> A: I kind of feel like that's the point…. Where are the hybrids?… Do you see a hybrid family? No, they don't use that word, far from it – our "creation," almost like they want me to find their created million-dollar family. And I can't.

That's the way it comes across…. They try to narrow it down a bit… [to] a single family that has one… [It's] Spring… It's very pleasant, it's very nice. I don't know what the point is here…I find it scary… they could *all* be them or could all be us and I could be looking for nothing… But… in this scene there are hybrids and I think the point of it is, I think **they've achieved their goal**. They've mastered the splicing and dicing, and test-tubing, and **they can fit in now**… You can't tell them apart. They're proud of that. [emphasis added]

And then the scene alters for the regressed abductee. The Greys originally show her a scene in color, and then they help her out by denoting the hybrids in black and white: [182]

A: … Like everything kind of stops…. Everything's in color, it stops. [The scene freezes on a man looking her way.] He turns his head and looks at me and he's like black and white, and that's one…. There's this little girl in a little pink dress… And the same thing happens to her. And they do this with a couple people [sic] and they're the ones that I missed and I couldn't tell the difference.

DJ: Do they look any different when you see them? Can you suddenly realize, "Oh yeah, that's one," or you still wouldn't know?

A: **There's only one way to tell and that is that energy field, that energy field around them but unless you can see it, you'll never know.** [emphasis added]

A Different Aura

The "energy field" around the people is obviously the **aura**, but the woman does not know the term. And her statement that seeing the aura is the only way to identify the hybrids is analogous to the coming examination in Chapter 5 for identifying the OPs (pre-Adamics, i.e., "1st Seed") among us – remember that they have <u>no soul</u>, and thus they have <u>no aura</u>. (Some hybrids have no soul… Book 2.)

She notes that only the man turned black and white – not his wife nor the kids. So families will be mixed, some human some hybrid, and apparently **they can interbreed**. So Dr. Jacobs continues to dig out some interesting information about the energy field that the Greys told her (during the regression) which is the only distinguishing aspect of the hybrids:

DJ: ….That it's the energy field that distinguishes them?

A: But I can't see it. I can't see it on anybody. But there's going to be a few people that <u>can</u> see it and will know. This is crazy. The ones who can see it or can distinguish… [if they] have an uprising about it, they would be subsequently terminated. So there's a power thing… this is not only going genetically… I feel that there's a political power or motivation as well in the underlying scheme… They're healthier… **It's kind of like an all-around superior model.** [183] [emphasis added]

116

So the alien agenda involving genetics has been producing a hybrid species of Man that is reminiscent of the Neanderthal to Cro-Magnon upgrade, and then the Cro-Magnon upgrade to Homo *sapiens*… in fact, the Greys <u>have</u> been here for a while doing this. [184] Is this reminiscent of what the Nazis were trying to acomplish?…(see later section.)

Key Point: We're Not Alone

Without belaboring the issue, it is <u>very</u> important to note the significant point made in Dr. Jacob's information is **that the hybrids, some of whom are walking among us, are so perfected that we could be sitting next to one on the bus, or in a restaurant, and not know.** And that applies to more than hybrids as the next chapter will emphasize.

Man is not here alone. And if you think he is, then consider why the US Government in 1969 passed **The Extraterrestrial Exposure Law,** [185] making contact with ETs an offense punishable by indefinite imprisonment with no appeal. Note that it isn't just talking about decontamination. The US Government is very serious about any citizens having physical contact with aliens … as if the aliens will communicate information that our government doesn't want known – this borders on the recent Patriot Act laws passed dealing with terrorism since 9/11. Could ETs be considered a 'terrorist threat'?

And it works the other way, too: suppose the aliens are malevolent and convince, manipulate or otherwise 'program' a human being to do something contrary to US national security? This suggests there are good and bad aliens… unfortunately true.

The Greys Replace the Anunnaki

As we have seen above, the Greys began doing their genetic manipulation on Man, some millenia <u>after</u> the Anunnaki created Man in their image… [186] and <u>after</u> the Anunnaki-sponsored Flood, and <u>after</u> the Anunnaki cleaned up the Nephilim mess. And <u>after</u> the Anunnaki left Earth (about BC 600). It is reasonable that the **Greys are a bio-cybernetic mechanical creation of the Anunnaki** to perform the desired abduction-upgrade and make it look like it is an ET issue. The Anunnaki are still involved with Man's genetic upgrade since they are still responsible for us (Chapter 11)… also see Chapter 8 in Book 2.

The Greys are also engaged in collecting all genetic seed for all the flora and fauna on the planet.[187] The reason given is due to the coming near-extinction of the current version of Man, such that the planet can be terraformed and the Earth can host a new (upgraded) human form. [188] It appears that this is the upcoming **Change** that faces Man. An abductee told Dr. Jacobs:

> The future for the aliens and hybrids is always a future on Earth where they will be integrated with humans. They offer no other possibility…. nonabductees will be kept as **a small breeding population** in case the hybridization program has unforeseen problems…. **Nonabductees are expendable** [genetics not acceptable – ed.] …. **the future will be played out primarily with aliens, hybrids and abductees**….. The new order will be insectlike aliens in control, followed by other aliens, hybrids, abductees, and finally, nonabductees. [189] [emphasis added]

Just what you always wanted to hear. No wonder Dr. Jacobs is not optimistic about the future, but remember: the Greys can plant false memories/info in their abductees. So only time will tell.

Dr. John E. Mack

The late Dr. John E. Mack, of Harvard Medical School, on the other hand was very **optimistic** about the involvement of aliens in our future. His book Abductions was written back in 1994 and profiles 16 cases that he personally investigated, not only by interview, but also by non-directive hypnotic regression to the actual abduction events – just like Dr. Jacobs did. What is interesting is that the two men, Jacobs and Mack, objectively analyzed the same issue and came up with **opposite conclusions.**

Dr. Mack felt that the intervention by the Greys in our affairs and in our future is a healthy one (and this represents the general thinking today) and that those abductees should be called 'experiencers.' He discovered profound changes in his patients, namely **spiritual transformations** – like the NDE experiences produce in people. [190] Most abductees are more altruistic, positive, sometimes psychic, and have a new, higher vision of themselves and humanity – their God is more of a positive 'god force.' [191]

Aliens' Observations

Peter, one of the abductees, in Dr. Mack's book (in his chapter 13) said: "….the aliens did not intend us harm and **their purpose was to 'get us to the point where we can interact with them consciously and not have it be so frightening for us.'"** [192]

In chapter 8 of *Abduction*, Mark, another abductee, shared that he has "….a dual human/alien existence but is closer to his alien connection or source than Joe [another abductee]." Through Mark, Joe discovered his own **human/alien double identity**. "…. Joe likened [Earth] to an **insane asylum**…. The alien beings appear to serve for both Mark and Joe as what Dr. Mack calls 'midwives', delivering them from the madhouse of our culture to another state of consciousness more compatible with the viability of the planet's life." [193] [emphasis added]

'Insane asylum' is not far off, and this issue will come up again. Earth may thus be a galactic rehabilitation center for wayward or defective souls. Abductees were all told that Man is destroying the Earth in his ignorance and greed, and that there is a Change coming and that we will need them to help restore the planet to a livable condition. [194]

So you get the point: something real happened for a lot of people, and some are led to believe it is in their best interest – as well as the planet's – and they want to serve. But what is this planet?

Dr. Jacques Vallée

A French astrophysicist who researched UFOs for a long time and brushed elbows with some of the major names in the field, Dr. Vallée was played by François Truffaut as the French scientist LaCombe in the movie *Close Encounters of the Third Kind*. Interestingly enough, Vallée wrote a book called <u>Passport to Magonia</u> (1969) wherein he is said to reveal key aspects of the UFO puzzle, and then left the field and refused to discuss it any more. Later, he said that "The abduction experience, in my opinion, is real, traumatic, and very complex." [195]   That it is.

Control System

One of the main tenets of his belief about UFOs is that they are part of a "control system" which is the means of rearranging Man's concepts.   He goes on to say the UFOs are deliberately presenting Man with absurd images, such as ETs wearing baseball caps and a paper starchart on the inside wall of a UFO!

> ….continually recurring "absurd" messages and appearances which defy rational analysis but which nonetheless address human beings on the level of myth and imagination…. The occurrences of similar "absurd" messages in UFO cases brought me to the idea that maybe we're dealing with a sort of **control system** that is subtly manipulating human consciousness. [196] [emphasis added]

And then he excuses himself:

> I do not want my words to be misunderstood: I do not mean that some higher order of beings has locked us inside the constraints of a space-bound jail, closely monitored by psychic entities we might call angels or demons. [197]

Why not say that? He <u>did</u> discover what is going on, although it is not a jail and they aren't demons. He then rephrases it:

> The UFO phenomenon exists. It has been with us throughout history. It is **physical** in nature and it remains unexplained in terms of contemporary science. **It represents a level of consciousness** that we have not yet recognized, and which is **able to manipulate dimensions** beyond time and space as we understand them. It affects our own consciousness in ways that we do not grasp fully, and it generally behaves as a **control system**. [198] [emphasis added]

The Control System is examined more in Chapters 12-13 and in Appendix C. And the abductees discussed earlier are also indirect recipients of those who effect the Control System. Their belief systems have been altered and, on some level, Dr. Mack found that they have been reprogrammed to accept and work with the UFO/ET phenomenon.

Virtual Reality

How close can you get without admitting it? Dr. Vallée describes where we are and then excuses himself and sidesteps the issue. He then explains more what he means by a 'physical' aspect to the UFO issue: he suggests we look at the world as a collection of events "… rather than a collection of material objects moving in 3-dimensional space…. In **virtual reality**, of course, you can't tell the difference." [199] [emphasis added]

Again, very accurate. When he was asked what he thought about the occasional "waves" of UFO activity, he replied:

> …it resembled a **schedule of reinforcement** typical of a learning or training process: the phenomenon was more akin to a **control system** than to an exploratory task force of alien travelers. [200] [emphasis added]

Exactly. In short:

A control system to develop human beings by those who run this virtual reality.

Wait until we get to Chapters 12-13; he has hit the nail right on the head.

Key thoughts

When we were less sophisticated, the Control System entertained us with fairies, elves and gnomes, and fiery chariots. In the late 1800's, they amazed us with airships. Now that Man has become more technological, they entertain us with UFOs and Crop Circles. Dr. Vallée adds:

> What does it all mean? Is it reasonable to draw a parallel between religious apparitions, the fairy-faith, the reports of dwarf-like beings with supernatural powers, the airship tales in the United States in the last century, and the present stories of UFO landings?
>
> I would strongly argue that it is – for one simple reason: *the mechanisms that have generated these various beliefs are identical.* Their human context and their effect on humans are constant…. *It has little to do with the problem of knowing whether UFOs are physical objects or not.* **Attempting to understand the meaning, the purpose of the so-called flying saucers… is just as futile as was the pursuit of the fairies** … The phenomenon has stable, invariant features [which]…. **vary as a function of the cultural environment into which they are projected.** [201] [emphasis added]

It will be seen in this section, with authors Moseley, Keel, et al, that there is a consensus that a part of the UFO phenomenon is more of an **interdimensional** nature than a physical 3D object (Think: the Greys). But the majority of them are physical 3D craft, and most are not from other planets.

Last Words

Jacques Vallée's last words on the subject are worth noting, considering that he was said to know the answer to the UFO riddle:

> …should we hypothesize that an advanced race somewhere in the universe in some time in the future has been showing us **three-dimensional space operas for the last 2000 years, in an attempt to guide our civilization?**

If so, do they deserve congratulations? …. Are these races only semi-human, so that in order to maintain contact with us, they need **cross-breeding** with men and women of our planet? Is this the origin of the many tales and legends where genetics play a great role: the symbolism of the virgin [birth] in occultism and religion, the fairy tales involving human midwives and changelings, the sexual overtones of the flying saucer reports, the Biblical stories of intermarriage between the Lord's angels and terrestrial women, whose offspring [Nephilim] were giants? From that mysterious universe are higher beings **projecting objects** that can materialize at will? [202] [emphasis added]

But we cannot ignore the facts, and after he analyzed thousands of them, he was forced to realize that it wasn't extraterrestrials visiting us, but something else was going on. Nineteen years later, in Dimensions, Dr. Vallée would make the following critical observations which are right in line with this book's revelations: [203]

The truth is that some UFOs may not be spacecraft at all.

[UFO behavior] is the behavior of an image, or a **holographic projection**.

…the extraterrestrial theory is not good enough, because it is not strange enough to explain the facts.

We are not dealing with successive waves of visitations from space. We are dealing with a **control system**…. A spiritual control system for human consciousness.

….[the phenomenon is] the means through which man's concepts are being rearranged…. I suggest that it is **human belief that is being controlled and conditioned.** [emphasis added]

Dr. Vallée dropped these hints in his book, Dimensions in 1988, and then officially said no more. He was much closer to the truth than he or we would like to believe… and there is more to it as we will see.

The Control System is further discussed in Appendix C.

James Moseley

Another prominent UFO researcher with a piece of the truth is called the **"Voltaire of UFOlogy."** [204] Moseley was known to keep UFO researchers on their toes with his sometimes satirical and biting observations of their work for more than half a century via his newsletter called *Saucer Smear*. He later founded a magazine called *Saucer News*, which was taken over by Gray Barker, who was a good friend of the afore-mentioned **Al Bender**. The connection is that Al thought he discovered what the UFOs were and before he could get the info to print, via Gray Barker, he was visited by 3 Men In Black (MIB), the real item, who shook him up so badly that he had health problems and almost constant headaches and he thus quit UFO research. [205] (See Chapter 2 in Book 2.)

121

Following years of UFO research, Moseley came up with a few heavy observations:

> Our supposed visitors are just too much like us – physically, emotionally, and mentally. They never seem to tell us anything we don't already know. **Their technology is only a very few years ahead of our own**…. Granted that intelligent life probably exists throughout the universe, it is still a weird coincidence indeed that **we are being visited by creatures who are almost** … **at our own stage of evolution**…. It is absurd to believe that a highly developed race would engage in silly genetic and sexual experiments with Earthlings….What is really happening, in my opinion, is that we are having occasional contacts with another realm of being – **another dimension**, or whatever. [206] [emphasis added]

Most researchers who studied the UFO data from the 50's – 70's noted the same thing: many contactee stories involved ETs who tended to look like us, speak English, or German, and were just a couple of years, it seemed, ahead of us technologically – **as would be the case IF those UFOs came from this Earth**. In addition, it is strangely coincidental that in the 1980s the Greys and Reptilians began to manifest… as if the perpetrators of the scenario knew they'd have to change their ETs and equipment observed to stay ahead of our cynicism.

And, lastly, Moseley leaves us with a summary of his work:

> Today, whereas most UFOlogists still prefer 3D "nuts and bolts" saucers and space people, I prefer 3 ½ D – 4D – 4 ½ D entities. Also, while some others believe that our visitors were around for a few years and then went away, I feel rather that, whatever this phenomenon is, **it has been a permanent part of the Earth's environment** at least since the dawn of recorded history, and **remains here now**. [207] [emphasis added]

That's two votes for the interdimensionsal UFO aspect. It is also suggesting an Earth-based aspect to the ET issue… And it will be seen that both Moseley and Vallée were very close to what is really being orchestrated.

Albert K. Bender

Having mentioned this man several times, it is appropriate to include a brief section on him. He thought he was dealing with ETs but in reality he was largely deceived by the Astral entities (Neggs) that will be examined more in detail in Chapter 6.

Al was a collector of odd stories and events around the country and world, just as Charles Fort was. After collecting his own set of paranormal oddities, he discovered the works of Charles Fort, which fascinated him greatly, but he was more attracted to the UFO anomalies which he discovered had been going on for centuries. [208]

In addition, Al lived in an old house with an attic that creaked and groaned during windy evenings, and whose floorboards creaked eerily as one walked across them. Combine this with a great love of authors like Mary Shelly (Frankenstein), Bram Stoker (Dracula), and Edgar Allen Poe. Al decided to convert his creepy attic into a "chamber of horrors" and he had

> …painted grotesque scenes and faces upon the walls… and after about eight months I had done so good a job that it almost frightened me …One wall of the room was still bare, so I soon filled it in with a complete drawing of the solar system…[plus] a sketch of what I thought the hidden side of the Moon would look like… Developing my horror motif further, I … [added] macabre items such as artificial human skulls, shrunken heads, bats, spiders, snakes, black panthers, and the like. [209]

The stage was set for interference. Unknowingly, he had **invited** what was to follow. As will be seen in Chapter 6, if you want to play the game, the Astral entities (Neggs) will oblige. His fascination with the occult, painting space scenes on his attic walls, and mixing it all with a horror theme was a direct invitation to be harassed with a UFO horror motif. And he was harassed … but not by UFOs or ETs.

Having a great interest in UFOs, Al started and ran a very successful UFO investigation bureau. At the same time, he was investigating and attending meetings with mediums, trying his hand at divination, and trying to perform séances in his house. [210] He was dabbling in the occult. Soon, he began to receive phone calls with no one at the other end of the line, and one late evening, leaving the local cinema, he was to be given his first 'visit' and a sample of many **headaches and vertigo** to come.

Arriving home late one night, after the cinema, as he went to his bedroom he noted a bluish glow coming from around and under the door. As he cautiously entered, it disappeared and then he smelled burning sulfur.

Sulfur and its odor are traditionally associated with what the Christians call the demonic. He innocently started out investigating UFOs, and wound up afflicted by the occult actions of the Neggs (to break him of the involvement). You want to play the game? They'll oblige. Bender just didn't realize that occupying oneself with things of the occult opens a door to unwanted deception and affliction – not UFOs or ETs. That doorway opens with fascination with horror movies, divination, séances, mediums, Tarot cards, and yes, Ouija boards – it is an invitation, and ignorance is no excuse.

Lastly, his friend and the publisher of his book, **Gray Barker**, suggests in the epilog that he understands what Al did and issues a subtle warning:

> If you, the reader, are experiencing anything similar to that described in this book, we sincerely warn you that it is in your best interests to find means of halting it. Your best human defense is merely **disbelief**…. If this method fails, you can always use the only ultimate weapon ever employed by Man – your **prayers**. Basically, I believe the phenomena described in this book can be considered negative or evil… And such cannot stand up against prayers. [211] [emphasis added]

Contact vs Disbelief

Disbelief seems to be a key to keeping ETs as well as the occult at bay. It is interesting to note that several times in the UFO literature, some researchers were told by government and military people that denying the UFO reality helps to keep it from becoming more of our reality. This sounds like something of a metaphysical principle, but in reality, were our government to admit the existence of the UFOs/ETs it would be tantamount to "inviting" them to participate in our reality – just as Al Bender's attic and activities amounted to tacit acceptance of another reality to insert itself into his daily world. Chapter 14 goes more into how this tacit permission can result in our reality and freewill being violated.

Thus, despite the Vatican okaying the ET concept, last chapter, our government is wisely keeping a lid on the issue for the following reasons:

> ...the two main reasons the government is withholding the truth about UFOs are the **religious** question, and the fact that **we do not have control** of the situation. 'They' are in charge....[and] if the Bible said that God created the Heaven and Earth, then what the hell do the aliens believe in? The thing that the aliens fear the most is that Man would find out that we are not the creation of an omnipotent supreme being, but possibly the creation of these aliens themselves – that **we are a genetic experiment**. [212] [emphasis added]

Denying the reality of the UFO/ET paradigm sends a message that we don't welcome it in our world. So, instead of disclosure, we should be asking <u>what</u> it is, <u>why</u> it is there, and <u>what</u> it wants – and if we don't like the answer(s), denial gives us an opportunity to prolong the inevitable and prepare for the ultimate confrontation when we're stronger. This also assumes that our freewill (to not be contacted) is being respected...

Open Contact?

Dr. Steven Greer keeps pushing for open contact with the ETs, but that may not YET be a viable scenario. We are a pretty primitive bunch of humans – many of whom cannot even calmly and logically think about the ET possibility, so what kind of chaos would ensue during and after an open public meeting with the aliens? Such a question was answered by the alleged alien contact of Daniel Fry back in 1949 and is significant nonetheless:

> If we were to appear as members of a superior race, coming from above to lead the peoples of your world, we would seriously disrupt the ego balance of your civilization. Tens of millions of your people, in their desperate need to avoid being demoted to second place in the universe, would go to any conceivable length to disprove or deny our existence.

> If we took steps to force the realization of our reality upon their consciousness, then about thirty percent of these people would insist upon considering us as gods, and would attempt to place upon us all responsibility for their own welfare. Of the remaining seventy percent, most would consider that we were potential tyrants who were planning to enslave their world, and many would immediately begin to seek means to destroy us. [213]

The solution suggested was to have the ETs contact the non-leaders of the world, and give the intelligent man-on-the-street the information and possibly the inconspicuous position of working with Them to help change the world. (Think: Gene Roddenberry.) The other alternative, which is already happening, is to have Them live and work among us to help steer the world in a more proactive direction by quiet work in multiple settings.

This avoids the more dramatic and misunderstood apparitions and humanoids seen at random throughout the world which give rise to tales of demonic entities ready to attack and eat Man. **We don't need fear**, and there isn't much to be afraid of – if the ETs were hostile, they'd have taken us over a long time ago because they have been here for centuries. That leaves one other possibility – the bad ETs can't get here, or haven't arrived yet – which in turn means **the good ETs are here protecting us** … no doubt there are coalitions on both side of the fence and the ET world is probably not all benevolent.

Yet, strange and nasty things have happened, most of which were investigated by John Keel and seem to involve ETs (but don't) …

John Keel

John Keel, who wrote *Mothman* (later a movie of the same name), was an internationally renowned UFO investigator with many books to his credit on UFOs and the occult, and he thought that the two were one and the same thing. He voiced an alarming theory:

> Demonology is not just another crackpot-ology. It is the ancient and scholarly study of the monsters and demons who have seemingly co-existed with man throughout history. Thousands of books have been written on the subject, many of them authored by educated clergymen, scientists and scholars, and uncounted numbers of well-documented demonic events are readily available to every researcher. The manifestations and occurrences described in this imposing literature are <u>similar, if not entirely identical</u>, to the UFO phenomenon itself. **Victims of demonomania (possession) suffer the very same medical and emotional symptoms as the UFO contactees**… The Devil and his demons can, according to the literature, manifest themselves <u>in almost any form</u> and can physically imitate anything from angels to horrifying monsters with glowing eyes. Strange objects and entities materialize and dematerialize in these stories, just as the UFOs and their splendid occupants appear and disappear, walk thru walls, and perform other supernatural feats. [214] [emphasis added.]

Interesting but **Neggs, Greys, demons and UFOs are not the same thing.**

The reason UFO contactees and victims of allegedly demonic activity sometimes share similar health problems is because both were subjected to the same EMF (electro-magnetic field) surrounding the phenomena.[215] And because that field was stronger than the body's weak bio-electric field, it can really disrupt it, and nausea, **headaches and disorientation** are common results. In short: the similarity is due to the fact that Angels (Beings of Light) and Aliens (imitated by Neggs which are **negative** Beings of Light) have a similarly empowered hyperdimensional source whose **higher energy can affect humans neurologically**.

Keel doesn't know how close he is to describing the higher energy that the Control System uses to replicate objects in our world, but that is examined more fully in Chapters 12 – 13. Suffice it to say, at this point that he has correctly identified a common effect, but infers the wrong conclusion. He goes on to almost describe what Earth really is (note the similarity to what Dr. Jacques Vallée said earlier about the Control System) when Keel says:

> I have gone through periods when I was absolutely convinced that [UFOs as] Trojan horses were, indeed, following a careful plan designed to ultimately **conquer the human race *from within***…. But I am now inclined to accept the conclusion that the [UFO] phenomenon is mainly concerned with undefined (and undefinable) cosmic patterns and that mankind plays only a small role in those patterns. That "other world" seems to be a part of something larger and more infinite. The human race is also a part of that something…[216] [emphasis added]

He is right, the human race **is** part of the Control System, but it is obvious from the rest of his analysis that he still suspects that our issues are somehow related to the demonic, trying to infiltrate, and that is not correct. He has mixed demons, ETs, UFOs, the little Greys and even fairies as paranormal effects of the (demonic) "other world." He is not right, but they are sometimes **effects of the Control System**. This is pointed out lest someone else gets the idea that ETs, UFOs, etc. are demonic. They aren't.

One last very significant observation that Keel makes will be explored more in depth in Chapter 12, but it bears presenting it here due to his discussion of ultraterrestrials and their harassment of Albert Bender, for example.

> The … ultradimensionals are somehow **able to manipulate the electrical circuits of the human mind.** They can make us see whatever they want us to see [shapeshifting] and remember only what they want us to remember. Human minds which have been tuned to those super-high-frequency radiations… [i.e., people with psychic abilities] are most vulnerable to these manipulations …. Many are driven **insane** when their minds are unable to translate the signal properly…. [but] not all ultraterrestrial contacts are evil and disastrous, of course. But there are many people throughout the world who are deeply involved in all this without realizing it. They have entangled themselves through other frames of reference [e.g., witchcraft, Ouija board, and séances] and , in many cases, have been savagely exploited by the ultraterrestrials in the **games** being played. These games have been thoroughly documented and defined … [and] the psychology of the … ultraterrestrials is well known and fully documented in the fairy lore of northern Europe, and the ancient legends of Greece, Rome and India. [217] [emphasis added]

Interesting to note that Keel connects the fairy lore and elementals with UFOs as does Dr. Jacques Vallée, and Keel also sees the connection with Al Bender's nervous breakdown at the hands of these 'beings' who allegedly occupy a world next to ours. He also identifies their ability to **shapeshift.**   All higher beings can do that, it proves nothing.

Remember that control was important to the Anunnaki, via the priesthood, and Dr. Vallée has also emphasized that. Man still needs to be controlled, for his own good and the preservation of the physical Earth. Man is largely controlled today through the Control System (as well as the Media).

Faked ET UFO Landing Coming?

While this book is not a lot about UFOs and minimally covers that issue (see Appendix A), because the Anunnaki gods had spacecraft and because there has been a recent [last 60 years] development of earthbound spacecraft, including Shuttles and other more Black Ops Craft (SR71 Blackbird, F117A Stealth fighter, B2 Bomber, the Aurora, 47B Stealth Drone… and **TR-3B**) post WW II, it is relevant to address a <u>potential</u> deception at this point.

Allegedly the new TR-3B, or Black Triangle.
(credit: Bing Images)

From what has been written about this craft, it ranges in size from 90 feet across to the width of three football fields and is what was seen over Phoenix in March 1997. It uses a spinning plasma field that negates gravity by 89%, and the three condenser balls (one at each corner) help guide the craft via the **Biefield-Brown Effect** as reported [218] … but not much else is known about it, except that it is a <u>global craft</u>, maybe not interstellar.

There may be a huge deception coming that even **Dr. Wernher von Braun** warned [219] about : some technologically superior Earth-based beings 'land' and, due to our TV programs, movies and books about ETs, we may tend to look upon them as technological saviors. After all, wasn't the movie *ET* cute, and wasn't the movie *Close Encounters of the Third Kind* very positive?? And how about *Paul*?

What if some UFOs are from Earth? Either from a covert advanced group on the Earth, or from underground beings (Nagas *aka* Anunnaki Remnant…) who have been here for a while, observing us and who now decide to come forth and put a stop to Man's abuse of the planet – which is also their home…? Supposing the **Earth-based UFOs** show up in mass and one of them lands, and out steps a being that looks just like us (because he is us), and offers to solve all our problems and install a One World Government, and they offer to throw in an updated One World Religion… Think about it… (Google: Project Bluebeam.)

Remember that **we are not here alone** and there isn't just one kind of 'Other' out there or among us (examples in Chapter 5 make this clear). And so the possibility occurs that these Others may decide to take to the skies, get our attention, and then pretend to be saviors who just happen to look like us (Anunnaki Remnant hybrids do look just like us), and who just happen to have the key to setting up a One World Government… **and** may help us avoid World War III, remove the many killer diseases, and remove the pollution. Based on their values. What if the TR-3B is the craft they use and they are benevolent?

Government Evaluation

Little known to the soldiers and officers of **Bentwaters–Rendlesham Forest** back in 1980, the US and Britain appear to have wanted to see just what the soldiers and other trained personnel would do if confronted with a UFO landing. Would they accurately describe what they had seen, record what happened, test for radiation, take pictures… or would they panic? (This would be a test of the 1962 Brookings Report – to see if Man is still fragile and cannot handle a confrontation with a real UFO.)

So, it is reasonable that a section of the Military, perhaps the Psy-Ops section, enacted a UFO visit and collected data on the personnel who went out to see the small, **black triangular** UFO in the woods. No one on the base was in on what was really going on – genuine reactions were wanted. The UFO came in once and again for observation, then disappeared. And interestingly enough, so did the files and collected documentation on the event which were filed with the British Ministry of Defence [sic]. The soldiers seemed to have passed the test – even if a bit confused to this day.

Reagan's Warning

Remember back on September 17, 1987, **President Reagan** was speaking at the UN, and was hawking his SDI or Star Wars Defense Initiative. He said:

> Our differences, worldwide, would vanish if we were facing an alien
> threat from outside this world. And yet I ask you … is not an alien
> force already among us? [220]

On another occasion, Reagan was previewing Steven Spielberg's movie *ET* in the White House movie-room, when he commented to Steven:

> There are probably only a handful of people in this room that really understand how true this really is. [221]

Soviet **Premier Gorbachev** also said in 1987: "The phenomenon of UFOs does exist, and it must be teated seriously."

It makes you wonder what Reagan and Gorbachev were privy to and whether officials perceive a possible alien threat – or were these statements "froo-froo" designed to support a later fake visit by fake ETs as suggested above…or promote SDI?

Lastly, the late **General Douglas Mac Arthur** suggested that our next world war might be fought in space around Earth…[222] and according to the **STS 48** video[223], we may be.

SDI and the Unwelcome Mat

So some form of SDI may actually be a reality, but publicly it was dropped in 1993. So what do we see in the **1991** STS 48 video clip – if it isn't a clever Photoshop® offering? The clip shows a UFO being fired upon [by an Earth-side source not in frame] and it does a 120° right turn to avoid the lethal energy shot. If that is Earth firing upon an ET craft, that is crazy. The ETs would have technology and fire-power way beyond what we have, so firing on them is like a caveman throwing stones at an M1 tank. Think about it, any ETs we see can be either benevolent or indifferent – a really hostile, advanced ET race would have made short work of us, <u>and long before now</u>.

> So what that says is that we are firing at other Earth-based craft since Chapter 12 reveals that we are in containment… no **STS** 3D ETs are visiting Earth. The little Greys when they do their genetic work operate via intradimensional portals – with permission. In Quarantine, negative 3D ET craft cannot come into Earth space and fire upon each other. The **STO** 3D ETs are here.

So all that says we are being looked after and our 3D and 4D Custodians probably are searching for ways to negotiate with an arrogant, violent bunch of humans who will not 'surrender' their illusion that (1) they control Earth and (2) it is their planet….and the **PTB** would shoot at those who want to assist Man while at the same time attending any negotiations with ETs. (Note: The Air Force gave orders in the 50's to shoot at UFOs.)

And because the PTB **Cabal** is largely USA-based, it holds a lot of responsibility to help or hinder any Interface with ETs, and it has been theorized that non-disclosure is largely dictated and controlled by the Cabal, not the military… It appears that the Cabal (PTB) currently values their power and control more than interfacing with ETs to clean up the planet and stabilize and empower the Human Experiment. [224] But that may change.

This could be a significant reason why SDI-type weaponry would be developed and used against any ETs who seek to promote a positive change on Earth. Just something to consider, and by the time that the nature and status of Earth is examined in Chapters

12-13, it will be better understood why the STO ETs (Custodians) proceed as they do.

Dr. Greer's Input

According to our "pro-disclosure" researcher, Dr. Steven Greer, there **are** Earth-based UFOs and he compares them to the real thing that Man has been allowed to 'recover':

> First of all, [real] extraterrestrial capabilities are extremely advanced... salient aspects of [their] technology have been taken out [of the UFO literature] so that people won't be discredited because it *is* so unusual. But then, if it *isn't* very unusual, most of the time this means it is an "alien-reproduction vehicle" [ARV] that is being manufactured by Lockheed and Northrup. People often ask, "How do you know the difference between a man-made UFO and an extraterrestrial vehicle?" It's very obvious if you are ever close up to one, because the entire *quality* of it is different. The ones that are extraterrestrial are extremely advanced, in the sense that they are "awake." **The actual craft itself has artificial intelligence and is conscious**. The beings on board are connected into it and can connect to you consciously. And the kind of light it gives off is like nothing you have ever seen on Earth: It is extra-ordinary. It looks like it is not of this world... [225] [emphasis added]

Man was allowed to recover space craft inserted into our reality and having met with some alleged 'owners' of the craft, Man has been able to **reverse engineer** the craft to a limited extent (Think: TR-3B). In sum, there are three types of UFOs: interdimensional/Grey (20%), Earth-based (60%), and the Neggs' illusions (20%). This will be clearer when Chapters 12-13 examine what Earth actually is.

Flying A Saucer

What does it take to **pilot an extraterrestrial UFO**? Dr. Greer's information above gives us a real clue: the craft is almost sentient, or as he puts it 'conscious.' It responds to the pilot who sits at the console, with his hands in pre-formed "hand-like" recessed impressions, (designed for the specific pilot), which the on-board computer 'reads', and the pilot may also have a headband or helmet which transfers his thoughts to the guidance system. [226] (Remember the 1982 Clint Eastwood movie, *Firefox*?)

> Both the orbs and UFOs are flown using "thought command" .... The thought command system on UFOs is connected directly to the pilots through a sort of **electrical "nervous system" on the craft**, which can be controlled by their own minds. The bodies of each crew member are likewise tuned into and connected to the nervous system built into the spacecraft .... It is adjusted specifically to the frequency of each crew member. Therefore the craft can be operated by collective thoughts... Thus there are no complicated controls or navigation equipment on board the [ET's] spacecraft.[227] [emphasis added]

So the ET pilot thinks about going to Earth, the system looks that up internally in its Navigation System, finds the coordinates, and like any good GPS system, or

Map-Quest ®, the craft sets the course and the pilot engages the craft with an expectation of speed/time to arrive. (The ship automatically uses what astronomers call "pulsars" as navigation aids, as suggested by **Dr. Paul LaViolette** in his book, *Decoding the Message of the Pulsars*, which can be used like space beacons.)

Disclosure Problems

Dr. Greer above is also heading up the organized effort to get the Air Force and/or the Government to disclose what they know about UFOs and ETs to the public. There has been a veil of secrecy clamped on the subject since the 1947 Roswell recovery of … whatever. While the official news release in July 1947 was that a flying disk had been recovered in the New Mexico desert, an immediate retraction was printed the next day that it was just a weather balloon, and they even later included "crash dummies" to explain the bodies found – **which were not part of the original account**. Later accounts of the crashed ship, by UFO researchers getting their information from leaks and anonymous informants, included the idea that there were bodies found in the wreckage… and weirdly enough, the Air Force then announced that they had used "crash dummies" to test high altitude parachuting effects on the human body… and that is what everyone was talking about. Even more interesting: there were **two craft** that crashed. How did two ET craft piloted as described above, with sophisticated hardware for interstellar travel, manage to hit each other? Or … were they shot down?

The Air Force even had Maj. Jesse Marcel Sr pose with the remnants of a weather balloon to cement the idea for the public (look closely at the picture):

Major Jesse Marcel Sr Exposes Roswell Truth
(credit: Bing Images)

131

An answer to the **Roswell crash** is that they weren't both ET craft. At least one was a terrestrial craft. One of them had oriental-looking 4' humanoids on board... source unknown. And the Army Air Force brought in the German rocket scientists from Alamagordo to evaluate what had been found. If it was truly alien, why bring in the Germans to see it... unless the government saw that these were not alien craft and they suspected the Germans might know something about it....? [228] The Germans denied any knowledge of the craft or technology on those craft.

Due to the **Blue Book** years (1952-69) of Air Force research, and government cover-ups (e.g., Condon Report, 1966-68), and the more recent (and still-in-effect) Brookings Report, (1962) even if the government wanted to disclose the truth – THEY CAN'T.

> How would citizens react to the knowledge that trillions of dollars have been spent on unauthorized, secret and unconstitutional [black] projects over the decades? [He means <u>expensive</u> secret back-engineering of UFOs, all the while denying they exist.] [229]

Consider that it could be worse than that. How would you like to be told that we have had exotic, back-engineered craft that could have been used to go to the Moon in a much safer way (and maybe did – See Appendix A)? It has been said that **Dr. Wernher von Braun** knew something and was always upset with NASA who forced him to use rockets instead of the technology that he and the Nazis had developed. [230] Has our government kept a 'gynormous' secret for too long and now they can't tell us because of the anger and backlash...? (As will be seen in a following section, the Government is not the enemy.)

By the way, here is what the Nazi technology produced in 1941:

The pre-Vril aka *Flugelrad*
(credit: Bing Images)

It has been theorized that this is what crashed at Roswell – at least one of the two craft (the other was 30 miles away at Corona). The **Vril** used fiber optics, transistors, Velcro and a turret sitting on a gear assembly... said to be found on one of the Roswell craft. [231] (That does not sound like advanced alien technology.) What if that is true? [232]

This is the *Flugelrad* craft in flight: (Note angle of 'wings' below and above picture.)

(Credit all: Bing Images)

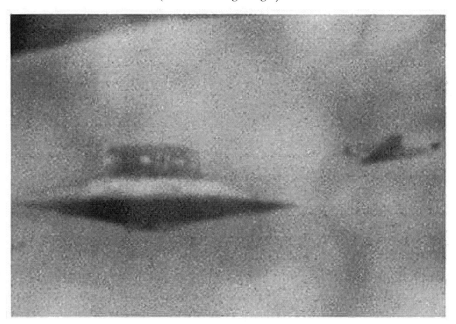

So it is obvious, despite the grainy photos, that the Nazis had exotic, field-propulsion craft. The *Balkenkreutz* (also called German Cross) can just be seen on the cabin of the craft.

These craft were largely experimental and while some used the counter-spinning magnetic fields to negate gravity, and others used the Schauberger vortex implosion technique (where the horizontal surface [consisting of adjustable wings, seen in picture, previous page] determined direction and air-flow). These were not nuclear nor were they using the ether (ZPE). Nor could the Vril fly to the Moon.

Later scientific technique, back-engineered from a crashed UFO in 1936 in the Bavarian Schwartzwald, and **Vril Society** input, led the scientists to experiment with anti-gravity via **the Bell** (*Die Glocke*) which was not designed to fly, but to test the levitation dynamics.

The Nazi development changed the shape of UFOs after the Bell 'power system' was perfected:

The Nazi Bell (*Die Glocke*) – note the Futhark Runes around the base.
(Credit all: Bing Images)

This powercore was put into a new design called the Haunebu:

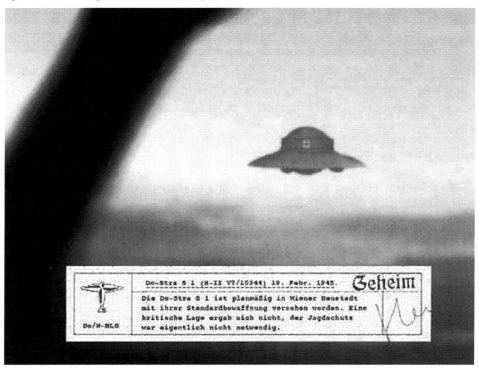

DoStra Haunebu I from a German Fighter Plane 1945
(*Geheim* means 'secret')

And there is another shot from **George Adamski's** files in 1957-60:

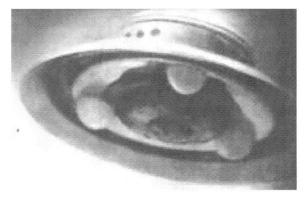

These both were called Haunebu I and they show the 3 energy condensers below the craft ... they were not gun turrets. Note the round magnetic housing between the condensers. (Note: it has no Iron Cross but is the same craft as above.)

It appears that **George was deceived**, and the saucer occupants were not Venusians.

(Credit all: Bing Images)

Another version of the Bell powerplant was put into the **Vril** (below). Note the condensers are gone:

Conceptual Vril 7 *Flugscheiben* (left and below)

This used 'magnetic reconnection' or counter-rotating rings of red mercury...

...and that allegedly led to a different Vril :

The Vril design is said to have given way to the Haunebu which used different technology, but achieved the same levitation effect.

These were not ready to fly and use in wartime, the Nazis were still testing and improving the power unit. As time went on, they built much bigger versions, such as the Haunebu II and III (below). The craft is real, but the **condensers** under the craft would not have 50mm

135

(Photoshopped) Howitzers. Yet, the underside armament concept might have been a prototype up until they discovered they could not shoot bullets from within the EMF (field) <u>below</u> the saucer. Guns could be mounted and fired from **the top**, however.

This was the later development, called the **Haunebu II,** twice the size of the Haunebu I. The real *Wunderwaffe*.

The Haunebu II *Flugscheibe*

And of course, they allegedly built an even bigger 120' version, the Haunebu III:

The Haunebu III *Flugscheibe*
(Credit all: Bing Images.)

Note the above also has Photoshopped guns on the underside, but is becoming a flatter, more aerodynamic shape… the **three condenser balls** were part of the directed energy that negated gravity and created a plasma field below the craft…similar to today's **TR-3B**. The original engineering design suggested **KSK** guns (little squares: *Bewaffnung*, on line 6) as *KraftStrahlKannonen* so they weren't Howitzers.

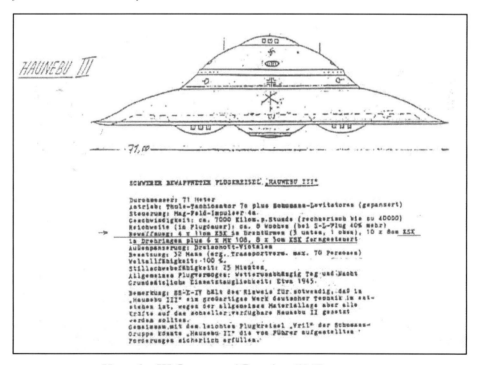

Haunebu III Conceptual Drawing (1945)

And as a matter of fact, the craft were so fast and agile that they were never caught in any aerial dogfights, but it is reported that they later did have *KraftStrahlKanonen* (KSK were more of an energy-microwave gun).

For that reason, it has been suggested that the next development, Haunebu IV, looked more like this (left):

A Conceptual Haunebu IV

Any potential armament would only have been **feasible in the top 1/3 of the craft**. With such a sleek and powerful craft, why didn't Germany win the war? Two reasons.

(1) The powerful electromagnetic field (EMF) around the saucer guaranteed that any bullets shot from under the craft would fly off-target, so Howitzers were not practical,
  and
(2) The German scientists deliberately held back fixing the armament issue of the craft as they knew Himmler would use it for <u>greater</u> evil.

> This was documented in an episode on the Military Channel. Note: Hitler was not the biggest problem, <u>Himmler was</u>, and as head of the SS he tried to have Hitler killed in July 1944 with a bomb in the War Planning Room. Why? Hitler was content to regain the land in Europe that had been the older **Germanic Confederation** of 1815–1866, as *Lebensraum* ("living space"). But, Himmler, Bormann and Goering wanted more.

Nonetheless, it is not documented what any current German craft look like, nor whether they still have the old ones… machines wear out. And the 3rd Reich probably disbanded and integrated into society… later generations often choose their own ideology.

Russian UFOs

It is suspected that as the Red Army came through the Eastern part of Germany in 1945, and outskirts of Prague, they would have discovered the underground facilities where the Haunebu and Vril (among others) were built and tested. That means they could have taken at least scientific plans back to the Soviet Union to tried and build their own UFOs, which it has been reported were called *Cosmospheres*. They did capture some Nazi scientists in those facilities who may have been forced to describe the basic principles, if not try to build such a field propulsion craft. (Before the war, the Germans and others were in touch with Nikola Tesla and Viktor Schauberger, so the rumors and basic concepts <u>were</u> in circulation.)

Allegedly, the Russian craft are more spherical, or elliptic, but we never see them:

Top Secret Russian UFO (HΛO) Development Program?
(credit: Bing Images)

UFOs and USOs

Another area of development removed the need for both Nazi submarines and flying UFOs – they found that if the craft was water-tight, the **field propulsion system** worked equally well in water. Air and water were two similar mediums and instead of *Luftscheibe* ("air disk") and a *Wasserscheibe* ("water disk"), they could have one craft that did both, a *Flugscheibe* or *Magnetscheibe*. [233] Or was this also disinformation?

Artist's Concept of a USO Emerging from the Sea
(Credit: Bing Images/UFO db)

139

Propulsion Systems

Lastly, regarding UFOs, it can be mentioned that there were many different types and shapes, not all capable of leaving the Earth's atmosphere. And yet, what is mostly seen nowadays, is not Haunebu, not Vril, but the **TR-3B, or black triangle** craft. To better determine whether this is an ET craft or a terrestrial one, we need to evaluate its propulsion system. A true, advanced ET UFO would truly be beyond our science, not crash due to random Earth scenarios, and it might be so advanced that it could not be back-engineered, or if it could be, there could be some component that we don't have (such as atomic element 115 that Bob Lazar mentioned).

The basic propulsion systems that the Germans experimented with were the following:

1. Viktor Schauberger and his **Repulsine: air** input, funneled into a vortex which resulted in a self-generating **implosion** that exits the device and explodes in the air. (Not practical for space travel.)
2. Karl Schappeller and his **ether-energy** device (Think: ZPE) which has magnets that generate 'glowing magnetism' that allegedly negated gravity and was another **implosion** device producing **'magnetic reconnection.'**
3. T.T. Brown and the **Biefield-Brown Effect** which is used in the B2 Bomber: a negative electrical charge is created at the back of the craft which creates a positive ('push') charge on the front of the craft, negating friction, sonic booms, and greatly reducing radar signature. If coupled with a plasma vortex under the craft, gravity is negated by 89% and you have the TR-3B. [234] **No jets needed.**

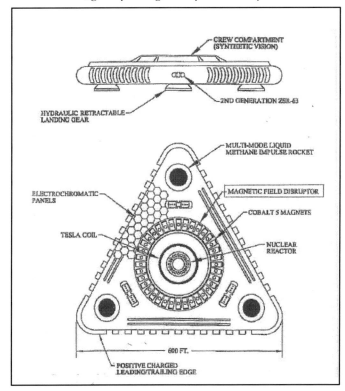

However, consider the illustration (left) – another example of creative **disinformation**. The three corner 'rockets' are not rockets but plasma condensers that help to steer the craft. TR-3B's are <u>always quiet</u> and jets would make noise.

Yet, note the **Magnetic Field Disruptor** in the middle of the craft. However, note the similar structure in the picture below…

(Credit: Bing Images)

A similar B2 Bomber **electro-gravitic effect** can be created in the TR-3B by the three variable-vectored condensers and an MFD. [235]

So, connecting the dots, we have

1. a history of secret projects (Think: Area 51) which turned out the black SR-71 Blackbird, the blackish B2 Bomber, the black F117A stealth fighter, and the black Aurora (which this author has seen), and the black Black Hawk stealth helicopter, and the blackish Apache attack helicopter…. And now a **black** TR-3B flying craft,
2. a flying triangle with plasma disruptor and **field propulsion** (electron/proton generation), technology that appears to be very close to that of the Haunebu,
3. and the following fished out of the ocean (from a smaller, winged prototype of some sort) showing a central magnetic power unit (MFD on the TR-3B?) :

Recovered Anti-Grav Prototype (note faint USAF symbol left wing)
(Credit: Bing Images/Black Triangles)

All that to say that the black triangles (TR-3B) do not qualify for exotic ET craft, and yet it is hard to know for sure who is building and flying them... Is the TR-3B propulsion the same as that of the Haunebu? – Even so, that wouldn't prove the Germans are flying them... the US recovered crashed craft over the years… and yet we find the following picture with a note in German:

The 'pinned text' says that it is "Die **Raumfähre** hat… mehr(?) mit der glob…." And that translates as "The **Spaceshuttle** has more [to do] with the global…" Did this replace the Space Shuttles we know about?

Normally, this (right) would be seen as a suspicious composite except for the fact that a TR-3B 'Astra' was photographed in flight (below)…

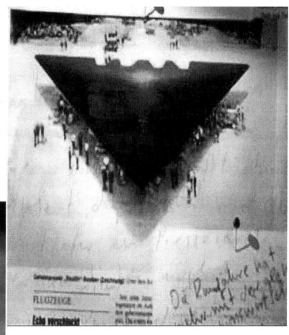

Area 51 Skunkworks Lockheed TR-3B Astra.

(Credit all: Bing Images)

…and they both have a similar aft (?) configuration. When researching the Internet, both pictures are identified as a TR-3B Astra (despite the German note) which is said to be a Lockheed creation. While it is largely a terrestrial craft, it has not been disclosed whether it is a German, a US, or a joint venture.

So we come to the key point in the discussion of UFOs as pertains to this book as a whole. This book is not about UFOs, and yet it is a fascinating subject which cannot be pursued too far without hitting a brick wall. And that is the point; one might spend years researching the UFO/USO subject and due to the disinformation out there today, all we can be fairly sure of is what the situation was 70 years ago – at the end of WW II. **Seventy years** since we knew the Germans had Haunebus whose propulsion systems seem to match that of today's TR-3B. That is not 70 years of progress. *Was ist los?*

The point is: there is enough disinformation, cover-up and error out there to make it impossible to resolve the UFO issue. While we can see that **they exist**, it is pointless to keep trying to get the answer, and all this chapter is saying is that the UFO confusion is just one more result of the disinformation in today's world. So what would be disclosed?

Grey Logic

The last thing we want to have is full disclosure, or overt contact with the ETs <u>at this point</u>. Either one could be disastrous to our civilization since the ET science, understanding of

God, and knowledge of our real history would certainly be different from what we are used to – as we were warned about in the 60's by the **Brookings Institute**. It would appear the ETs are aware of the fragility of the human psyche and respect the findings of the Institute to minimize throwing a naïve human civilization into chaos.

So why write this book? Three reasons: (1) Man needs to wake up and stop harming himself and the planet, (2) **semi-disclosure** helps prevent a total collapse if/when the UFO issue becomes more immediate, and (3) I was asked to write it to help seekers of Truth focus on 'graduating' from Earth. It will serve as **catalyst** for those who are willing to think outside the box that Man has been living in for centuries and become an Earth Graduate. The more enlightened will accept the new paradigm and move forward. The uninitiated will suspect something is now different and yet subconsciously they will be <u>protected</u> against a possible nervous breakdown because the Media and Government have been working a **reverse psychology** on them. They may have released the truth with disinformation in such a way as to show the thinking man or woman that things are not what they appear to be. (If the Government really didn't want people to think and wake up, would they allow *Ancient Aliens, Close Encounters*, or *Unexplained Files* on TV?) Many young people and older, smart thinkers are already fighting for what they 'know' to be true, having extracted it from the mish-mash of data out there.

Yet, the **Greys** are both a blessing and a curse. While they are performing genetic manipulation of Man's DNA to create a <u>better </u>hybrid race (Book 2, Chapters 8-9), they are also difficult to trust. They rarely communicate. How easy would it be to interface with ETs who can shapeshift, who know what you're thinking (so they tell you what you want to hear instead of the truth), who can plant false memories in your head, and their technology allows them to manipulate space/time? Part of the solution lies in Man's numbers being upgraded with enough of the **hybrid humans** (Indigos, Starchildren, etc) who have a higher IQ, are intuitive and more perceptive, and who are not imbued with limiting belief systems. Thus, they should be able to more easily see through deception and handle new (future) paradigms such that they would be better able to handle the ET presence.

So how do you undo the false beliefs in society? You don't. At least not peacefully. An effort was made in the 80's with ET-oriented movies to expand the public's awareness of aliens, but by the 90's we were back to the defending-the-planet-against-aliens concept – probably because it is more exciting and the human mindset finds war with aliens more entertaining. Think not? Consider the 2013 movie, *Ender's Game*. We're still at it.

The **actual solution** lies unfortunately, as Dr. Jacobs discovered, in the creation and release onto the planet of a better version of Man – more intelligent, more aware, less testosterone, and more able to assimilate new paradigms. It has been done many times; the latest was the replacement of Neanderthal with Cro-Magnon. It is now called **The Change**, and is further examined in more detail in Book 2, Chapters 8-9.

Government Denial of UFOs

While this is not a book about UFOs and it has in no way covered all the bases in that regard, it is significant that the US Air Force today repeatedly denies the existence of

UFOs – yet they used to chase them in their jets back in the 50's and had orders to **shoot them down** – which means the Air Force knew what they were, since shooting down real ET craft could have started a very short WW III – with the ETs!

If the USAF knows what they are, then they are not UFOs (i.e., unknown), they would be IFOs -- **Identified** Flying Objects. And then it would also be appropriate to deny the existence of UFOs since they are **IFOs**. And the Air Force has two warehouses full of evidence proving that UFOs don't exist. And something else:

We plan to be in space, and according to **Gary McKinnon,** we already are.[236] He hacked into NASA and Pentagon files around 2002 and discovered the names of non-terrestrial officers assigned to ships with names like "USSS LeMay" – he assumed that the 3 "S's" stood for [United] States Space Ship. He found a **Solar Warden** Program and pictures of ships.

(credit: Bing Images)

What is even more bizarre: instead of NASA saying that Gary hacked into our Simulated Fleet of the future where we game-play how an off-planet fleet would work, NASA and the US Government were angry and went ballistic seeking to put him in jail for 60 years. Huh? Again, I suggest that **they secretly want us to basically know**, and are working a **reverse psychology** on us – as Appendix A says. Or is it just semantics and we 'command the space' around Earth via satellites, missiles and Space Shuttles?

It is probably more than semantics. Consider the following timeline…

1938 UFO crashes in the Schwartzwald in Germany.
1941-43 Nazis build and fly Vril and remote fly 'foo fighters'.
1942 Large UFO hovers over Los Angeles, impervious to anti-aircraft fire.
1945 Germany surrenders, but scores of submarines and planes are missing.
1946-47 Admiral Byrd attacks Antarctica (December '46-Feb '47) with a small armada, and was soundly defeated. (Google: **Operation Highjump**) Looking for an alleged underground Nazi base in Neuschwabenland [now Queen Maud Land].)
1947 Craft crashed at Roswell (July)
1947 CIA established
1948 Air Force created (prior to 1948 it was the Army Air Force)
1952 68 UFOs buzz Washington DC (in one August nite)
1952 National Security Agency (NSA) established.
1952 Project Blue Book created (discontinued in 1969).
1953 Armed Forces Publication 146: a crime to release unauthorized UFO info.
1957-58 Admiral Byrd tries attacking Antarctica again (December); under the guise of **Operation Deep Freeze** and IGY. Defeated. Suspected Nazis are gone by 1957.
1961 National Reconaissance Office (NRO) created

1962 The Brookings Institute Report (against Disclosure).
1967 Outer Space Treaty – no WMD in outer space.
1969 Extraterrestrial Exposure Law.
1972 Wernher von Braun resigns from NASA (before Apollo 17 flight).
1972 NASA stopped the Moon Missions (last: Apollo 17).
1981 Space Shuttles initiated (terminated in 2011).
1983 Strategic Defense Initiative ('Starwars' SDI) proposed.
1986 Challenger Space Shuttle disintegrates.
1989 Berlin Wall comes down.
1990 First pix of Belgium Triangles taken.
1991 STS-48 video clip taken in orbit.
1998 International Space Station initiated.
2003 Columbia Space Shuttle disintegrates.
2000-02 Gary McKinnon hacks NASA and Pentagon computers.
2006 Pluto was reclassified (from planet to dwarf planet).
2011 SETI shut down (expensive exercise if they're already here).
2011 NASA stops the Space Shuttles (although Russia still operates hers, called **Buran**).
2012 Curiosity Rover lands on Mars (why not in the Cydonia area?).
2013 China sends Rover and Orbiter **Chang'e 3** to the Moon. (Appendix A.)

We have been busy searching the skies, Moon and Mars and still have not publicly announced any sentient life forms external to Earth. Other people in the Defense Aerospace Industry seem to know a bit more.

Rich Disclosure

The late **Dr. Ben Rich**, head of the Lockheed Skunk Works (Think: Area 51 and S4), shared a number of things in September 1992 during a presentation at the Air Force Museum in Dayton, Ohio. Sample statements included: [237]

"We now have the technology to take ET back home.

"We did the F-104, C-130, U-2 spyplane, SR-71, F-117 and many other programs that I cannot talk about.

"**We already have the means to travel among the stars**. But these programs are so locked up in black programs that it would take an act of God to ever get them out to benefit humanity.

"If you can imagine it, Lockheed Skunkworks has done it.

"I wish I could tell you about the projects we are currently working on. They are both fascinating and fantastic. They call for technologies once only dreamed of by Science fiction writers.

"**We now know how to travel to the stars**."

...and referring to Quantum Physics limitations in some equations that even Einstein could not straighten out, concerning hyper-luminal speed, Ben said, "There is **an error in the equations**, and we have figured it out, and now know how to travel to the stars, and it won't take a lifetime to do it."

And lastly, Dr. Rich, on his deathbed in 1995, shared one last jewel: He confirmed that there are **two types of UFOs** – the ones we build and the ones 'they' build. "We learned how to build ours from crash retrievals and **actual 'hand-me-downs.'**" [238] The ones we build and test-fly are called **Alien Reproduction Vehicles (ARV)** and are what people see from time to time and call UFOs.

> Another system called the **"Fluxliner"** culminated in the development of three different-sized vehicles. One was 7.5 meters in diameter, code-named "Baby Bear"... Next was an 18 meter version, code-named "Mama Bear"... The largest craft between 38-40 meters in diameter [120 feet] was code-named "Poppa Bear." ....The propulsion system was based on **Zero Point Energy** and it was said to be capable of **"light speed or better."** ....These "second space program" inventions were being developed in secret , while the above-ground relatively primitive Space Shuttle program was touted as progress to a fascinated American public. [239] [emphasis added]

Note: the speed of light is not an upper limit as Chapter 8 will reveal.

So Gary McKinnon discovered something very interesting, as well as Dr. Rich's statements may help explain why Dr. Werner von Braun quit the NASA Space Program (see Appendix A). And the government still denies things... for good reason.

No Disclosure

Denial is a very powerful weapon to give our government time to assess and cope with what appears to be a coming serious Change in our reality. Throughout history, people have proven to be fragile and prone to panic (Think: Orson Welle's *War of the Worlds* radio broadcast in 1938). Despite having been told at the start of the broadcast that it was just another show, people panicked and took to the streets with their guns! Many humans are unable to handle information that conflicts with the nice, little **prophylactic fantasy** that they live in. People as a whole would need to expand their thinking if we were ever to interface with beings (good or bad) from other planets.

Official public disclosure has not happened for the following reasons:

1. The public does not have a **need to know** (despite some curiosity at this point), and
2. Even if they did know, there is **nothing they can do about it**... except to realize that we are not alone, and it may not be <u>our</u> planet. (Herein is the risk of fear, panic, and nervous breakdown <u>and</u> the reason this book suggests a proactive alternative: wake up and get out.)

But public disclosure will not happen soon, for reasons already stated. In addition, according to the above-named Dr. Ben Rich, **full disclosure is not advisable**. It was originally his opinion that the public should not be told about UFOs and extraterrestrials.

> He believed people would panic and could not handle the truth, not ever. Only in the last months of his physical decline did he change his tune and begin to feel that the **"international corporate board of directors"** [i.e., the Cabal] dealing with the "Subject" could represent a bigger problem to citizens' personal freedoms under the Constitution than the presence of the off-world visitors themselves. [240] [emphasis added]

So, it appears that the government was doing **a wise temporary control of information**, and it almost broke free in movies in the '80s – but with the Indigos and ET hybrids beginning to insert among us now, disclosure seems even more remote than before … once **the Change** has taken effect, a more enlightened society will make a better decision as to what to reveal in the near future.

Two points remain and this gets interesting:

I. Breakaway Civilization

So if Gary McKinnon discovered a **secret space program**, and the Nazis developed flying craft like the Vril and Haunebu III, and Dr. Ben Rich told us that we already have craft that can go to the stars, and we are seeing Black Triangles (TR-3B) all over the world… are we being kept in the dark because (1) there is an ugly aspect to the exo-planet UFOs, or (2) because the very advanced breakaway civilization appeared to be a threat to the US and we raced to achieve parity, and we still are no match for them, or (3) we have achieved parity and united we face an external threat we cannot talk about ? (Think: Reagan's SDI Program.)

> **Note**: It is not because the Cabal is mean and wants to keep all the info for themselves. Consider: Could we already be on the Moon and are in a position to defend Earth (from whatever President Reagan feared)?

Maybe the stupidest thing Man has ever done was to send several space probes out past our solar system announcing our presence – what if underfriendly aliens find the probe and trace it back to Earth and pay us a visit? The plaque attached to the probe shows where we are. What if they see we are tearing up the planet and decide they want it for themselves…?

Could it be that until the Greys rework the human genome and insert the hybrid upgrade, that the large part of mankind is so far underdeveloped mentally and spiritually that the more advanced ETs don't want to deal with them/us? It is already a fact that ETs do not want to deal face to face with most humans because we carry **germs** and just like the sailors of Christopher Columbus that brought **smallpox** to the New World, and decimated the Indian population, the ETs are fully aware that human pathogens are very communicable. Not to mention the fact that most humans are fragile mentally and cannot handle the truth about ETs, the Moon, Mars and who is here with us on Earth already. For example, how many people could accept that Mermaids or Megalodon are a reality – even after the SCI channel ran programs and pictures of them?

147

Understand that the Greys interface with Man because they are **bio-cybernetic roboids** and are not susceptible to germs. Further consider that when humans are abducted and taken on board one of their craft, their clothes are removed because (1) they get in the way of the examinations, and (2) the clothes also can carry germs.

So, let's think more about this **hypothetically**. If the Nazis developed *Flugscheiben* and initially remoted themselves to underground bases in the Artic, Antarctic, or Chile, or Argentina…. They would not want to associate with "the unwashed masses of humanity" and would want to develop and protect their new civilization. (Think: Adm. Byrd defeat in the Antarctic in 1947.) A true, separate Aryan World. And if they had the ability to come and go from planet Earth, they might also be already working with those who (from **Aldebaran**) gave them a UFO in 1936 in the Schwartzwald, knowing that they would back-engineer it, build **the Bell** (*Die Glocke*) to test just the powerplant, and then insert it into the Haunebu working models.

Dr. Wernher von Braun and his compatriot Dr. Hermann Oberth, both answered a reporter one day at NASA who asked how they built such advanced rockets, planes, tanks, flying wings, etc – and Wernher's response was "We had help" and Dr. Oberth pointed to the sky. [241] When something crashed at Roswell, it was not surprising then that Wernher and a few top German scientists would be brought over from nearby White Sands to inspect the wreckage – to see if it looked familiar? It was said that Velcro, Kevlar, transistors, gears, and fiber optics found in one of the craft was not suggestive of ET technology [242] – but it was way ahead of the USA in 1947.

Is a **breakaway civilization** what the US Government cannot disclose, but several authors have already written whole books about? (Dolan, Marrs, Olsen, Farrell…) Or is that just fanciful thinking because we don't know what happened to the Third Reich?

> *What if Germany surrendered in 1945, but the Nazis didn't, as author*
> *Joseph Farrell has said?* [243] *The Allies neglected to invite a member of the*
> *Nazi Party to sign something legal. There was just Admiral Dönitz*
> *(acting head of the German Navy and Army) to surrender.*

Is it because the UFOs are directly associated with the existence of a more advanced group on the planet – and back in 1947–1952 when we couldn't even control our own skies over America – would that not give cause to deny a saucer was found and say it was really a weather balloon? And as the reality dawned on the Air Force (est. 1948 in response to the Roswell affair) and the NSA (1952), would the cover-up not be maintained especially if we were out-gunned, out-flown and no match for them? Would we not have a meeting with them (1954) to negotiate terms of a peaceful co-existence with them – "we leave you alone and you stop buzzing the USA and Washington DC?" Maybe we negotiated for access to some of their advanced technology… is that where Area 51 came from (in the mid-50's)?

Many interesting things to consider… yet, the Greys have the upper hand and are gradually **replacing this version of Man** who is largely inadequate to grasp and deal with the Reality of our current world in a way that is mature, respectful and proactive. The Brookings Institute reported (1962) that most people would have a **nervous breakdown** if unprepared for the reality of ETs and society would collapse in chaos. While it may not be that bad today after years of *Star Trek, Star Wars, ET, Close Encounters of the Third Kind, Cocoon, Taken* (2002 TV series) and *Paul*, there are still too many parochial narrow-minded people out there – and they are not reading this book. Nor do they watch *Ancient Aliens* on the H2 channel. They fear that *V* and *War of the Worlds* is the reality. Thus, there was only one way to **protect** today's sheeple and **proactively move** mankind forward, and that was by (1) denying what was really going on, and (2) creating a better version, a smarter, more intuitive version of Man so that a peaceful and competent interface with ETs could eventually occur.

The Hybrid Program is not about the takeover of Earth.

II. All Hybrids

And guess what? When all is said and done,

> **We are all hybrids -- descendants of the ancient Anunnaki and visitors from other worlds who were part of the Great Experiment (Chapter 1) – ET astronauts ourselves – from at least 5 Edens around the planet...**

Remember it was said that Earth was an experiment. STO ETs still care about us. No one on the planet today is a pure-bred human, created only by a God of the universe, as we were taught to believe. And if there were multiple ET groups making DNA changes over the centuries, trying new combinations of genes, then **Mankind is a mix of different alien humanoid breeds** – and something else very significant in Chapter 5.

The Greys don't care whether we know they exist or not, nor that we can be a lazy, ignorant, petty and violent species, **nor** that we can create inspiring music and art, and engage in many philanthropic outreaches. As **bio-cybernetic roboids**, programmed to do what they do, the Greys operate within the Quarantine and rework us genetically.

> **There is more on what the Greys are doing in Ch 8 - 9 of Book 2 (TOM) since what they are doing relates to Transformation.**

ET Summary

So Man is not alone, even today, and there has been an **on-going genetic upgrade** which appears to be making Man a better, healthier, more intelligent species. And if the Anunnaki are basically done upgrading Man via the Greys, then is the **Assimilation** into society already under way? (Book 2 addresses this issue in more detail.)

Genetics got even more mixed when other ETs came here, after the Anunnaki, and made genetic adjustments to the original humans... creating alternate versions and tribes in other locales (multiple Edens). In addition to the Anunnaki, there were also the beings from Sirius (according to the Dogon in Africa), Deneb, Aldebaran, and the Greys (according to Credo Mutwa, a Sanusi shaman among the Zulu). Interesting that Zulu means "people from the stars."

Dysgenics

And while it is not good news, the following is relevant and explains <u>why</u> the Greys are upgrading our genetics – particularly now:

> The Victorian Era was marked by an explosion of innovation and genius, per capita rates of which appear to have declined subsequently. The presence of **dysgenic fertility** for IQ amongst Western nations, starting in the 19th Century, suggests that these trends might be related to declining IQ.[244]

> *Dysgenics is the study of the cause of deterioration in hereditary qualities, and is highly susceptible to issues of political correctness.*

So several Western European nations conducted a study, involving Sweden, Netherlands, Belgium and Ireland, and discovered that (based on data that has been obtained and recorded since 1889), **the general IQ level has decreased by 13.35 points**, according to the same **2013 study**. So instead of the average person having an IQ of 100, it is now more like 85-90. And the significance of that is that the genetic markers in DNA that influence IQ potential in newborns, have been found to be declining… we are getting dumber as a species.

> *While it is said that 71-85 is 'below average' intelligence, the stigma is to be considered stupid, and for that reason, the IQ evaluation has irritated those who seek to say that we are all "created equal." However, "approximately 95 percent of the population scores an IQ between 70 and 130"[245] and that is far from equal – when those with IQ 70-90 have been found to commit more crime than those whose IQ is > 90. This IQ issue has societal consequences.*

The causative factors are said to be bad diet, drugs (Rx and recreational), chemicals in air and water pollution, and drinking, smoking and even obesity (because we exercise far less than our great-grandparents). Consider that our highly processed food, full of fat and sugar (because it enhances the taste), our junk food, fast food, and now, possibly, GMO grains…. Is it really wise to tinker with the way the original DNA was structured in our grains and vegetables? If our bodies do not get the nutrition they were designed for, the result is a lot of dysfunction and then illness. (See nutrition concerns in Ch. 14 and Index.)

The IQ decline is more easily explained in Chapter 9 where the plasticity and fragility of DNA is examined. The Victorians did not have cellphones, TV, cars, video games, **and** they often had to chop wood for the fireplace, ride a horse or walk 5 miles to their job which was often manual and was hard, manual labor for 8-10 hours a day – they were much stronger and more robust than we are today. There was no fast food, and in 1889, easy availability of liquor was absent.

Thus the Greys are doing us a favor by 'resetting' the DNA to a more healthy version of Man. So while the ET-UFO issue is fascinating, the Grey issue is more immediate and important. (See TOM Ch. 8.)

For the rest of the story on UFOs, see *The Earth Warrior* (TEW).
Real places, events and people set the stage for the docu-novel.

Chapter 5: OPs: Origins and Traits

It will be seen at this point that Man has two main sources of interference with his mental and spiritual development. Dual interference from the 3D physical realm via the Powers That Be (PTB) some of whom are descendants of the Anunnaki hybrids, and another from the soulless pre-Adamics who are still here. In the Astral realm, he has to deal with the Neggs (short for "negative guides") and occasional discarnates.

In the physical, Man has to deal with the "1st Seed" of Genesis 3:15, also known as the OPs (pronounced "Oh Peez") or Organic Portals. "Organic" because they are flesh and blood, living beings, and "Portals" because they have no soul and are occasionally subject to manipulation from the Astral. If they have no soul, they have no aura, and that is the easiest way to spot them, but they are also readily identified by their behavior, as outlined in this chapter.

As the chapter unfolds, remember:

No aura = no soul = no conscience

The point of these next four chapters (5 – 8) is to:

1. examine the OPs, what they are, what they do, how to identify them, and why they are a problem;

2. examine the Neggs and co-players in the Astral realm, and see what they do and why;

3. lastly examine briefly what Man is and how the OPs and Neggs contribute to his on-going deception, distraction, and keep Man off-purpose.

Ubiquitous OPs

This chapter is the first of two dealing with the OPs which are about 60% of the population on Earth. They don't have auras because they don't have souls; the aura is the physical 'reflection of the soul's energy – in fact, the body is contained within the soul, not the other way around. A soul means a connection to the Higher Self or Oversoul of which one is a part, and that in turn is connected to the divine hierarchy from whence commeth **conscience**. OPs have no conscience because they have no soul. Another word for them if and when they are dysfunctional is sociopath. They are not all bad.

If people saw auras, specifically the 1-2" etheric energy outline around people, they could verify this for themselves simply by observing people around them every day and taking a rough headcount. The fact that people don't see auras is why they don't know about the OPs, and this makes their existence even more of a secret -- and a problem at work and in a family.

Shown (left) is what the average person with an aura looks like – just the 1-2" etheric level. It is the bright white glow – easiest to see around the head against a dark colored background.

OPs do not have this energy glow around the head; they have what looks like 'heat waves' above their head, and only above their head.

Human aura
(credit: Digital Vision, and Kevin R. Brown, 1997)

While OPs are **not evil**, they can be a real nuisance, sometimes escalating to being a real pain, as they are very self-centered and STS (service to self) in their orientation to life, job, marriage, etc. For them, everything is about getting what they want, survival, power and ego – they have no compassion, no conscience, no altruistic tendencies, nor any interest in spiritual pursuits. They are usually the atheists since they have no soul and thus no connection with any Higher Power.

If one can identify them, and methods for doing so are included in these two chapters on OPs, they can be avoided and their negative effects minimized. If they make pronouncements for change and get their way, they can harm an unsuspecting society, or school, or church. (Think: Madalyn Murray O'Hair.) Methods for spotting them are given.

Valentinian Gnosticism Revisited

The idea of soulless people is nothing new. As was seen in Chapter 2, the ancients knew about these people 2000 years ago – they were called *hylics* by the Greeks. Even the Maya had a story about them in the ***Popul Vuh***, and Valentinian Christianity (Gnosticism around AD 140) also addressed the basic nature of Mankind, according to one of 3 aspects: [246]

> **The Elect**: the '**pneumatic**' or spirit-filled who were searching for a deeper Christian message because they lived via gnosis/insight;

> **The Called**: the '**psychic**' or mental man who was happy with what he knew (knowledge) and he walked by faith;

> **The Material man**: the '**hylic**' who was incapable of understanding any spiritual message, and did not have the soul-awareness of the other two types.

What is significant about this schema (from Chapter 2) is that in the early centuries AD, man was aware that **all men were not 'created equal'**, and that some men had souls and some didn't. *Hylics* didn't have a soul. [247] So they are not 'equal' to people with souls. And they may be doctors, lawyers and accountants because they can master details and many of them do serve a very useful function in society – but there is always the sociopath with a destructive orientation to society. Being a sociopath and having a soul are a contradiction – not that an ensouled person can't "go off the rails" and cause harm, but it is usually the conscience in the ensouled person that stops them from misanthropic behavior.

Somehow, perhaps deliberately in an attempt to 'level the playing field,' that information has been lost to the modern world. So much for truth.

For now, it is important to say that **we do not all have the spark of divinity within us**. And the assumption that we do leads to a number of errors, including marrying the wrong person, working for the wrong boss, or trusting the wrong person.

But what is important at this point is to stop and take a hard look at the "1st Seed" that was so often mentioned in the early part of this book. They were referred to as Organic Portals, hylics, and pre-Adamics – the result of the first Creation. And we were warned back in Gen. 3:15 that these people will be a source of problems for the ensouled humans as there will be enmity between the Two Seeds. Now it can be seen that the concept is more properly defined by whether they have a soul or not. So, it would be wise to know how to recognize these OPs to avoid them or contain them.

Why? For the simple reason that, while the OPs are not an organized conspiracy, they are the source of a lot of ensouled Man's troubles on the planet. And because the average person can't see auras, and easily spot the OPs, Man has decided that the problems on the planet are due to a conspiracy of Communists, or Jews, or Neo-Nazis, or Freemasons, Illuminati, or shape-shifting Reptilians.

Such thinking is misdirected, and because people don't understand Genesis 3:15, and can't see auras, their incorrect conclusion and placement of blame is understandable. Be aware that OPs are found in every country, every race, male and female, in every government, school and even churches – they are the problem within our society, not the Jews, not the Muslims, etc… *ad nauseum*.

The OPs don't even know what they are, much less that they are OPs. Thus, there is no organized conspiracy despite the fact that they all pretty much act alike, so it looks that way. And later it will be seen that there are different types of OPs, and so this disclosure in Chapter 5 is not about promoting a witchhunt, nor fear. It is to point out that there is another type of human on the planet with whom ensouled Man cannot basically get along… as the Bible said, it is unending strife because the two are naturally at cross-purposes. Genesis 3:15.

Organic Portals

So at this point, having raised the issue of the OPs, we need to take a more focused look at what they are. Again, there is a history and quasi-scientific investigation that has been made in their regard. 'Quasi' because this is a subject not readily open to scientific, hard evidence that you can hold in your hand and see that it is real – the main evidence for their existence comes from those who see auras. Anyone who sees auras will note that there are some people without auras. As the aura is the energetic reflection of the soul: no aura means no soul.

To those who don't see auras, the 'evidence' is meaningless. And to those who <u>do</u> see auras, they often go into denial and tell themselves that they just had an "off" day and can't see auras because they're tired…so they're not sure if they saw an aura or not… it was probably a 'retinal afterimage' they say.

Color in a World of Gray

It is frustrating to try and explain or prove the issue to people with normal vision. It is similar to a person who sees color because he has 'cones' in his retina, and he lives amid people who only have 'rods' and they see only black and white and shades of grey. He cannot describe the color red to them, for example, because they see it as just a dark shade of grey. They may even defend their limited vision by claiming him to be crazy, but he sees a whole world that is unknown to them.

The same applies to the 4D realm that surrounds us. There are reportedly things and beings that we cannot normally see, and as we will see in the next few chapters, **Man is not here alone** – there are Organic Portals (OPs), some discarnates, Neggs, parasites, Thoughtforms, and angels. And it is not cause for alarm, just because it is now pointed out. They have been here for a long while. And they are the reason the planet looks the way it does, and never "gets its act together."

Popul Vuh

Besides the Greeks and Gnostics identifying these people centuries ago as *hylics*, as is examined later, the same issue was understood by the Mayans and they wrote about it in their version of Creation, along with many of their ancient beliefs, in their *Popul Vuh*.

Normally, if this were the only source of information about soulless human beings, it could be easily dismissed as superstition and, coming only from the Mayans, it could be said that it was just 3rd world ignorance. In this case, however, what the *Popul Vuh* says about OPs agrees with what the Greeks said, with what the Gnostics said, and (in the next section), it agrees with what a current-day Russian researcher Boris Mouravieff said. The OP info is not BS from a backward country. It is truth that has been buried, most likely by the PTB or OPs themselves.

The following quote is reminiscent of the Anunnaki creation of Man – first the *Lulu* that could not pro-create, and then the *Adamu* who resemble the "wood" creatures below, and then the *Adapa* which could reproduce and was a lot like Homo *sapiens*. Check it out:

> According to the *Popul Vuh*, the "gods" had made creatures known as **"figures of wood"** before creating Homo *sapiens*. Said to look and talk like men, these odd creatures of wood "existed and multiplied; they had daughters they had sons…" They were, however, inadequate servants for the "gods."

To explain why, the *Popul Vuh* expresses a sophisticated, spiritual truth not found in Christianity, but which is found in earlier Mesopotamian writings. The "figures of wood" **did not have souls**, relates the *Popul Vuh*... In other words, without souls (spiritual beings) to animate the bodies, the "gods" found that they had created living creatures which could biologically reproduce, but which lacked the intelligence to have goals or direction. [*Adamu*]

The "gods" destroyed their "figures of wood" and held lengthy meetings to determine the shape and composition of their next attempt. The "gods" finally produced creatures to which spiritual beings [souls] could be attached. That new and improved creature was Homo *sapiens*. [Or *Adapa*.] [248] [emphasis added]

Sounds like a rewrite of the Anunnaki experience, and it should be as the Anunnaki went to Central America, as Viracocha, Quetzalcoatl, Kukulcan, etc. (see Chapter 11, 'Other Historic Anomalies')[249]... and they probably did the same 'teaching' there as the *Popul Vuh* continues the eerily similar point of view that Enlil had about the humans mating with the Anunnaki :

According to the *Popul Vuh*, the first Homo *sapiens* were *too* intelligent and had *too* many abilities! ... *they saw and instantly they could see far... they succeeded in knowing all that there is in the world...* Something had to be done. Humans... needed to have their level of intelligence reduced. Mankind had to be made more stupid. [250]

This is reminiscent of the issue with Enlil: the hybrid offspring of Anunnaki mating with humans was a threat to the dominance of the original Anunnaki who were limited in number, while the humans increased their numbers every day. Remember, Enlil's solution to the same threat was to let the coming Flood remove the problem. The Mayan gods said the same thing the Anunnaki said to this issue:

... are they not by nature simple creatures of our making? Must they also be gods? [251]

So as the Anunnaki also "dumbed down" their creation by removing abilities from Man's DNA, so too does the *Popul Vuh* relate a similar treatment of Man. Not only did Man not get to live as long as his creators, he was not to know what they knew, nor be able to do what they could do, and mankind has been pretty much kept ignorant – just as the God of E.Din (Enlil) wanted. **Nexus**: the Mayan gods were the Anunnaki.

And the connection with this chapter is that the OPs see to it that Man is dissed, harassed, frustrated, and blocked when he tries to reclaim his heritage, learn and do better. It should be noted that many websites' blogs are visited by OPs who login as 'Anonymous' and then proceed to attack and shred what someone else has offered as something noteworthy.

What you think are other humans, just like you, aren't just like you, and **they do not share the same motivations and goals.** Their job, sometimes with their controllers (Neggs) working against you, through them, is to stop you. And because you don't know any better, they succeed in creating wars when Man could be uniting, they create scarcity when there could be abundance, and they create fear when there could be peace, love and faith.

Why? To keep Man from getting it together and developing his divine potential – something they absolutely do not understand (because they don't have it).

> *Suppose the leaders of other countries and their military brass decided to declare a war… and the people didn't go along with it? To overcome this resistance, it would be necessary to control the media so that the people heard only what would get them to agree that attacking another country was the 'right' thing to do. And the leaders could keep it up as long as no one figured out what they were doing…*

It is fascinating that the Greeks, the Mayas and the Gnostics knew about this same OP truth which has been hidden from 'modern' Man. And yet, there is a current-day researcher who has also discovered it in her hypnotic regressions.

Backdrop People

New Age researcher, the late **Dolores Cannon**, discovered the OPs as she was working with her patients under hypnosis, and sometimes while speaking with the client's subconscious to better explain a problem. She called them Backdrop People as they are more like extras in a movie, and are just present to drive the humans' Scripts, or the Father of Light's Greater Script. She also was told that they have no path in life, no purpose such as soul growth – because they have no souls.

> This issue is further examined in *Amplified Science of Mind* (ASOM) in Appendices C & D.

In addition, the Russians have really done the most complete research into the issue.

Dr. Boris Mouravieff

Besides the Greeks and Mayans identifying these people centuries ago as *hylics and "figures of wood,"* there was a well-educated Gnostic, Boris Mouravieff, who was a Russian emigrant living in Paris in the 1940s – 1960's. He knew G. I. **Gurdjieff** and P. D. **Ouspensky**, but was not a pupil of either. Mouravieff wrote a version of Gurdjieff's 4th Way Teachings, calling his work Gnosis which consisted of 3 volumes. His primary contribution, although not the only thing he talks about in his three volumes, is to reinforce the concept of 2 races of Man on the planet: two races of humanity without regard for skin color, national origin or sex. He calls them **pre-Adamic** and **Adamic,** [252] or OP (Organic Portals) and ensouled, respectively.

> **Except for the lack of a soul in the OP, they would be almost indistinguishable from ensouled humans on the street, or TV.**

To people who cannot see auras, this information might be useless except that there are other ways to spot OPs that are pretty reliable. Of course, as with any skill, it takes knowledge and practice in the ways to spot them, and for your own well-being, the information is given in this chapter.

Why? You really don't want to marry one, if you have a soul, and you don't want them to head up your schools, churches and government. Proof to follow…

Creation revisited

Mouravieff's alternate, enlightened interpretation of the first two chapters of Genesis goes something like this:

> Genesis Chapter 1: the original 1st creation – without souls.
> Boris Mouravieff calls these humans **pre-Adamic man**.

> Genesis Chapter 2: another creation where the 'breath of life'
> (*ruach*) was breathed into *adamah* meaning "earth man" –
> Adam had a soul. Eve was created from Adam's rib and as a
> 'meet' (complementary/corresponding) mate for Adam,
> would also have a soul.
> Boris Mouravieff calls these humans **Adamic man**. [253]

To repeat: pre-Adamic man has been termed an Organic Portal for two reasons:

> **Organic** because they are flesh and blood,
> **Portals** because entities from the 4th can and do operate
> through them to serve an STS agenda.

A word of caution: just because the 4D entities can operate thru the OPs does not mean that the 4D entities created them. Nor that the OPs are always manipulated by 4D entities. The ability to manipulate the OPs is more due to the lack of higher energy centers (body chakras 4-7) that would normally support a soul inhabiting the body. With only the lower 3 chakras functional, the OP is a lot like an unfinished 2-story house, and no soul wants to inhabit an unfinished house… but without the upper 4 chakras, they are easy to manipulate.

That means that those things that a soul could normally do in a normal body (with all chakras functional), cannot be done in an OP body – even through the OP body looks normal, it isn't. These differences will be delineated in the review of "A" and "B" Influences below.

Note again that the creation of Man took place in two distinct stages and the pre-Adamic and the Adamic coexisted for a long time, probably intermarrying. [254] But the two were quite different in their ability to evolve:

> The prehistoric period is characterized by the coexistence of two humanities:
> pre-Adamic *homo sapiens fossilis*, and Adamic *homo sapiens recens*. For reasons
> already expressed, pre-Adamic humanity was not able to evolve like the
> new type. Mixed unions risked a regression in which the tares would
> smother the good seed so that the possible growth of the human species
> would come to a halt. The Flood was a practical suppression of that risk.[255]

Note that the Flood did not totally wipe out the pre-Adamics any more than it wiped out all the Nephilim, as was previously covered (Chapters 2-3).

Not All Men Are Equal

Again, Mouravieff noted that the pre-Adamic was limited in its awareness and developmental potential due to no higher energy centers (chakras) formed and active. [256] The pre-Adamic are really seen as Anthropoids, and the Adamic are considered real Men. And the two were anything but equal.

> We must also note that the other extreme, the equalitarian conception of human nature, so dear to the theoreticians of democratic and socialist revolutions, is also **erroneous**: the only real equality of subjects by inner and international right is equality of possibilities, for **men are born unequal**. …. these two humanities …. are **now alike in form but unlike in essence**.[257] [emphasis added]

And again, he cites the difference:

> The human tares, the anthropoid race, are the descendants of pre-Adamic humanity. The principal difference…. is that the [pre-Adamic] does not possess the developed higher centers that exist in the [Adamic]… which offer him a real possibility of esoteric [spiritual] evolution. Apart from this, the two races are similar. [258]

The Two Seeds of Genesis 3:15 explained.

Seeds of Prejudice?

Is it unfair or not "politically correct" to point out that all men (and women) were not created physically and mentally equal? Not knowing about their existence only protects them – it does nothing to serve you. As an analogy, would you prefer a dentist fully trained in the best dental school, or one that got his degree through the mail? Would you knowingly marry a woman whose genetics will lead to her having all children with Down's Syndrome? Would you knowingly get on a plane with only one pilot who was subject to epileptic seizures (that he also may have told no one about?) In short, the point is: in order to have confidence that what we are about to do will work and come out well, we need to know who/what we're dealing with – that is the purpose of licensing, by the way – to give some assurance that the person we're dealing with is competent, or "all there", as it were. OPs are <u>not</u> all there, some are "out to lunch" and I'm sure you have seen ditzy drivers, inept doctors/dentists, and even wondered about the person you married at times… or what your elected representative is doing in Washington.

It is not prejudicial to call a spade a spade. And you are a fool to tolerate 'differences', problems or inconsistencies that obstruct a society's or family's or church's well-being… if you do, you have just signed on for the lesson and it will blow up in your face, sooner or later. You must know who/what you are dealing with, and then stand up for what is the right thing to do. This chapter will help you learn to see these people around you – by their behavior.

A & B Influences

And it is this basic difference that the ensouled human should be concerned about. While the OPs are not blatantly evil, they do present a problem to a smooth functioning society when they do NOT have the same orientation to life that the ensouled humans do. The OPs are not interested in personal growth, nor are they capable of it, and since they have little or no conscience, their morals are often of the barnyard. They are not interested in doing what is right or appropriate, even if they know what it is -- they do what benefits them. Since they are not altruistic, they see no value in charity, service to others, or doing something because it should be done, even if one is not going to pay them for it.

'A' Influences (preference of the OPs):

> The pressure to reproduce, marry, watch TV, subscribe to popular magazines, vote, engage in political activities, memorize sports statistics, recite lines from movies, explain away weird phenomena with orthodox rationalizations, and the drive to pursue money and power. [259], [260]

> **OPs are not interested in abstract ideas, and they cannot be helped, changed, fixed, re-taught or enlightened.**

'B' Influences (preference of the ensouled humans):

> Piecing together the truth, observing one's environment for glitches and synchronicities, meditating on problems to solve them, developing one's individuality, paying attention to signs from one's Higher Self, analyzing and learning from one's mistakes, helping others, and seeking to develop independent thinking and creativity. [261], [262]

Perhaps more importantly, and this relates to Man's ability to evolve:

> Pre-Adamic man does not reincarnate. Not having any individualized element [soul] in himself, (in the esoteric sense), he is born and dies but he does not incarnate, and consequently he cannot reincarnate. He can be *hylic* or *psychic* but not *pneumatic*, since he does not have the *Breath of Life* [*ruach*] in him, which is manifested in Adamic man…. [263]

See why the teaching of reincarnation was buried along with the truth about OPs?

He's saying that the OPs have more of a collective group soul, like animals, and that their lack of higher centers (chakras) prevents them from being aware like ensouled humans, and thus from reincarnating. Reincarnation applies to souls, not to non-souls. When an OP dies, s/he follows the "dust to dust" regimen; again, there is no soul to go anywhere and they are thus not concerned with what happens to themselves when they die.

Mouravieff also says that the OPs serve what we nowadays call the Matrix Control System [Absolute III], and the ensouled humans serve the Christ Consciousness [Absolute II]. [264]

Lastly, Mouravieff confirms what was said earlier about mixed families and nations:

> Meanwhile the two races are totally mixed: not only nations but even families can be, and generally are, composed of both human types. This state of things is the … result of transgressing the Biblical prohibition against mixed marriages because of the beauty of the daughters of pre-Adamics. [265]

OP Appearance

This can be a sharp way of spotting OPs: they <u>tend</u> to be more handsome or pretty because they usually have no **karmic influence** to affect the way their bodies/faces look. It was taught that without negative Karma to endure, the OPs could be as naturally radiant and good-looking as is humanly possible. Although there are exceptions to this 'rule:' I have seen several fairly plain and 1 ugly OP.

> Physically the two races are virtually indistinguishable. Statistically there are minor physiological and perhaps genetic differences. Physiologically, OPs tend to be **more attractive and well-proportioned**. Because they exist on an emotionally primal level, natural selection has ensured that sexuality, physicality and attractiveness play a large part in their physical evolution. Also, unlike ensouled humans, OP bodies are conceived and develop independently of soul pressures and karmic burdens, so they are as attractive as probability allows… [266] [emphasis added]

As will be seen later, **Karma** is actually embodied by the 'Script' on Earth; while there are forces that act upon Man and OPs that can be called karmic, they are actually more Script-driven for the ensouled. OPs do not have Scripts.

Much space has been devoted here to what Mouravieff says about OPs as he was the foremost, modern-day researcher into the phenomenon. Much credibility in this subject comes from a careful study of his <u>Gnosis</u>, especially book III.

Yet Boris Mouravieff is not the only source of information on the OP phenomena. It also exists on the Internet on various websites. Just Google the term "OP" or "Organic Portal". Some of the sources are channeled information so caution is advised, yet most of the Internet material usually refers back to Mouravieff and his three volumes of information of the subject.

Two Seeds

So again, we come back to the evidence, which is growing, that there were <u>and still are</u> **two basic types of humans on the planet**. There are two different "seeds" upon the earth who have basically different, opposing, orientations to life. While Man and the OPs can both be STO or STS, there is a tendency for the OPS to be STS, whereas the ensouled person can be either.

Again, why should one be alert and avoid them? Well, shouldn't you know about and avoid a dishonest used car salesmen? Shouldn't you avoid a nice-looking man who is also a child-molester? Shouldn't you know that the Earth is not flat? Shouldn't you avoid close contact with anyone (OP or ensouled) who has HIV/AIDS?

In short, if you're going into the woods, wouldn't you want to know where the snakes are? Problems, potential and actual, should be avoided.

Genesis Revisited

At this point it is also relevant to emphasize that the pre-Adamic man represents the 1st Creation in Genesis 1. And this is significant because the Bible tells us that Adam and Eve had two sons, who would be 'Adamic' like them: the offspring had souls just like their parents. Then Cain killed Abel and was expelled from the scene – and he takes his wife from the Land of Nod. And is relocated to the New World.

The 'mark' of Cain was no facial hair.

This is important information. There is only Adam and Eve up to this point, with their two sons. Where did the rest of the people come from? To cut to the chase, it is suggested that the people in the Land of Nod were descendents of the pre-Adamics, from the 1st Creation, and Mouravieff would agree. [267] That means that Cain had a soul and his wife didn't. As they left for parts unknown, and did a lot of 'begatting' as the Bible says, they began the mixed marriage scenario and the furtherance of the OP and ensouled lines, with enmity between the two, just as Yahweh/Enlil said in the Garden of Eden when he expelled Adam and Eve.

That is a suggested, plausible scenario. It explains where the OPs came from and why, as Mouravieff says, we have mixed families. A family with Mom and Dad ensouled and the kids ensouled would make for the theoretically balanced marriage. Unfortunately, the ensouled Dad could marry an OP Mom, and the offspring can be a combination that brings peace or strife to the family. Ensouled parents would not know what to do with unresponsive, do-your-own-thing OP children, and OP parents would not care about nurturing their ensouled children and giving them spiritual values. Does this describe today's families' problems?

A family may have **both** ensouled and soulless humans by natural birth.

It bears repeating: The problem with a mixed family, where the parents are OPs, is that the **ensouled human** (ESH) children will not be cared for (nurtured and encouraged) as they could have been by ensouled parents. OP parents do not know what to do with ensouled children and their questions, deeper seeking and awareness (even psychic) issues.

Note that an ensouled man and an ensouled woman (unless they have defective genetics) will usually produce an ensouled child… but there is no guarantee. With an OP man and an ensouled wife, it could be either, but with two married OPs, the offspring will <u>usually</u> be **only** OP. The reason for this is that an incoming (incarnating) soul will normally choose ensouled parents – unless there are hard lessons to be learned at the hands of OP parents.

Therefore a recipe for a rough, insensitive or tempest-tossed marriage is for an ensouled human to marry an OP.

OP Characteristics, Basics

So, what are the general traits of OPs, and how can one reliably identify them? The basics are given here, with some advanced aspects.

First, the only way to be sure, and reliably know if someone is an OP is to determine if they have an aura or not. Second, the alternative is observation over a period of time and seeing if their **behavior** is congruent with general OP behavior. Third, if such consistent (daily?) observation is not possible, then consider whether they are congruent with ensouled human behavior.

Ensouled Human Behavior

The following four points are typically ensouled human behavior <u>not found</u> in OPs.

1. ESH's care about other people and may find themselves 'hurting' for another person. **Empathy**.
2. ESH's are interested in and pursue **spiritual** goals – meditation, yoga, even therapy and seminars to develop self.
3. ESH's **pursue truth** and dig to find out why things are as they are; this may include therapy and resolving "inner issues."
4. ESH's can have hunches, **intuition** and sense energy and act on it.

And of course, there are other things that are mostly characteristic of ensouled humans, but the four points above are the <u>major</u> attributes that immediately stand out. And of course, be careful: there are times when an ensouled human can act just like an OP and be selfish, uncaring, and use other people.

Major Aspects of OPs

While they generally remain something of a mystery, a few things can be said of them:

1. They have no souls and thus no connection to the god-force; thus they are not interested in spiritual issues or self growth
2. Their DNA does not permit soul growth or connection to higher realms due to higher chakras not being activated
3. Most of them are not bad or evil – some may be first-level souls (Pre-souls), or placeholder OPs
4. When they die, it is "dust to dust & ashes to ashes" time
5. Because they don't have a soul, they have no aura

6. Because they have no soul, they have no spark or glint in their eyes; they are flat and lifeless (they love wearing dark glasses)
7. Because they have no soul, they are not interested in religious matters **and** cannot discuss them
8. They have no conscience, no compassion, and exhibit low, if any, morals
9. Standing next to one, there is a sense that no one is there; as in no 'presence'; their energy is 'flat'
10. Their purpose is to distract and drain energy from the ensouled humans thus preventing them from connecting with their Higher Self (and achieving John 14:12)
11. They are mostly interested in food, sex, power trips and games
12. A psychopath is often a failed OP – they failed to mimic ESHs and survive in the ensouled world.
13. They blindly serve the orthodox teaching on anything; they do not question nor do they innovate.
14. They have no "inner issues" or problems that they need to work thru.
15. They often cannot 'get' jokes with a double entendre, and their humor is crude.
16. Some OPs are driven to control others... real 'control freaks.'

Physical Characteristics

An OP has only the 3 base chakras operative – chakras 1 – 2 – 3, and as such there is no fully developed energy pathway between all 7 chakras, so there is not enough energy to radiate as an aura. What is seen, however, is a kind of generalized or hazy energy field above the body – like "heat waves."

> *Caution:* a fuzzy or hazy aura does not mean that that person is a malicious or mischievous OP. Some are good. **Pay attention to their behavior.**

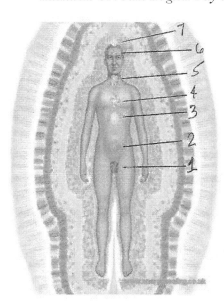

The basic human chakras are:

#1 – Root chakra – survival
    color: red   location: genitals
#2 – Power chakra – sex, power, money
    color: orange   location: navel
the person's lower back may ache if they have money/sex/power problems.
#3 – Self chakra – ego
    color: yellow   location: solar plexus
when someone is cowardly and wimpy, they are said to be 'yellow.'

Layers of the Human Aura
(Source:
www.differentlight.org/images/Aura.jpg)

163

Interesting that the chakras tend to relate to some of our physical issues.

Technically there are seven layers to the aura, each layer connects to a chakra. The innermost is the easiest to see (2nd page of this chapter).

The 3 basic chakras exist between the perineum and the solar plexus. The location and function of an ensouled human's chakras is identical to the OP's, except that the OP only has the first 3 chakras operative, and the ensouled human has all 7 operative, to some degree.

OPs cannot access the higher chakras because their **DNA is incomplete** and does not have the linkages via the **bionet** (Chapter 9). And with no soul, they don't need them. They can however, steal energy from the ensouled human to mimic the higher chakras, and when they do this they appear to be a full-scale human: all they are doing is <u>mirroring</u> the ensouled human and their attributes.

The missing OP (semi- or non-functional) charkas are:

4. Heart chakra – (**green**) compassion
5. Throat chakra – (**blue**) speak truth , wisdom
6. 3rd eye chakra – (**purple**) higher knowledge, insight
7. Crown chakra – (**white**) connection with Godhead, spirituality

Robotic OPs

Be it known also that there are some OPS that have been described as 'robotic' – real **control** freaks. They are very controlling, have no sense of humor, see everybody as something to be used to fit their agenda, there is no compassion, no remorse, and they are much more **aggressive** than the average OP. They fit very well in the military. If you marry one, they will tell you what to do and when to do it. Generally they are recognizable due to their tendency to talk down to people – as if you were 10 years old. The robotics are "OPS on steroids" figuratively speaking. No emotions. (Think: Mr. Spock on the original TV show *Star Trek*.)

Most OPs will start arguments with ensouled humans to get them angry and this provides an energy rush for them – they 'feed' off the energy you are radiating, as if they were an 'energy vampire.' Fear and lust also feed them (as well as the Neggs). Any strong emotion. You may even <u>win</u> the argument, but they got what they wanted and you will feel drained.

Energy Drains

Best of all, OPs provoking the ensouled humans into fear, anger or lust provides strong, radiated energy from the victim's 3 lower chakras – . This is often referred to as "**energy vampirism.**" [268]   And if they can start a war, that becomes a feeding frenzy, and it doesn't matter who wins – just as long as energy is produced that can be 'harvested' from the sheep who decade after decade put up with the manipulation.

Wouldn't it be nice if the PTB gave a war and no one showed up?

164

This is another reason to spot whom you are dealing with – so you don't 'feed' them. As a way of draining energy, OPs can trick unsuspecting humans into serving them, or solving their alleged problems for them, or believing false teachings that they promote. If an ensouled human speaks of spiritual wonders or experiences, the OP can laugh, deride and make fun of them – pooh-poohing any idea or pursuit that would develop ensouled Man's higher chakras. Sometimes the false teachings lead Man to spend a lot of energy in denying reality in a way that drains energy.

Such energy loss often involves others sending etheric 'cords' into one's aura as the 'physical' channels through which the energy is drained. [269]   These cords can't be prevented just by having a healthy aura but have to be proactively <u>blocked</u> by surrounding oneself with White Light <u>with the intention</u> to not be drained, nor affected by someone else's energy. The 'cords' usually attach around the 3rd chakra (solar plexus) and if one suspects that there may be one or more of these cords from other people, it is possible to visualize them being cut and even ask the Beings of Light to assist in removing them and cleansing the area where they were attached. This is not a game.

An OP Test

Here is a short test to see if from the description of 15 people whether you can tell which ones are the OPs. As will be seen in this section, there are some basic traits of the OPs (males and females behave alike) and some of the Ensouled Humans (ESHs) that almost always identify them. And yet, caution is advised in pre-judging, as will be explained.

Questions:

	OP	ESH
1. A person with dull, lifeless eyes; no spark of vitality in them.	_____	_____
2. A person who pretends to care.	_____	_____
3. A person who is only interested in money, sex and power.	_____	_____
4. A person who lies, cheats, and steals a lot.	_____	_____
5. A person who "eats, sleeps and drinks" religion.	_____	_____
6. A person who seeks personal, spiritual growth.	_____	_____
7. A person who criticizes everything you do.	_____	_____
8. A person who says they have been abducted by aliens.	_____	_____
9. A person who makes sacrifices for others.	_____	_____
10. A person who doesn't go to church.	_____	_____

	OP	ESH
11. A person who is very good-looking and has no problems.	_____	_____
12. A person who has a lot of health problems.	_____	_____
13. A person who is very controlling, insensitive and selfish.	_____	_____
14. A person who is suicidal.	_____	_____
15. A person who doesn't believe in God.	_____	_____

Answers:

There is 1 OP for sure (#1), and 2 probable (#11 and #13) – the rest can go either way.

Keep in mind that when the answer is "OP" that this signifies the usual, plain vanilla OP who does not have any higher centers (chakras) open. What you will see by the answers is that there are times when it is very hard to nail down just who is who. Hence

caution is strongly advised…

but with experience, even if one can't see auras, which is the safest method of spotting them, one will develop a 6th sense about the object of suspicion and usually be right – but it has to be based on (1) a <u>number</u> of traits, and (2) a "gut feel" that is developed over time.

Here are the answers with an explanation:

1. **OP** As was seen in the OP Aspects above (point #6), their eyes do not reflect any spark of life, which is actually the 'reflection' of a soul. They are usually brown-eyed as lifeless blue eyes are easy to spot, and brown eyes may also be so dark as to make it impossible to tell if they have an iris or not. Many OPs love to wear sunglasses, even indoors, as if they are aware their eyes are different.
2. **Both** Caring and not caring are not an exclusive OP trait, although many OPs do not have compassion or true caring as their heart chakra is not functioning – if it is, then the (Pre-soul) OP is trying to develop into an ensouled human, and their caring will be sporadic.
3. **Both** Ensouled humans can be just as 'primitive' as OPS and be focused totally on money, sex and power.
4. **Both** Lying, cheating and stealing are just as common in ensouled humans as is found among the OPs. It is a human inherited trait (Chapter 9).

   *Note: Later, I gave a personal example of a bad OP and a good OP. The bad OP has the above #2, #3, **and** #4 traits and if there is a person with all 3 traits, it is evidence to be very careful as they likely (90% chance) are an OP. I confirmed it for myself because I saw his lack of an aura. If a person, therefore, has too many negative traits, it is wise to be suspicious and leave them.*

5. **ESH** No self-respecting OP would be interested in religion as they don't understand what it is, why humans need it, nor can they discuss anything religious – they just don't have a clue. An OP can fake it, however, as in the case of my bad OP – for a personal agenda.

6 **ESH** Many ensouled humans are seekers of truth and enroll in classes and read books dealing with spiritual growth – to get closer to God. This is meaningless to an OP, as is religion.

7. **Both** It is often the assigned function of an OP to 'diss' and criticize whatever an ensouled human is doing, for the purpose of creating doubt and de-railing them. Of course, human nature leads people to be critical, and it is not the sole province of the OP.

8. **Both** Any human involved in the reproductive scenario can be abducted so that the genetics can be modified to (overall) improve the race.

9. **ESH** OPs don't sacrifice for others – unless it buys them something, or the 4D STS has directed them to do what looks like a sacrifice for some expected 'effect.' Sacrifice comes from the heart and that center is usually not open.

10. **Both** Ensouled humans avoid church because they hate God, or their mother made them go, or they call themselves an atheist . OPs are not 'fed' in church… they are bored there, but may be there to meet business prospects.

11. **OP** There are good-looking ensouled humans as well as OPs, so that was not the key phrase. "No problems" (that would come from Karma) defines an OP as OPs do not operate under any karmic laws, and so there is no major negative aspect in their life that bothers them. They do not have 'issues.'

12. **ESH** Ironically, many OPS are very healthy people. It is the ensouled who are suffering some 'karmic' lesson, allergic to something, or have a weak immune system. Not that OPs can't come down with a cold or the flu, but if they do, they go out to a bookstore or mall and play 'energy vampire' and get the energy they need to heal.

13. **OP** The key here is "very controlling," and they are masters at it. And at the same time they are insensitive and are controlling you for their agenda. This <u>can</u> be an ensouled human doing this, but it is not sustainable day-in day-out as the robotic OP does it most of the time.

14. **ESH** Do not hesitate to intercede for someone who is suicidal; your time and efforts could save their life. If they succeed at suicide, they will be sent back into the same lifetime (from the top) to handle what they thought they couldn't handle… and experience **Déjà Vu**. There is nothing we experience that we can't handle; suicide is a cop out, and the 'lesson' will have to be met. OPs do not consider suicide because they never get that depressed.

15. **Both** While anti-religion issue is often a giveaway (favoring an OP), there are hurting people (Charles Darwin was a soul) who resent God for not healing them, then blame Him, and assume He doesn't exist because He didn't answer them. (God <u>won't</u> remove your 'lesson' and if it is a physical health problem, it would be wise to spend some time seeing <u>why</u> the illness has gotten your attention, and change whatever needs to be changed.)
Some atheistic scientists are thus OPs.

Repeat: Some caution is in order as there are ensouled humans who can and DO act like soulless OPs… so no snap judgments should be applied.

I will repeatedly emphasize this caution because this OP material is not about a witch hunt. In fact, a lot of the OPs are good people, but rather 'primitive' as has been seen. Their main 'danger' to you is for you to be ignorant that they can and do operate to deceive, distract and derail you – as well as drain your energy.

OPs are best spotted either by seeing their lack of auras, **or their 'flat' eyes**, or by observing <u>multiple</u> facets of their behavior ('A' Influences)… all but the very best eventually betray themselves by their behavior. Those OPs who fail at fitting into society and emulating ensouled humans tend to be described as 'psychopaths' – they wind up hating ensouled humans and falling into dysfunctional, or criminal, behavior.

The following section can help recognize some problem humans…

Personal Experiences

Sedona Experience

I was in Sedona back in 1998 visiting a friend who had a very strange 10 year old son with flat black eyes; he appeared to be autistic, but his mother said he wasn't and had no explanation for his staring at me and refusing to talk, other than I was a stranger. As the day progressed, she complained of a general feeling of fatigue and an upset in her stomach area, and I offered to scan her aura (with my hand) and see if there was anything there. As I did so, I encountered one of these 'cords' and a weird, prickly kind of energy, and so I made several passes with my hands with the intention to remove the cord and any bad energy. As I did so, the son, who had been sitting on the couch, gave a loud yell as if he had been stuck with a sharp knife, and ran yelling "I hate you!" and crying to the bathroom, locked himself in, and would not come out. He had no aura.

I explained to her what had happened and that her son had been draining her energy, how he did it, and what she was going to have to do to stay free. She was not happy to learn that her own son was a parasite (I didn't know about OPs back then) and would drain her energy. However, she believed me since her energy had returned and her upset was gone. She felt fine and the son lost his energy source. I was amazed that it was that easy to remove.

Case 1 : A Bad OP – Shorty

At this point, it would be instructive to give a real example of an OP that was my room-mate for 3 years. We'll call him Shorty. Only base chakras open… he had no aura.

When he moved in, he had a boxy 4-door 4-cylinder sedan that was fine in the small town where he used to live, but he felt that it just wasn't "in" with today's women – it wasn't a "chick magnet" and being about 30 years old, this was important to him. So one day on the way to his college classes, he had an accident where a woman in a Suburban hit him in the left front and he ran off the road, and into a fence. He counted that a total loss, and took the insurance money plus some of his to get a more sporty car – A V6 Sebring convertible.

About a year later, he decided he didn't like the vehicle, and it still wasn't flashy enough to impress the girls, so he winds up in an accident identical to the first one - hit in the left front and counts the car as 'totaled', and he goes down with the insurance money (and some more of his) and gets a T-top, sporty V8 Camaro. The cops never caught on – nor did the lawyer of the other driver when Shorty decided to sue for $25,000 – after all, he needed to replace the two $10,000 outlays he had made, plus $5000 in legal fees.

All he got was $2000 and he bitched about it. I suggested one morning at breakfast that if he pulled the same accident for a third time, perhaps to get the ultimate "chick magnet" in a Corvette, the cops and judge would throw the book at him. He just looked at me. He never said, "What do you mean…?" but he never pulled it again. He moved on to other antics. Like going to multiple churches just to chase the women.

On another occasion, for Christmas past I had received a fancy glass jar with chocolate-covered maltballs in it, and I had put it up on top of the refrigerator, unopened. A few days later, I came into the kitchen and he was standing by the refrigerator eating something, and the jar had been opened and ¼ eaten. My intuition kicked in and I asked him what he was eating. He looked very guilty and said, "Nothing." So I asked him what it was he had in his hand, and he opened his hand to reveal 3 chocolate-covered maltballs, and I thought he was going to have a heart attack. I asked where he got them, and something an OP does real well is lie – up to a point. He said they were just lying on the counter. He found them.
I said, "You're lying" directly confronting him.
Shaking and glancing nervously from left to right, he said, "You're lying, too!"

I discovered over the years, there was never anything original that came from him – whatever I said, he parroted. In fact any argument with him was a waste of time, he could not even invent a response that wasn't a repeat of whatever I said.

Sounds like a moron, or a playboy, but he was mentally agile enough to get through college with a Masters, and figure out how to create an accident and make it look like the other person's fault. And he was clever enough to pretend he had a bad hand and he got one group of girls at college to do the research for his term papers, and another set of girls to type them for him. And then he dropped all interest in them.

One Sunday, he was on his way to church, and I asked which one, and he said St. _____. I asked why he was Catholic, and he smiled and said he was because his folks were Catholic but he didn't believe in any of it, he didn't tithe, and he just went to meet women. It was also impossible to discuss the Virgin Mary, Jesus, St. Paul, the Bible, anything – he knew nothing about anything. And cared less.

On another occasion, I was out with the landlady to visit a model home, and she got a call from him on her cell – to come quick, someone had just broken in the front door of our house. We asked him to wait there until we got there – and of course, he didn't. It looked like someone had kicked in the front door and did about $400 worth of damage to molding and sheetrock. Complicating things was the fact that the latch had been sticking for a few weeks and would sometimes keep anyone from opening the door – even with a key – from the inside or outside. Nothing was stolen. The interesting part: someone had used a key to roll back the deadbolt before kicking in the door. Of course, Shorty denied everything. We had the door repaired.

So, you say the guy was just an inveterate liar. To repeat: he didn't have an aura.

His room was a pigpen from day one. Never organized anything, laundry all over the place, books and CDs stacked in a corner, and the room was full of things given to him by well-meaning people who heard him say he was a "starving student," and so he had 3 ironing boards, 2 irons, 3 potted plants, 2 typewriters, 4 lamps, 2 non-working computer printers… and 56 CDs (we counted them) among other things. All given to him.

I got up one morning to find he was ironing a shirt in the upstairs hall and he had put the hot iron face-down on his shirt and ran downstairs to answer the phone. It was smoking. I unplugged the iron, and could not get the shirt unstuck from the iron, so I put them in the tub. I resolved to keep a fire extinguisher just inside my room. And he pulled the same stunt 2 more times – the shirt almost caught on fire – and that's when I blew up at him, and took the iron and hid it. When he asked me what I was doing, I answered that this was all because he was so dumb. He said, "You're dumb, too!"

We finally prayed and commanded the damage to stop, in Jesus' name, and that any/all lying and destructive spirits were not welcome in the house, and that they would wait for him outside. The next few weeks he was very quiet and docile and there were no further incidents, but he was getting surly without saying anything.

Finally he announced he was moving out. He was moving in with a woman who had 3 teenage kids and didn't care if he was a pig. Shorty was a constant nightmare and those are the kinds of things they can subject you to. They are insensitive and don't care about anything – except getting what they want: food, sex, and money.

Case 2: An Advanced OP – Wanda

'Shorty' was profiled above as a bad OP. He was very destructive and lied a lot – even if caught red-handed. He was a rather obvious candidate for an OP – even if I hadn't seen his lack of aura.

For those psychologists, psychiatrists and teachers who have had some in-service training (as I did), and who are reading this book, it can be said that his behavior mimicked that of an FAS (Fetal Alcohol Syndrome) person: the lying, taking things that didn't belong to him, and his use of other people to do things for him. And I might have stopped with that 'diagnosis' had I seen an aura around him. In any event, it seems that the treatment of him would be close to the same anyway: lock everything up and don't trust a thing he says.

After he moved out, in 2007, we had another interesting roommate move in. Also appeared to be an OP, no aura, but this one was a bit more sophisticated… a test from the universe perhaps? This one didn't destroy or steal – but those are not the only traits by which to judge an OP anyway. Just that we got past Shorty's destructive behavior only to deal with Wanda's (not her real name) power plays.

Wanda was a self-proclaimed queen – she moved in and took over. Her main characteristic was that of a spoiled woman – "high maintenance" as they say. She was recently divorced and had been used to an affluent lifestyle before her husband divorced her. So she now appeared to have a resentment against men in general.

Her basic behavior was to not tell you what she was doing, what her schedule was (when she'd need the bathroom), and then complain if we unwittingly obstructed her getting ready for work. I suggested we sit down and communicate. No. I asked if she could be considerate with her hours and kitchen and bathroom use. No. I asked if we could share some expenses to a mutual benefit. No.

She would never look me in the eye, and would go around behind my back and complain to the landlady about… something. Make it up. And she did. If I had to ask her to clean up her mess in the bathroom, she'd argue and threaten to move out. (Not an option, we needed the rent money.) Constant power plays.

She was Catholic, like Shorty, but not regularly practicing. Her mail came to a secret PO Box. She bought a locking doorknob to her room replacing the one we had there. And, lastly, she played head games; psychological maneuvers to get us to do things for her, or ignore her messes, or give her special consideration. Meanwhile she kept telling things about me to the landlady trying to drive a wedge between us (which the landlady was not buying and usually told me what had been said).

Of course, most of what has been just described is not uniquely OP behavior – and that is my point. **An ensouled person could just as easily act the same way**, for whatever justification. The dead giveaway was her lack of an aura – just a weird energy field around her, but not an aura. So most of the time I questioned whether she really was an OP… I didn't have to wait long for an answer.

The Dog 'Outs' Her

Things with her got even more interesting when we played host to some friends' small dog while they went on vacation. The dog had known us for years and liked to be with people, often watching TV with us. And as many people know, dogs are very honest; they have no agenda and they are open about whether they like someone or not.

<u>Every</u> time Wanda came home at night from her job, the dog would bark – good watchdog style, and then when he saw who it was, he would go ballistic – not just barking, but <u>snarling</u> and we had to hold him back for fear he'd try to bite her. He would not calm down, and when I picked him up, <u>he was shaking and bearing his fangs at her</u>. We jokingly said that the dog had 'outed' a bad spirit. We laughed about it, to ease the tension, but I didn't think it was a joke – the dog was deadly afraid of whatever he saw/sensed. Wanda had something with her and, besides no aura, all I could sense was a 'flat' energy about her…

Also interesting that we had 'babysat' the same dog back when Shorty (the other OP) lived with us and the dog never barked at him. So, OP was not the issue.

So I became curious: what was it with Wanda that was different? I renewed my efforts to see anything new or additional about her lack of aura, but was unsuccessful. Due to my research, it had to be one of two things:

either she had a bad spirit (entity) attachment that the dog saw or sensed,

or she was not an OP and was something else that looks human but wasn't.

To this day, I wish the dog could have talked and told me what he saw or sensed, but I soon got my answer...

Wanda Loses Face

On a following Saturday, soon after the incident with the dog, I went to use the bathroom and her room's door was open and I knew she was going to work that day, so I stopped at her doorway to knock and ask. She had her left side to me as she sat over in the corner of her room (15' away) working on her PC. Her peripheral vision apparently did not pick me up.

What I saw stopped me from knocking. I stood and stared at what I saw. It wasn't her –

it was her clothes and hair, but the face wasn't hers – it was dark brown, angular and reminded me some of Lt. Worf on *Star Trek*. High cheekbones, high, angled 2-part forehead, and a lower mouth/chin combination. At 15' away, the light was not playing tricks on me.

The picture (left) is a close likeness.

(Credit: artofwei.com/Bing Images)

A Klingon Female

I finally knocked. "OK to use the bathroom?", I said and she jumped, as I had taken her by surprise. She slowly turned toward me and I couldn't believe what I saw. It was humanoid, but she had apparently dropped her guard (thinking she was all alone, and had forgotten her door was open). As she slowly turned to me, her face morphed from the 'Klingon' face into her normal (also ugly) Wanda face. I was stunned: she was controlling how I saw her!

In that instant I knew what the dog had seen that terrified him, and I wasn't too charmed either. I knew intuitively what I was dealing with. She also knew that I knew. Her lack of aura was due to her being an alien of some sort. I swear I don't know just what it was I saw before she morphed back into "Wanda" but it takes some getting used to.

She moved out 2 days later. I have always wondered if she was one of the Earth-based Anunnaki Remnant? And I naturally wondered if she had had any impact on what I was writing as this book…? If she could control what I saw, maybe she also controlled what I was thinking/writing? (Baldy did not correct anything I had written when he showed up in December 2013 [see 'Genesis' section], so apparently there was no interference.)

We're Not Alone

What bothers me is the Others' brazenness – to ensconce themselves under the same roof! (She had bamboozled the landlady into taking her in as a roommate and, the landlady being passive didn't have the assertiveness to have her move on.) I didn't believe in **shapeshifting**, and yet that was what I saw her do. Her "Wanda" face was a projection, to cover what was not any better-looking, and in fact, I see now why her "Wanda" face looked the way it did – structural ugly is hard to hide. And that answers why she changed the original door lock – so she could not be 'surprised.'

Second issue that bothered me, was why was she <u>here</u>? She stayed to herself behind the locked door and turned on all electrical things she could find – running up a big monthly electrical bill, which she was finally obliged to help pay. Her purpose seemed to be to harass <u>me</u> (during the writing of this book) since she moved in the week I started the book, and moved out when the book was done. Perhaps also to be a source of "negative vibes" as that is what we felt when she was present; we felt nothing when she was away from the house.

Case 3. Homeowner Alien – Baseball Cap Joe

In preparation for making a quote for shutters to a couple who had just moved into a new home, I came to the front door, rang the bell, and introduced myself to the woman of the house. I was shown the many rooms where the shutters were to go, and so I set about taking and writing down measurements.

As I worked, I found myself back in the Master Bath area when a man came in and stood there watching me. The energy was not good, and while he had said nothing, I thought it best to explain what I was doing there. As I turned and faced him, I froze and my mind went blank. This time, it was obvious that what I was looking at (although there was no aura) wasn't an OP, nor was it robotic like a synthetic. The instant intuitive recognition was there: he was an alien and I didn't like him. His energy was creepy.

> *To this day, I have no idea why the "gods" chose to keep showing me these different people, unless it was for the purposes of this book… and since 2008, I have not been treated to any more of them.*

His face was very angular, eyes were angular, yellowish-blue, with very small irises, his forehead was not right (convex) with a crease down the middle – like someone had glued the two haves of his cranium together, leaving a seam, and my second thought was he was some unfortunate version of a Down's Syndrome, or maybe retarded. And he wore the baseball cap in the house. Yet, this home of his was a $400,000 model, and his wife was not working… something didn't add up.

I gathered my composure and managed to explain a few things and then I asked him a couple of questions, which he answered in a normal-sounding voice. Not retarded, not mechanical, quite glib and intelligent-sounding, and yet when I looked at him I got the creeps. As happened with the last man above in #2, my Source did a 1-second download and I understood that this "Hybrid, 2nd stage" had energetics that prevented him from having a normal-looking face, like "Wanda." (I was never told where he was from.)

He seemed to sense my discomfort and left the room and while I measured all over the house that morning, I never again ran into him. I'm sure most people don't notice these things, or if they do, they rationalize it all away and make some excuse for what they're seeing – a subtle form of denial that we are not alone and there are Others walking among us. That's Man's way of handling the unexpected, the different, the weird, etc… and then Man hurries back into his little prophylactic fantasy world he lives in. It's safer.

Case Analysis

So obviously, the question comes to mind: "Why am I being treated to all of these 'unique' experiences?" These were all between 2005 – 2008, right before I started officially writing the book. What am I supposed to do about it, or am I being somehow 'educated' for some future purpose? It does occur to me that Wanda showed up the week I began the book in January, and was still around until July, with it getting harder and harder to finish this book… The week I finished the book, she moved out. Coincidence? Perhaps the 'gods' were showing me things that they either wanted in the book, or as confirmation that what they said ("We are not alone here") is true.

None of these people have been "evil" or aggressive, and I have never felt threatened. It is just that it is not easy to get along with them – as if we and our way of doing things are 'alien' to them, and there are a lot of rough corners which easily play into disagreements. They do not fit in, that is for sure, and so I have ruled out that they are always here to help Man through some tough times. Maybe they're 'students' from other worlds…? Or Hybrids as Dr. David Jacobs has said.

Such is the general situation with OPs and it pays to learn about them and avoid the worst of them (Robotics), if possible. The best defense is seeing the etheric aura, and failing that, pay close attention to their **behavior**. The next best alternative is to watch peoples' eyes – are they alive or 'flat?' And learn to sense their energy. Then, listen to your intuition – ask your Higher Self to warn you when you are about to be targeted. And for God's sake, don't marry one.

Since the OPs are about 60% (!) of the population, it might be useful to see what therapists and counselors could do for ensouled humans who come to them with problems that are caused by OPs.

Encounter with Others

At the risk of sounding really odd, there were two other brief encounter during the years 2004 – 2006 that demonstrates that Other do walk among us. There are more entities here than Man, OPs, and Astral influences. I will make this brief, as it comes from personal, recent experience, but it is also relevant to an understanding that planet Earth is more than we think it is, and that we are not alone here.

Other #1:

I was shopping in a supermarket near home in 2004 about 11pm at night, and got in the checkout line behind a tall man in a light blue, one piece jumpsuit. He was carrying a lot of personal hygiene and hair dye products. So I looked at his hair. Standing just 3' behind him, I could not see any individual hairs, it all looked like a black energy field. I was tempted to touch it, but I was polite and didn't.

> *The checker was having a problem with the checkout equipment, and so I got to spend a lot of time in line behind this guy.*

I next noticed his jumpsuit. Light blue and not a wrinkle on it, no lint, so spots, no tears or anything, and I could not identify what kind of material it was. My eyes drifted down to his shoes… like running shoes, but one piece with Velcro straps. Again, I noted that there wasn't a mark on them, they looked brand new. At that thought, he moved from standing sideways to putting his back to me so that all I could see were the backs of his shoes.

Next I noticed his left arm, carrying those containers of personal hair stuff, and I noticed his left arm at the elbow was hinged in a funny way. The tendon that barely shows on most people when they hold their bare arm at a 90° angle was a pronounced 3" down his forearm… and at that thought, he used his right hand to pull his sleeve down.

Now I was dying to see his face. As we moved up to the cashier, whom I knew, she gave him a funny look and asked if he had his 'Rewards' card. His voice was very mechanical and he said he didn't. She gave him another funny look. I couldn't see his face, and when he took his sack of items, he kept his face away from me. He paid and walked away normally…

So I asked the checker if she had ever seen him before, and she said yes, but wasn't happy about it when he did come through… usually late at night. I asked what his face looked like, and she said there was **very little or no white to his eyes**, they were mostly black and of course we both heard his halting, mechanical voice. Something like the picture below…

175

(Credit: Bing Images/Prometheus movie: Black-eyed Engineers….)

Above is similar to what the synthetic human in the blue jumpsuit looked like… and that was it for that evening.

A few weeks later, I went into the same store, again around 11 pm, and I saw **the same man in the same blue jumpsuit** over by the Produce about 30' away. He had not seen me yet, so I was curious and moved over to the Starbucks partitions between him and me and I moved forward to peek thru a 1"crack between two of the partitions. My body was completely hidden. A normal person would not have noticed me.

I began studying him, now with his side turned toward me. Dammit, I thought – turn around so I can see your face! He did. And looked right at me. That creeped me out. He grabbed his stuff and went through the checkout before I could get up the nerve to follow him. (Or maybe I was 'controlled' to not follow him?)

I never saw him again, but the checker did and she was able to give me more weird aspects of the guy, and then she quit working there. I'm not sure what he was, but he wasn't an OP. It is possible he was a **Synthetic**, and except for hearing that from my Source, there isn't much information on them, nor what they're doing here. But how would a synthetic know what I was thinking? Can ESP have mechanical aspects?

Other #2:

I was in a local bookstore in 2005, sitting off to the side in the café, reading and drinking a Vanilla Chai Freeze. I don't know why I looked, but a short man came in the café and ordered some soup and drink, and then looked right over at me. Black eyes with little or no white sclera.

I thought , here we go again. He got his stuff and I went back to reading, he went over and put his stuff down on a table about 20' from me. I glanced up, nodded friendly-like, no response, and he picked up his stuff and moved it to the back part of the café where I couldn't see him. He also had no aura.

I have no idea what these 'people' are doing here, but they seem to know when someone is looking at them, and I suspect they can read our minds. I had no fear, no sense of weirdness, no sense of hostility from them…and I wasn't sent any thoughts from them, no thoughts suddenly appearing in my mind. I had the feeling that both of these characters were Synthetics.

All I can figure is that they were part of my 'education' during that period, and I could write about them, but I have never seen anything like any of them since 2005-2008.

OP Phenomenon

The OP represents a phenomenon that is now a normal part of living in the 3D Earth experience. Thus, at times they do serve a necessary function and it is mostly **caution** that is advised in dealing with them.

There is no need for fear, or cause for alarm – you have been living among OPs and the Others for centuries and most of them here are not up to any evil agenda. They are experiencing the Earth drama first-hand as are a lot of the Others who are also here. In any event, as will be seen in Chapter 12, the Earth is in quarantine and because Man has been protected by the more benevolent beings, in the last few centuries, there is no cause for alarm or panic at this time, either.

The problem is that Man is still unaware of who and what he is, what his potential is, and that he has been manipulated to stay ignorant, petty and violent for centuries, and that now there is a problem. A big one addressed in Chapter 14.

While the OPs aggravate the problem, the Neggs really seek to promote the problem (and get the OPs to do their dirty work for them), and Man is blissfully unaware that anything is going on – much less that there is a problem of monumental proportions.
As a result, Man is trapped, and doesn't know it.

OPs and Karma

Yet the OPs do have a useful function in the growth of ensouled beings, and that is why they have not been removed. Perhaps the most useful information on OPs has been saved for this section, coming at the end of the two chapters dealing with them.

Let's say that John Smith has some karma to work out on Earth and if he is to meet it and overcome it, someone is going to have to provide the **catalyst**. Someone is going to have to be the one to cheat him, or lie to him, steal something from him, or in some scripted karmic way, cause him enough pain that he has to notice the issue and not just blow it off, and secondly, he will be forced to deal with it, and thus grow spiritually.

Catalyst is often negative behavior from others. If members of John's soul group attempt to come back with him and do the negative things to him, (even meaning well as loving caring souls) under the Law of Karma, **they are incurring additional karma themselves**.

> *All souls are under the Law of Karma which is broader and harsher than Man would like to think. As a result, it would not make sense to try to solve John's problem(s) while embroiling his friends in new, additional karma… where would it end?*

Fortunately, the Higher Beings are several steps ahead of us with the solution: **Use OPs to provide the catalyst since OPs don't incur karma (because they don't reincarnate)**. And this is a role the OPs often fill as the physical hands and feet of the Neggs who see what John's karmic debt is and can work the OPs to deliver the 'lesson' or catalyst prescribed by John's Script – everyone must have a Script of Plan to work on when they come into the Earth realm, and the Script contains karmic elements, as well as tests, and optional points of choice for Exit (death). That way, John's ensouled friends don't have to work with his problems and complicate theirs.

> *Note: it should be clear at this point that trying to help another person who is going through a tough time, by removing his problem, even his illness if you are a healer, may be counter-productive: you have just removed his 'lesson' and he will have to face it later, anyway.*

> *That doesn't mean you don't care and ignore someone in dire straights; you pray for them and talk with them, and comfort them, and tell them that they ARE equal to whatever they are facing – but you don't remove the problem, nor do you do it for them.*

So OPs can apply anyone's scripted karmic lesson ("guided" by the Neggs) and no new karma is created. As was said earlier, the OPs tend to have defective DNA (which is why the soul did not move into the body), and this may manifest as typical OP behavior against you – but it may not always be karmically-oriented. Caution is advised as well as prayer. OPs can and do oppress, harass, steal, lie, etc and afflict you for karmic and non-karmic reasons, and the wisest thing is to pray against it – if it is not karmic, it should stop.

Karma is covered more in Chapters 7, 11 and 14.

OPs as Sociopaths

This is a very important part of the OP scenario, and while most psychologists and psychiatrists only deal with the occasional sociopath (and psychopath) that is referred to them (if the OP shows up!), they are not aware that the OP/sociopath can be very hard to handle, much less cure. And if the therapist deals with a psychopath (as Dr Peck does in Chapter 7), even he will not be aware that a psychopath is an OP/sociopath 'on steroids.'

Note that OPs don't go to therapy.

Remember that OPs do not have souls. The soul is the connection to a larger part of a person and can be seen as a soul-connection to the Higher Self, or Oversoul. If a person has no soul, they have no conscience. (Think: Ted Bundy, Charles Manson, and Richard Ramirez.) The absence of a soul is a condition as yet not recognized by professional therapists, and thus they do not know what the real problem is. A person without a soul has no 'inner drive' to care about other people, play fair, tell the truth and share.

>**A caveat here: just because someone has no aura does not mean s/he is a sociopath, or a bad person… but the potential IS there because s/he has no conscience.**

Rather than describe all the aspects of sociopaths, just be aware that OPs can be sociopaths. Many OPs are not good or bad, they are just…. there. And they are not to be hated, as will be shown later, they have a purpose (this is further examined in Chapter 13). OPs do not incur Karma, so they can "sock it to you" if that is what your Script calls for, and they will NOT incur any reciprocal Karma – which your best friend who has a soul would incur. If souls kept afflicting each other, that builds Karma (even if for a good purpose) and then neither can get out of here, forgiveness notwithstanding. This is one reason why there are so many OPs.

The other reason is they were the pre-Adamic race (see Chart 1A rev) and have as much right to be here as ensouled humans do. They fulfill a necessary function on the planet, just as bit players and walk-ons serve in a stage play, or like NPSc in a video game. They also serve as placeholders in case of a timeline split.

So, OPs are not to be hated as they serve a useful purpose. Their sociopath counterpart is to be avoided, and the psychopath is to be identified and locked up.

For a more in-depth view, please see The Sociopath Next Door, by Dr. Martha Stout.

Chapter 6: Astral Entities

This chapter may sound medieval and negative, but it has a positive 'twist' at the end. Concurrent with the last two chapters, it benefits one to know that we are not alone and <u>what</u> the other players are and what they are doing. Then we will see what this place is, and the significance of all this will come together in the last, summary chapter. So that one doesn't waste a lifetime here, one has to know what this place is, who is here with us, what Man really is and why he is here... **Earth is not an amusement park**. And when you understand what Earth is, you will automatically know that you want out. And by Chapters 15 and 16, you'll automatically know what is required to get out.

People must begin to realize that we have the opportunity to stop the negative aspects of living on planet Earth, rise above it all, and effectively take control of our lives despite the fact that there <u>are</u> entities "doing it to us" – both 3D and 4D – with the intent to trap and control us in our own ignorance. We can be our own worst enemy and we either do it to ourselves, or we invite it to be done to us, or we let it be done to us, all of which is almost the same thing. Through our ignorance and rebellion we have orchestrated our own confinement for our rehabilitation as will be explained later.

People today really need to realize that the Astral interference that people knew about centuries ago was not medieval nonsense or superstition, but it wasn't "demonic" as they assumed -- and it hasn't disappeared. I wish I could tell you that it has changed or disappeared, but it hasn't – and that is one of the reasons Man is trapped here. Today in the 3rd world countries, modern day shamen still see these Astral entities and successfully deal with them – and you can, too, without training for years to be a shaman.

What you don't know, and I discovered first-hand years ago, is that the negative entities in the Astral realm (the **Neggs**) are afraid of the Light, and if you stand your ground, invoke the Light, even use the name of Christ, you <u>can</u> overcome them. But they will return – unless <u>you</u> change. In fact, as will be seen later, you <u>must</u> if you are to get out of here. And, <u>you</u> must, because no one else is coming to save you.

This chapter is about clarifying the earth-bound denizens and function of the Astral realm. Let's begin with some definitions.

Terminology

Neggs

While the Neggs are explained more in detail in subsequent sections of this chapter, it is expedient to define the term as the "**neg**ative **g**uides" in the Astral who effect one's negative lessons, concurrent with one's Script. They are similar to the white, glowing Beings of Light, except that they are dark, have little Light, and they harass and oppress – subject to the limits imposed by one's Script.

They are <u>the</u> Astral entities that oppress and harass Man, and they are programmed to do so. Chapter 15 further explores <u>why</u> they exist.

The Neggs cause most of our problems in providing **catalyst** for Man's growth and change – see the section on Dr. Lerma at the end of this chapter. They can be also considered 'fallen angels' and the term 'Neggs' in this book refers only to them.

Neggs are not demonic, nor are they evil.

Lucifer

People like to use the word Lucifer to describe the god of this world. This is inappropriate – for two reasons. First, Lucifer is just a title and it means "Bringer of Light" and as such, it could be applied to a Jesus, to a Buddha, to a Krishna or anyone who brings enlightenment. Second, Lucifer is not god of this world.

Also note that Lucifer is not Satan, largely because Satan is an alternate name given to the leaders of those beings (Azazyel and Samayaza) that descended and had relations with Earth women, as the Igigi/Nephilim, whose spirits are now Earth-bound and denied reincarnation according to Enoch. But it can also be a name referring to Yaldabaoth, as the Gnostics believed. Satan, Azazyel and Yaldabaoth are synonymous in describing an unseen, mythical entity that hates Man.[1]

Another issue is that the word Lucifer has connotations today that are unfortunate despite its only used once in the Bible, in the Old Testament in Isaiah 14:12-20:

> How thou art fallen from Heaven, O Lucifer, son of the morning… how thou art cut down to the ground, which didst weaken the nations….thou hast said in thine heart …. I will ascend above the heights of the clouds; I will be like the most High…. They that see thee shall….consider thee, saying, Is this the **man** that made the earth to tremble, that did shake kingdoms? …
>
> But thou art cast out of thy **grave**… thrust through with a **sword**…
>
> Thou shalt not be joined with them in **burial**…
> [emphasis added]

Interesting to note that the context of the passage describes a man, not a supernatural being, such as Lucifer or Satan. The words in bold emphasize and belong to a person who fell from a high position where he could have done great things for his country or people, but didn't, and instead is fallen.

The NKJV Study Bible has a footnote that says the above passage "…uses the fall of Satan from Heaven to illustrate the fall of the Babylonian king." [2] The name Lucifer is derived from the Latin for 'morning star' and the only reference to a 'morning star' is in Revelation 22:16:

> I Jesus have sent mine angel to testify unto you these things in the churches. I am the root and the offspring of David, and the bright and morning star.

Contrary to what some people claim, Jesus is <u>not</u> saying He is Lucifer, merely that He is **a** bright morning star, **a** bringer of Light and Truth. And a Lucifer as a "bringer of Light" is not someone to fear or reject – unless Lucifer comes as a "system buster" to undo the corruption and ignorance with truth and Light.

Also note that Lucifer used to be the old name for the planet Venus which was first called the morning star, and then the evening star.[3] The Romans renamed that star, Venus.[4] So we cannot use Lucifer as a title for a god of this world, but only as a Bringer of Light or en**light**enment.

It is believed that Lucifer became a synonym for Satan (or "adversary") due to the early Christian writings that also vilified the serpent:

> … 'Satan' as a synonym for 'Lucifer' became 'official' among Christians in the late first and second centuries, with the theological writings of Church Fathers Origen (born 185 CE) and Saint Augustine (AD 354-430) – indeed, some theologians argue that Origen was the first to make this connection. [5]

And the connection is wrong. A "bringer of Light" is not necessarily the same as an "adversary." And specifically, Lucifer is not Satan, because Satan doesn't really exist. So where did the term 'Satan' come from?

Satan

Satan is reputed to be the dark god of this world who disagreed with God, left heaven and took many of the angelic host with him. As was mentioned earlier, the name Satan was also synonymous with Yaldabaoth in the Gnostic teachings. The name Satan originally meant 'adversary', and derived from the **Egyptian god Set** or Sata whence comes the word Satan into Hebrew. Note that Horus battled with Set just as Jesus battled with Satan…there are many similarities suggesting that **the Hebrews derived their word *satan* or *shaitan* from the Egyptian (and Islam) theology.** [6] And from Chapter 3, we already know who the Egyptian gods were… e.g., Ningishzidda (Enki's son) was Thoth, Marduk was RA…

> Traditionally, the Hebrew Shaitan … is seen as deriving from the ancient Egyptian god Set, but there is another, more unsettling and controversial association…. Hebrew scholar Professor Karl W. Luckert notes an interesting parallel between the Old Testament God and the **ass-headed Set** …the ancient Egyptians' nearest equivalent to the Judeo-Christian Devil… However, **the Egyptians had no out-and-out Satan figure, no irredeemable evil god with no function or purpose but to torment and entrap humans.**[7] [emphasis added]

> *Note that the Book of Genesis in the Bible never speaks of a Satan, nor his alleged demons… because it is folklore and not reality.*

So who was the Egyptian god Set, or Seth as he is sometimes called?

… Set ruled over a physical realm – an actual geographical location – that the Egyptians knew from their everyday experience to be night-marish….[they] recognized the hellishly inhospitable nature of the surrounding **'red' desert** – which was Set's kingdom. The Egyptians hated anything red …. [and] Set was called 'the red-skinned one.' [8] [emphasis added]

Set was also known as the god of lightening, thunder and earthquakes. And it is very

…interesting that Set also combined the characteristics of both Yahweh and Lucifer, especially his association with lightening. The Egyptian pharaohs also descended into the earth as the **serpent** Sata, father of lightening… [9] [emphasis added]

Egyptian God Set, Seth or Sata
(source: Wikipedia Commons Images.)

So what we have is a transfer <u>to</u> a Satan/*Shaitan*, of heat, lightening, the color red and association with a serpent, and characteristics reminiscent of Yahweh <u>from</u> the Egyptian god Set, Seth, or Sata.

*And wouldn't you just know it, **Seth was the son of Marduk** and Sarpanit (his hybrid earthling wife), was involved in killing Osiris, and Isis gave birth to Horus who avenged Osiris and removed Seth.[10]*

Enough said on the origin of the concept of Satan. And note: **No Satan means no Hell**. There are several viable candidates for the role of the putative god of this world: Sata, Yadabaoth, and Azazyel, not to mention Yahweh, Enlil and Marduk. Who it was exactly that was being referred to in antiquity is not clear, just that there <u>are</u> still entities who seek to entrap and restrain Man: the 3D PTB and the Anunnaki **Remnant** Dissidents.

*Remember that this book is catalyst and it is worthwhile to **consider** that the Neggs are enough to harass Man and that there doesn't have to be a "leader of the Neggs" – especially by the end of this chapter when you see how they work.*

Pictured: Note the 'horns' and 'tail' and the staff which would become a trident in later myth. His skin was reddish.

184

It is one of the points of this chapt er that there is a group of harassing 'devils' that have been accused of trying to manipulate and keep Man from developing his 'godhood', and they deserve full attention in this chapter. They are again examined briefly in Chapter 15.

But first, let's clear up a few more misconceptions.

Satan's Fall with Angelic Host

It is important at this point to clarify a traditional misconception that Satan rebelled in heaven and fell with about a third of the heavenly host. This is a garbled transmission of two different and very ancient (pre-Atlantis) events that got combined into one story.

1. **Satan/Lucifer did not fall**. The Igigi 'fell' and created havoc with their Rephaim, Anakim, Giborim hybrids and cannibalistic giants (Nephalim), etc., and would have probably wiped out Man if not for the Flood.

Note that the term Watchers is not used since the Beings of Light (angels) did not 'fall.' It was the bored and lusty Igigi in their ships orbiting Earth who descended and with Earth women produced the Nephilim.

> *The true Watchers in the days of Enoch/Noah were always the Beings of Light. The Igigi have been incorrectly called Watchers. Today, the Watchers are officially still the Beings of Light, but the Neggs assist.*

2. **The rebellion in heaven refers to the War of the Gods** -- ETs literally at war in the heavens, which involved the Anunnaki and Others (hence the connection with item #1 above) with other ETs as they fought for planets and territories, destroying the planet Marduk/Tiamat in the process (between Mars and Jupiter), and heavily scarring Mars.[11] In addition, the gods battling each other on Earth in their *Vimanas* is described in the Hindu *Mahabharata*.

Sitchin even recounts from ancient texts how the gods assisted Man in his human battles, as well as involving Man in support of the gods' battles. [12]   In fact, the Bible's Old Testament says how Yahweh [Enlil] assisted Man just as he did with Sargon in the 24th century B.C.:

> …Sargon attributed his long reign (54 years) to the special status granted him by the Great Gods, who made him "Overseer of Ishtar, Anointed Priest of **Anu**, Great Righteous Shepherd of ENLIL." It was Enlil, Sargon wrote, "who did not let anybody oppose Sargon." [13] [emphasis added]

Note from Chapter 3 that Enlil's king was Anu, and therein lies the link to the Anunnaki. These gods and their battles were later mythologized as the Titans, vs the Gods of Greece on Mount Olympus (Zeus, Aphrodite, Poseidon, Ares…), and later were renamed into the Roman pantheon of gods (respectively: Jupiter, Venus, Neptune, Mars...). [14]

It was the irresponsible Wars of the Gods (3D ETs), and their danger to the newly evolving earthlings as hapless bystanders, that caused the Quarantine explained later in Chapter 12 to be done. Not only did the Anunnaki fight among themselves, but they fought others on Marduk/Tiamat, Mars and Earth. [15] Whereas the residents of Tiamat had the power to blow up their planet (and did, creating the asteroid belt), the Anunnaki left the huge scar on Mars (*Valles Marineris*), blowing away part of its atmosphere and water. Apparently Zeus' (aka Enlil) thunderbolts were an advanced form of plasma discharge weapon. [16] (See Chapter 10 discussion of Nazca and the 'Candelabra'.)

4D STS Gang

The term 4D STS represents those entities/souls who are in the 4D (lower Astral) dimension and are Service To Self. This includes principally the discarnate souls who occupy 3D with an STS polarization. They are a hazard to Man since they can see us from the <u>lower</u> Astral. The <u>mid- to upper</u>-4D world is phase-shifted to where we can't see them and they cannot see us in 3D. The problems come in due to the Neggs and discarnates
who occupy the intradimensional area between 3D and 4D (the <u>lower</u> Astral) – they <u>can</u> see us and are the source of a lot of Man's problems.

The following is a brief overview of the five main entities of the Astral realm.

1. The **Watchers**, aka **Beings of Light**. Also called angels although they don't have wings, but are seen as bright spheres of Light and they work with the Neggs to serve ensouled Man's Script, providing catalyst for spiritual growth..

2. The ubiquitous oppressing **Negg** entity that is dark: either a grey in color or black and the color indicates just how negative it is. The darker the color, the more ability/power the entity has to influence its victim. It is easy to think of this entity as a 'dark' or fallen angel, although they didn't fall. Neggs don't hate Man but may 'take him out' if that opportunity is given them. They also answer the Ouija Board.

   Neggs are not evil, as shortly explained. They work with the Beings of Light who control just how far the Neggs can go, but don't discount them: they <u>can and do</u> seriously afflict people.

   A person suffering from a habit of alcoholism can be under the Negg's or a discarnates' influence and as such can be removed fairly easily. On the other hand, a person who dabbles in witchcraft and the occult comes under the purview of the more powerful Neggs (and Interdimesionals) who require more authority to remove.

3. The hapless **Discarnates** who are souls that died and are stuck in the lower Astral plane because they would not go into the Light when they died. They are also the ones commonly called **ghosts**, but not poltergeists – those are the Neggs doing what it takes to get your attention. They sometimes play games through the Ouija Board.

4. **Thoughtforms (TFs) and Parasites** which are passive entities, mostly reactive, and they attach themselves opportunistically to the aura to drain energy, or 'feed off' of Man's energy. They operate like bacteria or leeches. If they have sufficient energy they can influence Man's thinking or actions.

Because it was mentioned above, and will be better explained in Chapter 12, there is another, <u>rare</u> visitor from the Astral realm:

5. The greater anti-Man entities called the **interdimensional nonhuman beings** (see Chapter 12) who have the power and ability to afflict Man when they so choose, but this is not something they do on a regular basis. They are included because they do exist and can be considered an enemy of Man. [17]
They are probably what the Muslims call **Djinn**, or the Gnostics (Chapter 2) called **Archons** as the description fits both of them.

The following are not Astral but are described here for added clarity. These are largely 3D physical beings and also impact Man on Earth.

6. The **PTB** are included here just for the sake of clarity. They are 3D flesh and blood humans who <u>are known</u> to the public and who believe it is their right to rule business, governments and anything that comes their way. They usually have money and that is their power. Some may have hybrid Anunnaki genetics.

7. The **Elite** are humans but with an Anunnaki heritage, their DNA characterizes them as hybrids. They are behind the scenes working between the Anunnaki Remnant and the PTB. Their faces and names are <u>not known</u> to the public.

8. The **Greys** are an interdimensionally-operating bio-android that is here to perform genetic research and upgrades on humans. It is natural that there is a connection with the **Anunnaki Remnant** which has the responsibility to see to Man's development as a species. Their origin is not as ETs.

Without a playbill it is hard to tell who is doing what to Man, and that is why they are lumped under the term **STS Gang**. For practical purposes, due to the number of quotes where the terms 'Satan' and 'demonic' and 'Devil' are used <u>in the quotations that follow</u>, such terms can be replaced with the STS Gang term. We are mainly concerned with those that harass, deceive and oppress 3D Man, and that is largely the STS Gang.

If you think the lower Astral is crowded and a problem, you're right. That is the reason for the protective 'tunnel' when a soul dies and passes over to the Other Side (Chapter 16).

Islam and the Djinn

With all due respect to the Muslim-based people who may read this book, a brief word about the Djinn has to be inserted, even at the risk of muddying the water regarding the Astral realm. The Qur'an teaches that a proud and haughty entity named Iblis confronted Allah over His creation of Man, and refused to bow to him, as Allah requested. (See

Chapter 2 review.) He was also called Shaitan. So **three major religions on Earth have the same story** of a powerful entity who fell from grace, and allegedly took a large part of Heaven with him. Recall that the Gnostics also tell of a powerful entity (Yaldabaoth) who fought God, and was the explanation for Man's origin, and the source of his torment. However, the Islamic faith does not believe in 'fallen angels.'[18]

> *Before considering who the Djinn are, it is worth repeating for future reference, that the Djinn are most likely the Interdimensionals or Archons. All 3 terms describe a 4D STS entity that harasses Man.*

Just so that we are all on the same page, the Djinn are often portrayed in movies as genies living in a lamp that someone rubs, and out pops the genie to grant three wishes. The TV version was played by Barabara Eden, in *I Dream of Jeannie*. A **giant blue Genie** was a major star in the Walt Disney cartoon movie *Aladdin*, and the late Robin Williams played the voice of the powerful and sometimes goofy Genie.

> The word *Djinn* is Arabic and means "unseen or hidden." …. The word *Djinn* can be used to identify any nonphysical being that exists in another reality but we believe the Middle East used the term to describe a particular type of entity that exists between the multiverses (multiple universes) of matter and energy…. in a dimension close tour own, and they seem to have the ability to interact with certain people who live here when it suits their purpose. [19]

This may ring a bell:

> It was thought that when these djinn chose to show themselves, they would appear in the form of a snake…. [and] the djinn can take the form of any human or animal they choose…. [they often] **shapeshift** into hideous monster-like animals to frighten people or keep them away from what they consider their own property [territory]. [20] [emphasis added]

Serpents and shapeshifting again… where have we heard that? Are they the Neggs, covered in the next section? No, although the two could be confused with each other, but the Djinn are unique from the Neggs… Consider one more piece of information about them.

They inhabit another dimension, next to ours and have the ability to move back and forth. They are not Man's friends and are best avoided. They were created before Man, by the God of the Universe, and originally inhabited Earth with superior technology… thousands of years before Man was created.

> The djinn were … masters of this planet for only twenty centuries, and in that time were able to create kingdoms and societies with an almost super-natural technology. ….'*He (Allah) created Man from sounding clay. The angels from Light and the djinn from smokeless flame of fire.* (Ar-Rahman 55.15)" [21]

According to Islamic belief, the evil in the world is due to corrupt humans and Djinn who have turned their backs on God/Allah. Interestingly, "Demons, fairies, ghosts, demonic possession, and even sightings of extraterrestrial aliens are believed to be the work of djinn…"[22] Certain themes repeat themselves among mankind all over the planet… So what is the significance of the Djinn?

According to the Muslims who know more about the Djinn:

> Allah created three intelligent races in the multiverse: Angels, djinn and physical beings that include humans and all other "alien" races in the universe. Angels were created first, then djinn, who were placed on Earth as stewards and masters. They were most loved by God. The djinn are made of fire, and have long life spans and great power. They are able to manipulate matter and change form…. In their time… the djinn built great cities ruled by powerful kings…. Each group of djinn belonged to clans rather than states or countries… [and they] frequently fought, going to war over trivial matters. The wars lasted for thousands of years and polluted the environment…. their conflicts were turning it [Earth] into a wasteland.
>
> The djinn grew more powerful, using great and terrible weapons, eventually reaching the point of irreversibly damaging the physical universe. …. Allah ordered an army of angels to stop them, but the djinn gathered their armies and engaged the angels in a war that lasted a thousand years. … The older and more powerful djinn finally fell. The djinn were cast into a parallel world close to our own. [23]

While it sounds like the Wars of the Gods that Zechariah Sitchin and Sasha Lessin speak of, in their Anunnaki chronicles, it is also reminiscent of the fallen Watchers whom Enoch sees incarcerated in an Astral realm near Earth, and it is also reminiscent of Robert Monroe speaking of the **Interdimensionals**… and that is examined in Chapter 12. Suffice it to say that there are many accounts of beings, past and present, who are in a realm next to us, some of whom harass us, and others who don't care about us at all. As was shown in Chapter 4, Charles Fort and John Keel discovered that there really is something there… and it is better left alone.

The Djinn are collectively another term for 4D STS Astral entities that we cannot see – except if they choose to show themselves. Those with great power would be the **Interdimensionals** (best choice for the Djinn), medium power are the Neggs, and those with minor or barely any power, would be the discarnates. There is no easy answer, nor is one soon to be found, to this issue. We can't see what is in the dimension next to ours. It is one of the mysteries of this planet which does involve something real, but is beyond today's limited technology and ability of Man to precisely discern. Some of the starting points for research and contemplation are given within the chapters of this book.

The rest of the chapter will focus mainly on the Neggs as they are the most numerous and have the most interplay with Man.

The Neggs

Instead of referring to one of the Astral enemies of Man collectively as "the demons," as was ignorantly done in the medieval days, they are herein called the Neggs, short for "**Neg**ative **G**uides," because that's what they are. They are not demonic and so this chapter attempts to be more specific about whom we're dealing with whenever possible.

The Neggs have degrees of power, specialties, and even personalities. Some of them simply harass and obstruct ensouled humans. They rarely afflict the OPs, but they can enter or manipulate them to get them to say/do something that will cause the ensouled human(s) a lot of problems.

The Neggs are not evil *per se*, nor are they demonic, as defined by the Christian world. They are more of a 'general purpose' entity that <u>works with</u> the angels of Light, to harass, obstruct and influence in synch with their appointed function to deliver Man's training, or 'lessons.' Their job is to provide **catalyst** for Man's spiritual growth, and this will be seen at the end of this chapter and reviewed in Chapter 15.

The Neggs are fairly easy to remove during Deliverance (see next section) and they mainly deceive and cause physical ills. The Neggs are mostly associated with **oppression** whereas discarnates (and Interdimensionals) are concerned with **possession**.

> *It will later be seen that the Neggs are 'negative angels' doing the "dirty work" of the Beings of Light; so that the angelic host would not be just one type of being and have to alternately bless and curse, and thus be schizophrenic, the job of blessing and guiding was assigned to the Beings of Light and the job of harassing, oppressing and afflicting was given to the Neggs. The Neggs' sole function is providing catalyst. (See 'Necessary Evil' section.)*

Please be clear that the **Higher Beings** occasionally referred to are not 4D STS, and they do not enter bodies in this era; they do not possess, incarnate, 'Walk-In,' nor do they respond to invitations to channel. They penetrate everything and are benevolent. The Watchers, or Beings of Light, report to the Higher Beings.

Neggs' Operations

Because the Neggs are so important to understand how Man is afflicted, and because they are the source of <u>most</u> people's afflictions, it is important to know how they operate and what they can and can't do. Spotting their obvious and <u>very repetitious</u> techniques allows one to either change what one is doing, or come against them in prayer and stop them.

Neggs are not very clever or innovative and they don't have to be. The great majority of people never suspect the Neggs' activity in their lives, and so the Neggs don't need to come up with new ways to harass, influence and/or deceive. And this is also by design: since they work with the Beings of Light (Angels), the intent is that Man should begin to see and suspect the source of the interference, wise up and straighten out.

Neggs can operate directly on Mankind or <u>indirectly thru the OPs</u>. When they operate **directly**, it is to create health problems, confusion/deception, nausea, headaches, fuzzy thinking, and empower habits. They can also put ideas into peoples' heads, usually starting the thought with "I…..", as in "I think…." or "I don't like …" and that way the person thinks the idea is his. For example, when Peter hears Jesus say that He will not die but be raised up on the third day, Peter says "Oh, surely not You, Lord." Jesus, speaking to Peter, then tells Satan to "Get behind me." (Matt. 16:23).

Peter was manipulated to say what looks and sounds like a caring word in Jesus' behalf. Instead, Jesus sees where the comment is really coming from, and that it denies His agenda, and that Peter did not "take every thought captive" (II Cor.10:5) to consider that the counterproductive words of comfort might have been put in his head.

When Neggs operate **indirectly**, they first attach to an OP and get them to say or do what amounts to an attack on an ensouled human – verbally or physically. It is much more difficult (prohibited) for the Neggs to enter into an ensouled person and get them to do/say something, although they do succeed in planting ideas, as they did with Peter. Hence they often choose the oblique, or indirect, attack.

> *Be aware that OPs were not designed nor built with this harassment facility in mind, but due to the lack of higher centers, they were found to be easy to manipulate and very convenient for harassing the ensouled humans.*

Since there is no soul present in an OP, the Neggs can enter and use them indirectly to do what they cannot <u>legally</u> do with ensouled humans – all to further the general agenda of harassment, oppression, deception, confusion and blocking: catalyst for ensouled humans.

It is a violation of the Law of Freewill in the Father's Creation for any entity in an Astral realm to possess or manipulate another <u>ensouled</u> entity.

The basic Universal Law is: one body, one entity with freewill.

So to enter the body and manipulate the muscles, eyes, ears, vocal chords, etc. is not permitted with ensouled humans – <u>unless</u> the humans give permission (as in channeling, as did Jane Roberts who channeled *Seth*). If the Astral entity, regardless of level, tries it without the intended victim's knowledge and permission, any nearby Beings of Light have the automatic duty/right to intervene and stop or remove the intruder.

So naturally, the Neggs and other Astral entities try to **trick the human into going along with a deception**, or giving their OK, to be manipulated and may be ultimately possessed. The human would not normally agree but remember that Astral entities are clever and they will set the deception up in such a way as to get the human to go along with their proposal because the human is naïve, doesn't know any better, or is confused, or more commonly, has bought into an earlier lie that makes the subsequent Neggs' proposition look OK. More on this in Chapter 14.

Shapeshifting

In addition, the Neggs have the ability to 'shapeshift' or appear as something they are not. The New Testament said that Satan could appear as an angel of Light (2 Cor. 11:14), and that is true of the Neggs, too. If they think that the appearance of an angel, or the Virgin Mary, or Jesus will gain your trust, they can do it.

*Shapeshifting does **not** involve changing any molecular structure of the body of the one doing the shapeshifting. As will be seen in Chapter 12, vision/perception is based on holographic principles and the shapeshifter merely changes <u>what is seen</u> by modifying the holographic 'interference patterns' that the brain of the perceiver decodes and 'constructs' as a new reality in front of him. A form of mind control, like hypnosis.*

In addition, they can 'create' the illusion of UFOs whizzing thru the atmosphere – making right-angled turns at thousands of miles per hour. In reality, it is them, manifesting as a luminous sphere or whatever shape they think will capture your fancy. Hard to believe? Just consider the latest UFO reports of one big sphere becoming several smaller ones, and then reuniting. (Also see Chapter 4.)

They can also create Bigfoot, Loch Ness, Chupacabra and Mothman for our benefit. In ages past, they created fairies, elves, trolls, dwarves, etc. because that was the level of Man's awareness, education and superstition. Nowadays, they create some UFOs and some Crop Circles (see end of Appendix F).

Shapeshifting has also been attributed to the Greys. Amazonian natives while out on a hunt would one minute see a very large bird of prey up in a tree, and the next minute, it would be a Grey. [24] Abductees taken for examination by Greys are often left with a false memory of having seen a horse or owl with big eyes, when in reality they had seen the Grey's face.

Negg Tactics

In addition to fear and deception, planting thoughts in people's heads (claiming to be the voice of God) and shapeshifting, the Neggs have another procedure they use a lot. When you are reading something helpful, or someone is explaining something helpful to you, the Neggs can often follow this sequence to try and stop you:

1. **Block your hearing so you can't hear**, or
   block your eyes so you can't see what you're reading;

if that fails, and you did hear (or see)…

2. **Block your understanding** so that you can't use the info;

and if that fails, and you did hear/see and understand…

3. **Block you from taking action** – make you forget the info or diss it.

And just as interesting is an old saying: "If the devil can't make you bad, he'll make you busy." The Neggs can orchestrate events such that extra phone calls, people and emergencies intervene, then you'll get very busy, and then you'll become very tired and wind up saying or doing what they wanted you to say/do in the first place. Anybody seen that before?

Neggs Not Evil

As for the Neggs, they are doing their 'job', don't hate them or blame them... if Man didn't have weaknesses, they'd have nothing to poke and prod to get Man to make mistakes. This is where Man's corrupted DNA comes in – the genetic inheritance from the Anunnaki who could be petty, lying, domineering, violent, lusty and conniving. This genetic state is what the Bible refers to as being "born in sin"... receiving your ancestors' dysfunctional DNA... because the sins of the fathers <u>are</u> passed on down to succeeding generations... genetically.

The Neggs are not under a higher Negg's command; they answer to the Beings of Light, with whom they work. There is no Head Negg who orchestrates Negg agendas to afflict Man. Neggs are opportunists and seek openings, weaknesses, and invitations by unsuspecting humans – much as **bacteria** are not under the leadership of some Supreme Bacteria. They are all around and go where they can. They are all STS and have very little Light in them.

The Neggs are sometimes joined in their activities by unwitting discarnates (or Earth-bound entities). Discarnates were often tricked into serving when they died not knowing who or what they were, or generally said, they didn't have a clue what was going on, and they had very little Light or knowledge of the truth when they died. So they didn't know of the Father's love, and they didn't trust the Light, and they didn't know they had a <u>choice</u> about where they could go. So they stayed put and got trapped. This allowed them to be manipulated.[25]   More on that in Chapters 7 and 14.

Neggs' History

This planet has not always been oppressed by the Neggs and their puppets, the OPs. In fact, the OPs operated by themselves for many centuries, as *Lulu* and *Adamu* in different Eras, without the Neggs' presence or 'assistance.' The Neggs were not in existence before the Flood, and as a matter of fact are a fairly recent development along with what this place really is today, and **they came into being <u>along with the current Era (AD 900)</u>**.

> *Recall that there was no mention of demonic spirits in Genesis before The Flood, and that the Earth-bound spirits of the Nephilim and their offspring came on the scene <u>after</u> The Flood.*

What people knew just a few centuries ago about unseen entities that harass and oppress Man is still valid and is still going on now despite the modern trend to diss this information. How wise is it to ignore a part of reality just because you don't like it? And please note: Man's shadow side has been greatly empowered by his egotistical point of view that: (1) he has no negative side, and (2) there isn't anything unseen out there trying to trip him up. The fact that Man tends to think like that (New Age notwithstanding) is one of the reasons he is still here, as will be seen.

Neggs' Limits

The Neggs' 4 main weapons are fear and deception, shapeshifting – which they can't sustain for long as it takes quite a bit of energy -- and putting thoughts in peoples' heads.

Note that shapeshifting is deception. It is easy for them to put thoughts into peoples' heads because they can manipulate the aura, putting a thought in the 'mental level' of the aura, knowing that it will find its way through the higher mental chakra and drop into the person's awareness.

They are mostly limited to fear and deception, with the goal to influence or harass, although they can create serious physical problems thru drinking, drugs, and smoking.

> *Note that tattoos and body piercings (ear lobes are an exception) can weaken the aura because like acupuncture, they interfere with the body's energy flow ("chi") in the body's energy bionet and permit manipulation of body energies.*

Remember, like mosquitoes and vampires who avoid exposure to the Light, Neggs must leave at the use of Jesus' name (because the Higher Beings honor and often respond to the use of the name). And not only that, they work with the Beings of Light to effect Man's testing and tempting, within the limits set for each soul's learning process, as monitored by the Beings of Light. The Neggs are subject to limits as they perform their 'rehabilitation' or 'catalyst' function, and the Beings of Light are here to support and protect. This chapter's last section on Dr. Lerma will examine this aspect a lot more.

Necessary Evil

It bears repeating that the Neggs had to be created so that there would be a good entity (Being of Light) and a 'bad' entity (Negg) to effect Man's lessons. The alternative would have been chaotic: If there had been just the Beings of Light who one minute blessed you and the next minute oppressed you, that would have been much harder to administer. In fact, the Being of Light would then have been "double-minded" or schizophrenic and who would have been in charge of monitoring the Being of Light? It is simpler to have single-purpose entities doing a single function, thus their programming acts as their built-in system of "checks and balances." Angels bless and protect, Neggs harass and oppress... both working together in support of a person's Script (reason for being here). 3D is designed to work via polarity or duality thus forcing a choice from Man.

Man Gives Neggs Permission

Respect the Neggs to a point, and if they can 'hit' you where you're weak, note that you have the problem: you need to fix/change/stop something so they can't do that again. You need to take back the 'ground' that you have given them, knowingly or unwittingly, by realizing your mistake, asking to be cleansed by the Light, and not repeating the error.

For example, when you get angry and start to swear, or become sexually aroused, or watch a violent video, two or three or more Neggs will be attracted by the energy, appear near you, and then feed off your energy. [26] When you perpetrate, they react. **They do not instigate**, you do. So respect them up to a point where they become a nuisance, and then tell them to go... and clean up whatever it was you were doing that attracted them, i.e., take back any ground you have given them – it is effectively permission that you granted them. (See also Chapter 14) Your straightening out your thinking and behavior tells them that you are aware of them and intend to give them less opportunities in your life.

Again, for example, if you dabbled with Wicca or witchcraft, or the Ouija board, recognize that that gave them some ground because you were seeking power (witchcraft) or asking for a response (Ouija board), and so you entered their territory. You want to play the game? They will oblige – just be aware that you have given them permission to 'work' with you. What you don't know (and ignorance is no excuse) is that **they play by their rules**, not what you think is fair. So if they can get a toehold in you, and then a foothold, and then…the more you practice the 'black arts', or cooperate with the Neggs, the more ground they can take – until some people become very oppressed, and then finally possessed.

Playing games like *Pokemon* (short for "pocket monster") or *Dungeons and Dragons*, and the like in video games, is giving them permission to oppress. It is like walking into an HIV/AIDS ward in a hospital – you're asking for something to happen.

You can think of the harassment, deception and oppression as their 'job' although they are not altruistic – they are out to 'get' you, if they can… subject to the Beings of Light's approval (it has to synch up with your Script.) Remember in an earlier chapter, it was suggested that the ensouled humans would have to be stopped lest they develop their inner divine spark? In reality, the Neggs are the **catalyst** to move Man in the right direction, but Man has to wake up and realize that when he does the wrong thing, the Neggs capitalize on it. And if the Neggs secure a foothold, they may be aided by the opportunistic discarnate entities.

Other Entities

Thoughtforms

Throughout history, there have been thoughtforms (TFs) that have usually been created by negative thinking, as well as curses, so there are TFs of anger, sadness, confusion, and bitterness, and revenge for example. Note that Jung called them 'archtypes'. These float around in the lower Astral (4D) realm looking like a grey or black cloud (depending on intensity), waiting for the 'right chemistry' from a passing ensouled human. When a human comes near the TF, if the energy of the human is right, i.e., of the same type energy and wavelength, the TF is attracted magnetically to the person and can lodge in his/her aura.

> *Ever wonder why some people are always depressed? They don't need an anti-depressant -- they may just need a strong saltwater bath, or swim in the ocean. Salt cleanses the aura.*

Or a Negg may bring a negative TF to the unsuspecting human and try to 'plant' it in his or her aura.

A thoughtform is an energy 'cloud' that is attracted to a person of like frequency and attaches to and influences their aura, and may block a chakra. Very negative people will attract the negative TFs which just add to the person's negativity. And the more emotion and negativity the person exudes, the more it 'feeds' the TF, reinforces it, and it becomes a symbiotic arrangement. The TF does not have a life or will of its own; it is a passive bit

195

of sludge in/on a person's aura which can be cleaned by a salt water bath, or by doing Light meditation. Pranic and Reiki cleansing can also remove the problem TF.

> *If it is 'fed' by repetition, and not removed, it can drop <u>into the body</u> via a chakra and produce health problems.*

While the TF has no volition or consciousness of its own, it may be the product of several peoples' energy and it can be quite strong, such as a *tulpa*. When attached to a human, it can lodge in the emotional layer of the aura – which is why TFs don't attach to OPs – they have no aura. The negative energy can block the normal flow of *chi*, or universal energy, into/out of a person by clogging a chakra, and if not removed, the blockage can lead to health problems in the area of the body that the chakra serves.

Thoughtforms are analogous to a virus that has been released into a computer system. They can only attach and work where the person's 'firewall' (aura) is weak or non-existent. If a person's aura is healthy and strong, they cannot easily afflict such a person.

Discarnates

The spirits of deceased humans, aka ghosts, are also in the lower 4D realm. Some of them are not aware that they are dead and they are so attached to places and things that they do not move on into the Light, as do most souls when they "cross over." The spirits of the dead wander around at times trying to communicate with the living, and these are called ghosts; the malicious ones, called poltergeists, are really Neggs.

At any rate, when a soul dies, if they have no particular religious beliefs of the hereafter, they are easy prey for the other discarnates and some Neggs who can trick them into working with and for them. [27]   And this isn't hard to do. If the soul was addicted to drink or cigarettes (qv the entity *Seth* channeled by the late Jane Roberts), it is easy to point them toward a living person and suggest that they attach to that person who also likes drinking, and vicariously 'leech' energy and encourage that living person to drink more.

The Neggs falsely tell the discarnate that the Light is to be avoided and it may kill them.[28] While afflicting the living souls, the discarnates can also put thoughts in their heads and reinforce whatever negative habits they already have. [29] The discarnates have even been helped via the Neggs to influence living people to change things in the Bible – while scribes were copying the scrolls, to change a word or two, or just to rewrite parts of it. [30] This is further examined in Chapter 11.

So, the discarnates can be a real problem, just as the Neggs are. And they both need permission or opportunity to work their afflictions on Man. And they pretty much act without an orchestrated, conspiratorial agenda just as bacteria opportunistically infect and afflict.

Carlos Castaneda's Predators

Due to the don Juan Matus teachings promoted by Carlos Castaneda in a series of books, and due to its large following, it is appropriate to mention here that his teaching about *inorganic beings* and a *predator* in fact describe the Interdimensionals or Djinn (not the Anunnaki and not the Neggs). In Castaneda's final book, The <u>Active Side of Infinity</u>, don Juan challenges his apprentice to deal with the "topic of topics:" Predation. Don Juan explains it thus:

> We have a predator that came from the depths of the cosmos and took over the rule of our lives. Human beings are its prisoners. The predator is our lord and master. It has rendered us docile, helpless. If we want to protest, it suppresses our protest. If we want to act independently, it demands that we don't do so....
>
> ...the predators have **given us our system of beliefs**, our ideas of good and evil... They are the ones who set up our hopes and expectations and dreams of success or failure. They have given us covetousness, greed and cowardice.
>
> It is the predators who make us complacent, routinary, and egomaniacal... They gave us their mind, which becomes our mind. Through the mind, the predators inject into the lives of human beings whatever is convenient for them... Man, the magical being that he is destined to be, is no longer magical. **He's an average piece of meat**. [31] [emphasis added]

This pretty well describes what the Anunnaki did when they came in from the cosmos... humans in effect became their prisoners. But the manipulation of humans' minds and actions are descriptive of what the 4D STS Gang including strong discarnates do to Man, if they can. They have as much power as Man gives them. The Neggs <u>are</u> predators, although they didn't come from somewhere out in the cosmos, but they <u>can</u> manipulate Man's thoughts and emotions. It would be more accurate to say that the predators are from another dimension (Astral), surrounding this Earth, who have the power to imprison humanity in a daily, dull reality and keep Man entrained into his lower 3 chakras so that he is just a dumb sheep, or a "piece of meat." In short, Interdimensionals and/or Djinn as they both hate Man.

> *Note that Castaneda also says that Man is a "magical being" with a destiny that will be explored further in Chapters 7 and 9.*

Be clear that discarnates and Interdimensionals (Archons or Djinn) can oppress and then possess a person. Note that Neggs and Thoughtforms do not possess, but they can oppress. What is that all about? And how does one get rid of the affliction?

Deliverance and Exorcism

There is a major difference between deliverance and exorcism and it is related to WHO performs the service of setting people free from unseen oppressing influences. This section of the chapter is presented because (1) more and more churches are performing deliverances, and (2) there are some misconceptions about what it is.

A **deliverance** can be performed by anyone with the knowledge, experience, and ideally an <u>anointing</u> to perform such work. Not everyone is called to it, nor can just anyone do it, but many non-evangelical organizations also do the work. The format is generally unstructured as the ministers follow what the Holy Spirit tells them to do, and the results can be had within <u>hours</u>.

On the other hand, an **exorcism** is performed only by the Catholic Church and trained priests, sometimes assisted by laypersons. It follows a prescribed routine and is usually formal and can take from hours to <u>days</u> to complete.

The Deliverance Ministry

In general, deliverance is "setting the captives free" (Luke 4:18) and using the name of Jesus to do it. There is usually a pastor heading the group and there are usually several trained lay people to help administer the session. Usually the room is prayed over before the session, angels of the Light are invoked for assistance, and there is sometimes a prayer group working nearby interceding for the afflicted person. It is <u>not</u> necessary to know the names of the Neggs, discarnates or Interdimensionals to remove them, but the lead person ministering the deliverance <u>does</u> need to know what the afflicted person's problem is to speed things up.

For example, a problem with alcoholism involves a spirit or entity that is driving the person to drink. That entity may be a discarnate as Dr. Modi says [32] that influences the human person to drink and vicariously enjoys the intoxicating energy effect of the drink. So the entity is addressed, told to stop and leave, or it may be taken to the Light by a simple prayer.

Deliverance ministries abound in the Christian and evangelical churches, and are sometimes called Freedom Seminars, Fullness in the Spirit Workshops, Cleansing Streams … or some such name is given them. They are not openly announced as "deliverance ministries" due to the stigma attached to the idea that something unseen is oppressing people. A deliverance is usually done in less than an hour.

The Exorcism Ministry

On the other hand, exorcism is practiced almost exclusively by the **Catholic Church**, and involves one or more priests, trained laymen, and the Bible, rosary, a crucifix and holy water. It follows a set procedure called *The Roman Ritual of Exorcism*, [33] and involves the reading of the Holy Bible, prayers, psalms, and exhortations to the afflicting entity to leave the victim. A key aspect to exorcism is that the priest tries to address the "demon(s)" involved and learn their names to cast them out. The assistance of the Virgin Mary may also be invoked. The exorcism may involve hours and days, and the afflicted person may be kept in a locked room (see examples later in this chapter), and is sometimes physically restrained, until the entity gives up and leaves.

This is not just a passing fancy done by some kooks who imagine a thrill playing exorcist.

> By conservative estimates there are at least **five or six hundred evangelical exorcism ministries in operation today**, and quite possibly two or three

times this many…. [most] are considerably more modest, centered on an individual pastor or psychotherapist and taking on clients on a word-of-mouth basis. [34]   [emphasis added]

The whole point of this part of the chapter is that

1. The Neggs will empower Man's dark side if he is careless, and OPs in the media will pander to base interests with books, videos and heavy metal 'music', tattoos and

2. The need for Deliverance/Exorcism has increased <u>substantially</u> and it is not being taken lightly anywhere.

3. Humans with a soul can be oppressed and are rarely possessed.

As an example of what exorcism looks like, and what the oppressing Neggs and discarnates do, the two following sections offer some very powerful insights. And then the last section, dealing with Dr. Lerma, provides a surprise conclusion.

Dr. M. Scott Peck

Dr. M. Scott Peck is a medical doctor specializing in psychiatry, and has written several books on the subject of human evil. In his book <u>People of the Lie</u>, he notes:

> If we seriously think about it, it probably makes more sense to assume this is a naturally evil world that has somehow been mysteriously 'contaminated' with goodness, rather than the other way around. The mystery of goodness is even greater than the mystery of evil. [35]

He has no idea how close he is to the truth due to Man's inherited corrupted DNA and the many dysfunctional OPs. Since about 60% of the people around on any given day, in any given location, tend to be OPs, that makes for a decidedly negative potential. What is his definition of evil?

> **Evil** was defined as the use of power to destroy the spiritual growth of others for the purpose of defending and preserving the integrity of our own sick selves. [36] [emphasis added]

That does describe what sociopathic OPs can do if so guided by the Neggs entities. The Neggs do not lead Man into evil, but they can provide temptation and testing through their catalyst operations. Unfortunately, the OPs are much more active in promoting greed, power, lying, and self-centered activities which set people up for oppression.

Later in his book, Dr. Peck tackles the issue of **why bad things happen to good people**. He was studying two people who were both almost saintly and yet they fell prey to what he calls 'demonic' attack. He posits:

> …I have reason to suspect that the potential holiness of these two people

was one of the reasons for their possession. [37]

and

> I also mentioned a quality of potential holiness in the personalities of both patients. I wonder if they did not become possessed precisely because of this potential holiness. I wonder if Satan did not specifically invest its energy in attacking them **because they represented a particular threat to its [Satan's] designs**. [38] [emphasis added]

Very confusing. Was Mother Theresa taken over by 'demons' to prevent her from helping people? No. Was Buddha or Ghandi taken over? No. The above quote reflects a false assumption inherent in a lot of people. It is nonsense, but is an example of just how myth misleads us to believe in demons (who don't exist), but are somehow necessary, as the Gnostics discovered, to explain how this planet works. It is true that Dr. Peck does not know about OPs, but he should be able to recognize a sociopath when he meets one.

The reason bad things happen to good people is that they weren't really that good, you just thought they were, and they probably assumed they were, too. Or they may really be good people who have a special 'test' to pass. Later chapters further address this issue as it is important.

Just to round out the description of whatever entities are playing the role of Satan, it is worth hearing Dr. Peck give a list of attributes to help us better understand what kind of adversary we are up against. Dr. Peck sat in on numerous exorcisms, being friends in the past with Fr. Malachi Martin, a retired Jesuit priest who himself performed many successful exorcisms and educated Dr. Peck in the topic. According to Dr. Peck, the enemy has the following attributes: [39]

- Very self-centered, no real understanding of Love
- The notion of sacrifice is totally foreign
- No understanding of real science
- Thinks Man wants to be deceived as a natural state

The foregoing almost describes the OPs. Note that what Dr. Peck HAS described is the average sociopath. Instead he analyzes the putative 'demons':

They have several glaring weaknesses: "extraordinary demonic brilliance [coupled with]… extraordinary demonic stupidity. My observations confirm this." Agreed. Extraordinary pride and narcissism which overcomes its intelligence. [40] The enemy's weaknesses mean he is not all-powerful and should not be feared but **respected**, or maybe they are "…. more to be pitied than hated…. Yet one of my most profound impressions of the exorcism was of how **boring** it was --- that endless string of silly lies." [41]

> *And I repeat: that was done to wake you up. That is the ultimate purpose of whatever the Neggs do, and they can DO oppression until you finally wake up.*

And that is my point: instead of being Hollywood exciting, it is in real life, boring. I s uggest we can kick the enemy's butt and not put up with the lies and deception and oppression. That power comes from an understanding of who we really are, that we are not alone and can use His name (because the Beings of Light will honor it), <u>we say and repeat the truth</u>, and remember that the enemy is afraid of ensouled humans who stand up, call on the Light, and take their power back. More on that in chapters 14 -16.

Power of Truth

There is one very interesting point that Dr. Peck makes, and this is a shocker. He was assisting in an exorcism of a person called **Jersey** who had a lying spirit which called itself Josiah. During the exorcism, the lying spirit maintained that "…love is whatever you want to call it and does not require any translation into action." It had deluded Jersey into believing that and, of course, that is sometimes a New Age fallacy. Her release was achieved in the following way:

> It is no accident, I suspect, that the demon Josiah did not go away as we spoke about its basic fallacy [quoted above]. It went away only **after** the fallacy was exposed to Jersey in the here and now, and specifically when I wanted a cigarette every bit as much as she but was not going to break to have one because getting rid of Josiah was more important. In a sense I gave Jersey a very minor but still living example of sacrifice (or love) in action, and Josiah vanished so rapidly thereafter we didn't even realize right away that it was gone. [42] [emphasis added]

There is something to the saying that the truth sets us free. He notes elsewhere in his <u>Glimpses of the Devil</u> book, that **confronting the entities with the truth not only made them shut up, but often resulted in breaking their hold over the patient and set them free**. [43] As is said throughout this book, it is important to know the truth, and <u>get that Light in you</u>. It is also great protection against PTB manipulation in the Media.

Dr. Peck is not aware of the term OP, nor does he use anything like it, yet he perfectly describes one in the last half of his book under the patient's name, **Beccah**. She is insensitive, resistant to their efforts, cold, aloof, argumentative, possesses little conscience and has less compassion. She fired both Dr. Peck and her second therapist, and is considered 'lost' to any possibility of recovery. [44] But then, OPs (or sociopaths) don't recover or get better, and Beccah fits the mold perfectly – an OP may appear to be demonized, but they cannot be helped because they have no inner turmoil as do ensouled humans, and thus they don't get better. They will waste your time and drain your energy.

Dr. Peck often consulted with Fr. Malachi Martin, former chief Exorcist for the Catholic Church, and they discussed the issue of Beccah and evil:

> Malachi and I were both in agreement about the vital point that possessed people are not evil; they are in conflict between good and evil. Were it not for this conflict we could not know there is such a thing as possession. It is the conflict that gives rise to this "stigmata" of possession [in the case of an ensouled human]. **Thoroughly evil people are not in conflict; they are not in pain or discomfort. There is no inner turmoil**. [45] [emphasis added]

The late Dr. Malachi Martin's problem was that after years of Jesuit training to see the world in a certain way, he was left with an ecclesiastical "hammer", and when your only tool is a hammer, everything looks like a nail! He believed in demons.

I would suggest that the "evil people" he describes are in fact mostly OPs. Extreme OPs can appear to be psychopaths (sociopaths on steroids)... And the really good ones defy detection; they do not appear to be evil or psychopathic. This is not to say that the ensouled humans cannot also have evil behavior, coming from their shadow side (see Dr. Lerma's case with George later in this chapter), occasionally empowered by the Neggs.

Keep in mind that OPs are not usually abducted by Greys, nor are they possessed as ensouled humans are – there's no need. Some OPs do what their Astral 'controllers' guide them to do. Since the OPs do not have any higher centers (chakras 4-7) operating, they can be easily mind-controlled by controllers through the Astral realm.

Dr. Shakuntala Modi

It is worthwhile to consider one more educated expert's information, to get a rounded perspective on the Neggs and what they do to Man. Dr. Modi is another M.D. who practices psychiatry and discovered that classical psychiatric approaches to solving peoples' problems weren't producing results fast enough. By accident one day she found that one of her patients, under hypnosis, said he had a demon in his head causing the migraines he experienced. Shocked, she pursued it – not sure whether this was a subconscious, imaginary thing, or whether an entity was actually harassing her patient. In any event, she wanted to reach a healing state for her patient.

> Note: Keep in mind that Dr. Modi is not aware of OPs either, and because OPs don't go to therapy, not having any issues or oppression or inner conflicts, she would not be normally 'discover' them.

Over a period of time Dr. Modi came to discover that most people living have at least one attached EBE – an **earthbound entity** (sometimes a relative that passed on). Some have an 'attachment', as a thoughtform or parasite, and some have what she calls demonic spirits (which can be just Neggs, but Dr. Modi is not aware of the difference). The EBE is usually a **discarnate** entity. Thus, the attachment may be a Negg, discarnate or thoughtform, and the 'demonic' entity is one of the Astral entities playing a game, hoping you'll believe it's a dark entity. So, in essence, her work corroborates what has already been established, just the labels differ.

Dr. Modi gives a rather long, involved case with a patient she called **Ann** who came to Dr. Modi complaining of just about everything under the Sun: depression, chronic fatigue, poor memory, sleeping problems, vision problems, skin problems, muscle aches/pains, panic attacks, conversations in her head, headaches, irritable bowels, sinus problems, allergies, and hyperacidity. [46] (Reminiscent of Charles Darwin, whom we'll examine in Chapter 8.) Some of these issues get going due to karmic payback, and that aspect will be later examined, as well (Chapters 7 and 14).

202

It seems the Neggs can and do cause a lot of problems, and in Ann's case, there were over a dozen hypnotherapy sessions with Dr. Modi to relieve her problems, which were discovered to be **layered like an onion**, one on top of the other. No sooner had they discovered the cause of one problem, than the next presented itself, [47] and as they peeled back the layers, and released the entities responsible for each layer, Ann got progressively better and better, until she was set free – according to Ann's own journal.

One of Dr. Modi's patients shared a very interesting aspect of Negg interference and it bears repeating here since Dr. Peck also encountered the same issue in two of his patients. And it is also instructive in the extremely rare case of a saintly person who <u>does</u> undergo heavy oppression.

Special People with Light

Suppose a person came to Earth to achieve something special for others, and yet they are now in their 40's or 50's and feel frustrated, blocked, and either don't know what they were supposed to do, or they have tried to do what they felt led to, but for some reason nothing has worked. Several patients reported the following:

> [Some] demons are described as having a special purpose with the patients they are in. They want to stop patients from achieving the goals they set in heaven. According to the demons, these are the people who have **special purposes and missions on Earth**…. The demons claim that these people have certain God-given talents and goals while on the Earth. These are the people Satan and his demons especially watch for; a great deal of effort is exerted to stop them. When these people are born, it is not long until they have their own demons [TFs or EBEs] in residence.
>
> If they do not succeed by directly influencing and interfering with the individuals, then they try to stop them through other people around them, including their loved ones. These special-purpose demons are there for only one purpose…. **to stop individuals from fulfilling their God-given missions**.[48]   [emphasis added]

The Neggs know what the in-coming soul's purpose is, and they can see the amount of Light that the yet-to-be-born soul carries, and try to stop the person – if they don't have Heaven's protection. Other Neggs have said they wait for the soul to come down from the Light, and as it is making its transition (birth) to the physical world, they are able to tune into the in-coming soul's thoughts and know everything about his/her purpose <u>before</u> they even get into the womb! [49]

And just as interesting is another reported aspect of special in-coming souls:

> In very rare cases, I have seen people who have a **special shield or bubble** around them, completely protecting them. Under hypnosis, they report that they came from the Light with this special bubble, because they have a special purpose to achieve during this life. They are provided with this special

bubble or protective shield from the Light, which is around their souls and around their bodies both, so **they can be totally protected**…. all through the life from outside entities and influences, and [so] fulfill their purposes. [50] [emphasis added]

We can deduce from the foregoing that there are certain souls coming here whose projects are part of **God's Greater Script** which the enemy can't mess up. So the Neggs would also know what these special, protected souls are doing and ultimately one wonders if the Neggs don't see their own usefulness coming to an end…and they will be reverted to their original state, a Being of Light, when the Drama on Earth is completed.

One last quote from Dr. Modi's book will be expanded upon in Chapter 12. Under hypnosis, the patients sometimes would report seeing different types of entities who were able to get past their auric shield. Normally, the aura protects us from physical germs and spirit attachments, and sometimes from other peoples' negative energy. In this case, the entities

> ….said that they came in from **another dimension** that had the same vibrations as our dimension. One time, after releasing such an entity, [to the Light], we asked the angel, who was helping us, to explain it. The angel said that demons and angels can travel freely between two dimensions whose vibrations are the same; thus the demons can enter into a person even when the shield [aura] is strong and intact. It can happen only from certain points between the dimensions. [51] [emphasis added]

Initially this sounds impossible, as different dimensions should have different vibrations which would render them time/space 'phased' out of any possible connection with each other, and yet it may happen and is presented here as it corroborates the entities, called the **Interdimensionals,** that Robert Monroe spoke of (Chapter 12). This possibility is also examined in Chapter 16.

Dr. John Lerma

The last M.D. to be considered is Dr. Lerma who runs TMC Hospice for terminally ill patients in Houston, Texas. In his experience with the terminally ill, similar to the NDE patients, they are often visited by entities from the Other Side – both angels and dark entities (Neggs). And **herein lies some very good news**.

The patients receive information from these beings and are usually comforted by what they are told. Some of them pass the information on to Dr. Lerma. Among the many things related in his 2 books, Dr. Lerma reports that all people have a light side and a dark side [as undeveloped souls], but the dark side "…. is unlike what man perceives it to [be].

> Hell is the soul's <u>willful</u> separation from the Light of God." [52]

And that needs clarification:

> We create our hell, not God. God creates the way out of hell. They
> [the angels] said that man's not going to Hell. He or she is **already in hell**.
> We are trying to depart from it. [53] [emphasis added]

Sounds pretty New Age, but the meaning is that we have created our hell on Earth, with the help of the Neggs, discarnates and OPs. And as the patient said, we are trying to escape it. Man needs to get out – and that is the **Earth Graduate**. It was also made clear that **there is always a way back to God** and the Light, no matter how far one may have strayed – God does not judge. Even Dr. Modi discovered that when the Neggs were confronted, and found to be different shades of black, they all had a spark of their original Light down inside and <u>if she could get them to look within</u>, that spark activated and the 'demon' became its original self – an Angel of Light. [54] As was said earlier, the Neggs are playing a role and providing catalyst.

Even more interesting, and this relates to where later chapters are leading, Dr. Lerma heard something very interesting from several of his patients. George's story is perhaps the most comprehensive of the patient stories, and he shares:

> Around three in the morning, a bright light in the room woke me. Instead of nurses, I saw two floating apparitions to the left of my bed…. One entity was brightly white and about 8 feet tall with flowing golden hair. The one to his left was about the same height, but just a dark silhouette….darker than the darkness in the room. They appeared to be communicating and, after about 5 minutes, the white being turned toward me to let me know **they were here to help me** and the dark being remained silent. At one point the dark angel was coming toward me and then I saw a dark figure pop out of me. Both beings were now to the left of me and there was no sign of the beautiful, white apparition. The entire room was left an oddly bright black. They appeared to be conversing but I couldn't hear anything. I felt an unbelievable sense of fear. What were they doing and what did they want with me? I at last cried out, 'Why don't you leave me alone?'
>
> Just moments later, I noticed the dense shadow move back towards me. The apparition swiftly re-entered my body, bringing with him knowledge of my family's generational sins…. it was then that George experienced the birth of his own darkness in addition to his family's collective sins…. The **dark angel explained** to George that darkness was not evil as we are taught; it was merely **raw human energy used with negative intentions**. [55] [emphasis added]

It gets better and is incredibly significant to where this book's final message is going. George shared these thoughts with Dr. Lerma:

> "Dr. Lerma, I sensed that this life is about experiencing the extremes of positive and negative and everything in between, always remembering that choices …. [may] come with dire consequences. This darkness held the answer to my life-long question, and I was being given the intellectual capacity to comprehend…"

The white angel returned and asked him what he had learned. He could not remember anything.... [then] the angel [touched] his head and [opened] his mind to his whole life....

The angel told him, "It's not what you think. **We work together**. All that darkness is a side we all have. Your darkness was so dense and heavy that it took most of your body and mind and formed a dark entity.... God is always next to you.... We are here at the end of life when everything is made clear, to review and explain things to you." [56]   [emphasis added]

A major concept: **the Neggs and Beings of Light work <u>together</u>!**

According to the Book of Enoch, chapter 20, verse 7, Gabriel is one of the original Watcher angels whose job is to *preside* over Ikisat [**serpents**], over paradise, and over the cherubim. So there is some confirmation of this point.

Note: Be clear that the Neggs and the Beings of Light do work together, but this does ***not*** *include the Interdimensional entities who work only with themselves.*

The darkness is real and exists to 'train' us? So, **nothing is totally out of control**; God is still in charge and He is not surprised by whatever happens... The Neggs prod our dark side, or empower it, and we are supposed to overcome it. Catalyst. That would make Earth a kind of school... or a prison. Or is it something else?

Believe and Leave

At that moment, George said the room filled with a bright white light that penetrated to his soul.... George said that the dark figures outside him disintegrated, and the dark figure inside him just whizzed away and dissipated. ....several translucent blue angels went up thru the ceiling and one said "Don't be afraid. I am the Archangel Michael. We have tried and succeeded in battling the darkness with you. **Do you believe?**" George said Michael showed him how spiritual beings are continuously working to protect us from ourselves. By doing this, we.... have a chance to evolve towards God. [57] [emphasis added]

George had been a rough [gang] character throughout his life and had shot several people and was recently transferred to the hospice center from the Texas Department of Corrections. He was recently diagnosed with terminal lung cancer and was now handcuffed to the hospice bed. He did not believe in God, nor did he think he was worthy of any forgiveness from God for what he had done. Hence the angel's question: "Do you believe?"

Only Believe

Dr. Lerma warned George that if he didn't believe in God when he died, his soul could be trapped, or Earth-bound, and he would not go to Heaven. Dr. Modi corroborates that via her patients whose 'demonic' entities report:

Christians think that the Bible is the only book from God. We distorted the meaning in many places. Christians believe that you cannot go to heaven if you do not believe in Jesus. This is a trick we use to confuse people. The truth is that **if you believe in God, then you can go to heaven**. [58] [emphasis added]

In the end, George realized that he had been much rougher on himself than God would ever be; he was told to **forgive himself** and embrace and understand his dark side. His problem was that he only had a personal identity with his dark side. The **shadow** within us is "the extreme of our freewill." Then he said, "The Light destroys the darkness if we love ourselves. **Through self-love we can defeat the darkness within us**." [59]

He died peacefully.

If the Neggs (dark angels) work with the Beings of Light, then what about the Greys?

Respect

Back in December 2002, the Sci-Fi channel ran a series on TV called *The Abduction Diaries*. The featured abductee of the evening was a red-haired lady who was awakened in her bedroom, but not paralyzed as was usually the case. So she jumps out of bed and runs down the hall with the Greys right behind her. They corner her in the kitchen and in desperation, she cries out "Dear God! Help me!" (All you have to do is ask…)

Immediately a 9' tall Being of Light appears between her and the Greys – facing the Greys. The Greys stop and stand for a minute as if listening to the Light, but she couldn't hear anything. And then the Greys disappear, leaving the woman and the Being of Light in the kitchen. Then the Light turns to her and says:

"When you people respect yourselves, so will <u>we</u>."

Awesome. "WE!" The Being of Light was from the unseen realm, like the Neggs, and they and some Greys take orders from the Light. Remember what Dr. Lerma said – they work together. We do not know who we are, <u>what</u> we are, and that <u>we have authority</u> over these Greys – She learned to stand up to the Greys, say 'No!' and mean it. When you mean it, they get it.

> *The woman was never abducted again, by the way, and she later realized that they also respect the name of Jesus. Guess who the Being of Light served?*

As Fort and Keel said, the Neggs will 'mess' with you if they can. It would behoove us to wake up and become all that we can be, and walk the Walk -- including **respect** ourselves.

Serpent Respect

As was seen in the movie *The Fourth Kind*, the Greys are not the only ones doing abductions, and some of the Others are speaking Sumerian which gives a clue as to who they are. Little Greys don't yell things in Sumerian when they abduct people, as in the movie. Little Greys don't talk, period.

So, if there is a Reptilian or Anunnaki aspect to Man's harassment, it would be wise to consider why the Anunnaki Remnant Dissidents don't like Man. And that was pretty well covered in Chapter 3 – Man is rowdy, rebellious, petty and violent. Chapter 12 gives another reason the Dissidents seek to get rid of Man (think: Prime Directive).

Earth history unfortunately demonstrates Man's undesirable traits all too well. And the Anunnaki released disease on Man, and let him be hit with a Flood as a measure of their displeasure with their creation. Have we learned anything since those earlier times?

There is a connection between the woman being told that self-respect was a key to being respected. And it is simply this:

> *"If Man would respect himself and the planet, we as the Remnant Dissidents could work with that and work with the Insider faction to improve the lot of Man on the planet – as we used to try to do. But as long as Man insists on behaving like a chimpanzee, we will treat him as such and have no use for him."*

So Man is his own worst enemy.

Postscript

With all due respect to the reader, it was necessary to cover all of this material so that one understands that licensed, degreed experts are discovering Astral interference with Man and that there is some sort of harassment, oppression, and even the rare possession, being done to Man. The point in this chapter is not to be sensational or negative, but the Neggs are a good [necessary] part, as are the OPs, of the world we live in. Sufficient time has to be spent describing and explaining Neggs and OPs so that the yet-to-be-explained aspects of our reality can be appreciated.

Naturally, Man prefers to live in the belief that everything is OK, the world is safe, we're here all alone, and concurrent with the New Age beliefs, that there is only the Force and Man here on Earth. This is a nice but dangerous belief, as will be seen in Chapter 15 – and that is one reason why this book was written.

It is hoped that most readers will have the patience to read thru the first 11 chapters in sequence, thus gathering a better understanding of our world to better accept a major piece of the puzzle in Chapter 12. And if that weren't enough, the chapters following Chapter 12 build to a new and extended insight in Chapters 15-16.

Chapter 7: Man - Body, Soul and Spirit

Having covered the basics of OP nature and behavior, and having noted that OPs and ensouled humans do not always get along, the Neggs were examined for their effect on Man. Man is too important to not have catalyst provided by others in his everyday world. Why will be seen shortly. So it would be well to take a look at Man, what he is and <u>why</u> the Neggs, discarnates and OPs harass him.

Again, there is a basic difference between Man and the OPs – the existence of a soul. And Man's soul has a divine potential that is the crux of the whole issue.

Anunnaki Inheritance

Given that Man was created by ETs who shared their DNA with that of an existing Earth-based hominid, Man inherited a lot of <u>both</u> their behavioral traits. The 1962 Nobel Prize co-winner, James D. Watson, agrees that this is possible, although such discoveries are still in the process of being quantified:

> … there is a substantial genetic component to our behavior… [because] behavior…[was] critical to human survival, and therefore sternly governed by natural selection. [1]

Traits that ensured Man's survival, themselves survived in his DNA via Epigenetics (Chapter 9). If early Man behaved in a way that did not promote his staying alive, both Man and non-productive traits disappeared: it was called Survival of the Fittest.

Darwin Awards

As an interesting sidenote, Man did not always inherit intelligence from his ancestors, and there have been stories of **Man removing himself from the Gene Pool**, as documented and acknowledged each year by the Darwin Awards.

(Credit: Bing Images)

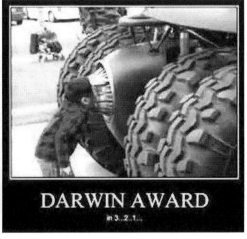

Three **classic and true stories** will demonstrate Man's unique ability to ignore the Survival of the Fittest axiom:

> The Boone & Scenic Valley Railroad [in Iowa] crosses 184 feet over the Des Moines River and its corresponding abyss.
> "Several years ago an adventurous pair decided to take their ropes and rappel off this architectural support… Our adventurers had to be completely fearless as they walked to the middle, tied off their ropes, and began to rappel down. But when the Boone & Scenic Valley Railroad came by on its daily tour of the valley, their one mistake became apparent. They had tied the ropes to the sturdiest support possible: the steel train tracks…" [2]

> This one shows that smoking is hazardous to your health and the story might be called The Ants' Revenge:
> "A woman was found burned to death, her body still blazing on a grassy area adjacent to her home… A lighter and a melted gas can were discovered nearby. After a lengthy investigation police turned up no evidence of foul play. They believe her demise was due to her habit of dousing anthills with gasoline while she smoked cigarettes..." [3]

> Last but not least, there is also proof that cellphones can be dangerous while driving, **and** while just standing around…
> " Police said a [Kansas] man was struck and killed by a train after his vehicle broke down on I-35. His attempts at repairing his car had failed, and he had stepped away from the busy freeway to call for help.
> As luck would have it, he chose to stand on the train tracks paralleling the road. When the train engineer spotted him standing on the tracks, the man was holding a cellphone to one ear and cupping his hand to the other ear to block the noise of the oncoming locomotive…" [4]

Yes, all three events actually happened, all four people removed themselves from the Gene Pool, and all won the Darwin Award. Is there something in Man's genetics that predisposes him to carelessness, stupidity…. and even violence?

The Gene Count

Dr. Watson also says that Man's tendency to violence may be based on one gene "interacting with environmental factors." [5] He theorizes that most violent individuals do possess a culprit gene which has been found on the X chromosome in men, which usually eliminates women from this trait – unless the gene occurs on <u>both</u> of the woman's X chromosomes. [6] (Think: Lizzie Borden or Lucretia Borgia.) The culprit was a mutated gene which produced faulty MAO (MonoAmineOxidase) coding.

The Anunnaki were known, according to the Sitchin material, to be warlike and had never-ending disagreements among themselves. They practiced incest, lying, and rape and suspicion and intrigue were a way of life with them. Perhaps the best description of them is found in the saying 'Might makes right' or 'The end justifies the means.' They were also intelligent, technologically advanced, and clever. It is these traits that have come down to us in Mankind today. Whatever their behavioral potential was, it is also ours.

And yet, our full potential was cut down or modified by the Anunnaki, since they did not want Man to be just like them. How do we know? As the most intelligent species on Earth, our genome should be the most complex, or at least our genes should outnumber the genes in the genomes of other animals. And this is not so… unless you add in the "junk DNA"…

> The current estimate is that humans who have an estimated 100 trillion cells making up our bodies, will end up with about 25,000 genes once they have all been identified. It is amazing to find out that a creature composed of only 959 cells, the Nematode worm, has around 20,000 genes… The mustard plant actually has even more genes than humans at around 27,000, while the fruit fly has 14,000, Baker's Yeast 6,000, and even gut bacteria E. Coli have … about 4,000.

> It is proposed by James Watson that our human abilities have evolved to make our genes multifunctional… Does that make any sense to you? How could a gene code for more than one specific effect? Would this mean that if we eliminate the gene that causes cancer, we accidentally eliminate the same gene which codes for cell division? I would suggest that there is probably much more to our introns and junk genes than we currently understand. [7]

And recent genetic research has discovered that the "junk" DNA [introns] actually does about 10 different functions in the genome. (See Chapter 9, 'Junk is Not Junk' section.) It is also suggested that Man's specialness can be activated by the 'rewiring' and recoding of the inactive DNA, and by rejuvenating the *telomeres*, as further examined in Epigenetics in Chapter 9.

DNA Mysteries

The size of Man's genome indicates that we should be capable of much more than we are, but until recently there was the curious issue of why **97% of the human genome apparently codes for nothing** and appears to be "junk DNA." Surely DNA is important, and useless DNA could not have evolved, as only the dominant, useful genes, behavior, and traits of any organism cause it to survive and replicate those traits in the DNA. So the design of Man did not include useless DNA.

> The genes of many lifeforms have an additional surprising feature. The genes contain stretches of DNA called **exons**, each of which codes for a particular protein, and **introns** which are stretches of non-coding DNA. The relationship between the inactive introns and junk DNA is not understood. Genes consist of alternating introns and exons, and the programmed genetic codes are contained in several scattered exons, rather than a continuous stretch of DNA. The largest part of the DNA consists of seemingly never-ending stretches of junk DNA. **In humans 97% of DNA consists of non-coding genes, while**

in … fruit flies only 17% of the DNA contains non-coding genes. [8]
[emphasis added]

Introns may seem useless, but it is illogical to think that a God of the Universe designed 97% useless DNA in Man, wasting space and providing genetics that don't do anything. And yet, a hominid genetics expert from another world might design DNA that way – for a purpose. So it was just a matter of further research before someone identified what the "junk" DNA did. The real question now is: <u>Why</u> was it designed that way, or did our once-useful DNA 'devolve' into the current state… or was it deliberately modified?

Is it possible that our genome is the same size as that of our creators, and because we were a threat to them, becoming just as smart after the human-Anunnaki interbreeding, which created *Adapa*, that somebody had to do something to "switch off" a lot of the genetic codes so that Man would be controllable? Is it possible that Man was useless as an intelligent slave and so was "dumbed down" via his DNA to make him manageable, ignorant and perhaps docile?

Extra 223 Genes in Man

It was recently discovered that Man shares 223 genes only with bacteria. These 223 do not exist in other lifeforms, such as flies, worms, dogs, cats, birds… At some point,

> "modern humans acquired an extra 223 genes not through gradual evolution, not vertically on the Tree of Life, but horizontally, as a sideways insertion of genetic material from bacteria… 223 genes is more than two thirds of the difference between me, you and a chimpanzee! [9]

God would not have put non-human genes in the creation of Man. Scientists cannot explain it and do not like it. "….these extra genes are a jump that does not follow current evolutionary theories" said a researcher at Baylor College of Medicine. [10] So maybe the theory of Evolution is wrong…? Or maybe the Anunnaki used something similar to virus vector engineering? And no one knows yet (2014) what the 223 genes code for.

Useless By Design

In a related article, another scientist discovered that the "junk DNA," or non-coding sequences are found in all living organisms on Earth, so they aren't unusual. It is just that Man, the pinnacle of creation, has the most junk DNA.

> After comprehensive analysis with the assistance of other scientists, computer programmers, mathematicians, and other learned scholars, Professor [Sam] Chang had wondered if the apparently "junk human DNA" was created by some kind of **"extraterrestrial programmer."** The alien chunks… all have their own veins, arteries, and its own immune system that vigorously resists all our anti-cancer drugs…

> Our hypothesis is that a higher extraterrestrial life form was engaged in creating new life and planting it on various planets. Earth is just one of them…

If we think about it in our human terms, the apparent "extraterrestrial programmers" were most probably working on "one big code" consisting of several projects, and the projects should have produced various life forms for various planets... trying various solutions. **They wrote "the big code", executed it, did not like some function, changed [it] or added new one, executed again, made more improvements, tried again and again.**

[They] may have been ordered to cut all their idealistic plans for the future when they concentrated on the "Earth project" to meet the pressing deadline. Very likely... the "extraterrestrial programmers" may have cut down drastically on big code and delivered [the] basic program intended for Earth. [11] [emphasis added]

That is as plausible a solution as the former one where the Anunnaki found *Adapa* Man to be an intelligent threat and so "dumbed down" his DNA. Some day we may know which version is the right one. But the fact remains that Man's DNA <u>was</u> manipulated, and the ETs (intelligent intervention) are more and more directly implicated by the recent discoveries in genetics. Darwin's old evolutionary world is less and less sustainable.

Brain Size Changed

As will be shown in Chapter 8, "...mitochondrial Eve and chromosomal Adam were created between 180,000 to 250,000 years ago." [12, 13]   Coincidentally, the Anunnaki were creating their slave worker, Man, about 250,000 years ago. Somebody had the knowledge and the skill to modify the body's DNA <u>and the brain</u>.

Scientists believe that humans underwent a major brain change around 200,000 years ago. What could have caused the sudden and dramatic change in human brains? ... There had to be a ... dramatic event that caused such a major change...There is emerging evidence supported by genetic and mitochrondrial dating, which seems to point to such an event... Keep in mind that the coincidental facts of mitochrondrial Eve and chromosomal Adam were both dated back to around 200,000 years ago. Just a coincidence, or another piece of the human puzzle that fits perfectly? [14]

So what was the change in the brain size?

Australopithicus	=	438 ml
Homo *habilis*	=	500-750 ml
Homo *erectus*	=	800-900 ml
Neanderthal	=	1534 ml (range: 1200-1700cc)
Homo *sapiens*	=	1395 ml (range: 1100-1300cc)
& Cro-Magnon		

most recent

(Source: Tellinger, p. 33-34, and Wikipedia/wiki/cranial_capacity.)

Modern Man does not have as big a brain as Neanderthal and yet is smarter than he was. So size is not everything. And what is even more interesting is that 99.9% of all human DNA is identical, so a lot of space has been wasted. Since dominant genes replace weaker genes (à la 'Survival of the Fittest'), how did do-nothing genes survive and replicate?

No Ape Men

While this subject was covered more in Chapter 4, it is fitting to mention that with all the paleontology and anthropology discoveries of the last couple hundred years, there have not been found any "missing links" or earlier versions of half-Man, half-ape that support Evolution.

> Piltdown Man was a hoax,
> *Ramapithecus* (Leakey's discovery) was just an ape,
> Nebraska Man turned out to be a pig's tooth,
> Java Man (*Pithecanthropus*) was just a large gibbon,
> Peking Man was the remains of an ape,
> Australopithecines (Leakey) was also an ape.
> Ardipithecus (Ethiopia) is also an ape.

And, referring to the Brain Table above, "…Homo *erectus* is considered by most experts to be a category that should never have been created." [15] And, again, Homo *habilis* is another category that "…had apelike proportions and should never have been classified as manlike."[16] Thus, **neither *erectus* nor *habilis* were evolutionary precursors of Man.**

What all this is saying is that except for Neanderthal, Cro-Magnon and Homo *sapiens*, there are no links to the apes, and the three versions of Man are unique: *Lulu*, *Adamu*, and *Adapa*.

And to clear up a remaining misconception,

> For about 100 years the world was led to believe that Neanderthal man
> was stooped and apelike. Recent studies show that this was based on …
> some Neanderthals who were crippled with arthritis and rickets.
> Neanderthal man, Heidelberg man, and Cro-Magnon man were completely
> human. [17]

And for what it may be worth, as something to think about, what if the creation of *Adapa* (Chapter 3) as Homo *sapiens* was perfect and pretty much resembled today's Man, and what if Cro-Magnon and Neanderthal were actually cases of genetic '**devolution**' <u>after</u> the creation of Homo *sapiens*? As will be seen in Chapter 9, modern Man shares no DNA with Neanderthal and perhaps this is why.

Terminal DNA

There does not have to be conflict between Evolution and Creation, but today's scientists need to remove the blinders with regard to Evolution-only. Some scientists refuse to seriously consider the Sumerian texts and the creation of the *Adamu*, which would answer a lot of our questions about Man's origins and heritage. 200,000 years ago something significant happened and Man was left with the genome of his maker, but severely cut-down, and Man was the proud possessor of some of the most undesirable Anunnaki genes. By design, the traits of arrogance, lust, lying, volatility, pettiness, and violence were not suppressed when Man served the Anunnaki as an unintelligent, subservient and primitive creature.

Today, Man is still trying to overcome his baser nature, and that was the whole point of what the Anunnaki did and why they did it – control: to keep Man from getting it together. **His DNA insures termination of his species by his own hand** -- just because Man cannot overcome his programming. His programming does not include what it takes to proactively change and sustain the change. And that is what the new Homo *noeticus* is all about, as was examined in Chapter 4.

It will be interesting to see what genetic advances are made in the next few years, and what types of humans 'evolve' and walk among us as a result of the altered genetics by the on-going Grey agenda.

The Ogo

Earlier in Chapter 3, it was brought out that Man was created by the ETs, and despite their exact nature and appearance, Man is their doing. Specifically, it was the Dogon tribe from Africa that cast another penetrating light on the nature and problem of Man:

> The Dogon refer to mankind as Ogo, the imperfect, the outcast. They say that the Ogo were rebellious and were unfinished as a creation. In order to make up for the rebellious – sinful – nature of the Ogo, one of the Nommo [an Oannes], named O Nommo, "Nommo of the Pond," [sounds like Enki] was **sacrificially crucified on a tree** to atone for our imperfect nature, died, and will return in an ark with the ancestors of men. [18]

Nommo is the name for the amphibians who also came from Sirius to set up civilization in Sumer. They as a group were also called Oannes/Annedoti and there is a link to the Anunnaki, suggesting a major connection of some kind to Sirius.

> Our own planet Earth is, significantly, 'the place where Ogo's umbilical cord was attached to his placenta…and recalls his first descent.' In other words, the Earth is where Ogo 'plugged in', as it were, to this system of planets. What Ogo the Fox seems to represent is man himself, an imperfect, intelligent species who 'descended' or originated on this planet … Ogo is representative of ourselves, in all our cosmic impurity. It comes as a shock to realize that **we are Ogo, the imperfect, the meddler, the outcast.** Ogo rebelled at his creation and remained **unfinished**…. And in order to atone for our impurity it is said over and over by the Dogon that the Nommo dies and is resurrected, acting as a sacrifice for us, to purify and cleanse the Earth. The **parallels with Christ** are extraordinary, even extending to Nommo being crucified on a tree, and… then being resurrected. [19] [emphasis added]

215

If you think that parallel is interesting, wait until Chapter 11.

It is said that the Nommo will return, as it was said that the Anunnaki will return, and Quetzalcoatl told the Mayans he'd return, etc… BUT, none of those who left have come back. And there is a reason they haven't been back as will be seen in Chapter 12.

Yet it was said that when the Nommo landed on Earth, they 'crushed the Fox' or Ogo and lessened man's rebellious nature… by removing some DNA from Man's genome?

> So perhaps man's brutish nature has already been sufficiently subdued in our distant past. Perhaps it was those visitors whom the Dogon call the Nommos who really did 'crush the Fox' in all of us, who all but destroyed Ogo, and have given us all the best elements of civilization which we possess. We remain as a curious mixture of the brute and the civilized, struggling against the Ogo within us. [20]

The Ogo within us is probably the Anunnaki genetic legacy… and Man probably has a mixed DNA as Others came and later (in other Eras – Chapter 15) genetically 'tinkered' with Man. There had to be a source for the oriental eye design, and the eye colors being limited to blue/brown/green … umless Enki was designing it all, including a beautiful green-eyed blonde called Inanna?

If the Nommo/Oannes were the Anunnaki, on the other hand, it would follow that at some point they would see the mess they made, mixing DNA as they did, and perhaps some of them would seek to remedy Man's 'fallen' nature (his shadow side) and try to upgrade his genetics, or 'crush the Fox' within us. On the other hand, perhaps the Nommo are not the Anunnaki and they came later to clean up what the Anunnaki left behind. And yet, today only the Greys are cleaning it up…

In any event, the Higher Beings saw what was happening and put a stop to it. The Anunnaki were last here about 600 BC as was reported earlier. The significance of that, and why they haven't been back, is the subject of Chapter 12.

As was seen, Man was created in at least 3 distinct stages – *Lulu*, *Adamu* and *Adapa*. *Adapa* had a soul, others didn't, and that has been so significant on Earth that it deserves special attention.

Ensouled Humans

So what is Man, body, soul and spirit?

Ensouled humans are **eternal** souls with DNA that permits connection from their magnetic center (aligned, coherent chakras) to the God Force – the divine spark referred to so many times. As souls, they cannot be killed and the worst that can be done to them (and has been tried in other Eras) is to <u>trap or contain</u> them, slow them down, or totally derail them… which <u>has</u> been done on Earth. This sometimes makes Earth a kind of prison planet, but it is more.

Spiritual Potential

What is significant is that **Man is multidimensional** and has a spiritual potential that OPs don't have, and the Dissidents through the Powers That Be (PTB) and OPs working within the RCF/Matrix (all covered later) militate against Man to suppress it. And yet, Man **will** spiritually evolve and eventually function as another Jesus/Krishna/Buddha – somewhere in the Father's Creation. The goal of the ensouled human is to eventually reconnect with Source and develop latent (potential) higher attributes – even psychic abilities. Jesus said it (paraphrased):

> "These things I do you shall do and greater…" John 14:12

Why is ensouled man such a threat? Because he has the spark of divinity which can be activated through his (to-be-rewired) DNA, but this is <u>received</u> when the time is right, and cannot be forced. Nor can years of meditation, yoga or Tai Chi force the DNA to develop or "rewire." Such efforts are noble, but soul growth depends much more on what the soul learns about self and the world, and since knowledge is Light, **the Light does the work**.

> *As will later be seen, in Chapter 9, DNA and Light are intimately connected, with scientists reporting that DNA releases biophotons upon stimulation of the DNA* [21]

When the student is ready, the transformation happens as a result of a spiritual energy 'potential' being reached, and this has been referred to as **kundalini** ("Serpent energy") moving up the spine to energize and transform the person – by connecting chakras. This can be dangerous if done without a teacher who knows what to expect and how to handle energy blockages in the student.

As the human soul comes into its own divine power, it is conceivable that it will be serving the Father of Light by "reigning" over some of the areas of Darkness – at least at some point there will be a confrontation.

Why Man is Oppressed

> *Note: Dr. Peck in the following quoted material makes some excellent observations on possession (which is very rare). Please note when reading the following selections that Satan, as identified by Dr. Peck, may in fact be (1) a discarnate entity as a wanna-be-Satan, or (2) the condemned spirits of the Nephilim and their offspring which were allegedly bound to the Earth and constantly seek a body to inhabit (since they were denied further incarnations), or (3), as will be seen later, the entity doing the possessing may be **an interdimensionsal being** seeking the 'pleasure' of 3D embodiment. Dr. Robert Monroe encountered several non-human intelligences during his OBEs who had zero like and regard for humans, and he was told to stay away from them by the more benevolent entities. (See Chapter 12.)*

During Day 3 of a long exorcism that Dr. Peck led, he began to wonder why what appeared to be a demonic spirit inhabiting his patient, Beccah, hated humans so much and he decided to ask it.

217

Note: It might have been an Interdimensional entity, a Negg, or a strong discarnate – it is hard to tell, and the entity never gave a clue as to what it was.

So speaking out loud before the possessed Beccah (not her real name) and the exorcism team, Dr. Peck began to speak what he felt was the truth of Beccah's situation – looking as much for <u>any reaction</u> as an answer.

> "….I think the basic reason you hate her is because she is a human being. I suspect you particularly hate her because she is a potential spiritual leader, but your genuine enemy is not just Beccah, but the entire human race. I believe the real question is, **Why do you hate humans?** I order you now in the name of Jesus Christ to tell me why you hate humans so much. Why is it your guiding motive to do everything you possibly can **to prevent humans from achieving their potential destiny?**" [22] [emphasis added]

Here we have Dr. Peck repeating one of the key issues presented in this book. And although he knew he might not get an answer from the very strong entity that had Beccah totally wrapped up, under its control, he thought speaking the truth might have an effect, as it had with Jersey (Chapter 6). So he continued and tried insulting the entity… which did not produce any response – because the entity was not Satan, and it was probably laughing to itself at Dr. Peck's ignorance. Dr. Peck noted that Beccah was far more possessed than Jersey and he realized that he might actually be dealing with a major anti-Mankind entity in her – not just some minor Negg or discarnate. [23] Beccah was restrained and just sat on the bed, weaving back and forth like a snake.

Higher Than Angels

So Dr. Peck really gets down to what he felt in his gut was the issue, and while it is not straight Church teaching, it finally elicits a response whereby the entity turns and glares at Dr. Peck as if to kill him:

> "So many times I have heard it said that God created us humans in His Own image. What does that mean?…. Even though most Christians think of angels as exalted beings, higher than themselves, it finally dawned on me that **this common Christian vision is wrong**. The reality, I believe, is that …. **God created us higher than the angels**, that it is not the angels who are superior to us, but we who are more fortunate than them. And that's why you hate us, isn't it …?" [24] [emphasis added]

Because this fits perfectly with the theme of this book and helps explain why we are "trapped" here on Earth, it is worth repeating the whole thing. Dr. Peck is so close to the Truth, he elicits a staring response from the entity. This revelation explains that Earth is not our home, and because Astral entities can't kill eternal souls, it also explains why they would choose to trap, deceive, and keep Man from fulfilling his potential. If the entity is related to the Djinn as an interdimensional, the next attack is going to make it angry:

Dr. Peck continues:

"You hate human beings so much because God decided to create them <u>higher than even you</u> ….and you simply could not stand it when **God decided to create creatures even more exalted than you**…. You refused to tolerate it. And that is why ….you have hated the human race from its beginning." [25] [emphasis added]

Dr. Peck then says "The [patient] had stopped writhing, intent on looking at me with murderous rage. I knew it would never admit the correctness of what I had just said."[26] While he has assumed the entity to be Satan, and that is not correct given the information in Chapter 6, it is most likely that of the Djinn, aka Interdimensionals (or even John Keel's *ultradimensionals*). Dr. Peck's appraisal of Man's significance as a created, high-potential soul is 100% accurate. Note that he mirrors the Gnostic view of Man and Yaltabaoth's hatred of same.

> *Note that a Djinn or an Interdimensional entity would hate Man anyway, and it would particularly hate Dr. Peck's constant badgering.*

Islamic View

And then interestingly enough, Dr. Peck adds a note:

> …. after Beccahs' exorcism I happened to discover it to be a standard doctrine of Islam….. that **human beings were created higher than the angels**. In fact, Mohammed himself proclaimed it in the second sura [2:34] of the Koran. [27] [emphasis added]

The actual passages in the Koran stating this important fact follow:

> When we said to the angels: 'Prostrate yourselves before Adam,' they all prostrated themselves, except Satan [Iblis], who replied: 'Shall I bow to him whom You have made of clay? Do you see this being whom You have exalted above me?....' Surah 17:62.

> and

> 'Satan,' said He, 'why do you not bow to him whom My own hands have made? Are you too proud, or do you deem yourself superior?'
> Satan replied: 'I am nobler than he. You created me from fire, but him from clay.' Surah 38:73.

For what it is worth, Jersey was set free, and Beccah remained possessed; Beccah was more completely possessed than Jersey -- what Fr. Malachi Martin would call almost 'perfect possession.' [28] In reality, Beccah was probably an OP, and had no soul; hence she would appear more perfectly possessed and <u>could not</u> be set free.

Exorcism Summary

In addition, Dr. Peck may have been off on the wrong path with the entity controlling Beccah. It may not have cared what Dr. Peck thought or said – especially if it was one of the non-human Interdimensionals that Monroe will later speak of in Chapter 12. It needs to be said that Beccah probably was controlled by one of the very strong anti-Mankind entities that Robert Monroe was urged to avoid when he did his OBEs. These entities evolved thru non-human ways, they think they're superior, and they do not like humans. They are <u>not</u> demonic or evil, they just do not like humans and consider them inferiors.[29] How do we see ants?

Nonetheless, one of them wanted to experience 3D and so was controlling Beccah.

The reason for not seriously considering Beccah's spirit to be an earth-bound spirit of the Nephilim is (1) we don't know if Enoch was telling it straight, or just giving us his best guess, and (2) the incarcerated Nephilim spirits were allegedly moved to another location as this Era started. By the way, (3) the Neggs don't mimic possession but **can** possess OPs, which is what Beccah appears to have been. Yet, if Beccah was an OP, the Neggs don't bother with such a game, thus the entity had to be an Interdimensional of some sort, or a really strong discarnate. A strong entity of any sort would not have answered Dr. Peck either because they and Astral beings are bound by the **Law of Confusion**: you have a 'right' to not know, and they are not authorized to 'teach' Man.

Yet the section above has value in that it reveals something that Dr. Peck discovered: **Man has more value than we have suspected (being created higher than the angels)**, and secondly that there are entities who can possess humans, especially OPs – if the human opens themselves to manipulation through Ouija Board, witchcraft, or channeling. Dr. Peck also taught us in Chapter 6 that telling the Truth to an oppressed or possessed person <u>with a soul</u> can set them free. The Light (Truth) can also set the Earth captives free…

Soul and Spirit

In the beginning there was God. Incredible potential. Order and chaos, Light and Darkness, Yin and Yang. A Designer. The One, the Central Sun… A concept so deep it is beyond the ability of 3D Man to fathom. So it is approached allegorically, and sometimes rejected by those who demand physical proof of something more intelligent and powerful than Man.

Evolution

Those who reject the existence of God claim that all current life that we see on Earth came from a primordial 'soup' which contained the building blocks (amino acids) of all life. And, supposedly, a bolt of lightning hit the soup, energizing it and causing new chemical compounds to develop, and over millions of years, and further lightning strikes (?), the first living 1-cell organism(s) emerged.

Why is this not still happening?

For some reason, the Second Law of Thermodynamics did not apply way back then, perhaps because no one had discovered it yet… That Law says that if any organism is left to itself, with no outside input, **entropy** is the natural result: all things tend to decay unless they are re-energized, or fed, or some external force keeps them going. "All systems, including living systems, decrease in order." [30] So the 1-celled creatures were brought to life, à la Frankenstein, by bolts of lightning and they did not fall prey to the Law of Entropy – until Man later also discovered it. How wonderful.

The foregoing is called Evolution which requires a huge amount of time for things to naturally "increase in order": particles would become single-cell organisms which would become multi-celled organisms which would become invertebrates… sea slugs, IRS agents, and eventually people.

In a brilliant piece of deduction which will forever go down in the history of Man and Evolution, Charles Darwin discovered that because a man looks structurally something like a chimpanzee, man must therefore have evolved from the ape. How exciting was that news? Anything was possible, so Charles said – given enough time. And yet, because of entropy, **time is the enemy of Evolution**. This issue will be dealt with more fully in Chapters 8-9 where today's genetics disproves Darwin's Theory of Evolution (but **not** Epigenetics, Natural Selection and Survival of the Fittest).

According to the theory of Evolution, if everything evolved from a 1-cell organism, and there was no God involved, then there is no design and no soul. Obviously, it would be a blow to Evolution if someone could prove the existence of the soul.

Weight of the Soul

Such was the plan of Dr. Duncan MacDougall in Massachusetts in 1907. The good physician reasoned that if the soul existed, it might have mass and thus it might have weight. If it had weight then when a person dies, they would weigh less. So he designed "…. a light framework built upon very delicately balanced platform beam scales" which were sensitive to 2/10 of an ounce. [31]

As a patient approached death, he had them placed on the special measuring "bed" and took their weight every hour up to the moment of death. Medically ascertaining that they were dead, he then took a last reading of the scales. What he found was that the overall **weight dropped three-fourths of an ounce**. The next patient lost half an ounce. The third patient lost half an ounce, and the fourth … well, the overall averaging of 6 dying patients yielded a net result of 21 grams for the weight of the soul. He published his findings. (There was a movie about this, called *21 Grams*.)

Naturally there were immediate detractors. But the good doctor admitted that the sample size was too small and there should be better controls and recording. [32] So he shifted gears and tried to x-ray the patient at the time of death, hoping to see something leave the body. What he found was that "….the soul substance gives off a light resembling that of interstellar **ether**." [33] These results were also inconclusive in that it was hard to replicate them.

Note: the existence and nature of "interstellar Ether" becomes significant in Chapter 9 when the subject of Subquantum Kinetics is examined. The Ether is pretty important after all. (Nowadays they're calling it Dark Matter…they can't say the word 'Ether'!)

The Germans Weigh In…

Leave it to the Germans to hear about this and give it a high-tech go. In 1988, the East German researchers measured the weight of over 200 terminally ill patients before and after death. Their results showed that the dying people lost an average of 1/3,000th of an ounce (.003 oz.). [34]   They published their findings in *Horizon*:

> "The inescapable conclusion is that we now have confirmed the existence of the human soul and determined its weight," said Dr. Becker Mertens of Dresden…. The challenge before us now is to figure out exactly what the soul is composed of….We are inclined to believe that it is a form of energy. But our attempts to identify this energy have been unsuccessful to date." [35]

While the foregoing account of the East German study has been questioned by several researchers, and no one can locate the alleged science journal *Horizon*, nor can the s cientist, Dr. Mertens, be located anywhere, I leave the above account for what is worth due to the off-chance that the East Germans may have done the research in 1988 or earlier, before the Berlin Wall came down, and subsequently with 1989 and the Wall coming down, such research may have been banned/discredited and the science team silenced. Dr. Mertens may be an alias and the actual research may have been done by the Russians.

While no one can pin it down as to precisely and consistently what the soul weighs, and some may weigh more than others, it is noble that some people were trying to learn what they could about it. Until recently, Science did not have any instrumentation capable of measuring or seeing the human soul, so its existence was hotly debated. Those who doubt the soul exists today are also the same ones who believe in Evolution and no Designer.

Yet there is a camera that does show a genuine picture of the aura (biophotonic emission of the soul), <u>not</u> a photograph of the hand's energy placed over a person's head.

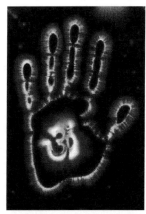

A Human Hand Emitting Biophotons
(source: http://hobbyphotographytips.com/wp-content/uploads/2008/05/kirlian-photography.jpg)

And shown left is also **Kirlian photography** [36] which shows the light energy field around the body. Remember that the aura is the energy radiation of the soul. This is reviewed again in Chapter 9 where biophotons are examined. Perhaps it will not be much longer before someone, besides psychics and those who travel outside their body, OBErs, and NDErs, can see the soul.

Consciousness

If one has a soul, s/he is also self-conscious or self-aware. If one has no soul (OPs), s/he is also conscious, but not self-conscious, so it can be said that self-awareness, or a sense of self, is related to the soul. Standard consciousness appears to be the ability to react/respond to one's environment as stimuli are relayed by one or more of the five senses. And since plants respond to sunlight, and some (Venus Flytrap) respond to insects, are plants conscious? Plants also react negatively to Heavy Metal music (by getting sick or stunting their growth), and they react very positively to soothing music – probably just a vibrational issue: jangling and discordant versus harmonious and smooth. Sound is energy and vibrations DO affect plants and people.

On the other hand, an enterprising anthropologist, Dr. Jeremy Narby, was researching DNA, ayahuasca and shamanism when he decided to question how consciousness fit into the human picture. He asked Fritz-Albert Popp (who contributed to DNA and biophotons research), if he had any thoughts on it and Popp replied:

> Yes, consciousness could be the electromagnetic field constructed by the sum of these [biophoton] emissions. But as you know, our understanding of the neurological basis of consciousness is still very limited. [37]

A person who is in a coma is not considered conscious and a loud bang will not arouse them. A person who is asleep can be aroused by a loud bang. What is the difference? A person in a coma is 'disconnected' from their sensory input, a sleeping person isn't. So standard consciousness is connected with being aware of, receptive to, outside sensory stimuli, and one of the five senses has to be activated, not disconnected.

So, OPs are considered conscious [awake] even though they have no soul: they look normal, they respond to the world around them. The OP is acting out of his lower three chakras. A Zombie on the other hand, operates only out of the lower, first chakra. And they are not considered really conscious since they don't readily respond to stimuli and they act as if they are largely unaware of their environment.

In a nutshell, awareness has to do with the **bionet** of meridians interconnecting the body with the etheric (first) layer of the aura, activated by the third chakra, the solar plexus – a key chakra connected with self (and ego). As Popp suggested, consciousness operates in the electromagnetic field immediately surrounding the body, fed by the biophotons running through the bionet, which is connected to and interconnects the five (and more) senses, and all empowered by the key third chakra.

This also relates, in a limited way, to plants: as shown by Kirlian photography, there is a bio-electric field around every plant and it is sensitive to light, sound – or vibrations in general. In the altered state generated by ayahuasca, shamans do communicate with plants – via the *maninkari* [elementals] that inhabit/care for the plants. That is how shamen knew which plants to put together to heal people. The plants told them. [38] So plants do have a limited consciousness and the American Indians weren't crazy when they spoke of the 'spirits' that inhabit plants, animals, rivers, etc – it is all connected.

223

Only modern man has disconnected himself from the living, bionetwork around him. What are shamen doing that is different? "In their visions, shamans [sic] manage to take their consciousness down to the molecular level." [39] Only modern, educated Man is so far into his head, trying to reason out everything, that he cannot connect with Nature. So modern Man doesn't respect Nature and we now have incredible pollution in our world – and dwindling oxygen (Chapter 14) – the only world we have and we are destroying it.

If that doesn't make your day, nothing will…

Soul

So what is a soul?

> **A spark of the Divine, The God replicating Himself, an eternal sentient, coherent Light energy being that is conscious of itself and its surroundings, intelligent, exists in multiple dimensions, and can evolve itself back to a connection with the Godhead**…

And it seems to have a weight. And if the aura pictures are correct, the state of one's soul (sad, happy, angry, jealous, etc.) manifests in the aura as colors reflecting one's feelings. Red reflects anger, blue reflects sadness, healing is reflected by green, and very intellectual analysis (say, computer programming) is reflected by yellow in the aura.

If you can weigh it, it has a slight mass, or physicalness. And it is who we are, because it is what animates the body. When John Smith dies, he is not there anymore. His body is, but his body is not who he is, and many NDErs (Near Death Experiencers) have said as much. The soul can leave the body and that personality is still intact – Robert Monroe in his Out of Body (OBE) experiences, documented in three books, demonstrated that.

So the soul exists, it has mass, and it is eternal. When it is not in the body, it resembles one of the Beings of Light that come to meet the NDErs at death, only not as bright. This is probably what the Bible calls our "imperishable body" in I Cor. 15: 44 and 52. Matt.17:2 is where Jesus displays his transformed body on the mount – resembling a Being of Light. As significant as that sight must have been to the disciples watching, strangely very little more is said about it and what it meant.

How do we know that the soul is eternal? Because souls were created in the likeness of The God, and God is eternal. And NDErs and OBErs all report that the soul is who they are -- an entity that goes on and on, having had many lifetimes. Also, it is believable that the soul is eternal since no one has come up with any evidence or teaching that the soul is born once into a body on Earth and then at the death of the body, the soul ceases to exist, too.

> *If someone believes that there is no more life after death, perhaps a person with that belief is confusing the issue with happens to the OPs at death. OPs have no soul and they DO cease to exist at death of the physical body.*

In addition, the soul normally enters the body just before birth, at birth, or just after birth. There is a soul hovering about the mother who plans to enter the body, but if the body is not genetically acceptable, or if the parents have recently decided to do/be something other than what the soul needs when it originally selected them, the soul does not enter and the baby may be stillborn, or function as an OP, with no soul. (Chapter 16: Interlife.)

Spirirt Power

What is the power source of the soul? What animates the soul? Even a lightbulb has to have electricity make it glow. This is getting very esoteric, but the soul is empowered by Spirit – capital "S" – not to be confused with the spirits that infest the Earth. "God is a Spirit." John 4:24. The Spirit empowers the soul via the silver cord, and the soul animates the body by transducing the energy from the Spirit through the bionet/chakra system.

The greater Spirit is manifest in numerous Godheads (or Oversouls) which link to many groups of souls (or Soul Groups) to which each soul belongs. Attaching each soul to its Soul Group is again that 2" thick silver cord, and in turn, the Group soul entity is attached to a particular Oversoul in the Godhead which is similarly attached to The Father of Light. The cords supply energy to the created souls from the Original Source, or the One.

Divine Hierarchy

The Father of Light and Souls exist in an organizational hierarchy – much like any well-run business enterprise. There are the Directors at the top, including CEO, then the Division Directors with their subordinate Section Managers, and below them in each Section is a Supervisor, and sometimes a lead person or Foreman. For example Accounting will have a Director of Accounting, then a Comptroller, then a Treasurer and Chief Accountant, then the staff within each major function. As was said, Souls cannot interface directly with the One anymore than bookkeepers deal directly with the company's CEO.

The Divine Hierarchy look like this:

> The Father of Light/The One
> > The Higher Beings
> > > Subordinate Beings including:
> > > > Masters, Avatars
> > > > Angels (Beings of Light) and Neggs
> > > > > Oversouls (Higher Self)
> > > > > Soul Groups
> > > > > > Souls

There is no Hell and no Satan (Chapter 6).

There is often a Board of Directors and that corresponds to the **Solar Council** which oversees our solar sysem. There is also a Galactic Council which coordinates the Solar Councils. Order and purpose permeate our Multiverse.

This concept is represented in the next page's Chart 3a of the Godhead.

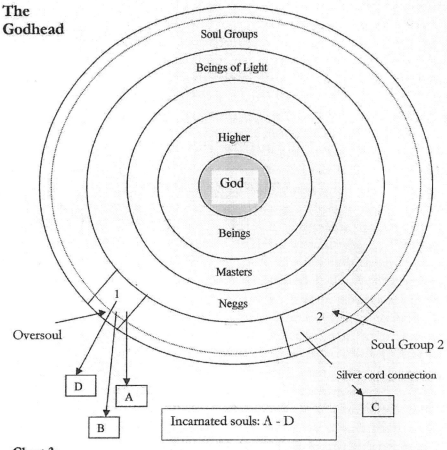

Chart 3a

Note1 that when soul A dies, his life is transported (recorded) to his Oversoul (or Higher Self) after his death. Soul B can access A's life thru the same Oversoul, during regression, but soul C cannot access/import the life of A during regression. B can also be aware of D, but D is not aware of C.

Note2 also, during the lives of B and D, if they are two aspects of the same soul, they are able to affect each other through sympathetic energy vibration (via their silver cords, explained in the text).

Note3 that soul groups may not be the same size, and that Oversouls inter-connect.

Guidance

Man as an individual soul, is connected to the Godhead via a silver cord. That is his connection to the Godhead for guidance… Nowhere are there any 'guides' or entities who are supposedly present in the unseen realm to guide Man. That is because the Neggs and discarnates present themselves as such and pretend to be Black Elk, Ramtha, Kryon, or Djwal Kuhl… or some such moniker that they think will impress you.

An ensouled human does not need any guide; he is expected to go **within** for guidance and connect with his Higher Self – which is all he needs. Such guidance takes the form of **intuition**, and is often called **Inner Guidance**, a hunch, insight, discernment, revelation or a 'gut feeling.' When ignored, it usually causes a feeling of unease, that something's wrong, and things do not flow smoothly.

Note that when a soul is in the Interlife receiving counseling and advice from much wiser Teachers, such counsel becomes part of the soul and his Script such that when s/he again incarnates, the assimilated lessons are ready for 'testing' and as such the soul gets to see whether s/he has actually learned the lesson(s) or not.

There is an excellent book that goes over listening to Inner Guidance called <u>Your Essential Whisper</u>, by LaRue Eppler. It explains why we have trouble hearing the still small voice of Guidance from within, and how to be able to recognize it and make it a working part of our lives.

> *By the way, please note that the reports of Near Death Experiencers, Out-of-Body experiencers (particularly Robert Monroe's), and the reports of hypnotically regressed patients (particularly Dr. Modi's) DO NOT report the presence of any so-called 'guides.'*

Soul Levels

Just as there are different OPs, there are different levels of soul not only reflected in the aura, but also in the orientation to life on Earth. As was brought out in Chapter 5, there is the Standard OP, the Robotic OP, and the Placeholder OP – not really an OP, but not a complete soul, either. The Placeholder is unique in that it can operate as a soul or as an OP. And the Pre-soul may have the option to become a more fully developed soul.

In any event, there is a kind of **hierarchy of souls** which reflects a soul's growth which is an expression of their experience and what lessons have been assimilated. While this is not cast in concrete, keep in mind that there are as many different levels of souls as there are types of flowers and variations within each flower group.

Baby Souls – these are the first-time souls, Pre-souls and may include the Placeholders. They are generally naïve and their aura is underdeveloped, often being an orange color (a mix of the lower three charkas which are the only ones really functional at this stage). They are the most timid of the soul types, often being afraid of germs and dirt – not having had much experience with Earth life. They tend to avoid crowds, not feeling comfortable with all that energy and being a bit unsure of themselves. For them, sex is scary and they are very concerned with avoiding social diseases. These souls are very concerned about appearances and want to dress and look right. These souls love Nature but are very prophylactic. These souls are drawn to a very basic, fundamentalist type religion and it is easy for them to believe in Hell and God's punishment. Aliens do not and cannot exist.

Young Souls – these souls have been around enough on Earth to know their way through the new experiences that the Baby soul is still learning to handle. Thus these souls tend to make up for lost time, and become involved in everything that catches their fancy. They join groups, sing, dance, party, try novel adventures (river rafting and sky diving, e.g.), and they are said to 'go for the gusto.' In their eagerness to experience it all, they begin to make mistakes, tromp on others' toes, and may even lie, cheat and steal. For them, sex is fun and they seek new ways to experience it. These souls are very concerned about appearances, too – do they look good enough, and have the latest designer this and that? These souls love Nature and seek to romp through the mud on off-road bikes.

These souls are drawn to a more progressive type religion yet they usually also believe in Hell and God's punishment. ETs may exist on other planets, but not here.

Mature Souls – these souls have been around even longer than the Young souls and are, in fact, back to work on the mistakes they made. As a result, these souls have begun to quiet down and tend to become introspective, trying to figure out what things mean and how they can get the upper hand over the ailments they often have. They are often found in New Age and New Thought churches, seeking better information on how to handle their lives, their health, and their finances. For them, sex is a responsibility and they take it seriously. These souls pay attention to their appearance and make it reflect who they are; dressing is a statement about their real self or what they value. These souls love Nature and seek to understand Mother Earth and work with others to heal the environment. These souls are drawn to a think-for-yourself religion which is really a search for spirituality and they are exploring different religions and teachings to find answers to their life issues. They doubt there is a Hell and think Karma is probably true. ETs are real and here, but don't talk about it.

Old Souls – these souls are the most interesting, and can be real characters. They have mastered most of the issues that Mature souls are still working on, and they have come to a greater awareness of the Oneness of all things and all people. They could also be called 'last timers' as they are either doing clean up work (righting wrongs, forgiving others, etc) or are in some sort of teaching capacity for other souls who are still learning basics. For them, sex is no big thing and ironically, they can be bawdy, laughing at it all. These souls are very laid back about appearance, not shaving if they don't want to, wearing comfortable clothes despite how others are dressed – yet they are clean. Styles don't impress them and they do what they want (without offending others). These souls love Nature and work with her, and would rather be alone in the woods communing with her than sitting in church or shopping in the Mall.

These souls are found in a New Thought church, or something like Baha'i or esoteric Gnosticism, or none at all. They know that spirituality is more important than religious rote, and they know there is no Hell, and they know that Karma is real. They know ETs are real, and are here among us to help, guide and protect… they may have met some.

As was said, this is just a general way to get a handle on four of the many stages of **soul growth** – there are a lot of souls who are still going through the first two stages and may wind up being defective and as Dr. Newton relates (later this chapter in the section on The

Body); if they never develop the intent to be/do/have something more significant or spiritual in life, they will go from being recycled, to possibly being 'disseminated' – or having their energy rearranged. Such rebellious souls may become defective if they try to party forever, or run power trips on others as a way of living.

Many souls are a mixture of levels, depending on their individual ground of being – more advanced in some areas than others, and it depends on just how much they are willing to accept of their reality.

Multidimensional Souls

Another aspect to our soul is that it is multi-dimensional: we exist concurrently in other times and places, other timelines and dimensions. [40] Since all aspects of self are inter-connected, the undeveloped aspects of one's self can and do affect the mood and peace of the other aspects. [41] This is akin to the 'nonlocality' phenomenon of Quantum Physics.

The term here is specifically "aspect" and not "fragment" since fragment refers to parts of one's soul that have split off, or became fragmented due to trauma. John Jones in 3D Earth may experience a trauma and a small part of his soul will **fragment** (to escape the negative energy impact of the trauma); whereas Bob Jones may have many other **aspects** of himself including: (1) one in a parallel dimension, (2) one 300 years ago on Earth, and (3) one 1200 years in the future on Earth, to name a few.

Each person in this reality has other aspects in other realities that influence each other, as indicated by the dotted lines in the following Chart 3b.

Reincarnation/Past Life Scenario

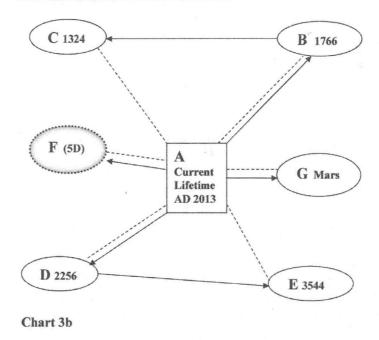

Chart 3b

All potential 6 soul aspects (B – G) of the one person (A) are linked thru the Higher Self (dotted lines). **Arrowed** lines represent "linear time" access. **Dotted** lines represent 6 (direct) energetic soul links and there are energetic interactions via the Higher Self along these lines ('cords').

The above is a representation of the Multidimensional nature of the Ensouled Human Being. Man A in 2008 may also exist concurrently (simultaneously) in lives B, C, D, E in this dimension, but in 4 different timelines, and he also exists in the fifth dimension in life F. Note that he may also have a life on Mars in the 3D realm.

When hypnotically regressed, and asked to go **back** in time to see who he was 'last time' he will encounter lifetime B (AD 1766) and then lifetime C (AD 1324). If he is asked to go **forward** in time, he will encounter lifetime D (AD 2256) and then the lifetime E (AD 3544). All in the 3D realm, for the purpose of illustration here.

Allocation of Soul Aspect Energy

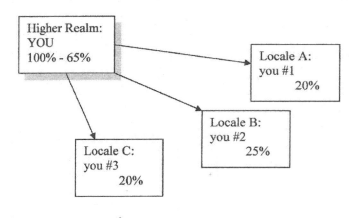

Allocation of Soul Energy

Chart 3c

Note in the above diagram that YOU as a main Soul (or Higher Self) in the Home Realm decide to experience 3 other realms or timelines. This requires an allocation of your energy to 'replicate' yourself into those other 3 realms… and you don't want to spread yourself too thinly! For the average soul experience, a 20% allocation is sufficient (as the Higher Self is quite powerful and has a lot of energy), and in a difficult realm, an allocation of 25-30% may be appropriate… this is an "energy bank" that you can draw on to meet higher energy demands of the lifetime for health, reserve stamina, and mental prowress. Note that when the 3 aspects are allocated, the YOU still has 35%.

If an advanced soul, from say the 6th level, decides to project into the same 3 realms, it may require less energy allocation due to a presence that just observes and "anchors the Light." Ironically, it has a greater energy well to dip into and could allocate 20% which for it would be equivalent to "you #1" above allocating 40%... much more than necessary.

Different soul levels have different levels of useful energy – a Baby soul has a lower PFV, is underdeveloped and so the energy is 'rougher', cruder and not as refined as that of an Old soul, and a soul from the 6th level is even finer than that of an Old soul, and requires less to perform equal to any soul in 3D. Ascended Masters can project into many realms at the same time if necessary, and their energy being so much higher and finer, it is like a battery recharging a Baby soul if called upon to heal that Baby soul. The healing works because energy always flows from the higher potential to the lower.

Effects of Multilevel Aspects

And just what interrelationships and effects do the different aspects have on each other? They are still connected through the Oversoul to each other.

Oneness suggests:

> Your presence is called forth to interact with them [other soul aspects] at the levels at which *they* experience self-awareness. Your responses are influenced, vibrationally, in each of their worlds in much the same way as theirs are in yours. In this way, multiple variations on the same scene actually *happen*, yet each of you perceives it from your own unique vantage point. [42]

Be clear that one soul aspect affecting another does NOT refer to karma. The interaction is limited to an "energetic" effect that is transmitted via the 'cords' that connect soul aspects to the same Godhead, and the effects may be relayed down cords to another aspect – if the receiving aspect is of a lower vibration. In the universe, energy is always flowing and it always flows from a higher potential to a lower potential. Higher vibrations tend to block (overpower and cancel) weaker, negative vibrations which is why avatars and gurus are seldom affected by lower/negative vibrations around them. Thus, they often serve to raise the vibrations wherever they are because their higher (faster) vibrations seek to bring others 'up' to their level.

What Chart 3b is showing is that **all** 3D lifetimes are generally concurrent, or synchronous; although **individual** lifetimes/Scripts usually happen linearly (as a closed loop). The ongoing, multiple aspects are not happening linearly, although they can be retrieved that way in hypnotic regression. Note that when A is regressed hypnotically to look for his last prior lifetime, it may actually have been B (and is thus not on-going any longer because he is now at A), **or** B could also be another aspect of his same Group Soul whose lifetime is ongoing and is not the same exact soul aspect as A, but is seen as 'him' because the two soul aspects are part of the same Soul Group, and they are all each other. All are One. This atter is an example of "**imprinting**" where a soul aspect imprints the life experience of another soul aspect to gain the experience, even though s/he did not actually live it.

Confusing initially, but these are the variations that exist depending on how time is looked at: linearly or cyclically/spirally. In the cyclical (no time) view, they are all happening concurrently. In the linear view, it is A then B then C....

<u>Oneness</u> explains...

> As each of you *creates* alternate variations on the identity of others, with whom to interact at your own custom-made levels of awareness, these alternate aspects of consciousness and the circumstances they encounter combine to influence the energy fields of each of you. For that reason, it is altogether possible and often likely that your **mood shifts**, quite suddenly, in ways you find hard to explain.
>
> An adverse reaction on the part of an alternate aspect of self, playing a role in a diminished environment, adds a sour note to the resonance of the collective *you* identity.... You are largely unaware of the complexity of the composite that, in actuality, is co-creating your experience of reality.... Those of you who continue to experience **chronic depression** are often simply at the effect of the adversities encountered by parallel aspects of self in the vibrationally diminished realities of others.
>
> Many of you are "moody" and subject to unexpected fluctuations in the way you feel that have <u>little or no relation to the circumstances of your life</u>.... Chances are, you are feeling the influence of the multiple layers of vibrational input being provided by the countless levels of reality in which you, in actuality, are present. [43] [emphasis added]

And you thought the Neggs and OPs were all you had to deal with. Now you can also be affected by other aspects of yourself in other realities. How to know where the 'problem' comes from? You don't, but prayer and hypnotherapy might help identify the source of the problem and relieve it.

> *It isn't important to know exactly where the problem comes from – and dabbling in the occult, looking for answers, can lead to more problems, hence the Biblical injunction against it (Deut. 18: 10-12). Man is merely expected to handle whatever he gets, as catalyst, and that means going within (as the Gnostic Gospel of Thomas, v. 70 said).*

Offloading Others

And lastly, in this regard, be aware that a lifetime of constant depression, fatigue and unexplained negativity may also be due to a very esoteric and rare reason: You have taken on (through prior agreement, before birth) the task of **offloading the karmic strain** of another soul aspect (say, soul M) who otherwise might not be able to make it – you are sent the <u>extra</u> pain and upset that would otherwise be too much for that other soul. Yes, they still have to undergo the karma and whatever pain that their script may entail, and you cannot handle all their karma for them, but you can and do offload <u>some</u> of their stress, pain and negative energy.

This is permitted because (1) it is an act of compassion, which we are all learning, (2) you are strong enough to handle it for them, and (3) the soul M may have taken on more than s/he could handle but doesn't want to start over. There is nothing in the **Law of Karma** that says a soul with heavy karma must also be able to handle <u>all</u> the upset and pain that go with it – at one time. That soul must experience the extent of the pain/loss/upset etc that goes with the Script to experience the significance of the lesson, but they need not suffer past the point that they can endure. Karma is not about breaking a soul.

Naturally, as can be guessed, soul M took on more than he could reasonably handle, and it is an act of Love that his brother (another soul aspect from the same Soul Group) cares enough to help sustain soul M, and learn a few things in the process himself.

Different Realities

Sometimes reality seems to shift to another level… or timeline.

> There is **simultaneous presence of every being at countless levels**. And it is natural …. to emerge with consciousness at the next higher level of density, once the work has been achieved. One's awareness of the transition may not be apparent until it becomes blatantly obvious that the rules of "the game" have been radically altered. Ultimately one realizes that one is not now present in the same world as one once was. [44]

Normally, the shift is *seamless*….and as one normally ascends the changes are not noticed, but the reality that one notices of the "here and now" is "…. an ever shifting personalized reflection of one's vibrational [PFV] state." [45]

> The focus upon a particular scenario and one's perception of that reality as the "here and now" is determined by one's ability to deal with the life lessons being presented at a given level of awareness…. one is technically **bouncing between realities all the time**, depending on one's state of beingness in the "now moment."
>
> ….
>
> For those of you who are experiencing a virtual roller-coaster of occurrences representing extremes of ease and difficulty, that very state would be indicative of **jumping levels of reality** in rapid-fire succession. These *symptoms* would indicate an individual who is completing life work on many levels simultaneously and is experiencing ascension at a radically accelerated pace. [46] [emphasis added]

Obviously, we are more complicated than we suspect, and that is the point. We are multidimensional beings and normally we are not affected by our other aspects' experiences; we usually wait until we merge our soul aspects back to the parent Soul to assimilate different realities.

There is more but suffice it to say that **we are multidimensional beings** whose location and 'education' are orchestrated or coordinated with our various aspects by our Higher Self. The Higher Self is that part of us that has been called 'superconscious' as opposed to the subconscious, and it can be addressed in hypnotherapy and some of the answers it gives, in a different voice, are very informational – when it answers. And that is on a 'need to know' basis, and it usually says so if that is the case. The Higher Self is the point of our soul consciousness that links us to our Soul Group, and oversees where we are located and when/how we merge different aspects into an existing soul.

Man's Purpose

Concurrent with an overview of Man, his soul, spirit and the body, in preparation of the later chapters of the book, it needs to be examined WHAT Man is doing here. Contrary to what the New Age people say, it is not to have fun and boogie, nor can we develop our godhood abilities (experience personal power over creation). That would defeat the purpose of the Earth School.

There are people, as will be said again, who think something is wrong with their lives if they aren't happy. Man is not here to have fun and be happy – that is one of the **worst** teachings of our time, although we are not here just to suffer either – unless we fight our lessons. If Man can have fun and be happy at times along the way, great, but to expect that life is all about trying to have fun and be happy, is a setup for an upset! It won't happen for most souls – because they are here to learn.

The last chapters (12-16) explain what Earth really is and why we are really here. All people havea reason for being here. And it varies from person to person.

Some people are here **to work out a specific 'lesson'** (not always karma), but they need to experience that their attitudes and behaviors (STS) aren't working – even if they didn't directly afflict anyone else with them. In another Realm, to which we really belong, even though they weren't dysfunctional or defective, the obstinate souls' ego got the better of them, and they were found to be out of harmony with the rest of the entities, and their behavior or attitude was disrupting. So the 3D Earth is a good place to work that out because you get to be in a context of your equals. What you put out will come back to you; we mirror each other.

Some people are here **to teach** others; they are more advanced souls who can teach and advise other younger souls.

Some people are here **to heal** and bring new, healing modalities to people, especially as Man pollutes the planet, and new diseases emerge.

Some people are here **to correct**: discover that they are dysfunctional: rebellious, resistant, self-centered, violent, greedy, lying, etc. And the gods who run this place will see to it that that person inhabits a body with enough Anunnaki legacy genes to cause the difficulties they are to learn from – and overcome! Such states will put them in a context of their equals – to better experience what they do that doesn't work.

Some people are here (as advanced souls) just **to anchor the Light**. They outflow positive energy which has the ability to cancel negative energy.

Ultimately, the purpose for everyone is **to come to one's Self**, as did the young man in the story of the Prodigal Son. In this case, it is about developing all aspects of mental, emotional and spiritual maturity to be of more service to the Light in the ever-growing and expanding Multiverse. There is a home for all souls, and it isn't to stay on Rehab-Earth. The goal is to become an **Earth Graduate** as will be shortly examined.

The Body

A discussion of Man and his different aspects would not be complete without looking at the body – note I didn't say his body. The body is rather an entity unto itself, in addition to having some mix of genetic inheritance from Man's creators, as earlier discussed. What may shock some people is that **the body has a life energy and intelligence of its own**, and does not need a soul to govern it. This is why it is sometimes very difficult to lose weight, stop drinking, or stop smoking – not all addictions are Negg-based.

The medical community has known about the body's innate intelligence for years – it is called the *Vis Medicatrix* – the ability of the body to heal itself if given the right food, enough clean water, sunlight, and clean air. Of course a lot has been made of the power of visualization and positive thinking to help heal one's body, but this is just the soul and the body working together. **It is important for the soul to have a good relationship with the body.**

Be aware that the soul can leave the body permanently during a coma and not return, yet modern medicine can keep the body alive for months. And as was already discussed, the OPs do not have a soul and are walking around like normal (ensouled) people energized largely by the first 3 chakras.

Conflicts

What does one do if there seems to be a battle to get the upper hand and break a habit? What is one expected to do – fight the body, force it to submit, or resign oneself to a 'rebellious' body? And what if the brain/mind doesn't work right?

Dr. Michael Newton had a few interesting insights during his regressive therapy with some patients who had 'body' problems:

> There are certain displaced souls who have become so contaminated by their host bodies that that they require special handling. In life they became destructive to others and themselves…. There are souls who slowly become more contaminated from a series of lifetimes, while **others are totally overcome by the body** alone….
> Contamination of the soul can take many forms and involve different grades of severity…**A difficult host body** might cause the less experienced soul to return [home] with damaged energy where a more advanced being would survive the same situation relatively intact…. The soul has a great

capacity to control our biological and emotional reactions to life but many souls are unable to regulate a dysfunctional brain. [47] [emphasis added]

This relates to our genetic inheritance where the "sins" of the fathers are passed on to their progeny. And some souls DO choose to handle a wayward body or a dysfunctional brain (due to some malformation during fetus gestation) for some specific soul growth opportunity. (Think: Dr. Stephen Hawking, a brave soul.) So we are not all born perfect and not all souls are equal in acquired knowledge and ability.

Rearrangement of Energy

What happens if a soul cannot overcome the body and get control? Dr. Newton was speaking with a Counseling Entity on the Other Side (via a hypnotized patient) regarding this issue, trying to defend the soul's inability to overcome the effects of the body:

> S: (patient) Yes, [I am] in a restoration area …we deal with those who have become **atrocity souls**.
>
> Dr. N: What a terrible name to call a soul!
>
> S: I'm sorry you are bothered by this, but what else would you call a being associated with acts of evil that are so serious they are **unsalvageable** in their present state?
>
> Dr. N: I know, but the human body had a lot to do with…
>
> S: (cutting me off) **We don't consider that to be an excuse**. [48] [emphasis added]

Serious stuff. Man is expected to get the upper hand, and if he can't, perhaps this is what Jesus meant when He said "If thy right hand offend thee, cut it off…. [rather] than thy whole body be cast into hell [torment]." (Matt 5:30) And then what happens if a soul is so damaged that they cannot function and resists a return to Earth to work out the issues?

> Dr. N: If they won't come back to Earth, then what do you do?
>
> S: These souls will then go the way of those souls we consider to be **unsalvageable**. We will then **disseminate** their energy… we call it the breaking up of energy… We break up their energy into particles… and it is changed and converted.
>
> Dr. N: Then what happens to those souls who refuse your help?
>
> S: Many will just go into limbo, to a place of solitude. I don't know what will eventually happen to them. [49] [emphasis added]

So, if the New Agers say, "Life is just a big party, have fun and forget about tomorrow…. You're here to feel good!" My condolences, these souls will be back… or disseminated.

There is just one struggle here on the planet, and that is on a personal level: you need to find out <u>who</u> and <u>what</u> you are, and <u>where</u> you are. **Think outside the box that was created for you by others**. The tools are always available. The truth wants to be known. The Eternal One has a purpose for each soul and it isn't on this planet. When you figure it out, then live according to the Divine Law until departure time. **Then you can be released**. There is no point in living 200-300 lives on Earth to sample all possible levels of life here. They are <u>all pointless</u> to experience, and **no one needs more than one lifetime on Earth** to get the message. Souls repeat the Earth experience because they are resistant. [50] [emphasis added]

Taming the Body

There is something that can be done with regard to the body, however.

The body forces you to experience empathy, hate, remorse and all other emotions, together with desires and passions, to confuse you, make you forget yourself, become **a dumbed-down version of yourself**…. The more you let [emotions, desires] be your masters, **the stronger you will chain yourself to this world**, which is contrary to your duty, yet do not loathe them, **respect**. I channel them to a place where they can be used for something substantial. [51] [emphasis added]

As for the goal of being more spiritual in this lifetime, there seems to be a 'force' that would hold us back and 'contain' us:

It is connected to the operations of **your physical body which rebels every time you reach higher to that realm**. Physical body has the task to let you experience this reality and whenever you search for the other [spiritual realm], it resists. It is its duty, so **respecting it and gently taming it is the best approach**. Also beings [Neggs] will accompany your thoughts and try to divert them, again it is their duty, show respect and that will be recognised [sic] by them. Never see them [Neggs] as malicious or evil, they only react to your actions. There is not a force which does not want you to be what you really are, the opposite is true but they also have their tasks that they must fulfill. This is about a material part of you. [52] [emphasis added]

Note the emphasis on respect in the above quotes.

Channeling *Chi*

A useful way to get out of the strong desires and energies of the lower 3 chakras, for example, when it is obvious that a strong lust or anger is arising, is to do the following exercise. This is called Channeling the *Chi*— **the mind can and does direct the *chi*** (Book 2, Chapters 10—11). The sooner this is done when one feels the bodily drive into strong emotion, the better.

Sit quietly and close your eyes. Focus your attention on the lower part of your body, specifically the genital area. Visualize the growing energy of lust or anger as a red cloud surrounding that part of your body. Feel it. Imagine you can command that energy cloud to rise up into the area of your heart (heart chakra) and visualize the energy turning from red to a beautiful shade of green surrounding your heart area. Focus on your heart area and feel compassion. The original energy will transform under the higher vibration of the heart chakra.

Repeat until all energy has transformed and you feel a more peaceful, compassionate energy.

The reason this works is that **the mind can direct/control the energy (*chi*)** in the body.[53] When you think of an area of the body, *chi* automatically heads in that direction, and the mind can increase/decrease the flow. Moving a denser (red) energy to the higher heart chakra vibrationally transforms the red energy to green energy, and lust or anger is replaced by compassion.

Energy Awareness

While speaking of moving energy, be aware that your energy affects other people around you. In fact, you may be receiving others' energy as well as sending them yours. This may result in your feeling 'up' while in a room with others who are in a positive mood.

Having a bad day? Your low vibrations may bring others down, too, even if you don't say anything. Just as you bring on new habits and make yourself well/sick with same, so too can you affect others.

> *Remember that in the universe the way energy works is that it flows from the higher potential to the lower. God empowers His creation through this principle. In the same way, if one is run down and needs energy, being around other people will have the effect of raising one's energy level, and slightly dropping theirs.*

Also as you grow spiritually, your **words** gain more power to affect people because they carry more focused energy. And be careful – suppose an ascended Master were walking among a crowd of people and suddenly had a fit of anger – how many people would get sick, dizzy, or worse because they were suddenly hit with his higher focused energy?

If you care about others, have forgiven them, know your Self, show compassion no matter what you're feeling, and **respect self and others**, you will have achieved a level of spiritual growth that practically guarantees that you get out of here at death – "even unconditionally loving each secular soul you come into contact with, not just the extra and special souls" as an old friend Fr. Ernie used to say.

Watch your use of energy as you grow spiritually. You are held accountable for it.

Preview: Earth School Graduate

In other words, Man is much more than a first glance would suggest, and this may be why Robert Monroe was told by one of the Beings of Light that although the Earth school is a rough one, "The graduate from the human experience is very respected elsewhere." [54] More specifically, Monroe adds:

> The first point in consideration of human structure certainly should be the note that a small percentage [of souls] have never been thru the experience… Some may have had physical life experience in other parts of time-space and in another physical form, but this is their first run as a human…
>
> Human existence on Earth is an interesting anomaly. **It has some peculiar qualities that are unique in the development of intelligence and consciousness.** As a result, human life has many attractions. To some it is like attending a vast amusement park… a playground where standard rules (non-earthly) are suspended for the moment. They desire human existence simply out of curiosity… Many… decide it is an ideal opportunity to try an experiment conceived in their periods of contemplation…
>
> Still others find that the limitations imposed by physical incarceration as a human also engender concentration of energies available only in that state. **This is the only point available to apply such energies.**
>
> By far the greatest motivation – surpassing the sum of all others – is the result.
>
> **When you perceive and encounter a graduate, your only goal is to be one yourself once you realize it is possible.** And it is. [55] [emphasis added]

He goes on to say that one of the outcomes is the ability to translate Prime Energy into any manifest form, and "…second, to become a first-order generator thereof." [56] And this is not easy to imagine in our current state, which is akin to never having heard a song, and not knowing that we can sing – how would one ever want to sing, much less know what it is, or be able to learn it? [57]

So, in general, Man is quite a complex, fantastic and valuable creation and this issue will be amplified in Chapter 15 when we examine more why we are here.

Chapter 8: – Old Science

It was said earlier:

<u>Almost</u> everything you think you know about Earth History, Physical Science and Religion is false. The three main areas will be examined in this Part III in an attempt to expose the common misinformation we have all bought into and correct it.

Whereas the errors in Religion and Earth History appear to have been done on purpose, the Science aspect is more of the nature of continued 'flat Earth' thinking principally in the area of Physics. Biology and Chemistry are **not** included in the list of errors because scientists all over the world are able to replicate and prove/disprove what these two fields report as truth. It is different with Physics, especially Quantum Physics, which tends to be more abstract and rife with questionable theories.

This is again in an attempt to gain more Light, to gain 'escape velocity' to get out of here. It is hoped that the reader will not only question the reported errors, but will also question the suggested answers and come up with either reinforcement or positive change to his/her own truth. The worst thing would be to blindly accept anything from anywhere as truth; so if this section makes the reader think, it will have done its job.

Cosmology

Until the time of Copernicus in the mid-1500's, Western Man had believed the Earth was flat and the center of the Universe. Moreover, it was believed that the Sun revolved around the Earth – after all, all you had to do was look: the Sun appeared to circle the Earth each day – which was flat because it looked like it. And Tycho Brahe reinforced the notion.

Copernicus stunned the Church and scientists in 1543 with his heliocentric model of the solar system – which put the Sun at the center and the Earth revolving on its axis and circling the Sun. He escaped punishment by the Church for his heresy as he died shortly after he published his work. Later, Johannes Kepler and Galileo Galilei would develop Copernicus' ideas.

In 1616 Galileo went to Rome to defend Copernicus' ideas and point out that heliocentrism did not contradict Scripture. He was tried by the Inquisition, found "vehemently suspect of heresy," forced to recant, and spent the rest of his life under house arrest. The Inquisition's ban on reprinting Galileo's works was lifted in 1718. It would take the voyages of Columbus and Magellan in the 1400-1500s to prove that a sailing ship would not fall off the Earth

Anaximander World Map Ca 550 BC
(courtesy Wikipedia Commons, in the public domain.)[1]

241

if it sailed out too far. The former world view of the Earth was summarized in a version of a world map of the time… shown above.

By the 1st century AD, Pliny the Elder made the statement that everyone agreed on the spherical shape of Earth, although there were many arguments about how the oceans would stay on a sphere. [2] In addition, while it was not Galileo's doing, it took the Greek philosophers Pythagoras in the 6th century BC, and Parmenides in the 5th, to recognize that the Earth had to be a sphere. But it was not universally accepted dogma until Columbus and Magellan sailed into the unknown and proved that Earth is a sphere.

The point being that Science moves very slowly to adopt new ideas, and sometimes jumps to the wrong conclusion based on appearances or flawed experiments – such as the Michelson–Morley experiment to prove the existence of the ether, which will be discussed later. And sometimes, objectivity is replaced with personal, subjective motives that one seeks to prove, as in the following case with Charles Darwin. Sometimes the truth is just ignored while following the Scientific Method.

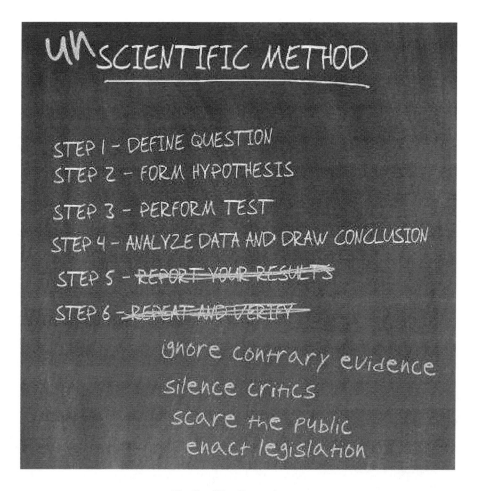

(Credit : Bing Images)

Evolution and Charles Darwin

And in all fairness →

Two classic pictures of Charles Darwin   (Credit: Bing Images)

Today's younger scientists are beginning to question the Darwinian Theory of Evolution especially as they are finding evidence of a young Earth, and DNA intricacies that suggest an **intelligent design**. There seems to be no question about two other Darwinian theories, such as Survival of the Fittest, and Natural Selection, but the Theory of Evolution has really caused a stir among thinking people, younger scientists, as well as the Christian groups who believe that Man was uniquely created by God. But remember, that Evolution was and IS just a Theory, not a fact, not Law.

Man wants to believe that he is special and perhaps unique, and he is, but that has no bearing on who created him on Earth. His specialness derives from the nature and potential of his soul operating through his DNA.

To better understand how and why Darwin developed the Theory of Evolution, it is helpful to understand a little bit about Charles Darwin himself and why he so intensely sought to disprove God's existence.

Charles Darwin was a physically sick man whose wife was a good Christian and Charles wanted God to heal him. Charles had a lot of health problems that truly defied diagnosis and cure. No one could accurately diagnose or heal him. So Charles turned to God, and his wife prayed with him. When God didn't heal him, Charles scientifically concluded that since the prayers were not answered, they must not have been heard because there probably wasn't Anyone up there listening. He reasoned that there must be no God, but he wasn't 100% sure so he remained an **agnostic** until his death. Despite rumors to the contrary, he never converted to Christianity, but he did still occasionally attend church.

Due to his severe health problems, he often could not sit through a church service, and for therapy, he'd walk to church with his wife, and continue walking until after the service when she rejoined him for the walk home again. Sometimes he would not meet her after church and a search would find him passed out in a nearby park. For more therapy, and to get away from the sometimes damp English weather, he sailed away to southern seas to regain his health. [3]

While in the Galapagos Islands, off Ecuador, he observed nature so keenly that he developed 3 striking theories: The **Theory of Evolution**, The Theory of **Survival of the Fittest**, and the Theory of **Natural Selection**. Nobody argues the last two – they are a given. In fact, in Chapter 9, it will be seen that **Epigenetics** is a modern term in genetics that explains the Selection and Survival theories.

And ironically, as Chapters 3 and 4 showed, Man did "evolve" from the Ape (Homo *erectus*), but it was an assisted evolution.

> *By the way, if evolution had been the only force at work, moving Apes to Man, then why are there still Apes? And why isn't it still happening?*

Creation Evidence

But Charles' friends (including scientists) urged him to rethink his position on Evolution, in which he said Creation came into being without a God, and thus there was no design to Creation. It was all a case of some bio-chemical laws randomly at work in the uncontrolled Universe. They pointed out to him that the **human eye** shows design and design means a Designer. Charles would not initially look at the evidence: there are 4 key parts to the eye that if not present, the eye doesn't work – and the 4 parts are distinct (they do not all touch each other), functional elements that are related to each other, but none of which directly, physically influences the 'evolution' of the other two. Thus the eye could not 'evolve' out of interactive evolutionary necessity.

The Human Eye

Three of the four key elements are: the **iris**/pupil (shutter), the **lens** (focuses light on retina), and the **muscles** that allow the eye to adjust quickly.

> In the nineteenth century, the anatomy of the eye was known in detail…. different colors of light, with different wavelengths, would cause a blurred image, except that the lens of the eye changes density over its surface to correct for chromatic aberration. These sophisticated methods astounded everyone who was familiar with them. Scientists…. knew that if a person lacked any of the eye's many integrated features, the result would be a severe loss of vision or outright blindness. They concluded that the eye could only function if nearly intact. [4]

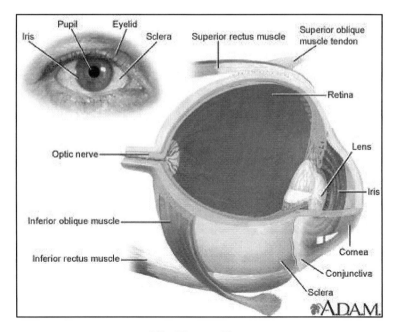

The Human Eye
(source: http://apps.uwhealth.org/health/adam/graphics/images/en/1094.jpg)

More than that, the 4th element, called the **retina**, consists of a patterned dispersion of rods and cones which appear to be designed to facilitate "spatial acuity." [5]   The **rods** facilitate vision at low light levels and the **cones** (3 types, no less) determine color and facilitate high spatial acuity. Why would two types 'evolve'? For what purpose?

There are more rods in the eye than cones, and both types are clustered more densely at the back of the eye with the highest cone-clustering (150,000 cones/sq mm) right at the fovea, where the eye's main focal point is. There are less rods and cones as one moves from the back of the eye toward the front. There are 150,000 rods per square millimeter – more densely packed than their digital camera counterpart, pixels. In addition, the structure of the individual rods and cones shows design, wherein the cell membranes fold in and create multi-layered photoreceptor cells, and each has photopigment molecules. [6]

Interesting that other species also have rods and cones in their eyes, but their physiology is different – wouldn't nature have evolved a simple photoreceptor that worked and then kept that same design? And how would nature **evolve** a photoreceptor cell – how would it know what "vision" was and how to "evolve" to it from a simple cell?

And through it all is a 5th element: a link to the **optic nerve** transmitting the 2-dimensional image which is upside down on the retina to somewhere in the brain, allegedly 'righting' the image by the way, so that we can see things right side up. And according to today's quantum physicists (Pribram and Bohm), if the world around us really consists of holographic frequency codes, that makes the brain a "frequency decoder" and we may be projecting our perceived reality "out there," instead of seeing it somewhere "in" the brain. [7] And that is not Evolution but **Design**. (Ch. 12 and Apx. B.)

… our 'physical' reality is made up of **holograms** that give the illusion of three-dimensional objects when they are, in fact, nothing more than **frequency patterns**… you are actually watching holographic television, and your brain/lower mind is the TV set… the brain is decoding frequency patterns and turning them, into holographic images that we 'see.'[8] [emphasis added]

So when you touch a wall, your hands relay the information from the wall's frequency patterns to the brain and that information is decoded as "solid, cold, and hard." More on this in Chapter 12. It is enough for this part of the book that vision appears to be holographic, and that the nature of vision being much more than pure mechanics or optics, lends weight to the argument <u>for</u> Creation, since it speaks of intelligence behind a <u>design</u>. (See **Appendix B**: Vision & Holograms, and people with different vision.)

> *Note: the very first eye in the very first human somewhere in the Beginning had to have had a Creator. The Anunnaki did not create the eye; they merely manipulated the genetics.*

Darwin Semi-Confesses

After quite some years, Darwin still sought support for his Evolution of Man, despite his scientist friends advising him that he was in error. And Darwin knew something wasn't 100% solid with his Theory of Evolution, and he said as much in <u>The Origin of Species</u>:

> To suppose that the eye with all its inimitable contrivances for adjusting the focus to different distances, for admitting different amounts of light, and for the correction of spherical and chromatic aberration, could have been formed by natural selection, seems, I freely confess, **absurd** in the highest degree. [9]

Nonetheless, he then proceeded to try and figure out how the eye might have evolved anyway. Man always hates new, original breakthroughs that challenge his established ideas. It is called **cognitive dissonance**. So he wrote to Asa Grey, a famous Harvard professor, for encouragement. Instead Asa wrote back that he seriously doubted that natural processes could explain the formation of the eye, and that no part of the eye is of any use without all the other parts. [10]

And that situation also exists in the biochemistry of a lowly beetle.

Other Creation Evidence

Another killer evidence for Creation was the **Bombardier Beetle**: inside its abdomen are two sacs of fluid which mix just before being expelled from the anal part of the beetle – a hot fluid created by chemical reaction once the two fluids come together. It is very effective for deterring the beetle's enemies.

Again, that indicates <u>design</u>: the fluids are kept separate and cause no problem by themselves – but if stored in the mixed condition in the beetle's body, it would fry the beetle. [11]

A great example of design is also the **Giraffe.** It has been argued that the long neck was designed to allow the giraffe to eat leaves high up in a tree. However drinking water is a problem: the giraffe has to bend over, with straight legs and its head below its body, to drink from a pond. There is a mechanism much like **peristalsis** in its long neck that carries the water UP its throat and into its body.

http://en.wikipedia.org/wiki/File:Flickr_-_Rainbirder_-_Reticulated_Giraffe_drinking.jpg

If the giraffe had evolved, wouldn't a short neck have been more 'practical,' and wouldn't its food have been more ground level, and thus it would not have needed the unique water-carrying action of its long neck?

> …The giraffe is equipped with… a coordinated system of blood pressure control. Pressure sensors along the neck's arteries monitor the blood pressure, and can signal activation of other mechanisms to counter any increase in pressure as the giraffe drinks or grazes. Contraction of the artery walls, a shunting of part of the arterial blood flow to bypass the brain, and a web of small blood vessels (the *rete mirable*, or "marvelous net") between the arteries and the brain all serve to control the blood pressure in the giraffe's head.[12]

There is no conceivable natural, evolutionary, explanation for this marvel. Additionally, there are symbiotic relationships between plants and insects that indicate design: the fig wasp and the fig tree, and a bee designed to utilize the orchid. [13] Note that the Bible said that the plants were created <u>before</u> the insects and animals… Why would a fig wasp nest and insert its eggs into a fig… why not a peach? Because the fig nourishes the hatching wasps and the peach would not… unless designed to do so.

Thus we can begin to say that **design means there is a Designer**.

Darwin's Health

Dr. Modi gave a rather long, involved case with a patient she called Ann in her book, examined in Chapter 6. Recall that Ann came to Dr. Modi complaining of just about everything under the Sun:

> … depression, chronic fatigue, poor memory, sleeping problems, vision problems, skin problems, muscle aches/pains, panic attacks, conversations in her head, headaches, irritable bowels, sinus problems, allergies, and hyperacidity. [14]

Now, let's postulate that Charles Darwin's contribution to science was affected by his severe health problem(s) as was his concomitant religious position of an agnostic. It is worth repeating here that this great thinker, who deserves a lot of credit and respect, nonetheless had such severe and mysterious health problems that the physicians of the day could not diagnose nor alleviate them. They are presented in light of Ann's similar problems in Chapter 6:

> For over 40 years Darwin suffered intermittently from various combinations of symptoms such as malaise, vertigo, dizziness, muscle spasms and tremors, vomiting, cramps and colics, bloating and nocturnal flatulence, headaches, alterations of vision, severe tiredness/nervous exhaustion, dyspnea, skin problems such as blisters all over the scalp and eczema, crying, anxiety, sensation of impending death and loss of consciousness, fainting, tachycardia, insomnia, tinnitus, and depression. [15]

With a few exceptions, the description of Darwin's health problems could also be describing Ann's in the earlier paragraph. At least the extent and mystery of their afflictions is very similar, even if the exact symptoms are different. As Drs. Modi and Peck both point out in Chapter 6, if someone has a special proactive task to perform in this world, the Neggs will do their best to stop it, and it is thus possible that Darwin came here to proactively advance the scientific information on Man, and might have produced a different Creation-based theory, had he not been so afflicted health-wise. He was disappointed in God for not healing him, and thus became a **determined agnostic** whose doubts about God produced an Evolution-based theory instead.

Or, is it possible that, since the sins of the fathers are visited on the offspring, as was earlier discussed, that Darwin's problem was genetic and a prior ancestor(s) gave some ground through genetics (a weakness) for him to be afflicted? Such things are called 'generational curses' and do exist. [16], [17]

> *Or maybe it was a combination of Neggs **and** DNA… In any event, Darwin is due a lot of credit for persevering in the face of incredible health problems and for being as productive as he was.*

Genetics Bespeaks Design

In a recent book examining the discoveries by today's geneticists, Stephen Meyer emphasizes that there is increasing evidence for Intelligent Design in all genetics, thus suggesting a Designer.

> Intelligent design does not answer questions about the nature of God or even make claims about God's existence… It simply argues that an intelligent cause of some kind played a role in the design of life… the theory of intelligent design does not affirm sectarian doctrines… the virgin birth … predestination… salvation, original sin, or the reality of reincarnation. [18]

Meyer shows that intelligent design is scientific as its postulates are being proven by in-depth genetics research. What is therefore suggested is that something intelligent designed Man, and being intelligent, there must have been a purpose to such design. This book maintains that we should some day come to recognize the ET assistance in

Creation, and Sitchen and Tellinger have already suggested a purpose behind Man's design on this planet.

The key point here, again, is that we are not alone. Not only are there the 4D supportive angels of Light, but there are also the Neggs whose 'job' it is to afflict us. It looks like the 3D progenitors of Man are also still here, if only as a skeleton crew, observing and tweaking as necessary.

Carbon-14 Dating

Since a lot of Evolution's dating of fossils, rocks and organic material depends on the use of Carbon 14 (C-14) dating techniques, it would be well to briefly examine the value of such a technique. Is it reliable?

C-14 is used to measure the percentage of unstable carbon isotopes in once-living objects. It is known that every 5,730 years half of the isotope breaks down into a 'daughter element' and thus at that rate, in just 29,000 years very little would remain of the original isotope in the object being tested, and thus after 50,000 years, there would be no point in bringing the object into the laboratory. [19] **So C-14cannot be used on really old objects**.

It is admitted, even by the dating technique's originator, Willard F. Libby, that the technique is **not dependable when dating things beyond 5,000 years old**. (After The Flood, which could have altered the C-14 content of trees, bones, etc, its use is questionable.) And things that are beyond 50,000 years in age, like the dinosaur bones, would not have enough C-14 left in them to measure. So why are we told that dinosaur bones were carbon-dated back to 65,000,000 years ago?

Of course, the dating paradigm depends on a steady, constant rate of decay, with no addition or deletion of parent or 'daughter' material, and it is important to know how much daughter material was originally present so one can set the starting date. [20]
The biggest problem with the C-14 dating system is that it has proven to be **unreliable**. Many thousands of things have been C-14 tested with shocking results. For example, a Saber-toothed Tiger supposedly one million years old, was C-14 dated to 28,000 years old. [21]   And there are these oddities:

1. Mollusks (living) test dated at 2,300 years dead.
2. Mortar from an English castle less than 800 years old
   test dated at 7,370 years old.
3. Seal skins (fresh) test dated at 1,300 years old. [22]

The C-14 system depends on the idea that there have been NO globally catastrophic events in the past 50,000 years. If conditions on Earth were very different in the past, and especially before the Flood, then C-14 is nearly worthless, particularly for ages beyond 5,000 years. [23]

From the *Bulletin* of the Geological Society of America (vol. 69, January 1958) Curt Teichert writes, "**No coherent picture of the history of the Earth could be built on the basis of radioactive datings**." [24]

So C-14 dating cannot help Man discover the 'when' of past objects, and it does very little to support the claims of Evolutionists. Perhaps they should use Helium or Radon as a measurement index (Chapter 10).

Einstein: Genius or Fraud?

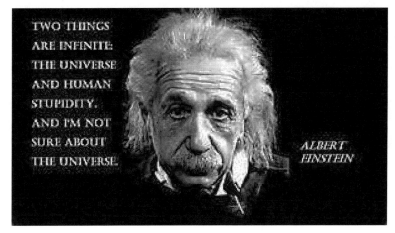

TWO THINGS ARE INFINITE: THE UNIVERSE AND HUMAN STUPIDITY. AND I'M NOT SURE ABOUT THE UNIVERSE.

ALBERT EINSTEIN

Einstein was in some ways a very smart man and there are a lot of great sayings attributed to him. However, as with all scientific progress, early theories are often overturned.

(Credit: Bing Images)

Besides Darwin, it is coming to light more and more, that many of Einstein's postulates and theories are flawed. Specifically examined in this section are: his famous (allegedly plagiarized) formula $E = MC^2$, Black Holes, the Big Bang, and the Expanding Universe. All seriously questionable, including his General Theory of Relativity (GRT) and Special Theory of Relativity (SRT), as will be seen.

Let's keep in mind that Einstein did have a background in physics and mathematics, and was very good at it. He worked as a scientific **patent clerk** and it was his job to examine in-coming patents for electrical and electromagnetic patents, so he had exposure for years to many new ideas in these fields. His own work in the field of **photoelectric phenomena** did earn him a Nobel Prize in 1921, so he wasn't a dummy, but it has been suggested that he 'borrowed' a lot of his ideas from others' patent applications and that is why when challenged to defend his ideas, he rarely did – and he let others speak for him. [25]

It is strongly suggested that he did not debate or answer because the ideas were not fully his, he just liked them, and failed to answer Walter Ritz, Georges Sagnac, and Ernst Gherkin, to name a few. [26] In addition, Paul Gerber called him an outright **fraud** and his long-time teacher in math and physics called him "**a lazy dog.**" [27]

We may have been idolizing a man who was just clever at postulating physics concepts, but was **not the genius** he was reputed to be. He was probably the "poster boy" to give credibility to the fledgling field of Quantum Physics, at that time 5-10 years old, and we all need heroes….

According to Ben Rich, who headed Lockheed Martin's Skunk Works (where many exotic aircraft were developed), and where they successfully created electrogravitic craft that fly, he explained the issue with Einstein, saying,

> There is an **error in the [traditional] equations** [dealing with space travel and the speed of light] and we know what it is and we now have the capability to travel to the stars…. We now have the technology to take ET home…. [and] it won't take someone's lifetime to do it.
>
> ….they had, for example, determined that Einstein's equations dealing with relativity theory were incorrect…. [and he] went on to say that they had ***proved*** [sic] **that Einstein was wrong.** [28] [emphasis added]

Nonetheless, Einstein was clever. Let's examine some of his concepts.

Photoelectric Effect

This one is a winner. Take a metal plate, and bombard it with photons. As the photons strike a metal plate from a left angle, they cause electrons to be ejected, flying off to the right. Electrons emitted in this manner may be called *photoelectrons* being the result of light energy being carried in discrete quantized packets (ie, ***quanta***). This discovery was a critical forerunner of quantum theory and earned Einstein a **Nobel Prize**.

$E = MC^2$

While Einstein is reputed to have been a genius, and this formula is attributed to him, does anybody see the **inherent nonsense** in it? The formula says that mass at the speed of light, squared, becomes energy. It doesn't take a PhD in Physics to see that squaring the speed of light is an incredible speed – so fast it is hard to grasp: 34,596,000,000 miles per second.

The usually stated speed of light is 186,000 miles per second. Fast. Earth is 93 million miles from the Sun. So, light from the Sun reaches Earth in 8.3 minutes. Now it sounds slow, and that's an aspect of relativity for you.

Einstein also theorized that no object could go faster than the speed of light as it would become energy; mass would increase with the speed of light, and convert back into energy.[29] This appears to be wrong following the redo of the Michelson-Morley experiments which DID prove the existence of an Ether.

The point is: Why square the speed of light? Why not 1.5 times it? Why not cube the speed of light? Given that subatomic particles sometimes operate at close to the speed of light, could it be that exceeding the speed of light produces not only an energy conversion, but at higher rates of speed, there might be a **time shift** and one finds oneself in a different timeline, or dimension? Time is relative to a person's velocity. Einstein did theorize that the faster one travels, the more time slows down for that person… so would exceeding the speed of light move one backward in time?

It is suspected that squaring the speed of light results in a sufficiently large number that, like Evolution requiring 4.5 billion years to operate, somewhere in that increase of speed past 186,000 mps, Mass could become Energy. But the point is that no one knows just when, or at what speed Mass does become Energy. Perhaps it occurs **at** the speed of light… E = MC?

Now the interesting part. The energy to mass conversion formula was **not** developed by Einstein, but came across his desk as a patent clerk examining the work of an Italian physicist, DePretto in 1904. [30]   In fact, according to professor C.L. Kervan, "…**it is a mistake that matter can be transformed into energy**…. The nucleons do not disappear, but are found in the fission products. If some neutrons are expelled, they are not destroyed. For matter to disappear, it must be opposed by anti-matter." [31] So Einstein took DePretto's formula and added a superscript '2' to it… but according to Dr. Kervan, **Einstein is still wrong.**

All of that to say that Einstein was not correct in everything, and yet parts of his mathematical theorems dealing with astrophysics are correct and are used by NASA to compute and anticipate trajectories – except for what Dr. Ben Rich said in Chapter 4.

But the speed of light is a significant issue in this chapter, and Einstein assumed there was no Ether based on a flawed light experiment in 1887. He was wrong (and Book 2 really delves into that issue).

…In Einstein's Defense

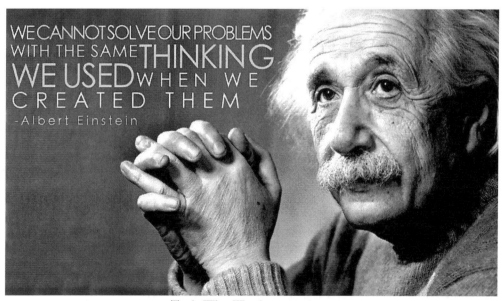

Truly Wise Words…
(Credit: Bing Images)

Let's look at the man from the 40,000' level and recognize a couple of salient facts – in 1905 Quantum Physics was in its infancy – if it were to survive, it would have to prove interesting, theorems would have to be seen as valuable and probably true, reflecting an abstract yet reasonable explanation of our real world, and there would have to be a focal point in one person, spearheading the new discipline – ideally a genius.

Einstein was chosen by a group of his peers to represent the new field – and with a clever methodology: whereas his peers did not want to lose their university jobs, and whereas most wanted the field to prosper, they would (and did) present their theorems through Einstein such that if the ideas or postulates proved false, Einstein took the heat for it and the background group would go back to the drawing board. Only they could explain their work.

This actually did happen and is the reason why when Einstein was challenged to explain his theorems and some aspects of Quantum Mechanics, he couldn't and didn't --- as was said earlier in the initial section – i.e., "he failed to answer Walter Ritz, Georges Sagnac, and Ernst Gherkin, to name a few." He was not a genius, he was a spokesperson… and a decent mathematician. And he did win a Nobel prize, but he was not the god he was made out to be – "Oh, you're an Einstein!" people say when duly impressed. Perhaps such appellation needs to be tempered with the facts of an average intellect in Physics and Math.

Speed of Light

The speed of light has been called a constant and represented in mathematical formulas as 'c'; it is said to <u>never</u> vary -- if measured in a pure vacuum, and Space is not a vacuum. Yet recently it has been shown to vary according to the medium through which it passes, and it has been shown to be **decreasing** with the passing years. [32] Light, like sound, <u>does</u> change speed (slows down) in water, and when it passes by huge stars with very strong EMF, it can bend and accelerate into the star's field. In addition, the alleged constant speed of light was measured several times by the same equipment 16 years apart and it was consistently found to be **decreasing**. [33]

Back in 1887, two researchers (**Michelson & Morley**) began to reason that space was not empty and that just as a plane can fly faster <u>with</u> the wind and lose speed flying at 90° across the wind, light might do the same thing in what had been theorized to be a substance called 'Ether' that somehow filled all of the universe. What was needed was an experiment to shoot 2 beams of light – one <u>with</u> the Ether current and the other <u>against</u> it and record the arrival times of both. The results surprised everyone. [34]

> The experiment, conducted in 1887, found no ether currents; the conclusion was that no ether exists. The consequences of this interpretation have haunted scientists for more than 100 years. In 1986, the journal *Nature* reported on the results of experiments conducted with more sensitive equipment. The bottom line: A field with the characteristics of the **ether <u>was</u> detected**, and it behaved just as the older predictions had suggested it would…. [35] [emphasis added]

> This experiment, and others since then, suggests that the Ether does in fact exist, just as Planck suggested in 1944… it just does not come in the form that Michelson and Morley expected. [36] [emphasis added]

Michelson repeated the experiment many times in 1920-1926 and discovered that there is an **anisotrophy** (speed depending on direction), and thus validated the Ether postulated earlier. It just isn't mechanical; it is electromagnetic.

And another more modern-day researcher, Professor **Reginald Cahill** of Flinders University, produced a paper in September 2008 on the same subject (his paper can be found at www.ptep-online.com/index_files/2008/PP-15-04.pdf) and the updated results are summarized as follows:

> Professor Cahill adduces both theoretical and experimental evidence for the anisotropy of the speed of light in vacuo, and reassesses a number of older experiments, such as the Michelson and Morley experiment, showing clearly that they too, besides not being null as usually reported, actually detected light **anisotropy**. Professor Cahill's own recent experiments with modern technology detected the anisotropy of the speed of light to first order accuracy. [37] [emphasis added]

> *Note:* **anisotropy** *is the directionally dependent characteristic of light -- i.e., light speed can vary according to the direction and medium in which it is measured.*

So the speed of light is not constant any more than the speed of sound is. The anisotropy of light was suspected and subsequently verified. And the speed varies with the direction in which the light is moving through the Ether field.

Light Limits

Can one exceed the speed of light?

> There is a problem with breaking the speed-of-light barrier. **The theory of relativity** says that the rocket power needed to accelerate a spaceship gets greater and greater the nearer it gets to the speed of light. We have experimental evidence for this, not with spaceships but with elementary particles in particle accelerators... [like CERN]. We can accelerate particles to 99.99 percent the speed of light, but however much power we feed in, we can't get them beyond the speed-of-light barrier. Similarly with spaceships: no matter how much rocket power they have, they can't accelerate beyond the speed of light. [38] [emphasis added]

As for the first part of the quote, it would appear that there is a problem with the Theory of Relativity, because **the light barrier has been broken**. [39] As for the last statement, it would appear that no one has ever been able to move a rocketship anywhere near the speed of light, so the statement is a little curious... How would they know for sure? The mass of a particle and the mass of a spaceship are orders of magnitude different... How can they be compared?

Superluminal Pulses

Recent research into the speed of light has involved lasers, the 'Ether field' and particle beam generators. Specifically, a Russian scientist, **Dr. Eugene Podkletnov**, developed an electro-gravitic beam generator which sent gravity beam pulses across two parallel laser beams and measured the effect (and timing) of the gravity pulse on the laser beams.

> His research team was able to measure the speed of their gravity beam pulses by using an oscilloscope to mark the moments when the gravity pulse momentarily dimmed two laser beams directed across the beam's path. Knowing the distance between the laser beam cross-points and the times registered for each successive dimming, they were able to determine the speed of a gravity pulse... Podkletnov's team found that the pulses were traveling at **sixty-four times the speed of light!** [40] [emphasis added]

With that kind of speed, one doesn't need to postulate **Wormholes** to cross the Universe. And **Wormholes are an idiot idea** anyway: How would one be created, just where you want it, how would you control where it exited, and even more significant: How would you keep one open while moving through it ... Where would you be if it collapsed on you while traversing it?

The evidence is astounding and has been replicated to insure that it wasn't an error in calculations or procedures. This means that faster than light space travel is possible (with an **electrogravitic drive**) and "...at the same time refutes Einstein's **outmoded** Special Theory of Relativity." [41] Can it be explained?

> ... the high speeds of these pulses becomes understandable when considered in the context of **subquantum kinetics**... [which says that] a light wave should have a speed of c, the velocity of light, relative to the local ether rest frame. Now, suppose that the field gradient of the advancing gravity potential wave accelerates a slug of ether to a high velocity relative the surrounding laboratory ether reference frame... say that it attains a **velocity of 63 c**... this should be possible since **the ether is not bound by the same speed limit rules that apply to electromagnetic radiation**... [so] if a light ray or shock front was moving within this ether wind slug in the same direction as the ether wind... this light ray would be traveling at **sixty-four times the speed of light**, 63 c for the speed of the ether wind slug plus 1 c for the light ray moving forward **within it**. [42] [emphasis added]

Not only has light used a carrier not bound by the same rules as light, but the solution to this enigma is found in the new branch of Quantum Physics called **subquantum kinetics**. Dr. Paul LaViolette's book Secrets of Antigravity Propulsion nicely describes this field and why it is supplanting the older, outmoded physics. It is microphysics based on discoveries made recently which promise to answer the questions about the subatomic world that traditional Quantum Physics has trouble with because it keeps trying to fit everything into the General Theory of Relativity – and parts have been demonstrated recently to be wrong. [43]

255

So much for absolute trust in Einstein-clad theories. The new supplants the old and Man moves forward.

Ether and Dark Energy

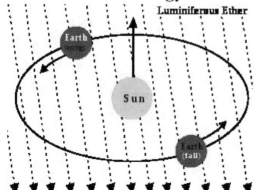

Luminiferous Ether

Could the Ether be the universal field of energy that permeates and connects everything in our world? Is this the substance (call it what you will, even **Dark Energy**) that underlies the functioning of nonlocality as well as ESP? Ether will soon be seen in this chapter to provide the framework for a formidable challenger to Quantum Physics: Subquantum Kinetics.

Credit:
http://en.wikipedia.org/wiki/Cosmic_ether

The Ether was called luminiferous aether as it was hypothesized that the Earth moves through a "medium" of aether waves that carries light. The concept of the Ether goes way back to Hendrik Lorentz and his "Theory of Electrons" of 1892.

It was enhanced by Henri Poincaré in 1905 and **rejected by Einstein** at the time. It was thought to move throughout all space and pervade most matter, in addition to which it was 'flowing' in one principal direction most of the time ... see Michelson & Morley experiment above and the concept of anisotrophy.

So the Special Theory of Relativity which depends on a Light constant is also flawed, according to Georges Sagnac. [44] **Einstein did not believe in the Ether**, nor did he think the Universe was expanding, but he did believe in the Big Bang and Black Holes... the former didn't happen, and the latter is not what we think it is. (Three out of four wrong: he was right, the Universe is not expanding.)

When physicists rejected the Ether explanation for the underlying strata of the Universe, they threw the proverbial baby out with the bathwater.... Later as Michelson reestablished the validity of the Ether concept, and Sagnac later verified it, physicists suddenly 'discovered' **Dark Matter and Dark Energy** – perhaps it was too embarrassing to admit that the Ether was OK after all.

Miscellaneous Theories

Big Bang and Expanding Universe

It is said that our Universe originated with an explosion of proto-matter which is not defined, nor really explained. It is an assumption that the Universe is thus expanding as a result of material, atoms, particles and coalescing matter into larger spheres, and following some laws of celestial mechanics, matter eventually aggregated into galaxies and solar systems…

Not all physicists agree with this. Dr. LaViolette, a prominent astrophysicist, asks what was the source of energy to power the Big Bang? [45] In addition, physicists argue for the expansion of the Universe based on the cosmological **redshift** – light shifting into the bottom of the visible spectrum (infrared) as a way of 'proving' that the stars are receding… In reality, Dr.s Hubble and LaViolette both suggest that the Universe is not expanding, and that the redshift is a function of **"tired light"** [46] wherein the photons lose energy and slow down.

Fritz Zwicky first proposed the tired light phenomenon to explain the redshift effect by stating that as photons in the universe gradually lost their energy, and since a photon's energy and wavelength are related, a reduction in photon energy translates to a reduction in wavelength (ie, visible spectrum). [47] Thus the redshift is not caused by receding galaxies; it is due to a Universe with spiraling Galaxies that are not all running away from each other, but which contain **photons that are running out of energy**. [48] Dr. LaViolette proved this in a paper in 1984.

Black Holes

It was initially hoped that String Theory would help decode the nature of Black Holes, but physicists and astronomers cannot understand the disorder found within Black Holes. There are many singularities found with Black Holes, and confusion as to what they contain inside, and while they have been able to mathematically describe the disorder, the scientists still do not know what a Black Hole is.

In fact, the so-called Black Hole at the center of our galaxy, known as Sgr A*, is not a Black Hole but should be called **a "mother star"** as it gives birth to matter and **genic energy** within our galaxy. This is explained by Subquantum Kinetics whose postulates have held water for over 30 years, and DO offer a meaningful understanding of what a Black Hole is versus what a "mother star" is, and what it does. [49]

> Unlike a conventional Black Hole, a mother star does not need to swallow matter in order to generate its enormous energy efflux. Rather, both energy and matter spontaneously created within its depths and the ensuing outward [genic] energy flux prevents the star's mass from unrestrained collapse. [50]

Conventional Black Hole theory is founded on a general relativistic concept of space-time warping. But there is no warping of space-time around a celestial body, according to Subquantum Kinetics – space remains Euclidian. The huge mass of a Black Hole is supposed to warp space-time – this is one of Einstein's major points supposedly substantiating his General Theory of Relativity (GTR).

> Bending of light as it passed a very heavy object (e.g. the Sun) and red shift of light in a strong gravitational field…. were the so-called "classical tests." …. Einstein's GTR explained bending as a "curved space-time effect"

[however...] Even the so-called Red Shift in light rays passing a strong gravitational field of the Sun could not be confirmed... 80 years later [1989] scientists agree that any red shift observed is not explained by the GTR.[51]

In addition: **Nikola Tesla denounced Einstein's** concept of warping space. [52]

While a lot of Einstein's theories have been shown to be false, it still looks like he was **the "poster boy"** for the fledgling Quantum Physics field which was perhaps 5 years old when Einstein made his GTR and Special Theory of Relativity – to continue to receive funding for the exploration of theories, something had to be shown for their work, and it looks like some of their ideas came off the wall, unproven, not holding water, and some, like Wormholes today, are just nuts. But that is how a fledgling field is funded. And then some financiers are convinced to fund **supercolliders** where the hunt for obtuse and abstract particles can be continued... when Subquantum Kinetics has explained the nature of our universe for the last 30 years... but "don't bother me with details," they say.

Einstein Met Tesla in his Lab
(Credit: Bing Images)

Subatomic Particles

It has been recently found that some new particles are 'created' by the observer looking for them -- not discovered. According to **Jahn and Dunne**:

> They believe that instead of discovering particles, physicists may actually be *creating* them. As evidence they cite a recently discovered subatomic particle called an **anomalon,** whose properties vary from laboratory to laboratory. Imagine owning a car that had a different color and different features depending on who drove it! This is very curious and seems to suggest that an anomalon's reality depends on who finds/creates it. [53]

According to Wikipedia,

> ... as study continued the number of negative results [to prove the existence of anomalons] continued to grow. By 1987 interest in the topic had waned, and most research in the field ended. However, some research continued and in 1998 Piyare Jain claimed to have finally demonstrated them conclusively, using **larger** accelerators at Brookhaven National Lab, and CERN, and combining that with a **thin** detector which he claimed was key to the problem of detecting the anomalons. More recently he has claimed that the particles in question are actually the elusive *Axion*, long thought to be part of the Standard Model but unseen in spite of decades of searching. [54]

In addition, Jahn and Dunne believe that

> ...we live in a 3D construct created out of interconnectedness, sustained by the flow of **consciousness**, and ultimately as plastic as the thought process that engendered it... In a holographic universe, consciousness pervades all matter... [and] ... **reality is established only in the interaction of a consciousness with its environment** ... [which consciousness can be] anything capable of generating, receiving or utilizing information. Thus, animals, viruses, DNA, machines (artificially intelligent or otherwise), and so-called nonliving objects may all have the prerequisite properties to take part in the creation of reality. [55] [emphasis added]

In short, Jahn and Dunne state that "...subatomic particles do *not* possess a distinct reality <u>until consciousness enters the picture</u>." So the next question is: <u>How much</u> does the effect of the observer in Quantum Physics influence what the subatomic particles <u>do</u>? Or are we just being deceived by those who **control** this reality from above 3D? (See Chapter 12.)

Einstein Rebutted Again

In a 2008 issue of *Mental Floss* magazine (vol. 7 no. 5) for Sept/Oct 2008, scientists have been examining an abandoned uranium mine in Africa (home of the Anunnaki mining operations, as the reader will recall from Chapter 3). Says the article:

> Einstein once declared that **c** [the speed of light] never changes and that nothing can ever travel faster than it. Today, however, a tiny patch of land in Africa may prove that this famous constant also isn't so constant after all. [56]

The mine is in Oklo, in Gabon, and bears all the signs of having been mined, processed and then dumped there. Along with some odd type of glass that can only be produced by incredibly high temperatures – such as that produced by fission.

> The strangest part about Oklo was that its nuclear signature was just a little bit off. This is where Oklo confronts Einstein. As scientists scrutinized the site's byproducts, they began to discover **small discrepancies in some of the elements' atomic weights**... For example, the atomic weight of samarium at Oklo wasn't matching up with the atomic weight of samarium in the rest of the world. It was as though these elements had been assembled in a different factory than all the other elements in the world... the more carefully scientists examined the site, the more these little discrepancies started chipping away at core tenets of physics.[57] [emphasis added]

And in particular, the "fine structure constant' called **alpha** which defines how different parts of an atom bind together – a fundamental, unchanging constant of $1/137$ – did not apply at Oklo. The teaching in physics is: If the value is higher or lower, atoms do not form and life would not exist.

> In 2004, scientists tried making theoretical calculations using a slightly different value for alpha, and the data for Oklo fit perfectly… The only problem is that alpha is considered a "fundamental constant"… the number should *never, ever* change. If it did, physics itself would experience a mini nuclear meltdown… every calculation about the Big Bang and the nature of the universe is based on a fixed value for alpha. [And] alpha is related to other constants in the universe – most notably c, the constant for the speed of light and the cornerstone of Einstein's theory of special relativity. **If alpha varied in the past, then so did the speed of light.** And if either of these things is true, then cosmologists and astronomers know a lot less about the universe than they thought. [58] [emphasis added]

And that appears to be true: scientists are now acknowledging the varying speed of light, and a possible **"fickle" alpha constant**. This might explain how the universe allegedly expanded faster than light just after the putative Big Bang, but it means **there is a whole new world of post-Einstein physics**. But then, Einstein had it coming:

> …Einstein himself once used tiny discrepancies in Isaac Newton's calculations to overthrow Newton's laws of motion. [59]

Not even Einsteinian physics is sacred. And it will be seen why the world we think we live in is so hard to analyze and why trying to write its laws of operation in concrete is futile. **The fact that constants can change in Physics is a red flag** which is very relevant to what Chapter 13 reveals.

And if we think the Universe operates with 'constant' parameters, what does that do to the concept of time travel?

Time Travel

Steven Hawking adroitly addresses this issue.

> Again, since time and space are related, it might not surprise you that a problem closely related to the question of travel backward in time is the question of whether or not you can travel faster than light… if you can travel with unlimited speed, you can also travel backward in time. [60]

The Quantum Physics proof of that statement is involved and will not be examined here, except to say that the faster you go, approaching the speed of light, the more time slows down for you… If you moved **at** the speed of light, time would stand still, and theoretically if you **exceeded** the speed of light, it should 'reverse' time and you'd be going backwards because you were 'losing' time, or running 'negative' time. Linear time is a continuum: from + at one end to a 0 in the middle to − at the other end.

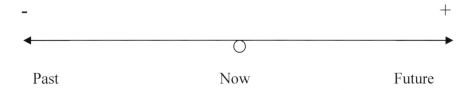

Bi-directional Linear Timeline Flow

The Grandfather Paradox

Time travel can also be related to moving to another timeline, and while that is a subject for another chapter, let's correct the idea that Jack cannot go back in time and kill his grandfather because, it is said, Jack would never have been born. The Multiverse is smarter than that. So, as far as going back in time, Steven Hawking once asked an interesting question:

> "If time travel to the past is possible, why haven't beings from the future come back to visit us?" [61]

> *Answer: What makes you think they haven't? And if their intentions are not honorable, what makes you think they'd announce their presence?*

The Multiverse offers 2 ways to view the past:

a) the 'dynamic time' system: if time travelers go back in time, and they want to modify the existing timeline's past, they may do so but it <u>creates an alternate timeline</u> and they may become observers in it if they changed something in the original which causes them to cease to exist. They may not be able to get back to their original timeline.

b) the 'static time' system: If time travelers want to see their same timeline in the past, they may do so with phase controls that make it impossible to modify anything, and no one will even see them so there is no impact upon a developing culture. This is the safest way to view the past.

Method (a) above is done by staying within the current 3D timeline; method (b) is done by shifting into the lower 4D realm to observe the 3D timeline… much as a 3D person can observe the 2D world better from 3D.

In essence, time travel involves similar technology to using a 'wormhole' to cover vast distances without using hyperlightspeed. Since the 3D world is all about limits, the issue is resolved, as Einstein correctly said, by taking it to a higher level. The wormhole concept works better by slipping through a 4D **space**/time anomaly in 3D and time travel is using a 4D **time**/space anomaly in 3D.

Quantum Weirdness

Nonlocal Communication

Another aspect of Quantum Physics that bears examining is **Nonlocality** -- what Einstein called "spooky action at a distance." The phenomena occurs when a positronium atom decays and shoots off **two photons in different directions**, when the physicists measure the two particles, they have identical angles of polarization – and if one of the twin particle's spin is changed, the other particle compensates for what the first one did – and no one told the second particle what was done to the first one. This suggests an interconnectedness…. or **'entanglement'** which is what the metaphysical world has said for centuries. And yet, Einstein argued against this "spooky action at a distance" because it endangered his SRT (then unknown to be flawed). [62]

> It is one thing to say that physical measurement of the first particle's momentum affects uncertainty in its *own* position, but to say that measuring the first particle's momentum affects the uncertainty in the position of the *other* is another thing altogether. **Einstein, Podolsky and Rosen** asked how can the second particle "know" to have precisely defined momentum but uncertain position? Since this implies that one particle is communicating with the other instantaneously across space, i.e. **faster than light**, this is called **the EPR "paradox".** [63]

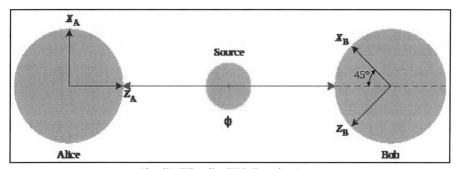

(Credit: Wipedia: EPR Paradox.)

Splitting a particle and sending the two halves in opposite directions, then changing the Spin of the particle at Alice, the compensating Spin will automatically be done at Bob.

So how can this phenomenon be explained – according to Quantum Physics, or Subquantum Kinetics… or by anybody? The answer is very important to Chapter 13. **Nonlocality** is predicted by Quantum Mechanics which says that the Universe allows interconnections that are not local. The quantum connection (communication) between particles can exist "…even if they are on opposite sides of the Universe… as if they are on top of each other."[64] Since the GRT does not allow superluminal communication, Einstein 'approved' the concept of nonlocality even though Quantum Physics cannot explain how it works. Subquantum Kinetics <u>can</u> because it uses the Ether (aka Dark Energy aka ZPE)… the Field or Matrix interpenetrating the Universe (see below).

Of course the example above, if you will note, involved TWIN particles from the same positronium atom. Such 'spooky' action does not apply to all particles in the Universe, but it is an example of nonlocal communication – because the particles are twins, they are *de facto* interconnected.

Such connectedness is accounted for in **Subquantum Kinetics** when examining the electromagnetic model of the Ether [Chapter 9]. [65]

So, it was once a popular idea that there is nothing faster than the speed of light… kind of like the idea that the Earth was flat. Let it be considered that **thought is faster than light**; one can picture oneself 'flying' from Earth to the Crab Nebula in a second, and the physical light would take another gazillion lightyears to get there. Or, one can visualize being at the Sun and, in less than a second later, visualize covering the distance from the Sun to the Earth – whereas it requires 8.3 minutes for light to do the same.

There is also the 'nonlocal' effect above of communication between subatomic particles which appears to be instantaneous, and not limited to the speed of light. [66] In a nonlocal universe, everything is connected and communication is instantaneous. In other words, when things in the universe appear to be separate, especially if separated by 40 light years, for example, they are really interconnected (at least by the Ether) and the Whole is connected at a higher level than we on Earth as limited humans can see much less fathom.[67] Perhaps it is a sort of **Divine Matrix**, as Greg Braden said.

The Quantum Net

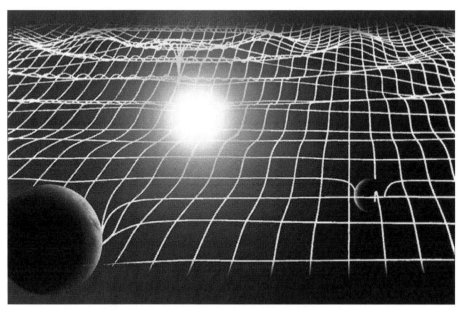

The Sun, Earth and Moon in the Field
(Credit: Bing Images)

According to the latest reports, **we are all interconnected**, and at some upper level of our being, via our soul-connections, we are all One. Of course the mystics have been saying that for centuries, but there is research that connects us all through a 'divine matrix' or coherent **Field of intelligent energy**, according to Greg Braden. Discussed earlier, this is called **Nonlocality**:

> **Dean Radin**....has been a pioneer in exploring just what it means for us to live in such a world. "Nonlocality," he explains, "means that there are ways in which things that appear to be separate are, in fact, not separate." There are aspects of us, Radin suggests, that extend beyond the here-and-now and allow us to be spread throughout space and time…. Whatever we choose to call that mysterious "something," we all have it; and ours mingles with everyone else's as part of the field of energy that bathes all things. This field is believed to be the **quantum net** that connects the universe….[68] [emphasis added]

Excellent term. Since everything and everybody is connected, we all affect indirectly what other people think and do…and this has been called the "**butterfly effect.**" A heavy rain causes a flood in China, which causes a part of the land to sink, which affects the tectonic plates causing them to shift, and then there is a seemingly unrelated earthquake in Mexico City the following week.[69] The flood did not directly cause the earthquake, but led to a series of unseen events that, like so many dominoes falling, may have precipitated the earthquake.

The quantum net, Braden's **Divine Matrix**, and the Ether of Subquantum Kinetics sound like they are all the same thing. Chapter 9 will include the **Bionet** in this group.

And that includes humans, too – we are all One and interconnected at the soul level, and that is one of the great messages of the mystics as well as the message brought back to Earth by those who experience the Near Death Experience (NDErs). Not only do we affect each other, we affect the plants, animals and the planet with our thoughts, energy and actions. [70]   Not only is this related to the 'butterfly effect', but it is another version of the **"100th Monkey"** – we are all interconnected via the torsion fields of the Matrix and when enough people learn something, or accept something, it is easier for others who follow to learn it, too. And this, in turn, is related to *memes* which are viral-like ideas that permeate a society – perhaps the phenomena of the meme gathering acceptance, like an **archetype**, and thus strength, is how the '100th Monkey' effect works.

Aspects of our oneness are also explored in Chapters 7 and 9. Everything is connected to everything else, and that especially includes Man's apparent ability to influence the subatomic world.

Scientists working with photons from a positronium atom above questioned WHY the particles adjust to each other. Is there a Law operating in **the implicate order** that maintains a balance, or that says twin particles must stay aligned…? That is the subject of exploration for some of today's physicists, and yet part of the answer already lies with Subquantum Kinetics which has much to say about the Ether and its basic operation.

Cat Absurdity

A really weird aspect of Quantum Physics today is the conundrum called **Schroedinger's Cat**. This deals with whether a cat inside a sealed box is dead or alive, in the paradox's simplest form. Quantum Physics entertains the notion that the cat is neither alive or dead until the observer opens the box to see... in other words, the cat's status is a **probability wave** which will collapse when the box is opened and the cat will be either dead or alive... but neither state is real until the observer looks at the cat. This is because Quantum Physics believes in the observer's ability to influence outcomes ... and is exactly what they have experienced while trying to determine a particle's location <u>and</u> properties. It can't be done – you can measure one or the other but not both at the same time as the measurement 'contaminates' or interferes with the actual state of the particle.

There are other physicists who think the cat is either dead or alive whether you look or not. They consider probability waves to be subjective nonsense.

Quantium Bayesianism

Just when you thought it could get no weirder, there is another physicist who got fed up with the probability waves – a form of mental masturbation that Quantum Physics sometimes indulges in, after all, some of Einstein's theories were based on "thought experiments." [71], [72] – Dr. von Baeyer has rejected the standard model of probability waves and sees the Schroedinger Cat paradox differently in terms of his Quantum Bayesianism (**QBism**):

> ... run the [Cat] experiment – but don't look inside the box. After an hour has gone by, traditional quantum theory would hold that the atom's wave function is in a superposition of two states – decayed and not decayed.... By insisting that the wave function is a <u>subjective property</u> of the observer, rather than an objective property of the cat in the box, QBism eliminates the puzzle. [QBism] theory says that *of course* the cat is either alive or dead (and not both). [73] [emphasis added]

So some physics professors have reached a point where more common sense reigns, but they still like to say that "... one's personal state of mind makes the world come into being.... By interpreting the wave function as a subjective belief and subject to revision by the rules of Bayesian statistics, the mysterious paradoxes of quantum mechanics vanish. " [74] Sounds like the **anomalon issue** (Jahn and Dunne above) and the Observer Effect (Chapter 12) again.

Bayesian Statistics' probability is subjective, it measures the <u>degree of belief</u> that an event will occur. And most proponents of the QBism system maintain that until an experiment is performed (and someone looks to see if the Cat is dead or alive), the probabilistic outcome does not exist.

> Asserting that Schroedinger's Cat is truly both alive and dead is an **absurdity,** a megalomaniac's delusion that one's personal state of mind makes the world come into being. [75]

But here we open a new can of worms that mirrors what the New Agers want to believe:

we can <u>create our day</u>, as was suggested by **Dr. Joe Dispenza** in the movie, *What the Bleep*. The apparent 'fact' that Quantum Physics supports the idea that the observer can influence what particles do, and thus produce *anomalons* in the laboratory (i.e., produce what we expect to see via the **Observer Effect**), or as was once believed, influence the action of particles in the Double Slit experiment, lends weight to this idea. **The Observer Effect,** as it is called, is due to something else, as will be seen in Chapter 12

> *But let it be stated that affecting the **subatomic world** by thought is not out of the realm of possibility – because the energies of particles are less than the energy of our thoughts (which are torsion fields as is more fully examined in Book 2).*

Double Slit Experiment

This has been a conundrum for physicists since it was first discovered in 1803 by Thomas Young. Picture a photon projector and in front of it 10 feet away is a barrier with one vertical 1" slit in it which reveals a wall behind it.

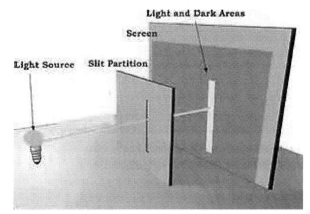

When a **single** photon is fired at the slit, the pattern on the wall shows where the photon hit – as a spec of light. That says **light is a particle**.

(Credit images: Bing Images)

Now open a second vertical 1" slit just an inch from the first slit, and fire another **single** photon at the barrier –

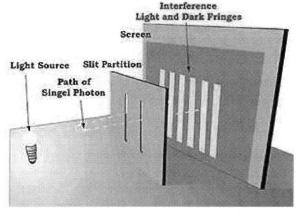

…the pattern on the wall shows a wave-like pattern. That says **light is a wave**.

Is it both?

Why is the pattern on the wall different based on whether there is one slit open or two?

What is even more weird, and what Thomas Young did in 1803 is to put the slits in a line with the single phtoton:

(Credit all images: Bing Images)

Interference Patterns

Screen

bright

dark

bright

dark

bright

dark

bright

dark

bright

S_1

S_2

It produces the same interference pattern of alternating dark & light as when light passes through just the single slit. Note that **multiple single-photons** were fired through the single slit in the picture above -- naturally the 'dark' bands say that more photons hit there than in the 'bright' (less dark) bands.

Someone may wonder what would happen if three slits were used… it produces almost the same interference pattern as the double-slit.

Double Slit

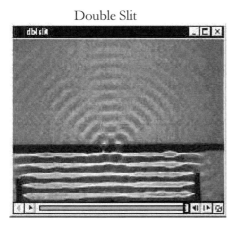

Triple Slit

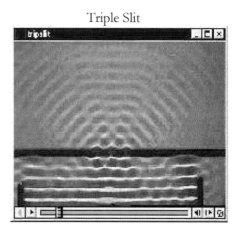

Is light a particle or a wave? The only 'resolution' so far is to consider that light can behave as a particle or as a wave – but how did the photon 'know' there were two slits, and thus change its 'behavior?' This is definitely quantum weirdness. (Chapter 13 may hold the answer.)

Light is Photons (*Quanta*)

Having rasied the interesting issue of Light, it would be hard to leave this chapter without verturing a definition and explanation of what Light is. While it behaves like a particle and a wave, it is basically just electromagnetic (EM) radiation… in the **EM Spectrum** between ultraviolet and infrared light, or in the range of 400 nanometers (nm) as UV, or 400×10⁻⁹ m, to about 700 nanometers as IR:

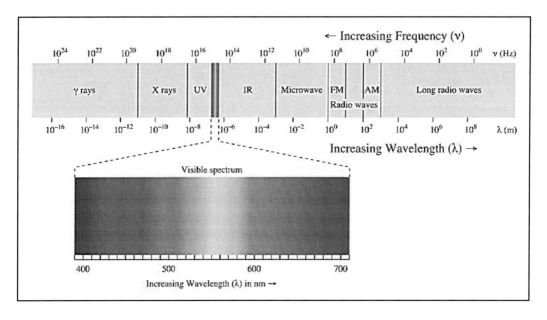

(Credit: Wikipedia: http://en.wikipedia.org/wiki/Light#mediaviewer/File:EM_spectrum.svg)

The very first section of the EM Spectrum shown is γ (gamma) – these are the dangerous **gamma rays** put out by the Sun. Next, **X-rays** are all familiar to us when we visit the dentist. Less intense is **UV** (ultraviolet light) then VISIBLE light, and then **IR** (infrared light). Beyond that, we get into microwaves, radio waves…

The photons are all up and down the Spectrum – when a particle or *quanta* (energy packet) has an energy signature of a certain wavelength and frequency and energy of 1.24 eV (electroVolts) the energy packet, *quanta*, becomes visible – if the energy is greater at 1.24 meV (megaVolts) it is a gamma ray. If the energy signature is less, it is a microwave or radio wave – **the same *quanta*, but with a different frequency and wavelength.**

For example, when the eye sees color, it is because different wavelengths of *quanta* are bouncing off an object, and the retina reacts with a rod (black & white only) or a cone, and the intensity of the *quanta* hitting the cone determines the color. **The *quanta* coming into**

the eye has no color component. Note that **the color blue has less wavelength than red** and that is why neon signs in red are easier to read at night than blue signs.

Rewind: The difference in wavelength is also why the police cars alternately flash blue then red from their light cluster as it has a disruptive effect on some people – the brain has to react to 400 nm then 700 nm then 400 nm....etc. And this (while you look at it) they say momentarily interferes with the ability to think clearly.

So in a later section of Chapter 9, it will be revealed that the DNA also releases *quanta*, called **biophotons,** and these communicate with different parts of the body/mind complex.

> In fact, in Book 2, Chapters 12 and 13 examine the electromagnetic 'sea'
> that we all live in, and the EM components are sometimes called *chi*, Light,
> torsion waves, Æether, the Matrix, and bio-energy.

Quantum Neggs

At the risk of sounding medieval, there is another possible explanation for the Nonlocality experiment, and even for the Double Slit experiment. The Neggs are also in the room watching this experiment. Since their agenda is to distract, confuse and amaze humans, perhaps they are responsible for the behavior of the electron(s)? And before dismissing that idea too quickly, let me remind the reader that Charles Fort did research on fish, rocks, and slime (among other odd things) falling out of a clear sky – for years. On perfectly clear days. Remember also what was pointed out in John Keel's research into Mothman and Bigfoot: **some unseen entities <u>are</u> playing games with us** – these things such as fish falling out of a clear sky and a Mothman monster scaring people are not natural, and yet they happen. No one has ever caught a Mothman, nor a Bigfoot, and they won't. It is all an illusion to entertain, scare, or amaze us – and it works. Thank the Control System.

The possibility of the Neggs playing games with subatomic particles could be merely a modernized, 'scientific' version of fish falling from the sky, or fairies that appear out of nowhere. It seems that as Man has become more sophisticated and technological, so are the illusions that are presented to him. About 100 years ago, it was mysterious Airships, fairies and elves, then as we became more technological, the illusions became UFOs (breaking the laws of physics with 90° turns at 4,000 mph!), cropcircles and little Greys.

> *Notice:* **Mermaids** *are not included in this issue. They are an alternate*
> *line of 'evolution' from Man, started by the Oannes (Chapter 3).*

The reason for suggesting Negg interference is due to the **Control System** aspect of our world as Dr. Jacques Vallée said. He suggested that there is an <u>interplay</u> with us (via UFOs, Crop Circles, and Greys) that is designed to cause us to wonder, analyze and grow (see Appendix C).

> *Instead of Neggs, it may be the 'gods' who run the Control System.*

The whole point of this chapter is to be wary of men in white coats who make 'expert' pronouncements. It would be well to objectively reconsider any hard and fast rules – such as that of the speed of light. Science is constantly advancing and overturning previous pronouncements, so **we can't totally castigate Einstein – he was postulating theories as physicists tried to figure it all out**. However, he was not a genius: a genius would have gotten most of the theorems correct. He got many wrong. For a more current-day set of heroes, one may look to Dr. Feynman, or Neils Bohr, or Dr. Brain Greene, or Dr. Paul LaViolette who is ahead of the pack and whose work is being validated every passing year.

Just as Newtonian Physics was great to explain the physical world of the 1800's, it has been found to be inadequate in describing relativistic events, [76] and has been superseded by Quantum Physics when digging into the deeper aspects of how the world works. Now it looks like Quantum Physics is about to be obsoleted by **Subquantum Kinetics**…

Nonetheless, Quantum Physics has been very useful for showing the wonder and awe of the created universe – and such is the point of three fine books, The Tao of Physics, The Dancing Wu Li Masters, and The Holographic Universe. Note that it is not religion that is being confirmed by Quantum Physics, but a more spiritual understanding of the Multiverse and the design, metaphysics and intelligence behind it.

Chapter 9: – New Science

Having made an issue of **Subquantum Kinetics** in the last chapter, it is time to explore the subject and see what is new and why it works so well. It will give the spiritual seeker some additional information about the wondrous world we occupy. Its developer, **Dr. Paul LaViolette**, an astrophysicist, has made numerous predictions (26+) about the fabric and operation of the Universe based on System Theory, the Ether and nonequilibrium thermodynamics. And he has been right! The Quantum Physicists are so heavily invested in their own theories they can't see that he has solved what they are still wrestling with – but then again, sometimes the quest is what it is all about…

Subquantum Kinetics

Subquantum Kinetics (SQK) begins at the subquantum level of matter, with already established principles, and postulates further well-ordered reaction processes, collectively called the *transmuting ether*. It does not depend on observation of the physical world as a starting point, as does Quantum Physics.

> The **transmuting ether** [is] an active substrate that is quite different from the passive mechanical ethers considered in the eighteenth and nineteenth centuries. It further proposes that the concentrations of the substrates composing this ether are the energy potential fields that form the basis of all matter and energy in our universe. The operation of these ether reactions causes wave-like field gradients (spatial concentration patterns) to emerge and form the observable quantum level structures and physical phenomena…[1] [emphasis added]

SQK begins with a mathematical model of (subquantum) ether processes, then computer simulates the model adjusting it to generate quantum level phenomena, and then compares the results to actual observations.

> Because it begins with a single action system model as its point of departure, for describing essentially all observable physical phenomena, subquantum kinetics qualifies as a unified theory. By comparison, conventional physics begins with many theories conceived independently from one another and later attempts to "sew" these together. But the result is far from unified, being instead a self-contradictory agglomeration. [2]

As time goes on, Quantum Physicists will realize that their postulated Dark Energy and Dark Matter are the same Ether substrate that SQK deals with. After all, the Universe and its subquantum components is only one consistent thing, not a multiple of different things, so SQK and Quantum Physics cannot develop radically different definitions of particles, waves and theories and both be right.

SQK Operation Basics

While this chapter is not a treatise on SQK and why it works, it is amazing how elegant yet simple it is. While Dr. LaViolette was initially inspired and intrigued by a self-repeating chemical wave phenomenon called the **Belousov-Zhabotinskii reaction** (below), which led to an insight into the transmuting Ether process, a more basic model called the **Brusselator** led to the development of what was to be Model G.

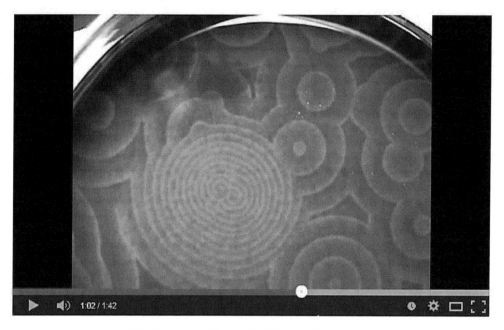

The Belousov-Zhabotinskii Reaction
(Credit: YouTube: search: "BZ Reaction":
https://www.youtube.com/watch?v=3JAqrRnKFHo)

Model G describes the basic function of the Ether substrate and consists of **etherons** which interact with each other in a repetitive cycle, a non-ending 'dance' of subatomic particles, diffused throughout space, and is described by just 5 basic kinetic equations.

$$A \rightarrow G$$
$$G \rightarrow X$$
$$B + X \rightarrow Y + Z$$
$$2X + Y \rightarrow 3X$$
and
$$Y \rightarrow \Omega$$

Model G [3]

According to Dr LaViolette's explanation: the model refers to the recursive conversion of X etherons into Y etherons and back into X etherons. A and B are input Ether reactants, as well as Z and Ω are output Ether reactants. G, X and Y are variable Ether reaction intermediates. Concentration patterns of these three variables form the particles and photons that compose our physical Universe. [4]

272

Simple and elegant, SQK has no plethora of particles as in Quantum Physics which has: 18 quarks, 18 antiquarks, 8 gluons, including 3 the massive U particles (U+, U-, U⁰). So far 47 particles in Quantum Physics are not enough to describe the Universe and together describe the "particle zoo." [5] It is done in SQK with 6 basic particles.

Lastly, a brief comparison of Quantum Physics issues with those of SQK:[6]

Advantages of SQK

Classical field theory	**SQK**
1. Plagued by the field-particle dualism.	Problem does not exist.
2. Plagued by the wave-particle dualism.	Wave aspects incorporated.
3. Considers antigravity an impossibility.	Considers antigravity flight.
4. Natural events are inherently indeterminate.	Commonsense notion of causality.
5. Allows disruptive naked singularities.	Avoids this problem.
6. Universe emerged from nonexistent state.	Universe emerged from preexisting ether substrate.
7. Cannot explain how subatomic particles originate.	Subatomic particles arise from ether substrate.
8. Quantum electrodynamics and General Relativity contradict each other: Cosmological Constant conundrum.	All fields encompassed by 1 internally consistent theory. Gravity is explained.
9. Universe is expanding due to redshift.	Redshift not due to expansion; it is due to "tired light" phenomenon.
10. Black Holes are matter-consuming.	Black Holes are "mother stars" which birth matter and energy.
11. Fails to explain the excess heat coming from the Earth's core.	SQK attributes it to **genic** energy.
12. Fails to explain source of supernova explosions.	SQK genic energy explains this.
13. Posits existence of **quarks**, but cannot produce proof.	SQK uses 6 basic **etheron** elements to source all matter.
14. Posits existence of **strings** within quarks which cannot be proven/discovered.	SQK etherons are basic elements and are all that is needed to explain the Universe.

Lastly and most significantly, conventional physics was impacted by the theories of Darwin, and does not recognize an unobservable, causative spiritual realm, much less a God. While Einstein postulated the existence of multiple dimensions to make his GRT and STR theories work, and String Theory nowadays uses multiple dimensions to explain string function, that is not the same thing as a spiritual realm which overlays our world and Higher Entities who help 'run' this 3D realm.

On the other hand, SQK is based on general systems theory which admits the possibility of an unseen spiritual realm. It harmonizes with mystical teachings, Yin and Yang, higher consciousness, and *Chi* for example. And that is one of the reasons for including SQK in this chapter – as it helps to explain the underpinnings of this Earth and where we find ourselves, all examined in Chapters 12-13.

Man is a special creation and Earth is a special place in which to grow and learn lessons. To that end, his DNA was constructed to be rather plastic (Think: Epigenetics) and reflect his spiritual growth and any developing capabilities. The next section examines the recent findings in this regard, including both the German and Russian advancements in the field of genetics.

Genetics and DNA

In this section, it is of high importance to show the recent discoveries and the mystery of Man's DNA, and consider what he may have inherited from the alleged Anunnaki creation.

Because Man is considered special, so should his DNA also be. But this is not physically so. A researcher in 1975, Mary-Claire King

> …. was able to infer that human and chimpanzee DNA differ in sequence by a mere 1 percent. In fact humans have more in common with chimpanzees than chimpanzees do with gorillas…[7]

And that is not a good thing, seeing that chimpanzees can be very aggressive and murder their own kind. [8] But then, so did the Anunnaki. Perhaps we'll never know the source of that proclivity in Man…

One would also think that since Man has 'evolved' from a bipedal hominid, from Homo *erectus* to Neanderthal to Cro-Magnon to Homo *sapiens*, that it would result in evolving his DNA… But did it? Each of the aforementioned species was an upgrade, not an evolutionary mutation.

Studies of Neanderthal DNA show that we are genetically **distinct** from them. [9] And there is **no genetic evidence to indicate the Neanderthals interbred with Cro-Magnon**, [10] although it is possible Neanderthal women found Cro-Magnon men desirable but such mating probably didn't happen and if it did, it would not show up in any mtDNA analysis. [11] However, since Cro-Magnon is a subspecies of Homo *sapiens*, that interbreeding possibility is a given. So how did "evolution" happen? The point of all this is that the lineage of Man is not a nice straight line nor does it have predictable aspects; there are jumps and mutations and their causes are not immediately obvious.

> **Note** that Darwininian Evolutionists will say that modern Man has some Neanderthal DNA because (1) Evolution is assumed to be linear, (2) the Theory of Evolution says it should be there, and (3) they ignore that all Hominids (Erectus, Neanderthal, Homo *sapiens*…) will have stretches of identical DNA that are the same because they are part of the same Family-Genus-Species…

It should be obvious that traditional, Darwinian Evolution depends on linear, gradual

274

change and not "jumps and mutations" as have been observed. Jumps would suggest "assisted evolution" and that is what today's researchers into DNA are discovering that the facts suggest.

Score One for Sitchin

According to the latest DNA research based on mtDNA (the mother's DNA which transfers intact to each newborn), Man originated in Africa... score one for Sitchin. The father's DNA has mtDNA from his mother but does not pass it along to the offspring – only the mother's mtDNA and the father's sperm (<u>nuclear</u> DNA) carries forward into the newborn. Thus the lineage of Man is traced using the mother's DNA. So what would be interesting is to sample DNA from all over the planet and see if Man's origins and lineage can be ascertained.

That was done by Cann and Wilson. They found that the human family tree has two branches – one that has only groups **within** Africa, and the other group contains some African groups and everybody else. Thus it is recognized that modern Man arose in Africa which had been suspected for some time. [12]

> By making a number of simple assumptions about the rate at which
> mutations accumulate through evolution, it is possible to calculate
> the age of the family tree – the time back to the great-great-great-great
> ...-grandmother of us all. Cann and Wilson came up with an estimate
> of about 150,000 years. Even the most distantly related currently living
> humans shared a common ancestor as recently as 150,000 years ago. [13]

Anthropologists were outraged at those numbers. Everyone "knew" that Homo *erectus* left Africa 2 million years ago. And Neanderthals were 'supposed' to live about 700,000 years ago, yet current-day re-calculations put it at 30-40,000 years ago. So another researcher did with the Y-chromosome what Cann and Wilson did with the mtDNA – Peter Underhill found again that the family tree was rooted in Africa and that the family tree was more of a bush and Man's origins dated back to 150,000 years.

Score Two for Sitchin

Back in Chapter 3, Sitchin told us that the Anunnaki created Man about 200,000 – 250,000 years ago, and the more recent versions created by them that could procreate were created in the 150,000 - 200,000 year range.
However there are some problems, not with the dates, but with the mingling of the species as the supposed evolutions took place. Watson tells us:

> We have seen how the Neanderthals failed to interbreed with the new
> arrivals [Cro-Magnon] in Europe, and the same seems to have been
> true whenever Homo *sapiens* encountered Homo *erectus*. Whenever
> they met, the former displaced the latter. And the **disappearance of
> the last Neanderthal, around 29,000 years ago,** represents the
> extinction of the last of the nonmodern descendants of Homo *erectus*. [14]
> [emphasis added]

No Neanderthal Link

Teilhard de Chardin once commented that "… when true Homo *sapiens* in the forms of Cro-Magnon, Grimaldi, and Chancelade men – representing our three modern dominant racial types – appear on the evolutionary scale, there is no evidence that these modern types evolved gradually from the Neanderthals which preceded them." [15]

And again:

> Neanderthal was so far below the fully human Cro-Magnon that de Chardin could not understand how the first could logically have evolved into the second. The gap was too wide and the jump was too quick in the fossil record. Relatively speaking, **Cro-Magnon man seemed to have suddenly appeared on the earth.** [16] [emphasis added]

Obviously, Man has had help and is <u>still being upgraded</u>. For what it is worth, James D. Watson, winner of the Nobel Prize for his work in Genetics, has this to say about the issue:

> … the Neanderthal branch [of the human evolutionary tree] is a long way from the modern human limb. If …Neanderthals and moderns had indeed interbred [when they encountered each other], Neanderthal mtDNA sequences would have entered the modern human gene pool. That we see **no evidence of such** … input implies that modern humans eliminated the Neanderthals rather than interbreeding with them… [and] studies of Neanderthal DNA have shown that **we are genetically distinct from Neanderthal.** [17] [emphasis added]

Neanderthal Disappears

In fact, most people will have a hard time understanding that Neanderthal suddenly disappeared while Cro-Magnon man came abruptly on the scene. They were here at the same time, but no interbreeding. And since this was not a gradual phase-out of the old and phase-in of the new, it was obviously not Evolution at work. Geologically speaking, the replacement happened overnight – **with no genetic link between the two**. This can only mean there was <u>intelligent intervention</u>.

> It might be conjectured that Neanderthal man was either exterminated or hauled off the Earth to make room for the new slave race, and perhaps to prevent breeding between the two subspecies. Whatever the precise truth of this might be, we do know two facts with certainty: modern anthropology has discovered a **sudden replacement** of Neanderthal with modern man, and Mesopotamian records state that intelligent planning by an extraterrestrial race lay somewhere behind that dramatic event. [18] [emphasis added]

And as will be seen early in Chapter 5, in a reference to the Mayan *Popul Vuh*, **Man was modified by the 'gods' for a reason**, and it was not to be in Man's favor at that time.

The Neanderthals dominated Europe for thousands of years, but by 30,000 years ago, they were all gone, underline{replaced} by Cro-Magnon, and there was no interbreeding since the Neanderthals did not contribute any genetics to the gene pool of modern humans. [19]

In searching backwards for the convergence point where the most recent ancestor would be found for all current sequences, they found an ambiguity. Both mtDNA and the Y-chromosome had undergone natural selection resulting in a favored mutation at the convergence point.

> Was [the ambiguity] produced by evolutionary **tinkering**, or something much more significant in the overall scheme of human prehistory? …. The coincidence suggested forcefully that at the moment in question (150,000 years ago), **human populations did indeed undergo a radical genetic alteration,** one capable of affecting mtDNA and Y-chromosomes simultaneously. The phenomenon involved …. is called a "genetic bottleneck." [20] [emphasis added]

What is missing is the concept of 'assisted evolution.'

Score Three for Sitchin.

What they are saying is that 150,000 years ago, there could have been underline{several} different mtDNA sequences and underline{several} different Y-chromosome sequences, but "….today's sequences are all descended from just **one** of each. All the others went extinct…" [21] It looks like there was 'manipulation' of some sort, after all.

> Independent archeological information supports this hypothesis [that modern humans wiped out the Neanderthals]. It would appear that, around 50,000 years ago, modern humans suddenly became *culturally* modern: we see in the remains from this time the first indisputable ornaments, the first routine use of bone, ivory and shell to produce familiar useful artifacts…. **What happened?** We shall probably never know. [22] [emphasis added]

Was Man trained to make pottery, clothes, raise food, make fire, write and make cuneiform tablets….? According to the Sumerian tablets, Man was taught a lot of things, including warfare.

According to the Sitchin material, it underline{is} clear what happened. It is strongly suggested that the eventual *Adapa* was helped along genetically, from the original Homo *erectus* to Neanderthal to Cro-Magnon which was a subset of today's modern Homo *sapiens*. And such species that did not work out, like Neanderthal, were 'removed' and replaced with other 'more viable' versions of Man – and such, as we will see, is **still happening today.** Homo *sapiens* appears to be in the process of genetic upgrade to Homo *noeticus* via the current-day little Greys' abductions.

Score Four For Sitchin

Nobel laureate Francis Crick, who discovered DNA, in the late 1970's proposed the theory of Directed Panspermia. This said that the seeds of life on Earth were the result of other intelligent civilizations sending life here in robotic spaceships. Not asteroids?

Shooting down the Evolutionist theory, it was discovered that all living organisms on Earth are built with just 4 amino acids and the arrangement of them, by the hundreds in the chromosomes of the organism, determines what the organism is and what it can do.

> "...All living things use the same four-letter language [A, C, G, T] to carry genetic information. All use the same 20 letter [amino acid] language to construct their proteins..."

> If life had developed by chance – through trial and error – as Darwinists propose, then it was more likely that different numerous codes would have evolved in different parts of the world, under different conditions. **Yet there is no evidence for an evolutionary process.** Using complex statistical calculations, Crick found that chance alone could not account for such a condition. Thus he concluded that life must have originated elsewhere and been transported here. [23] [emphasis added]

While he wasn't ready to say that UFOs and ancient astronauts existed, he was subtly saying that alien civilizations probably visited Earth in the distant past and considered Earth to be a kind of "cosmic wildlife park." [24] Said Crick:

> Perhaps we are under some sort of discreet surveillance by higher beings on a planet of some nearby star. It is not clear exactly how these cosmic game wardens would do this without our detecting them, but with a higher technology such supervision [via cloaking] may be relatively easy. [25]

And then he realized he was uneasily associating himself with science fiction and quickly explained that he wasn't crazy:

> The whole idea stinks of UFOs or the Chariots of the Gods or other common forms of contemporary silliness. Against this I can only claim that whereas the idea has indeed many of the stigmata of science fiction, **its body is a lot more solid. It does not really have the major feature of most science fiction**, which is a great leap of the imagination... Each of the details which contribute to the required scenario are based on a fairly solid foundation of contemporary science... [26] [emphasis added]

That shows that some scientists can be progressive and open-minded, and once again, Sitchin is vindicated. And if the Vatican has as much said that ETs are our brothers (in Chapter 3), why is there so much resistance to facing reality? We can't even handle it on a simple, limited basis as the next section shows...

DNA Irregularity

We have been told for years that the Indians in North America came across the Bering Strait ages ago when there was a land bridge between what is now Alaska and Russia's eastern coast. From there, the tribes allegedly spread out over the North American continent.

Nice story but recent DNA analyses tell a different tale. In 1994 a team of scientists from Emory University analyzed the mtDNA from many Indian tribes across America and found "… four major varieties, each of which had components associated with groups **in Asia**." [27] Good, that corroborates the traditional story.

But there was **a fifth group** discovered among the Ojibway, the Navajo, the Sioux, and some other tribes that was different. It was reported that "… the only place this [fifth] group shows up is among **Europeans**." [28] [emphasis added]

The conclusion? Not everything is as nice and neat as the scientists would have us believe. Not all North American Indians came from Asia. Some have European roots.

Junk is Not Junk

There are certain aspects of DNA itself that are only now being understood, such as the presence of 'junk' DNA – repetitive sequences which apparently do nothing. Only 3% of the human genome is known to code for proteins (i.e., the reproductive functional part of the genetic code) which means the other 97% does what? [29] Part of this issue was covered in Chapter 8; the remainder is the next issue in this chapter.

In a very enlightening, and recent, book reflecting the latest discoveries in Genetics, Stephen Meyer explains how even the so-called **'Junk' DNA actually does something** and is further evidence for Design in Creation, refuting the pure Evolutionists.

> *The discovery in recent years that nonprotein-coding ['junk'] DNA performs a diversity of important biological functions has confirmed [the prediction that designed organisms should have DNA that performs a function]…*

> …recent scientific discoveries have shown that the nonprotein-coding regions of the genome direct the production of RNA molecules that regulate the use of the protein-coding regions of DNA… [listing 10 functions]… In some cases, "junk" DNA has even been found to code functional genes… Indeed, far from being "junk," … the nonprotein-coding DNA directs the use of other information in the genome… [30]

It will later be discovered that some of the stretches of 'junk' DNA are for the express purpose of replacing worn-out DNA sections, almost like a 'DNA spare tire'.

DNA Discoveries

DNA Transposons

The basic building blocks of DNA are 4 amino acids, coded A,C,T and G, which when they are arranged in a multiplicity of combinations, contribute to the complex genetic coding making up the human genome. But there is something really unique about DNA and it isn't just the code sequences.

> … only 3% of human DNA is composed of the 30,000 genes that encode the physical body, and the other 97% was, until recently, considered to be "junk DNA," with basic sequences that repeat over and over like a broken record – sequences that remain the same for each DNA molecule under study, hence our 99.9% genetic similarities to each other. However, scientists are now aware of the existence of over a million different structures of "jumping DNA" or "transposons" in this remaining 97% of the molecule. Scientists named it **"jumping DNA"** [because] … these one million different proteins **can break loose from one area, move to another area**, settle down, and thereby **rewrite the DNA code**. "… the primary structure of DNA <u>does</u> actually change." [31] [emphasis added]

And this plastic changeability is part of the miracle of Man's inherited divine qualities that PTB entities on Earth want to suppress.

DNA Transmission between Organisms

The following information from Russia, dramatic as it is, depends on the existence of a "DNA life wave" also described as a 'torsion wave' which somehow "…transfers the energetic DNA code of a duck into a hen." [32] Seriously. (See endnote.)

> The duck was placed in a five-sided room about the size of a hatbox with a parabolic domed roof, and on each of the 5 sides of the room, a funnel was placed with the tip pointing away from the center [of the room]. Then narrow copper pipes were routed between the open ends of each funnel and on into a second room, which was shaped like a rectangle, and had the hen placed within it. A roughly two gigahertz electrostatic generator was placed inside the five-sided room. The idea behind this experiment was that the electrostatic energy would generate powerful **torsion waves** that would strike the duck's DNA, causing the waves to pick up the duck's characteristic patterns. Then, just like a pyramid, each funnel would capture these waves and direct them through the copper pipes to the adjacent box.

> After as little as five days of exposure, the rapidly-developing embryos within the pregnant hen would be genetically reprogrammed at the DNA level into duck-hen hybrid creatures that would hatch and live a normal, healthy life. [33] [emphasis added]

Part Chicken, Part Duck: A Chuck
(source: http://www.monkeytypesthebible.com/uploaded_images/chuck-771837.jpg)

Note the **webbed feet, longer neck and duckbill** on a chicken in the picture. They didn't use Photoshop. What happened? In Gariaev's own words (aka Garjajev):

> [The] hybrid chickens of [the] hens [in this experiment] had typical features of a duck – a flat beak, an elongated neck, and larger internal organs... The weight of a one-year-old hen-duck hybrid was 70% higher than the weight of hens grown from irradiated eggs. The second generation of the hen-duck hybrids retained all changes... without further re-radiation. (http://www.emergentmind.org/gariaev12.htm) [34]

Absolutely far out. What does this mean for fertility treatment, or for cloning?

What this means is that we are only touching the tip of the iceberg in DNA research and that Man was created with some really heavy-duty, far-reaching, highly-potentiated material – we are not just skin and bone, or a mass of cells strung together, that evolved without a design. Our DNA has an electromagnetic aspect to it, or the "torsion waves" would not have been able to pick up DNA characteristics and impart them to the electromagnetic signature of the Chicken. This also suggests that Rupert Sheldrake's concept of **morphogenetic fields** around all living things is a reality.

In the following sections, the information is presented to give the reader a deeper sense of wonder about the human body and how special we all are – reverence for the human form should be the norm, and that of itself could preclude the tendency to destroy other human beings. And then add to the DNA information that we are all One, connected at the Higher Soul level, and there could be a revolution in Man's consciousness which would change the world.

Of more recent interest are the scientific experiments with DNA which show how fragile and malleable it is, as well as its unique properties. This section will just show a few aspects of DNA that communicate its 'specialness' and mystery. All the more to gain a better feel for how unique and special Man really is, and why it is a shame that Man does not respect himself and his potential...

DNA Features

DNA Auto-repair

One of the fascinating aspects of DNA is that it has the ability to detect mutation or error and correct itself. This is why we don't see more birth anomalies than we do, and why our species is not evolving extra fingers, eyes, or losing fingers and hair, for example.

> There is a profound and fundamental reason for the limits of variation and adaptation, which are confined strictly within the species. The simple reason is that the DNA faithfully replicates its information and protects its own integrity. Of most profound impact in organic chemistry was the discovery that enzymes within the cell **actually repair any errors or damage in the DNA**! The profound nature of this discovery was emphasized by professor D. H. R. Barton (Nobel Prize for chemistry): "The genome is reproduced very faithfully and there are enzymes which repair the DNA, where errors have been made or when the DNA is damaged." **Evolution won't work, because stasis is maintained within living systems**. [35]
> [emphasis added]

Epigenetics

Having said that, it is important to point out that one of the latest DNA discoveries has shown that our DNA can and does change to **adapt** to our environment (a form of *Natural Selection* and *Survival of the Fittest* combined). Epigenetics describes the way plants and animals acquire changes in their DNA <u>during their lifetimes</u> – before passing the changes on to their offspring – and <u>before</u> the changes are fully coded in the parents' DNA: "While the person's underlying DNA code never changes, epigenetics programs genetic modifications that can be passed on to his or her offspring." [36]

> *Remember, "The [genetic and dietary] sins of the fathers are passed down to the succeeding generations..."*

This is not mutation; it is a case of the reproductive sperm and eggs receiving the new genetic code which manifests in the offspring due to the action of an epigenetic marker attached to the gene. The DNA is more like hardware while the **epigenome** is the software that tells the gene to switch on/off. Current research indicates that the epigenetic marks can fade in the offspring and DNA will revert to its original programming...if the epigenetic change is not crucial to the existence of the organism. Thus a major factor in permanent genetic change is still that of natural selection.

The great hope in current research is that the epigenetic marks can be influenced to switch on/off and aid in the management of disease by suppressing or activating appropriate genes. As Chapter 3 pointed out, HIV/AIDS may be controllable by suppressing the coding for protein on the outer shell of the T4 white cell – to which HIV attaches before doing its dirty work… If this can be epigenetically controlled, as in the case of the **CCR5*delta*32 mutation**, and influence the macrophage to lose 32 base pairs, it is conceivable that an epigenetic change in Man can subvert the operation of HIV and render Man immune to it. Naturally one wonders if this is how the Anunnaki stopped the *Suruppu* and *Asakku* diseases…?

> Epigenetics has made scientists realize that the old nature-versus-nuture debate isn't just passé; it's unhelpful… Genes influence our behavior to a great extent, but thanks to epigenetics, we now know that the environment can change our genes, too. [37]

In addition, we now know <u>why</u> Man can be more complex than other creatures on Earth but possess a less or equal number of genes. Epigenetics is the reason. [38]

DNA, Bacteria and UV Light

As is pointed out later with respect to DNA's ability to morph, due to sound and or light, and having just said that it has the ability to repair itself, there is an exception to this. It has been found that the DNA in bacteria and other pathogens that have been subjected to UltraViolet Light Type C (or UV-C) has been 'deactivated' and the bacteria cannot replicate and cause disease.

> As UV light penetrates through the cell wall and cytoplasmic membrane, it causes a molecular rearrangement of the microorganism's DNA, which prevents it from reproducing. Specifically, UV-C light causes damage to the nucleic acid of microorganisms by forming covalent bonds between certain adjacent bases in the DNA. The formation of such bonds prevent the DNA from being unzipped for replication, and the organism is unable to reproduce. In fact, when the organism tries to replicate, it dies. [39]

In this case, the UV-C light bathes the whole organism and affects <u>all</u> of its DNA, whereas (above in the section "DNA Auto-repair") the minor amount of affected DNA might cause cancer but the organism would still live and replicate. The point being how sensitive or fragile DNA really is – to sound, light, EMF, chemicals in the food we eat…

DNA and Behavior

A person's basic behavior tends to be set while in the womb, due to his DNA, according to the latest findings.

> From the moment we become conscious as a child, the programming of our reality begins. In fact it begins in the womb through the mother. We already start with a 'body' that carries its inherited reality programming through the DNA, and this usually includes genetic subservience to authority and a sense of "I am small and insignificant." … the minds of vast numbers of people are

prisoners of their body's genetic programming and responses… In such people an inherited genetic trait like alcoholism will be repeated in their own experience. **Those with a consciousness more powerful than the genetic programming will be able to override it and avoid the repetition**… the programming of a body hologram – its "library of experience" – is passed on through the DNA to its successors in the line. The body holograms contain all the information accumulated by all the expressions of that DNA since the line 'began….'
[When a person is born] the incoming consciousness has to cope with all those inherited programmes, beliefs, and assumptions of reality… "Do you wonder any longer why people are so easy to manipulate when they inherit that genetic programming to start with?" It said that most people expended so much energy coping with the inherited responses, reactions, desires and demands of their body **hologram** that they had little left to look up and see beyond the illusion. [40] [emphasis added]

The point was made elsewhere that our DNA does influence who and what we are and what we can do. It affects our hair/eye color, our ability to see colors, our ability to move, think and learn, our IQ, and it affects our basic nature – sanguine, phlegmatic, etc. And in the following sections dealing with German and then Russian DNA discoveries, this will become more apparent. It even affects our language ability.

DNA and Intelligence

For years it has been argued that IQ is the result of heredity (genetics) and environment. Today's scientists decided to test that premise by evaluating identical twins who have been separated at birth and raised by different parents, some poor, some rich. They have the same genes but experience different environments. The results were surprising.

"Identical twins reared apart are almost as similar as identical twins reared together… By the age of 16 these adopted-away children resemble their biological parents' IQ just as much as kids who are reared by their biological parents… [thus] genes have a crucial role in intelligence. [41]

Despite assiduous research, however, **specific genes for intelligence have not been found, and IQ remains a big mystery.** Yet, genes play a big role, based on studies with twins, and the suspicion is that there are many genes involved that together act to determine just how intelligent a person can be – not that they will in all cases actualize that potential, just that it is there. It would seem that a person's environment makes the difference in whether the potential is fulfilled or not.

[Dr. Turkheimer] found that the strength of genes' effect depended on the socioeconomic status of the [identical twins]. In children from affluent families, about 60% of the variance in IQ scores could be accounted for by genes. For children from impoverished families, on the other hand, genes accounted for almost none… Turkheimer posits that poverty brings with it powerful environmental [and nutritional] forces that may shape intelligence from the womb through school and onward. But when children grow up in

284

the relative stability of an affluent home, gene-based differences can begin to make themselves felt. [42] [emphasis added]

In short, the overall conclusion was that "…genes played little role in the variance of scores among poor children and played a far stronger one in more affluent children." [43] In addition, it was found that **breast-feeding** children could positively result in a boost in IQ – if the children had a particular variant of a certain gene. [44] Research is on-going and frustrating as the issue is so complex.

> *It will eventually be discovered that the incoming soul's "ground of being" imprints the DNA with the IQ potential – assuming no genetic defects to stop the brain from "wiring" more connections to functionally serve a high IQ.*

German Research

Biophotons

In a book entitled Vernetzte Intelligenz ("Intelligent Network") by Fosar and Bludorf, the authors maintain that light is the most important food in the world for our bodies. They liken the DNA to a "Living Internet" where the light is communicating information throughout our bodies over a Bionet using **biophotons**. [45] Photons are small **quanta** of light emitted by the DNA, hence the "bio" aspect of the phenomenon.

> *Note: their book has not been translated into English (as of 2013) and all their subsequent quotes are from their own, personally-written English article, entitled "The Biological Chip in our Cells."*

Another German scientist, Fritz Popp, was the first to discover the phenomenon of **biophotons** which aid in cell repair and coordination of various body parts.

> Photons switch on the body's processes like a conductor launching each individual instrument into the collective [orchestral] sound. At different frequencies they perform different functions. Popp found with experimentation that molecules in the cells would respond to certain frequencies and that **a range of vibrations from the photons would cause a variety of frequencies in other molecules of the body**. Light waves also answered the question of how the body could manage complicated feats with different body parts instantaneously or do two things at once. These "biophoton emissions," as he was beginning to call them, could provide a perfect communication system, to transfer information to many cells across the organism. But the single most important question remained: where were they coming from? [46] [emphasis added]

The passage suggests we may be healing with light or microwaves in the future… and Book 2 explores the progress that hjas been made to date (2014).

More than that, **every** living organism emits a natural light radiation, called **biophotons**, which coincidentally contribute to the structure and existence of the **aura** – the EMF or "light body" around the physical body. (Chapter 7) Earlier it was pointed out that OPs do not have an aura and it is now suggested that their fuzzy energy field (instead of an aura) is produced by an insufficient biophoton emission, or one of a different wavelength. This suggests different DNA.

> *Remember the Chuck that was created by radiating a chicken with DNA from a duck? Now you know how it was done – sending the biophoton field and its info from one animal to another. (Think: morphogenetic torus.)*

Fosar and Bludorf report that not only do we emit light, we also <u>take it in</u> from the environment. [47] And we nourish the body with light as well as by the food and water we ingest. They say, ".... the looked for light memory of the body is nothing else than the DNA. It is well known that the DNA is most deeply involved into [sic] the bio photon [quanta] radiation." [48]

Antenna & Superconductor

They further say that DNA is "an ideal electromagnetic antenna" and an "organic super-conductor." It is a great 'antenna' since if it is stretched out, it is over 2 meters long, and it ".... has a natural frequency of 150 megahertz." [49] As a superconductor, it operates at normal room temperature (unlike most superconductors that require extreme cold), and since all superconductors store information, so does DNA.

> *"Junk DNA" may be storing information that we don't even know about; could the Greys' abductees have had information or programming stored in their DNA?*

According to David Icke, DNA being a transmitter and receiver has the potential to constantly affect and <u>be affected by</u> the energy fields around us. [50]

The Bionet

The significance here being that light waves ("*chi*") speed along the 'Intelligent Network' of DNA within our bodies to communicate like an Internet inside the body. This is how acupressure works. When you think of throwing a ball, the message is sent to the arm and all muscles involved – and some people can still walk and chew gum at the same time. The body's internet multitasks.

> For example the ability of superconductors to store Light was just discovered in recent time…. surprising, but …. light…. is not anything seizable [sic]. Light is pure electromagnetic energy, divided into small **quanta**, so-called photons, which…. constantly move with [the] speed of light. [51]

Since DNA is a kind of electromagnetic antenna, sending and receiving light, would it not then also be **susceptible to electromagnetic radiation**? This is actually the case, and was just examined in the Chicken – Duck experiment.

> Independent of the biochemical function as a protein producer the DNA is a complicated electronic biological chip that communicates with its

286

environment, as [the] latest research from Russia found out. [52]

Fritz Popp was really on to the secret of DNA, but at the time he published his findings, the discovery of hormones and the birth of biochemistry eclipsed his work, and his findings were swept aside with the certainty that "….everything could be explained by hormones or chemical reactions." [53]   So, Western science took another step backwards; the first being the adoption of the Theory of Evolution. As we have seen and will see, there is a reason that the Light keeps being buried, and half-truths are promoted vigorously as the complete truth.

Signaling Molecules

Chemicals as hormones, enzymes, (neuro)peptides, and neurotransmitters among many others serve as chemical messengers in the body and brain. They are often referred to as 'signaling molecules' or 'Redox Signaling' and are the major study in the new fields of **psychopharmacology** (prescribing chemicals to effect specific changes in the body/mind), and **psychoneuroimmunology** (using chemicals to condition the immune system).

In fact, it is known that just 4 common atoms can be combined to form very important Redox Signaling Molecules – H_2O (water), NaCl (table salt) and N_2 (nitrogen) are the most common sources and can dissociate and recombine to form H_2O_2 (hydrogen peroxide), HO_2 (hydrogen superoxide), HOCl (hypochlorous acid) and NO (nitric oxide). More common chemical messengers are insulin, testosterone, estrogen, adrenaline and histamine.[54]

While some very physical, chemical means of effecting change have been found operative in the body/brain, let us not forget that **Man is much more than the sum of his parts**… or chemicals. Ensouled Man is a true *gestalt* and only the OPs are just "the sum of the parts." It is the soul operating the body, albeit via emotions, that provoke the chemical messengers to be released. There is a psychosomatic aspect to the human as well as a somato-psychic aspect; one affects the other.

It is clear that both biochemicals and biophotons are the means of communication in the body's biological Internet, or **Bionet** which includes meridians and chakras… shown below.

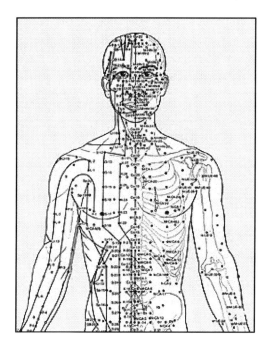

The Bionet: Chi Meridians – Accupuncture Points
(source: http://www.tibetanacademy.org/Images/acumansmall.gif

*What Popp discovered led to another researcher's development of a cure for cancer called Rife Technology after its inventor, Royal Rife. It uses light and parts of the **electromagnetic spectrum** (keyed to the 'vibration' of the cancer) to bombard the cancer with light (electromagnetic) radiation. The developer died and his equipment has disappeared.*

Popp discovered what he called a "radiation theory of DNA" -- confirmed by both the Germans and the Russians. He found that DNA

> ....emitted a permanent current of photons, from only a few to hundreds. The number of photons emitted seemed to be linked to an organism's position on the evolutionary scale: the more complex the organism, the **fewer** photons being emitted. [55]   [emphasis added]

This was not expected – the more complex and large an organism, the <u>more</u> DNA it would have per square inch of its body and should emit <u>more</u> biophotons. Plants and lower animals emitted about 100 photons per square centimeter, and humans emitted only 10 photons. He also found that people who were dying were losing Light – "their Light was going out." By the same token, MS patients had too much Light. In a state of stress, photon emission went up, which explains the deleterious effects of stress on the body. [56]

Popp reasoned that light was important to the healthy functioning of the human body. Naturally it dawned on him that he had a potential cure for cancer. And he also tested the quality of food for its biophoton emissions and found that "… the **healthiest food** had the highest and most coherent intensity of Light." The Japanese refer to the energy value of food as "*hado*" and there are charts showing the relative amount of natural 'worth' or *hado* (also called *ki*) and how long its value lasts. Obviously, food losing its energy quotient causes it to spoil and be of little or no value.

DNA and Language

Another interesting aspect of DNA is the faculty of DNA to transmit traits and abilities from person to person – including language ability and the DNA 'presets' a kind of resonance and coding based on the language a person speaks.

> ….it is possible to set the structure of the genetic code in relationship with each existing language of mankind….the structure of the DNA does not correspond to the human language structure, but **the human languages follow the genetic code in their structure** [of] the rules! [57] [emphasis added]

Even more astounding is that DNA has a genetic code which follows the same rules as our human language; **the language we speak is, to a certain extent, controlled by the DNA code.** What he is saying is that even before humans first spoke, their DNA could have been coded to 'create' or support a certain linguistic style. [58] So if researchers were looking for the original language spoken by Man, they could have identified it from today's DNA – if it weren't for the Tower of Babel event. In order to scramble languages, it was thus necessary to alter the DNA to support a different syntax and lexicon. [59]

Dr. Watson corroborates this finding with his comment on what the press has called "the **grammar gene**."

> As we discussed in the context of human evolution… in [year] 2001 mutations detected by Tony Monaco at Oxford in the **FOXP2** gene were found to impair the ability to use and process language. Not only do those so affected have difficulty articulating, but they are stymied by simple grammatical reasoning… FOXP2 affects behavior by shaping the very organ at the center of it all… if I am right, many of the most important genes governing behavior will indeed turn out to be those involved in constructing … the human brain. [60]

So there is a genetic component involved in our behavior and our ability to process language, and it is suspected that the genetic-cellular-behavioral-linguistic interfaces are complex.

Human languages did not appear coincidentally, but are now said to be a reflection of our DNA, and since there are different languages, there had to be different DNA (in the FoxP2 gene) … so were there multiple Adams and Eves, or what event happened to give different Men different DNA and thus different languages? Remember the Tower of Babel?

What this suggests is that the Anunnaki were such masters of genetics that they knew where and how to alter Man's DNA in the brain to effect the language changes; i.e., set up new neural pathways and stored vocabularies with inherent grammar reflected in the DNA. It would be interesting to see if current-day researchers could employ **hypnotism** or **encephaloprogramming** techniques to give a person a new language and total control of it within a few hours of alteration in a language lab.

Hypercommunication

Maybe we can give a fifth point to Sitchin for that one, too. Sitchin says this about language and DNA:

> Did the Almighty, who had revealed to Moses the secret of the alphabet, then **use the genetic code as the secret code of the alphabet?** The answer seems to be yes. If this conclusion seems outlandish, let us read the Lord's statement in Isaiah 45:11: "It is I who created the Letters [of the Hebrew alphabet] ....Whoever was involved in the creation of Man was involved in the creation of the letters that make up the alphabet." [61] [emphasis added]

So what? Note that the genome in Man (<u>without</u> the ability to reproduce, as was stipulated by Sitchin back in Chapter 3) had 22 paired chromosomes. Sitchin suggests it is not a coincidence that the Hebrew alphabet has 22 letters. Interesting that Man's genome has 22 paired chromosomes plus the X/Y factor, or chromosome 23, denoting sex/procreation. Coincidence?

Fosar and Bludorf add:

> The arrangement of the elementary bases in the DNA follows a grammar, an immaterial plan, which is similar to the structure of our languages.... the analogy between the structure of the DNA and the human language is most pronounced just in the parts of the giant molecule, which are not used for protein synthesis.... designated so far as "silent DNA" ['junk' DNA] .... the "silent DNA" – figuratively spoken – speaks a language! .... this code is rather actually used for communication, more exactly – for ***hypercommunication***. Hypercommunication is a data exchange on DNA level using genetic code. Since this code possesses a structure, which is the basis of all human languages, also higher information may be transported, which is able to come up to human consciousness and to be interpreted there. [62] [emphasis added]

So it would appear that there is hypercommunication using the genetic code found in "junk DNA", and the elements or messengers of this data exchange are the hormones and biophotons communicating over the body's Bionet.

This all suggests <u>design</u>, not random evolution.

Junk DNA is not junk. Just because the conventional scientific world cannot figure out what it does, and doesn't have the equipment to test it (as Popp built his own equipment to make his discoveries), that doesn't mean it doesn't do anything. My God, we're still in the stone age in the scientific world: if a tree falls in the forest and a scientist is not there to hear it, it's assumed to not have made a sound. It's true that we should not jump to conclusions and formulate hasty (possibly erroneous) conclusions, but by the same axiom, if it walks like a duck, looks like a duck and quacks like a duck, it probably is a duck! And yet, some scientists will not believe until the duck bites them on the… nose.

Russian Research

DNA and Holograms

Pjotr Garjajev (aka Gariaev of 'Chuck' fame earlier) has also made some fascinating corroborations of the foregoing information, as well as 'pushed the envelope' a bit further to reveal even more interesting aspects of our DNA.

> The DNA chromosomal continuum in living systems has wave attributes. The well-known genetic code [A-T, G-C] is a code for protein synthesis and nothing further. Chromosomes in vivo work as **solitonic holographic** computers under use of the endogenous DNA laser radiation. [63] [emphasis added]

Garjajev's statements are founded on scientific experiments, not theory. So now there is a link between DNA waves and holographic information:

> If one modulates a laser beam by a frequency sample, then one may affect with this the information of the DNA waves and so the genetic information itself…. [and] **one can use quite easily words and sentences of the human language**…. DNA substance in vivo [in living matter] reacts to language-modulated laser light, even to radio waves…. One may design devices with which through suitably modulated radio or light beam radiation cell metabolism may be affected, even the repair of genetic defects is possible without all the risks and side effects of [chemotherapy]. [64] [emphasis added]

If sound affects our DNA, what is the sound of Heavy Metal at 120db doing to our DNA?

Psychoneuroimmunology

This is suggesting that under hypnotherapy, there is power in the spoken word, or in laser-mediated light, and the Russians have tested that and found:

…the **DNA is able to react directly to the spoken word**. [65]

This is another aspect of the new field of psychoneuroimmunology (see section 'Signaling Molecules' earlier) – the effect of the mind and word on the immune system – healing akin to hypnotic suggestion. Both chemicals and the mind can affect the immune system, but the Russians have taken things way down the field.

It has been demonstrated that a hypnotized subject's arm can be touched with the eraser

291

end of a pencil, be told that that is a lit cigarette, and immediately a welt/burn will appear where the pencil touched his arm. Just as easily, a burn can be made to heal through the power of suggestion. And lastly, it has been observed that patients with **MPD**, Multiple Personality Disorder, demonstrate different physical attributes and memories when each of the personalities comes forth: one personality has asthma, another has no asthma but needs strong prescription glasses, and yet a third has eczema – which does not appear in the case of the other two personalities. [66]

According to the Russian research, **words have power:**

> … the higher developed an individual's consciousness is, the less need is there for any type of [healing] device: once can achieve these results by oneself…. One can simply use words and sentences of the human language." [67]

Lastly, **DNA can be programmed by light**, or more precisely, by laser.

> The Russian scientists irradiated DNA samples with laser light. On screen, a typical **wave pattern** was formed. When they removed the DNA sample, the wave pattern did not disappear, it remained…. the energy field apparently remained by itself. This effect is now called **phantom DNA effect**. It is surmised that energy [from the environment and space] still flows through the activated wormholes [sic] after the DNA was removed. The side effects encountered most often in hyper-communication in humans are inexplicable **electromagnetic fields** in the vicinity of the persons concerned.
>
> Electronic devices like CD players and the like can be irritated and cease to function for hours. When the electromagnetic field slowly dissipates, the devices function normally again. [68] [emphasis added]

All this is to say that **we are much more than we think we are**; we can do more than we think we can; and there are other places in the Father's Creation where we can use our developed abilities… IF we can wake up and overcome the entities who seek to keep Man from developing his connection to the Godhead and from being a realized human being as a Jesus …or Buddha, or Krishna.

DNA and Language, Revisited

Remember, only 3% of our DNA is used for coding proteins involved in the reproduction of our species. The other 97% which is considered to be "junk DNA" by Western researchers, is very much part of our language ability and a process now called **hypercommunication**.

First, our genetic code found within that 'useless' 97% of our DNA, serves as data storage and communication. And, the genetic code follows the same rules as the language we speak.

> They found that the alkalines of our DNA follow regular grammar and do have set rules just like our languages. So **human languages did not appear coincidentally but are a reflection of our inherent DNA**. [69] [emphasis added]

Apparently there is a sequence (called a 'grammar' or 'rules') to the way our 'junk' DNA arranges itself and that can be correlated with the language we speak – whether the language is complicated like Russian, or less complicated like Spanish. Russian has 6 grammar cases, German has 4 cases, and Spanish does not use cases. (And, FYI, the Basque language has 12 cases… what were they thinking?)

> **Cases** are grammar constructs that change the endings of words in a sentence, usually the nouns. So, the Russian word Karandash is the noun for pencil….
>
> In the sentence, "I write **with** a pencil," 'with' triggers the Instrumental Case ending, and Karandash becomes **Karandashom**.
> If I say "The lead is **in** the pencil", the word 'in' triggers the Prepositional Case ending, and Karandash becomes **Karandashe**.
> And if I say, "The pencil**'s** color is red" that tiggers the Genetive Case ending and Karandash becomes **Karandashov**. And so on…
>
> Now don't you love case-free English, French, Spanish…?

Thus the DNA coding sampled for these 3 native speakers would show differences consistent within their language types. That is, all native Spanish speakers would have a similar genetic coding for language, and all native Russian speakers would have a similar genetic coding for their language – but those two codings would be consistently different, in some way, from the English-speaking person.

That raises two issues:

1. What happens to the genetic coding when a person speaks 2 or more languages? It would seem, consistent with what has been said, that the DNA coding would diversify or gain a complexity – unless it is compart-mentalized…
    And why when a person speaks 4 languages, do the languages and vocabulary not mix and mingle as one language is being spoken?
    And does this explain what happens when a person from, say the Philippines, tries to learn English, they can **never learn English perfectly**, and will always speak English with some Filipino grammar superimposed on English? (Think: the Tagalog word 'sa' serves for he or she… similar to Spanish 'su'…)

    BTW, "This" in Spanish is Esta and in Russian it is Eta…. Hmmm.

2. Can a new language be programmed into the DNA overnight – as was Allegedly done at the Tower of Babel, and where in the DNA would it be 'stored?'

Second, the issue of **hypercommunication** really is describing access to knowledge that is outside of one's usual 'database' – in essence, inspiration or intuition. It has also been suggested that were the DNA researchers to compare the DNA of a known and proficient psychic and with that of a normal, non-psychic, person that the DNA would be different in key areas of the 'junk' DNA – that the psychic has 'coding' for the abilities s/he has.

DNA is a key to Man gaining advanced (paranormal) abilities. He already has the Bionet for it and plenty of unused DNA, let us hope that with power comes wisdom and compassion, and that that is why we are so constrained in our current situation on Earth. Man must come from the heart not just the head. Let's see why…

The Human Heart and DNA

As a wrap-up, Joseph Chilton Pearce has some corresponding and interesting comments on DNA, the heart and the brain.

We all know we have brain waves that can be measured, and we have most of us had an EKG or an EEG taken – showing that there is a slight electromagnetic field around the body. Pearce says that the heart puts out an energy field shaped like a **torus** (doughnut-shaped field), and the strength of the field (which can be measured from 3 feet away)

> …. produces 2 and a half watts of electrical energy with each heartbeat at an amplitude forty to sixty times greater than that of brain waves – enough to light a small electric bulb. This energy forms an electromagnetic field [em] that radiates out some twelve to fifteen feet beyond the body itself. [70]

The torus also appears to be **holographic** – meaning that "…. any point within the torus contains the information of the whole field." [71] And that signifies that at any infinitesimal point in the heart's torus, all frequencies are present. There's that holographic aspect again… one begins to get the idea that a lot of our world is a hologram, or hologram-based. And that is one of the key subjects of Chapter 12.

At this point, notice that the heart of a duck would also have a torus containing info reflecting its duck DNA… and what if this toroidal info could be transmitted to a chicken…would it affect the chicken's toroidal DNA via some morphogenetic field? (See 'Chuck' in earlier section.)

Book 2 deals with this aspect of toroidal fields and the Morphogentic interfaces between Living things.

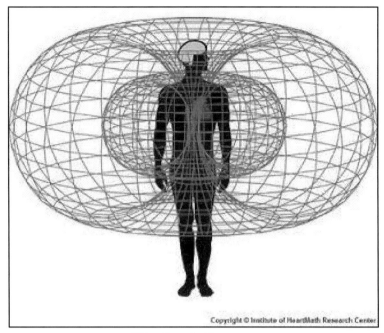

The Heart's Torus

Pearce goes further to make the connection with DNA:

> The heart radiation saturates every cell, DNA molecule, glia, and so on, and helps determine their function and destiny. From this viewpoint the heart seems a **frequency generator**, creating the fields of information out of which we build our experience of ourselves and the world. [72] [emphasis added]

and

> When brain and heart frequencies **entrain**, they enter a synchronous, resonant, or coherent wave pattern…. Our heart maintains an intricate dialog with our brain, body and world at large and selects from the hierarchy of em [electromagnetic] fields the information appropriate to our particular experience. This dynamic feedback influences and modifies the very fields of energy from which we spring. [73]

It would be interesting to verify that the heart, body and brain are communicating with each other over the Bionet discussed earlier. Perhaps there is a way to synch up an encephalograph (brain) with a machine recording a cardiogram (heart)…. ?

And lastly, he writes that

> …. **em** fields can act on our physical health both positively and negatively on a cellular level…. physicians in Holland use em fields to heal cancer. **DNA is em-sensitive**, allowing some em fields to regulate DNA, RNA, and protein synthesis, as well as to induce cell differentiation and morpho-

295

genesis. Rupert Sheldrake's **morphogenetic fields** may involve electro-magnetic energy as well as nonlocal effects beyond current knowledge.[74] [emphasis added]

This should give us new cause to think about what a cellphone apparatus connected all day to our ear is doing to the brain cells just 1/2" away. The cellphone EMF radiates strongly in a plume up to 2-3" (in all directions) from the antenna. [75] Brain cells are delicate and the EMF of the cellphone is impacting the braincells' energy [76] – perhaps interfering with their normal em function – overriding the normal, lower em field of the brain cells with a stronger more dominant field. Only time will tell what such a situation is producing.

What is really important to see is that the human being is a beautifully complex, integrated organism with sophisticated DNA, a Bionet, interacting electromagnetic fields, and a brain-heart connection that actually gives every human the ability to linearly reason (brain) about something and then to appropriate the more holistic capability of the heart's intelligence. **Half or more of the cells in the heart are neural (glial) cells like in the brain**, and the heart uses this foundation to sense and regulate the bodily functions so that the brain does not have to be consciously controlling body temperature, digestion, breathing, and hormonal regulation, for example.[77]

So if Man could "pull it all together," reprogram his DNA, set new neural pathways in his brain, use more of the power of his mind, what could he do? Is anyone on the threshold of being and doing more?

Paranormal Abilities

Note that certain people in today's world have been able to walk on water, levitate, know what is behind closed doors, put their hand thru the glass of an aquarium without breaking the glass and remove an object, put a quarter inside a sealed can of Coke, disappear, and read people's minds. Such were the demonstrations of **Criss Angel**, featured on satellite TV in 2007 on a program called *Mind Freak*.

One of Criss' most astounding bits of 'magic' was going into a supermarket, with a video camera recording everything. **No breaks in recording**. He went into the produce section by the oranges and lemons. A woman was asked to select an orange, another person was asked to select a lemon and a store clerk was asked to select one egg from a carton of eggs selected by another person. Criss took the selected egg in one hand and took the selected lemon in his other hand, focused in heavy concentration, and quickly brought his two hands together. Instead of a broken egg, just the lemon was left. He then took the selected lemon in one hand and the orange in the other, and as before, with heavy focused concentration, he brought his two hands quickly together – and only the orange was left. He had the boy carefully inspect the orange, showed it to the camera, and it was solid. He then asked for a knife and carefully cut the orange open – to find the lemon inside it. He carefully cut the lemon open to find the egg inside – which was opened and inside was a live chick. Absolutely awesome. Obviously more than magic.

Perhaps a relevant question is, Did Criss do these things himself, with advanced abilities that he somehow developed, or were they done through him by the Neggs with the agenda of deceiving and/or entertaining people? Or is he an alien? And yet his public demonstrations are a <u>reminder</u> of what ensouled Man can do when plugged into a Divine Source, as was the man called Jesus.

A Britisher, **Derren Brown**, followed suit the same year with his TV program called *Mind Control*. He deftly performed a lot of mental feats, such as removing a man's memory and putting it back, with the wave of his hand; knowing what someone was about to say with very high accuracy; and being able to manipulate buyers into buying something they didn't want. He could also correctly tell if people were lying, and he could correctly read their minds to identify a secret word known only to them.

Darren admitted on the show that he was astute at reading body language and using the power of suggestion to manipulate people, and yet the mind-reading episodes (unless staged) showed significant psychic ability.

If Darren and Criss actually performed their above-named feats from an innate ability, that suggests that their DNA is different. Or are they among the Others walking among us who look human but have 4D abilities that we don't have?

4D Abilities

These things are psychic abilities normally attributed to the 4D world and renowned quantum physicist **Michio Kaku** has a potential explanation: "…feats of wizardry could be explained if one could somehow move objects through the fourth dimension." [78]

A psychic **Henry Slade** was performing feats of magic that were astounding back in 1877:

> First, Slade was given two separate, unbroken wooden rings and asked to join them without breaking them… Second, he was given the shell of a sea snail…could Slade transform a right-handed shell into a left-handed shell? Third, he was given a closed loop of rope made of dried animal gut. Could he make a knot in the circular rope without cutting it? … Slade was also asked to remove the contents of a sealed bottle without breaking the bottle. [79]

Needless to say, he did these things, just as Criss Angel performed some of his marvels. While Criss will not say where he got his knowledge and just how he puts a quarter inside a sealed can of Coke, Kaku has a basic explanation from Quantum Physics:

> …. in three dimensions it is impossible to convert a right-handed object into a left-handed one. Humans are born with hearts on their left side, and no surgeon, no matter how skilled, can reverse internal human organs. This is possible… only if we lift the body out of our universe, rotate it in the fourth dimension, and then reinsert it back into our universe… [it] can be performed only **if objects can be moved in the forth dimension**. [80] [emphasis added]

The point is: if we were in 4D (within a 3D construct), feats of magic and mental wizardry just await the person who knows how to use the fourth dimension to disappear, walk on water, turn water to wine, put an egg inside a lemon inside an orange …. While this may be our heritage, or destiny, personally, I'm glad this knowledge is not more available, because its common use could lead to chaos if used by spiritually undisciplined people.

What Earth really is and why most of us can't all activate our divine abilities will be better explained in the last 4 chapters. However, remember that the chapters on OPs disclosed that there are Others here among us – they look like humans but aren't, and would they not be able to manipulate reality to amaze us… for their agenda? The Anunnaki literature recounts how the **Anunnaki hybrids** were able to do things that the humans could not do. Hence it is important to start recognizing truth and acquiring a sense of discernment so that you will have the option of identifying false agendas and rejecting them.

When one reflects on the errors of Science, History and Religion one will have a sense that all is not what it seems, and one will learn to question and research issues. Hopefully better discernment of lies vs truth in the future is a by-product of that awakening process, and that builds Light in a person's soul – the Light one needs to get out of here.

Chapter 10: -- Earth History

Geologic Timetable

A lot of what we call Earth History is based on traditional suppositions fed us by those who believe in and promote the idea of Evolution. Geologists, archeologists, and historians to name a few, want to sustain the notion that the planet is 4.5 billion years old, and that Man went thru stages of evolution from a basic hominid to what he is today. To prove this, the geologists who believe in Evolution also devised a geologic timetable to support the Theory of Evolution -- but the timetable is based on the <u>assumption</u> that the planet is 4.5 billion years old.

The timetable below does not reflect any hard, scientific fact – in fact the Earth evidence presented in the Section " Young Earth Evidence" shows the opposite of an old planet.

<u>Period</u>	<u>Time (mil. of years)</u>	<u>Life Forms</u>
Quaternary	0 - 1	Rise of Man
Tertiary	62	Rise of Mammals
Cretaceous	72	Seed-bearing plants Dinosaurs
Jurassic	46	First Birds
Triassic	49	First dinosaurs
Permian	50	First reptiles
Pennsylvanian	30	Shells, insects
Missippian	35	Crinoids
Devonian	60	Plants, fish
Silurian	20	Earliest land animals
Ordovician	75	Early bony fish
Cambrian	100	Invertebrates
Pre-Cambrian	???	Bacteria-algae-pollen?

Simplified Geologic Time Scale
(source: The Young Earth, J.D. Morris, p.8)

Anybody notice that the years don't add up to 4.5 billion? They total 600 million, and no one knows for sure how long each period was, so there are some 'guesstimates' in the list. In addition, the fossil record shows that Dinosaurs and Man were here <u>together</u>, [1] and there is a human footprint form in Permian rock! [2] The timescale was arbitrarily decided on, and subsequent students in Biology and Geology have come to accept the Chart.

In addition, the Geologic Timetable with its emphasis on geologic strata, or layers of Earth across the centuries, has given the wrong impression of coal formation and the age of rocks and fossils.

Coal Formation

One problem with using geologic strata as proof of Earth's age is that adjacent layers in coal strata, for example, have been assigned ages that easily span millions of years; strata level 1 is said to have been deposited first, and then after much time passed, strata level 2 was deposited, and so on with stratas 3 and 4... Coal mines were formed from peat or the decay of living organic matter, especially trees. In some coal mines, up to 50 different coal seams are stacked on top of each other, each layer supposedly taking a lot of time to create. Or so we're told...

In many coal mines across the US, there have been found '**polystrate trees**' – trees which fossilized intact, before decaying, and they extend thru more than one layer! This suggests that there was rapid, continuous coal accumulation – it had to be rapidly formed because the peat forming around the tree could not take millions of years to form without the tree disintegrating before the coal was created. The trees must have grown in place and then there was a rapid sedimentation and coalification while the tree was intact – because that is what is found: complete (fossilized) trees extending thru several coal layers and into the shale layer. [3]

Coal does not take millions of years to form. It has been created in the laboratory in a matter of just weeks – under artificially created pressure and heat. [4] The video (The Young Age of the Earth. Glenn Aufderhar, in Video bibliography) shows that two scientists took a 1" cube of fresh-cut wood and put it in a high pressure chamber, generating intense heat, and when they removed the cube several weeks later, it was not charred wood – it was in fact coal. If it had been left in longer, and subjected to the moisture found in the Earth when coal is created naturally, it would have been more 'glossy' looking.

The generally accepted geologic and historic explanations for our planet sometimes need closer scrutiny than we at first suspect. Another error concerns the dinosaurs and Man: it is said that Man came along quite a bit after the dinosaurs – Man was supposedly Cenozoic and the dinosaurs were, at the latest, Mesozoic – something like millions of years apart.

There is geologic, fossil evidence to prove that Man and the dinosaurs were here at the same time... dinosaur tracks alongside Man tracks in Glen Rose, Texas. Sometimes the Man tracks are inside the dinosaur tracks. [5,6]

The point being that the geologic timetable has been constructed to agree with the concept of Evolution and does not necessarily reflect the true chronology of Earth's history.

Oil Formation

The traditional story is that the remains of plants and animals decomposed into organic material that became trapped in rock strata and then heat and pressure transformed the decaying material into hydrocarbons, then coal, oil and natural gas. [7] This is called a biological origin.

Recent discovers of oil at the 30,000 foot level have discovered oil, and the question is: How did plants and animals get 6 miles down in the Earth? Current experiments in the laboratory have shown that oil also has an **abiotic** origin: at extreme temperatures and pressures, oil can form without organic material. [8] The Russians have argued and proven that petroleum can originate from minerals deep in the Earth, and later experiments have shown that synthetic oil can be made from minerals alone. [9] *Mobil1* anyone?

> [The] … Gas Resources Corporation in Houston Texas… produced octane and methane by subjecting marble, iron oxide and water to temperature and pressure conditions similar to that 60 miles below the surface of the Earth. [10]

More amazing is that **some oil reserves have been found to replenish themselves** (abiotically):

> Gulf of Mexico oil field Eugene Island 330, for example, saw its production drop from 15,000 barrels a day in 1973 to 4,000 barrels a day in 1989, and then suddenly spontaneously reversed and was pumping 13,000 barrels of a "different aged" crude in 1999…. In fact, according to Christopher Cooper of the Wall Street Journal, "between 1976 and 1996 estimated global oil reserves grew 72% …. And considering the doubling of reserves in the Middle East alone, …. it would take a pretty big pile of dead dinosaurs and prehistoric plants to account for the estimated 660 billion barrels of oil in the region." [11]

> *Of course this assumes that a depleted oil field was not 'rejuvenated' by an adjacent inflowing oil field, or that the figure above for the increase in global oil reserves is not due to the opening of new oil fields…*

In any event, the fact that petroleum can be created **abiotically** as well as coal – in the laboratory, and neither one requires millions of years to develop, is the important point. This is very significant when Chapter 12 reveals what Earth really is.

Carbon-14 Dating Revisited

Dating rocks, fossils and petrified trees based on the decay rate of Carbon-14 (C14) in them is based on the assumption of Uniformitarianism – that things decay at the same rate forever. Restated, the ***assumption*** is that the rate of aging, or decay, of C14 in any tested object was constant throughout all the history of the Earth. It is merely an assumption. In reality

> ….the [C14] method is valid only for 'recent' times. Even the most devoted advocate would not claim that it has anything at all to say beyond about 60,000 years before the present time, and its inaccuracies are well-known. On the other hand, the [C14] technique *does* have some application in the most recent few thousand years. [12]

So C-14 cannot be used to try and establish the true age of the Earth, nor as a way to determine which geologic strata fossils belong to. Whether the Earth is young or old must be evaluated based on other criteria, and caution is advised.

Say the scientists:

> Neither the old-earth nor the young-earth idea can be scientifically proven by geologic observations, and likewise, neither can be disproved. [13]

The young Earth argument will not go into whether or not God created the world and all in it within 6 days since we don't know what length of time was represented by a "day" in the Genesis account. We're looking for as much physical evidence as possible to see whether the Evolution or the Creation model is supported by the physical evidence on Earth. It is not necessary to try to substantiate the Genesis account; today's recent evidence speaks for itself.

In any event, the planet looks a lot younger than its alleged age of 4 ½ billion years old, and more progressive scientists today are considering dating the Earth at a lot younger age.

Young Earth Evidence

To avoid making this a long chapter, it is sufficient to list only 9 issues that today's scientists have discovered about the Earth that make them think that it is as young as 10,000 – 20,000 years old, and possibly as old as 2 million years old. The difference in age arises in the aging/dating methods discussed earlier which are still subject to criticism.

The main arguments in favor of Earth being somewhere between 10,000 years to 2 million years old contradict the Evolutionary model. The old Evolutionary model needed 4.5 billion years to allow for evolution from a primordial sea of goop to evolve into Man; the Evolutionist thinking being that that is enough time for *something* evolutionary to have happened. Young Earth scientists, and their number is growing, believe that the evidence presented below suggests other than an old Earth.

Fossils

First, **there are no intermediate stages of dinosaurs** which would show a dinosaur species evolving into a new species. In addition, there are eggs and adults but no juvenile forms of the same species. The absence of 'transitionary fossils' kills Evolutionary theory [14] because over a very long period of time, there <u>should be</u> transition fossils. The fact that there aren't any means the dinosaurs weren't here for that long, and thus there are some real 'holes' in the Evolutionary Theory <u>and</u> the Geologic Time Scale.

> The fossil record shows no evidence that any basic category of animal has ever evolved from or into any other basic category. [15]

and…

...the curious thing is that there is a consistency about the fossil gaps: **the Fossils go missing in all the important places**. When you look for links between major groups of animals, they simply aren't there...[16]

And lastly,

All paleontologists know that the fossil record contains precious little in the way of intermediate forms; transitions between major groups are characteristically **abrupt**. [17] [emphasis added]

"Abrupt" suggests intervention, as if the new group had external help to produce an 'upgrade' or variegated replica of the original group – like hummingbird to condor.

If the dinosaurs were here for millions of years (Triassic – Jurassic – Cretaceous), then why are there no intermediate forms or transition skeletons found indicating that Evolution did take place? And why are there so few dinosaur bones found?

Findings in the fossil record contradict **the Darwinian view that species arise gradually over long periods of time**. In fact, there is no evidence for the gradual appearance of one species out of another. There is no evidence of intermediate species, linking one form to another... [18] [emphasis added]

In addition, there is no fossil evidence to 'document' the transition from reptile to bird (Triassic to Jurassic), nor is there any evidence to show how the finned fish evolved. [19]

Population

Second, calculations regarding **Earth's population statistics supports a young earth**. It is noted that at a population growth rate of 2% per year, which has been observed for almost a century, and given a current 6+ billion population, it has been calculated that it would only take 1100 years to reach the present population from an original pair of humans. And that isn't counting wars and death. [20] Even if wars and death are included, and plagues, wars, mass weaponry, crowded cities, abortion rates and famines are included, the population growth rate hasn't changed much. [21]

Even more interesting is to do the math from the other end: assume Man has been here for a million years, and use the 2% growth rate per year, and then estimate how many people would be on the planet today:

The number is so large, it is meaningless, and it's approximately the number which could fit **inside** the volume of the entire Earth.... there should be about 10 to the 8600th power, or 10 with 8600 zeroes following it.... [and if that's true,] where are their bones? [22]

Anthropologists tell us that **Man has <u>not</u> been here for a million years**:

....civilization dates to only five thousand or so years ago, at the beginning of human history.... Archeologists have shown that in a variety of places around the world, **very advanced, modern cultures sprang up suddenly, almost simultaneously.... Human culture from its very start was advanced, and humans have always been intelligent**. [23] [emphasis added]

Sitchin would agree. And according to the Sumerian accounts, Man as we know him, civilization and all, was begun right after the Flood – about 8,000 years ago.

No Bones

Third, if Man has been evolving for millions of years on the Earth, **why are there so few bones found?** Starting just 1 million years ago and using a 2% growth rate, yet finding today a population of 6+ billion, where are all the millions of bones from those who must have died? [24] The same question can be asked of the dinosaurs, also supposedly here for millions of years.

Magnetic Field

Fourth, the **Earth's magnetic field has been decaying at a constant rate** since it was first measured in 1835, and using that rate (with 1400 years half-life) and extrapolating backwards, it can be determined that the magnetic field must have been much stronger in the past. Such a field is necessary for life on earth as it stops harmful cosmic radiation from killing lifeforms. Yet if the field were too strong, using the doubling factor every 1400 years, just 100,000 years ago life would have been life living on a dense neutron star here – impossible. [25]

So, either the decay rate is not constant, or if it is, the planet is not more than 10-12,000 years old.

Helium

Fifth, **the amount of helium found in the atmosphere is a clincher for a young Earth**.

Helium is produced below the Earth's surface by a process of radioactive decay. According to the latest scientific measurements, 13 million helium atoms escape into the atmosphere every second. And the amount of helium atoms escaping the Earth's atmosphere into space is 0.3 million per second. Thus helium is accumulating at a very rapid rate... doing the math, based on the amount of helium in today's atmosphere, delivers a figure of 2 million years old maximum as an age of the Earth. That is, assuming that the rates of escape have been uniform... but what is weird is that helium is in abundance in the rocks, and not in the atmosphere, so the Earth is much younger than 2 million years old. [26]

Sediment

Sixth, sediment on the ocean floor is another good measure of age of the Earth. Since the Earth has been covered with water from Day 1, and water is constantly eroding the continents, **there should be a lot of sediment on the ocean floor. There isn't**. The rate of sedimentation has been found to be a fairly consistent 27.5 billion tons per year. Yet the amount of measured sediment on the ocean floor today stands at 410 million billion tons. Simple math arrives at a maximum possible age of 15 million years (assuming a uniform rate, and no biblical Flood).[27]

Salty Ocean

Seventh, **salt in the ocean should be getting saltier** with the years and if the original ocean was salty, 3-4 billion years ago, shouldn't it be <u>too</u> salty now? The scientists studying the ocean asked themselves the same question and set about determining the 11 types and amounts of salt input to the ocean and the 7 types and amounts of output – i.e., the ways that the ocean can gain and lose salt. These were quantified and, using the minimum and maximum values that they developed, the maximum age of the ocean can only be 62 million years old. That is not saying that the Earth is 62 million years old, just that it couldn't be any older than that. [28]

And that is not considering whatever the Flood of Noah's day may have done to alter the rate of salt gain/loss…

Meteor Dust

Eighth, meteoric dust from space has been accumulating on the Moon and Earth since the beginning, and it was feared in the early 1960's that if we tried to land on the Moon, there **should be a foot or more of dust** and that could adversely affect landing and takeoff. Measurements back in the '50s and '60s indicated that meteorite dust was coming onto the Earth and Moon at the rate of 14 million tons per year. That dust includes a lot of iron and nickel. It was inferred

> …that if the Earth has been here for 5 billion years, then there should be enough such material here on Earth to form a layer over 150 feet thick. No one expected to find such a layer, of course, since the Earth's surface is continually mixed by rain, wind, erosion, etc, but it *did* bother scientists that **nickel is so rare on Earth.** If the Earth is old, and the rate of accumulation [per the Uniformitarian assumption used by Evolutionists themselves] has been the same throughout Earth history, there ought to be more! The Earth's nickel content is much more compatible with a young Earth than with an old Earth. [29] [emphasis added]

So what about the Moon? There is no rain, wind or erosion comparable to Earth – what falls on the surface stays there. Later when Man went to the Moon, the dust layer was found to be **only an inch or so**….

> Given the measured rate of influx, this small amount of dust could easily accumulate in a few thousand years, but if the Moon is old, something is wrong. [30]

Of course this argument has been revisited with better and more modern scientific measurements of dust influx, and it has been found that the rate of fall onto Earth and the Moon varies quite a bit, and is <u>not</u> consistent. It falls alternately in both heavy and light cycles. Nevertheless, if Earth is supposed to be 4.5 billion years old, and even if the influx varies, there would have been many cycles of influx resulting in <u>more dust and nickel</u> than we have today on Earth.

Continental Erosion

Ninth, and lastly, there is **the erosion of the continents** (via streams and rivers) which has been consistently measured and calculated to be 27.5 billion tons per year – see 'Sediment' in #6 above. Now it is known that the total land mass above sea level for the last 70 million years (since the last geological upthrust) is 383 million billion tons. Simple math tells us that "[at] present erosion rates, all the continents would be below sea level in 14 million years!" [31]

This last point may not be a valid way to evaluate the age of the Earth as much as it levels a devastating critique against the story that **Uniformitarians** tell. The assumption that decay and erosion processes have proceeded at a uniform rate throughout the Earth's history is just as spurious as the Evolutionary assumption that given an incredible amount of time, all life on Earth could have evolved from a single cell organism in an on-going, uniform process. What really happens over a long period of time is called **entropy** – natural decay, and it has been institutionalized as the Second Law of Thermodynamics.

Thus, **Evolution's worst enemy is time and is not its ally.**

And there are other tests, but the true significance of <u>what appears to be</u> a young Earth will be discussed in Chapter 12. It is also interesting to note that the Jewish culture has been counting years since their inception, and according to them, this is the year 5775 (2014) which tends to suggest that the Flood might have occurred about 6,000 years ago.

> *One may also be struck by the fact that all 9 evidences above do not yield a consensus where all 9 point to the same, or roughly the same, age for the Earth. It is suggested that such would be the case if Earth went through different eras and between each there was a* ***"Wipe and Reboot"*** *or terraforming done before starting the next Era. As weird as that sounds, it has been done, and Chapter 12 offers the rationale for that.*

Chronology Alteration

There are other ways besides geology in which Earth history has been misrepresented, or altered. What is worth considering, is that the chronology of Western Civilization has been seriously altered to give the impression that Man has been on Earth a long time. The following information is not mainstream in the US, and since it has been seriously presented by a man with high credibility and credentials, it is a proposition that does deserve <u>serious consideration</u>. It explains a lot.

> *It should not be accepted in toto until the current, on-going work is done. Much as one cannot judge a painting until it is finished, and Dr. Fomenko is still researching and writing his 7-part tome, it is still worthy of critical evaluation, but it is a critical element among the major points of this book.*

The Chronology Alteration information is presented here because:

(1) it fits with the overall theme of this book, dealing with our general deception by Astral entities, the Elite, and the Anunnaki Remnant, whose purposes are well understood and have been previously stated,

(2) its basic, underlying information has been found to be true, even if the conclusions reached seem far-fetched,

(3) as it is true, all people should know about it — as an impetus to getting out of here.

So consider the following as a **serious** possibility.

Dr. Anatoly Fomenko

Dr. Fomenko is perhaps the first person to notice that something was wrong with history as traditionally reported and taught in our schools. He sought an explanation and applied scientific, logical, linear analysis in a methodology to determine if what appeared to be strange **patterns**, repeated themselves in other historical accounts. What he found was that too many historical accounts all had similar people, events, scenarios, as well as similar elapses of time between the similar events, and he discovered that most historical events, from the ancient to those of just 500 years ago, all seem to have been fabricated on a similar template. He analyzed many historical events, and compiled and compared data until he had enough to present his shocking theory.

Dr. Anatoly Fomenko then wrote a 586-page book called History: Fiction or Science?, vol. 1, which is where he reveals, and reasonably proves, that Western Civilization's chronology has been greatly altered or fabricated. But before examining what the book reveals, let's first look at his credentials:

> Dr. Anatoly Fomenko is a Full Member of the Russian Academy of Sciences, Full Member of the Russian Academy of Natural Sciences, Full Member of the International Higher Education Academy of Sciences, Doctor of Physics and Mathematics, Professor, Head of the Moscow State University Section of Mathematics of the Department of Mathematics and Mechanics, Laureate of the 1996 National Premium of the Russian Federation (in Mathematics), as well as the author of 180 scientific publications, 26 monographs, and textbooks on mathematics. [32]

Peer Review

With that said, the man is a well-respected professor at prestigious Moscow State University and would hardly jeopardize his credibility and future with a bunch of woo-woo ideas -- as incredible as his conclusions appear to be. One of his esteemed peers, Alexander Zinoviev, read his work and had this to say:

> I familiarized myself with the works of A. T. Fomenko …. and they

impressed me greatly. The authors [occasional co-author G.V. Nosovskiy] reveal a way of cogitating that manages to fuse austere logic with dialectic flexibility....They flabbergasted me with their sheer disquisitive might as well as the research results which, in my opinion, can by rights be called the greatest discovery in contemporary historical science – what A. T. Fomenko and his colleagues had learnt over the course of their research was the fact that **the entire history of humanity up until the XVII century is a *forgery of global proportions*....** a falsification as *deliberate* as it is *universal*.

.... a new, blatant, global and premeditated falsification was already in full swing. Prior to becoming familiar with the writings of Fomenko, **I had already known that the falsification of the past was a rather common phenomenon inherent in human existence. However, I was [not] aware of the scale of this fraud....** [33] [emphasis added]

Departmental Review

There are two esteemed, logical, analytical professors at Moscow State University telling us that much of the 2000 years of **the Western history of humanity has been forged**. And this includes Russian history as well. The first, Zinoviev, himself is quite distinguished, published, and winner of numerous awards. He supports Fomenko's findings, as does another contemporary of Fomenko's, A. Shiryaev, who is quite distinguished himself and is the Department Head where Fomenko works:

> A.Y. Shiryaev is a Corresponding Member of the Russian Academy of Sciences, Doctor of Physics and Mathematics, Head of the Probability Theory Studies Department of the Moscow State University Department of Mathematics and Mechanics, Head of the Probability Theory and Mathematical Statistics Department of the V.A. Steklov Mathematics Institute of the Russian Academy of Sciences. [34]

All this to say that Fomenko is a very credible man and so are those who reviewed and support his findings. None of them want to be considered kooks, and they are not pulling people's legs. They have discovered something worthy of note.

A.Y. Shiryaev has this to say about Fomenko's work:

> The author of the book suggests a new approach to the recognition of dependent and independent narrative (historical) texts based on a number of models .... with the aid of empirico-statistical methods and ...extensive statistical experimentation with varying quantitative characteristics of actual texts.... The verification of these models (statistical hypotheses) by sub-sistent chronicle material confirmed their efficacy.... one has to note that **the author's principal ideas are perfectly rational from the point of view of contemporary mathematical statistics** and ....the scientific results obtained by the author are most remarkable indeed.... The concept offered by A.T. Fomenko is novel and somewhat startling, and ... deserves

a meticulous study. [35] [emphasis added]

The Publisher's Review

That's a very technical, and cautious, way of saying that he likes it. In addition, the publisher also found it amazing but credible:

> *History: Fiction or Science?* is **the most explosive tractate on history ever written** – however, every theory it contains, no matter how unorthodox, is backed by solid scientific data…. **This version of events is substantiated by hard facts and logic**…. The dominating historical discourse…. was essentially crafted in the XVI century from a rather contradictory jumble of sources …. whose originals had *vanished* in the Dark Ages ….and the allegedly *irrefutable* proof resting upon the power of ecclesiastical authorities. **Nearly all of its [Western Chronology's] components are blatantly untrue**! [36] [emphasis added]

Now you know where we're going and why so much time has been spent establishing the credibility of Dr. Fomenko and his work. The reason for providing all the foregoing credibility is to provide a foundation for the incredible discovery in <u>this</u> chapter that supports and even more incredible discovery in Chapters 12-13.

Methodology

Before sharing some of his most interesting discoveries, it is relevant to share his methodology – so that it will be obvious that he didn't just use statistics to support some off-the-wall idea he had about Man's history.

One of Fomenko's simplest methods is statistical correlation of texts. His basic assumption is that a text which describes a sequence of events will devote more space to more important events (for example, a period of war or an unrest will have much more space devoted to [it] than a period of peaceful, non-eventful years), and that this irregularity will remain visible in other descriptions of the period. For each analysed text, a function is devised which maps each year mentioned in the text with the number of pages (lines, letters) devoted in the text to its description (which could be zero). The functions of the two texts are then compared.

> For example, Fomenko compares the <u>contemporary</u> history of Rome written by Titus Livius with a <u>modern</u> history of Rome written by Russian historian V.S. Sergeev, calculating that **the two have high correlation, and thus that they describe the same period of history, which is undisputed**. He also compares modern texts which describe different periods, and calculates low correlation, as expected. However, when he compares, for example, the <u>ancient</u> history of Rome and the <u>medieval</u> history of Rome, he calculates a high correlation, and concludes that **ancient history of Rome is a copy of medieval history of Rome**, thus clashing with mainstream accounts. [37] [emphasis added]

Using such methodology, Fomenko arrives at the conclusion that somebody used the same, or a similar, **template** to describe <u>many</u> supposedly disparate historical events <u>and</u> their accompanying personages.

Astronomical Evidence

Dr. Fomenko examines recorded astronomical events associated with historical claims to see if the data align with actual historical claims. For example, was there something that could astronomically be considered a Star of Bethlehem about 2000 years ago, and was there an eclipse soon (32 years) after that is alleged to happen during the Crucifixion of Christ?

After examining much astronomical data, kept by the Greeks, the Romans, the Chinese, etc., he found **only one pair** of such astronomical events separated by 32 years in the *Almagest*:

> He associates the Star of Bethlehem with the 1054 AD supernova (now Crab Nebula) and the Crucifixion Eclipse with the total solar eclipse of 1086 AD. Such a pair of astronomical events separated by 32 years (the approximate age of Jesus at the time of his death) is extremely rare.

> He [thus] argues that the star catalog in the *Almagest*, ascribed to the Hellenistic astronomer Claudius Ptolemy was actually created between 600 and 1300 AD.[38]

This issue is more fully examined in **Appendix D**.

Methodology Applied

The following diagram shows what Dr. Fomenko discovered applying his methodology to two kingdoms, supposedly separated by centuries and miles.

Note that the zig-zag lines represent timelines, the distance in time between major people/events, the nodes' distance from the center line (just a reference point) represent the number of years between nodes. For example, Manassah (50) and Justinian (47) are indicative of the number of years (50 and 47) between predecessors:

> From Constantine III to Justinian I was 26 + 47 years = 73 years
> From Jehoahaz to Manasseh was 31 + 50 years = 81 years

> Thus the points 47 and 50 are almost equidistant from the center line, as are almost all other nodes…

Plotting the years as distances from the center line repeatedly shows a pattern that has been statistically verified as having a huge correlation or significance, and thus Dr. Fomenko concludes that not only this example, but literally hundreds of others, were fabricated on a template. Similar people, similar events, similar time between events, etc. suggest a farbrication of sorts, and the diagrams "mirror" this fact…

The conclusion being that <u>real</u> history between hundreds of events over hundreds of years with different personages would not have had so many high correlations in terms of the years being very similar between key events/people. But, this situation would exist even if the real history had been altered, and certainly if it were fabricated.

Parallelism between two kingdoms <u>separated by centuries</u> that is more than coincidental: [39]

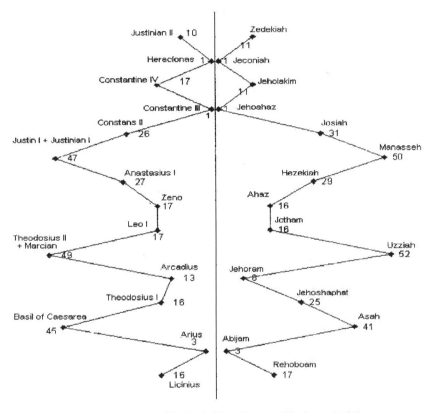

Parallelism between the Kingdom of Judah (10th-6th centuries BC) & the Eastern Roman Empire (4th - 7th century AD): [39]

(source: http://upload.wikimedia.org/wikipedia/en/0/07)

The above is an example of what Fomenko calls "a secondary parallelism", i.e., according to his theory, both dynastic lines represent **two different "reflections" of one historical sequence of rulers** who lived after 10th century AD. Note the amount of effort required to achieve accurate match - 7th century Byzantine emperors are shuffled, some of them are merged together, two long fragments are removed from each dynasty (years 841-767 BC and 565-641 AD, respectively); two religious leaders - Arius and Basil - are inserted in the list of emperors with rather arbitrary "reign durations." Parallels between individual rulers' biographies are normally rare and superficial. [40]

These two events, separated by 2-3 centuries should not have the same, duplicate schema. That they do, plus hundreds of others that Dr. Fomenko tests, suggests that a template was used to backdate and modify historical events. Why will be seen in Chapters 12-13.

Basic Axioms of Fomenko's New Chronology

1. Human evolution has always been linear, gradual and irreversible;
2. The "cyclic" nature of human civilization is a myth, likewise all the gaps, duplicates, "dark ages" and "renaissances" that we know from consensual history are fantasy and **hoax;**
3. **We know little if anything about history before AD 900;**
4. The chronology that we take for granted was invented in the 16th and 17th centuries;
5. Archaeological dating, dendrochronological dating, paleographical dating, Carbon 14 dating, and other methods of dating ancient sources and artifacts are erroneous, non-exact and dependent on traditional chronology – and thus involve circular reasoning;
6. **There is not a single document that can be reliably dated earlier than the 11th century;**
7. Ancient Rome, Greece and Egypt civilizations were crafted during the Renaissance by humanists and clergy;
8. The Bible was still being written until the Council of Trent (1545-1563); (this had to stop with the invention/use of the printing press)
9. The false chronology was largely manufactured by Josephus Justus **Scaliger** about 1583-1606, and completed by Jesuit Dionysius **Petavius** in 1627-1632. Years were back-adjusted and are off by a consistent cabbalistic factor of 333 and 360. [41]

Needless to say, these items will raise some eyebrows, and yet, if one has the time to examine Fomenko's methodology and the results, significant, reasonable doubt will be raised that the historical chronology that we have always believed is true.

In addition, Dr. Fomenko's theories comply with the most rigid scientific standards as a whole:

1. There is a coherent explanation of what we already know;
2. His theories are consistent and can be replicated;
3. The predictions can be confirmed empirically;
4. He documents everything thoroughly. [42]

So, let's examine some of the more startling discoveries from Dr. Fomenko's work, as they relate to the theme and purpose of this book. The following are some of the major points that he calls The New Chronology in Volume 1 of his projected 7-volume set:

New Chronology

Scaliger and Petavius

The chronology of Western Civilization, especially Europe, was the work of two men: Josephus Scaliger (1540-1609) and Dionysius Petavius (1583-1652). Scaliger started it, Petavius joined him, and after Scaliger died, Petavius concluded the work. Using Roman history as the backbone of the chronology, the essence of the Classical and Middle Ages are the Scaliger–Petavius version, simply called **"Scaligerian Chronology"**.

The groundlaying works of Scaliger and Petavius of the XVI-XVII century present the ancient chronology as a table of dates given without any reasons whatsoever. It is declared to be based on ecclesiastical tradition. This is hardly surprising since "history has remained predominantly ecclesial for centuries, and for the most part, was **written by the clergy**." [43] [emphasis added]

It is further believed that Eusebius and St. Hieronymus were also responsible for some of the historical data. In short, it required educated men who could read and write to perform the task of documenting history's chronology – and that meant a lot of it was done by the Catholic Church. [44]

Controlling the Truth

Let's hypothesize here. Suppose a fledgling religion, not more than 300-400 years old wanted to cement its position the world. In order to acquire as many converts as it could, it would also seek to promote a history of itself and its world that was as flattering as possible – even to make itself look as old as it could. Yet, there might be people who knew how old the church really was, what the original Christians had really taught, and what things the Church had sought to rewrite in its favor, so it would be necessary to develop a **'remedial outreach program'** (Inquisition) that would convince people that they were wrong and that the Church was right – even if the Church had to brand them as heretics, then torture and kill them.

At that point, it could rewrite history as it sought fit – if it could get rid of actual historical evidence to the contrary. It might even be expedient to sack and burn a few libraries at Alexandria, Rome, and elsewhere. Perhaps it might also be expedient to physically wipe out Cathars and Knights Templar to promote silence and acquiescence to the Church. Apparently, Prince Machiavelli's phrase, "The ends justify the means" was taken literally.

Books were destroyed by an edict of the Trident council. Alexandria's library was sacked and burned <u>several times</u>. The suggested reason is because the documents in the libraries contained text and history that did not agree with the Church-approved history which now said that the Church had been in existence since the 1st Century. Hence, the Church could proudly claim Peter as the first Pope… when it was really with the Council of Nicea called by Constantine in AD 325 that the fledgling Church began to organize.

And secret societies were formed in retaliation to preserve what they felt was the truth.

Part of the problem was that scrolls and documents were handwritten and could be changed at will to suit powerful peoples' purposes. That came to a halt in 1450 with the invention of the **printing press**, and it is under- standable why the authorities were anxious to control this new device… once multiple copies of something were run off, and distributed, history, facts and events could no longer be changed – unless the books were burned… [45] Dr. Fomenko says that there have been no inconsistencies and 'phantom duplicates' detected in analyses run on the time period AD 1600-2000, or since the printing press.

And it gets better…

AD 900 Limit

The many historical coincidences (chart sample above) are statistically impossible. And when one does the math and eliminates false histories, as Dr. Fomenko has done, it is discovered that we don't know anything concrete about history on Earth backwards of AD 900. [46]

> The entire part of the Scaligerian textbook preceding 900 or 1000 AD consists of **phantom duplicates.** Their medieval **originals** are in the time interval of 900-1600 AD…. The "Scaligerian textbook" contains no un-expected duplicates starting with the XVI century AD and later [due to the printing press]…. In general, the outline for the global chronology of Europe was created in the XVI-XVII century, in the works of J. Scaliger and D. Petavius. [47] [emphasis added]

and

> ….we have come across traces of **a fairly deliberate creation of artificially elongated "history"**, which the chronologists of the XVI-XVII century were actively involved in. [48]

And again in an article on the Maya, another author eerily corroborates Dr. Fomenko's hypothesis:

> … the Maya culture had its heyday from about AD 250 to 900, when the civilization mysteriously collapsed. [49]

> *In addition, the Viking and Chinese recorded histories also have a 'gap' about AD 800-900. Something happened which is examined in Chapter. 12.*

What that means is that backwards of AD 900, we really can't be sure of what happened when, if at all, **and** between AD 900 and AD 1600, a lot of the chronology was manipulated to the tune of 500 years at a time… How much of our history is fabricated?

Bible Timeline Fabricated

If all this is true, then it also follows, according to Dr. Fomenko, that "…all the events of both the Old Testament and the New Testament – fit into the interval between the X century AD and the XVI century AD." [50]

Another source corroborates Dr. Fomenko's thesis.

> Important to our story is the fact that the *Encyclopedia Biblica* reveals that **around 1,200 years of Christian history are unknown:** "Unfortunately, only few of the records [of the Church] prior to the year 1198 have been released." It was not by chance that, in that same year (1198), Pope Innocent III (1198-1216) suppressed all records of earlier Church history by establishing the **Secret Archives** (*Catholic Encyclopedia*, Farley ed., vol. xv, p. 287). Some

seven-and-a-half centuries later, and after spending some years in those Archives, Professor Edmond S. Bordeaux wrote *How The Great Pan Died*. In a chapter entitled "**The Whole of Church History is Nothing but a Retroactive Fabrication**," he said this (in part):

> **The Church ante-dated all her late works**, some newly made, some revised and some counterfeited, which contained the final; expression of her history… her technique was to make it appear that much later works written by Church writers were composed a long time earlier, so that they might become evidence of the first, second or third centuries…

The evidence that the Church wrote its own history is found in Diderot's *Encyclopédie*, and it reveals the reason why Pope Clement XIII (1758-69) ordered all volumes to be destroyed immediately after publication in 1759.[51] [emphasis added]

Whether the reader can believe it or not, the foregoing is nonetheless a tantalizing issue, and one that is currently undergoing further investigation by Dr. Fomenko. Perhaps even the lack of records about a historical Jesus has to do with what is called the Dark Ages…

The Dark Ages

According to Dr. Fomenko, due to Scaliger's manipulation of the chronology of Western Civilization, **there were no Dark Ages**, merely the shifting of history and information with it – all to make the Church look older than it really was.

> The historians of the 18th – 19th century gave rise to the peculiar concept that the medieval period was that of the "Dark Ages." The "great achievements of the classical age" are said to have faced utter decline and vanished… The great literary works of "antiquity" are all supposed to have been kept stashed away as deadweight until their resurfacing during the Renaissance. Moreover, these "antique" texts were allegedly kept by ignorant monks whose prime responsibility was, as we are now told, the destruction of "heathen literature." [52]

and

> We are of the opinion that what we see isn't a degradation of "the great legacy of the past" but, rather, the *naissance* of civilization that gradually created all the cultural and historical values, which were cast far back into the past due to the chronological errors that lit a spectral light in the "classical age" and **left many medieval periods bare**. [53] [emphasis added]

Corroboration also comes from contemporary John Keel :

> …man's own record of his early history was systematically destroyed by conflicting [religious] factions. The Library at Alexandria, Egypt, which housed thousands of years of history was sacked and burned [three times]. The remnants of early cultures were wantonly destroyed. And then **we were given a new**

history, generously dictated by the ultraterrestrials, and we bogged down in the Dark Ages for a thousand years. [54] [emphasis added]

In other words, there was no "Dark Ages" period and due to Scaliger's shifting the actual historical events backwards about 1000 years, **this left a gap that could not be explained**, and so it was assumed that mankind had regressed (into the Dark Ages) and instead of constant progression in the Arts and Science, there appeared a curious 'gap.' Keel suggests that the ultraterrestrials influenced the historical rewrite.

The ultraterrestrials that Mr. Keel refers to were covered in Chapters 4 and 6 – but probably they were the unseen Anunnaki Remnant operating through the Elite who were largely Church hierarchy when Scaliger and Petavius were busy formulating a history for mankind. As will be seen, the Elite of that day and age, largely the Church, under the shadow influence of the ever-present Anunnaki had a reason for doing so – besides glorification of the Church. If Man did not have a continuous history before AD 900, because the Higher Beings had done a "Wipe and Reboot" (in which the Maya also disappeared), it would be necessary that someone create a history for Man such that he plugs into whatever he's doing without the distraction of a major mystery.

And that is the reason for going into this part of Dr. Fomenko's discoveries. On the surface, it is interesting that someone has found that our history of civilization has been manipulated, and that coincides with an earlier statement that "…almost everything you think you know about Earth History…. is false." And, in Chapter 12, it will be shown why the manipulation of our history, science and religion were done.

Chronology Summary

Was it somebody's desire to not only make the Church look older (a minor point), but to serve a much more important reason: to make it seem that Man had been on the planet much longer than he really had been?

Thus Dr. Fomenko sums up the revelation, promising 6 more volumes to complete the analysis, and gives his overview of his first book:

> …. virtually all of the old documents that have reached our age are copies from ancient originals, presumed lost…. It seems that earlier documents simply failed to have survived until the present day. However, the over-whelming majority of XI – XVI century originals either got destroyed, or were subjected to **tendentious editing** in the XVI-XVII century, during the creation of the Scaligerian Chronology. Whatever meager genuine evidence of antiquity escaped such editing (or rewriting in the light of the veracious [sic] Scaligerian chronology) are declared to be forgeries or creations of ignorant authors…. [yet] **many of the documents declared fake nowadays turn out to be original…. In our opinion, nearly all of the events described in the ancient chronicles really *did take place*. The question is one of their exact *location and timing*.**
> This is precisely where chronological and geographical confusion began, aided by the **deliberate distortions** of the Scaligerite chronologers, which

led to the "elongation of history." [55] [emphasis added]

So **Western chronology is largely a forgery backwards of the printing press**, and backwards of AD 900, almost nothing is known for sure. It is herein suggested that the Dark Ages did not exist because Man went through a "Wipe and Reboot," and thus no one was on the planet at that time. If the founding Church intelligentsia somehow knew about that, from the Anunnaki Remnant, aka the Roman gods, it might behoove them to elongate history and try to cover up the unaccountable 'gap' in Man's real history.

And it is possible that the Church <u>did</u> know inasmuch as the Roman Empire revered the Roman "gods" who were still here and were playing games with Man, up until the Empire morphed into the Roman Catholic Church – all prior to AD 700. Wisely, the Church sought to put all the gods' (Anunnaki) interference and influence behind it as Man was "reloaded" onto the planet about AD 900 (similar to Man regaining the planet after The Flood).

Other Historical Anomalies

Aztec, Maya and Olmec

Just as the Sumerians were taught civilization by the Anunnaki, both the Aztec and Maya civilizations were visited by Quetzalcoatl), a 'feathered serpent' who was benevolent and taught the natives much. Such a being is important as he is a connection between the Anunnaki and Egyptian cultures and the Central American cultures. According to Sitchin, Enki had several sons, and the sixth one was called NIN.GISH.ZID.DA ("Lord of the Tree of Life") who reigned over **Egypt** as Thoth. [56], [57]   When Marduk/Ra came back to Egypt about 3100 BC to reestablish his power, Thoth had to go, so

> …taking along **a group of his African followers** [Nubians], he went all the way to the New World, to become Quetzalcoatl… The first calendar instituted by him in Mesoamerica (the [Mayan] Long Count calendar) began in the year 3113 BC…[58] [emphasis added]

So the giant **Olmec** heads represent Nubians from Africa. No one knows what the Olmecs called themselves, but they developed the multi-wheel stone calendar and gave it to the Mayas. What were they tracking? (The Aztecs had a different calendar: a large round disk with a tongue sticking out of the middle.) Don't confuse the two calendars.
(Credit: Bing Images)

Zechariah Sitchin with Olmec Head

Interestingly, when the **Aztecs** traveled south through what is now Mexico, they had begun their journey up in the area of what is today Arizona. They met resistance everywhere they went and were denied setting up a place to live because they were so warlike and abusive of other tribes. So they maintained their journey southward, asking the gods for a sign to tell them where to stop and build their city. Their shaman was given a vision of an eagle sitting on a nopal (cactus) holding a snake in its mouth. As they neared Lake Texcoco in the central part of Mexico, they saw an eagle sitting on a cactus with a snake in its mouth – and it was on the edge of the lake. They stopped and began to build their city <u>on the lake</u>, and called it **Tenochtitlán.**

They built their city on the lake using the same technique that Enki used to build his house on Snake Marsh (Chapter 3). And their tribal legend said that they came originally from a place to the East called **Aztlan**. Atlantis? Not only does Mexico today make use of their serpent vision on the Mexican flag, but the country's name reflects their tribal name.

(Credit: Wikipedia: Tenochtitlan)

The Aztecs called themselves Mexica, where the "x" is pronounced like "shh." Mexica became Mexico, and the "x" changed in pronunciation to an "h."

The Aztecs' city **Tenochtitlán** bears an eerie resemblance to the **Mississippian Culture's Kincaid** settlement (AD 800-1500) [59]– mounds, buildings and all, and it is suggested that after Atlantis sunk, the survivors made it to the South Central USA, founded the large Mississippian Culture and later an extreme group, called Aztecs, left and headed South into Mexico.

(Credit: Wikipedia: Mississippian Culture: Kincaid)

Mayan Pyramids

Steep Steps at Palenque

It was noted earlier that the Anunnaki were taller than humans, in addition to being repulsive-looking. It was also pointed out that the Anunnaki Elite tended to stay atop their ziggurats and pyramids – out of the view of the populace. Since they were 8-9 feet tall, they would have had a longer step or stride and that would explain the steps on most Mayan pyramids: they are very awkward for humans to climb as they are bigger and steeper steps.

(source: http://images.search.yahoo.com/search/images?p=palenque%20pyramids)

In addition, the pyramid stairway had a very steep angle to discourage humans from climbing up, as shown on the following page.

And some pyramids, like the main one at **Tikal**, have a modern man-made set of stairs up the backside so that humans can climb to the top, whereas others like *El Castillo* at Chichen Itzá have a steel cable strung up the stairs to use as a railing. Clearly the builders did not need such aids and the stairs were deliberately designed to accommodate them, indicating that they were bigger than humans.

Carefully Climbing Palenque
(source: http://images.search.yahoo.com/search/images?p=palenque%20pyramids)

Note in the picture above that everybody is on their hands and knees because the slope is too steep for standing ascent.

Nazca Mysteries

A little farther south, on the plains of Chile, there are the enigmatic Plains of Nazca with what appear to be 'runways' etched into the soil. In fact, the pictographs etched into the soil (monkey, spider, hummingbird, etc) were done by the early humans in an attempt to re-attract the gods, who did use the area and then 'marked' it:

1. The 'runways' were actually directional guidance like a map, which is why they can only be appreciated from the air – they point to important places in the old Anunnaki world, including Sumer, Tiahuanaco, Machu Picchu, Malta, Baalbek, Tikal, Aztlan, Great Zimbabwe, etc. The length of the line indicates the distance. Removed is the coding box that said (electronically) <u>what</u> it pointed to. The Anunnaki flew their craft up to the wide end of the line, downloaded the directional info, and took off.

2. Other geometric designs were informational and territorial markers, such as the giant circles within triangles. Reminding the natives of their power, the 'Candelabra' (trident) on a hillside also represented the plasma-microwave type weapon, [60] similar to the one that the god Neptune carried as a symbol of his power/authority.

Ancient, ignorant savages who knew nothing, eh?

3. There are many *puquios* or water wells in the area, some at the end of the 'runways' and others scattered across the Plain. The wells were engineered to permit access to the underground water, and there are shafts, vaults and pipes which extend for many kilometers <u>below</u> the surface – obviously an engineering feat beyond the level of the local natives at the time. [61]

At one point, the Nazca area was important enough to build the *puquios* for the natives because the Anunnaki also used the area as a base, so water was a necessity. Larger traces of their presence were carefully obliterated when they left… about the same time as Puma Punku was destroyed.

Peruvian and Bolivian Mysteries

The major sites of ET activity in South America were Tiahuanaco at Lake Titicaca, Machu Picchu, and Sacsayhuaman all in Peru, and Puma Punku in nearby Bolivia. The Anunnaki were as much collecting gold in Peru as they were in South Africa. And factions fought each other for control of the resources. Note the trident on the hillside at Nazca…

Trident of Power - Nazca Hillside   **Stacked Toroidal Plasma in Physics**
(credit: both: www.crystalinks.com/nasca.html)

And if that weren't curious enough: consider these glyphs from Kayenta, Arizona:

www.everythingselectric.com

What did the ancients see that inspired their artwork? Plasma weapons?

The stoneworking is evidence of advanced tools in **Puma Punku**. Laser-like cuts and perfect holes were made by granite and diorite – very hard rocks. The Puma Punku stonework was not done by a primitive people with stone tools .

Says researcher Witkowski:

> When taking into account modern construction achievements, we face the truth that *many of the construction methods that were applied at Puma Punku have absolutely no equivalent anywhere else in the world and would even be <u>hard to reproduce in our time</u>.* [62] [emphasis added]

The precision used in making the H-shaped blocks is on the order of 1/10th of a millimeter, and the blocks have almost 80 surfaces each. Amazing stonework for diorite which is harder than granite. The drill holes on the left block (below) are perfectly smooth and exactly the same width, depth and distance apart. And then the blocks' surfaces integrated with each other to make a very sturdy wall, or launching ramp, with a complex design.

Advanced Stonework at Puma Punku
(Source: http://images.search.yahoo.com/images/viewes....puma%2Bpunku%2)

Clearly, an advanced civilization with impressive technology did the stonework which formed part of a <u>base of operations</u> with a complex of buildings and large, flat stoned areas. The Anunnaki had such technology. It was destroyed in a small battle.

Sacsayhuaman was more of a fortress with huge boulders weighing many tons that fit so perfectly together that one cannot get a piece of paper or a knife blade between them – almost like they were lifted into place, then heated and 'molded' into shape.

This advanced stonework is also true of the huge structures at **Ollataytambo** not far from Sacsayhuaman.

Fortress of Sacsayhuaman
(source: http://www.world-mysteries.com/mpl_9.htm)

The Temple of Sacsayhuaman was a major activity center for the Anunnaki. Across the valley is **Rodadero** -- a giant rock hill with numerous stairwells and benches carved into the rock, purpose officially unknown. (It was a communications control center.) Again, the large stairsteps are not made for humans.

Serpent Culture

There is much fascination with serpents around the world, and there are many buildings, statues and earth mounds with a serpentine motif, as in Ohio. Even some statues of Mother Mary in the Catholic Church show her standing on a globe which is encircled by a serpent, and under her feet are two black horns. Eve was tempted by a serpent in the Garden of Eden. The symbol of the medical profession is the *caduceus* or a pole with two serpents entwined facing each other below a double-winged sphere. Moses lifted up a bronze serpent on a pole in the wilderness to heal his people (Appendix E). Egyptian pharaohs and Tibetan Nagas wore a stylized cobra on their forehead, the *uraeus* (symbol of the 3rd eye, or wisdom). **Kundalini** is said to be an energy at the base of the spinal column, coiled like a serpent that climbs up one's spinal column giving a person enlightenment, and this was one of the major purposes of the Serpent 'worship' cults. These groups promoted enlightenment via techniques to get the kundalini 'serpent' to rise up the initiate's spine, as well as dispensing esoteric knowledge to the initiates. (See Appendix E.)

Serpent Worship

There is a Mayan pyramid called *El Castillo* at **Chichen-Itzá** where twice a year, the Sun's rays hit the stepped stones lining the stairs going up the pyramid, creating the illusion of a serpent created by the shadows... by design. Such advanced knowledge of archeo-astronomy is beyond what a primitive Mayan people would know just by watching the stars at night. The serpent appears at the Equinox... how did they arrange that?

Pyramid of Kukulcan
(source: http://www.world-mysteries.com/chichen_kukulcan.htm)

It is also interesting that each side of the pyramid has 90 steps and there are 5 more at the top – indicative of the days in a year. Note that there are 7 'triangles' comprising the serpent's body, said to be symbolic of the Seven Sisters of the Pleiades.

The pyramid's Serpent image is to venerate **Kukulcan**, (aka Quetzalcoatl aka Viracocha), a benevolent god who taught the Mayan and Aztec cultures much. Chichen-Itzá was the Mayan cult center of Kukulcan. [63] Ningishzidda (Enki's son) was **Quetzalcoatl**, and **Viracocha** and Kukulcan.) [64] What is really fascinating are the serpent designs on the walls and columns **inside** the house at the top of the pyramid where the 'head lizard' stayed when he visited the Maya.

Serpent Origins

Serpent wisdom images and groups basically started with the Anunnaki and Sumeria, inasmuch as the Anunnaki existed on Earth long before history was recorded. When it finally was written down (in Sanskrit, cuneiform or otherwise), the Serpent tradition was found to extend to include Atlantis, Mu and Agartha among other places whose cultures also interfaced with that of the Anunnaki. [65]

Enki, and Anu their king, possessed spiritual wisdom, as well as deep medical and anatomical knowledge, in addition to looking like humanoid reptiles. Enki was even known as a Dragon, or Serpent of Wisdom, and later was given credit for starting the **Brotherhood of the Serpent**. [66] So when Man later chose to venerate his benefactors, the result was the Serpent imagery and worship cults <u>all around the world</u> because the Anunnaki flew to and visited many cultures around the world. (Appendices E and F.)

Of course, the Anunnaki traveled all over the world – from Sumer to Peru, to Chile, to Mexico, to India and to North America, so there are ruins and artifacts that mutely attest to their ancient presence. They were largely seen as benefactors and it is very likely that these beings were responsible for developing Man's knowledge of astronomy and mathematics (and hence the accurate stone calendars), agriculture, weather, writing, medicine, war/battle, religion, and basic government. [67]

Quetzalcoatl: Feathered Serpent
(source: http://www.crystalinks.com/mayangods.html)

And each area of expertise had a specific ET 'god' associated with it and that was the origin of the panoply of gods, such as would later be known to the Greeks, then the Romans. Zeus (Enlil) was the god over all the other gods, while Poseidon (Enki) was the god of the sea, and Ares (Marduk) was the god of war, for example.

So what we have is "walking serpents" founding civilization and being known as the 'People of the Serpent', or Chanes. [68] The People of the Serpent were called **Quetzalcoatl**, or "feathered serpent" as most of them had the appearance of a serpent with Quetzal bird feathers adorning them. **Note their height,** and reptilian appearance.

A noted author, Edward Thompson, who wrote <u>People of the Serpent: Life and Adventure Among the Maya</u> (1932), determined that

> …the People of the Serpent were the founders and ruling dynasty of the Olmec and Toltec civilizations, which gave rise to great Maya centers such as Chichen Itza. His conclusion was that the People of the Serpent conquered 'not by force and strange weapons, but by binding the primitive peoples to them by force of their power and wisdom.'

> What we see here is the arrival among the indigenous peoples of Mexico of what appears to have been an elite group, remembered as being **serpentine** in nature or appearance. [69] [emphasis added]

Again, this is significant, as the Anunnaki were serpentine in appearance, and it was the same group of beings in the Yucatan and Peru that occupied Sumer – since the Anunnaki lifespan was several thousands of years and they did have airships that could rapidly move them over great distances.

> They used their knowledge, organization skills, and great wisdom to unite tribal communities with a common cause – the foundation of civilization. In return, these priest-kings, lords or rulers were seen as divine and remembered by later generations as gods or great wisdom-bringers. [70]

And it was a minor step from there to where the people developed Serpent Cults, as underground groups of believers who retained the truth of those early years and what had been done for mankind. This even extended into a Current Era with the Gnostic Ophite groups[71] of which **Pythagoras** was a foremost initiate, and his name even means "I am the Python [serpent]." [72]

In addition, another "feathered serpent" known as **Votan** set up a town called Huehuetlan and established a treasury of statues and artifacts establishing a connection to his 'gods' – which was promptly destroyed during the Spanish hunt for gold and conversion of infidels in the area, such that by AD 1691 nothing remained of Votan's legacy. [73]

The point being that not all of these "feathered serpents" were bad – unlike nasty **Huitzilopochtli** (and **Texcatlipoca**) who chased Quetzalcoatl out of town and re-instituted human sacrifice. As we will see, there were some Anunnaki who were antagonistic toward Man (and still are).

And lastly, it was Votan who established a secret society for the furtherance of his teachings. In another form, this secret society continued into the 20th century and was called Sh'Tol Brothers in the Yucatan. [74]

Serpent Organizations

It is said that Ea, or Enki, was the founder of the Brotherhood of the Serpent, sometimes called the **Great White Brotherhood**, whose function was to free the human race from the oppression of its Custodians.[75]   Unfortunately, while Enki's heart was in the right place, Enlil and Marduk (both in the role as Yahweh) controlled public relations and so 'villainized' Enki that he lost the trust and following of mankind, and his title of Prince of Earth was changed to Prince of Darkness. Enki later became equated with Satan, the Devil and the keeper of Hell – as was explained in Chapters 2 and 6. That is the origin of evil on Earth.

> Ea [Enki] appears to have compounded the blunder [creating the Brotherhood] by founding and empowering the early Snake Brotherhood which, after its reported defeat, continued to remain [sic] a powerful force in human affairs, but under the domination of the very Custodial factions that Ea and the original Brotherhood were said to have opposed. History indicates that **the Brotherhood was turned under its new Custodial "gods" into a chilling weapon of spiritual repression and betrayal**, despite the efforts of many sincere humanitarians to bring about true spiritual reform through Brotherhood channels all the way up until today. [76] [emphasis adde d]

Note: the **Custodians** *as described by Bramley, appear to be the same as the Anunnaki Remnant, who are small in number, but consider themselves leaders of the human Elite who mostly see Man as a nuisance.*

And Bramley goes on to document the ways in which these Custodians have set about **"preserving mankind's status as a spiritually ignorant creature** of toil throughout all history. During all that time, and continuing today, the Brotherhood and its network of organizations have remained intimately tied to the UFO phenomenon." [77]   In fact, there is a report in the UFO literature, among abductees, that some of the UFO occupants wear **a triangular patch with an S-like Serpent** inside it on their uniforms. [78]

For the most part, in the Western world, the ancient serpent wisdom was carried forward by the Templars, the Freemasons and Rosicrucians who went underground to protect their knowledge which was vehemently repudiated by those in orthodoxy whose goal was to control mankind. [79]   In Europe, the wisdom was spread by men like the Count of St. Germain, Kolmer, Cagliostro and Hayyim Jacob Falk. [80]   In the Eastern world, the Serpent Wisdom was maintained by the Nagas (India), the Djedhi (Egypt), Lung Dragons (China), and the Quetzalcoatls in Mesoamerica. Collectively, they were united in the Great White Brotherhood [81] prior to its imposed internal polarization. (Appendix E.)

It seems the battle for Man has never quit, and that is the point of this section. The enslavement did not go unnoticed by the Higher Beings, and something was done about it, around AD 800-900, and that is why the Anunnaki who left Earth cannot return. But there are some still here…

Anunnaki Remnant

The last section of this chapter briefly looks at the current aspect of the Anunnaki and examines the credibility of their presence and current agenda.

It is an important historical note, worth emphasizing, that not all of the Anunnaki left Earth in 650-600 BC. A hybrid Remnant stayed behind and its two factions (positive **Insiders** and negative **Dissidents**) have been the ultimate behind-the-scenes controllers of the planet via the Elite (who in turn, try to guide the PTB). The two Remnant factions cannot agree on what to do with Man, one wants to help us, the other wants to kill us – just as did Enlil 10,00 years ago! The reason the Remnant is allowed to remain on Earth is that they are here for almost the same reason we are. To learn respect, compassion, and management of resources. The Remnant works through proxy humans called the **Elite** just as they always have, and many humans are not aware that a larger agenda is at work.

The Remnant sometimes work directly among us since some of them (Anunnaki hybrids) also look just like us and no one would suspect unless they can see auras. These of course are not the Naga component <u>in the flesh</u> since the Nagas look like a cross between Lt. Worf of *Star Trek* fame and a human – dark skin color, angular face, black hair – and have a general disdain of Man. **Nagas** also can **shapeshift** and appear as humans when needed… this is the source of the Djinn legends in Chapter 6. Remember that vision is holographically-based and a more advanced mind (or machine) can project and control what you see. No molecules change (See Chapter 12).

As for the Nagas and the Indian scene, it is reported that **Lord Shiva** had an earlier incarnation as the **horned** nature god Pashupati and was 'Lord of the Animals,' including serpents. **In fact, he had two horns upon his head and carried a trident** [82] — reminiscent of the god Neptune, and the 'Candelabra' carved into the side of the mountain in the Nazca plain. The trident is associated with the Anunnaki, specifically Ninurta, as a formidable weapon and was described as the 'Divine Thunderbolt'. [83] That is the connection with the Nazca design on the hillside.

Summary

Again, it all comes down to what this place really is and who is here with us. And Man's repetitive history provides clues that offer not only a description but an exposé of an advanced agenda. But it is not possible for the average person to discover what Earth is despite years of study and reflection in history, archeology or ancient writings. The answer would have to be given to people, as it was to me. But most people are likely to diss the answer because it conflicts with what they think they already know – they have been **conditioned** to not hear. Mention UFOs or mermaids, for example, and people laugh.

> *One of Man's most frustrating ways of reacting arises when he is told something that disagrees with what he already believes. His standard (and programmed) response is:*
> ### *I don't like it,*
> #### *therefore it isn't true.*
> *As a result, Man does not wake up, and that is the goal of the PTB who consider it their mission to rule: Lords need Serfs.*

And yet, this chapter has made an attempt to examine the mis-understandings and errors present in what we think we know about Earth history, and why a lot of the information is an inaccurate assumption – based on other assumptions that are also inaccurate. For example, the Geologic Timetable is inaccurate, C-14 dating isn't reliable, and yet we believe that Man has had a slow, gradual evolution And thus, the Young Earth Theory and Dr. Fomenko's Chronology will seem quite bizarre to people who think that Man has been here for millions of years and that we have a totally accurate history line into the ancient past.

The reality of this Earth and its history is something that the more open-minded will appreciate, and yet I still recommend that the reader treat it as **catalyst**: contemplate it, research it (any and all of the references given, for starters), and evaluate what it may offer for focusing one's spiritual walk.

Chapter 11: -- Religion

Foreword

Because this can be a very sensitive subject for some people, it is emphasized that Man DOES need religion, a Faith, and a connection with Something larger than himself. In no way is this chapter (or book as a whole) denigrating ANY religion *per se*, and it is not trying to trash Christianity, nor promote Islam. The God of the Universe is real, He loves Man, and there have been Beings sent throughout the centuries to guide, protect and inspire Man. Religion is a part of our lives and being because Man is more than just a body; he has a soul that is connected to the Father of Light and that needs feeding and sustaining through the power of prayer and the Word.

However, what this Chapter seeks to do is remove the froo-froo, disinformation and false teachings to present a clearer view of **Man as a special being** – which was also presented in Chapters 7 and 9. He is not just a flesh and blood sinner, although he is imperfect, but he is on his way to becoming all that his divine potential can deliver. The Bible has a lot of value for one's spiritual walk but cannot be taken literally, as shown herein.

Please do not be offended, as no offense is intended, just a clarification of some errors, mistranslations and false teachings so that one can (1) further research them if wanted (most corrections are footnoted), and (2) one can focus on the more beautiful and inspiring parts of the Bible (Psalms, Proverbs, Sermon on the Mount, and Corinthians [issue of Love]) and dwell in Truth instead of fantasy.

Why? False beliefs are an albatross around your neck when you die. (Chapters 14-15, and end of Introduction, 'Annotation'.)

Purpose and Origin of Religion

As was pointed out earlier, religion was initiated by the Anunnaki as a way to (1) give Man ethics and morals, and (2) failing that, control him. Even the Anunnaki recognized there was a divine power/intelligence in the universe – as any sentient and advanced being would. The problem, early on, was that humans were deliberately limited in their mental processes (until the *Adapa* version was developed) and the humans haplessly worshipped the Anunnaki as gods.

Giving Man religion was an attempt to move humans in a direction that promoted morals and the Anunnaki gave Man many Do's & Don'ts as recorded in the Torah (think: Mosaic Law) hoping that humans would get the message and be more self-directed and realize that there was a mono-theistic God of the universe who reigned, not just the Anunnaki.

That didn't work until *Adapa* because *Adamu* and his predecessors were not too bright, to put it bluntly. In addition, Enlil had a problem with the constant racket that the humans made when they got together after their day's labor. Singling, dancing, shouting, banging drums, yelling during games and contests – it was not to Enlil's liking. Thus he tried to cut their numbers, hoping less of them would make less noise, and he ordered food to be withheld to promote famine. When that didn't work, he tried *Suruppu* disease, and later another disease called *Asakku* disease. [1]

The Flood changed everything. And following the deluge, Enlil reluctantly decided to accept the humans as useful but instituted Religion and genetically-chosen human priests to keep the people in line – after The Flood, the humans were descendants of Noah's hybrid human line, and were intelligent enough to be taught agriculture, medicine, metal-working, astrology… and morals/ethics which were the foundation of the religion. They were also taught writing and instructed to write down the instructions for food preparation, medicine, business transactions, etc.…

But all was not working in Sumeria. The humans needed a physical in-your-face god to look up to; they were not following the deeper religious precepts they were taught. Thus Enlil and his staff resorted to meeting the humans on their level – and gave them a god of rain, a god of healing, a god of war, a god of the sea, the mountains, etc… and Man became superstitious.

Much later, another human hybrid would meet with Enlil on the mountain and physically deliver Ten Commandments to the people who were still headstrong and rebellious. And that was basically the origin of the Torah and kosher food preparation, as well as Gematria and Qaballah. All given to guide Man.

Then the Anunnaki were invited to go home, about 600 BC, and Man was left with whatever had survived of the Laws (Hammurabi), History (Epic of Gilgamesh, *Atra Hasis*, and *Haggadah* among others), and verbal accounts passed from generation to generation. Eventually these were written down in the Torah and much later, the Church gathered significant writings from the Greater Mesopotamia region and selectively formulated (about AD 325, at the **Council of Nicea**) the official teachings of Christianity.

What we have today, for religious tradition, emerged from the surviving accumulated philosophy and religion from millennia past. Because some of it was 'adjusted' to meet fledgling Church designs (see Fomenko, Chapter 10), groups wishing to keep the original teachings intact formed their own 'societies' such as the Essenes, Gnostics, Knights Templar, Cathars and the Rosicrucians. Many of these groups were persecuted in an attempt to create a "straight vanilla" version of the Truth – as promoted by the Church.

Many true Anunnaki original teachings and Man's early history were lost in the several sack-and-burns that the ancient **Library of Alexandria** underwent. And when the Church found even in the Middle Ages that too many people still knew of the older esoteric teachings, a public Program of Correction (aka The Inquisition) paid terminal visits to many people in an attempt to control and stabilize the "accepted Church doctrine." Those visited who didn't recant and confess to heretic views and change their ways, saw Saint Peter earlier than planned.

Lastly, in the AD 1500 period with the invention of the **printing press**, changes and forgeries made to religious documents (which had been prolific in the 1000 years since The Council of Nicea) came to a halt. More significantly, the Church of England commissioned an "official" version of what was becoming accepted orthodoxy (since AD 325) and in AD

1604 King Jimmy authorized the King James **version** of the Bible. How was this version different from what was originally taught Man by Enki which was passed on to the Essenes?

> *Remember, Enki taught the truth to his progeny and for that Enlil demonized Enki and his teachings. Thus Enki became a Satan and the Brotherhoods of the Serpent Wisdom were later branded anathema by the Church.*

One thing was for sure: any reference to the Anunnaki and their influence on Man was being removed from History and Religion. Human priest-kings 'adapted' the Anunnaki-given "Dieu et Mon Droit" (trans. 'God and my right [to rule]' – which was decreed by the Anunnaki) to suit their own human purposes. And now, Man does not have whatever the original teachings were, such that should ETs arrive and examine our religious beliefs, they will wonder about our Child's Garden of Misinformation. This Chapter is an effort to get people to consider the urgent need to upgrade Religion to a more modern, workable view of Man, the Universe, God and our place in it. If we could upgrade pagan worship to a more organized, proactive religion, surely we can recognize spiritual truth in what modern Physics, Near Death Experiencers, and traditional esoteric writings suggest, and upgrade Religion as **Bishop John Shelby Spong** suggests, to a more dynamic, truthful version of our world and why we are here.

Failing that, we are left with Religion to control Man; blind teachings taken solely on faith, a religion in which Man does not have a say and is not supposed to think.

Control

Another way to confuse and manage Man is with religion – just get a few different versions going around the planet, and with Man's natural tendency to proclaim that his version of anything is the correct one, and his tendency to violently promote his society, his religion, or his science as the best one, there can be wars to further distract and occupy his time. Also a great way to control Man: threaten him with Hell if he doesn't behave.

Remember that the Anunnaki found that the *Adapa* revering them as gods was semi-effective for controlling the humans. Just threaten the humans with God's vengence for misbehavior… And as it was pointed out, the Anunnaki gave the desired version of ethics, philosophy and religion to the 'chosen' human leaders (priests) who in turn imposed the societal rules and procedures on the populace. This involved setting up a **human priestly class** who administered the "Word of God" (Anunnaki desired behavior) to the people since the priests were privy to what the Anunnaki wanted.

The religious teachings were designed to control, and can still be found in today's Bible:

> Render unto Caesar the things that are Caesar's.
> If someone wrongs you, turn the other cheek.
> The meek shall inherit the Earth.
> Resist not evil.
> Tithe 10%.

And of course :

The Ten Commandments.

Interestingly, the Bible also says "Resist the devil…" (James 4:7) so if we are told earlier to "…resist not evil" (Matt. 5:39), does that mean the devil is not evil??

The teachings above are music to a tyrant's ear – if the populace follows these teachings, the abusive ruler can do whatever he wants and the sheep should not complain nor resist. The ideal religion says the humans are to be <u>passive and compliant</u>… and yet the man called Jesus was not that way: Did he not take a whip to the money-changers in the temple, and later curse the fig tree? Those are not the actions of a passive or compliant person who meekly accepts whatever happens as OK…

At any rate, **fear of the gods** was instilled into the people so that they would cooperate and do what was wanted. Back in those days, it was an easy matter to have one of the Anunnaki show up and create rain, blast a hole in the ground to create a well or lake, or disappear people. God was immediate to the people and very tangible to the rowdy humans. Enlil gave the order to let The Flood terminate humans, not The God of the universe. [2]

Because there were many Anunnaki in charge of many different aspects of Sumerian life, the people began to equate floods with one god, rain with another god, food/crop production with another god, education with certain god, and so on… until there was an assortment of gods. This is the origin of **pantheism**. Enlil was the supreme Anunnaki god, who would later be called Yahweh, or the vengeful, irascible God of the Old Testament [3],[4] and later demand that only he was their God, with "no other gods before me."

Enlil's Defense

And in Enlil's defense, it needs to be seen that the humans were just a means to an end, the Anunnaki did not come to Earth to start a civilization – they just needed **slave workers** to mine the gold and uranium, work the crops, and build the buildings. Humans were later used to fight the wars between Anunnaki factions. When those tasks were done, the usefulness of the humans was at an end, and the Anunnaki wanted to go back home. They could not take the humans with them. So what do you do with them?

What Enlil was thinking of was the **Galactic Law**[5] that said no new creating of sentient beings was permitted in their space travels… for exactly the reason that Enlil was angry with Enki: once you create a sentient race, even an upgrade of an existing one, you are responsible for them! And that is also why the Anunnaki Remnant is still on Earth.

Some humans have **defective** DNA because it was tailored to limited needs – note the number of criminals with two "X" chromosomes, as well as children with Down's Syndrome, people born color-blind… Some humans also are **dysfunctional** – they are petty, violent and ignorant and do things commensurate with emotional/hormonal drives that they do not understand, nor can they control them – drinking, smoking, drugs, rape, and shooting other people.

This is why Enlil thought it best to terminate the humans since they were not genetically outstanding and a lot of them could not be taught or trained. They had built dumb slaves on purpose. He knew that over time, the unstable genetics would **de**volve, and that was why the earlier Neanderthal had to be removed, along with the Nephilim – hence the famines, the diseases, and finally The Flood. All to cut Man's numbers to something more manageable and in harmony with the Earth's limited ability to support an increasing population.

When the numbers get too high, unemployment and food sources become a problem and action has to be taken… even today we have a warning in the 1980 Georgia Guidestones:

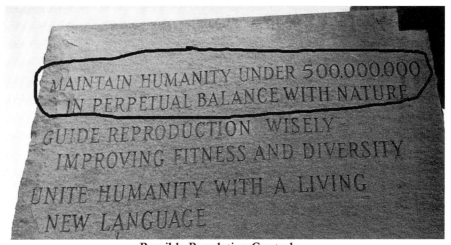

Possible Population Control
(source: http://en.wikipedia.org/wiki/File:Georgia_Guidestones)

Not only is population control listed, but genetic engineering of the human is also seen. A One World Government, One World Religion and a One World Language are suggested.

Enlil promoted order, structure and reason. When Enki got too involved with his creation, the two brothers began fighting and Enlil turned on Enki for trying to lead Man into developing his spiritual potential (via the Serpent Brotherhoods), and Enlil then cast Enki as a Satan in the Earth… and the Church has continued the image.

Enlil thus was not a bad guy, he just couldn't handle the rowdiness so often manifested by this unfortunate and DNA-limited creation. They were noisy, smelly, undisciplined, not too bright and **needed action and sound to entertain them**. Even today's youth have trouble sitting still in class, always have to have something to listen to, sing along with, someone to text to… Humans have inner 'drives' that told Enlil that they would not make it as a species.

> *Not that the Anunnaki were pure and holy either, and they squabbled and fought – which is what Enlil realized: Anunnaki genes in a primitive, wild hominid made for a great physical worker, but the genetics were worse than what the Anunnaki had!*

Since a **Remnant** was constrained to remain on Earth and learn from their mistake (Enki

333

is here and Enlil is not), and learn how to shepherd a fledgling sentient race, humans are still receiving guidance indirectly from the Anunnaki **Insiders** who want us to succeed, via the Elite. Unfortunately, the Anunnaki Remnant **Dissidents** pander to the PTB (3D humans) who want to see us **not** make it. Such is the reason for stupid events on the planet, like government shutdowns, promoting GMO food, chemtrails, putting fluoride in the water, and rampant diseases, for example.

The Anunnaki Remnant are here for almost the same reason we are, and Enlil wanted to avoid that. Both humans and Anunnaki are to learn respect and care for others and the planet.

Anunnaki Religion

Some Anunnaki taught Man to practice **blood sacrifice** as a way to worship, and in return, Man venerated the creator gods with the Serpent cults – all around the planet. Such were the teachings to the Maya and Aztec by **Huitzilopochtli** and to the Toltecs by **Tezcatlipoca** who was the brother of Huitzilopochtli. Similar teachings were given in India, China, Peru, Britain and Egypt. In the Americas, the one benefactor in all this was **Quetzalcoatl**, also known as Kukulcan or Viracocha (in Peru). They were all **"feathered serpents,"** but with different agendas: Huitzilopochtli and Tezcatlipoca promoted human sacrifice and Quetzalcoatl tried to stop it. [6] Some sacrifice continued with the Serpent worship cults.

Note that Man received partial Anunnaki DNA <u>and</u> the religious 'programming' which was designed to (1) keep Man in fear of the gods, and (2) keep Man subservient and dependent on the gods through their chosen human priests. Man was not to question but blindly accept and obey, and millions of people today still do that with their religion.

Examining Religion

Let me suggest this:

If you can't examine your religion, you don't have much of a religion.

If some of the teachings won't stand the light of day, and no credible antecedent for them can be found, AND it all has to be taken purely on faith, you may be living a lie. And this is a crucial issue – false beliefs are keeping Man in bondage and will get Man nowhere when he dies. And that goes for the New Agers as well. They may all be **recycled**.

While it is not in the purpose of this chapter to trace the origins of today's religions from the days of the Anunnaki, it is relevant to examine some of the aspects needing revision in a major religion, Christianity. Why Christianity? Because its roots and development can be, and have been, traced back through Egyptian theology, Mithraism, and Judaism, and pagan religions of the Middle East – the home of the Anunnaki. [7] As one of the "oldest" Western religions, and most likely to be found among this book's readership, it deserves special attention if people are to know the truth and be set free.

Christianity

And while on the subject, it bears saying that the Roman Catholic Church (called the Church herein), which was the formal instigator of Christianity in AD 325, is due a word of thanks for trying to resolve the chaotic religious scene of the early pre-Christian centuries. In an effort to unite Man under one banner, one religion, and erase wars based on religious differences, the Church expanded its hegemony over the civilized world by absorbing other peoples and their often pagan religions into one… theirs. So before we go throwing stones and accuse the Church of using a mish-mash of theology from pagan religions, be reminded that it was an attempt to establish one culture, one religion, and to unite Man under God instead of under the sword which the former Roman Empire had done but could not sustain. In fact, has anyone noticed that the Roman Empire apparently morphed into the Roman Catholic Church? There are interesting similarities:

The Roman Empire		The Roman Catholic Church
Caesar	→	The Pope
The Senate	→	The Cardinals (Vatican)
The Roman Army	→	The Jesuits / priests

Unification

In order to include or absorb a pagan society, and stop it from attacking Rome, it was a clever idea to try to conquer the pagan people first by creed/faith and show them that whatever their main cult teaching was, the Church also had it (or a similar teaching) and the two cultures could come to terms believing in the same basic God… those pagan cultures that didn't assimilate were smashed and absorbed under the sword anyway. The unification concept was a good one – the violent method of implementing it left a bit to be desired.

Instead of a lot of little local despots and tribal factions, it was advantageous to include one's neighbors in the empire that one was building – not just for the sake of empire, but that Man might co-exist in a relative state of peace and make progress in agriculture, philosophy, science, societal matters, and medicine. A lot of little states meant a lot of potential little wars and one and his family might not survive against a bigger, united enemy (like the Huns or Vandals), and survival was important.

But there were some scattered pagan remnants that adhered to other teachings no matter what the Church did. The Church was trying to move forward, beyond the Anunnaki l egacy, even if they had to create a new religion. Groups like the Gnostics, Cathars and Knights Templar sustained beliefs and teaching contrary to what the Church was trying to establish. Don't think the very early church fathers didn't know about the Anunnaki, even though they were cleverly disguised as the pantheon of Greek gods and, later, as the Roman gods.

335

Anunnaki Hybrid Remnant aka The Gods

Many Anunnaki began leaving Earth about 610 BC and most were gone about 560 BC.[8] And yet there was a **hybrid Remnant** that stayed on and controlled Man (via the priestly group) the same way the Anunnaki gods had done earlier. The Remnant initially took the form of the Greek gods who were real, not myth, and who later were given Latin/Roman names, [9] and thus <u>the Church would have known about them</u>.

Greek God	→	**Roman God**
Apollo (Enki)		Apollo
Dionysus (Ningishzidda)		Bacchus
Eros		Cupid
Heracles		Hercules
Zeus (Enlil)		Jupiter
Ares (Marduk)		Mars
Poseidon (Enki)		Neptune
Hades		Pluto
Odysseus		Ulysses
Aphrodite (Inanna)		Venus

There are more gods but the above is a sampling of the names used first by the Greeks and then later changed into Roman gods. The older Greek temples were actually one of the resting places of the Anunnaki gods as they traveled from place to place, surveying their domain. In the past, they resided atop ziggurats in Sumeria, atop pyramids in the Yucatan, atop Machu Picchu and then Mt. Olympus in Greece – places that were not easily accessible to Man. But what is interesting is that the "… Roman gods arose from a void with no mythological tradition associated with them." [10] That means that there had been no Roman precedent for a pantheon of gods, but Romans were told to adopt the worship of the same Greek gods <u>but to change their names, except for Apollo</u>.

> *Apollo was one of the Greek or Roman gods, thus he appears in both pantheons.*
> *The Greek and Roman gods were the Anunnaki or their hybrid descendants.*
> *Note that* **Enki** *got around and was known by several names – depending on country.*
> *Also* **Marduk** *was Mars, Ra and Nimrod.* **Inanna** *was also Kali and Ishtar.*

Also interesting that there were allegedly two sets of Greek gods: the **Titans** (TI.TA.AN in Sumerian which means "Those who in Heaven Live") and the **Olympians** who were another set of gods that defeated the Titans. [11] Besides the wars between the gods in heaven, the Olympians had also earlier taken on the **Giants** (Anakim, Rephaim and Giborim…) running amok on the Earth and removed most of them. The squabbles and infrastructure wars between the Greek gods were actually the wars between the Anunnaki.[12] And Sitchin informs us that the Titans were the Rephaim thus resolving the whole issue of who was whom. [13]

Anunnaki manipulation has always been with us, and continues to this day through the

Elite (and their 'cutouts' the PTB) – minus an obvious pantheon of gods that we can see. Anunnaki manipulation of Man is also similar to the treatment of Man by the Greek gods – testing, playing and aiding/obstructing Man.

And it was thus for many other human civilizations around the globe, in different Eras, who also had their pantheon of gods. While it started with the Sumerians, it spread to the Greeks, the Celts, the Japanese, the Mayans, the Egyptians, the African tribes, and the Chinese, and in a number of cases around the world, **the same god** appears **but with a different name.** [14] Enki was said to be Quetzalcoatl, Kukulkan, Viracocha and Ahura-Mazda for example.

The problem was that the Anunnaki gave Man basic religion and fear of the gods, and goddess worship – of Inanna (hybrid Anunnaki), later called Ishtar, Astarte, and Asherah – the same goddess with a different name. Other famous goddesses were: Isis, Hathor and Semiramis. Little wonder that the Virgin Mary was the Church's goddess (originally for the benefit of the absorbed pagan tribes) and has remained a mainstay of the Marianist sect.

History Gap

As Chapter 10 showed, there was some significant modification of Christian history, and there is **not much concrete Western History backwards of AD 900**. It is as if Western History, and perhaps Man's only history on this planet, started in the AD 800-900 time frame. After the departure of the Anunnaki,

> **the Maya suddenly disappeared, the Viking outposts in North America disappeared, the Greek and Roman "gods" were no more, and even Chinese history is very vague about history backwards of AD 900**.

Something happened, and Chapters 12-13 will explore the result.

Yet other researchers have determined that there is a bigger historical problem than that:

> Important to our story is the fact that the *Encyclopedia Biblica* reveals that **around 1,200 years of Christian history are unknown**: "Unfortunately, only few of the records [of the Church] prior to the year 1198 have been released." It was not by chance that, in that same year (1198), Pope Innocent III (1198-1216) suppressed all records of earlier Church history by establishing the **Secret Archives** (*Catholic Encyclopedia*, Farley ed., vol. xv, p. 287). Some seven-and-a-half centuries later, and after spending some years in those Archives, Professor Edmond S. Bordeaux wrote *How The Great Pan Died*. In a chapter entitled "**The Whole of Church History is Nothing but a Retroactive Fabrication**," he said this (in part):
>
> > **The Church ante-dated all her late works**, some newly made, some revised and some counterfeited, which contained the final expression of her history… her technique was to make it appear that much later works written by Church writers were composed

> a long time earlier, so that they might become evidence of the first, second or third centuries... [15] [emphasis added]

That is a serious deficit in the evolution of the Christian faith, and **the Church is well aware of what their clerical ancestors did and has said as much throughout the *Catholic Encyclopedia*.** After so many centuries of promoting a certain 'party line' or teaching, it is very difficult to get it turned around without doing major damage to the religion as a whole. Dr. Fomenko in Chapter 10 explained how that came to be. Yet the new Pope may be able to make some proactive changes before too long...

Religion is Culture Absorbed

Most people have not studied the history of religion and as a result do not see that many cultures borrowed their religious concepts from each other, reworked them and claimed them to be their own. [16] Merging religions was a great way to merge cultures and build an empire. It is worth repeating:

> This is particularly true regarding cultures that have merged thru invasion. ...throughout the past 6,000 years of known history peoples have migrated and moved all over the place, so much so that it is impossible here to name the migrations. During these various migrations...invaders absorbed the cultures they invaded. To do this, they usually had to **make the presiding cultural gods into either sub-deities under their own god or gods, or into demons and devils.** This is precisely what has been done throughout the world, whether one realizes it or not. [17] [emphasis added]
> ...
> What few people realize is that **the principal God/Devil of the Old Testament [is] also derived in this way,** from older traditions, specifically the Egyptian, Indian, and Zoroastrian. In fact the God/Devil construct comes in part from[a] derivation of the Dual God of Persia, Ahura-Mazda/Ahriman, or the Egyptian Horus/Set. [18] [emphasis added]

As was stated earlier in Chapter 6, the Horus/Set battle is very reminiscent of the Jesus/Satan battle, and the etymology is very close, too: the name Jesus sounds a bit like Horus, and his name was also spelled Iusa. Horus was called the Krst. The word Satan derives from the Egyptian Set who was also called Sata and Set-anup. [19]

Just because traditions in religion are ancient doesn't mean they are valid and based on reality. Religions took the forms they did to match someone's agenda... and that was usually **control.**

Ways and Means

If the Church was going to create a new religion and establish a beneficent order on Earth, the old teachings and history had to go, and a new world with just Man and God, no animal sacrifice, and no stories about gods and ETs, had to become the norm. And in the shuffle, the information about the OPs who had been called *hylics* by the Greeks, was suppressed – to our detriment.

338

Push came to shove and the suppression got out of hand with the murder of the Cathars and some of the Knights Templar, the sacking and burning of the Library of Alexandria, and anyone in Europe who contradicted the Church was often fatally visited by the Inquisition. The idea was **to force unanimity** – at any price… perhaps a salient application of the Machiavellian concept of "The ends justify the means." And the Church was not alone in using force to convince people to follow the Church; occasionally proponents of Islam and Judaism followed a similar route.

As suggested earlier, in order to successfully convert pagan believers, it also meant incorporating some major pagan ideas (Easter and Christmas) into the new Christianity being formed. While this will not be a comprehensive look at the origins of Christianity, as was mentioned earlier, the phrase "almost everything you thought you knew about… Religion is false" receives major emphasis in this chapter.

Isn't it time to upgrade religion… Isn't Man outgrowing a 1500-year old religion? The proof of that would appear to be the **growing apostasy** in the civilized world, and Bishop John Shelby Spong will address that all-important issue later.

Highlights Examined

It is important to take a look at some of these religious beliefs and promote the truth such that when people die, if they have removed their false beliefs, they will not be shackled by them and wind up going to a context where the (false) beliefs are dominant: i.e., **recycled** back to Earth because they are attached to Earth beliefs. This will be corroborated in later chapters. Some history and resulting beliefs need to be examined.

For example, a major readjustment of Church teaching was when Copernicus and Galileo showed the Church that Earth and Man were **not** the center of the Universe; that also means that Man was not the unique creation of God. Galileo was incarcerated.

Protestant Reformation

The first area of concern was the Catholic Church and its resultant Inquisition – as mentioned in the last chapter, but that was not the only oppressive issue making the rounds in Europe. A much more interesting and far-reaching event was the action by Martin Luther that resulted in the Protestant Reformation. Much of the Christian teaching and issues raised in this chapter were not the doing nor the teaching of the Catholic Church but the result of Martin Luther's protest against the Catholic Church.

While the Catholic Church was guilty of the **Inquisition**, it served the purpose of control to bring many disparate ideas, pagan beliefs, and actual heretic teachings in line with desired Church teachings. And if rebellious people sought to disrupt society and the Church, the Church had to do something to stop them, and for those who would not listen or recant, sometimes the only answer was death to the perpetrators. That is how important it was to establish order among rebellious humans (Think: Enlil's complaint was similar).

The other Church area that got out of control was **Indulgences**, which was money paid to the Church in concert with the Confessional. If properly done it could be very effective in relieving a confessor of his burden of sin … but the Medicis got involved and it became more important how much money a sinner could pay than how much spiritual relief was obtained. And this was an area about which many Catholics complained, thus fueling the flames of the Reformation. [20]

Thus it is important to see that the Church was not the pariah or ogre that some authors have made her out to be. Many priests and Bishops take their role of spiritual leader seriously and the Church has always been truly supportive of those who support and attend to her teachings and outreaches, including the Seven Sacraments. Opus Dei and the Jesuits also create value for society, yet some see this as a 3-way conspiracy to dominate and dictate… but the suspicious "free-thinkers" are the very ones with whom the Church has had issues throughout history. The Church is run by humans who are not perfect, and the absence of a moral leader in the world would be a return to a kind of pagan, do-your-own-thing, as some New Agers prefer.

Martin Luther

Martin Luther was a German Catholic priest who was very interested in mystical teachings and traditions and became progressively unhappy with the Church. He had his own sins and was not comfortable renouncing nor confessing his and thus could not avail himself of the confessional. He was aware of the "boomerang" effect of one's sins causing problems for the sinner, and he sought an alternative way to negate one's karma. He thus sought another way to find salvation, thus creating a new form of Christianity, and problems for the Catholic Church. Thus, **he is responsible for millions of today's Christians believing in redemption through Christ**, something the Catholic Church was not teaching. [21] The Church taught salvation through Faith, Work, Confession and the Sacraments.

He could have reinforced the good tenets of the Church and eliminated the Medici commercialism, but instead he "…taught the false idea that a person has no personal control over his salvation." [22] It was all due to God's grace and the only thing a Christian could do was profess a belief in Jesus Christ whose death on the cross paid for one's sins. It will later be examined that neither the Church nor Jesus in the Bible said that his blood was paying for Man's sins. Paul said that, or whoever wrote Paul's letters, which is still questioned by some Christian scholars.

> Because Luther's confessionals were unsatisfactory, he felt compelled to invent another way to escape the **karma** …the punishments of his monotheistic God. Luther therefore developed the idea that God would allow Jesus' pain and suffering on the cross to become the "boomerang" for everybody. In other words, by "believing in Jesus," you will not spiritually suffer for the bad things you have done … because Jesus has already suffered for you…. Luther's method amounted to "**quickie salvation**" and works and Confession were no longer needed. [23]

Luther also had a personal seal which amounted to his initials "M L" with the Rosy Cross …reflecting the **Rosicrucian Order**. So the Catholic Church launched a Counter-Reformation to unsuccessfully obviate the heresies, and the major thing the Reformation did to the Church was break the back of the Inquisition. The price to be paid for all this 'new thinking' was more materialism, and the evolution of "humanism." [24]

So what ideas crept into Christianity that birthed in the aftermath of the Reformation? Let's examine a few major issues that serious people are questioning today…

Jesus Died for Your Sins?

Jesus is said to have died on the cross, as a sacrificial sin offering for all mankind. Before deciding whether it's true or false, let's look at this teaching in today's more enlightened view, and then decide, based on the ethics and some new facts surrounding this teaching. The teaching is **attributed to Paul, not Jesus**, in the New Testament. **Nowhere in the New Testament does Jesus say He has come to die to remove mankind's sins**. Jesus said he came to set the <u>captives</u> free … by the Truth. It had nothing to do with sin as we'll see.

> "You shall know the truth and it will set you free." Jn 8:32

If it were that important a mission, you'd think that He'd have made it very clear to His disciples, as He (allegedly) made it clear that He was to die and be raised up on the 3rd day. By the way, if Resurrection was a part of God's Plan and God revealed the prophecy to Isaiah (Is. 53), **why does Isaiah not mention the Resurrection**? Is not the Resurrection <u>the</u> more significant part of the whole Cross scenario?

Research indicates that it was Paul who said that Jesus was a sin offering – and the idea was repeated by the author of Hebrews, whom many consider to be **Bishop Clement of Alexandria**, since the Greek style of writing, in vocabulary and grammar, matches the Bishop's. Paul did not write Hebrews. In Hebrews 9:28 is a key phrase:

> So Christ was once offered to bear the sins of many…

In contrast, Paul considered himself to have been enlightened by Christ himself on the road to Damascus, and the author of Hebrews (in verse 2:3) considers his knowledge of Christ to be secondhand. [25] And so the Christians point to Paul's Epistle to the Ephesians, and verse 5:2, as Paul's statement that Christ was a sin offering. And while Ephesians may have been written by Paul (or someone claiming to be Paul, since there was a lot of forgery in those days) [26],[27] Paul was establishing doctrine that was repeated in the Book of Hebrews. If Paul was wrong, then Hebrews was wrong. And **Paul did not know Jesus**, and never met Him nor heard Him speak personally while Jesus was alive.

> *It is unknown whether Hebrews was written before Paul wrote his epistles (AD 50-59), yet it is generally thought that since Hebrews does not mention the destruction of the Temple (AD 70) but the imprisonment of Timothy (Acts 13:23) <u>is</u> mentioned, a date for Hebrews between AD 60 and 70 is reasonable… <u>after</u> Paul's epistles. So Hebrews is probably repeating Paul.* [28] , [29]

Paul says in I Cor. 15:17 that if Christ is not risen, your faith is in vain. In short, is it more important that Christ rose from the dead than that He died for peoples' sins? And nowhere does the Bible suggest that the specific Resurrection act is related to our sins being paid for.

No Vicarious Atonement

It is very simple.
The Bible says "God is Love." Agape, unconditional Love. All the time.
The Bible says "God is the same yesterday, today and tomorrow." Unchanging.
So…
Would a loving God, who doesn't change, sacrifice his only 'Son' to pay for sins…
Would an Earthly father do that? If God doesn't change, how would Jesus' death on the Cross allegedly change God's mind about Man and now He is all love to Man – since the Cross? That sounds like an Earthly god, like Yahweh/Enlil. (Chapter 1). Would a loving God get mad at Man and send a Flood to wipe them all out? Yahweh/Enlil did.

It looks like the Christians are confusing Enlil with the loving God of the Universe.

No Scapegoat

The man called Jesus actually came to set the captives free – from what this place really is. Not to be crucified for them. (See Appendix D.)

There is a problem with believing that Jesus paid for one's sins. If He did, then one's sins are no more and there would be no reason to come back to Earth again and again to learn or 'pay for' what one did wrong. Yet we know from many professional hypnotic regressions over the last 20 years that this **soul recycling happens,** even to Christians. We also know it happens from what the **Near Death Experiencers** say. If Jesus paid the price for your sins, that should get you out of here… right now! Yet, souls **do** come back, even Christian souls, as reported by the NDErs and Dr. Modi's patients. You come back! How can that be if there is nothing more to pay for?

This is one of the areas that needs updating to get in sync with the reality of eternal souls reincarnating – which was **a teaching of the original church.** It was removed in a proactive effort to get people to straighten out their lives NOW, in the belief that they had just one life and then Heaven or Hell was their reward. Scared straight. People need to know that **Karma rules** and you either get it together or you will keep coming back and back until you do… and that is not endless fun and games here – the gods that run this place will progressively "tighten the screws" to get your attention until you do straighten out… but 51% is good enough – **you don't have to be perfect.**

By the way, the Koran shares the information that Jesus did not die on the Cross, but was healed. (Surah 4:157). It is rumored that the man called Jesus went back to India and spent the rest of His days there until dying of natural causes at the age of 117. So if He didn't die, He certainly wasn't a "sin offering" for Mankind. **(See Appendix D where this issue and Dr. Fomenko are connected.)**

Need to Rethink

Many adults have not seen through the illogic of the sins on the Cross issue…the same way they could not see thru the **Easter Bunny, Santa Claus or the Tooth Fairy** when they were younger. But in this case, as adults, they <u>want</u> to be free of their sins, they like to believe someone else can pay the price – they do not want the responsibility. (Christianity teaches that Man <u>cannot</u> pay the price and so there had to be a Jesus.) And that is the heart of the matter – **Jesus paying for your sins is promoting irresponsibility:** it means that you don't have to learn your lessons and be worthy of entering Heaven. You can be an ignorant, petty person and Jesus will love you and take you in. Really? I suggest that Heaven is no place for rowdy souls who haven't learned their 'lessons.'

> *In point of fact, as will be seen in Chapter 15, it is because we are rowdy, petty, lie, cheat and steal that we are here. It was our dysfunctional behavior that got us 'contained' here, and <u>no one</u> is releasing any of us until we clean up our act. There is no vicarious atonement, great as it sounds… but it bought many converts to the new Church.*

What a surprise the believers will get on the Other Side. Because it is a <u>false </u>belief, the Neggs <u>can</u> recycle you, like this: you die, thinking your sins are gone and have no more to learn or pay for, and so you expect to go Heaven and be with Jesus – but that isn't possible because after you became a Christian, you stopped working to learn and grow spiritually, and may have done very little additional to be a better person – falsely thinking Jesus paid for it all! Now the Being of Light will inform you that you go back to learn what you didn't learn.

Surprise. You bought a lie and now are **recycled**.

That is why it is said: "You shall know the truth and the truth will set you **free**."

And it is too late to fix anything. When you are put back in a body, you are given 'amnesia' and can't remember whatever truths you discovered on the Other Side, so you cycle back again and again – never figuring out what is going on – and you may buy into more lies, or the same ones, the next time around. And then comes the crowning irony: a book like this comes along, inviting you to think, investigate and grow, and if you diss it, you stay in the Earth recycling loop. The real gods prefer that you wake up and **free yourself from Earth**.

You don't have to believe this book, just be willing to consider these things, use it as **catalyst** and do your own research, and your own thinking – outside the box that was created for you by others. There is Truth out there and it is not hiding.

Rewind: Karma, Reincarnation & Recycling

Karma is about learning – see Chapter 7's explanation. Remember that simultaneous or concurrent lives bear no karma to each other – any karma belongs to, and stays within, the individual <u>soul aspect</u> lifetime being linearly reviewed.

Multiverse karma is more like the Golden Rule – what you do to others (good or bad) will come back to you, but not as in "an eye for an eye." Instead of karma, Man is more like "meeting himself" and the lessons in his **Script** which may or may not be based on karma.

Reincarnation and **recycling** are the two main devices for incarnating souls in this current Earth realm:

    Reincarnation means you can incarnate in a different body, in a different time for <u>new</u> experiences. This has to be <u>earned</u>: if old lessons have been learned. The new Script applies here.

    Recycled, however, is what happens for most people – due to what this place is, and that is revealed in Chapter 13. Recycled means you can't get out of here, and you are basically trapped… one of the 'proofs' is **Déjà Vu** – you <u>have</u> been here, you <u>have</u> seen it, and you <u>have</u> heard it and done it before. There is no new Script in this case.

This is covered more in Chapter 14; refer to the section on 'Life is a Film.'

Vicarious Atonement

So wouldn't vicarious atonement be a lie because you <u>do</u> have to learn from your own mistakes ("sins") and <u>cannot</u> impute (dump) them on Jesus? Or on anyone. If a fledgling church were trying to impress people, win them over, and offer them something better than what they already believed, <u>and</u> if that same church knew how base and corrupt Man could be, what could be better than to offer their potential converts the promise of all their sins being paid for by a sacrificial god-man?

Please be clear on this:

Jesus never said He was paying for anybody's sins.

Paul is the one who, as a practicing Jew and **ex-persecutor of Christians**, emphasized the teaching of vicariously paying for sins in the New Testament. And remember that Paul's letters were written BEFORE the 4 Gospels, meaning they could have influenced the writing of the 4 Gospels. And also remember that **Paul did not know Jesus** and never heard Him teach. So, how accurate is Paul's message?

Ethics of Vicarious Atonement

Now the ethics aspect. Consider: what kind of a God would condone killing His own Son, whom He loves and is without fault, just to appease His wrath? Sounds like an Aztec god. Does a loving, <u>earthly</u> father kill his innocent son to remove the sins of his daughter? What kind of perversion is that? And, does anyone seriously believe that sacrificing doves or bulls can atone for Man's sins? **Sacrifice is pandering to Enlil (Yahweh).**

Or would a loving, wise God (Abba) care about each of His created souls <u>learning</u> and growing through their trials and mistakes ("sins"), to where they reach a more spiritually mature, compassionate, approach to life? The Father of Light loves his creation and does <u>not</u> operate by Enlil's dictum, "An eye for an eye."

Savior Myths

If you are looking for a savior god, one who was a "son of God," or at least a god whose exploits exceed those of mortal Man, you have a lot to choose from:

> Krishna of Hindostan, Buddha Sakia of India, Osiris and Horus of Egypt, Zoroaster of Persia, Baal of Phonecia, Indra of Tibet, Tammuz of Syria, Mithra of Greece & Rome, Ahura-Mazda of Persia, Attis of Phrygia, Adad [ISH.KUR, son of Enlil] of Assyria, Beddru of Japan, Cadmus of Greece, Quetzalcoatl of Mexico, Fohi and Tien of China, Adonis of Greece, Prometheus of the Caucasus, Mohammed of Arabia, Lugh of Celtic fame, and Apollo of Greece/Hyperborea.

What is interesting is that most of these 'saviors' or gods are found in myths coming out of the very part of the world where the Anunnaki ruled and gave Man religion. [30] Most of them were not myth but real, 3D beings.

Could Christianity and two of its key traditions be based on myths from ancient cultures conquered by the Church? Easter and Christmas are known to be "cleaned up" pagan celebrations. **Easter** was in celebration of Ishtar (Spring equinox), and **Christmas** was in celebration of the Sun's rebirth (Winter solstice). [31] Even the Twelve Days of Christmas are associated with the traditional 12 signs of the Zodiac. [32]

Nothing is quite what it seems…

Jesus or Horus?

And then according to Albert Churchward in Of Religion, there was Horus in Egypt:

> Jesus was the Son of God, Horus was the 'son' of God in Egypt….
> Jesus was the Light of the World, Horus was the Light of the World.
> Jesus said he was the way, the truth and the life. Horus said he was the
>   way, the truth and the life.
> Jesus was born in Bethlehem, 'the house of bread'. Horus was born in Annu,
>   the 'place of bread'.
> Jesus was the Good Shepherd, Horus was the Good Shepherd.
> Jesus was the Lamb. Horus was the Lamb.
> Jesus is identified with a cross, Horus was identified with a cross.
> Jesus was the child of a virgin, Mary. Horus was the child of a virgin, Isis.
> Jesus had 12 disciples. Horus had 12 followers.
> Jesus was the Morning Star [a Lucifer]. Horus was the Morning Star.
> Jesus was the Christ. Horus was the Krst.
> Jesus was tempted on a mountain by Satan, Horus was tempted on a mountain
> by Set. [33]

Coincidence? The Horus story "…predates the Christian version by thousands of years." [34] Is it possible that the story of Jesus Christ is a repeat of Horus and/or Krishna? [35] If so, **the real Jesus was later mythologized.** (See Appendix D.)

Having said all that, it is important to point out that there is power in Christ's name (prayers in His name <u>are</u> often answered), and that during deliverance ministry activity even the Neggs (or alleged 'demons') don't deny that the name has power. And neither do I, but I used to wonder what Jesus' <u>real name</u> was... The man later called Jesus was real – what hurts the Christian cause is the fact the contemporaries of the alleged Jesus never wrote about him – such as Philo, Suetonius or Pliny the Younger. And Josephus' entry in the *Antiquities of the Jews* has been proven false – by serious Bible-banging scholars. Maybe someday the whole story can be revealed …minus the myths of antiquity.

Some claim it <u>has</u> been told… What if Jesus wasn't his real name?

Apollonius of Týana

We might consider the man called Apollonius of Týana (4 BC – 102 AD), born in the region of Cappadocia (Turkey) during the reign of Augustus, **whose father was the god Apollo**. He was the subject of Philostratus' biography <u>Life of Apollonius</u> (written in AD 210). The biography is considered reasonably credible since Philostratus was a personal friend of Damis, who was a follower of Apollonius.[36] Even if, as some detractors say, Damis was fictional, Apollonius <u>did</u> have followers and Baha'u'llah the founder of the Baha'i Faith, Sir Francis Bacon and Voltaire all recognized Apollonius as an exemplary philosopher, teacher, healer, and Miracle-worker. [37]

He wandered around teaching, healing, and doing miracles, about the time that Jesus was supposed to have done his miracles. Philostratus' book was suppressed by the orthodox clergy as the Church gained momentum with its story of Jesus, and whereas many copies of the story of Apollonius could be found in Alexandria, the copies were harder to find after the libraries of Alexandria were sacked and burned. [38] It looks like the Biblical life of Jesus was modeled on that of Apollonius, and Jesus' birth and death events were a composite of earlier people and myths.

Temple Bust of Apollonius of Tyana
(source: http://www.truthbeknown.com/apollonius.jpg)

Unlike Jesus, there is evidence to prove that **Apollonius actually existed**... Apollonius was born in the reign of [Emperor] Augustus... In the Augustan age, historians flourished; poets, orators, critics, and travelers abounded. Yet not one of them mentions the name of Jesus Christ , much less any incident in his life. Jesus left us nothing in writing, although there is a growing speculation that the Gospel of Thomas was written by his hand... If indeed [Jesus] existed, he traveled only to Judea and Egypt. Apollonius traveled extensively and wrote extensively. The Emperor Marcus Aurelius admitted that it was to Apollonius that he owed his own philosophy, and **erected temples and statues in his honor.** No statues or temples were erected to Jesus. [39] [emphasis added]

Also said of the Emperor Aurelian:

Aurelian vowed to erect temples and statues to [Apollonius'] honor, for was there ever anything among man more holy, venerable, noble, and divine than Apollonius? He restored life to the dead, he did and spoke many things beyond human reach (The Magus by Francis Barrett). [40]

Apollonius' Fame

It was said that many temples and statues were erected to Apollonius in many places, "...including his own town of Týana, even though the later Christians destroyed many of them." [41] It is odd that Apollonius' reputation was identical to that of Jesus, and he was well-respected and even revered in many places, and yet the Christians almost demonically turned to destroy Apollonius' works and suppress his legacy. Apollonius was not a rival to Jesus, nor did he threaten the fledgling Church in any way. [42]

Says another expert in the origins of Christianity, regarding Apollonius:

...Hierocles, the pro-consul under Diocletian (284-305 AD), ...wrote the "Philalethes" (AD 303) **exposing the Apollonius-Jesus connection**. It should be noted that Philostratus' account makes no mention of any Jesus Christ, not even as a rival to Apollonius, who purportedly lived precisely at the time alleged of Jesus. [43] [emphasis added]

However, Apollonius' factual life was in danger of usurping the Church's idea of Jesus, and this bothered early Church fathers like Justin Martyr (2nd century AD):

How is it that the talismans by Apollonius have power over certain members of creation, for they prevent, as we have seen, the fury of the waves, the violence of the winds, and the attacks of wild beasts. And whilst Our Lord's miracles are preserved **by tradition alone**, those of Apollonius are most numerous, and actually manifested in present facts... [44] [emphasis added]

Thus the biography of Apollonius was suppressed by the Church and "...the books of the New Testament did not appear until at the very least 100 years after The Life of

Apollonius." [45] So most of the writings about Apollonius were either destroyed, hidden, or just suppressed until after those living (who knew of Apollonius) had died before the Church promoted the new savior, god-man, Jesus. Apollonius himself could not be used as the role model since the Church had to embellish the god-man with various pagan elements to make it acceptable to the many converts it hoped to acquire. [46]

Connection with Dr Fomenko?

If as Dr. Fomenko says, history was backdated several hundred years, is it possible that the Inquisitions of the 1100-1600 AD era were right on the heels of Apollonius' time and his works… which is why people knew about him? If he existed in the 1000-1100 AD era, could that be why the Inquisition had to be used to promote the fledgling Church – free from non-Catholic history? Would that not be a great idea to backdate history – to distance Apollonius backwards 800-1000 years from the time of the Inquisition? That way future people would not connect the two, and what if the story of Apollonius could be buried altogether?

Jesus as Apollonius

In addition, nowhere in the writings of Apollonius is there a mention of anyone called Jesus or Saul/Paul. Conversely, the contemporaries of the alleged Jesus such as Philo, Suetonius, Plutarch, Pliny the Younger and Cornelius Tacitus **do not specifically mention a Jesus**, nor is the Josephus reference trustworthy: it has been found to be an insertion, suggesting fraud in the early Christian church [see below]. [47] While there is often a 'Yeshu' or 'Chrestus' found in some of the ancient texts, the mention is usually a brief 1-liner and it is unclear who they are referring to. Certainly if Chrestus was as important as Jesus was alleged to be, wouldn't there be more said about him? Apollonius was as noteworthy and significant as was Jesus, but Apollonius was well-known and Jesus wasn't. Strange, unless Jesus was Apollonius and the Catholic church changed his name… (the issue is clarified in Appendix D).

Apollonius The Nazarene
(source: http://www.interfarfacing.com/apollonius.jpg)

Similarity?

Jesus (source: Bing Images/Jesus)

The picture of Apollonius above is reminiscent of a lot of pictures of Jesus. In fact, there is a book by a young boy (four-year-old Colton Burpo) who died, went to Heaven, then returned (NDE) and told people what Jesus really looked like. [48] Then Akiane Kramarik painted the picture (below left) which Colton approved:

Akiane's Picture of Jesus   **Image on Shroud of Turin**

For what it is worth, some people may wonder if it matches the Shroud of Turin image, and that is included above. You be the judge… In addition, Appendix D has an analysis by Dr. Fomenko on Jesus that could be of interest…

Could the life, activities and teachings of **Apollonius** have been used to establish the life of Jesus, as appears to have been the case with the lives of **Horus** and **Krishna**? Certainly if the written records of Jesus were lost and only the oral tradition survived, would it not have been a plausible effort to 'reconstruct' the life of Jesus based on any one of the exemplary three saints mentioned? Do not all avatars do basically the same thing and teach the same things?

And yet the Church did not wipe out Apollonius' teaching, as many of his teachings and writings were taken East into India for safe-keeping. In 1801 a major text was brought back and translated to English. [49] Nor were his followers scattered after his death. Apollonius had started a church and had followers called *Apolloniei* which survived several centuries after his death, and they were probably connected with the Therapeuts and **Nazarenes** as Apollonius had contact and ministry with them during his life. [50]

Many of Apollonius' followers were also to be found in the fledgling Church, especially after The Council of Nicea (AD 325) met, so he may be said to have had an effect on the Church inasmuch as his life mirrors that of the new god-man, Jesus, including his writings, and then the Church embellished the newly-hatched Nicean teachings with "…serpentine myths and traditions of the oldest [pagan] order." [51]

Paul as Apollonius

It is interesting that there are many similarities between the missionary activities of St. Paul and Apollonius, with both men having visited the same cities and having performed the same works.

> **It is very likely that 'Paul' is a version of the name Apollonius since Apollonius' nickname was 'Pol'** *and visited the same places the Apostle Paul was said to have visited, and Pol did the same things Paul did.* [52]

There is historical corroboration:

> **Apollonius** is a Greek name, the Latin Romanized version would be **Apollos**. Apollos over a period of time as well as convenience morphed to **Paulos**…in its English format is **Paul**… Apollonius was born in Tyana [Turkey, just 30 miles from St. Paul's Tarsus]… both Apollonius and Paul were in Tarsus at the same time in their youth, as Newman points out, Apollonius and Paul were also at Ephesus and Rome at exactly the same time…

> In the Greek text, Apollonius is commonly written as Pol as well as Apollos, "Apollos" of the New Testament [Corinthians] – the eloquent "Jew" whose preaching and baptizing at Corinth and at Ephesus preceded the work of the Apostle Paul…

> The companion of Apollonius was **Demis**… and [Timothy] **Demas** was the companion of Paul. [53]

It is reasonable to think that Apollonius could have served as **the role model** for both Jesus and Paul. And current-day author Ms. Atwater has something to say in this regard…

More Bible Insights

In her excellent book on *Near Death Experiences,* P.M.H. Atwater corroborates much of what has been said in Chapter 1 and this chapter: [54]

> The Holy Bible and Christianity did not develop as the masses are taught. The Sinai Bible (the oldest known) contains the first mention of Jesus, beginning when he was 30 years old. When the New Testament of the Sinai Bible is compared with modern-day versions, 14,800 editorial alterations can be identified. **Paul was actually Apollonius of Tyana**, a first century wandering sage…. Restructured writings of Apollonius became the Epistles of Paul in AD 397. Early Gospels never mentioned a virgin birth. Christ's suffering, the crucifixion and the resurrection did not appear in the Gospels until the 12th century…   [emphasis added]

Ms. Atwater further points out that today's Christian scholars know about The Great Omission – crucifixion/resurrection missing from earlier versions of the Bible – and The Great Insertion is when the Church put it into the Bible via the Gospel of John.

The Church was very busy, and very selective.

Religious Tolerance

The Church dissed an important aspect of Apollonius' teaching: He was tolerant of all other religions and sought only to help people perfect whatever their form of worship was. It was only important that a person have the integrity and dedication to their professed belief – whatever it was.

Secondly, Apollonius did not travel to other lands with the goal of proselytizing. He understood that **the Father will hold people responsible for whatever their belief or professed faith is, and how well they served it** – NOT whether they believed in the 'right' religion.

This is a point of view to keep in mind in the later section on Bishop John Shelby Spong. Inasmuch as Apollonius communicated with the gods who run Earth and watch over Man, and he was divinely empowered – meaning the gods (Enki) were pleased with him – his attitude towards all religions could warrant serious attention… and copying.

Reasons to Reject?

It can be seen what the Church was trying to do in creating a god-man without any blemish when one reads more deeply about Apollonius. While everyone agrees that Apollonius was a **flawless model teacher and healer**, following the true Pythagorean Way with no black marks against him, [55] if the Church had promoted him by name, it might have led people to fall back into their old pagan ways or leave.

Apollonius was known to **venerate the Sun** every day, [56] he believed in **reincarnation** (as did Origen), and he supported the Gnostic message that **Man could find God within**, through Knowledge. In addition, it appears that Apollonius was not only a Pythagorean, but one of his main sources for his spiritual teachings was **Orpheus**, since the two statues of Apollonius and Orpheus were often found together in many temples. [57] These issues were anathema to the Church. A hybrid god-man, son of Apollo, would not do as a role model.

Further, and perhaps most significant, as Apollonius means "son of Apollo", [58] then Apollo being one of the gods, and such term was often applied to the great men of antiquity (Gilgamesh, Sargon, Alexander, Zarathustra, Noah, etc) suggests that Apollo, and thus his son, were in fact genetic **hybrids** and that bloodline with its special DNA is what gave Apollonius his special powers – just like Alexander the Great and Moses who were hybrid descendants of the Anunnaki *Adapa*. That fact would be enough for the

Church to reject him – even though his words, behavior, and writings were as pure and as spiritual as the teachings of a Jesus. In fact, Jesus' teachings are almost verbatim what Apollonius taught and wrote.

> *In short, if this conclusion is correct, the Church just wasn't taking any chances and had to distance itself from the Anunnaki legacy.*

So the Church could not accept the actual Apollonius as their basic role model, but recreated a new god-man role model for humanity that was more in reach than Apollonius was: the teaching of a fully human Jesus that was 'Christed' by the Father when he was baptized, would be easier to accept and follow. It is hard to emulate a hybrid god-man and so **Man was reduced to worshipping and not emulating.** [59] And yet, Apollonius was something of a god and was worshipped as one, [60] so the issue is complicated. It lies in the main fact that **the earlier Church knew what Apollonius' lineage was**, and that he wasn't 100% Man, so the brief ministry of Jesus had to be used, probably amplified with Apollonius' exploits. Remember: Apollonius and Jesus were said to have historically taught and done the same things… And don't all avatars teach and do the same things, anyway?

> Apollonius was called Son of Man because his mother was human.
> Apollonius was called Son of God because his father was Apollo (Enki).

Is this the origin of the term?
Apollonius spent his later years in Tibet, Kashmir and India, where he died well over 100 years old. He never married, and if Apollonius was the role model for Jesus that spikes the story that Jesus was married and sired a Merovingian bloodline…

Christianity's Irregularities

Josephus' Entry Was Forged

Lastly, Gardiner raises the existence-of-Jesus issue, as have many other researchers, which continues to this day, despite the huge amount of books written about Jesus in the last 100 years. Ironically, since there is nothing concrete about Jesus the man, the many books are basically rehashing the same old information from the four gospels and Gardiner suggests that many of those books would have been better off staying as trees.

> …when we come to examine [the books], one startling fact confronts us. All these books relate to a person concerning whom there does not exist a single scrap of contemporary [1st century] information – not one! Nobody can say with any conviction in truth, and not faith, that Jesus was a real person. [61]

And before someone points out **Flavius Josephus'** *Antiquities of the Jews* (18.63-64) as an irrefutable source, to repeat: it is widely accepted (by serious Christian Bible scholars) that this passage was subject to a forgery wherein several lines were added (to what Josephus had already written about a messiah) that purport to describe the Jesus as the Messiah, and his rising on the third day. [62] Another researcher has echoed the same findings on Josephus:

...there are only two brief paragraphs that purport to refer to Jesus. Although much has been made of these "references," they have been dismissed by scholars and Christian apologists alike as **forgeries**... No less an authority than Bishop Warburton of Gloucester (1698-1779) labeled the Josephus interpolation regarding Jesus **"a rank forgery**, and a very stupid one, too." [63] [emphasis added]

And for those who may be interested,

[Joseph] Wheless, a lawyer, and Taylor, a minister, agree with many others including Christian apologists such as Dr. Lardner, that it was **Eusebius** [an early church father] himself who **forged** the passage in Josephus.[64]   [emphasis added]

It's getting so you just can't trust anyone anymore...

Now, let's see how well the Word of God holds up to close scrutiny – after all, if it is truly the inerrant word of God, it will have no errors, inconsistencies or contradictions.

The Word of God

Epistle Shuffle

In addition to the question of the dates of the gospels, it came to light that Mark was the first written gospel, then Matthew (based on Mark), then Luke, and then John. [65] And earlier we had the epistles of Paul which **actually** <u>predate</u> **the four Gospels**. Other researchers have noted that **Paul doesn't mention an historical Jesus**:

There still remained the problem that the real Paul doesn't mention an historical Jesus. But once again the solution was simple. Place Paul's letters **after** the gospels. Now when readers come to Paul they naturally assume that he is talking about the historical Jesus portrayed in the earlier books. Modern spin-doctors could learn a thing or two from these Literalists! You've got to admire their ingenuity. [66] [emphasis added]

As a matter of fact, repeated for emphasis, Paul wrote his letters <u>before</u> the four Gospels were written.[67] And then they were inserted <u>after</u> the four Gospels as if Paul had written them based on his knowledge of Jesus (whom he really never met), and the preceding four Gospels. What a sham. Is this why Peter and James allegedly would not let Paul preach/teach in Jerusalem and forced him to take his teachings on the road?

But if Paul didn't exist, and Jesus didn't exist, maybe Peter and James also didn't exist, and the issue of Paul versus James and Peter is a non-sequitur. As said earlier, Paul may have been based on the missionary journeys of 'Pol', or Appolonius of Tyana. They both went to the same cities <u>at the same time</u>.

353

In addition to *Hebrews* <u>not</u> being written by Paul, the *Acts of the Apostles* only speaks of 3 of the disciples – how is this revealing the acts of the <u>twelve</u> apostles? *Acts* was written to establish Peter as the founder of the Church. Paul never accepted the authority of Peter. [68]

> In the third century CE the holy forgery mill of Literalist Christianity continued to churn out documents to add to the New Testament. More letters were created that portray Paul as a Literalist, such as *2 Thessalonians* and *3 Corinthians*. Letters were also forged in the names of Peter and John. The *Second Letter of John* gives up all pretense that it is trying to communicate anything about Jesus…. During the first three centuries CE **every book that now makes up the New Testament was hailed by someone as sacred scripture and derided by someone else as a forgery**…. Literalist Christians also adopted the Tanakh, which had been so vociferously rejected by the original Gnostic Christians, and made it their Old Testament… [69]
> [emphasis added]

The Tanakh (OT) was rearranged by the Christians to appear to be one long preparation for the Messiah Jesus, so that the Old Testament ends with Malachi's saying that "… I will send the prophet Elijah to you…" and thus the New Testament picks up with John the Baptist preparing the way for Jesus.

Except for the first 5 books (the Pentateuch), the Old Testament of the Christian Bible is **in a different order** from the same books in the Jewish Tanakh. I would suspect that the Jews have a better idea of the correct order of <u>their books</u> than those who rearranged the books of the OT for the Christian Bible.

Bible Structure

While the Bible is an inspired document, and parts of it are beautiful, there is a very big structural flaw that has gone unnoticed for centuries. The Old Testament (OT) has nothing to do with the New Testament (NT) and the two should never have been put together as one book.

> **Binding the OT with the NT is like binding <u>Moby Dick</u> and <u>Pinocchio</u> into one book because they both deal with the ocean and a whale.**

Case in point, mentioned earlier, was in the Book of Isaiah where it is taught that Isaiah was foreshadowing Christ (Isaiah 53) going to the Cross. Nice try. Isaiah was describing an archetypal messiah in general, and he was not the only one writing such material at that time – **Jewish history is replete with messianic literature**. The whole point of the NT teaching about Christ is that He rose after the crucifixion – His <u>resurrection</u> is the whole key to Christianity. And Isaiah's version missed it.

> **Isaiah says nothing about a resurrection.**

Thus, Isaiah was not describing Jesus… or the Holy Spirit goofed and forgot to mention <u>the</u> Resurrection to Isaiah.

In fact, in the approximately 400 years between the OT and the NT, there were <u>hundreds</u> of messianic documents written and they foretold (hoped?) that a messiah would come and save their people. The Jews were always looking for a messiah who would sacrifice for them. Jesus was not <u>that</u> Messiah. The Jews know it and they are still waiting…

In addition, the NT has little to do with the Torah which is actually a separate religion – the Jews do not include the NT in their holy writs, neither Torah, nor Talmud, so why do the Christians include the OT in their Bible? Is it to make Christianity look older than it really is? If so, why didn't the Christians include the Apocrypha as did the Catholics?

Moreover, the Old Testament provides a biblical gloss that makes serious study impossible – one has to turn to the other scrolls, epics and writings from Sumeria, or to the *Haggadah*, to pursue details.

> One gets the impression from reading the Old Testament, particularly Genesis, that no one was really in charge. There is a lot of argument and debate with God; there is much confusion in the Garden of Eden where an omnipotent god has to search for Adam and Eve. The role of Satan or Lucifer in heaven and on Earth is obscure. The activities of the Nephilim are barely touched on and then forgotten. [70]

Remember: around AD 325, a committee originally put the Bible together, according to their own agenda, and then centuries later (AD 1611) a King Jimmy modified it – that's why it's called the King James <u>Version</u>. Just because something is ancient and traditional doesn't mean it's true. It may just have served someone's purpose in its time.

Misquotes in the Word : Pickles and Camels

In the OT Book of Jonah, the Bible tells us that Jonah was in a whale, and it is doubtless something that the God of the Universe <u>could do</u> if He wanted. But if you happen to be aware of **Aramaic idioms**, as are scholars George Lamsa and Rocco Errico, you learn that there was an idiom in that part of the world that said that if you were in a problem, you were "in a fish," and if the problem was huge, so was the fish – or you were in a whale of a problem.

We have a similar saying here in the USA: "Jack, can you help me out? **I'm in a real pickle!**" Will people 1000 years from now think that there were huge pickles that could hide a man inside? (If so, they'll claim they all came from Texas.)

In another example of ignorance of Aramaic idioms, Jesus is alleged to have said "It is easier for **a camel to go thru the eye of a needle**, than for a rich man to enter the kingdom of Heaven." Again an error in translation and scholars have postulated camels kneeling to squeeze through a narrow gate in the wall of a city, etc ….Silly. All because they don't know.

In Aramaic, the word for camel is gámla and the word for rope is gamlá-- accented and spoken differently. Thus Jesus' statement should read, "It is easier for a rope to go thru the eye of a needle, than for a rich man to enter the kingdom of Heaven." It makes slightly more sense when the proper translation is used.

Enough mistranslations abound that Dr. Lamsa wrote a book about it: <u>Idioms in the Bible Explained and A Key to the Original Gospels.</u> Worth checking out.

Confusion in the Word

Paul in ACTS

Paul was traveling to Damascus when he was supposedly knocked off his horse/camel by a bright light. He recounts the event <u>twice</u> in the Book of Acts:[71]

Acts 9:7 says "And the men which journeyed with [Paul] stood speechless, **hearing a voice** but seeing no man." (KJV, Study Bible)

Acts 22:9 says "And they that were with me saw indeed the light… but they **heard not the voice** of Him that spake to me." (KJV, Study Bible)

So, Paul heard the voice both times, but the 2nd description in Acts 22 contradicts what happened for the men with him. Did the writer of the Acts 22 passage forget what he said in Acts 9? In addition, there is this aspect of the same scenario:

Acts 26:13-14 says "At midday…. I saw in the way a light….And….I heard a voice speaking unto me, and saying **in the Hebrew** tongue…" (KJV, Study Bible) or if we change Bibles to the NIV:

Acts 26:13-14 says " About noon….I saw a light from heaven… And…I heard a voice saying to me in **Aramaic**…" (NIV, Study Bible)

The Scofield/Reina-Valera says "Hebrew" and the Promise Keepers (NIV) says "Aramaic." NAS says "Hebrew", and the Living Bible (NLT) says "Aramaic."

Which is the correct version? If this is really God's word, we have a problem. **Hebrew and Aramaic are not the same language.** You say this is a nit-picking point, but how many other places in the Word were mistranslated? If this were truly the Word of God, would it be contradictory and confusing? And which version would The God endorse?

> *Is it for this issue that Christian **Apologetics** was created – to apologize for and explain the Word of God? Why not just correct it?*

Gospel Fictions

The Gospel stories are largely fictions written by the Church fathers and could rightly be called "Gospel Fictions." [72]

> The gospels are **all priestly forgeries** over a century after their pretended dates. Those who concocted some of the hundreds of 'alternative' gospels and epistles that were being kicked about during the first several centuries C.E. have even admitted that they forged the documents. Forgery during The first centuries of the Church's existence was admittedly **rampant,** so

common in fact that a new phrase was coined to describe it: **"pious fraud."** Such **prevarication is confessed to repeatedly in the Catholic Encyclopedia**. [73] [emphasis added]

Shocking, but plausible. This could explain why the gospels were written so long after Jesus' death (100 + years), instead of during His time. And consider…

There is a reason for those years of silence: the construct of Christianity did not begin until after the first quarter of the fourth century [AD 325 = Council of Nicea] and that is why **Pope Leo X (d. 1521) called Christ a "fable."** [74] [emphasis added]

Christ is Profitable

Lastly, consider the words of Pope Leo X quoted earlier: "What profit has not that **fable** of Christ brought us!" [75] Even the online Wikipedia reference to that quote indicates that it is genuine:

… the earliest known source of this statement is actually a polemical work by John Bale *Acta Romanorum Pontificum* [of] 1574: "For on a time when a cardinall Bembus did move a question out of the Gospell, the Pope gave him a very contemptuous answer saying: All ages can testifie enough howe profitable that fable of Christe hath ben to us and our companie." The Pope in this case being Leo X. (http://en.wikiquote.org/wiki/Pope_Leo_X)

This suggests that even by the time of Pope Leo X, or the 1500's, it was the case that the Jesus character had been so mythologized that even the Church hierarchy was doubting His reality.

And yet, **there is truth and beauty in the Bible** – it is **not** a worthless book. It just is the "inspired word of Man" – or sometimes the inspired and modified Anunnaki word. Remember that they were the source of religion for Man and its purpose was control.

And yet, our understanding of Jesus' ministry needs a serious update because we have all been misled by a current "politically correct" Christianity which was designed to be something different when it was first formed. Those times have changed, people have become smarter, but Christianity has not changed.

There are many Bible scholars who are waking up to the illusion, including **Bishop John Shelby Spong** who has said that he rejects the concept of Jesus' death on the cross for our sins, the virgin birth, and the Bible as the literal, revealed word of God.[76] And judging by the last few pages examining the Christ myth above, we <u>need</u> a new Christianity – one built on truth, Light, brotherhood and Love. Bishop Spong's concern is that if we don't seriously overhaul Christianity and make it relevant for today, it will die. And today, **apostasy** is a real issue, gaining ground with each year….

A New Christianity

Bishop John Shelby Spong of the Episcopalian Church has written many books promoting the necessary 'death' of an archaic Christianity and he discusses at length what elements the new Christianity should have to truly serve Man, and not just be some lifeless ritual that serves no one spiritually.

> The reformation needed today must, in my opinion, be so total that it will by comparison make the Reformation of the sixteenth century look like a child's tea party… I believe that Christianity cannot continue as the irrelevant religious sideshow to which it has been reduced… [and] **the way Christianity has traditionally been formulated no longer has credibility**. [77] [emphasis added]

He goes on to say that modern man now perceives reality differently than Man of even 200 years ago – the advances and knowledge in science alone (see Chapter 9) make one question the Bible. The virgin birth is seen today as artificial insemination, and we know that "being born in sin" refers to one's corrupt DNA from one's ancestors, and we also question the existence of a Devil and Hell.

The Darwinian view of life has also affected the Christian world. Besides the standard "No-Creation, All-was-Evolution-from-a-Primordial-Soup" teaching, Darwin also brought to Man the realization that things are still evolving – the Creation is not perfect, nor is it complete. [78] And now that we know more about the likely Creation of Man by ETs and its total possibility via our knowledge of genetics, limited though it is compared to that of the Anunnaki, we have begun to look at the world in a different light.

Blasphemous Sacrifice

Bishop Spong also deplores the teaching that a mighty God, like an oriental potentate, has been offended by the behavior of His offspring and so decrees that His Son shall be sacrificed so that "… His offended dignity has been satisfied." [79] Says Dr. Spong, **It is a barbaric thought that a loving God of the Universe cannot forgive His fallen creation without shedding the blood of other parts of the living creation**. A sacrifice of a faultless man. Out of such teaching came the eucharist where we then eat His body and drink His blood. Doesn't anyone see the barbarism in this? Make no mistake, the RCC taught that the wafers and wine were the "transubstantiated" body and blood of Christ… but the concept is still **cannibalism**.

> Seldom did Christians pause to recognize the ogre into which they had turned God. A human father who would nail his son to a cross for any purpose would be arrested for child abuse. Yet that continued to be said of God as if it made God more holy and more worthy of worship… **I would choose to loathe rather than to worship a deity who required the sacrifice of his son.** [80] [emphasis added]

Jesus, Apollonius, Horus, Krishna and Quetzalcoatl did not condone blood sacrifice.

Jesus as Rescuer

So any reformation of Christianity must be a re-think of everything we have accepted or believed to date. "We must be able to move beyond what we have traditionally said that Jesus is." [81]   And the same celebrations of birth, marriage, death, and so forth, which have been part of the church till now, can and should be continued – **the church should be a community support structure that celebrates, confirms, and <u>enlightens</u>**.

> *Unfortunately, it is hard to find pastors and priests who are truly enlightened enough to lead a flock in **spiritual** growth. What they are usually good at is ritual performance, and not true understanding of Man as a spiritual being.*

The image of Jesus as rescuer (sin sacrifice) has to go. [82]   And as far as the Gospels and their picture of Jesus goes, they can't be used literally.

> One must never identify the text with the revelation or the messenger with the message. That has been the major error in our two thousand years of Christian history. It is an insight that today is still feared and resisted. But let it be clearly stated, **the Gospels are not in any sense holy, they are not accurate, and they are not to be confused with reality**. [83]
> [emphasis added]

It should also be pointed out that creating in Man a "savior mentality" and an expectation of someone coming to save him, <u>weakens Man</u>. If Man wants to play the role of a victim, then he opens himself to someone else playing the role of a rescuer, telling Man what to do, and disempowering Man. In any event, Man then does not take responsibility for himself and he gives his power away. What power? That of making choices and growing up so that he is a responsible being, and not a wimpy, passive victim.

Even the New Age writers are echoing the need for change:

> Once before… two thousand years ago, in a backwater of the Roman Empire, one man tapped into the prevailing hysterical messianic expectation and the result was Christianity. Theology and personal belief apart, the effect of this was to create generations of **happy slaves** who believed they came into the world as sinners and required the Church to order every detail of their lives. From that point of view, at least, Christianity has been a huge success. But now it is largely losing its grip, [and] **something new, but similar, is required**. [84] [emphasis added]

What is required is more of a Gnostic approach – which is what we had until the Church threw the baby out with the bathwater. Reminds me of a song: *Everything old is new again.*

Necessary Change…

Sounds familiar. And this Bishop Spong is quite brave to come forth and speak what has to be said. He still considers himself a Christian, but is not buying into the mindless rhetoric and ritual that have so characterized the religious scene. And I suggest that this mindless rhetoric is comfortable and easier to do than to be a real spiritual beacon for a congregation – and that is why there is resistance to Dr. Spong's ideas and why the mediocre version of religion continues to this day. What Dr. Spong would prefer is **a real, one-on-one relationship with the living Christ.**

Man is going to have to go inward to seek the Kingdom of God, and his connection with the divine. It comes down to faith in the unseen and a belief in Something greater than we are which looks out for us, and cares about us. And this all assumes that we can discover who and what we really are, what our potential really is, and find a way to actualize it. Traditional religion does not do that. Hence, what is wanted is a spiritual path, not a religious path. **Spirituality not religiosity.** Maybe the Tao? Or Unity?

It is time for a change. Man has been following the traditions set up hundreds (and thousands?) of years ago by people who were told what to believe by the gods who were in fact ETs. They used religion to control Man and he wound up believing what he was told and not what the ultimate truth was… because he wasn't evolved enough for the truth. We must today stop running around believing things because that's what others have believed before us. **We must stop living in the box that was created for us by others.**

Such things as messiahs, avatars, sin, sacrifice, revelations and Endtime scenarios all need to be reviewed and updated or removed.

Endtime Scenario Illusion

Religion has also been used to promote a fallacious Endtime scenario, whether to give people false hope in a coming Rapture, or to give people fear of a coming Apocalypse, it is big business. And false.

Apocalypse and Rapture

In a very insightful book by **Steve Wohlberg**, End Time Delusions, he describes how the idea of the Rapture came to be, and why Man is being taught that there is a coming Apocalypse. To expose the illusion, Wohlberg examines two main supports for the supposed Endtimes: (1) the coming 7 years of Tribulation and (2) the Acpocalypse with its pre-, mid- and post-millenial Rapture concepts which co-exist in confusion because no one can agree on what the Bible really said.

In fact, the Bible does not literally speak of a Rapture. Even the book of Thessalonians just says that believers will be "caught up" in the air to meet Him on "the day of the Lord..." whatever that is. (Thess. 4:17) Of course, this has been promised throughout the years, and it makes for good press. The fact that it is Paul's teaching is suspicious, since he was a ringer and his teaching was different from what Jesus/Apollonius taught.

The following will not be a biblical exegesis; it will suffice to show that the idea of the Rapture was created by one man in the 1800s, and that there is no "7 weeks" (years) of Tribulation period yet to come. This is important enough to examine closely.

360

Seven Year Tribulation theory

Wohlberg informs us that there is no "seven year" concept nor a "seven years of tribulation" anywhere in the Bible.

> Amazingly the entire theory is really based on a rather speculative interpretation of two little words in one single verse....in Daniel 9:27....and the two words are "one week." [85]

In Daniel 9:24-27, Gabriel divides the seventy weeks prophecy into 3 periods:

> ".... seven weeks (verse 25), sixty-two weeks (verse 25), and one week (verse 27). $7 + 62 + 1 = 70$.... So far we have seen 69 weeks fulfilled. That leaves "one week" left, otherwise known as the famous "70th week of Daniel." [86]

The significance of the 70th week is that there has been a huge **gap** between the end of the 69th week and the 70th week – which was explained away by the creation of a new (non-Biblical) concept: **Dispensationalism**. It was clever but false.

The GAP

After the GAP, allegedly comes the 70th week of Daniel, the so-called Tribulation, and then the Rapture. The GAP is also called **Dispensationalism**. To better explain this, a Scottish Presbyterian minister **Edward Irving** around 1830 began to teach ".... the novel idea of a two-phase return of Christ, the first phase being *a secret rapture before the rise of antichrist*." It is hotly disputed where he got this idea, but it appears to have come ".... from a young Scottish girl named **Margaret MacDonald** who first 'saw' it during an ecstatic 'revelation.'" [87]   Sounds like the Neggs were at it again...

The Rapture

So Irving developed and taught the idea of a Rapture, and somehow passed it on to **John Nelson Darby** and both of them became champions of a pre-tribulation Rapture and of a coming Antichrist during a period of Tribulation.

> In light of ... careful research, it seems Margaret MacDonald's pre-Antichrist "rapture revelation" is **the real smoking gun** behind Darby's theology. Regardless, the essential pre-tribulationism of Margaret's doctrine soon became a **weapon of mass deception** in the hands of Darby and his dispensationalist followers. [88] [emphasis added]

John Nelson Darby later became known as the Father of Dispensationalism, which teaches that God deals with Man in special periods, or ages. Accordingly, Man is now in the "Church Age" which will conclude with the Rapture. Then Daniel's 70th week (the Tribulation) will supposedly kick in during which the Antichrist will persecute the Jews.

> His [Darby's] most striking innovation was the timing of a concept
> called the Rapture, drawn from the Apostle Paul's prediction that believers
> would fly up in the air to meet Christ in heaven. Most theologians under-
> stood it as part of the Resurrection **at time's very end**, Darby repositioned
> it at the Apocalypse's very beginning, a small shift with large implications....
> Darby's scheme became a pillar of the new Fundamentalism. [89]

This is the kind of disinformation that the Neggs promote thru the OPs.

Summary

Wohlberg points out that this is a prophecy about 70 weeks, and in Jewish prophecy a day
was symbolic of a year, so 70 weeks would be 490 days, or 490 years. The first 69 weeks
would be 483 years, using the same conversion. This 483 years was also the time period
from the captivity in Babylon down to the arrival of Christ. So "69 weeks" were fulfilled.
Now there is supposedly just one week (7 years left) to account for.

That 70th week (7 years) was accounted for by Jesus: His ministry (3 ½ years) and then the
additional ministry after the Resurrection (3 ½ years). [90]

> The entire prophecy of Daniel 9:24-27 covers a period of "seventy weeks."
> Logic requires that "seventy weeks" refers to **one consecutive block of time**,
> in other words, to seventy *straight, sequential weeks*. The truth is there is no
> example in Scripture (or anywhere else!) of a stated time period starting,
> stopping, and then starting again. *All* Biblical references to time are consecutive:
> 40 days and forty nights, 400 years in Egypt, 70 years of captivity. In Daniel's
> prophecy, the "seventy weeks" were to begin during the reign of Persia and
> continue to the time of the Messiah.
>
> Logic also requires that the 70th week follow immediately after the 69th week
> If it doesn't, then it cannot properly be called the 70th week!
> **It is illogical to insert a 2,000- year gap between the 69th and the 70th weeks.**
>
> Daniel 9:27 says nothing about a seven-year period of "tribulation," a "rebuilt
> Jewish temple," or any "antichrist." [91] [emphasis added]

So the 70th week was part of the other 69 weeks and has already happened.

Dr. Fomenko on the Apocalypse

As we saw in Chapter 10, Dr. Anatoly Fomenko has analyzed Western Chronology and
discovered that it was greatly 'adjusted' by two educated priests, Scaliger and Petavius.

In addition, he and his team examined the Bible with the same set of historical,
sociological and very advanced mathematical tools, and made an interesting discovery
with regards to an Apocalypse: What if **the book of Revelation actually belongs in
the Old Testament?**

If the current location of the Apocalypse in the Bible is chronologically accurate, then its frequency column graph of the names… would have to look like the lower graph [shown in chapter 5 of Dr. Fomenko's book]. *However, the actual frequency graph for the Apocalypse is entirely different!* [graph 5.43] … In other words, *the absolute maximum of both graphs is not in the New, but the Old Testament books, currently separated from the Apocalypse by several hundred years.* Thus, we revealed an explicit contradiction to the frequency dampening principle, soundly confirmed earlier in reliably dated and chronologically correctly ordered texts… As a result we will find the chronologically accurate order of "chapters" in the Bible….It is interesting that …**we discovered that the New Testament Apocalypse appears to be near *the Old Testament prophecies*… in particular, the Old Testament prophecy of Daniel**, which is in perfect conformity with a well-known viewpoint that the prophecy of Daniel is "an Apocalypse in many ways similar to one from the New Testament." [92] [emphasis added]

So, the Apocalypse really 'synchs up' with the Book of Daniel and belongs in the Old Testament – **it has already happened**. Dr. Fomenko supports Mr. Wohlberg.

Alternates to Religion

The New Age has spawned a couple of interesting alternatives to religion which some seekers have picked up on, and they both deserve a brief examination.

I. Course in Miracles

While the channeled book Course in Miracles (CIM) is mostly innocuous, it earns a place in this discourse due to the fantastic technology that made its deception possible. It could therefore just as easily have been put under the Science section, but because it deals with spiritual growth, the issue is religious in nature.

In 1965, Helen Schucman was a psychiatrist who thought she was going crazy when she started hearing a voice telling her to write down all that it said. When she asked who was speaking to her, the voice said it was Jesus and He wanted her to write a book for Him. It is obvious that she had problems with the first 5 chapters, as they do not 'flow' at all, and are very choppy. She had to adapt herself to listening and writing what was given, and apparently the other end of the 'line' was discovering how to proceed with her.

Incredible that this large book was dictated through her, from 1965 to 1972, hearing a voice that no one else in the room with her could hear, and it was interesting that she often developed **headaches** and often had to stop transcribing for a few days at a time.

Voice to Skull (V2K)

The truth of the CIM book is that it truly was dictated by a voice that only she could hear. She never suspected that it wasn't Jesus speaking to her and yet today we know about **V2K** ("Voice to Skull"), or PsyOps devices that were perfected by the military in the 60's and 70's to send messages directly to a soldier's head without using a radio. The message would appear as words in the receiving person's head, and only they could hear it. Someone standing close to them could not hear it; the message was neurally 'implanted' in their head via a microwave carrier wave that would simulate brain wave patterns in the transmitting device to synch up with and activate the brain waves of the receiving person in the auditory part of their brain. [93]

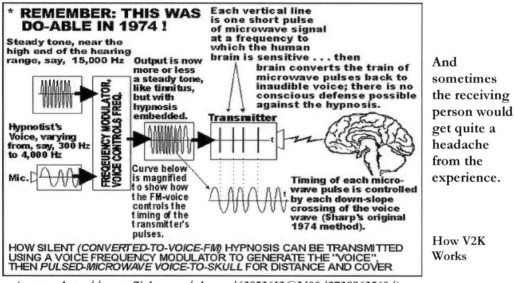

And sometimes the receiving person would get quite a headache from the experience.

How V2K Works

(source: http://www.flickr.com/photos/63853612@N00/2738963560/)

Patents exist today for this V2K technology, and it has been around since the 60s. It was an outgrowth of **MK-Ultra** research and the later attempts of the US to counter the Russians' use of psychotronic equipment in the 60's against the US Embassy personnel in Moscow. [94]   The military has considered using it to beam the 'Voice of Allah' to Iraqi terrorists and command them to stop fighting and go home. [95]

And yet, if studying the CIM material leads one to be a more compassionate, patient, humble and forgiving person, by all means, please continue.

II. Create Your Day

It wouldn't be right to ignore a major New Age teaching that has people running around trying to "create their day" – after all, they have been told they can do it (viz., the movie *What the Bleep*). They are also living in an illusion – such power to create one's day would not be given to immature, petty people in a 3rd dimensional realm. Remember why you're here – to grow, learn and perhaps serve. How does allowing you to create whatever you want, when you want, teach you patience, compassion, humility, respect or thinking of others?

Creating your day is a selfish STS teaching. Me, my and mine. Sounds like an OP (as a sociopath) agenda. Just think what it would be like to have 5,000 new adepts all running around creating their day (at each other's expense – because they're not aware or considerate), and you get to be in their reality. Who gets to have the signal turn green just for them? Who gets to 'manifest' the parking space just where they want it? This easily borders on a violation of someone else's freewill and that is why 3D human beings are not permitted to do it – but the idea sure sells books doesn't it?

Religion vs Spirituality

Lastly, with regard to religion, it was suggested that we become more spiritual instead. What does that really mean? (See Chapter 16) Many people in today's world think they are spiritual if they chant, meditate, do yoga, become vegetarians, or channel higher masters… but is that really it? Wasn't the original idea (Gnosticism) to go within and connect with one's Higher Self and manifest higher and more loving behavior to one's fellowmen?

Something to think about is what our more advanced neighbors in space do with respect to religion or spirituality. It is suggested that an anthropomorphic view of God will not work because that is Man's personal and naïve idea that stands to be shattered when ETs show up and tell us who or what God really is. So what would a more advanced concept of God look like?

Cutting to the chase, here is what an advanced set of (benevolent) ETs might teach us:

> There is a Central Sun, or powerful, bright living Intelligence that inhabits the center of our Universe. It is a Force in creating and sustaining all life via the unseen intradimensional network of Energy permeating all Space. On a sentient level, it has created a Hierarchy of beings, from Higher Beings to Beings of Light (angels) to Group Souls to Higher Selves to individual souls who 'play' in the Father of Light's Drama. It is an all-permeating Intelligent Energy that acts/initiates and recycles based on vibration with the ultimate goal that this Father of Light, or the One, eventually experiences Itself through its Creation to which it has assigned the attribute of Freewill (in this part of the Multiverse).

> The highlight of Its creativity was the creation of parts of Itself, smaller sparks of intelligence, called **Souls** for whom the Hierarchy exists and guides into greater participation in parts of the Creation which are largely unknown to said Souls, but in which they will one day serve or work with in the Great Drama.

> This is to say that true Science underpins the ETs' concept of God, 'spirituality' as such does not exist, and the interaction of all beings is governed by adherence to Universal Law. **The Law of One** and the Law of Love are the two greatest, and there are others such that one's actions are governed by knowing that we are all connected, we are all One, and what we do to another is also done to ourself. Thus Love, compassion, respect and patience for others is the hallmark of a greater understanding and is a measure of soul growth. In short, higher ethics.

Of course, underdeveloped beings, and those without souls, do whatever they do not as evil, but as egoistically, soullessly unaware of a Greater Way. And in a Universe of Freewill, OPs have as much right to be here as the souls do, but the souls have a responsibility to follow the Law of One despite whatever the beings of lesser (or no) Light do. It is not necessary to correct those without a soul as they cannot be 'reached' and will have to be avoided or eventually contained.

A truly advanced Soul is humble because they are not controlled by the ego and they know Whose power and awareness is flowing through them, that they are a small part of the One, and with the greater awareness comes a responsibility to walk in the Way of the One. Doing that "rewires" one's DNA.

Does that not sound like the **Earth Graduate** of Chapters 7, 15 and 16?

Action Item

For those who seek to move from Religion to Spirituality, or who want a church of like seekers who want to learn more metaphysics, such as what Mani or the Gnostics knew, then the two main **New Thought** churches of today are recommended: Unity and/or Religious Science. **Unity** (not Unitarianism) is out of Lee's Summit, MO, and has always been Christ-centered, offering Lessons in Truth and seminars in personal growth. **Religious Science** promotes a more scientific understanding of Man's relationship with the One and our world. Both often have workshops that teach the principles of Prosperity and Healing. New Thought churches are not always called Unity or Religious Science, they may be called something like a **Center for Spiritual Living**.

Summary

So there is no Endtime to come as the Book of Revelation speaks about. **It has already happened.** History has been altered, we appear to have a young Earth, and we're in a new Era. The sad truth is that this place might go on and on as it has been, wallowing in deception and mediocrity.

Man is a very special creation when coupled with a soul. We need to think outside the box that was created for us. It is healthy to question Science, Religion and even History – especially since the winners write history their way.

The reason for exposing the religious errors is so that one's belief system doesn't work against them with false expectations in this world AND when they die and cross over. This is better explained in Chapter 14. Ignorance is not bliss and keeps one shackled to this world.

Chapter 12: HVR Sphere & Perception

At this point, there are a few more preliminary, relevant pieces of information to consider, and then this chapter will clarify what this place is. Please note that Chapters 1-12 were to examine what you think you know and expose the errors and truth of some major issues. That was to make sure we're all 'on the same page' when starting this chapter.

This chapter will draw on the information presented in the first 13 chapters, with particular emphasis on the last three. Chapter 14 will then examine why we have a problem and what form the numerous problems take, and Chapter 15 will give the final summary, clarifying the nature of Man and Earth.

This chapter's following sections are relevant to understanding the question that has been put forth since the beginning of the book:

> What has to be true about this place for it to look the way it does?

By now it should be easier to accept that this is not our planet, we are not here alone, and we don't belong here. But, why do we need to get out? And, to peak your curiosity, the above question can be rephrased:

Are you really living on the planet you think you are? [96]

The answer is not found in the 'box' most people live in and this chapter is going to turn upside down what you have assumed for years to be true. That was one reason for going through the review of a lot of religious issues, earth history, and physical science – a lot of it isn't true or even relevant to what Earth really is – and **that** is why most people cannot see what Earth is and so get trapped here. If it weren't for some discoveries in the world of Quantum Physics, some of the answers would still be conjecture, but the answers are not all in Quantum Physics... some are found in an examination of perception. Even the perception of subatomic particles...

SubQuantum Physics

Many new and fascinating things have been discovered in Physics in the last few decades. Things that tell us that we're not living in the world we thought we were... at least the world of Newtonian Physics is inadequate to explain the subatomic and underlying aspects of our world.

Several of these issues, previously explored in past chapters, are bilocality, nonlocal communication, the Quantum Net or Divine Matrix or Ether that connects all of us, epigenetics, paranormal abilities, and the unseen Astral and subatomic worlds. Particularly relevant is the issue of what effect an observer has on his environment.
Let's start with that.

Observer Effect

It is hard to accept that an observer's consciousness can affect the outcome of experiments with subatomic particles, but today's physics has been discovering that. It <u>suggests</u> we have some power to affect the world around us. Not to manifest Reality, but according to physicist David Bohm:

> ...if subatomic particles only come into existence in the presence of an observer, then it is also meaningless to speak of a particle's properties and characteristics as existing before they are observed. [97]

Naturally, Einstein disagreed because he theorized that subatomic *quanta* exist as waves, <u>until</u> we look at them. But, just as interesting and relevant is the creation of **anomalons** in the laboratory:

> Unlike Bohm, Jahn and Dunne .... believe subatomic particles do *not* possess a distinct reality until consciousness enters the picture.... We're [not] examining the structure of a passive universe.... Instead of discovering particles, physicists **may actually be *creating* them**. [98] [emphasis added]

One of the cases in point was when the Russians discovered *neutrinos*. For many years the particle had been proposed but no one could find one. Then one was found in 1957, and physicists determined that if it had mass, it might help explain some thorny problems, and then in 1980, lo and behold the Russians discovered the neutrino had mass. Laboratories in the US did not agree and could not find any mass associated with the neutrino. Note: when it was reasoned that the neutrino should have mass, lo and behold the neutrino was found to have mass – in all but US laboratories.[99] The US still cannot resolve the issue... What is that saying, "You'll see it when you believe it?"

Perhaps it is our limited perception of our world that needs a closer examination so that we don't misinterpret or misunderstand what we think we see.

Perception

Being more aware of <u>how</u> we perceive is critical to an understanding and accepting of the revelation of what this Earth is. We take what we see for granted, not really considering how we see, what perception is, how perception is related to the **holographic** essence of the world, and how one's perception can be manipulated (especially by **hypnosis**). And it was suggested in Chapter 9 that one's DNA has a bearing on our ability to perceive.

Besides the obvious DNA-based effect of color blindness, there is also the aspect that our DNA coding has 'permitted' us to see only a limited range of the light spectrum. We humans cannot see what dogs and cats see that cause them to stare across the room, snarl, hiss or cower at what looks like empty space to us. There are parts of the world around us that we cannot see and we may not really see what we think we do see...

Remember that **shapeshifting** *is not moving one's molecules into a different* *configuration; it is all about mentally controlling what the observer 'sees.'*

Let us take a look at holograms, hypnosis and perception in this light. It will help to understand what this place really is.

For an additional examination of Vision and Holograms, see **Appendix B**.

Holograms

Holographic images, or projections, are a fascinating aspect of the real world around us. Holography signifies "the whole in every part." While it is not necessary here to go into what holograms are and how they operate, it is enlightening to hear that our **vision and memory operate in a holographic way.**

Vision is reportedly holographic as there is no way for the actual images 'out there' to be displayed on a 'screen' inside the back of our heads (in the brain's so-called "vision center"). In fact, there is no "vision center" nor is there a one-to-one correspondence between the object we see and the image's representation in the brain. [100]

> [Karl] Pribram discovered that not only did **no** such one-to-one corres-
> pondence exist, there wasn't even a discernable pattern to the sequence in
> which the electrodes [sensing brain activity in volunteers] fired. He wrote
> of his findings, "These experimental results are **incompatible** with a view
> that a photographic-like image becomes projected onto the cortical surface." [101]
> [emphasis added]

Pribram also discovered that memory, like vision, was holographic – or more precisely, distributed. This meant that **the brain was using some kind of internal holographic processing** and there would be no more correlation between brain electrical activity and what was being seen, than there would be any meaning in the interference patterns seen on a piece of holographic film. He found that the neural activity in the brain operates as a wavelike phenomenon "… creating an almost endless and kaleidoscopic array of **interference patterns**, and these in turn … give the brain its holographic properties." [102]

So the image of Tank sitting before all those screens in *The Matrix* with their green, vertically flowing symbols was not so far-fetched. The concept is correct; our brains interpret whatever the holographic symbols are 'out there' in the world around us and, get this, **we spatially create the image of the object 'out there' as if we are projecting it in front of us** – how else could we navigate to it to touch it? We're part of the hologram. [103]

*The brain decodes the hologram and **the mind** enmeshes and actualizes us into what we 'see.'*

Allegedly, the patterns of holographic interference work as the following brilliant drawing illustrates…

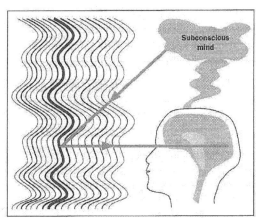

Figure 48: Subconscious mind creates the wave or thought patterns and the conscious mind 'observes' them into the holographic illusions that we take to be the 'real' world. It is only an illusion, a figment of our implanted belief and imagination

Figure 49: If we could see the 'world' before it enters our eyes it would be a mass of wave patterns – thought fields. Through the collective mind we transform these fields into an agreed 'reality' – the landscape we think we see all around us. In fact, it is within us, within our own minds

Holographic Vision
(Source: David Icke, <u>Tales from the Time Loop</u>. p. 351)

What if there is nothing out there but clouds of holographic **"interference patterns"** that our brains decode and 'construct' as reality in front of us? David Bohm, a foremost physicist, thinks that the entire universe is a hologram. If that is true, then how does a camera take a picture of an object: Is it the actual object on the film or a set of the holographic interference patterns? The **camera has no brain to filter and decode the patterns.** Thus, according to the holographic theory, the camera also photographs the interference patterns and like the real object, our brains decode the swirls on the photo and we 'see' the object... [104]

Tricky Vision

As was mentioned in Chapter 8, the eyes consist of multiple parts, some not touching each other, and if any key component is missing, vision with the eyes doesn't happen. As Appendix B explains, some people can 'see' with other parts of their bodies. But the real 'smoking gun' as far as the true nature of vision goes, is that the eyes have a **blind spot** – both eyes have a small section of the retina where there are no rods/cones and thus no image is relayed to the brain from that area – that should produce a 'hole' in the image we see. It doesn't because **the brain 'fills in' the picture** and we see a complete image!

Vision is much more than electrical pulses transferred to the back of the brain, into the visual cortex, where there is NO movie screen upon which the world is displayed – and by the way, the scientists tell us that the image in the brain is replicated upside down... and **the brain rights it** for us! What is the upside-down image displayed on? How did the brain 'know' to right the image? And since the optic nerve does not transmit photons, how are electrical pulses converted to images?

So far, the brain is doing <u>at least two</u> manipulations of what we see… Is there a third? Is it translating the holographic "interference patterns" as well? Do we really know <u>how</u> we see? Read **Appendix B** about the Chinese who 'see' with their fingers and noses, and the special women who have a different cone in their retina and see more than the average person … and you decide.

Hypnotism and Perception

An interesting question to ask oneself is: Are there things 'out there' in our reality that we cannot see (1) because our DNA does not permit seeing anything but the standard visible light spectrum, or (2) because we have been subconsciously conditioned to not see them? Or both?

Case in point is the story of the hypnotist who demonstrates our ability to see 'through' solid objects, or see things that are not there. In this case, Tom was hypnotized and told there was a giraffe in the room. He gazed in wonder at it (obviously creating it in <u>his</u> reality). Later, more interesting was when, still under hypnosis, the hypnotist had Tom sit on a chair, and he put Laura right in front of him, standing up. But Tom had been told she was not in the room, and when asked if he could see her, despite Laura's giggles, Tom said no.

> Then the hypnotist went behind Laura so he was hidden from Tom's view and pulled an object out of his pocket. He kept the object carefully concealed so that no one could see it, and pressed it against the small of Laura's back. He asked Tom to identify the object. Tom leaned forward as if staring directly thru Laura's stomach and said that it was a watch. The hypnotist nodded and asked if Tom could read the watch's inscription. Tom squinted as if struggling to make out the writing and recited both the name of the watch's owner (which happened to be a person unknown to any of us in the room) and the message…. Tom had read its inscription correctly. [105]

What do we really know about our ability to see? Do we really see the world around us as it actually is? You will soon find out we don't.

Another interesting aspect of holograms is that they appear to exist **in layers**.

> Interestingly, holograms also possess a fantastic capacity for information storage. By changing the angle at which the two lasers strike a piece of photographic film, <u>it is possible to record many different images on the same surface</u>. Any image thus recorded can be retrieved simply by illuminating the film with a laser beam possessing the same angle as the two original beams. By employing this method…. a one-inch-square of film can store the same amount of information contained in fifty Bibles! [106] [emphasis added]

And as was said earlier, memory appears to be holographic and DNA processes and communicates via waves of light or biophotons – interacting with the cells of the body, including those in the brain. So **vision is holographic because the real world 'out there' is holographic**, <u>and</u> we store and retrieve memories holographically.

Then it can be said that the physical universe might appear to be a giant hologram to us, as physicist David Bohm said. [107] I would suggest, in keeping with Occam's Razor, that our world is 3D physical, but our perception of it (i.e., vision in the brain) is akin to holographic processing. **That makes us part of the 'hologram,'** unconscious of the actual perceptive mechanism, but able to function physically within it.

So the famous Double Slit experiment (end of Chapter 8) is a result of internal holographic processing due to the Control System: the hologram was changed to reflect 2 open slits and a normal wave resulted. A single slit constricted the light within the hologram so that it 'appeared' to be a particle when it was actually still a wave, but focused or condensed.

Earth as a Holodeck

And of course, those who watched *Star Trek* years ago, during the Captain Kirk era, should remember that aboard the Starship U.S.S. Enterprise NCC 1701, there was a big room called the Holodeck. It was empty, and had all black walls with yellow or orange calibration (grid) lines running up and down and across it. It was about 30' wide by 60' long and maybe 20' high. The crew used it to run computer **simulations**. That is a key word.

What was interesting, and this is very relevant, was that the crew could activate a computer-supplied simulation of a jungle, or forest, and the trees were real – one's hand did not go through them. And coming to a precipice, the drop was more than to the floor of the Holodeck, and if one came to the top of a hill, the view across the landscape extended way beyond the 30' wide walls of the Holodeck. Last but not least, one could get seriously wounded, killed, or trapped in the computer simulations if the security protocols failed.

Star Trek Holodeck
credit: www.crystalinks.com

The overall scenery (on and near the walls) was said to be **holographic**, and the parts you could touch, like the trees and rocks, were provided by the ***replicator*** technology. And somehow these two technologies were coordinated by the ship's computer to provide a 3D realistic experience. [108]

Physicist William Tiller thinks our reality is similar to that of the Holodeck – he thinks the universe is a kind of Holodeck "…created by the 'integration' of all living things." [109] This means the universe is comprised of **reality fields** sustained by a flow of consciousness – and consciousness again seems to be the key… but, whose consciousness?

> If [our] universe is a holodeck, all things that appear stable and eternal, from the laws of physics to the substance of galaxies, would have to be viewed as reality fields, will-o'-the-wisps no more or less real than the props in a giant mutually shared dream. All permanence would have to be looked at as illusory, and only **consciousness** would be eternal, the consciousness of the living universe. [110] [emphasis added]

> *Note that holograms, simulation and Virtual Reality are further examined in Appendices B and C.*

Manipulated Perception

There is the possibility that anomalous events, those that defy easy, scientific explanation, are the **reality fields** and that the universe is sustained as a stable construct that is **not** subject to modification by our individual consciousnesses. That is, the reality fields occur within a limited conscious agreement with other sentient beings – if we all see a purple elephant in the room, we can all agree that that is part of our reality. [111] Unless of course, some Higher Beings are manipulating what we see, hear and think, and entraining us into a group (mind) **simulation** – for agendas that we are not aware of.

What the consensus of quantum physicists dealing with this issue seeks to promote, knowing that it can't be empirically proven (yet), is that **there is no reality beyond that which is constructed by the "integration of all consciousnesses"** and that the holographic universe could be a **construct** reflecting our coherent sculpting by our subconscious minds. [112]   But here again, that assumes that we in 3D reality have some power to create and manifest with our minds, but even with 100,000 minds 'efforting' to create something collectively does not mean that it is possible for humans in this 3D reality… it just means that we mutually agree on our observed, coherent Reality.

Key Concept 1

What is about to be explained here is that it IS true that we are living on a 3D Earth Construct that is contained in a 4D Holographic Virtual Reality (HVR) Sphere. That is to say that the original 4D Earth has been replicated and simulated as a 3D Construct and is protected by enveloping it in a 4D energy field of some sort – which is transparent (*Gegenschein*), and so we think we're in a 3D universe. The Simulation is an advanced form of 'interactive' hologram effected by the Control System. (See next chapter and Appendices B & C for more.)

Created by the Higher Beings above the 4D realm – we are in a Virtual Reality Sphere, or Simulation of their design, replicated by special holography, which is subject to their consciousness and computer. It is run by an incredible 4D Bio-plasma computer. Our physicists happen to have discovered some of the principles and lower-level mechanics of the Sphere: subatomic particles, the holographic nature of reality, entropy, the dual nature of light, biophotons, and the nonlocal communication property of DNA.

Again: Are you really living on the simple little planet that you think you are?

Charles Fort and Robert Monroe discovered what Earth really is and both described it in the following sections.

Fortean Sphere

The famous **Charles Fort** often questioned the scientific dogma of his day, 1912. He wondered where all the strange objects falling from the sky came from, and he wrote 4 books documenting the oddities and speculating on their source. During his writings, he also kept coming back again and again to the idea of **a 'shell' surrounding this Earth**.

> …whether there be a shell-like, evolving composition, holding the stars in position, and in which **the stars are openings**, admitting light from an existence external to the shell, or not, all stars are at about the same distance from this earth as they would be if this earth were stationary and central to such a shell, revolving around it. [113] [emphasis added]

Intriguing, but nonsense you say. And Fort would agree with you, and yet it was an idea which clearly fascinated him. He was no uneducated man, totally mystified by science and the world. It was his unique ability to go toe-to-toe with the astronomers and scientists of the day – demanding answers to the oddities he had recorded. He was considered an *enfant terrible* of science – questioning everything. [114] In math and astronomy, he could hold his own. And yet, he repeatedly questions the presence of something surrounding the Earth:

> The **Gegenschein** -- That we have indication that there is such a shell around our existence. The Gegenschein is a round patch of light in the sky. It seems to be reflected sunlight, at night, because it keeps position about opposite the Sun's. The crux: Reflected sunlight – but reflecting from what? That the sky is a **matrix** in which the stars are openings, and that, upon the inner, concave surface of this celestial [transparent energy] shell, the sun casts its light, **even if the earth is between…** [115] [emphasis added]

The Gegenschein
(credit: NASA: _http://apod.nasa.gov/apod/archivepix.html_ _and below_)

It is recommended that the reader check out the above NASA link to three samples:
2008 May 07: The Gegenschein over Chile. (sunlight)
2006 December 26: The Gegenschein. (sunlight)
June 25 1999: The Gegenschein. (sunlight + Sun)

Interesting that in his book <u>New Lands,</u> written in the 1920's, he used the word **matrix**.
But he is making a very interesting point that science still today cannot answer:

> Suppose the Gegenschein could be a reflection of sunlight from anything
> at a distance less than the distance of the stars. It would have **parallax**
> against its background of stars.
> _Observatory_, 17-47: "**The Gegenschein has no parallax.**" [116]

So Fort is saying that since its perceived shape and size does not change with any change
in our position from which it is viewed (i.e., a parallax), that it must be reflected off the
surface of something consistent in shape. If it were reflected off dust in the atmosphere, it
would have size and shape distortion depending on the viewing angle – <u>but it doesn't</u>.
Fort was no neophyte to astronomy and certainly would have known the difference
between sunlight reflecting off dust in the upper atmosphere, and swamp gas, Moon
dust, or whatever the standard argument of the day is for what he personally observed.

Note that **NASA** has pictures of the Gegenschein (above) – Fort wasn't imagining things.
As will be seen shortly, Fort was on to something, and while he knew the Shell wasn't a
metal thing, and that there are no holes in it to simulate stars, it <u>is</u> real, and is also what
bounces back our radio and TV transmissions:

...not enormously far away, there is a shell around this earth... According to data collected by the Naval Research Laboratory [1925], there is some-thing, somewhere in the sky, that is deflecting electro-magnetic waves of wireless communications, in a way that is similar to the way in which sound waves are sent back by the dome of the Capitol, at Washington. The published explanation is that there is an "ionized zone" around this earth... the [term] "ionized zone" is not satisfactory... From Norway [there were] short-wave transmissions... reflected back to earth... as if from **a shell-like formation**, around this earth, not unthinkably far away. [117] [emphasis added]

And yet, we keep up the ruse that we are looking for extraterrestrial life with our SETI radio telescopes... Wouldn't any ET radio transmissions to us be reflected back, too, from their side of the same 'barrier?' Why is this expensive game being played?

*As Robert Monroe shortly discloses from his OBE ventures, there are no **3D** lifeforms out there... most sentient life in the universe is in the 4D and above realms. And that makes sense if you understand that the soul has almost unlimited potential 'out there', yet is constrained here on Earth.*

There is a very advanced (energy) Sphere around this Earth as we will see, functioning in 4D+ but only reflects light in 3D. It is interesting that an open-minded skeptic of the 1912-1932 Era first voiced the concern that Science was ignoring the Gegenschein, and not giving us all the answers... In fact, knowing Fort from his writings, he was 'baiting' the scientific establishment with the idea of a shell whose holes were the stars, but the bait was not taken. And as will be seen, there **is** something around the Earth, and another researcher, Robert Monroe, also ran into the Sphere's walls – literally.

Out of Body Experiences (OBEs)

A trip into the unexplored aspects of the actual world around us would not be complete without looking at what **Robert Monroe**, of The Monroe Institute fame, had to share with his experiences of our reality. Some of his discoveries, like those of Quantum Physics and holograms, directly relate to what this place called Earth really is. This section will be rather comprehensive as it directly relates evidence for the theme of this chapter and book.

It should be understood that Monroe became a true seeker and an accomplished OBEr and kept a journal over the years that he traveled, noting where he went, what he saw and did, and some of the interesting things he learned about our reality. His ability to leave his body was not intentional at first; it was something he discovered was happening to him, and in an effort to learn more about it, and control it, he began to investigate it. It turned out that what he thought in the beginning were lucid dreams were much more than that. We are not in a dream-like reality, much as some aspects appear to be that way, but as Dr. Vallée said, we are in a kind of **Control System**.

Different Realms

The first thing Monroe noted (especially in his first book, Journeys Out of the Body) was that there are levels of reality (Locales) once one has left the body, and those nearest this Earth experience are less than wonderful. According to his classification system, **Locale I** is the one we live in – the here and now, the world of the physical senses. **Locale II** is the first level one sees when initially out of the body – the immediate Astral world, and it has

....depth and dimension incomprehensible to the finite, conscious mind. In this vastness lie all of the aspects we attribute to Heaven and Hell.... It is inhabited, if that is the word, by entities with various degrees of intelligence with whom communication is possible.... You think movement and it is fact...Communication is instantaneous. [118]

Locale II is a natural environment to the Second Body (soul). Reality there is made up of deepest desires and frantic fears, and there is no way to hide what one is thinking or feeling – it is all exposed, and is sometimes ".... unleashed in full force." [119] Note that wild, undisciplined people dying and going to this realm would suffer the effect of their and others' emotions. This is where ghosts reside.

....the areas of **Locale II** "nearest" the physical world.... are peopled for the most part with **insane or near-insane, emotionally driven beings** [or discarnates]. They include those alive but asleep or drugged and ... quite probably those who are "dead" but still emotionally driven.... **it is not a pleasant place to be**. It is a level or plane where you "belong" until you learn better. I don't know what happens to those who don't learn.... It is here that one meets all sorts of disjointed personalities and animate beings.... Only by cautious and sometimes terrifying experimentation was I able to learn the art or trick of passing thru the area. [120]   [emphasis added]

Locale III is the upper end of Locale II and is where the 'next timers' reside... getting ready to reincarnate/recycle.

Locale IV is the uppermost area contained within the HVR Sphere, assumed to be home to the Interdimensionals, as well as 'last timers' or graduating souls.

Note that the locales are not discretely defined, and there are no barriers between them, other than what appears to be a shift of energy which would tend to contain entities of like vibration in their appropriate, resonant level; ie, Transdimensionals vibrate higher than Neggs so the former would tend to be found in a higher vibrational milieu within the HVR Sphere that is most comfortable for them – avoiding lower coarser vibrations of Locale II.

Locales and Barriers

Locale I –   in Chart 4, this is our everyday 3D Earth (L1).

Locale II –   in Chart 4a is represented by L2: **home to the Neggs, discarnates and**

Thoughtforms (H-band and RCF/Matrix).
L2 = lower Astral.
Locale III – in Chart 4 is represented by L3: **souls awaiting incarnation/recycling.**
L3 = mid-Astral.
Locale IV – in Chart 4 is represented by L4: inhabited by **Transdimensionals, and the Graduating souls.**
L4 = upper Astral.

B1 and **B2** are symbolic of a change in energy state, a functional barrier, between L2 and L3 and L4, effectively containing entities to a region commensurate with their PFV comfort level.

B3 is a significant physical 4D barrier that allows passage to/from 3D Earth within 3D, but keeps most entities in the 4D+ realms from interfering with humans in 3D. This is the barrier that quarantines HVR Earth from the rest of the 4D+ Cosmos where most life is.

The **Gegenschein** that Charles Fort spoke of would have been shining off the barrier B3 as the outermost barrier, also related by Monroe that he hit several times in disoriented OBE attempts to return to his body. The Moon would be the other side of the Gegenschein (reflective barrier) since the reflection appears <u>between</u> Earth and the Moon.

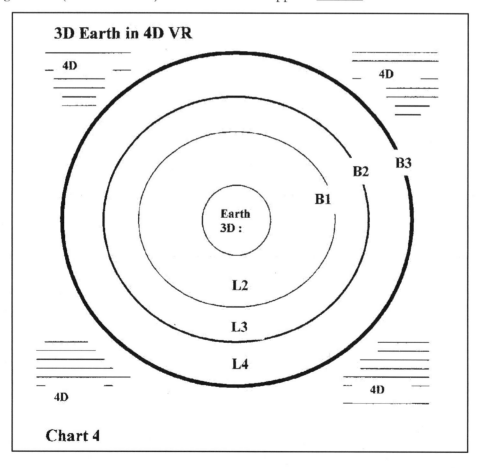

The above chart is a conceptual view of the HVR Sphere including the elements described in this book, and attempts to conceptualize the levels that Robert Monroe encountered. Note that the chart is greatly simplified but it adapts Monroe's Locales/Barriers concept, and the **"fields upon fields"** concept that Morpheus described in the movie *The Matrix*, to better depict the HVR Sphere.

The chart above is a general, high-level view of the 3D Construct in the 4D realm that we are calling the HVR Sphere. The outermost barrier B3 is the one that keeps the HVR Sphere in **quarantine** and protects it from external 4D+ entities.

H-Band Noise

Another thing Monroe noticed, and it required some time to understand it, was what he called the H-Band Noise – a region of **thought pollution surrounding the Earth (in lower L2)**. It is uncontrolled or disorganized human thought that accumulates as a form of "messy energy" whose amplitude is governed by the degree of emotion attached to the thought. He found that it was best to pass through the H-Band field as quickly as possible to minimize the 'noise' and its negative effects on one's peace of mind. [121] The effects of these **thoughtforms** were discussed in Chapter 6. See also: RCF/Matrix.

The H-Band is probably the realm that inexperienced psychics inadvertently tune into thinking they are getting info from the **Akashic records**. Such information can be erroneous and deceptive due to the game players over there.

Obstruction & Harassment

And yes, Monroe saw and experienced "tormentors", as he calls them. He had learned to pass through the Locale II area, but before mastering that, he was subjected to harassment by the indigenous entities there:

> In non-physical trips to Locale II, often there is a "layer" or area which one must pass thru, as mentioned earlier. It seems to be the part of Locale II closest to the Here-Now [3D Earth], and in some way most related. It is a grey-black hungry ocean where the slightest motion attracts nibbling and tormenting beings. It is as if you are the bait…. move violently and fight back then more excited denizens come rushing in to bite, pull, push, shove. Could this be the borders of Hell? …. They seem subhuman, yet have an evident ability to act and think independently. Who and what are they? I don't know. I haven't taken the trouble to stay there long enough to find out. [122]

It would be a sure bet to conclude that he is describing the realm of the **Neggs**, and/or discarnates in the closest Astral level (L2) to us.

On other occasions when Monroe went to slip out of his body, he was met with something sitting on him, preventing him from completely leaving his body. "They weren't vicious, just troublesome." [123] He sometimes called out to God to help him get rid of the things, and the best that showed up once was **a Monk** who peeled them off of him and carried them away. On another occasion, he <u>was</u> viciously attacked by something in the dark before he could drop off to sleep, but he figured he must have inadvertently slipped out of his body. He later noted in his journal that he felt that there was no person or religion that he knew of that would have been effective against whatever it was that attacked him. His only defense during the fight was to maneuver back over to his body and drop back in. [124] This was an **Interdimensional**, mentioned later.

He later discovered that if he slowly slipped out of his body, and then quickly zipped into the upper Locale III area, he was free from them.

A Personal Simulation

Monroe mentions another experience he had while out of body, and that was with what he called an *Inspec* (short for Intelligent Species) – they closely resemble the Beings of Light, or angels of the Light. They have a way of teaching that is something like a **virtual reality**:

> A favorite quick and learn-forever method of theirs was simulation. It was based on their ability to create and place into a human consciousness – mine – **an earth-type situation so real and so overwhelming that I could not tell reality from illusion**. I don't know the limits of such simulation talent or technology. Nor do I know the extent to which they employ the technique…. **once into the simulation, it became absolutely and totally real – and I lived it.** [125] [emphasis added]

At any rate, going through the simulation, if he did it wrong, the simulation would stop and automatically reset itself to the beginning again, and run once more – until he got it right and chose the correct action. If he got it right, the simulation ended. [126] Reminiscent of the movie *Groundhog Day*… and in agreement with the principle in this book that if you don't make progress in this lifetime, you will repeat Earth.

One important aspect of his simulations, like *Groundhog Day*, was that he knew he was repeating, even though it was very real… his seeing the same scene over and over again amounted to… **Déjà Vu**. And that is a clue to being in a simulation… which means that being recycled is reliving a simulation.

> **If the Inspecs can manipulate a simulation for Monroe, so can the Higher Beings who run this HVR Sphere and oversee the Inspecs.**

Key Concept 2

What is very important about Simulation is that it takes place in a virtual reality, which can be holographically created and manipulated. And the *Inspecs*' putting Monroe through a simulation that was so real that he could not tell he wasn't in the physical, real, solid, 3D world is very revealing. Just like us: we think we're in a solid 3D experience on Earth… but are we? How would we know… unless we occasionally see pixels or gridlines in the landscape, and objects that have been part of our world are suddenly not there any more, or in a different location…? Missing time is a big clue. People you know whom no one else remembers…

The mystics have said for centuries that all is *maya*, or illusion…perhaps holographically created? Could a Virtual Reality on the scale of the Earth be created holographically? (What is scale to ascended beings?) Of course, you will say that when you touch a tree, it is solid… but what if your sense of touch is programmed to interpret the subcodes within the holographic 'tree' vibration as 'solid?' Is this a partial key to how the avatars and yogis of the Far East walk through walls – because they know that they aren't really solid?

How do we know we're not in a simulation on Earth? Robert Monroe, and the late Stuart Wilde, gave us some more answers in following sections… but first it is necessary to complete the overview of Monroe's discoveries as they help to describe where we are.

Limits

On a number of his OBEs, Monroe journeyed to distant realms, and even looked for another 3D world like ours. Says he of things he learned from his jaunts:

> You can go anywhere in any time: past, present, or future via OBEs….
> **There is no speed of light limitation [to a soul without the body]**.
>
> **If there are intelligent beings in the <u>physical</u> [3D] universe, we failed to find them**. Either they were hidden, or more likely we didn't know what to look for. [??] In the <u>nonphysical</u> [4D] universe it was an entirely different matter. We encountered hundreds, if not thousands, **most of them non-human**. [127] [emphasis added]
>
> *As was said earlier, the speed of light is not a limit; thought is faster. And* ***all movement OBE is by thought or intention***.

Key Concept 3

He found that **"The graduate from the human experience is very respected elsewhere."** (See end of Chapter 7.) Monroe was so told by an *Inspec* when he asked of what value the human experience was. It seems he'd draw from it even should he return to a <u>nonhuman</u> incarnation. [128] The lessons, growth and experiences were something that many other entities did not want to subject themselves to – and when you realize what this place is, you'll see why. Graduating from the Earth School takes a lot of focus, discipline, respect and effort – all recognized by the Higher Beings (See Chapter 15).

Key Concept 4

Multidimensional Souls

He confirms that Man exists in multiple locations concurrently, and that there is no such thing as time. Souls are inserted into different realities from the Realm that we are originally from. Inserting (birthing) into a 3D Construct is an open possibility.

He then sees himself helping himself in another lifetime. His specific comment was: "That meant, therefore, there were <u>three versions of me</u> at the same place at the same time!" [129] There were 3 different characters (not 3 clones) in that lifetime who played 3 different roles, and this is consistent with what was said about our multidimensional aspects coming together to support or merge (Chapter 7).

> *The Monk that rescued him earlier was a higher aspect of himself that came back to rescue him and carry off the tormentors.*

Another time, Monroe on an OBE was speaking with an advanced being about a woman he knew and the subject came up again:

> We are trying to show that she is multidimensional, and this is why she is able to see as a great circle of self, of many forms, of the self. It appears to her to be like many selves extending from a circle and between. We are trying to show her **there are many, many dimensions of one human self**. [130] [emphasis added]

On another trip, he was asking a higher entity of the Light about souls that come in pure (no Karma) to the Earth, and the answer was "A lot have no previous human experience, though they have plenty of some other type – both physical and nonphysical."[131]

The Barrier

On several OBE trips, Monroe encountered a **barrier** (which had to be B3 in Chart 4), that extended in all directions – he was trying to get back to his physical body and ran into an impenetrable wall or force field of some sort. He tried to go around, under, over and got nowhere. So he stopped and even asked for help but none came. No angelic help. No *Inspec*. No one came to his aid. He finally got the idea to go in the opposite direction and that worked, but why it did he never resolved, and he was never told what the barrier was. [132] It seems he somehow got disoriented and hit the barrier going in the wrong direction.

> **That means that even as a soul, we cannot get out of this HVR Sphere – unless we die, or "graduate out."**

Obviously it was a barrier to something, keeping him from leaving the HVR realm in which he found himself… which is why no one came to help him; he was expected to think, turn around and go back. Since **he didn't find any 3D beings on any of his journeys,** and he hits a barrier, it appears that <u>the barrier is keeping him inside something</u>, and that Sphere will be very shortly discussed.

It is suggested that Monroe's barrier is the 'Shell' of Charles Fort, and the Sphere shortly mentioned by Stuart Wilde. Note that Monroe hit the barrier (B3) while doing an OBE in 3D (still within the HVR Sphere) – it is invisible in 4D but reflects light in 3D. In the last section on "Limits" Monroe told us that **all life in the Multiverse occupies 4D and above, and he found no sentient life in 3D**. Thus the barrier is designed to work for

4D+ entities, but might not stop 3D physical beings from going to/from planet Earth within the HVR Sphere. There is a problem with this as we'll soon see…

Nonhuman Intelligences

Monroe met numerous intelligences that were also in their Second Body (Light-energy body) and they could shapeshift into something more comfortable for him to look at, but **the great majority wanted nothing to do with a human**. The only beings that sought to assist and protect him were Beings of Light, which he called "intelligent species" or *Inspecs*. And the (once human) *Inspecs* usually steered him away from the nonhumans as they explain: [133]

> *And there are also the nonhuman intelligences. We have tried to steer you away from them, as much as we can. These are the* **Interdimesnsionals** *(Chapter 6).*

> Why?

> *Some early encounters with some of us did not work out well. They do not regard humans in the way we thought they might. They have a sense of superiority because they have evolved in a different way.*

> So there are no big brothers in the sky?

> *Not in the way we humans dream that there are. The difficulty is that* **these intelligences have abilities in the manipulation of energy that we cannot yet conceive of.** *And they use them without the restraints we put on ourselves….*

> I see …. Are there a lot of these intelligences?

> *Too many in the physical universe. Trillions perhaps. And there's the other one.*

> The other one? The other nonhuman intelligence?

> *Would you believe that in all of our history, ours and yours, we have encountered only one nonhuman intelligence with an origin not in time-space…* [134] [emphasis added]

What is interesting about this exchange, to repeat and emphasize, is that **most of the life in the Multiverse exists not in our 3D realm, but in the 4D+ dimensions**. And like the Neggs in the lower Astral surrounding Earth, some of them are not too friendly to many different species there are, no one really knows. Some apparently are

> from the same galaxy as we are. Others seem to be **from other energy systems and times**… All have certain elements in common … they have scarcely any interest in who and what we [humans] are, and finally, communication with them is an impossibility because we don't understand their methods of doing so. [135] [emphasis added]

So it is apparent that Man is not alone and there are others here in the 3D Earth realm, even on the Earth, and probably underground as the 'stagehands' who help run this Drama. The significance of the non-human intelligences' treatment of Man is that (1) that is how Man treats lesser lifeforms on Earth, and (2) since Man doesn't respect himself, why should Others respect Man? They treat Man like we treat ants.

So, he did run afoul of entities that inhabit the space close around the Earth (in the lower Astral realm) – the same ones this book is referring to as the Neggs. And he did encounter the Barrier.

But the question remains, <u>What</u> is this place that we and they inhabit?

Holographic Virtual Reality -- HVR Sphere:

The Earth is contained, quarantined in an energy Sphere off which Fort's *Gegenschein* reflects, conceptually shown below:

The Earth in Conceptual HVR Sphere
(source: www.gafnews.com/sites/)

In addition to the HVR Sphere, which has already been revealed, there is another part without which the Sphere cannot operate – the **Control System**. Every School must have a Curriculum, and the Control System is the Curriculum, delivering lessons (catalyst) to the souls-in-training here in accordance with their Scripts. These two aspects, plus the Quarantine, and the Simulation are now further examined.

Wilde Corroboration

The initial introduction to our reality comes from a brilliant English writer, the late Stuart Wilde, who first examined the idea that we are contained in a sort of Sphere. While he was not the first to theorize its existence (Rudolph Steiner holds that honor), Wilde developed the idea and examined its implications. Similar information later came from Robert Monroe, Charles Fort, David Icke, Michael Talbot, lately from Nick Bostrom [136] and Jim Elvidge. [137]

The realm to which Man normally belongs is <u>not</u> in this 3D Construct; his normal home was <u>not</u> visited by Robert Monroe in his OBE journeys. This Earth is a version of the original 4D world allegedly visited by the Anunnaki, and Sirians, etc. centuries ago. Thus it is **a very sophisticated Simulation**, and **holographic replication**, set in a 3D realm still within 4D, and so the Anunnaki 'history' and cuneiform tablets are still part of the Erath scene.

Key Concept 5

In addition, **the Earth is basically quarantined from the normal cosmos by being a 3D holographic-type Construct within a 4D Virtual Reality**, or Holographic Sphere for short, if you will. If one connects the dots and resolves the minor differences in what the other seven men have been saying, this is the result. And it is accurate as will be seen.

By the way, Robert Monroe, in running the personal simulations presented to him, was <u>alone</u> even when he thought the other people in his drama were real. [138] They were part of the simulation, and can be considered OPs (or NPCs).

According to a well-known physicist, Brian Greene (featured in Chapter 13):

> One future day, a cosmic census that takes account of all sentient beings might find that the number of flesh-and-blood humans pales in comparison with those made of chips and bytes [OPs], or their future equivalents. And, [Nick] Bostrom reasons, if the ratio of **simulated humans** to real humans were colossal, [say, 60%?] then brute statistics suggests that we are not in a real universe. The odds would overwhelmingly favor the conclusion that you and I and everyone else are living within a **simulation**…[139] [emphasis added]

And as was said in Chapter 5, the number of OPs on Earth appears to be about 60% of the population. The next chapter further addresses Greene's ideas supporting the proposition that we are living in a <u>very sophisticated</u> Simulation.

In fact, Charles Fort knew we were 'contained' by something, John Keel suspected it, and the late Michael Talbot delivered the message that many aspects of our world/universe have holographic explanations to them… David Icke correctly identified the low-level STS consciousness aspect of the "Vibratory Prison" (as he calls it) or 3D Matrix surrounding us, Nick Bostrom suggests that our lives are lived in a type of computer simulation (not a version of the *The Matrix*), and Engineer Jim Elvidge suggests that

> … I would have to conclude that we are not biological willing participants but rather spiritual entities [souls] occupying an **advanced machine** some-

where in the universe.[140] [emphasis added]

And next Stuart Wilde will introduce us to what he called The Sphere and this chapter calls the 3D Construct … but first we need to realize that our Sphere is **contained**, by Monroe's Barrier which refelcts Fort's *Gegenschein*.

4D Reality

There is support for Wilde's theory of the quarantining Sphere from the channeled entity RA (a 6th level entity with integrity and credibility):

> Questioner: What is the position of this planet [Earth] with respect to the
> progression of cycles at this time?
> RA: I am RA. This **sphere** is at this time in **fourth-dimension** vibration. [141]
> [emphasis added]

And on another occasion, also in January 1981:

> Questioner: What is the density level of our planet Earth at this time?
> RA: I am RA. The **sphere** upon which you dwell is **third density** in its
> beingness of mind/body/spirit complexes. It is now in a
> space/time continuum, **fourth density**. [142] [emphasis added]

The Morphing Sphere

Wilde had been a student of higher consciousness, or enlightenment, and while traveling it had a surprising effect on him as one day he noticed his hotel walls morphing from solid to fluid, changing color, and beings occasionally slipping in and out of perceived reality. [143] If you're not on drugs, and he wasn't, that will get your attention. Says Wilde,

> …I have had many very strange experiences: beings morphing in and out of
> my perception, some human looking, some not; walls that bend and wobble;
> the strange unexplained scents of flowers; flashes of light; and doorways,
> endless doorways. **All around us are worlds more intricate than you can
> ever imagine**. There is dark and light. The tales we have been told of the
> spirit worlds and the afterlife are vaguely true in part, yet wildly inaccurate in
> other aspects. [144] [emphasis added]

There have also been people who reported seeing **gridlines** stretching over the countryside and trees and buildings missing where they used to be… as if the fabric of our world morphs and is not solid but somehow plastic. This may sound like something out of *The Twilight Zone*, or the *Star Trek* Holodeck, but such is a part of the underpinnings of our reality that some gifted people occasionally see. (Chapter 13 image).

Wilde describes the Sphere thus:

> ….a prison created by our minds and for our minds. In the olden days, it
> was called the **Reflective Sphere** [Rudolph Steiner]…. It's everywhere.

It is deep inside all our religious teachings and our New Age philosophies – it is in every spiritual practice that was ever invented.

The Sphere tricks you mercilessly. It's very callous.
The world is lying to you.
The trick is unbelievably clever. It is so total, so complete.
It's all around you as a diamond-shaped **net in the etheric**….
The transdimensionals in nearby etheric dimensions also trap you….

Almost everything you have been taught is 'round backwards. [145]
[emphasis added]

Sound familiar? David Icke, another Britisher, said something similar back in Chapter 4 and called it the "vibratory prison." [146]   According to Icke, this prison is run by a form of higher consciousness from the 4th dimension; entities who seek to 'manipulate' this 3rd dimension by controlling the human mind. The attempted control is allegedly performed by 4D STS entities, but in reality, **benevolent HVR Sphere control is maintained by the Higher Beings through their designees, the Beings of Light and the Neggs, via the Script for each soul – set up before every soul incarnates**. (OPs do not have Scripts.)

Quarantine

In addition to being a 3D Sphere in the 4D realm, it was necessary to protect Man with a Quarantine when the HVR Sphere was created. That is why the Sphere was constructed – to get Man away from external STS 4D+ ETs and other interdimensional entities who sought to use and control Man. A way had to be found to protect ensouled Man from the 4D+ entities who could harass Man, drain his energy, and purposely derail his spiritual progress. The solution was to put the HVR Sphere in a quarantine:

> Questioner: I would like to ask, considering [Man's freewill]…how can the Guardians quarantine the Earth?
> RA: I am RA. The Guardians guard the freewill distortion of the mind/body/spirit complexes of **third density** on this planetary **sphere**. The events which required activation of **quarantine** were interfering with the freewill… of mind/body/spirit complexes [i.e., Man]. [147] [emphasis added]

Note that RA just said we're in 4D but our 3D Construct is 'guarded' here. The corroboration should be completing itself…

But the Quarantine is not fool-proof:

> Questioner: Is there any effort … to stop the [3D and 4D interference with Man]?
> RA: I am RA. **Every effort is made to quarantine this planet**. However the **network of guardians**, much like any other pattern of patrols on whatever level, does not hinder each and every entity from penetra-

ting quarantine, for if request is made in light/love, the Law of One will be met with acquiescence. If the request is not made, due to the slipping thru **the net,** then there is penetration of this net.

Questioner: [How are the intruders stopped from coming thru the quarantine?]
RA: I am RA. There is contact at the level of light-form or light-body-being... **guardians** sweep reaches of your Earth's energy fields to be aware of any entities approaching...and [they] are hailed in the name of the One Creator. Any [good] entity thus hailed ... will of freewill obey the quarantine...

Questioner: What would happen to the entity if he did not obey the quarantine after being hailed?
RA: I am RA. To not obey quarantine after being hailed on the level of which we speak would be equivalent to your not stopping upon walking into a solid brick wall.

Questioner: ...What would happen to [him or his craft]?
RA: I am RA. ...The vibratory level of those able to breach the quarantine boundaries is such that upon seeing the love/light net it is impossible to break this Law [of One, which includes non-interference]. Therefore, nothing happens. No attempt is made. There is no confrontation. **The only beings who are able to penetrate the quarantine are those who discover windows or distortions in the space/time continua surrounding your planet's energy fields.** Through these windows they come. These windows are rare and unpredictable. [148] [emphasis added]

Key Concept 6

So the HVR Sphere replicating as 3D is not only in 4D, and in Quarantine, but there is a kind of 'energy net' around the Earth, referred to herein as a grid that acts to repel 4D+ 'outsiders' who have a lower (STS) vibration. Note that the 3D effect of the Quarantine does NOT serve to keep Man on the planet – however, he may be a "sitting duck" should he try and leave the planet and travel to other planets, even in this solar system. If there are beings whose level or technology allows them to enter 3D, and they are not benevolent, Man may have a problem. That is one reason that Man would have had to have protection to and from the Moon, or Mars, and such may be a reason that Man has not been back to the Moon in 41 years.

Are the dots connecting yet?

Monkey Business

Man's pettiness, violence and diseases are not wanted elsewhere in the Multiverse, let alone this solar system, and he will have to learn to function with all the integrity, compassion and **respect** he can generate before he will be ready to interact with other intelligent, benevolent entities who are in some cases, much more advanced. God help him if he has to interact with advanced, <u>malevolent</u> entities whose technology could make short work of him and his spacecraft.

It does not dawn on Man that a lot of the ETs see him, in comparison, as a **wild monkey** learning to drive down the freeway – other ETs using the same space would be quite annoyed at Man for his lack of discipline, respect and knowledge. Thus he is in quarantine as much for his own protection as to provide a safe space to mature as a species.

The Prime Directive

Recall that there was something called the "prime directive" in *Star Trek*. The U.S.S. Enterprise and its crew were not to interfere with, nor influence in any way, the developing cultures on other planets. It meant: *Non-interference with developing beings.*

It is also a **Galactic Law** that any advanced space-faring race that can create or manipulate sentient beings genetically (aka the Anunnaki) are responsible for their 'created' or modified offspring. **Since the Anunnaki Remnant is still here (including when the Earth was moved into the HVR Sphere about AD 800-900), they are required by Law to see to our proactive development. In so doing, they also grow.**

The Law says that advanced races are bound by laws and ethics:

> …"creator gods" such as these … are bound by laws and ethics to see to the future well-being of the races they choose to create. So the Nibiruans were stuck with us Cro-Magnons, like it or not. **They had to civilize us and culturalize us** [sic]. They knew from experience that we didn't like the looks of their species, so they couldn't control us directly as kings or whatever… eventually they hit upon the idea of religions whereby they could **control** us through ideologies based on fear and guilt. [149] [emphasis added]

Knowing that the Anunnaki were real and that the majority left Earth before it was moved into an HVR Sphere, the small Remnant would be involved now in our development. This bears repeating: The Anunnaki Remnant are still here – and operate as overseers, but in <u>two groups</u> (Dissidents and Insiders) that, like Enlil and Enki in Chapter 3, still disagree on what to do with Mankind. **They are here for almost the same reason we are**: to learn how to respect other life forms, how to care for a planet, and because we may share a lot of their DNA, they have some personal issues to overcome like we do: lying, lust, greed, impatience, anger, violence, pettiness…. They are being trained in what to do with the responsibility of a creation (which is what Enlil wanted to avoid), and the humans are learning responsibility for the planet and respect for others.

Regardless, some day Man may be in the same position as the Anunnaki with regard to any sentient beings he 'creates' out there — if he ever gets out of here.

So, in concert with the Higher Beings, the Anunnaki have also had direction and help, since they are among the "lesser creator gods" out there, and the HVR Sphere would also be intended to provide the protection and safe haven concurrent with a Prime Directive so that the Anunnaki could do their assistance/learning without external interference, **and**

389

it reflects the intent for Man to grow and realize what he is, and move into that potential.

Summary Concepts

At this point it should be emphasized that the Sphere is transparent, and the stars can be seen through it. Who knows, the Simulation may one day insert 3D beings on some close planet as training for us in how to get along with ETs…

Since it is a 3D-within-4D energy Construct, keeping out other 4D+ entities, it also has the ability to reflect the Sun's light in 3D, as Fort noted when he examined the phenomenon called **Gegenschein**. Having seen the Gegenschein, it appears to be a diffused reflection <u>between</u> the Earth and the Moon. As a force field, it is 4D transparent (Monroe didn't see it when he hit it) and yet its particles also reflect 3D sunlight, suggesting that the energy is coherent across several dimensions even if the particles are not. Agreeing with Charles Fort, it is not dust or cosmic particles that are reflecting the Sun; the effect is different and not subject to **parallax distortion**.

Nexus: It is being called an HVR Sphere, short for **Holograpic Virtual Reality Sphere**. The Sphere is a Virtual Reality 3D Construct, the Earth is the Simulation as a 3D Construct within the Sphere.

The reason for calling it **Virtual** is that Earth in the Sphere works as a 3D <u>Simulation</u> and yet the Sphere containing Earth is actually in 4D, and we are accommodating to the 4D realm but are not quite there. Like Criss Angel and Derren Brown (Chapter 9) seem to demonstrate, if you know what this place is and how to visualize and focus, and you have the DNA, you <u>can</u> effect small miracles. For that reason, it is referred to as Virtual.

> *Note: Man was originally in 4D. That is the realm to which he belongs. It was necessary to contain Man in a 3D environment where he would not have his psychic (4D) abilities so that he would be forced to learn "lower level" lessons while having the vibrations in the HVR Sphere adjust and prepare those who were open to the move back into 4D.*

It is a simulated **Reality** because Earth was **replicated** in a **Virtual** Sphere, and souls needing rehab were moved into it, birthed here, and soulless OPs (NPCs) and orchestrated events consistent with a person's Script drive the catalyst to provide growth. Beings of Light and Neggs help drive the lessons.

> NPCs – in a video game, they are **Non-Playing Characters** controlled by the computer. Until now they were called OPs.

Earth just went through a "Wipe and Reboot" somewhere in AD 800-900, and then our Era started over again in the Sphere. This is not a human-type holographic reality, nor is it a dream, as in lucid dreaming. **It is a 3D Simulation in a 4D Realm**… Monroe, Fort and Wilde all got it right. We are physically here and are going through a slight ascension which is where the Higher Beings adjust the vibration level of the Sphere, entraining those souls who can adjust, into a higher level of awareness… and they will 'graduate' <u>back</u> to their original 4D Realm.

When the Earth was surrounded by the outer energy grid, or Monroe's Barrier, or Fort's Shell, or Wilde's Sphere, it automatically locked out any external 4D ETs. The Anunnaki were the progenitors of Man and their little Greys were invited to enter the Sphere to make genetic adjustments, to assist Man in overcoming his baser nature. But making genetic adjustments to living humans has been like trying to paint a moving freight train, and some of the Greys' machinations have been discovered in hypnosis despite blocking human recall of abduction events.

The outer energy grid of the Sphere has been slowly but inexorably raising the vibrations of the Earth. Many souls will not want to grow, nor can they with a low PFV return to their original 4D Realm, and so the Higher Beings will reset the HVR planet (i.e., "Wipe and Reboot") and continue the training of the remaining more open-minded souls who will be joined by whatever hybrids the Greys have been genetically 'building.' Souls are always sequestered in a level they will be comfortable with. The more resistant may be moved to another 3D planet (or another timeline or another simulation).

Increasing Vibrations

In raising the vibrations, the Higher Beings intend to entrain those souls who are ready into a higher awareness. The HVR Sphere resonance at L1 would be about 3.5D and the outer locales may be almost at 4D... this is all to work on the denizens of 3D Earth, and affect the Earth and Man. If a soul who is ready to become an Earth Graduate waits at the outer edge of the HVR Sphere, and the outer edge attains a 4D resonance with that soul, that soul will automatically find himself 'popped' out of the HVR Sphere and will find himself automatically back in 4D – our original home.

Thus, the Schumann Resonance at L1 should be found to be increasing. This has been a gradual process, but many are not adapting to it – thus the 'harvest' to the original 4D realm will not be large.

> The Earth's Schumann Resonance has traditionally been 7.8Hz. Lately it has been measured at 13 Hz and rising. The higher vibration level can entrain resistant people into a state of anxiety and forgetfulness.

Note that the souls that accept and move with the increasing vibrations (The Flow) are automatically 'qualifying' themselves for return to the 4D timeline. No one is running around selecting who goes and who doesn't – Man **selects or deselects himself** by virtue of his PFV – which is why the Knowledge is so important: right now Man has a choice but is not aware of it. Soon it will be too late.

The illusion is that Earth is our home, but this is a royal illusion. It would be nice if just waking up spiritually were enough to get one out of here, but it ain't so. One has to **assimilate the Light**. Knowledge is Light and it is the Light that sets us free. While both Icke and Wilde see the Earth situation as a trap, Icke thinks Love is the answer – we should love our unseen jailers. Wilde, on the other hand thinks we can call on God's Gladiators (Beings of Light) to help us escape from this zoo. [150] In reality, it is going to be **knowledge** that gets Man out of here, because until he <u>knows</u>, he can't make a choice and do what it takes to leave.

Spheres of Influence

The Sphere was spoken about in the 15th and 16th centuries in occult writings, and people called them "**invisible spheres of influence that surround Earth and humanity…**" [151] Stuart tells us that a painting from that time shows a soul leaving the Earth plane for other worlds:

> In the painting, there are **zigzag lines** that we associate today with brainwaves and electricity. How they knew is a mystery. The great Austrian metaphysician **Rudolph Steiner**, who dominated the scene in the 1920s and 30s, also spoke of the influence of the Sphere that surrounds humanity. He spoke of **the Sphere** before electromagnetic fields were properly understood, and certainly before quantum theory was properly worked out. [152] [emphasis added]

So the Sphere is not really anything new, it is just unknown and people do not suspect that they are surrounded with a controlling, 'constructed reality' that influences them. This is also what Morpheus was talking about in the movie *The Matrix* when he said that there was a layer of fields, "**fields upon fields**" that exercise complete control over humanity. People are oblivious, even after seeing the movie, that **there is a superior force like an electromagnetic field that controls their lives by controlling what they see and hear**, similar to the sections on holographic vision and the V2K (Chapter 11) information.

In this case, it is a low electrical (Hz) field, commonly called ELF or extremely low frequency, that is transmitted into the atmosphere around Earth by the Sphere which can entrain human minds into any mental state desired. A manmade example was the Russian KGB which operated a psychotronic transmitter called the **Woodpecker** (until the demise of the former Soviet Union) at a very dangerous 10 Hz level, designed to promote neurological disturbances in any population toward which the transmitter was aimed. [153] Using the 16Hz frequency,

> …. a mental state such as aversion, panic, suicide, paranoid schizophrenia, mania, manic depression, and a host of other psychological behaviours [sic] could be induced with the flick of a switch…. In 1997, the Russians … developed satellites that could change the behaviour of an entire country by blanketing that country from space with UHF or microwave mind control beams. [154]

ELF was also found to be able to cut or damage DNA.[155] So it can happen and has been done. (See Brain Waves in Glossary.)

> *Those who have a higher consciousness (greater awareness), and thus carry more Light, and whose PFV is higher, are much less affected by ELF, and not entrained by it.*

The Sphere is a sort of **hyperdimensional** energy grid, generated by an Astral 4D version of a computer (outside our Sphere), much as **Dr. Modi's patients reported seeing**. Even Robert Monroe while out of body hit the inside of the HVR containing wall and didn't realize what it was. That says that there is a Sphere with actual limits or walls that contain us and even in the Astral, or etheric, body we are unable to just get up and walk out. We have to 'prove' we are worthy to be released, and as said just earlier, your PFV can automatically 'pop' you out... That amounts to a Quarantine as suggested earlier. Perhaps 'containment' is a better term. And yet, depending on your point of view, it could also be a prison.

Transdimensionals

Wilde discussed the issues of control, Astral beings, thoughtforms (TFs) and humanity with a very knowledgeable scientist who has done some research into the 'fields upon fields' that Morpheus spoke of. There seems to be a **layered dimensional reality** around us that even Robert Monroe encountered (see Chart 4) and he called them Locales I-IV. It seems that these TFs, Neggs and other **Interdimensional entities** are able to live and function there. Said Wilde:

> What I found so fascinating was that our reality, while not computer generated [as in *The Matrix*], is in effect very similar. We are in **an electronic prison**, an electromagnetic field that is being controlled ….
>
> In September 2000, I met a very knowledgeable scientist who also talked about the **fields upon fields.** He said that they have come about as a result of humanity's emotions and thought forms over the ages; but the fields also have their own identity, their own evolution. He said the fields feed off humanity for sustenance….[and] attempt to sustain a false immortality. He said the fields' intrinsic nature is one of **control**….
>
> The fields have become stronger and stronger as the world's population has increased dramatically since World War II…. **Inside the fields are entities that have evolved within it.** Whether these entities are birthed inside the field or whether they are **transdimensionals from another dimension** who are attracted to the field for sustenance, we don't know as yet. [156] [emphasis added]

And even more unsettling is that entities can enter the HVR Sphere…According to RA, quoted earlier:

> **I am RA….The only beings who are able to penetrate the quarantine are those who discover windows or distortions in the space/time continua surrounding your planet's energy fields.** Through these windows they come. These windows are rare and unpredictable. [157] [emphasis added]
>
> *This is one of the best reasons for doing a "Wipe and Reboot" – it removes accumulated Astral influence, pollution, and levels the playing field for the next Era.*

Fields upon fields, realms upon realms, and I would suggest that the entities spoken of above **are** the transdimensionals. Also called ultradimensionals by Keel and **Interdimensionals** by Monroe. There is also reason to think that this same group may also be the **Djinn** as known by the Arabs. Certainly they are not the Neggs or discarnates.

Wilde is describing the **layered Astral realm** and, of major importance, the Neggs and the Interdimensionals who populate it. The beings that hassled Robert Monroe when he first tried to go out of the body. The ones who play games (Ouija Boards) and cause fish to fall from the sky, and manifest some UFOs and Bigfoot and Mothman – to amuse, amaze and scare. Monroe also spoke about the need of these beings to feed on our provoked energy output (usually anger or fear) which he called **"Loosh."** [158]

Remember that even Dr. Modi reported that her patients often saw **other beings that were said to come from other dimensions.** [159] And according to some very esoteric teachings, these entities can be benign or mischievous… none of them are said to be evil. That means they could be Angel-like, Negg-like entities, Avatars, transdimensionals and God-knows-what-else – even the alleged Djinn (which may also be the Neggs playing a game)… If that doesn't confuse you, nothing will. Or have another go at the last **Nexus** paragraph above in the Section called 'Summary Concepts'.

Key Concept 7

There is a coherent picture forming that this is not our planet, we are not alone, but we are being 'controlled' – even if ultimately in our best interest, i.e., to provoke spiritual growth. (See Appendix C where Dr. Vallée examines the **Control System**.)

> *Note: no doubt this is why the Higher Beings allow the disinformation and manipulation that go on here: ultimately we have to wake up and rise above it, **whether we understand it or not**. In short, it can be a very exacerbating form of* **catalyst**.

The Higher Beings have created this 3D HVR Sphere in 4D, and in Quarantine, effectively placing themselves between us and God. They run the Sphere and manipulate its concomitant Control System. That means that objects, characters and events can be inserted into the HVR Sphere as needed – to provide catalyst for true soul growth. Some UFOs, and most Bigfoot, Mothman, Mermaids, and Fortean anomalies fall into this category. Nessie does not -- she is a plesiosaur from another Era. And a lot of UFOs are Earth-based creations – from the Anunnaki Remnant (aka Naga), or from Man with back-engineering guidance provided by entities inserted by the Control System.

> When Dr. Wernher von Braun was asked how they developed such advanced rocketry and *Flugscheiben (saucers)*, he pointed to the sky and said "Sie haben uns durchgeholfen." [160] We had help.

We often appear to be like cattle in a pasture who think that the pasture is all theirs and yet have no idea why they're there. But cattle don't have souls for one thing and we are not powerless like cattle – we do have access to Beings of Light (angels) and a direct line (prayer) to God the Father. And cattle don't pray – but there are billboards where they do encourage people to eat chicken!

Why Create an HVR Sphere?

We are 'constructively' trapped in the HVR Sphere until we wake up, desire to move forward in the Father's Creation, and **prove ourselves worthy to be released**. [161] Man is an important creation and while he <u>is</u> contained, the means of escape have been provided … if Man will open his eyes and look.

Consider that **souls have been placed here for 'rehab' purposes** because at some point, somewhere else, they insisted on doing what they wanted, when they wanted, the way they wanted – playing god – their way, and their behavior was not acceptable to others in the realm where they were. If you were a god, or Higher Being, wouldn't you devise a place where wayward souls could be 're-educated' by finding themselves in a context of their equals and experiencing what they, themselves, were like? Would you not protect it from outside interference? Would you not provide teachers to inspire and show a better way? Would you not have a Control System providing Curricula to amplify each soul's Script? Would you release such 'unbalanced' (off-center, inappropriate and sometimes extreme) souls to the more civilized realms in **4D** that other beings enjoy? Do they not put criminals in prison to keep them from harming the society around them? Do they not admit mentally unstable people to sanitariums and mental wards in an effort to rehabilitate them?

Sad, but as long as Man does not know who he is and why he is here, he'll never get out of here. [162] He must have Knowledge (Light) to graduate from Earth, and that is obstructed by those 3D human PTB who think they run this place. He can plug into all the 'feel good' philosophies there are out there, and kid himself that life is about having nonstop fun, and feeling good, but he is living in a self-imposed illusion. What has been called a

Prophylactic Fantasy

in this book. And as long as he is deluded, and can't handle reality, this HVR Sphere will be his home… until of course the planetary pollution (or disease) puts an end to the current Era, and the real gods do a "Wipe and Reboot", reset the ecosphere, and start it all over again.

The concept of the controlling Sphere, as a vibrational prison, or as a school, <u>does</u> explain why the world looks the way it does, and this is covered more fully in the next chapter.

Summary

Concurrent with the information in the last two sections, Key Concepts 1-7, and a repeat of this book's major related ideas can help to focus better on the overall HVR Sphere concept.

Evidence Suggesting an HVR Sphere

While it is fairly conclusive, the evidence for our being in a 3D simulation, holographic reality, which is within the 4D realm is supported by the following 13 concepts developed throughout the book:

1. Young Earth Evidence – if the Earth is 4.5 billion years old, then why doesn't it look like it ? Refer to the list of scientific evidences in Chapter 10 that show Earth has had at least had one "Wipe & Reboot" so that it looks young. A "**Wipe and Reboot**" is what is done before Man starts over each time – in a new Era – and this last time in an HVR Sphere, for reasons already given. The Flood 10,000 years ago is considered a "Wipe and Reboot" event.

2. Stuart Wilde's Sphere – his perception is reinforced by that of Charles Fort, Robert Monroe and Rudolph Steiner. Wilde's spiritual awareness, documented in many of his books, led him to experience a perception of our reality that is best described by living in a sort of Sphere wherein Man can be monitored and controlled. The Sphere's outer shell is an energy barrier, functioning as a quarantine against 4D+ entities, and yet it only reflects sunlight in 3D where it is not an obstacle to Earth access (due to there not being any significant entities to block in 3D).

The barrier reflects The *Gegenschein* – not only discovered by Charles Fort, but as mentioned earlier even NASA has photographed it, and it does exist without parallax – meaning it **is** consistently reflected off of something between Earth and the Moon with permanence, substance and a consistent geometry.

3. Moon & Mars Trips – Many people dispute that we ever went to the Moon, and they question that we have a Rover on Mars taking pictures. If they're right, no Moon trips in 1969-72 and no Rovers on Mars would corroborate that Man cannot get outside of the Sphere, and its quarantining grid, any more than Robert Monroe could. However, we know that Man can venture out away from the Earth, because the Sun's light and particle emissions can affect Earth, not to mention asteroids which are not stopped by any 3D barrier. The 2009 LCROSS explosive rocket that bombed the Moon demonstrated that the Moon is accessible from/within the HVR Sphere.

4. Jacques Vallée's Control System – The Control System discussed in Chapter 4 and in Appendix C must have a closed environment in which to function – one from which Man cannot escape from 3D if the control is to be effectively applied. Control cannot be exerted on an Earth where Man can come and go between dimensions (even via OBE) as he wills – thus the HVR Sphere, the Barrier, and the Quarantine. Catalyst (objects, people, and events) can be inserted into the HVR Sphere as the Higher Beings see fit.

If Man is allowed to establish bases on the Moon or Mars, that would be still within 3D and the Control System would still apply – its boundries will just have been extended. To date, over the centuries, Man seems to be pretty much contained on Earth and such off-planet ventures have not been commonplace, probably because of the logistics involved in overseeing his development as a soul before he is allowed to leave Earth.

5. Fortean Anomalies – fish and rocks falling from the sky should register as something unusual with humans… yet most either don't believe it happened or they run in fear from the information. What if the Control System is doing it – like They did elves, fairies and airships – to get Man's attention? Why? To cause him to realize that Earth is more than he thinks it is… wonder and awe often move Man into better science and spiritual learning.

But Man is often stubborn – he ignores what he doesn't like, or blows it off … and gets recycled.

6. HVR Sphere Simulation -- a self-contained, quarantined Sphere which has a Control System, just as a computer has an Operating System, is the unity that drives the holographic simulation in which Man finds himself today. Several advanced thinkers, Bostrom and Elvidge, have echoed and reinforced the Simulation concept, as have several movies, *Groundhog Day*, *The 13th Floor*, and *The Matrix*.

7. Chronology Altered – Dr. Anatoly Fomenko's discovery that backwards of AD 900 very little can be known about the history of anyone's civilization, and his major discovery that all of Western history's chronology was modified by 2 priests using a template during the 1500-1600's, suggest that something significant (a "Wipe and Reboot") happened in the AD 800-900 period. As was shown in the last chapter, even the Classic Maya <u>civilization</u> disappeared – overnight. The only reason for back-dating history would be to make it look like we and the Church have been here a long time (when we haven't) so that no one suspects that Earth is not what it seems.

The chronology would have to be altered to make it look like we have been here a long time IF someone on Earth who was responsible for shepherding Man after AD 700-900 knew that we had been removed from 4D reality, and Earth was placed in a 3D Construct for the reasons discussed throughout this chapter.

8. OBE Experiences – Robert Monroe's OBE experiences – hitting a barrier, harassment by Astral entities, not seeing any other 3D beings until he ventured into an alternate 4D realm/timeline. These experiences exactly describe trying to function within the alternate reality that is herein suggested and takes on the form of an HVR Sphere.

9. Simulation & Recycling -- The *Inspecs* also ran simulations on Monroe that he could not tell weren't real. He had to repeat each **simulation** until he got it right, or figured out what they were trying to show him. A 3D simulation in 4D could behave similarly, like a *Star Trek* Holodeck.

Simulations that one has to repeat are called **recycling**. Souls on Earth are recycled until they get it right. When a significant part of Mankind does not understand the lessons, or has significantly contaminated the ecology, or is about to destroy the planet, the gods suspend day-to-day operation of the Control System, move Man and the OPs into a holding area, and reset the planet, i.e., clean it up and then put mankind back on Earth (with no memory of the suspension). BUT, this sometimes results in a "gap" in linear history – the last one is referred to as The Dark Ages. (Hence the point 6 above to rewrite history.)

10. UFO maneuvers – They defy 3D laws of physics suggesting that they are illusions or interdimensional objects, and note that there are <u>no longer</u> any 3D **ET** UFOs. The UFOs break the laws of physics in the 3D world -- 90° turns at 4000 mph, sudden stops and instant acceleration, not to mention disappearing – but all possible in an HVR simulation.

The Simulation operates under different Laws than our Newtonian Physics. Whereas the genuine 3D UFOs are powered by anti-gravitic/electromagnetic propulsion, that creates a field around the craft that 'shields' it from the 3D laws of physics. As a result, right-angle turns <u>are</u> possible, fantastic acceleration, and even the ability to 'cloak' and remain invisible are all part of the advanced physics possible within the HVR Sphere (as permitted by the HVR Astral Bio-Quantum Computer).

11. Paranormal Abilities -- Note that certain people have been able to walk on water, levitate, pass through solid walls, know what is behind closed doors, put their hand through the glass of an aquarium without breaking the glass and remove an object, put a quarter inside a sealed can of Coke, and physically disappear.

The fake versions of these things are illusions performed by master magicians, sometimes 'helped' by unseen Astral entities. The genuine versions of these things are called psychic abilities normally attributed to the 4D world, suggesting that as we grow and return more toward our original 4D orientation, our (para-)normal abilities could be more empowered. (See Chapter 10.) So, could 4D entities be walking among us demonstrating these abilities (remember Wanda in Chapter 5)?

12. OPs and Catalyst -- The OPs exist usually as bit-players in supporting roles to the main Drama acted out on Earth by the ensouled beings. They are largely puppets and Placeholders and 'portals' through which the HVR Sphere may provide **catalyst** to help ensouled Man to grow. The more extreme OP versions are called sociopaths who also have no aura, thus no soul and thus no conscience, but even they have a role in the Earth Drama.

13. Quantum Physics – would agree that the world we think we see/know is not what we take it for. Such things as nonlocality, biophotons, holographic vision and memory, virtual particles, light being both a wave and a particle, and the feasibility of time travel, all speak to the essence of the **hyperphysics** of the 4th dimension. And the Control System, operating on the HVR Sphere from outside the Sphere, would use hyperphysics to replicate and operate this 3D Earth Simulation.

An HVR Sphere is concurrent with the essence of hyperphysics and control.

Science moves ever forward, and just as the concept of an HVR Sphere would have been utterly foreign to scientists 100 years ago, so today we are at least considering it, and perhaps 100 years from now it will be an accepted fact. Just as we left Newtonian physics in the 3D world, we have had a new physics to try to describe our world, quantum physics, where things are not really solid, time is not always linear, and particles respond to the observer watching them. And quantum physics is now being challenged by **subquantum kinetics**. [163]

Man is a marvelous creation and it has been Somebody's intent that he is protected and guided through his 'lessons' to evolve spiritually from caterpillar to butterfly. Ultimately, this is an opportunity to become **Earth Graduates**, and it should not be taken lightly.

The quarantined 3D Sphere, with the protective grid, and the Neggs to provide catalyst, and the Beings of Light to oversee, answer prayer, and guide, and the potential in his DNA says that **sentient, ensouled Man is an important creation** – enough for today's 'caretakers' or Watchers to have performed a few more genetic upgrades. Just as they replaced Neanderthal with Cro-Magnon, so Homo *sapiens* is nowadays being replaced by Homo *noeticus* (aka the Indigos). If our current DNA limits us from making progress as a species, then the upgrades are being done for our benefit; the PTB will not be able to deceive and control the *noeticus* human who discerns and knows more, and thus the PTB Lords will have few if any Serfs to rule. That is why the PTB prefer to keep Man ignorant.

Chapter 13: -- Virtual Reality & Simulation

In the last 15 years there have been a number of books and movies dealing with the concept of virtual reality, simulation, and holograms. Those that are of the most interest with regard to this book's theme are listed in the Bibliography.

The following is an analysis of four current-day movies dealing with simulation or virtual reality, and their significance to the **Earth HVR Sphere** of Chapter 12. The Holodeck of *Star Trek* fame was discussed in the last chapter as it is much closer to where we are, and relates more closely to other relevant issues discussed therein.

The concept of the HVR Sphere will be more fully defined by the end of this chapter.

Groundhog Day – deals with a TV anchorman, Phil, whom the gods keep cycling through the same day over and over until he finally learns compassion and seeks to care about and assist other people. The unique thing about this movie is that every time the gods recycle him, he gets to remember what he did the day(s) before (and there were <u>many</u> as he is there long enough to learn to play the piano well). He keeps trying new things to get out -- including staging his own death, which doesn't work. He is recycled (**Déjà vu**) in a controlled environment/reality which is effecting the **Simulation**.

The Truman Show -- deals with a man, Truman, who from birth was the subject of a "reality" TV show and who is '**contained**' in an apparent seaside town where he lives and works. In reality, the set is under a huge steel dome (note: half **sphere**) which contains the "world" in which everything happens in front of almost 5,000 cameras that follow Truman everywhere on over ten thousand days of his life. Since his birth, he has been the "star" of this reality drama and <u>everyone else</u> is an extra or actor who is in on what is really going on. Only Truman does not know that his 3D world is a fake set. While there is no script, only Truman is free to do whatever he wants – except leave or find out who/what he is. Like Phil, Truman doesn't know what is going on, nor can he easily walk out. This is **Manipulated Reality**.

The Matrix – deals with a young man, Mr. Anderson (later 'Neo'), who was "living" in part of the Virtual world run by machines and who is rescued and becomes part of the real world. He serves to undo the Matrix because he, unknowingly, is the predicted "one" to do it. The Matrix is a **Virtual Reality** which seems real to the humans who are asleep, dreaming their lives, serving as a power source for the machines who run the virtual reality. The humans are manipulated in the virtual world, but are kept happy because (1) they don't know where they really are, (2) the Matrix supplies all their fantasies, and (3) the machines need the human life energy to run their world. Humans are happy, except Neo who has always sensed that something was wrong with the "world" and so he becomes the "chosen one" to end the enslavement of mankind.

The 13th Floor -- tells the story of a group of people who believe their world is real, but in fact it is a **Virtual Reality Simulation**. In turn they have created another world into which they can move (reminiscent of the technique in the movie *Avatar*) and they can fully experience that realm that they know to be not real. In fact, at one point, one of the characters drives out of town, through the road barricades and off into the uninhabited desert, comes up over a hill and cannot believe what he sees: the unfinished set of the simulation in which he finds himself –including the gridlines where scenery had not been 'painted.'

Scene from The Thirteenth Floor
credit: The Thirteenth Floor, Columbia Pictures, Roland Emmerich. 1999

What is amazing is that the *13ᵗʰ Floor* main character, Douglas, is a character who with a techie friend in 1998 creates a 1937 Simulation via computer, but is unaware that his 1998 world is in turn simulated from a higher, future level in 2024.

Neo, like Phil and Truman, has to find out where he is and overcome to get out. Douglas in the *13ᵗʰ Floor* does not have to overcome, but he does have to wake up and realize where he is. Phil had to overcome his arrogance and insensitivity, Truman had to overcome his fear of water, and Neo had to connect with something higher in himself and thus overcome the Matrix' programming. In most cases, the message is: (1) that we are 'contained', and (2) we are not aware of who we really are, yet may be more than we think we are, and (3) we need to get out of here.

This book's Introduction said it: This is not your planet, You don't belong here, and you need to wake up and get out. These movies are a similar wake-up call.

Reality vs Virtual Reality

Before getting into the sections on VR versus Simulation which follow, it would be helpful to define reality.

Reality is an **agreed-on** physical structure that surrounds us, which we can see, hear, taste, touch and/or feel. It is not defined by what we can see or touch – it is really defined by a consensus of multiple people agreeing that the reality they share is "real." It affects our five senses the same way it does everyone else's five senses, and thus there is **agreement** that what we all see around us is our reality. Our common **experiences** are the basis for the agreement. Differences in peoples' experiences source disagreements.

Physical 3D reality can also be replicated somewhere else – real houses can be built and lived in, food can be grown in the ground, and rocks are hard and water's wet. Thus another aspect of reality is that it **consistent**.

If someone sees a pink elephant in the room, or a giraffe as Tom did in Chapter 13, that **is** that person's reality – but no one else can verify it. Such is the case with Virtual Reality – it is rarely shared by many people at one time, a notable exception being the Fatima apparition of 1918, which was a very high level simulation.

Another way, besides agreement, to know if one is interacting with reality or a virtual reality is to consider the **source**. [1]   We know that houses are real because we can see them being built and we know the source of the materials and labor. We know cars are real because we know the source and can see them being built if we travel to Detroit and take a tour at GM. That is, they are not apparitions, they are solid to the touch. The problem comes in if there are things in our world that we can't see but are real (there are people who still today deny the existence of germs and Astral entities), and other things that are here and can be seen, but are not real (some UFO sightings, Bigfoot, Mermaids and Mothman are apparitions, just as fairies and elves were years ago).

Conversely, we did not see the Earth being built, nor can we see the source of the wind, nor can we see gravity… so we hypothesize about something we all agree is real, but we have no idea where it came from nor how it got that way.

Truman has a similar situation that we see but he doesn't: the Moon in his world never moves, and because it has always been that way, he doesn't question it. In a similar way, the Earth in 3D Simulation, within the 4D realm, is something that we have always seen and so don't question it. Check out the furor 500 years ago when people were told that the Earth wasn't flat; the HVR Earth Sphere revelation may have a similar effect.

> **What if:** in the Simulation 500 years ago, the Earth <u>was</u> flat because that was the known world, and it wasn't necessary to simulate more as no one went far over the mountains or across the sea?

And if, say, half of our world that we assume, and agree on, to be real isn't, how would we know? That is the issue with the HVR Sphere in which Man finds himself today. It looks real, feels real, and everyone agrees that it is there – and it **is** our 3D reality. But it is contained within a Sphere like Truman's world, for observation. Truman is in a drama, playing a role, and that agrees interestingly with what Shakespeare said about Man and this world **Stage.** Just as Truman is watched, so is Man.

> *Remember that Man used to be aware that there were beings called The Watchers, who still exist by the way. A lot of people don't like this idea because then they'd have to be responsible for what they do.*

First let's examine Virtual Reality, then Simulation, and then pull a clarification of their interrelationship...

I. Virtual Reality

The most intriguing aspect of virtual reality (VR), in any form, is that it is very hard to remain objective and remember that it is not real. It is a little easier to remember that a video game is a game because the game exists on the computer <u>within one's surroundings which don't change and are not part of the game</u>. On the other hand, there are helmets that people can wear which provide sensory inputs to the brain and the subject sees, hears, smells, and may feel or taste whatever sensory input is fed the brain – just as if it were actually happening.

What is the difference between actually eating a steak and drinking fine wine, versus having it all pumped into your brain through neuro-stimulation as was done for Cypher in *The Matrix*? The sensation and satisfaction are there, and isn't that one reason why we eat the steak and drink the wine? How can we tell the difference, and is that important?

This line of thinking is not new. Rene Descartes, in the seventeenth century, entertained the possibility that

> ... all our beliefs might be false. In his *Meditations,* he aims to find a secure foundation for knowledge and... shows that all of our beliefs are susceptible to doubt. He begins with the **unreliability of our senses**, but decides that this doesn't quite do the job. He then considers the possibility that **we may be dreaming** everything up. In fact, there is no sure fire way to show that we are not dreaming. But... we could not always have been dreaming since the contents of our dreams could not be generated from dreams alone and so must come from some other source. He then considers that a **malicious demon is systematically deceiving us** such that every one of our beliefs is false... [2] [emphasis added]

Wonderfully archaic – but he <u>was</u> on the right track as we saw in the last chapter and the Control System. (Appendix C.)

While this book does not support the theory that demons are responsible for Man's false beliefs and thus his problems in life, it does support the position that there are influences on Man from the Dissidents, occasional discarnates, the ubiquitous Neggs, and a possible RCF/Matrix, and that a lot of Man's beliefs <u>are</u> false – by design. And don't forget the new, man-made technology to manipulate thinking called V2K examined in Chapter 11.

To recap, the problem with VR is that it cannot easily be distinguished from reality without a **reference point**. And if one is immersed in the virtual reality, there is no fixed point of reference, such as the room one is in while playing a VR game on one's computer. And a lot of people don't care (like Cypher) – it is an escape, which *The Matrix* movie adequately shows.

But, if as in *Groundhog Day* Phil's case, he is allowed to remember that he was here before (each prior day repeats) and what he did yesterday that did not result in getting out of the repeating drama, then one can see that (1) one is trapped, and (2) the way out has to be discovered – usually through trial and error. Any trap is to be overcome, not passively accepted.

Be aware that in the first three movies above, only Neo is working through a **Virtual Reality** (because he [Mr. Anderson's body] is not physically in the scenario), and Phil is working through a **Simulation** (because he is physically inserted into the daily repeating scenario). Truman also thinks he is in the real world, but his world **is** 3D, and it is fabricated or contrived, a movie set, a **Manipulated 3D** reality contained in a steel half sphere – like Earth which is in a complete Sphere. All three people are part of the **context** of their lives, so that is not a clue to where they are.

In addition, all four protagonists are **contained**, as we are on Earth. Watching the four movies, we realize eventually that they are contained, and they don't know it. Gradually the first three do what it takes to get out (as dictated by the parameters of the VR or Simulation). Neo destroys the Matrix, Phil learns to love and serve, and Truman over-comes his fear of water and sails to the edge of the dome in which he has been trapped. Douglas is helped out of his Simulation by someone from the higher Simulation in which he is contained.

> *Note that Phil did not lucid dream at night – he was* not *in control which is one of the aspects of Lucid Dreaming, to be examined at the end of the chapter.*

But what happens when Man on Earth, who is living in a 3D simulation similar to the one Phil was in, also doesn't know where he is, what he is, and can't wake up?

That is the point of this book. This chapter is suggesting that Earth is a real, 3D world but instead of being contained under a steel half-dome as in Truman's world, Earth is contained within a more sophisticated high-energy Sphere in 4D – all orchestrated and monitored from outside the HVR Sphere. Fort's *Gegenschein* reflects off this field's energy barrier somewhere between the Earth and the Moon, and Robert Monroe actually hit the barrier in several of his OBEs. Shakespeare was right: Earth amounts to a **"Stage"** in quarantine, for reasons given later herein, and in Chapter 15.

Rewind: VR Exegesis

While several dictionaries consulted did not define the term "Virtual Reality" or even "virtual" as used in this chapter, it is acknowledged that many people use the terms Virtual Reality and Simulation interchangeably and that shown by the *Star Trek* Holodeck: the Simulation is the Virtual Reality as long as one drama is playing. If the Holodeck were to play multiple simulations, or multiple dramas <u>at the same time</u>, then each drama would be a simulation within the Holodeck Virtual Reality – and that is what Earth is. Technically a Simulation must run in a Virtual Reality whose environmental resources support the Simulation(s).

VR Criteria To Consider

Before going to the next section, it might be useful to share seven ways we can know if we are in a VR or a Simulation. These are things to look for in a Simulation of our world and in the events around us…

1. Constants and Laws Change

It has recently come to light (Chapters 8-9) that the constants of Physics and including the Laws of the Universe are not so constant. The speed of light, C-14 dating, and the alpha constant are not constant, and entropy does not always happen (The Second Law of Thermodynamics). Any parameters and 'constants' can be changed at any time in a Simulation, as well as they could wind up in corrupted code that normally drives a stable part of the Simulation. If "internal consistency" is not there, then it is very suggestive of a Simulation whose inner 'programming' occasionally misfires [3] and this is examined by Dr. Greene in a later section.

Hints that this is not a real universe would come from imperfections in the Simulation.

> "…It is unlikely that we would find an obvious imperfection such as a fuzzy border on the other side of a mountain, which has never before been observed. Imperfections in the observable universe would be subtle and almost undetectable. They will be found [however] in the laws of physics." [4]

And just so, it has been observed that there has been a change in the speed of light, the alpha constant in decay rates, and The Fine Structure Constant also seems to have changed – this is the ratio of the speed of light, the charge on the electron, and Planck's Constant. [5] Constants should be the same everywhere in the universe, but that is Man's idea, and perhaps the Simulation operates with different but not antagonistic laws in different parts of the universe…? It will take further deeper analysis with more advanced equipment to get to the bottom of this issue. And if we are in a Simulation, it may be adjusted so we can't figure it out, no matter what we do. Or They ('the gods' aka the Higher Beings) may just restart us…

2. Things Disappear

Objects, buildings, trees and fixed parts of the landscape may change location, size, orientation (N-S-E-W), color – or just disappear. On-ramps that used to be there are now gone, motels that used to be there are gone, and if you get out, walk around and physically check, you may find that there is absolutely NO TRACE of them ever having been there. The same may apply to people; you go back to a town and try to look up Sally Smith, and no one knows her or who she was…such mysteries were a favorite for Rod Serling on *The Twilight Zone.*

3. Synchronicities

This one is a real kicker: things just happen to work out at the right time in the right way! The right people show up, or you meet some one just "by chance," and you just happen to see/hear the very piece of info you were looking for... easy for the Simulation to manage as They can insert the right people, or right objects at the right time, or orchestrate events to produce a synchronicity.

4. Auric Information

This one is added for those who can see auras, the etheric energy envelope around people, usually 1 -2" above all parts of the body. When you see peoples' auras appear and disappear, or one day John has an aura and the next day he doesn't, this might make you think you have switched timelines to another locale where the same person who normally has an aura, now doesn't. That is a possibility, but it is also indicative of an ensouled person leaving that body (as in *Avatar*) and the Simulation. Whereas these people without auras have been called OPs, they may in fact be NPCs -- Non-Playing Characters controlled by the Simulation computer.

5. Scenes Repeat or Freeze

This should be an obvious clue, and it rarely if ever happens. For example, sometimes on the *Star Trek* Holodeck, the simulation could hang up, or freeze, and the player could get stuck in the simulation. It is theorized that if this actually does happen, hopefully it is localized to a small area of the planet, and the gods would stop everything, suspend time, fix the problem, wipe memories of the glitch, and then start the scene again. How would we ever catch this?

6. Déjà vu

Experiencing Déjà Vu is a key sign that one has been **recycled** back into the exact same lifetime – same drama, same family, same 'test' all over again that one failed to handle the last time. That can only be done by resetting and rerunning the Simulation. It looks familiar because it **is** a repeat of a former simulated scenario. (This is examined again by Mouravieff in the next chapter.) The 'rerun' may be isolated for the soul as a "fractal simulation" as happened to Phil – while he repeated his years of reruns, he was fractally isolated from the rest of the 'normal' world that he had occupied until the first day of reruns. It may involve a suspension of time, such that as Phil completes his innumerable reruns, when he rejoins the 'normal' world, it is just one day later in that world.

7. Fortean Anomalies (yes, again)

Since rocks and fish falling from a clear sky are not normal everyday events, could they not be products of the Control System... designed to make us re-examine our world? Such weird events would be easy to create in a controlled HVR Sphere, or Simulation. If Man doesn't pay attention to fish and rocks, maybe he'll notice UFOs...?

II. Simulation

Reality can be simulated – there are fake fruit and flowers, called *realia*, used as non-spoiling decorations on dining room tables. We use mannequins to display clothes, and some wallpaper reproduces park scenes, etc., and of course there is *trompe l'oeil* in the art world – an arch painted on a wall appears to be looking down at a seascape in the Aegean. Not everything we see is real.

There is also a more sophisticated simulation called **holography** where people, objects and places can be simulated – not only in the Holodeck on *Star Trek*, but at Walt Disney World, and in laboratories and such is technologically generated and sustained.

Simulation seems real but isn't. And it usually has a <u>purpose</u> and it often involves <u>repetition</u> – as in a flight simulator (learning to fly), or as happened with Phil's day repeating itself, and even a special simulation that was given to Robert Monroe as reported in *Far Journeys*. [6] The VR itself <u>usually</u> does not involve repetition because it is the 'container' or matrix in which the simulations run. Witness the *Star Trek* Holodeck which plays out a scenario without endless looping of scenes – but even that is usually under the control/request of the players.

If Man is **recycled** to the same lifetime (as suggested in Chapter 14), the whole VR, or **a fractal part** (a subset) of it, then becomes the simulation and Man is expected to do better the next time around, overcome, and get out.

Simulation and VR Include OPs

Keep in mind that a simulation such as the one in *Groundhog Day* necessarily involves OPs (NPCs) as the only required actors in the drama. It would not be fair, nor necessary, to involve and recycle real, <u>ensouled</u> human beings into your simulation – unless there were a karmic entanglement that required two or more souls to work out their differences.

So what Phil experienced the first day he was in town was the real town and the real people (ensouled <u>and</u> other OPs). Then each succeeding day was a repeated performance with the simulated town and simulated people (for years in the loop) until he got the message and became a more loving and less cynical person. He could not kill nor be killed as it was a special simulation whose ground of being (ground rules) obviated that. Needless to say, while he spent 'years' in the simulation, only one real Earth day had passed and later his real life moved forward – now with the girl of his dreams. So when he awakens at 6:00am on the first day that the radio does not repeat Sonny and Cher's song, he awakens in bed with the real girl and in the real town – on <u>day two</u> of his total visit for the newscast they were to do. It is no longer a simulation.

> **Or is it? What if everybody was in a larger Simulation which appeared to be their 'normal' lives? And when his fractal simulation is done, all their lives go forward and the girl does not remember her NPC / OP experiences in his fractal simulation…**

The simulation that Robert Monroe experienced in his OBE was a repeated, orchestrated experience where he had to choose the proper course of action to handle his small plane on fire. His initial solutions were all rejected (as were Phil's) until he finally made the right choice.

> *It is observed that about 60% of the people on Earth are OPs and that very few ensouled people are present. This is based on the occasional headcounts made throughout the 3-year period when I saw auras. Most people on this Earth are OPs – now recognized to be NPCs.*

III. VR or Simulation?

Let's stop and summarize and clarify. Here are the 3 keys:

1. A Simulation must run within a container, a context, a Matrix, and that is called Virtual Reality.

> Please be aware that the explanations of things in this chapter fit that definition; if one is trying to fit the explanations into what one already thinks is VR or Simulation, confusion may result.

2. At all times the Creators of the HVR Earth Simulation are considered to be synonymous with Higher Beings aka 'the gods.' At no point is it said that aliens or ETs run this Earth Simulation.

3. Now we have to re-examine OPs and see them as NPCs – Non-Playable Characters controlled by the Simulation computer.

> **Also please note the "Nexus" points-of-connection in the following sections; they are a kind of summary restatement for clarity.**

Rewind: Simulations

Whereas a Virtual Reality is a <u>total</u> Simulation, it is generally (by definition) a total, all-inclusive environment. A VR may consist of multiple, related, or fractal Simulations to comprise the overall VR. A Virtual Reality that contains no running Simulations is just like a scenario 'painted' in a *Star Trek* Holodeck with no people or animals. It doesn't move, and thus is as useful as a CAD-CAM drawing that doesn't rotate.

On the other hand, in our everyday world, a simulation can be run within a real-life context, on a PC or Flight Simulator pod at American Airlines, that is not within a VR. And it may be reset (i.e., different Eras) and repeated as many times as necessary until the student gains mastery, and that is generally the <u>purpose</u> of a simulation. The VR **is** the <u>containing</u> **context**, but the simulation usually happens as a **content** within one's everyday reality. For example, the *Matrix* is the VR, but Neo's ability to fly is a simulated aspect within his VR.

For another example, suppose you are hiking through the wilderness (Important: no one else around) and you encounter a Bigfoot. Is it real? You stand and watch it, and it watches you – but doesn't attack. The Bigfoot simulation was inserted into your 'real' (VR) everyday world for whatever reason. They want to test you – will you try to shoot it, chase it, photograph it, or try to communicate with it? It is a fractal simulation – within the larger 'real' world you think you already occupy…

Trapped in Simulation

Another aspect of simulation, demonstrated by the *Star Trek* Holodeck, is the aspect of the simulation hanging up, or freezing, and your getting stuck in the simulation.

> One of the most compelling features of the Holodeck (for the viewers, not the participants) was that the program on occasion would get stuck, or freeze, and the "real" player would get stuck in the "fictional" story. Thus the question of what was truly real came into question in an important way, since if the player couldn't get the program to work or stop [or find the Holodeck exit] then he or she was going to be stuck permanently in another world – a false world… [7]

What usually happens in our HVR is that we get so 'plugged in' to the drama, and addicted to the sex, money/power, drugs, drinking, revenge, etc that we attach ourselves to this place and must go through it again – that is commonly how we trap ourselves in our HVR Simulation. (The gods do not do it to us.) The concept is that at some point the player absorbs or merges with his 'reality' and becomes one with it, as we have on Earth. At what point can the player, or Man, back off and realize that it is a Simulation, master it and walk out? What if the HVR Earth simulation has become so real, so absorbing, so addictive that Man no longer has the ability to get out, or as Monroe would say, Man cannot achieve the Escape Velocity? [8]

Earth HVR Simulated Sphere

That is the official description of this place and each part requires a more full examination

HVR – officially Holographic Virtual Reality. This is used as the general catch-all name for our reality (in this book) whose part are better defined as follows…

Holographics –
much more sophisticated than Man currently produces – what we experience is driven by a kind of advanced bio-plasmic computer in 4D with such speed and resources that it completely oversees this 3D Construct. Very much like the *Star Trek* Holographic-Replicator technology, the Holographic part establishes the location and grid that is 'painted' with Replicator-type technology. When you touch a rock or drink water it **is** real, but the Replication process can just as easily disappear objects, too…

In addition, the holographic part of the HVR scenario is that vision and memory are holographic.

Replicator --

> this is a function, integral with the Holographic part, that actually creates Matter from the subatomic strata (Ether) in which we live, move and have our being. The Holographic part is much like CAD-CAM and spatially draws the objects to be, and the Replicator initiates 'creation' (subatomic rearrangement) to manifest molecular objects.

> *It would have been impossible to explain how the HVR works 100 years ago as we did not have the current technology as a reference point. And what They are really doing is still further removed from these concepts as the HVR Sphere and the operation is integrated with living Higher Beings trained to run the bio-plasmic computer… still a concept beyond even the Kurzweil Singularity. The HVR computer is a living computer.*

"Virtual Reality" in HVR --

> the reader will be aware by now that Earth Sphere **is** a sophisticated VR with occasional fractal subsets of Simulations (like Bigfoot above) into which Man is <u>actually inserted</u> (as opposed to experiencing the VR from outside as Neo did in his pod in *The Matrix*). That is why it is so hard to verify that this is an HVR, but is one of the reasons for the confusion in Quantum Physics today.

> *So why bother? We have to live our lives anyway, what difference does it make?*
> *Answer:* **This is not our home, we do not belong here, and the Father of Light does not want us to spend forever here** *– when we graduate, He has a place for us when our lessons have rendered us humble, respectful, compassionate and ready for further training to serve – in short, STO-oriented souls.*

Simulated –

> meaning that we are not floating on a 3D rock in real space that was the product of a Big Bang. The HVR can be thought of as a Simulation (as does Nick Bostrom), [9] but the longer more complete name, Holographic Virtual Reality Simulation, is intended to remind one of the salient aspects of the HVR. Our reality is simulated and synchs up with the Script with which we entered the Earth.

Earth Sphere –

> In Chapter 12, Earth is often referred to in a kind of shorthand as just the Sphere, as it does encompass us and is the 3D Construct – constructed by the bio-plasmic replication process. (Note that it is unknown so far how much of our solar system and galaxy are part of the 3D Construct. Yet it is known that the Earth Sphere is quarantined as hinted at by the Fortean *Gegenschein* and the 6th level entity called RA.)

> See below (under Silby) for a Summary Description of the HVR Sphere.

The Scientists Speak Up

This last section on Simulation is a compendium of what the scientists, philosophers and mathematicians are saying about the likelihood of our being in a Simulation, as just described.

Dr. Nick Bostrom, Oxford philosopher

… believes in a literal simulation, not a *Matrix*, and thinks people are patterns within it who can be programmed to appear sentient. He discounts the importance of pixels/gridlines in a landscape as the super beings could just paper over these glitches and delete same from our memories. The proof of a Simulation would be us evolving to where we can create simulations ourselves. [10]

Roughly, his argument proceeds in 3 parts as follows:[11]

> **i.** Human descendants might not survive long enough to achieve an advanced civilization capable of creating computer simulations that host **simulated people** with artificial intelligence (AI) comparable to the natural faculties of their ancestors.

> **ii.** Such ancestral simulations might be intellectually or culturally prohibited in some way, even a modest interest could *plausibly* generate billions of **simulated people** (for research, genealogy, reenactment, nostalgia, recreation or other reasons).

> **iii.** Informing an **artificial person** that they are living in a simulation would defeat the authenticity of the simulation — better that they genuinely go about their daily business, for all intents and purposes, given a high-fidelity historical reproduction of the *real* world. Barring extinction (i) or prohibition (ii), it is much more likely than not, that we are living in such a simulation — and should it come to pass that we, ourselves, run such simulations, **it is all but certain**. [emphasis added]

This is brilliant, but not all the people are simulated. There are real, ensouled humans in simulated bodies, and there are OPs who <u>are</u> just simulated. He is on the right track. And according to Dr. Brian Greene "…sentience cannot be simulated"[12] and that means real souls have inserted themselves into the Simulation which contains viable human forms.

Jim Elvidge, Electrical Engineer

This scientist was quoted earlier and he agrees that we live in a programmed reality which reflects intelligent design. [13] As support for that thesis, he offers:

> **The parameters of our world are tuned for our existence –**
> Just the right distance from the Sun, water, air, and a Moon to control the tides and a precise eclipse of the Sun,

> **There is a non-random, or pre-planned aspect to the events in our reality –**
> This is due largely to the Control System – inserts designed to teach and inspire, (Charles Fort would love it)

The Programmers make frequent modifications to fine-tune the program and its data structures –

> Note the anomalistic changes in the Laws of the Universe… Chapters 8-9, where decay rates are not constant, the Sun is now heating the Earth, and *anomalons* which appear as the observer expects,

They have included "easter eggs" for our enjoyment –

> Hammers made by Man found in old coal strata, the Antikythera mechanism, ancient models of planes from Peru, and the Nazca lines…

All of this is possible because our world is not linear, it is "quantized" or **granular**. Says Elvidge, "It takes an infinite amount of resources to create a continuous reality, but a finite amount to create a quantized reality." [14]   Bits and pixels are not even allocated in a Virtual Reality video game until the character moves and changes the scene, and then the new scenario is built just as the character moves into it – and this is really noticeable on a PC that is too slow for the game!

Speaking of granularity in a quantized world, it is important to note that the granularity of our reality has been measured and found to be 1.6×10^{-35} meters and 10^{-43} seconds. **Planck length** and Planck time.[15] And the human eye at 12 inches can handle resolutions of 5×10^{30}.

What this means is that the actual quantum mechanical granularity of our reality is much smaller than our eyes can detect.[16] Says Elvidge, **the very fact that our reality is quantized is strong evidence that our reality is programmed.**

> In order to program a virtual reality, there must be quantization. It is impossible to develop a program with unlimited resolution.[17]

In closing this reference, suppose that we have a video game with a tree that uses 5 MB of storage. If you allow your players to zoom in on the tree, by a factor of 100, then the tree now has a storage size of 500 MB, and if you allow the player to cut into the tree, that has to be modeled, and the storage size for the tree could jump to 90 GB… very unwieldy even by today's standards.

So, Elvidge proposes something that Dr. Jacques Vallee would approve of:

> Advanced intelligence has pervaded the universe, is monitoring us, and is either toying with us by presenting themselves in a slightly futuristic manner, or coaxing us along developmentally. [18]

Yes, the Higher Beings <u>are</u> coaxing us via the Control System.

Professor S. James Gate

… a professor at Cornell University, while analyzing the Superstring mathematics that have accurately defined their operation, noticed something very unusual in June 2012 which suggests a design to our universe. It was corroborated by Neil deGrasse Tyson:

>...theoretical physicist S. James Gate has discovered something extraordinary in his String Theory research. Essentially, deep inside the equations we use to describe our universe Gate has found **computer code**. And not just any code but extremely peculiar **self-dual linear binary error-correcting block code.** That's right, error correcting 1s and 0s wound up tightly in the quantum core of our universe.[19]   [emphasis added]

This is almost the smoking gun but it does not prove conclusively the existence of an HVR Simulation – yet. Physicists have yet to be able to demonstrate an experiential model of Strings in the laboratory – all they can do is postulate based on observations and known facts. Yet, again, the discovery is shocking as there would be **self-correcting code** within a Simulation just as there were error-detection and self-correcting routines within all the computer programs that I wrote in my 35 years in data processing. Such routines show intelligent design and would not have evolved naturally in the fabric of space.

With this discovery, we are 90% home in establishing that our world/universe is a Simulation. Dr. Greene is about to add another 5%...

Dr. Brian Greene, Professor of Physics

Dr. Greene really challenges our sense of reality when he suggests that our experiences do not provide absolute proof that what we see, touch and hear is real. And the proof today comes form VR helmets that send sensory inputs to the brain providing the sight and sound of whatever VR games we are playing. Same issue exists with being hypnotized to 'see' a pink elephant in the room. He tends to agree that we may be in a Simulation and would not be able to tell the difference if our world were really real, or a supercomputer firing electrical impulses into our brains. [20]

The only way to know was if the 'world' we think is real began displaying glitches, say, a piece of sky missing, an off-ramp that goes straight into a clump of trees, or the universal laws of physics begin to change, and this state of anomaly was discussed earlier.

While the physical world may be simulated, he points out that the human brain would require an incredible supercomputer, faster than anything we now have, or even will have in the next 20 years to simulate the brain. This suggests that the **simulated humans** (OPs) are not just simulated, they are controlled by the 'Players' who have created the Simulation, thus being a kind of 'avatar' (NPC) to play in our world. The souls coming in would have the basic brain as designed for the basic human in the Simulation, but the ensouled human would have a slightly greater potential running the mind through the flesh and blood vehicle's brain. Mechanical operations, preprogrammed into a brain in a simulated human, do not equate to the same kind of brain functioning that a sentient being has… thus the leap to a sentient android may not be possible, despite *The Terminator* series and Ensign Data [android] in *Star Trek* (sorry, Kurzweil). [21]

Dr. Bostrom made a telling statement with which Dr. Greene agrees:

> ...if the ratio of simulated humans to real humans were colossal, then brute statistics suggests that we are *not* in a real universe.[22]

And Chapter 5 has already pointed out that the current headcount of OPs in our world is about 60%. Again, that would be what a Simulation is all about – 'puppets' to drive the Greater Script and ensure that ensouled humans get their lessons (Karma).

Referring to Nick Bostrom's theory, Dr. Greene remarked that Logic alone cannot ensure that we are not living in a simulation. **In fact, the odds are overwhelming that we may be in a simulation because our reality itself allows for the creation of realistic computer simulations!** [23]

And the *coup de grace* is Dr. Green's analysis of what we could look for in our world to confirm/deny that we are in a Simulation. Hang on to your hat.

In any simulation, there would have to be an internal element that seeks to maintain consistency in the simulated world, and **self-correct itself** if something exceeds established control parameters. What did Professor Gate (just above) discover?

This quote is very significant, please bear with its length as it capsulizes what is happening in Physics today, and reinforces the Simulation concept:

> Simulators ... would have to iron out mismatches [between different disciplines used to create any simulation: biology, chemistry, electronics, psychology...] arising from disparate methods, and They'd need to ensure that the meshing was smooth. This would **require fiddles and tweaks** which, to an inhabitant, might appear as sudden, baffling changes to the environment with no apparent cause or explanation. And the meshing might fail to be fully effective; the resulting **inconsistencies** could build over time, perhaps becoming so severe that the world became incoherent, and the simulation crashed.

> ... the simulation would proceed by a single set of fundamental equations, as mathematical input [for] the nature of matter and the fundamental forces... simulations of this kind would encounter their own **computational problems**... [because] the computations would necessarily invoke approximations [since there cannot be an infinite number of decimal places]... So, it's still possible that computer-based calculations would inevitably be approximate, **allowing errors to build up over time**.... Round-off errors when accumulated over a great many computations, can yield **inconsistencies**.

> ....cherished laws might start yielding inaccurate predictions... a single widely-confirmed result might start producing different answers.... So you'd closely re-examine the theory, coming up with alternate new ideas to better describe the data. But, assuming the inaccuracies didn't result in contradictions that crashed the program, **at some point you'd hit a wall**.

> After an exhaustive search through possible explanations.... An iconoclastic thinker might suggest a radically different idea. If the continuum laws that

physicists had developed over many millennia were input to a powerful digital computer and used to generate a simulated universe, **the errors built up from the inherent approximations would yield anomalies of the very kind being observed…**[24] [emphasis added]

… And the simulated scientists in the simulated universe would be puzzling over the same issues that our 'real' world scientists puzzle over today. Of course, the Programmers could stop the Simulation and fix the glitch, wipe people's memories, and restart the Simulation … and isn't that why the Earth has had numerous Eras? (Often accompanied by a "Wipe and Reboot?")

Lastly, Dr. Green suggests a scenario very close to what we have today:

> I suspect the novelty of creating artificial worlds whose inhabitants are kept unaware of their simulated status would wear thin to the Programmers [observers]; there's just so much reality TV you can watch.
>
> …. Perhaps simulated inhabitants would be able to migrate into the real world or be **joined in the simulated world** by their real biological counterparts. In time, distinction between real and simulated beings might become anachronistic. Such seamless unions strike me as a more probable outcome.[25] [emphasis added]

And that is the point of this book: the OPs are here, the ensouled humans are here, the Others are here (Chapter 5), and the Laws of the Universe seem to defy consistent analysis – at least the neutrinos put physicists through a merry chase in different countries and their nature is still not decided.

Nexus: And this is what appears to be happening in our world: it looks like those who built the Simulation have found a way to enter into it and help us along – they create the better art, music and books…. to inspire… Or play a game as we would using the Sim City software… perhaps the Programmers can insert themselves (which is the theme of *13th Floor*), and like *Avatar* interact with the other characters… Or a Rehab Facility in 4D sends wayward and dysfunctional souls into this Simulation to experience themselves at the hands of others like them… a kind of Virtual Correctional Facility….?

And what if a computer built by Man could simulate the real world? Has that been done, and what were the results?

Seth Lloyd, Quantum Computer Scientist

Dr. Lloyd contends that the universe is the ultimate and original information processor. Every atom and particle register information. Dynamic exchanges of energy and information occur all the time between subatomic particles. But the universe is significantly more powerful than the best digital computer today, and **the universe is so complex that no earthly computer can accurately model it.** In fact, the universe operates in a digital <u>and</u> analog mode, and there is only one type of computer that Quantum Physicists have developed that does both: **a quantum computer.**

A quantum computer operates using the laws of Quantum Mechanics.

The universe is basically quantum mechanical, and a digital computer cannot adequately simulate that. Each atom in a quantum computer is called a **'qubit'** and can register a '0' state or a '1' state – at the same time [superposition]. [26] Thus, Spin UP = 0 state, spin DOWN = 1 state, and a horizontal spin is neutral (either 0 or 1). We discovered back in Chapters 8-9 that Quantum Physics was weird when it proposed the Probabilistic Dual State of Matter: until we open Schrödinger's Box, we don't know if the cat is alive or dead and so both states theoretically exist at the same time. (See Glossary: Qubit.).

Since the universe consists of *quanta*, discrete particles of matter/energy, the way to simulate it is with a quantum computer. **In fact, the universe is indistinguishable from a quantum computer which in turn is a universal quantum simulator**. [27]

> Thus it could be simulated efficiently by a quantum computer – one exactly the same size as the [modeled*] universe itself…. Indeed an observer that interacted with the quantum computer via a suitable interface would be **unable to tell the difference between the quantum computer and the system itself**. [28] [emphasis added]

Double-talk? No, he is saying that the universe is a quantum computer, which in turn, as he said above, is a **quantum simulation**. If A = B and B = C then A = C. So the universe is a quantum computer … which is what is used to simulate a quantum universe, thus if it looks like a duck, walks like a duck, and sounds like a duck, it probably IS a duck. OR it acts like a quantum simulation because it is simulated on a higher-level, more powerful quantum computer, herein called a Bio-plasmic Computer (operating from 4D).

> ***Note:** If our modeled universe is a really small construct and fits within the large memory allocated by the Simulation Quantum Computer, then we are in a Child universe within the larger Parent universe. Our universe is just scaled down.

In our world, a professor of nuclear engineering, Dr. David Cory, built a quantum computer at MIT that is able to perform quantum simulations involving billions and billions of **qubits** (in 2005 – probably more now). Cory's quantum simulators are far more powerful than any classical computer could ever be. They map the behavior of elementary particles onto the qubits and operate quantum mechanical logic, dealing with 'spin' as a state of the qubit, processing billions of quantum interactions per second. [29]

> **All that to say that a "simulation of the universe on a quantum computer is indistinguishable from the universe itself."** [30]

Does that mean that we are living in a Simulation, according to professor Lloyd? He says not necessarily…

Nexus: it does mean that advanced beings with a quantum computer big enough to perform scalar calculations could simulate our universe, and that is what Elvidge, Greene, and others are saying. And this chapter is suggesting that **the Creators of the Simulation**

have found a way to enter into their Simulation… [31] (See movie, *Thirteenth Floor*.)

> Because of the power of quantum computers to simulate physical systems
> [like the universe], a quantum computer that can perform 10^{122} ops on 10^{92}
> bits has enough power to compute **everything we can observe**. [32]

He has all but said it. And he even has a pretty good idea of how big the 4D Bio-plasmic
Quantum Computer running our Simulation would have to be, assuming that it is, or
mimics, a quantum computer. A reasonable guess is that the Higher Beings are using **a**
computer that is a bit more down the road from a simple quantum computer….
But conceptually the same since it would have to manipulate (Replicator) and monitor
(Control System) **quanta** in the Simulation.

Craig Hogan , Professor of Astronomy & Physics

Dr. Hogan is a professor at the Universdity of Chicago, and the director of the Fermilab
Center for Particle Astrophysics.

German scientists working at the Fermilab on the GEO600 team have discovered a sound
when trying to measure **gravitational waves.** At least their giant GEO600 detector which
should be measuring gravitational waves is picking up a sound that suggests that space-time
"stops behaving like the smooth continuum Einstein described and instead dissolves into
'grains' just as a newspaper dissolves into dots as you zoom in…. If the GEO600 result is
what I think it is, then we are all living in **a giant hologram**." [33]

Dr. Hogan is best known for his theory of **"holographic noise"** which derives from
quantum fluctuations in spatial position or distances that fluctuate and that is what the
gravitational wave dectector picks up. Stars, objects, molecules and atoms all move and as
they do, they produce sound. In addition, gravitational waves are produced from violent
events like supernovae and mergers of black holes and neutron stars … what he calls
"microscopic quantum convulsions of space-time."

> The idea that we live in a hologram probably sounds absurd, but it is a
> natural extension of our best understanding of Black Holes, and something
> with a pretty firm theoretical footing…..[It is]helpful for physicists wrestling
> with … how the universe works at its most fundamental level. [34]

He then explains how light bouncing off the holograms on 2D credit cards recreates a 3D
image … the effect is 3D but the source is 2D.

> In the 1990s physicists Leonard Susskind and Nobel prizewinner Gerard
> t' Hooft suggested that the same principle might apply to the universe as a
> whole. Our everyday experience might itself be a **holographic projection**
> of physical processes that take place on a distant, 2D surface." [35]
> [emphasis added]

Does this sound like Charles Fort and his *Gegenschein* in Chapter12? Fort, Wilde, and
Monroe all postulated a 'shell' of some sort around the Earth, which reflects light, and

The Earth in Holographic Containment
(source: www.gafnews.com/sites/)

which transmits the light of the stars – but what if the 'shell' is reflecting the 2D universe and transmitting it as 3D? It would as our world is contained in and subject to a Simulation controlled by the Control System – which makes the stars appear to be distant and real… but they may be just 2D projections of the Control System on a shell located far enough from our HVR Sphere that we can't tell they are part of the Simulation. And weirdly enough, when the Control System 'moves' the stars and planets (simulated sidereal movement) it makes a sound that can be heard… that is the essence of what Dr. Hogan has discovered.

And last but not least, there are other sources that support the Simulation idea.

Wikipedia (various compiled sources)
… discusses whether Simulation computers can actually run a simulation where computers within the simulation can't do what the Simulation computers can do… in short,

> No-one has shown that the laws of physics inside a simulation and those outside it have to be the same, and simulations of different physical laws have been constructed. The problem now is that **there is no evidence that can conceivably be produced to show that the universe is *not* any kind of computer,** [thus] making the simulation hypothesis unfalsifiable ….[36]

So we cannot prove that we are <u>not</u> living in a Simulation. However, the onus resides with other pro-Simulation authors:

George Dvorsky
…a science contributor to the IO9 website, says that recent experiments may be shaping up in favor of Simulation:

> …a team of physicists say proof might be possible and that it's a matter of finding a cosmological signature that would serve as the proverbial **Red Pill** from the *Matrix*. And they think they know what it is. According to Silas Beane and his team at the University of Bonn in Germany, **a simulation of the universe should still have constraints, no matter how powerful**….[and] these limitations… would be observed by the people within the simulation as a

kind of constraint on physical processes….And to help isolate the sought-after signature, the physicists are simulating quantum chromodynamics (QCD)…. [also referred to as] the "lattice gauge theory". [37] [emphasis added]

This also includes inserting a test within QCD for the **GZK cutoff** – to see how and why **high energy particles operate in ways other than predicted**.

> *GZK Cutoff:* **Greisen–Zatsepin–Kuzmin** *limit is a theoretical upper limit on the energy of cosmic rays which should fall within set parameters, and distant cosmic rays that should have weakened by the time they get to Earth have been measured way* <u>above</u> *what physicists expect. This appears to be an anomaly of our Simulation.*

Ed Grabianowski

… another science contributor to the IO9 website, who says that "…**the odds are nearly infinity to one that we are all living in a computer simulation.**" He argues that we already have computers with enough processing power (i.e., Cray Supercomputers) to run a credible Simulation – the trick is that "the computer only simulates what it needs to." [38]

Nexus: In short, it isn't necessary to display all the scenario at once – just those parts where the conscious being (soul) finds himself – as a matter of fact, that can be seen to be a processing technique of Virtual Reality video games on a slow PC – as the character moves to the right, for example, the player has to wait until the program 'creates' the tree and rock necessary to the scenario. Obviously, our Earth HVR Simulation is <u>very sophisticated</u> and very fast and can serve millions of souls all over the planet –because the planet was created (replication), Man (souls) was inserted along with the OP "bit" players, and the Drama was initiated by a very sophisticated Control System which undoubtedly includes feedback to it.

Says Mr. Grabianowski, "[Simulation] actually explains a few of the trickier things about quantum physics, like why particles have an indeterminate position until they're observed." [39] And then he gets on board with the OP scenario: "There could be just a few active simulation inhabitants, with the rest of the world filled with "non-actor" or NPC characters controlled by the computer. Their actions are only simulated as [when] you perceive them…." [40]

Nexus: We are quickly approaching the 98-99% mark confirming that we live in a very sophisticated Simulation.

Brent Silby, Advisor in Philosophy

… of UPT School in Christchurch New Zealand, reminds us that the simulation might just extend beyond Earth… "… all the planets, asteroids, comets, stars, galaxies, black holes, and nebula are also part of the simulation….. **the entire universe is a simulation** running inside an extremely advanced computer system designed by a super intelligent species that live in a parent universe." [41] This is possible, he says, because the universe operates on a finite set of laws and thus it can be simulated by a computer.

If we accept the possibility that advanced beings <u>can</u> create a Simulation, then it is likely that we do exist in a Simulation… **of their design and for their purposes**. The reason for this is that there will likely be many simulations but just one original universe. So statistically, there is a higher chance that we are in one of the simulations as opposed to being in the original universe. [42]

Objection to Simulation

Even Silby plays 'devil's advocate and raises a common objection to our living in a Simulation by saying that the argument has traditionally been that if we could create a simulation, we would. Same thing applies to advanced beings. A corollary argument has been that if high-tech beings can create the simulation, should they, would they – or would they have higher morals and not do it?

Morals really have nothing to do with the issue. The issue is probably more one of scientific curiosity – Can we do it? What would happen? Well, in our world, we have created simulations – called **Sim City, Sim City 3000 and Sim City 4.** Of course these simulations are void of simulated humans in a 2D version, and the 3D version, **SimCity Societies**, still lacks people. And these are quite sophisticated packages, generally applicable to modeling new communities with a full range of civic services, economic and ecological concerns, and the latest Sim version offers societal values to consider: productivity, creativity, prosperity, spirituality, authority and knowledge. [43]

Create Paris the way you want it…

(Credit both: Bing Images)

Sim City 5

Sim City 2

… or invite a monster to romp through your city.

This borders on creating your own video game!

Nexus: The mere possibility that we, or future humans, will have the ability to simulate a scenario, a world, or a universe, does not mean that we/they will do it. Agreed. But that is not exactly the issue raised by this book. As will be seen in Chapter 15, Earth was created the way it was by the Higher Beings for the purpose of retraining wayward and defective souls. It requires a Simulation running in a VR subject to a Control System, with self-corrective feedback to do that.

A summary statement at this point would look like this:

HVR Earth Simulation Definition

The 3D Holographic, replicated Earth is real, contained within the quarantine "shell" (*Gegenschein*) as a 3D construct, actually sitting in 4D, and the "computer" running the Show is a semi-sentient, Bio-plasmic organic computer-like organism with a feedback Control System as part of its main Operating System. Objects on Earth are quantized and materialized within the holographic framework by a subatomic process (Replication) similar to what was described in the *Star Trek* Holodeck. To protect Man, the Earth and its immediate surroundings (the Sphere) are enclosed in a high energy barrier allowing very controlled exit and entrance.

Man is inserted as a soul into this environment for lessons and comes in with a Script that says what he can do and not do. He interacts with OPs who are NPCs. Beings of Light and Neggs help administer the individual soul's Script within the framework of the larger Greater Script – which reflects the purpose for the HVR Sphere.

Note that a soul's Script is controlled within the Greater Script, just as individual application programs on a PC are controlled by the Operating System. For example, MS Word must operate within the confines and structure of the MS XP operating system, for example, and use its resources. Anything not prohibited by the Script to the soul is considered "freewill."

The HVR is subject to manipulation by Higher Beings ("They") who monitor phases of the Greater Script, and Man's individual Scripts, coordinating all with the Beings of Light and the Neggs. They can insert objects, people and events as deemed necessary… sometimes called synchronicities. They can also disappear things and remove people as needed, and They can perform a "Wipe and Reboot" to clean the Stage and reset the Drama as a new Era if necessary.

Thus Earth is not Man's home and he is expected to learn and graduate.

> *Repeat: Higher Beings are not ETs or aliens. They are a mid-part of the Divine Hierarchy that exists between Man and The Father of Light, or the One. In sequence, above Man are the Angels/Beings of Light and the Neggs, then Soul Groups/Oversoul, then a multi-level hierarchy of Higher Beings, and then the actual Godhead/Father of Light/One.*

HVR Sphere Clarification

There are a couple of very important aspects of our Simulation to understand.

1. Despite different Eras, the **3D Earth is physically real**, and its various components have been constructed, even 'planted' over time. (Think: Great Pyramids.) The Simulation is not re-designed from scratch every time a new Era is started, just re-activated. The physicality of Earth, the dirt, the rocks, mountains, mystery carvings and pyramids, were all created there via the Holographic-Replicator technology as real objects, during the Era in which they belong, and they stay with the constructed Earth. It is a little like originally writing a computer program, even a SimCity version, where the program produces an initial scenario, and then subsequent updates to the code add and delete things adding to the final descriptive state of the City… and in our case, most of what was initially created as 3D Earth is still here, and some objects get added and deleted with the activities of Man during each subsequent Era.

2. If there is a "power failure" related to the technology of the Simulation, **what has been created does not disappear**… i.e., everything we see and work with every day is not being generated "live" as we go and disappears if sections of the Simulation should   momentarily lack power. The Simulation has created a 3D Earth that does not disappear because it is locked into 3D space-time within the VR Sphere, and its 'power' has never failed.

    > As a computer analogy: the physical state of the Earth is recorded in Working Storage – backed up on an external storage medium.

    However, occasionally the Simulation running is suspended when it comes time to do a "Wipe and Reboot," because things have gotten off-track (planet too polluted, or not enough souls to energize and coherently sustain a positive vector in synch with the Higher Being's intent and new souls are not entering the Earth realm) so the Simulation is halted.

3. The Gods-in-Training (some are graduated souls from the Earth School) can and do **add to and delete from our Simulation**, usually clandestinely. This is generally in support of the Control System whose purpose is to entrain Man into a higher state of thinking… more awe, wonder, inspiration, often via mystery. Objects can be inserted, people can be inserted (OPs, to be sure), bodies created and souls inserted, and even events can be orchestrated to serve the Greater Script, or Plan for Mankind in each particular Era. (Eras tend to have a theme, a level of awareness, and specific drama to experience and handle.)

4. The **whole universe that we see is the Simulation**, not just the Earth. The parts that we can access, like going to the Moon, will be parts of the Simulation that are made real for us as we need them… the rest of the planets and Galaxies that we cannot reach <u>are</u> holographic projections (thus it would be wise to rethink the 'redshift' phenomenon) – What could be the lesson from what we think we see

there? Said another way: Is a simulated Universe expanding and receding or is it made to look that way? In a similar way, a solar flare from the Sun is displayed for us, as part of the hologram of the Sun, and then the physics of its effects on Earth are programmed to 'affect' our planet.

The beauty of this technique is that it isn't necessary to Replicate subatomic material into <u>all</u> the stars and planets we see... just those that we could get to... <u>when</u> we get there.

Perforce, this also suggests what was said earlier, in Chapter 12, that there is no 3D sentient life visiting us in UFOs. Most sentient life in the Universe is in 4D and above, and the Quarantine (a space-time 4D vectored energy) keeps them from randomly visiting us.

5.   It also follows then, that **the Simulation operates with a subset of the Laws of the real (4D) Universe** to which we belong, and in which this 3D Simulation is operating. This is why Quantum Physicists are 'guilty' of analyzing the **Imax Theatre**, and thinking that they have a handle on Multiverse reality. Subquantum Kinetics is closer to the truth of our situation.

Rewind: HVR Earth Simulation Genesis

For those who still doubt that we are in a Simulation with all the trappings described above, or would like a better overview, let us look at it from another point of view. This is also the way I was given the information.

The Higher Beings wanted to set up a place where They could contain souls, safe from incursion from outside interference, harassment and curiosity, and guide them through specific lessons to empower their soul growth. Leaving souls in bodies to wander around a 3D planet and letting them randomly interact with each other had not worked even though the planet had the Angels in 4D around them to oversee and guide them. Avatars had been sent over the centuries to walk among them but the Anunnaki legacy genetics predisposed the humans to rebellion, pettiness and wars no matter what was taught them. And in remote times, other races came into the Earth and would work with the genetics and experiment with humans to try their hand at creating a better form. This resulted in (1) more division among humans who were overly sensitive to "us versus them" appearances and (2) different religions from each race's 'creators.' It was AD 800 and something different had to be done.

The goal was to provide a closed environment where the 'lessons' took the form of catalyst to evoke true soul growth. The souls were running amok and recycling back to the Earth School too many times. What was ultimately decided was to set Earth apart but not in 4D, the natural home of souls, where the ensouled humans would still have their 4D abilities and could override and cancel any lesson at will. So the **Earth world would be 3D to support limited soul powers**. Secondly, there would be positive and negative catalyst, provided by two types of Angels that would work together. Third, there would have to be an overriding Control System (C/S) which would be the "master program" that ran the place, into which each soul coming into the Earth would have a Script that was like a subprogram of the C/S to effect that soul's lesson(s) for each incarnation. And because the C/S had to run in a 'closed environment' (like a computer application runs in a controlled environment [i.e., a partition within the computer Mainframe]) the 3D Earth could not be left open to interference from any external source, and so the Earth was created as a 3D Construct within the 4D Realm, but surrounded by a Barrier or high-energy field Quarantine.

To provide catalyst, the C/S was designed to be able to insert people (NPCs), and objects (Airships, UFOs, and Antikythera mechanisms, for example), and orchestrate and coordinate events (meeting one's soulmate, or key OPs to administer lessons, for instance) that would appear synchronistic even coincidental. Each soul's Script was linked to the C/S pulling resources and orchestrating itself – which is why specific points of entry had to be pre-programmed (i.e., soul's date, time and family at entry).

So at first the original 4D Earth was surrounded with the containing energy Sphere, whose C/S was to impute 3D laws and characteristics to the Earth, and surrounded Earth with the Quarantine and called it the 3D Construct. Outside the Construct was the Moon and the rest of the 4D Galaxy. An interesting effect was the reflection of the Sun off the energy field surrounding the Earth. The *Gegenschein*.

Additionally, there had to be an overall controller of some sort to orchestrate the 4D Earth, energy barrier, 3D laws, Scripts, and coordinate the OPs/NPCs and Angels subject to the intent of the Higher Beings who were doing all this…. That meant a Master Program run from 4D as nothing in 3D had enough scalable power to simulate and replicate people and objects and coordinate events that reflected the freewill of the ensouled humans in the Sphere. **That hit a brickwall**. The 4D Earth could not be subsumed into the coherent energy matrix of the 3D C/S – the two different vibrations were not compatible and 3D Laws could not manage the Sphere-embedded 4D version of Earth.

The opposite had to be done.

Thus the 3D Construct was replicated within a Simulation run from 4D providing all the necessary elements of the 3D Earth scenario, the C/S and Holographics and Replication all integrated (and phase-controlled to give a sense of time passage) within the Simulation such that the ensouled humans would not suspect that they were not on a real Earth. As a precaution, the souls incarnating would not be allowed to remember anything preceding their incarnation as they might remember what they knew prior to birth in a body and either confusion or rebellion could result.

Like any Simulation, it operates with Laws and controls, feedback loops (individual Scripts must mesh with the Grand Script) and self-correcting routines. As Dr. Greene theorized earlier, because the Simulation is subject to 3D (finite) definition, mathematical formulations and the inevitable rounding limitations, the Simulation occasionally shows what should be unchanging constants to be changing, and occasionally replicated objects disappear, or fractally-generated scenes hang up...

If the humans succeed in seriously polluting their environment, or the Simulation develops a scenario contradiction due to multiple segments with self-correcting codes, the Higher Beings have to perform a "Wipe and Reboot" – halting the Simulation, suspending 'time' for the souls, cleaning up the planet, resetting and recoding the programs that developed anomalies. Before the souls can be put back, they also have to have their memories reset (Think: neutralizer in *Men In Black*) and then they can be re-inserted back into the Simulation... sometimes in he case of a coherent society that was developing and had a known continuity of historical events, if the event had to be deleted (due to corruption or wrong vector) this results in a gap in the Earth scenario timeline, and such gap has to be accounted for by back-adjusting the history that people thought they had. (Think: Scaligerian Chronology, Chapter 10.)

Because the Simulation is 4D-generated and controlled, it is easy to insert and disappear objects and people... for the purpose of amazing, inspiring, or motivating the curious humans to try and emulate what they see. Such was the purpose for inserting Beethoven, DaVinci, Mozart, and Pasteur, for example to deliver the "next step" in the Grand Script for Man. Occasionally 4D entities would enter the Sphere for observation, and find that radar or bullets could shoot down their visible craft, also providing Man with scientific technology ahead of his social and spiritual development. Inserts were also made to contain and try to deflect inappropriate use of such technology as weapons.

The C/S is all about moving Man forward in science and spirituality to improve his world, such that following the Grand Script, Man reaches the ability to leave the planet. At such point, the Simulation will expand to grow Man in the interactions with what are called ETs – also inserts – as he learns respect, compassion and cooperation with others.

Lucid Dreaming

Because some readers are going to mention another alternative to Simulation, it is necessary to address and quash one last idea.

A recent philosophical consideration in today's world is that of lucid dreaming – Man supposedly living in a dream state and yet is controlling what he experiences. Instead of trying to control the world we live in and "create one's day," a better alternative is to stop avoiding reality and learn to handle whatever comes up. Catalyst for growth cannot be controlled anyway. Does the student control the school? Lucid dreaming does not offer any skills for handling this reality – it is a denial of reality or an avoidance.

The issue is briefly explainable, however, because many people who think they are lucid dreaming are in fact doing what Robert Monroe did – going Out of Body (OBE) – and experiencing another realm. It often happens to people who are asleep, and they don't know that that was what they were doing. And it is still avoiding <u>this</u> lifetime and its lessons.

Summary

So, there are several ways to know if we're in a Virtual Reality or Simulation but it will take patience and keen observation as Those who put this place together were/are quite expert at it. It is interesting to note that, as was the case back in the days of the Greek and Roman gods, Man is still being "interfered" with, manipulated, or at the very least watched as the stars of all 4 movies above were. Fascinating to contemplate.

The answer is not apparent upon casual observation, although some people are able to <u>intuit the answer</u>. However, the evidence is there, providing we stop rationalizing inconsistencies (glitches) and synchronicities (miracles) as Truman did so often.

As was said in other chapters, one of the ways to determine whether one is in a simulation is to learn to see auras. If everyone around you has no aura, that is a safe bet that you're in a simulation because the OPs are playing a role (as NPCs) in a Drama of which you, and other possible souls, are the 'stars' and it may be just for your benefit (Karma).

Without seeing auras, there is one other way. If you find that you can't communicate with others, they don't listen, no one cares what you think, you can't 'reach' anyone to help them…. or if you always lose, you can't get what you want, and if you do, it is taken from you (losing all the time)…. or you're deathly sick and a Being of Light shows up and asks you if you want to continue… pay attention to such occurrences, inconsistencies, and statistical impossibilities. No one can lose all the time, and sit back and ask yourself if there is something to be learned from a situation, especially if it keeps repeating itself in your life experience.

Insight: is this why waking up and discovering what this place really is earns the respect of the *Inspecs* aka Beings of Light, and other souls? Note that the Higher Beings, the gods, the Ones who operate this Simulation want us to learn and assimilate our lessons to become souls who now DO the right thing – then you get out. Knowledge is the "booby prize" if you don't walk the better walk! Knowledge is the beginning, DOING is the ticket out of here… as the Earth Graduate.

To repeat: you don't have to be perfect to get out of here.

Simulated Last Thoughts

Ultimately, it may not matter to most people if we are in an HVR Simulation not – the lessons are there to be learned. However, knowing that it is a Simulation can take the 'edge' off our failures and negative events – knowing that it is catalyst, a test, and something we are to go THROUGH.

And if we learn what we are supposed to learn, and it **is** an HVR, we will be released – like Phil. The worst case scenario would be that it is **not** an HVR, and we are just being manipulated on a 3D rock by any passing ETs…who, with superior technology, could easily subjugate the planet and turn Earth into a prison planet. I prefer the Simulation as it has a purpose and, because it is contained, we have a safe place to learn our lessons, and it also means we are supported in getting out of here -- as a graduate.

The only negative aspect of this issue for ensouled people is being **recycled** in an HVR/Simulation because we don't wake up, we don't master the 'lessons' that are being given us, and it goes on forever, or (as is now the case) we are about to destroy the planet's ecological balance and the gods have to do a "Wipe and Reboot," clean up the planet, and start us all over again. Ultimately, if we refuse to wake up, stay dysfunctional and not move forward, the gods may "disassemble" us, as Dr. Newton suggested. [44]

For those who "have ears to ear" and assimilate the message, this book is designed to prevent the negative scenarios. In the meantime, the next chapter examines WHY we need to get out of here.

> **Note**: for further examination of the Simulation issue, please see *Quantum Earth Simulation* (QES, Ch. 8), wherein 11 additional scientific **anomalies** are reviewed which suggest that we may be in a very sophisticated Simulation. The last of the 11 is very strange: noise from the edge of the universe appears to be "coded information" and has yet to be resolved or explained.

Chapter 14: -- Challenges

This chapter examines major obstacles to our knowing the truth, being healthy, and getting out of here. While the Neggs do harass and sometimes oppress Man, Man does a lot of the damage to himself, and this is especially true with respect to the environment. It is important to take a look at what challenges exist and deal with them, to the extent possible, so that Man is less hampered by ignorance, false beliefs and manipulation by others.

Yet those three are major aspects of the world we live in. So the question was put: What has to be true for the world to look the way it does? That was basically answered in the last two chapters. You are not living on the planet that you think you are. We are in an HVR Simulation and ignorance, false beliefs and manipulation are part of the scenario. And we are being watched to see what we do with it.

> And with the future discoveries of Science, and credible spiritual sources, it may turn out that Chapter 13 will have to be modified to reflect new information. Sobeit if that contributes to our knowledge and understanding.

Thus we can say that these are the general challenges facing Man here:

1. Living in a Simulation
2. Disinformation and Deception
3. Manipulation by Man and Others
4. False Beliefs
5. Violation of Freewill
6. Subconscious Sabotage
7. Environment and Health
8. Anunnaki Remnant

Living in a Simulation

While most people don't know where they are, being in a Simulation is not necessarily a problem. They have to handle whatever comes up in their lives anyway so for many people it doesn't matter whether we're in a Simulation or a real 3D planet like most people assume. The Simulation is very advanced and for all intents and purposes of the Higher Beings who run it, events, opportunities, plans, failures, diseases, etc are just as real as if it weren't a simulated reality. Except for one thing: as a school or rehab center (take your pick), the processes that ensouled humans must undergo must be subject to observation and control, kind of like lab rats being tested.

We are much more important than lab rats but there are events and tests that we have to go through (and that's a key word: <u>through</u>) and handle them. The Drama is not real, as the smiling Chinese sages have said for centuries, but it is relevant and is often tailored to the individual by the Beings of Light and the Neggs, working from the Script with which we entered this domain. If we are here to learn something, the lessons must be part of our Script, and they cannot be left to chance to become more/less than the Script demands. Such control is orchestrated by the Beings of Light and our progress is monitored. There are no accidents.

For example, suppose Joe is a new National Park ranger and his boss wants him to learn and master whitewater river rafting. So he goes to Colorado, selects a school on a big river, and a 6' rubber raft, and the instructor makes sure Joe has the equipment he needs, and he will spend a little time going over a map of the course, explaining the pre-programmed obstacles. If Joe has the time, the instructor offers to sit Joe down in a room with a computer VR simulation of the river to get the feel of the course and its challenges.

When Joe has absorbed the knowledge of what the course demands, he is advised how to handle the paddle, how to keep his balance, and is warned about the kids on the shore in two locations who throw rocks at passers-by. Joe now knows what he has to do, and is taken to the start of the course on a swiftly–flowing river 80' wide and 10' deep, with 4 sets of rapids with big boulders, tree branches sticking into the river from the shore, and a couple of sandbars.

Unknown to him, there will be a helicopter overhead observing his progress to make sure he doesn't get into serious trouble… if he flips over and loses his raft and paddle deep in the rapids, he may need help getting out of the river. Otherwise, if he is alert, knows what is coming, he can be reasonably prepared to meet the challenges… and if he succeeds, he is given a certificate as a River Graduate. If he fails the first time, he will be going though the VR simulation until he is reasonably proficient at that, and then he may try an easier river, or just go back and do the same river again.

Our lives in the HVR Simulation also have the same elements: a body instead of a raft, obstacles, preparation in the **Interlife**, and the option to play a virtual scenario in the Interlife of what our 'chosen' lifetime would look like. Instead of a paddle, we have a certain skillset (abilities that we have either developed or were given to us), obstacles on the river are replaced with tests that we must handle, and the Beings of Light stand ready to intervene and 'rescue' souls who bite off more than they can chew. The soul will be asked if it wants to continue, or be counseled instead of quitting.

Positive Aspects

The advantages of the Simulation are that we are protected (in Quarantine) from potentially curious and harassing ETs, and as souls we can't be killed, and we are observed and helped as needed. If things get screwed up, or we just cannot figure out what to do, or if we have contracted a terminal illness, the Being of Light will show up and discuss options with us.

> I was in the hospital in January 1965, dying of pneumonia. One lung was full of mucous and the other was ½ filled and I was not expected to make it through the night. Lights were turned out at 9 pm and I fell asleep. I was awakened sometime during the night by a really bright light, and it was so

bright I didn't open my eyes, I just assumed it was the night nurse, looking in on me.

I was asked how I felt, and not knowing what was wrong with me, I said OK. Then I was asked if I wanted to continue… and I said yes.

I awoke the next morning feeling great, I could breathe freely and I was hungry. The pneumonia was completely gone and my lungs were functioning normally – which two hours later freaked the doctor out… he could not say 'miracle.' Wondering where my breakfast was, I walked over to the door, it was locked, so I unlocked it (from the inside) and went into the hall – my room was directly in front of the nurses' station… they saw me and screamed. I didn't know I wasn't supposed to make it through the night… but I had had help.

So I thanked the nurses for their 'greeting,' and thanked them for looking in on me last night. They told me that my door was locked and no one visited me last night. It still didn't dawn on me what had really happened, and months later I would wonder about Their 2nd question: I was asked if I wanted to continue? Nurses don't ask that.
We have a choice about living or not? And I kicked myself months later for not opening my eyes to see Who that was at the foot of my bed!

Negative Aspects

We are contained and cannot get out of here until we learn our lessons, pass our tests, and show that we are worthy to move forward. Tests that we fail, must be met again and again until handled. If we fail, and it is an important test, we receive additional counseling or training in the **Interlife**, and depending on what we still need to learn, we may be **recycled** into the same lifetime, or (because the Higher Beings are not ogres) we may be given an opportunity to learn the same lesson **reincarnating** in a different body and realm. Things are negotiable until one steps into the body, just as Joe had better be ready to handle the river once he is loaded onto it – running the river is not the time for negotiation.

Lastly, a possible downside of the Simulation is that it has so many OPs – and they are not always easy to deal with – especially if they are your parents (as was my case).

It is all drama and is designed to be handled. **Our opinion about what we got doesn't count** for anything, we are supposed to move <u>through</u> it, handling it.

Disinformation and Deception

This is part of the Earth scenario because so many OPs (NPCs) and undeveloped souls are here. In fact, Chapters 8 – 11 pretty well covered the errors, lies, deception and disinformation that we have been experiencing here. We are not expected to fix/stop/change it – just handle it. You really need to get that.

Rewind: We are not expected to fix/stop/change anything — just handle it.

The way to handle it is to get enough truth into you that your discernment kicks in and warns when someone is running a deception, or your intuitive side (which will grow if listened to) warns when something or someone doesn't 'feel' right. And this is part of the waking up process that souls go through here…often by being taken advantage of, manipulated and undergoing violations of our freewill – those lessons learned become part of the soul and can serve in future incarnations. Thus it behooves souls to read and learn as much as they can about our world, people, Science, History and Religion to prevent being used or misled by others.

Manipulation

Disinformation and Deception naturally are what is used to manipulate people – to get you to say/do things that seem to be OK, but which are actually a violation of your freewill. You are given information that is not true in an effort to coerce you into making a decision that had you had the real facts, you would not have made. You were compromised. The used car saleman said, "This car was driven by a little old lady on Sundays to church. It's a creampuff!" And while the body looks great, later you may find out it was the Little Old Lady from Pasadena that owned the car, and the rings are shot.

You have freewill to choose based on the facts. To the degree that you are manipulated and compromised in making a decision, your freewill has been violated. And if you believe that you're saved and die and expect to now go to Heaven, a Being of Light may show up (Neggs can shapeshift and trick you), and tell you that you have to go back, or you can follow him to "just the place for you!" And you may wind up contained in a grey, foggy realm where you can't meet and mingle with other souls… I saw the place in an Out of Body experience and don't want to go back.

But deception, disinformation and manipulation are permitted here as part of the training ground: to wake you up and get you to seek truth, Light and Love. By letting you experience darkness, you will come to appreciate the Light that much more. And if you question why some experiences are so rough, remember:

Steel is not made without fire.

Don't get all bent out of shape over events on Earth. Souls have freewill to experiment, and the OPs often follow the Script that you are in – to provide **catalyst** for your growth.

Life is not a puzzle to figure out.

When people ask, "Why is this happening to me? I'm a good person. I don't deserve this!" that is a restatement of the time-worn "Why do bad things happen to good people?" Perhaps now you have an inkling that (1) they aren't as good as they think they are, or (2) they have a special test to go through that reflects something that they may have learned, but the Higher Beings sometimes submit the test again just to see if you <u>really</u> learned the lesson. Their purpose is not to jerk you around, or needlessly test souls for the heck of it – **the purpose is to show YOU whether you still have it all together**! And They will not send anything to you that you cannot handle – it is just your opinion that "it shouldn't be happening to <u>me</u>!" You might want to take a look at what that is all about… what is your ego's point of view? Are your expectations in line with the reality of your life?

Ok, enough sermonizing, but the points are valid and bear stating for those who are Young Souls (Chapter 7) and have not assimilated the above realizations.

False Beliefs

This is a very important area, and is largely why this chapter was written. We'll spend some time here. It is important to inspect some of our cherished beliefs – even those we got from our parents, teachers, friends we admired, 'experts' or the Mainstream Media. Remember:

> **If you can't look at it, you can't handle it,**
> **and if you can't handle it, you're not getting out of here.**

As we saw, the OPs, the PTB and well-meaning but naïve souls all can promote false religion, science errors, and false Earth history. Why? Control, or to get what they want.

If humans can be made to believe things that aren't true, they will wander in a sea of deception and confusion – not knowing who they really are, what their divine potential is, and best of all, if different groups of men serve different gods, they can be manipulated into going to war – each for their own god or cause. (Think: Hegelian Dialectic.) Keep them distracted and confused. And if they have too much idle time, better start a war so that their numbers can be brought down, people can be ordered around, and somebody gets to make money off the sale of armaments and, of course, from the reconstruction that follows the war. Blow up everything they have and then sell them new stuff. Great economics. If necessary, install Martial Law to **control** the populace. Or promote microchipping everybody…

Still think Earth is not an insane place? See now why it's quarantined?

Does Man ever learn or see through this situation? Rarely. Because the programming is too good, too complete – partly due to prevalent thoughtforms, group mind, and corrupt DNA. We also expect 'experts' to tell us the truth, when they may not know either. The Earth's low-vibration energy that sustains low-level awareness works to entrain all on the surface into their lower 3 chakras, and Man will never know he can do/be/have more because the higher chakras don't have enough energy with which to resonate to reach and sustain a higher consciousness.

> *This why the Earth Graduate is so respected – s/he broke free*
> *of the illusion and disinformation.*

Such resonance is like two tuning forks sitting side by side. They are of the same material and tonal quality – say, middle C. If one is struck to get it vibrating and placed next to the other (non-vibrating) one, within about 30-40 seconds, both tuning forks are vibrating the same. That is **entrained resonance**.

Man is also entrained by subliminal messages on TV and the effects of music and video games. What are you listening to?

Multiple Beliefs

Another little-known way to chain yourself to planet Earth, i.e., to be recycled, and really support chaos in your life, is to believe multiple systems at the same time.

This is something that some New Agers pride themselves on: the ability to embrace multiple philosophies, teachings, symbols, practices, etc… Sounds good, doesn't it? After all, the more things you can embrace, supposedly the less upset and arguments you will have, thus you should be at "…peace with all men because you believe all things…"
Red flag!

Case in point was a real New Thought minister who read and devoured as many different religions, philosophies, and teachings as he could – including the latest Quantum Physics discoveries – all supposedly higher teachings and facts about our world. He felt he was really enlightened and just had to share something different every Sunday morning, perhaps to enlighten his congregation, but surely to entertain them as well.

However, he was one of the most unstable people I knew in that he could waffle back and forth on almost any metaphysical subject, and he did not have a firm foundation in truth. His favorite quote was "What is truth?" He thought truth was relative and while he certainly did not believe in the Neggs, he did have a statue of Kali on his office desk – he said he venerated her. He could not understand why his congregation did not grow, a very close friend died, and the church developed a strange energy.

He believed that Kali was the goddess of new beginnings, even if it meant destroying the old. A slight misunderstanding. Kali is about change and can be dark and violent, including annihilation. If Kali has a dual nature, it would be wise to exercise caution before venerating (inviting) her to participate in your life. Things are not always what you want them to be (another false New Age teaching) – they are what they are.

Doesn't enlightenment accept all things? No. A master will permit you your folly, after cautioning you, so that you learn – it is a freewill universe. A fool will learn in no other school than that of "hard knocks." Not all things are appropriate, as examined later.

So what is the problem with following multiple teachings, multiple paths? How does that actually **dis**empower a person and lead to their being recycled?

Incompatible Beliefs

Let me give you another personal example from my life and what it did to me.

Let's say that you like the warmth and love in Christian churches, but also want the New Age deeper teachings, and you like Yoga and Tai Chi, admitting to the teachings of *chi* and *kundalini*, and your goal is to really get it together – hopefully approaching an inner knowledge base like Jesus or Buddha must have had… You think.

And that is the problem: your head thinks these things are compatible with ultimate Truth and even tells you that you are clever to have assembled a very eclectic mixture that is more enlightened than other enlightened people…The ego has a part in this deception, too.

As has been said about the power of words, many words together make a system, a philosophy, even a religion that has a certain **energy signature**, or vibratory quality, because different words have different energy. Having used a real aura camera years ago to test the vibration (energy signature) of different teachings, it is possible to visually quantify what the vibrational signature of the Bible is, versus the Tao, versus the Book of Mormon, and various New Age books. The Bible was a beautiful crimson color (Love).

Bottom line: not all teachings are harmonious with each other. And whatever system you belong to (ascribe to, or practice) will bring to you whatever is concordant with that system.

For example, some one who subscribes to **Christianity** will immerse themselves in the fellowship and love, tithe, and may believe in laying on of hands to heal, and certainly believe that Jesus cast out devils – thus there will be a belief that devils exist. In addition, most Christians believe that their sins are gone, and that they are to be meek and humble people, they live just one life and then go to Heaven.

On the other hand, someone who subscribes to the **New Age**, believes he can Create His Own Day, manifest riches, says there are no devils, channels Astral masters, and he may not tithe. Knowing so many alleged deeper truths, New Agers don't believe they have any sins, and they may deny making any mistakes – leaning sometimes toward Wicca in that they can do whatever they want, "…as long as it harm none." Some don't even believe in Karma and Reincarnation. And because they know so much more than the 'sheep' in Christianity, they tend to reinforce their ego and are anything but humble.

Thus, an ignorant seeker may say, "I want the love and warmth of the Christian church, but I also want the truth of the New Age church… thus I will support both churches, both systems… I can balance them, and just tune out the parts I don't like." **Red flag!**

That person has just signed on for the lesson. Because they're following a mish-mash of teachings, with different vibrations, and different corollary experiences, they have a jumble of energy, it is not focused, and may be so discordant as to produce illness and even insanity in a worst case scenario.

> *Note: that can happen because the Neggs see what you're doing and will support you in whatever lesson it is that you seek to learn – even unwittingly creating and experiencing chaos and ill health.*

You cannot believe in one system that teaches reincarnation (New Age) and no demons, and believe in another system that teaches no reincarnation (Christianity) and the existence of devils. The teachings have energy, as well as **archetypal resonance** and you will attract to you experiences and people that play out BOTH teachings. Like confusion and chaos? That's what you signed up for.

To further clarify, as a Christian, submitting oneself to the Thoughtform (archetype) of Christianity, you will have (attract) Christian experiences to you – Bible studies, tithing, healings, prayers, etc. – and because Christianity is a powerful archetype believing in the demonic, you can attract those experiences, too.

You get whatever goes with the package called Christianity.

Think not? I invite you to look at Padre Pio's life in the monastery. He felt that a true follower of Christ should be suffering as Christ did. So, he not only had the Neggs physically attack him in his 'cell' at night, [1] leaving bruises and marks all over him, but he also had the stigmata. [2] (In his palms instead of correctly in his wrists, because that is where he thought Christ should have them.)

"Aha!" you say – "because he believed it and 'it is done unto you as you believe!'" All I have to do is watch what I believe, and if I don't believe in the devil, I can still be a New Age Christian [sic] because, accepting the New Age side of things, I know the truth."

Sorry, but that is a clear case of mental masturbation.

You lose. It really doesn't work that way. The Neggs execute <u>all</u> the archtype(s) that you choose.

Archtypes

If you are a Christian, the archetype is so strong, you do not personally have the power to override the parts you don't like and create it the way you want it. By trying to merge Christianity and the New Age into your own system, a new, unique one, you are trying to create a new archetype (i.e., religion) and unless you have the power of a Jesus or Buddha, you can't do it. What you <u>will</u> attract is **chaos** – some of Christianity and some of the New Age, and as shown above, the two systems are not compatible. You will pull the 'devils' to you as you are meditating and seeking to channel higher entities – and even the Neggs and discarnates in the 4D world ARE higher, since you are in the 3D world. Good luck.

The Mormons joined forces with each other to create a Mormon archetype, but that took the concerted effort of hundreds and thousands of souls, and even then, it is nowhere near the strength of the Christian archetype. So are you as one person going to create your own archetype…?

As a New Ager, you will also experience being very uncomfortable in the Christian church when they talk about Jesus dying on the cross for your sins, since you don't recognize sin, nor vicarious atonement for same. And over in the New Age church, you may come to dislike some others who think they are creating their days and manipulating stop lights. They think they have superior enlightenment compared to you, and very few people are as loving as they are in the Christian church. You will experience **stress** through discordant resonance in both churches: you subscribe to <u>two archetypes that energetically fight each other</u>.

For more on archtypes, please see Carolyn Myss' book <u>Sacred Contracts</u>, and the works of Carl Jung.

Why would you want to create stress and chaos in your life?

And even worse, when you die, no one system 'owns' you, you may be your own person, and yet you do not have the truth to make a proactive choice for yourself as to where you can now go, based on the Truth, and so you get **recycled**.

Changing Paradigms

You say that that can't apply to you because you are an educated, thinking person, maybe even 'enlightened.' And as proof, you offer the switch you made from Christianity (or whatever) to Buddhism. Then you had the strength of character to switch again to a New Age church. No one controls you, you say.

See section on 'Subconscious Sabotage' later as some New Thought churches can violate your freewill.

All you did was **change one matrix for another**. And every matrix, or paradigm, is a way to control people. It just takes longer to see some of the controls after switching to a new paradigm… the love-affair has to wear off before you'll see that most belief systems are engineered to do the same thing: <u>control</u>. Your **mindset** is your belief system, the matrix that you live in. And we all do it – to explain the world we live in to ourselves – so that we'll be safe and the world will be more predictable (thus safer), and maybe if we get it really figured out, we can control it – "create our own reality." The ultimate deception.

Sorry, no one 'creates' their own reality in 3D. Your Script dictates the basis of your reality, but you can **attract** blessings/curses to you. Remember, you need truth/Light to get out of here and avoid being recycled. This is why it is so important to seek/attain true knowledge.

Knowledge protects.
Ignorance enslaves.

Escape Velocity

The reality is, your false belief systems are your <u>biggest</u> problem. And this is why so much time has been spent in this book going over truth and error. Truth has Light. True <u>knowledge has Light</u>. False beliefs have very little or no Light. When you die, if you don't have enough Light, or true Knowledge, you don't get out of here. 'Escape velocity' is reached with 51%, or better, Light **in** you. The more false beliefs that the Neggs, OPs and PTB can push your way and get you to accept, the less Light you have, and the reason you don't get out of here at death is because with all that false 'knowledge,' you are not of any use in the Father's kingdom. So you can be legally 'recycled.' (More on this in this

437

Chapter's 'Life is a Film' section.)

Man does not need more than one lifetime's experience on Earth to get what this place is all about. As multidimensional souls, with other aspects in different timelines and realities, the goal is to experience different parts of the Father's Creation – not to spend 100 lifetimes on planet Earth. Yet, that is what can happen because Man does not know how important spiritual growth is and so wastes his/her time here – still subject to the exacting doctrines of Karma/Reincarnation or Script/Recycling. (More in Book 2.)

> *By the way, The Law of Karma only applies to the planet Earth School.*
> *It is not operative elsewhere in our (simulated) Galaxy.*

These Laws serve to keep Man bound to this planet because (1) he doesn't know <u>why</u> he is here, and (2) he cannot live a perfect lifetime and (3) the Neggs, if they can, will see to it that he creates more 'Karma' for which he must come back… Man <u>can</u> overcome these issues if he knows what is going on. That is a purpose of this book.

> *A little secret: you* **can** *handle anything that is thrown at you, you just don't know it and that is one thing the lifetimes are designed to prove to you. You are much more than you think you are.*

Truth Rules

Part of attaining the escape velocity to get out of here is to realize the Truth, which imparts more Light to one's DNA. If one's Light quotient (also measured as PFV) is greater than that of the planet, AND if one stands up to the 'Beings of Light' (**if** it is the Neggs in disguise), and asserts one's rights, AND doesn't agree to something that violates his/her freewill, one can be set free. A lot to consider.

> "You shall know the Truth and the Truth will set you free…"   (Jn 8:32)

> … but first it may anger you! That is what they don't tell you – and if
> you have been trying to assimilate the information in this book, you
> know what I mean!

A lack of knowledge and belief in the wrong things are all that stand between you and gaining mastery of your life – and getting out of here. You <u>will</u> <u>choose</u> to get out of here when you know the truth about yourself and this place. But you can't choose until you know, hence the trap.

Light and Freedom

> If you bring forth what is within you,
> what you have will save you;
> If you do not have that within you,
> What you do not have within you [will] kill you. [3]
> > Book of Thomas : 70

He was speaking of Light.

To get out of here, you need Light, and your personal light must be greater than that of this planet to leave, or you stay here. So you **must bring forth what Light you have and seek to gain more**. You also stay here if you don't know that you have a <u>choice</u> to leave (even if you already have enough Light), and if you let the Neggs pretend to be Beings of Light and convince you that you have a (false) Karmic debt to pay.

Your Light can be kept low by buying into the emphasis on sex, violence, power, money and melodrama which keeps a lot of people in their first 3 chakras – they may never get out of here. A lot of people today think that life is about having fun – not learning, growth or service. It takes more than fun to develop one's Light through the other 4 (higher) chakras. Developing or feeding one's energy through all the 7 major chakras is what builds one's Light, raises one's vibration, to exceed the planet's vibration, and thus gets one out of here.

Feeding Your Chakras

How do you feed the energy of your chakras? Simple. Do those things that stimulate the higher chakras 4 -7. Chakra 4 is about Love and compassion. Chakra 5 is about telling the truth. Chakra 6 is about listening to your intuition, hunches, even meditating. And chakra 7 is built in meditation, service and devotion to Higher Ideals, and as the lower 6 chakras de-energize and lose dominance, the 7th chakra will strengthen in one's connection to the Godhead, or the Oversoul.

If you watch violent sexy movies you are feeding the 1st chakra. If you worship money and power, you are feeding the 2nd chakra. And any ego-trip or ego-based activities strengthens chakra 3...

Light and Knowledge

The higher one's consciousness, the more one is aware of the Truth, and the less one can pretend that Love and Knowledge aren't important. In fact, a failure to be loving when it is appropriate really weighs heavily against that person; it means a lesson was not learned, an awareness was not reached, and the 'lesson' will have to be repeated, sooner or later.

Love is important but so is Knowledge.

> It is not necessarily a feeling that one has that can also be interpreted as an emotion, but rather... the essence of Light which is knowledge is love, and this has been corrupted when it is said that love leads to illumination. Love is Light is Knowledge...
> To love you must know. And to know is to have Light. And to have Light is to love. And to have knowledge is to love. [4]

And elsewhere, Laura Knight-Jadczyk makes the clarification:

> Knowledge is a function of consciousness, and all knowledge that IS knowledge and not assumption, prejudice or illusion, increases consciousness.[5]

To get scientific for a minute, it needs to be examined that Knowledge and Light actually **are** related. Light has a vibration, or more properly, even intelligent Light, is comprised of photons. Steven Hawking says:

> Today… we call a **quanta** [a discrete packet] of light a photon. **The higher the frequency of light, the greater its energy content.** Therefore, though photons of any given color or frequency are all identical, Planck's Theory states that photons of different frequencies are different in that they carry different amounts of energy. This means that … the faintest light of any given color – the light carried by a single photon – **has an energy content that depends on its color.** For example, since violet light has twice the frequency of red light, one quanta of violet light has twice the energy of one quanta of red light… [and] is twice as large as the smallest possible bit of red light energy. [6] [emphasis added]
>
> **FYI:** *police vehicles use **blue and red lights** because of the mental effect it has on the driver's perception: the brain is momentarily 'stunned' and cannot reconcile the wavelengths coming from opposite ends of the visual spectrum.*

DNA emits photons of light (Chapter 9). So light has a frequency and the higher the frequency, the greater the energy, so people with a higher consciousness would have a higher frequency, a brighter aura, and thus carry more energy. To those who see auras, this translates as more Light – more biophotons coming off in their aura. And because they are of a higher consciousness, they know more, and that affects their PFV and their DNA which results in more light – thus, they have Light.

> **The Higher Beings do not keep you here – you keep yourself here by virtue of your own low Light. You self-select yourself. Both the Higher Beings and the Elite want you to 'graduate'… it is the PTB who want you to stay here.**

So, how much Light do you carry? Think you know the Truth?

Test Your False Belief Quotient

The following questions are common statements found in our world, the New Age movement, and sometimes in the Eastern and New Thought worlds. They are either true or false. This test is offered as an aid to help you discover how many of the erroneous beliefs you have accepted that are or are not true. At the end of the test, score yourself, and the answers are given and explained.

Caution, as can be seen in the first few statements, they are designed to elicit a "Yeah, but…" response indicating that you have bought into something that you think is true because you can see other possibilities in the question(s). If you can identify the apparent contradictory aspects of a statement, you will achieve some degree of clarity…

Questions:

	T	F
1. All people create or manifest their reality; i.e., "create their day," whether they realize it or not.	___	___
2. The mind can make you sick or well.	___	___
3. Things often happen by accident, for no reason.	___	___
4. Karma is paying for what you did to others; it is payback.	___	___
5. If you think and/or say what you believe long enough, sooner or later it will become your reality.	___	___
6. Words have power.	___	___
7. Unseen entities in the lower Astral realm can and do cause our problems.	___	___
8. All information received from the 4D Astral realm is from higher beings who speak the truth.	___	___
9. There are shape-shifting reptilians who are conspiring to take over the world.	___	___
10. You are the source of all your thoughts.	___	___
11. Man as a soul was created to be higher than the angels.	___	___
12. In reality, there is only the Force and Man.	___	___
13. There is a Heaven and a Hell, and angels and demons.	___	___
14. Sending Love and Light always works to improve things.	___	___
15. The end of the world is near; Apocalypse is near.	___	___
16. Man is all alone on Earth and it is his planet. So he is here to have fun and do whatever he wants.	___	___
17. There are human beings on the Earth who have no soul, and thus do not understand and share the goals of humans with a soul.	___	___
18. The Quija Board is harmless fun and no real communication ever takes place with it.	___	___
19. Man really went to the Moon in 1969-72 .	___	___

	T	F

20. Most UFOs are illusions like Bigfoot, Mothman and the Loch Ness 'monster.'   _____ _____

21. A person who is good and loving, although somewhat ignorant, will still go to heaven.   _____ _____

22. If I don't like something in my life, I should ignore it, thus denying it power, and it will then go away.   _____ _____

23. Jesus paid for our sins and believers are now going to Heaven.   _____ _____

24. If I am a healer, I should heal as many people as possible.   _____ _____

25. When I go Out of Body (OBE) at night, I am visiting other timelines or dimensions.   _____ _____

Now let's see what the answers are, and how close to leaving you might be... a 10-15 correct is marginal, 15-20 is sufficient to get out, at 21-25 – what are you doing still here?

Answers:

1. **False.** Popular illusion promoted by OPs and confused teachings. You can <u>attract</u> your day, but not create it; you do not have the power to do that in 3D reality. Such power is 'monitored' (because technically your soul does have the potential), it is not allowed in 3D as it would create chaos in the Rehab center. Your life is geared to your Script.

2. **True**. The mind directs the *chi* and can thus heal the body. Negative thoughts which generate negative emotions can make you sick by upsetting hormonal balance, shutting down the immune system, or causing you to eat/drink something that makes you sick.

3. **False**. There is always a cause, even if unseen, and it may come down to someone's "premeditated carelessness." If it really wasn't caused by human negligence, it may have been caused by the Neggs. In any event things don't just happen by themselves. (Chapter 6)

4. **False.** Karma is <u>meeting yourself</u>. Just because you knifed someone in a past lifetime does not mean you have to be knifed in this lifetime; what you need to 'meet', discover and resolve is that part of yourself that caused you to knife the other person. See Chapters 7 and 11.

5. **True** – to a certain point. You still do not create your reality; you attract it. After you fill a figurative 'box' with enough energy or sustained desire, the desire can manifest. Persistence often pays off.

6. **True**. And the word spoken by an awakened person has much more 'power' than that spoken by an unawakened person. Words have a <u>vibration</u> (energy) that either empowers

or diminishes people. (Chapter 9 showed how words can affect DNA.)

7. **True** – but not always. We sometimes set ourselves up for disasters and problems, and it is part of our growth to know when we're doing it and when others are doing it to us. In most cases, not doing what we should be doing results in the Neggs administering corrective catalyst; ongoing refusal to make corrections in our path results in further 'hits' until we finally stop and pay attention. See Chapter 6 and Neggs' function.

8. **False.** Every entity above Man's 3D level is "higher" than Man but that doesn't mean that discarnates for example know the truth, let alone can tell you. Caution and discernment are advised.

9. **False**. There <u>are</u> reptilians and the Neggs <u>do</u> shapeshift, but the shapeshifting reptilians are as much an illusion as Nessie, Mothman, and Bigfoot…. whatever the Neggs think you'll buy into. The PTB and Remnant do the conspiring, and the Greys, Neggs and Others do the shapeshifting.

10. **False**. The Neggs and discarnate entities can and do put thoughts in your head – as well as the two-legged 3D humans using V2K technology. (Chapters 6 and 11.)

11. **True**. Man's divine connection is destined to put him, like Jesus, in charge of realms in the Father of Light's Multiverse, which is why the Neggs, discarnates and Dissidents are obstructing Man from being all he can be, and blocking his destiny. (See Chapters 6 and 7.)

12. **False**. How nice it would be if this were true – no struggle, no confusion, just ascension to higher realms… only yourself to overcome. A lie straight from the Neggs. And yet the God Force does exist and can be synch'ed up with as one gains awareness. See answer 11 above.

13. **False.** This belief will get you recycled when you die, as you are "not ready for a higher realm yet…You need to go back and perfect yourself some more…" See Chapters 7 and 11 on karma and reincarnation. There is an Interlife where teaching, reflection and planning are done, but no Heaven as is commonly pictured.

14. **False**. If you send Love and Light to OPs, or those controlled by the Neggs, you have just empowered them; the opposite of what you intend may happen. They have the ability to change the 'intent' attached to energy and can misuse what you send.

15. **False.** The Mayan calendar was off. The world does not end, Man does not disappear; it is just the culmination of a cycle and the "harvest" may be performed by a timeline Split if the gods don't do a "Wipe and Reboot" and start a new Era. (Chapter 15.) 2012 was a Galactic eclipse; we crossed the equator of our Galaxy (and we are still here).

16. **False**. Man has never been alone on Earth, it is not his planet, and he does not belong here. How much "fun" is a sanitarium where the inmates are doing whatever they want? See Chapters 12-15.

17. **True**. Check out Chapters 5 and 6. There are several different types of humans

without souls (auras) and they are a source of Man's problems…discussed in Chapter 5. Also see Genesis 3:15 and Chapter 2.

18. **False**. The Ouija Board <u>is</u> a means of connecting with "game players" on the Other Side – the lower Astral realm. They love an audience and will give partial truth, as far as they know (limited in 4D – they do not know everything), and as much as they think you will swallow. You want to play a game? They'll oblige and the lower Astral is full of tricksters. (Chapter 6)

19. **Really?** Please check out 8-10 NASA pictures of Earth from the Moon and ask yourself why they show the Earth in several different sizes? (Remember that the Earth is 3.67 times the size of the Moon, so would the Earth as seen from the Moon be the same size as the Moon as seen from Earth – as seen in many NASA pix?) This issue has been examined better in Appendix A.

20. **True**. UFOs are not "unidentified," they are <u>identified</u> and should be called IFOs – some are created by the same entities (Neggs) who brought you Crop Circles. More distraction, deception and confusion. 80% of the UFOs are illusion, and some are Earth-based. (See Chapter 4.)

21. **False.** Love is not "all you need." Sorry, Beatles. Light is knowledge and yours must be higher than this planet's level, or you come back. Knowledge changes your Light level and gets you out of here. Very nice, loving people who know nothing are not useful elsewhere in the Father's kingdom, and they fall victim to other entities who diss Earthlings. They may be recycled.

22. **False**. Denying your reality means you deny your lesson(s) and will have to repeat them. What you resist, persists and may cause you additional problems. (See also section 'Subconscious Sabotage' this chapter.)

23. **False**. Karma and your Script rules, not vicarious sacrifice. Each soul is to learn from his/her mistakes ('sins') and grow to be an Earth Graduate – thus responsible for 'saving' him-/herself. See Chapter 15.

24. **False**. An illness means something is wrong and the person suffering needs to see what s/he did wrong to cause it. A healer removing the sick person's 'lesson' may have to answer for inappropriate use of their gift. Ask first, and <u>if it is not karmic,</u> and the person understands their illness, you can attempt a healing – but ask "if it be the will of the Father of Light."

25. **False**. Robert Monroe proved this one (Chapter 12) – a real OBE stays within the HVR Sphere, and most people experience a lucid dream. When he scanned the universe it was because he was permitted to travel with his Oversoul which showed him different realms. (See Chapter 7 and soul aspects.)

Vibratory Reactions

Earth normally reflects a low vibration in its traditional 3D state – but since this is now a

3D reality construct in 4D, the Higher Beings can apply localized "vibratory medicine" to the Sphere and treat the Sphere with loving, positive vibrations, thus increasing its vibrations and physically entrain Man upwards against the pull of 3D density and efforts of the OPs and Neggs. Of course, Man is free to resist.

Are the dots connecting yet?

Reaction

Also note that as the vibrations increase on the planet, that those souls for whom the increased vibration is more than they are comfortable with, will react in unpredictable ways. Since we usually try to drop back to a level we feel comfortable with, it is expected that those who are resistant to moving forward with the new vibrations will champion a return to the 'good old days,' and seek the lifestyle and values of earlier times.

Others will go into **denial** and keep trying to live as they have always lived, making excuses for their increased irritability, mistakes, rebellion and memory losses. But the 'old ways' don't work in an environment with higher vibrations.

Still others will **feel a loss of control** and take out their frustrations on the road and more erratic driving will be seen – in a futile attempt to prove (to themselves) that they are still in control or 'free' to do whatever they want.

And still others will **get a gun** and try to solve their problems with it.

Man's refusal to 'go with the Flow' or Quickening, and swim with the current will also result in increased societal tensions, misunderstandings, crime, drinking, drugs, smoking and a renewed search and dogmatic adherence to beliefs that <u>were</u> comforting when times were less stressful. Even if the beliefs no longer work because they are out of phase with the energy of our re-entry into the fourth dimension, let alone the fifth dimension. And that is a danger.

If you have false beliefs when you die, that **mindset** stays with you and colors what you do over there; so you may not be able to go where you'd like, or may wind up somewhere other than where you planned on.   Note:

> **Robert Monroe verified that your mindset determines where you can go when out of the body**. [7] So you want to get it right -- before you leave the body!

Déjà Vu

Recycling can be facilitated by the Laws of Karma and Reincarnation – if you didn't make enough spiritual progress in the lifetime which you just exited, the Being who reviews your life will find problems, or stagnation, and if your life substantially made no progress, they can plausibly put you in one of their 'Astral training schools' in the Interlife (to effect changes in your soul's vibration), and then later move you either into another body – or even back to the very same lifetime you just left. Yes, the <u>exact same lifetime</u>. **Recycled**.

Don't believe that? That IS **Déjà Vu**. You <u>have</u> been here before, you <u>have</u> seen this before or you <u>have</u> heard that before, and you <u>have</u> done that before… Time as we know it does not exist; it is a linear construct for the 3D planet Earth's HVR Simulation.

Déjà vu means you were recycled.

Let's qualify this issue of false beliefs, false learning, a bit more…

Life is a Film

According to Boris Mouravieff (of our Chapter 5, OP fame) again:

> The life of Man is a film… Incomprehensible as it may seem, **our life is truly a film produced in accordance with a script**. This film goes on continuously, without ever stopping, in such a way that, at the time of his death, Man is born again. **What seems absurd is that he is born in the same place, at the same date where he was born before, and of the same parents** [i.e., recycled]. **So the film goes on again**. Each human being then is born with his own particular film [script]…
> **The repetition of the film is not reincarnation**, although these two are often confused…
> It thus happens to him that, faced with certain events, he will feel that he <u>has</u> already seen or lived those events…
> The human personality is not a reality in the proper sense of the word, but a possibility. It plays a role in the film to which it is attached, from which it will not disappear until the moment of the Second Birth [death].[8] [emphasis added]

Note the following diagram, which represents the progress of two lifetimes:

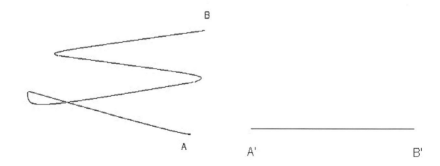

The above diagram shows a lifetime on the right where no progress was made, and the end of the life (B') is the same level as the beginning (A'). This flat line means that not much was learned, there was no soul growth, and the person basically wasted their lifetime, and will have to repeat it.

On the left is a lifetime that made considerable progress, with a few twists and turns, setbacks and reversals, but ultimately winding up with more Light and more spiritual progress than the lifetime on the right. The ending must be "higher" than the beginning if the film is to not repeat; otherwise you can visualize the end of the film as attached to the beginning of the film (a giant loop) – and it repeats in a life where nothing or very little was learned.

The teaching is that Man is born (into the film/script), and as he progresses and applies himself to the better 'B' influences (in Chapter 5), the film stops being linear and begins to assume a **spiral** path upwards. The personality is associated with the indestructible real Self and will be transfigured by conscious application of spiritual growth, and the personality [ego] morphs into an Individuality.

> As long as Man lives in the wilderness [of 'A' influences], self-satisfied and immersed in lies and illusions, the film will unfold with mechanical inflexibility, and the personality will remain entirely unchanged. [9]

And a person who has made no progress in their life/film, gets **recycled**. If you didn't pass 3rd grade, do you get to go on to 4th? As below, so above.

> The crossing of the Second Threshold represents the Second Birth, the birth of Individuality. As Man becomes more and more integrated with his "I", growing his Individuality, he becomes progressively integrated with the Cosmos and acquires "gifts" appropriate to his individual nature. Simultaneously, he progressively participates in real, objective existence which finally characterizes his being. **This is liberation from the bonds of the film.** [10] [emphasis added]

In theory, Man can stay in the repeating loop of his life/film/script until the end of time. As long as he is happy with himself, oblivious to the truth and higher forces, attributing his virtues to himself, attributing his problems to others… he is among the "living dead" that Jesus described as those who "believe themselves to be alive." [11] They repeat the film, since it stays **linear** and the end meets the beginning in a giant loop… and hence they are **recycled** (and may later experience Déjà vu). Of course, if the soul is defective and repeats this behavior for lifetimes, s/he may be disseminated, as Dr. Newton said in Chapter 7.

On the other hand, the person who seeks Truth, spiritual growth, and acts on intuition and follows the 'B' influences (Chapter 5), has turned his film into an upward spiral, where the end cannot meet the former beginning. Having done that, he is breaking the cycle of repetition and does not return to that lifetime/script. In fact, he can't because his 'magnetic centers' or chakras have grown and he is now watched and assisted by Higher Beings who are adept at setting up circumstances (via the Control System of the HVR) as stepping stones to further growth.

> We should know that, at the end of a spiral (incarnation), a comparison is made between the film as it was conceived at the time of birth and what it has become at the time of death. The balance sheet between these two states

is drawn up, as in accounting, by listing assets and liabilities, followed by a profit/loss statement. This will show the result of the elapsed life objectively.[12]

If enough progress is made, Man is said to cross the Second Threshold, and moves forward to a new life experience, and experiences the Second Birth of Individuality. If some, but not enough, progress was made, he <u>may opt</u> to start all over again, not reworking the linear film, but reworking the semi-spiral version with the goal of assimilating the lessons and growth that eluded him the last time.

Occasionally a very shallow spiral will have to be reworked, relived, or redone.

Getting Out of Here

Now you know why,

> **if you don't know what this place is, and what is expected of you, you will not get out of here. You can be trapped and not know it.**

> The best slave is the one who can say, "I'm no slave, I'm free!"

Because you will not know <u>why</u> you are here and thus will not do what it takes to get out of here. If you knew what this place really was, you would WANT to get out, and you would <u>automatically</u> know why you're here, and you would <u>automatically</u> do what it takes to get out.

The Neggs, discarnates, OPs, PTB and Dissidentss love 'company' that they can manipulate. That's why you don't know what this place is. **They are not going to tell you**. Lords need Serfs, Rulers need Slaves, as well as Teachers need Students.

Oh, I know. It is said you can get out when you become a more loving person. (See question #21 above in the Test.) You heard that "Love is All You Need". Great song. It won't be enough to get you out of here, though. You have to have Love <u>and</u> Knowledge.[13]

But you say, "I'm having fun, drinking, smoking, sex, travel...and I don't harm anyone..." Why should I want to leave?

> This is not your home.
> You do not belong here.
> You are not the top of the foodchain.
> The Father has a purpose for you –
> and it isn't on this planet.

Remember what the higher entity said who spoke through one of Dr. Newton's hypnotized patients: Souls who are dysfunctional and do not get it together may be **"disseminated."** Souls cannot party here forever – if today's pollution doesn't get you, then the <u>real</u> Life Review will, or the "Wipe and Reboot" will.

Please be aware that life is not about feeling good; no one is here for that purpose. In fact, that is not even a purpose. **Life is about waking up, overcoming, and getting out of here… becoming an Earth Graduate.** Why would you want to stay in an insane asylum, or a rehab center?

Violation of Freewill

Quite bluntly, the PTB, the Neggs, discarnates, OPs and your neighbors have violated your freewill and you agreed to it at some point in your life.

Initially some people will disagree with that because (1) they don't know how subtle and persistent the PTB and OPs can be, and (2) people think they're in control of their lives. Without congratulating them, these STS entities can be considered <u>masters</u> at deceiving and tricking you into giving your power away. And this violation principally surfaces when you die; and then what you didn't learn and still don't know <u>can</u> harm you and you may wind up some place other than where you intended. Your mindset needs to include enough knowledge and awareness to discern who's there, what they're doing, and enough self-respect and integrity to stand up and say no.

> *But the sheeple nowadays have been lulled into a false sense of security – they let Harry, Tom or Dick handle their political/societal affairs for them while they sit on the couch, eat their burrito, and laugh at Seinfeld. Meanwhile Harry, Tom and Dick are making off with the Country right under their noses… often lying about what they are doing, but the people go along with it. Lazy people get the kind of society they agree to.*

Violation of freewill cannot happen without some **deception** that convinces us that there is no danger to us and gets us to think it is OK to do something. Then you go along with the idea/suggestion/urge. You have accepted BS without knowing it – all they have to do is <u>get you to agree</u> (for <u>whatever</u> reason) to what is promoted, and if you don't care, or you don't know, **you have given your power of choice away**, and cannot then do the right thing. Then the Neggs capitalize on your ignorance, and even though it is frowned on to violate another's freewill in this universe, the Neggs have gotten away with it <u>because you agreed to it.</u> The fact that they lied to you and got you to agree through deception doesn't hurt them – <u>You</u> have the problem, not them.

This is also something that is done by the PTB who 'spin' history, promote confusion, and manipulate public opinion. Societal trends and attitudes that would not have been acceptable 50 years ago are now gaining acceptability due to the promotion of the idea that we're now in the 21st century and thus should be more progressive and open-minded. Case in point: Gays <u>and</u> the spreading of HIV. About 52% of the American public has HIV, including heterosexuals, and the CDC knows it can't be stopped or cured, so we ignore it, we no longer tell the public what the infection rate is ("don't want them to worry, they're probably going to get it anyway, so why bother?"), and we thus promote same-sex marriage with the understanding that it is "an alternate lifestyle," and because we are now more enlightened, it is OK… "Get with it people!" is the injunction. We did the same thing with alcohol and tobacco – we couldn't stop it (Think: Prohibition) and so we 'legalized' it and put a tax on those commodities. All of that not to denigrate the Gays, but to show that society, for better or worse, has a history of going along with things that can be harmful to our health – alcohol, tobacco and HIV are not the hallmarks of a healthy society. But, loving and respecting the Gays, is.

> **Caution: Gays are not the problem, HIV is, and it seems to have started with the Black Gays first. Regardless, they are our brothers and sisters and we should still care for them.**
> **See Chapter 15 and Section on "Handle Sex Orientation."**

If there were a conspiracy to wipe out Man, HIV would be the way to do it, and cause minor damage through alcohol and tobacco, to say nothing of what drugs do to people's DNA and health. If there were a conspiracy to remove Man from the planet, you'd want to get his approval (so he doesn't rebel) and understanding that fluoride is OK in the water – doesn't the ADA sanction it? (European countries have rejected it.) You' d want to promote the idea that **GMO** food is OK, and that **Chemtrails** are helping to protect us from the Sun's UV rays… In other words, get Man to agree to things that are harmful, that abuse him, so that if the gods step in, the perpetrators can say, "Don't blame us – they agreed to it!" The other defense is to say "Well, we told them – right there on the Georgia Guidestones!" Then, when a society falls, the people are caught off-guard and claim they didn't know what was going on.

And ignorance is no excuse because all one has to do is stay aware and **ask.**

By the way, parents, teachers and pastors regularly violate people's freewill by using their authority position to get you to believe what they want. Kids are lied to about Santa Claus knowing if they're good or bad and thus manipulating the kids to do what the parents want. Teachers can unknowingly teach the wrong thing (see section on science errors in Chapter 8) and violate the kids' right to know the truth. And lastly, preachers used to threaten people with Hell and damnation if they didn't do what the preacher thought was right.

> **Your freewill can still be violated even if you're not aware of it.**

Subconscious Sabotage

This is a biggie for some New Age people, please pay close attention. This is a form of **violation of our freewill** – although while it is being done to you, it seems harmless.

Mr. D found a New Thought church where the guru/minister would lead the whole congregation in a guided meditation at the beginning of each service, every Sunday. They'd sit quietly, eyes closed, breathing deeply, while the guru would lead them into a relaxed state – also known as 'alpha' wherein the subconscious mind is very susceptible to suggestions. After a few minutes of relaxation, the guru would repeat affirmations for 5-10 minutes, such as,

> "There is no negativity in my life"
> "I do not entertain negative thoughts or people"
> "Nothing negative happens to me"

"I speak only positive words and ignore the negative ones"
"Nothing negative is real in my life, I focus on only the positive"
…etc.

This is a real 'catch 22': if you have problems, you can't solve what you can't see.

… after a few Sundays of that, guess whose subconscious, programmed while in 'alpha', is PROGRAMMED to ignore any negative input in their life? Guess who cannot handle and resolve negative events because they don't exist for him? Guess what effect it had on his marriage as he could not deal with anything negative in his life, and work out solutions to problems with his wife…? Guess who could not deal with problems with vendors and employees in his company…? Did he listen when told what the problem was? No. Would he go for "deprogramming" under hypnosis to become a normal person again? No.

This is real, people. And is one of the dangers of the 'guided meditation' in some New Thought churches – which really amounts to **hypnotic suggestion** and some day, when Man wakes up, it will be seen as a violation of freewill, and may involve misdemeanor prosecution for practicing irresponsible hypnosis with naïve subjects.

Be careful with affirmations and evaluate the content of some 'guided meditations.'

Global Problem: Earth's Ecosphere

This is the last challenge we will examine. Just in case people are unaware of the scope of problems facing Man, here is a quick list of the most common ones – the point being that **a quick review** of these issues will drive home the point of (1) just how many there are, and (2) how precarious is our living on the planet that is collapsing under us.

And because this is a very negative subject, I will minimize it, just to point out the major news headlines (with URLs) and include a key explanation, if necessary. Especially note the **bolded text.**

Pollution:

Oxygen has decreased overall on the planet over the last 100 years by 20%.
The Pacific floating garbage patch is twice the size of Texas and cuts oxygen generation.
http://search.yahoo.com/search?ei=UTF-8&fr=att-portal&p=oxygen+levels&rs=0&fr2=rs-bottom

The North Pacific Trash Vortex
Plastic garbage dumped at sea comprises an area **bigger than the size of Texas**. The plastic contains toxic chemicals harmful to marine life, and there are also old but intact nets that trap dolphins and sea turtles who die because they can't get free.
http://www.greenpeace.org/usa/campaigns/oceans/follow-the-journey/trashing-our-oceans

Significance: the ocean's surface has always contained millions of phytoplankton to (1) provide a food source for marine mammals, and (2) provide oxygen in the atmosphere. We now have **25% less oxygen** on the planet than in 1890. According to NOAA, if we lose another 8% nobody will be breathing.

Ozone layer depletion worse.
As the ozone layer depletes, Ultraviolet-B (UV-B) radiation increases – no longer stopped by the atmosphere, and skin carcinomas increase, as well as the phytoplankton (oxygen-producers) are killed by the UV-B radiation. As the phytoplankton die, so do the krill and that helps starve the penguins and whales. (www.umich.edu/~gs265/society/ozone.htm)

Significance: I often wonder what the real estate developers are going to breathe while they try to spend their millions of dollars made while overdeveloping the country and **cutting down trees and shrubs** …we already don't have enough clean oxygen, and then we wonder where respiratory problems come from… They cut down a 40 year old oak tree and put back a 2 year old sapling… This is the version of mankind that doesn't work and is leading to his replacement for the sake of the planet.

Dead Zones Multiplying Fast, Coastal Water Study Says
This is from a 2008 report on the 'Dead Zones' around the world – areas in the seas where life is no longer supported due to the severe pollution – Man is creating it faster than Mother Nature can clear it away.
There are now more than 400 dead zones, up from just over 300 in the 1990s.
http://news.nationalgeographic.com/news/bigphotos3669583.html

Environment:

Russian Lake Disappears, Baffling Villagers   May 2005
A lake disappeared overnight and left a giant muddy hole, with trees fallen into it.
http://news.yahoo.com/s/nm/20050519/od_nm/odd_russia_lake_dc

Glacial Lake in the Andes Disappears.
A five-acre lake has disappeared in the Andes in Peru, and no one knows why. There were no earthquakes. June 2007
http://www.foxnews.com/story/0,2933,285314,00.html

Nine Major Earthquakes in World since January 2010
Beginning with Haiti 1/12/10 as a 7-magnitude to another 7.2 in Baja California on 4-4-10, the planet is shifting a lot of crust.
http://earthquake.usgs.gov/earthquakes/eqinthenews/

Earth Loses its Magnetism
(Molly Bentley BBC News UK Edition in San Francisco)
The geomagnetic field around the Earth is weakening and satellites in orbit are affected by the change in Earth's core and substrata reflected in a weakening magnetic field. Satellites are being damaged by increased solar radiation normally stopped by the

magnetosphere which is now weakening.
(Sunday Times, Johannesburg SA, Sunday 18th July 2004)

Sunshine study finds world's darkened since '50s.
The dimming trend is not understood, but reaches 37% in places around the Earth – less sunlight. Part of it is pollution, but it increases 2.7% per decade. 2006.
http://www.houstonchronicle.com
article is http://www.chron.com/cs/CDA/ssistory.mpl/nation/2566165

Alabama Tornados in 2011
Dozens of tornadoes devastated the South in a massive storm system that has reduced neighborhoods to rubble and killed at least 337 people across 7 states, the AP reports. Some tornados were a mile wide and traveled hundreds of miles before stopping.
http://www.huffingtonpost.com/2011/04/28/alabama-tornado-photos-2011-storm_n_854879.html

Japan Killer (8.9) Earthquake of March 2011
We are still two years later trying to clean up and stop the **radiation leaking** from the worst nuclear power plant disaster Man has ever seen. The radiation plume has contaminated Hawaii and California (by air, rain…). Japan's coast suffered devastating 30' tsunamis.
http://www.huffingtonpost.com/2011/03/11/japan-earthquake-tsunami_n_834380.html

Traditional Warning Stone on NorthEast Coast of Japan
(credit: http://landscapetsunami.wordpress.com/2012/08/07/tsunami-warning-stone-2/)

Traditional warning stone, one of many, around Aneyoshi, Japan – the 1939 tsunami rose to 117 feet – what were they thinking at Fukushima with a 30' wall?

Significance: The NorthEast coast of Japan has been known for decades to be a danger zone for <u>large</u> tsunamis and there are 100-year old stone markers warning of this fact. So why was the nuclear power plant (Fukushima) put right on that coast? Wouldn't it have made better sense to put it on the NorthWest side of Japan's coast and run powerlines to wherever the power was needed? In addition to destroying the oxygen, this is another example of Man's being unfit to competently manage the planet's resources.

Vanishing Wildlife:

Another 2000 American **White Pelicans have vanished** from the Chase Lake National Wildlife Refuge, preceded by 27,000 several weeks ago. They did not fly off and no one knows where they went. (Charles Fort would love it.) www.deluthnewstribune.com June 17, 2004 in Medina, N.D.

400 Dolphins Wash up Dead off African Coast.
In Zanzibar, over 400 dolphins washed up dead on the coast and no one knows why. Autopsy revealed they weren't poisoned. 4-29-06
34 Whales Dead, Beached in N.C. Jan 17, 2004

Jumbo Squid Wash Onto California Beaches   2004
500 Humboldt squid washed up dead on Newport Beach shores.

Are Microwaves Killing the Insects, Frogs and Birds?
Many cities are experiencing the same phenomenon, around the world: no insects, no birds, no bees, no ants. Fish, birds and bees in particular are disappearing and due to **our heavy cellular microwave use, it is believed to be the culprit.** Man making money at the expense of nature.
http://rense.com/general81/emfs.htm March 2008.

Dying Frogs A Sign of Biodiversity Crisis
(Rachel Tompa at UCBerkley , reporter; published in Proceedings of National Academy of Sciences, week of Aug 12, 2008)
"Devastating declines of amphibian species around the world are a **sign of a biodiversity disaster** larger than just frogs…" said Professor David Wake at UCB. **"We are in a mass extinction spasm right now…"**
http://www.precaution.org/lib/08/prn_mass_extinction_spasm.080813.htm

Unprecedented Bat Die-off in NY and VT
Thousands of bats are dying of an unknown cause… they control insects. Maybe the bats are dying because the insects (their food) are being killed by the microwaves?
www.rense.com January 2008.

Whales Dying in Record Numbers Near Argentina
Since 2005 over 308 whales have died of unknown causes off the coast of Argentina, and 88% of them are under 3 months old – not much future for this population.
http://news.discovery.com/animals/whales-dying-in-record-numbers-near–Argentina.htm

Disease:

Rising Threat of Infections Unfazed by Antibiotics
(Andrew Pollack, New York Times, March 1, 2010)
Many germs are evolving and developing immunity to existing antibiotics. Hospitals are also cited as a breeding ground for drug-resistant germs, notably MRSA and C-Diff. http://finance.yahoo.com/insurance/article/108931/rising-threat-of-infections-unfazed-by-antibiotics?mod=insurance-health

As was pointed out earlier, Man's very existence is in jeopardy. Before the Anunnaki Remnant can remove Man from the planet, the superbugs may do that first. There is the prevalence of killer diseases running around the planet. One or two could be a coincidence, but 15+ is a bit suspicious:

> HIV/AIDS, SARS, MRSA (drug-resistent flesh-eating staph), H5N1 and H1N1 (flus), West Nile virus, E. coli, Morgellons, Hantavirus, Malaria, Ebola, *C-Diff*, Acinetobacter baumannii, Klebsiella pneumoniae, and Enterobacter aerogenes.

And, no, **Man is not developing new antibiotics to take care of the bacteria**. Every new vector that is developed in the latest antibiotic, is countered by the bacteria and they develop a resistance to it. [14] Case in point, *Clostridium difficile* (C-diff) which is resistant to standard antibiotics, and is a growing problem in hospitals – you go in for one thing and come out with a superbug infection (e.g., one of the last 4 named in the above list) which can't be easily killed.

According to one report, C-diff has been "…growing by more than 10,000 cases per year" and it played a role in more than 300,000 hospitalizations in 2005. [15] Let's hope the hospitals and clinics are scrubbing down better nowadays.

Antibiotics

Antibiotics have been misused and mis-prescribed for years, according to an earlier cited article. Upset patients with just a cold (viral infection) go to the doctor and demand a prescription which is usually an antibiotic which is good only against secondary bacterial infections. And as the patients begin to feel better, they stop taking their Rx, which allows the remaining bacteria to develop a resistance to the antibiotic.

Not only do the bacteria build a basic resistance to the antibiotic, but so does the body until that drug becomes largely ineffective. The other heavy use of antibiotics has been to give **tetracycline** to cows and chickens to keep them healthy; Man later eats the chicken, their eggs, and drinks the milk and wonders why a doctor's prescription of tetracycline is no longer effective against germs in his body, and consequently is no longer prescribed.

And "…**the major pharmaceutical companies are withdrawing from research into antimicrobial drugs.**" [16] There are no more vectors left with which to hit the bacteria without also compromising the patient's health! A new methodology, such as

bacteriophage therapy or **probiotics**, [17] will have to be developed, but that is very expensive and so far, only the Russian are investigating phage therapy seriously. [18]

Other Issues

In addition, there are **Chemtrails** (not contrails) which fall to Earth in the water and soil and people are allegedly contracting Morgellon's Disease. These are nanofibers below the skin caused by high density polyethylene fibers designed to replicate and grow in the atmosphere…. But what is happening when the fibers fall to Earth and get into our water…?

In recent years (2012-2013), there is occasional atmospheric spraying. (Chemtrails are contrails that do not disappear in 10 minutes – they are **chemical nanobots** that fan out and help block harmful radiation from the Sun, now that our ozone layer has been weakend by decades of fluorocarbon vapors.) [19]

And then there is **Mad Cow Disease** caused by *prions* in diseased cattle, deer and other 4-legged ruminants (and Man still eats red meat). Less of an issue now than it was 10 years ago, but is still an occasional find in deer and sheep, and some cows.

Speaking of cows, it has been noted that **cow milk** has IGF-1 factor in it (which is meant to blow a 60 lb calf into a 400 lb cow, but is also enlarging our young, growing kids when they drink a lot of milk…). It is healthier to drink an **organic** milk that has Omega-3 in it, and those brands are available in the supermarket. Goat's milk is healthy, too.

In vogue nowadays are **tattoos** – everybody seems to be getting one, even a small one hidden under clothing. Beware that the color tattoos were often made with **heavy metals**: the color blue from cobalt, red from mercury, yellow from arsenic… Do you really want that in your body? There are some colors made with non-toxic sources – ask for them.

Dental fillings are made with a silver amalgam, part mercury, and over time the mercury may leak out and get into the bloodstream. Mercury is a poison and predisposes the person to allergies among other things. Same warning for **flu shots** made with a mercury 'fixer' called Thimerasol (aka Thiomersal). If you need a flu shot, ask your doctor for the version that you **inhale**, it is free of Thimerasol.

Note that **Fluoride** belongs in your toothpaste, not your drinking water. Europe has removed it from their drinking water. Warning: some bottled water brands are filtered tap water and still have fluoride. FYI: German and Russian concentration camps used fluoride in the camp drinking water to keep the prisoners docile.

Aspertame also known as **Nutrasweet** or **AminoSweet** contains phenylketonurics which cause some people problems because their body cannot assimilate phenylalanine. Always check the label of the soft drinks to see which sweetener has been used.

Don't let **bottled water** sit in the car on hot days – if the plastic heats up, it can leach BPA into the water, and that is a carcinogen. Same goes for buying water in plastic bottles stacked in front of a supermarket – in the Sun all day. Not good.

And don't forget the potential **cellphone EMF radiation danger** to braincells. If the cellphone has enough power to go through the walls of the building where you work, connect with a cellphone tower across town, it has too much power to be held up to your head 10-12 times a day, 24x7x52. Incredible as it seems, there are people who attach a mini-cellphone to their ear so that (for convenience's sake) they always have their cellphone irradiating their delicate braincells. [20] (See Darwin Awards in Ch 7.) It is safer to use an earbud or the speaker phone until the issue has been clinically resolved.

Brave New World

Lastly there is another challenge we will all have to deal with in the coming years – Man is making great progress in understanding and replicating the human brain, and creating electronic devices that go way beyond V2K (Chapter 11). Science is trying to tell us that technology is Man's best friend, but it has a dark side to it if it is run by the soulless scientists and PTB who see Man as simply a bio-mechanical being who has no soul and is simply chemical responses to external stimuli. This is the pro-Evolution gang on steroids and is dangerously close to implanting humans with all sorts of microchips (RFID) – for control. (Think: Kurzweil's *Singularity*.) That issue has never disappeared from the planet, and now it comes alive with the 'approval and sanction' of modern technology.

Look out. **This is another reason the ensouled humans will want to get out of here**. Let the Anunnaki control freaks have the planet… ensouled humans need to avoid what the Earth is becoming. The rich and powerful have been steadily funding the research to give them the electronic control over mankind… Do you want to be part of that?

World Without Borders

And how do you keep the sheeple from waking up? Control the Media? Already done. Fluoridate their water? Already done. Control the source of new ideas? Aha – underway! Note that all of the **bookstores** except one are now gone – you cannot just walk into a variety of bookstores and browse and discover some new documentary or revelation… and when that last bookstore is gone, the discovery of new books and ideas will be limited to a browse online – if you know what to look for. And if 'progress' goes so far as to stop printing books and require that one identify themselves, sign up for Kindle or Nook, and download an eBook, certain books can be denied to people, or at least they have a record of who bought what.

Same thing with **video rental** stores. Again, it used to be possible to explore the DVDs at Blockbuster and discover something interesting without looking for anything in particular. The current move is to require selection of videos by remote control via one's TV – and the selection of videos is not exhaustive like Blockbuster was… try finding some throught-provoking videos with your remote (e.g., *The Fourth Kind*, or *Iron Sky* for starters).

Lastly, the **Internet** will have to be locked down or seriously controlled to keep people from sharing ideas, discovering noetic and spiritual websites, and blogging topics that the PTB frown on. Note that the original internet was started for Universities, the Military and

Government users. The current Internet has become so crowded and open to hacking the above 3 named areas, that a second, new internet was created (again just for those 3 users) and it's called I2 – all fibre-optic and super fast. It is rumored that Microsoft's IE 6 – 7 – 8 Web browser already has the code in it to seriously control logon and future use of the Internet.

Where will future 'seekers' get their inspiration, knowledge, and answers?

Anunnaki Remnant Challenge

Historically speaking, the Anunnaki have always been with us – outside the HVR Sphere before AD 900, and nowadays inside and underground. The preceding chapters have explored their creation of Man, the Dissident faction seeking to obstruct Man and their aiding and abetting today's PTB, the Remnant actions on this planet in the guise of the Quetzalcoatl group (Kukulcan, Huitzilopochtli, Viracocha, Votan, etc.), and lastly their residence as the Nagas.

The **Insider** faction of the Anunnaki Remnant, on the other hand, has sought to assist Man and develop his ability to grow, stand alone, and get out of here. This Elite agenda is concurrent with fulfilling their purpose for being here – which is almost the same as Man's. Both groups are to learn respect, responsibility, compassion, and develop knowledge. The Insiders have an additional function that Man will also adopt one day: as fledgling creators, they are responsible for their creation… just as a mother is responsible for her child.

The **Dissident** faction denies any responsibility for Man, having washed their hands of him when they found him to be unruly, noisy, petty, and rebellious (Chapter 3). Having tried to remove Man via famine, diseases and The Flood, he has persisted and they do not accept their role as mentors and they give counsel to the PTB for ways to control or in some cases get rid of Man. This is the big difference between the two Anunnaki factions.

However, both factions agree on the fact that Man is a big problem. They disagree on what to do with him, but they both agree that Man has to be contained on the planet – his pettiness, disrespect of lifeforms, violence as a solution, and disease are not wanted 'out there.' As a result, both factions are also confined to the planet to work out a solution and deal with their 'lessons' as novice creators.

Current Situation

The Dissidents have maintained for centuries that the rehabilitation of Man is hopeless and so they have put their support into the PTB efforts to control Man. The PTB don't realize that the Dissidents seek to remove Man and them, too. And Man does it to himself: lying, cheating, stealing, pettiness and violence are the signature aspect of too much of mankind. Thus, the Dissidents want Man removed and have so argued, reminding anyone who'll listen that they were here first and took better care of the planet than Man has. It is hard to argue with that issue. Man has been his own worst enemy.

If it weren't for the Higher Beings insisting that sentient lifeforms be respected, preserved, and given impetus to improve, Man would be gone from the planet by now.

The Genetic Solution

So who's winning? Is anything proactive being done? Why don't the two factions 'duke it out' with their superior weapons and the winner takes over the planet with his agenda?

Neither Anunnaki faction is free to remove the other and to constructively resolve their differences and their problem with Man is why the Remnant is still here. The Council looked at the problem from their higher level and saw that the current version of Man (about 1100 years ago – before the start of this Era) was hopelessly stuck due to the devolution and deficiencies in Man's DNA. Hence a request was made of the Remnant to use their bio-mechanical Greys to begin a "5th column" solution to the problem by covertly upgrading Man's DNA such that the "caveman" mentality that had spelled disaster for Neanderthal did not repeat itself this time.

This has meant tracking families for generations to see if the genetic tweaks are working; That means abducting and taking samples. But trying to modify the DNA of a living, moving hominid has been a little like trying to paint a moving freight train! Hence the night visits, the paralysis, and the blocks placed on memory – all to minimize the disruption. Thus new humans are being born among us since the 1980's and are often called the Indigo children, or sometimes Homo *noeticus*.

Needless to say, the Dissidents don't like it; they have gotten used to being superior and controlling Man, and if they can get rid of Man, their problem is solved, they get to go home. In addition, the coming **new Homo *noeticus* is not controllable**. Lords need serfs and the serfs are gradually disappearing. The Indigos seek to get along with each other, tell the truth, they are healthier, they work with Nature and clean up the planet, and they often promote new spiritual trends. They are the Dissidents' worst nightmare.

In addition, the Indigo presence on the planet, along with that of the Wanderers, and all Lightworkers in general, are empowering the positive coherence that will entrain more of mankind into a more proactive society. It has already started: Since when do you successfully land a big commercial jetliner in the icy Hudson River and no one dies? Since when did this country elect a Black president (despite the KKK and White Supremacy groups) – which race the PTB have been abusing for decades? And what happened to the axis shift and the Nostradamus "1999 terror from the skies….?" Did anyone notice that the December 2004 tsunami was nowhere near as bad as it could have been? We did not have the 20-50' tidal waves that were feared. And in another interesting note, we are in the peak of the Sun's eleven-year ramp-up to what is usually strong solar activity… and the Sun is pretty much quiet. Things are different.

Yet souls need to wake up and get out of here, largely for all the foregoing reasons, plus the Father of Light has a better way to occupy you elsewhere in the Kingdom (see Index: Areas for Service). That means people must seek to become Earth Graduates.

Chapter 15: -- The Earth Graduate

So what was this book? Brain Candy? An oblique attack on the Catholic Church or the Christians? An attack on the earthly Powers That Be? Not really. This book could have been about the subjugation of Earth, who did it, how and why, but that isn't important now.

As a result, this book is not an exposé of the Elite and does nothing to stop them. The problem is the PTB, composed of OPs and dysfunctional humans. It is a source of information for those who already suspect something is wrong and seek a better, more peaceful, loving world. This book is about getting out of here and gives just enough confirmation in Chapters 8 – 11 of what is wrong in an attempt, not to change it, but to supply the Light and assist perhaps a few thousand more people to wake up and become **Earth Graduates**.

Chapters 1 – 11 built to a semi-conclusion in Chapter 12, amplified it in Chapter 13, and then Chapter 14 identified the challenges which suggested we leave Earth. Now Chapter 15 summarizes this book's major points and suggests that we leave Earth as an Earth Graduate. Chapter 16 gives pointers on what it takes to raise one's Light to the level of "escape velocity."

By now it can be seen why almost everything you think you know about Earth History, Physical Science and Religion was false. This is not our planet, not our home, and we're not alone. 3D humans who think they run this planet don't want Man to leave. Yes, these aspects sound weird, even bizarre compared to what people think is reality. That is just a measure of how conditioned people are to NOT pay attention to where they are, what they are, and where they're going… And that, as this book has attempted to show, is by design.

Summarization

What is needed is a coherent summary of the many points the book made, and there are two aspects to that: a high-level and a low-level.

The High-level View

A major view of Earth from the 40,000' level showed that the Earth used to be in 4D as that is where most life in the Universe is. In its time, Earth was a repository of flora and fauna also found on many other planets; some considered Earth a zoo, some saw it as a botanical garden, and each of the major life forms was found on Earth: reptiles, insects, birds, fish, and mammals of all types. The flora and fauna found on Earth could be transplanted throughout the Galaxy by those wanting to experiment with creating their own unique ecosphere… thus, Earth was something of a Genetic Home Depot – whatever you needed to stock your ecosphere, it was found already balanced and working on Earth.

But all was not peace and harmony or fun and games. Earth also had mineral resources and most importantly, water in abundance. There were Others from Sirius and Orion who decided to take what they wanted from Earth, since there was no one to guard it, and the Earth was run on the honor system: take what you want but leave some for others. Except that there were Others who were more like pirates –not evil, but just determined to take what they wanted when they wanted it, and argued that that was OK because this Universe operates on the Freewill system, and it was their Freewill to do what they wanted.

While Earth was not inhabited, there was a small Caretaker contingent, more of a scientific support team from different worlds, watching over the ecosystem. Mars was inhabited, there were groups of beings underground on Venus and occupying several large moons circling Saturn and Jupiter. At this point, Earth and Mars did not have moons but they were about to receive them. The solar system had been a peaceful place for millennia, but then the Others discovered it. They wanted to build a base on Earth and mine some of its resources, and the Caretakers, outnumbered and outgunned, were not in a position to enforce a 'no.'

Needless to say, the Others disagreed among themselves as to who would get what, and there were some disputes, and then celestial shoving matches, and finally a cosmic war (described in the *Mahabarata,* no less) that occurred in our solar system as ships fired upon each other, the planet between Mars and Jupiter was blown up, Mars was severely scarred (Valles Marineris) by a plasma disruptor (also shown on the hillside at Nazca – think: Neptune's Trident), and Mars and the Earth were the scene of several battles. Very advanced warfare was either done with plasmic disruptors, or by grabbing a large asteroid and electromagnetically 'throwing' it at the enemy – one such asteroid was deflected and careened into the Earth temporarily destroying most life on the planet.

The Caretakers succeeded in bringing the desecration to the attention of the Galactic Council who sent forces to stop the destruction. Mars inhabitants and what was left of their water went underground, having lost a large part of their atmosphere, Earth had lost Lemuria in one of the battles, not to mention that the Garden was now ruined as a result of the meteor impact and the atmospheric dust circling the planet for years. The Earth was declared offlimits and as a precaution, since the Council would not allow a defending army to occupy the Earth, a Moon was moved in from another part of the Galaxy, partially hollowed and it became an observation and defense post – to protect the Earth from further disruption. The same was done for Mars, and is the origin of two artifical moons circling that planet.

The Council ordered the reconstruction of the Earth as a repository for significant flora and fauna and was able to terraform it back to normal within about a decade of our time. Meanwhile the Others were kept out (via a passive quarantine) – there was nothing for them here anyway. Time went by and one group of the Others, later called the Anunnaki, petitioned the Council to mine Earth resources up to a point agreed on by the Council, and they were permitted to return peacefully to Earth and set up a base in what is now South Africa. They also set up headquarters in what is now Iraq.

There were Others who saw this and grumbled about it, occasionally sending 'science' envoys to Earth, which almost always ran afoul of the Anunnaki. The Anunnaki had a major base on an island continent in the Atlantic, and in the Middle East with a large pyramid which served as both a beacon from space (its sides were polished marble), and as a power generator. Meanwhile, the Others had set up working bases in the Bolivian and Peruvian highlands, namely Sacsayhuaman, Puma Punku, Machu Picchu, and Tiahuanacu.

Over time, squabbles over resources occurred again. Push came to shove, and small battles broke out, with the Anunnaki destroying the South American bases, and the Others destroying what has been called Atlantis. The Anunnaki were also using weapons of mass destruction to wipe out and control the humans, and it was about 2024 BC that two Middle East cities were destroyed with nuclear bombs. That also got the attention of the Council (whose sentries were now observing from the Moon).

And it was about 600 BC, our time, that the Council forced the Anunnaki to withdraw from Earth, but because they had created sentient life, intelligent hominids (*Adama, Adapa*, etc), a portion had to stay behind to oversee their creation, according to Galactic Law. While they were on Earth, the Anunnaki had created several versions of a strong but semi-intelligent human as a worker force, but in so doing had created one brutish version whose genetics were devolving and they could not follow instructions, and they had to be removed and be replaced with a more stable version, called Cro-Magnon. Enlil the commander of the Anunnaki never wanted to be responsible for Man and tried several times to wipe out humans, but he was always foiled by the Science Officer, Enki.

So a small Remnant stayed on Earth, at first playing the role of gods in an effort to guide Man, and the Greek gods morphed into the Roman gods, but Man was so rebellious, stubborn, petty, violent and devious (all Anunnaki genetic traits mixed with those of a wild Earth hominid) that the Remnant petitioned the Council to let them also leave Earth, saying that humans were hopeless. They admitted they had created a mule instead of a horse, but the Council was adamant that the Remnant had to learn from their mistake and see if they couldn't correct it – according to Galactic Law, a 'creator race' is to shepherd their creation, educate and nurture it.

The Council also examined the Earth situation and decided to take things a step further to help both humans and Anunnaki – further incursions on Earth by space pirates and any ETs were to be prevented at all cost. Thus the Council enlisted the wisdom and power of the Higher Beings to take 4D Earth, replicate it as 3D and create a Simulation in a Quarantine so that in a new Era in a protected environment, the humans would learn their lessons, and the Anunnaki would learn theirs – which involved the humans. That was done about AD 800-900 , our time.

In addition, genetic upgrade of Man with the use of the **Greys** was begun since the Anunnaki were still held responsible for Man's genetics. Man had suffered too much with largely dysfunctional genes inherited from the dysfunctional Anunnaki… not to mention whatever was the base genetic structure of the primitive hominid that was used with which Anunnaki genes were mixed.

So the Earth was by itself as a normal planet in space before AD 900, at the latest. Due to all the visits and activities of the Others, many edifices and objects were left on the Earth, and these were left when the 4D Earth was replicated into the HVR 3D Simulation. It is reduced to a 3D holographic replicated planet, still in 4D, which means it is not the original 4D Earth, but a Simulation subject to 3D laws thus limiting the greater abilities of souls while on Earth. The Quarantine primarily keeps Others from entering and disrupting the HVR, but it also keeps the Earth's low vibration from afflicting nearby space.

That's the high-level view, and I agree that it is not that useful, but it is the basic scenario that has led to where we are now and why. It was merely a background because some people want to know. The more important and useful information is yet to follow.

The Low-level View

For best coherency, this section will be an overview of the salient information given, chapter by chapter. Then there will be a one-page Grand Summary.

Chapters 1 – 4

These chapters are being combined as it was merely for historically comparative purposes that the different versions of creation vs evolution were offered. There was some truth in many of the reported issues, but since that was the Earth in 4D (before the HVR Sphere), it is just given for background purposes.

Those that were called the Anunnaki did exist and they did create Man on the planet. Several versions, some better than others. Those versions that didn't work out, because they were not physically strong enough to do the labor, or they weren't intelligent enough to follow instructions and think about what was the next step in a sequence of instructions, had to be removed, and up until Man was given the ability to procreate, it was fairly easy to control the humans. Allowing them to procreate did remove the onus on the science staff of cloning and birthing additional workers, but when they escaped into the wilderness surrounding Anunnaki encampments, they would breed unchecked and their numbers and noise increased.

A significant part of these chapters was the Chart of Creation, Part 1A in Chapter 1 – this shows who was created when. It also points out that there were soulless humans created early on, and later in Chapter 5 it was seen that the Greeks and Maya knew about them. Basically there are two types of humans on the planet – ensouled and soulless.

The Anunnaki did mine the resources and shuttle them up into orbit where the waiting freighters and their crew would ship them back to their planet. Because the original Anunnaki were serpentine in appearance, that gave rise to Serpent wisdom and cults in the inhabited world because the Anunnaki were wise, and sought initially to develop the ethics and faith of the humans under their tutelage. Special human priest intermediaries were developed to serve as leaders of the humans, privy to what the Anunnaki leaders wanted. In this capacity, the rules and regulations evolved into a religion, and you followed the rules or the gods would remove you. Many of the humans escaped from time to time and formed their own independent tribes and their own pagan worship rituals.

The **ziggurats and temples** atop Mayan pyramids were where the Anunnaki lords stayed when overseeing a region. They interfaced with the humans though their appointed human priests as a lot of humans found them ugly. Science officer Enki later discovered he could create a **hybrid** that looked human but had Anunnaki genetics and mental capabilities, and thus later generations of Anunnaki like Marduk, Inanna and Apollo looked human and were more acceptable to the humans. Sometimes the Anunnaki hybrids interbred with the humans (usually the *Adapa* humans) and this produced humans with advanced abilities, such as Sargon, Alexander the Great, Apollonius and later, Moses.

A significant part of Chapter 3 was the Vatican opening up to the idea of sentient life on other planets and their theory that any ETs smart enough to get here would also have a better understanding of God and Man's place in the Universe.

Lastly, it was brought out that appearance of unknown beings and objects might be part of a **Control System** designed to entrain Man into a more advanced technology and religion. To that end, avatars were sent to guide Man (Christ, Buddha, Krishna), and advanced technology was inserted into Man's world (airships, UFOs) to encourage and inspire him.

Chapter 5

A very important part of living and surviving on Earth is to realize that there are two basic types of humans – ensouled and soulless. The Greeks called the soulless *hylics* and later Boris Mouravieff called them Pre-Adamics. They are also called OPs (Organic Portals) since they are flesh and blood (organic) and the Astral Neggs can operate through them (hence, they are a kind of portal into our world). It is nothing new but the information has been buried or ignored in today's world, perhaps because some of them are sociopaths. The sure way to identify them is by the presence/absence of an aura, and since most people can't see that, the information is ignored in favor of just saying that all humans are alike and some are just dysfunctional and misanthropic.

The major differences between ensouled humans and the soulless humans was emphasized, and the point was to identify them by their behavior – being careful to note that even the ensouled may have OP-like behavior. The key element and drawback of an OP is that they have **no soul** (and hence no aura) and thus they have no conscience – which explains their insensitive behavior.

Lastly, it was emphasized that there are different types of OPs and some of them serve a very important function on the Earth nowadays. They are bit players in the Greater Drama and often provide catalyst for the ensouled humans – providing lessons that if an ensouled human A did a negative act to another ensouled human B, it would incur negative Karma for soul A, and then no one gets out of here. OPs do not incur Karma as it is a construct only for souls in the HVR Earth realm. And OPs are also the NPCs of the Simulation.

Chapter 6

The most important information in this chapter was that of the Neggs, the counterpart to the Beings of Light, or Angels, who according to Man's Script see to it that he gets his lessons in this lifetime. The Neggs and the Beings of Light work together both knowing what a person's Karma is and what his Script says he can do and not do – a person is born with a Script; it is the basic lesson plan for this life. OPs don't have scripts. A very young, undeveloped soul has a more simple Script, as the lessons are often more basic, and there is less freedom compared to an old soul who has learned much and has more leeway (i.e., originality) in his/her Script.

The Neggs are not demons and they are not evil. They are Beings of Light who still have a point of Light way down inside, but it is suppressed while they administer the 'dark side' of a person's lessons. The Angels administer the blessings, protect and guide a person while the Neggs administer curses, and seek to derail and cause harm. The Neggs do not have free reign to do whatever they want, whenever they want – the Beings of Light oversee them and that is why the two work together.

It is worth repeating why this arrangement exists. If there were only Angels who could bless and afflict, guide and deceive, or heal and kill that could be a rather schizophrenic being. It was deemed to be much simpler for the Angels to always be 100% proactive, and for the Neggs to always be 100% negative. It is simpler to have a separate Jeckyll and a separate Hyde. However, there is nothing the Neggs can do that exceeds Man's ability to handle it and overcome… it is just that Man hasn't discovered that yet. But don't underestimate them: the Neggs are playing hardball – they are sometimes out to take you out, if they can. Yet their efforts are often moderated and mollified by the Beings of Light, per your Script.

Your job is not to avoid Neggs, nor seek to be a warrior and kick Negg butt, nor is it to be so holy, or gain so much Light, that they can't see you (as has been falsely said).

> **Your job is to master the body, discover the truth, and understand what this place is, how you came to be here, and how to return to the realm to which you really belong… Show that you are worthy to be released.** [1]
> **An Earth Graduate.**

Chapter 7

It is important to understand that an ensouled human is a special creation. The soul carries with it a connection to the godhead, or Oversoul which is your immediate Source knows truth and Light. The soul is eternal and cannot be destroyed (except by Higher Beings as Dr. Newton discovered when discussing really defective souls). When an ensouled human dies, their soul passes over to the Other Side for a lifetime review, to evaluate what they need to learn next, and then after possible schooling in the Interlife, the soul is put into a new life somewhere in the Universe… it doesn't have to be back on Earth, but if the important Earth lessons weren't learned, it most likely will be a **recycling** back to Earth, and might even be back into the same lifetime that the soul failed to master. As the soul repeats a lifetime, there will be episodes of **Déjà Vu** – because s/he has been there before, has done that before, has seen and done that before…

If a soul has done well in a lifetime, they counsel with a more advanced Teacher and choose another incarnation – even in another timeline, realm or type of body.

The ensouled human has a terrific potential that scares those beings who do not have souls. After achieving a certain level of knowledge and personal growth, the soul can serve in a number of capacities in the Father of Light's kingdom… and may wind up running a sub-realm somewhere, guiding and controlling what goes on there. Obviously, the soulless would seek to stop souls from growing if they can – hence the darkness, disinformation and deception on Earth. The soulless will obfuscate, disinform, derail and destroy whatever they can --- to try and avoid the inevitable. And they are here on Earth, too. While they do not know why they fight the Light, subconsciously they create a small Hell on Earth, usually as sociopaths, or OPs, and it is the job of the ensouled person to identify those people, and rise above the mess that they create. It often cannot be stopped/changed/fixed because that is the nature of Earth – the OPs (NPCs) provide catalyst, and as soon as an area of 'darkness' is removed, another springs up. But that doesn't mean that one should ignore darkness and ignorance – it really counts FOR you in your life review if you succeed in overcoming and stopping any form of darkness.

The soul is a spark of the Divine, and is multi-aspected, meaning that it usually splits and incarnates into different realms for different experiences. This is a **Multiverse**, and while one aspect of a soul A is on Earth, another aspect of A may be on Mars, or maybe in a different time or dimension. What happens to soul A aspect 1 on Earth may influence how soul A aspect 2 on Andromeda may feel – the two are connected and for no reason that aspect 1 is aware of, the experience of aspect 2, if traumatic enough, can impact aspect 1 – especially if the two aspects are what is often called a **Twinsoul**.

Lastly, when a soul comes to Earth, to be born, it comes with a purpose (often represented by its **Script**), and it will already have chosen a body and a family and a country and a time in which to be born. Usually the soul does not enter the baby's body until <u>at birth</u> (so abortion is not killing a soul, just denying a 'house' for it to live in while on Earth). And as a lot of people have found, but not understood, the body has a life/mind of its own – e.g., try and control habits! – and if the soul does not enter the body, the body can still live and move forward – as an OP. The soul may back out if the body/mind of the baby has a defect that would preclude that soul using the vehicle to meet its lessons. However, some souls choose a defective body to learn patience and overcome prejudice or limits.

Scripts are not 100% controlling, nor are they cast in concrete. Most have **points of choice** in them, where the soul must choose a path and that 'rewires' the Script for another set of potentials and opportunities. A lot of scripts have several options for how the soul can exit the body and Earth realm (i.e., via death). If a Script gets off track, the person may receive a visit from a Being of Light, and may or may not remember what was decided, but the Script can be modified for new lessons, or the soul may opt to die in his/her sleep and start over. Be clear: **no one makes a soul do anything**, options are always discussed and consequences reviewed and then the soul (who is usually rougher on itself than the Angels or Teachers would ever be!) decides what it wants to do… and that may succeed or fail. It is all a learning process.

Chapters 8 - 11

These chapters dealt with the **Trilogy of Errors** (Part III of the book) that was referred to when it was said: "Almost everything you think you know about Physical Science, Earth History and Religion is false." The keyword is 'almost' as not everything is false or wrong, but there are a lot of errors – promoted by the PTB working in concert with the OPs (and hence the Dissidents) to keep humans simple and dumb.

The 3D rulers, the PTB, cannot have an educated public, a well-informed public, a public who knows the truth – such a bunch of smart sheep are impossible to rule. Lords need serfs. Dumb serfs who can't even balance their checkbooks so they can be told what to do. Sorry, but that is not a conspiracy, it has just been the Agenda of the PTB for centuries (due to their Anunnaki mindset) and with today's technology, they are about to enforce and control information via the Media and Education. Even today, there is a 'spin' put on events that even though many people saw something happen, the public is told what it really meant, who did it, and to forget it… Anunnaki control has never left the planet.

How's it working so far?

So why does **Science** have errors? Well, Biology and Chemistry don't because anyone anywhere on the planet can replicate experiments in those fields, and there is no 'deeper' or "Quantum Chemistry" as there is in Physics wherein the underlying truth of our universe can be misconstrued. And that is why Chapter 8 seeks to open people's eyes …

And it is so important that it has been necessary to diss and ignore the astrophysicist who has the answers that Quantum Physics is still looking for – his Subquantum Kinetics has solved the riddles of Quantum Physics which is still, comparatively, dealing with a flat Earth. Hence, Dr. LaViolette has been given some coverage to amplify that the truth can be known and we don't need to invent non-productive theories about Strings and Higgs Bosons.

Chapter 9 also presents new information on DNA, general genetics, epigenetics, and the Bionet in the body. It also examines the power, energy and intelligence of the Heart as a way to amplify the teaching that ensouled Man is a special creation.

The second part of the Trilogy of Errors is the disinformation about our planet's **History**. The geologists think the planet is old because that is what Evolution needs to work out its theory, and they are using an unreliable measuring tool in C-14 … but it is interesting that coal and oil do not need millions of years to develop, and **Man and the dinosaurs were both here at the same time:** fossils show both footprints in the same strata.

Dr. Fomenko has shown that a lot of Western history contains 'phantom parallels' and errors suggesting that someone backdated a lot of Earth history before AD 1600 and it was thanks to the printing press that the last 400 years haven't been modified. Even if Dr. Fomenko's corrected timelines are off, adjusted for the chronology error he feels is most plausible, there are questions in our assumed history timeline that don't hold water. Why did no contemporary of Jesus write about him? Why are we told that the American Indians all originated in Asia and came across the Bering Straight, when some Indians have European DNA? Why are we told that the Mayans built their pyramids, when the steps of most Mayan pyramids are way too steep for a human to navigate? And why are we never shown what is **inside** the temple at the top of the Chichen Itza pyramid?

Why are we not shown the anachronistic glyphs on the walls of the Egyptian pyramid at Zoser (Djoser) at Saqqara in the Abydos temple (helicopter, submarine, jet plane) ? Interesting (in the image below) are the "boxes" or picket fence squares below what appears to be a helicopter – the same "boxes" have been recorded during satellite fly-overs on Mars. They aren't hieroglyphs, so what are they? The helicopter looks to be following a submarine, and below that is an aircraft of some sort – reminiscent of the small 2" gold planes found in Peru. And below that is what appears to be a glider…

Glyphs Inside Pyramid of Djoser

credit: http://www.mysteriesofancientegypt.com/2012/10/the-helicopter-hieroglyphic-symbol.html

There is a lot of effort and money spent to keep Man's real past on Earth hidden…because a think tank (The Brookings Inst.) back in the 60's suggested that humans would find the truth about themselves and their planet too hard to handle…. Or could it be that the PTB cannot maintain power over the sheep if the sheep wake up?

Religion was the third part of the Trilogy of Errors, and was a hard chapter to write. Many things had to be removed so as not to totally offend the faithful. Yet certain hard truths that can all be verified, by inspecting the Bible, or history were left in. The objective was not to offend anyone, but point out inconsistencies and omissions just as was done in the Science and History sections.

Religion was designed to control Man because he does need a system to live by, whether it is ethics, religion, or behavior-oriented, Man has been too wild because of the inherited Anunnaki genes. Without a code to live by, whether it is Christian, Muslim, Buddhist or Hindu, as does pagan Man, a tribe, city or nation will devolve into chaos and cease to exist. Religion has overall been a proactive organizing influence – even if Man had to be threatened with Hell, and even, unfortunately via the Inquisition, killed if he would not comply. Yes, it is that important to establish rules and order on this planet, without such it would be a planet of chaos. Thus the Elite and Church are not to be hated for what they did; with a bit of analysis it will be seen that they did what had to be done at the time.

*This book is not for the "unwashed masses", it is for those who know something is wrong, that we're **de**volving as a society, and who are smarter than the average human. They know there is more that they are told to be doing or learning, and they want to, but they may not know what they are to do with the advanced awareness. This book is for them.*

I repeat, don't blame the Elite. They have no nasty conspiracy to lock us all down and deny our freedoms. The Elite don't really have a choice in what they have to do (in the coming years) because the humans are still ignorant and unruly, and destruction of society and the planet, by those who use people and resources for their own end, will not be allowed. (The PTB are a different story, and are not the Elite.)

In a way, the recommendation by Rev. John Shelby Spong is a great idea – upgrade (all) Western religion to reflect the global and latest scientific views. Just as Christianity, merely as an example, is now outmoded and the Bible has errors and inconsistencies, we need a more intelligent Religion that the growing, thinking populace can adopt. The longer we wait to do this, the more apostasy will grow, and Man will abandon what faith and ethics he does possess.

Chapters 12 - 13

At this point, the reader is given an introduction to vision, holograms and hypnosis to emphasize that we can all be tricked into seeing things that are not there – as well as not seeing things that are there. Vision and perception are holographically based.

Leading up to a revelation of what this planet really is, it was important to review the *Star Trek* Holodeck, and **replication** as a methodology which works with **holography** to create a virtual world. Then a review followed of what Charles Fort, Robert Monroe and Stuart Wilde had discovered about our world. Fort made a big deal about the *Gegenschein* which reflects off something around Earth, and Monroe did many OBEs and actually hit the wall surrounding Earth that Fort wrote about. Then Wilde described "…walls morphing and seeing gridlines over the landscape…" – all as a lead-in to what this place really is.

Further analysis supporting Chapter 12 was given in Chapter 13, suggesting ways to know if we are in a Simulation or not, and containing a breakout of the key aspects of same.

The HVR Earth Simulation definition was given in Chapter 13.

Chapter 14

Because ensouled Man is to become an Earth Graduate, and that is the goal for all souls, then graduating from the planet (or School) is very important. As impetus for getting out of here, reasons for doing so are given by showing how controlled/manipulated Man is, followed by a brief review of why the planet cannot continue to support Man much longer, and he will have to leave, graduated or not. Those who don't graduate (learn from their Scripts and grow spiritually and mentally), will be recycled.

Following the reasons it does not look profitable to stay indefinitely on Earth, a further explanation is given, referring to Mouravieff's data, of what recycling can do to a soul and how this translates into the common experience of **Déjà vu**. Lastly, there is a brief review of environmental and health issues to pay attention to, to (ironically) lengthen one's stay on Earth with the goal of being healthier to make sure one can complete one's lessons.

The Basic Twenty-two

Now that the first 14 chapters have been capsulized, an even shorter version follows. It was asked earlier, What has to be true for the planet to look the way it does? The following suggest the conclusion in Chapters 12-13 is correct.

So here is what is concurrent with Man being quarantined in an HVR Sphere:

1. The planet is a **young planet**, maybe 400,000-500,000 years old – science bears it out. The Earth is not hollow but there are large caverns which are occupied by those who assist the Control System.
2. The **chronology** of Western Civilization has been seriously modified with the goal of making it look like we have been here a long time, and we know nothing, really, backwards of AD 900.
3. Man's **DNA** has been cut down to just the basics, to control him; and much of his 'junk DNA' can be re-programmed to do greater things.
4. The Anunnaki **genetic legacy** was retained in Man by the Higher Beings who control and direct the HVR Sphere.
5. There are no 3D ETs in a 4D VR realm, and some UFOs are illusions, or interdimensional. Some are Earth-based craft.
6. There is no Mothman, Bigfoot, Mermaids or Chupacabra – they are also illusions produced by the **Control System**.
7. **Karma** operates within a person's **Script** and as such is orchestrated to produce a specific lesson/growth in that person.
8. **Reincarnation** is an option -- provided you're not recycled. **Déjà vu** is the clue that you <u>have</u> been recycled.
9. There is no coming Apocalypse, nor Endtime, but 2009-2016 seems to portend a shift to a new Era.
10. The **OPs** exist and have no aura or soul; they are largely puppets and Placeholders and 'portals' through which the HVR Sphere may provide catalyst to help Man to grow.
11. Man has an eternal, **multidimensional soul**; different aspects inhabit different places and 'times' concurrently.
12. **Neggs** exist but are subject to the Light and Higher Beings. They provide negative catalyst to spiritual growth.
13. Religion was largely created by the Anunnaki to proactively control Man's behavior.
14. With the HVR Sphere's vibrational enhancements, Man can wake up and surpass the teachings of conventional religion.
15. **Vision and memory** are both holographically-based.
16. Man is not alone here but the Others are part of the **Greater Drama**.
17. Darwin was correct about Natural Selection and Survival of the Fittest – now called **Epigenetics**.
18. **Subquantun Kinetics** will replace Quantum Physics because it is simpler and adequately defines our world.
19. **Serpent Wisdom** groups all over the planet sought to preserve important metaphysical teachings of the Anunnaki.

20. There is **no Hell, no Satan**, no demons – but if your belief system requires it, the Neggs will create same for your growth… Be careful what you ask for. (Belief = asking subconsciously.)
21. The Elite are not the PTB, but the PTB allegedly report to the Elite.
22. The Higher Beings running the Simulation sometimes have to stop the the Show, or Drama, and clean up the planet, called a **"Wipe and Reboot,"** and then restart an Era with Man reinserted.

This is part of what has to be true for Earth to look the way it does. The Basic Twenty-two. Now let's look a couple of minor points to round out the basic concepts.

Earth Eras

At this point, it would be relevant to clarify what has been meant by 'Era' inasmuch as the periods that Man has been living in are generally consecutive, time-wise, but the Eras are separated by the oft-suggested "Wipe and Reboot" thus inserting gaps in the chronology.

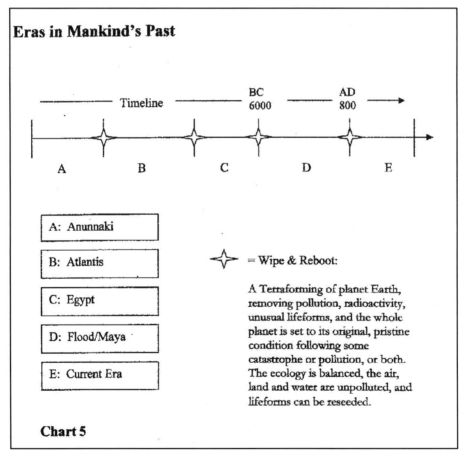

Eras in Mankind's Past

Timeline ──── BC 6000 ──── AD 800 ──→

A   B   C   D   E

A: Anunnaki

B: Atlantis   = Wipe & Reboot:

C: Egypt

A Terraforming of planet Earth, removing pollution, radioactivity, unusual lifeforms, and the whole planet is set to its original, pristine condition following some catastrophe or pollution, or both. The ecology is balanced, the air, land and water are unpolluted, and lifeforms can be reseeded.

D: Flood/Maya

E: Current Era

Chart 5

The above Chart 5 is a basic diagram showing a number of past Eras, principally characterized by a dominant race/civilization. Eras have no fixed length. What happens in one Era is often left for the archeologists of the succeeding Era to discover – hence the Anunnaki <u>were</u> here, but that was another Era. Eras are terminated when it gets out of hand: either too much violence or too much pollution, or the Greater Script (covered shortly) is tending to go off-track.

In Chart 5, note that when the current Era E was begun, around AD 800-900, by AD 900 Man had lost several hundred continuous years of history, and the history that pertained to the end of Era D, which began with the Flood and ended with the Maya disappearing, left a curious gap – which Dr. Fomenko explains in Chapter 10. A history was provided for Man by back-dating and copying salient history from the beginning of Era E (AD 900-AD 1500) to make it look as though we had a more continuous history with the past. This resulted in duplicate historical elements, called **"phantom parallels."**

The dinosaurs were removed at the end of Era B. The Flood was the "Wipe and Reboot" that closed Era C. The start of Era D is approximate. December 2012 was not the end of the world. The Aztecs, Maya and Hopi have all spoken of preceding 'Worlds' or Eras that ended by fire, water, calamity, etc and they like to say that we are in the 4th or 5th World – depending on source. So the concept is not new.

Man's Corrupt DNA

Where does Man's corrupt but unique DNA come from? "Corrupt" as in: the incomplete DNA with its transmission of traits that lead to violence, sickle-cell anemia, color-blindness, lactose-intolerance, allergies, Parkinson's and other diseases, **but** "unique" in that it also can transmit aptitudes for playing piano or mastering several foreign languages, and a physical agility to be proud of.

First, it needs to be said that whether or not the Anunnaki gave Man potentially corrupt DNA (carrying their own negative traits), souls have been around for a long time and when a soul incarnates into a body, that body takes on the soul's level of development, also called an 'energy signature.' The soul's energy and karmic debts **imprint the body** with that soul's energetic signature: shy, angry, naïve, fearful, intelligent, vindictive, irresponsible, loving…. even handicapped or birthmark aspects. And that in turn 'rewires' the DNA to sustain/reflect the orientation. And if the energy is too strong, or discordant, as in the example of anger, the body rebels and besides hormonal imbalances, cancer can be the result of cells receiving dysfunctional signals on the Bionet that was discussed in Chapter 9.

Mind, emotions, DNA and soul energy are all interrelated. Interesting that the mind and body are interrelated, and feelings and the spirit are interrelated.

Conditioning

Man has also been conditioned to reject the truth through constant reinforcement by the Media, by the churches, and by the schools, so that anything that does not fit into the "established teachings" about science, history or religion must therefore be erroneous. In addition, the Media is filtered today such that any unusual news that would make you wonder and begin to research a subject doesn't show up on the 10 o'clock news any more. It used to.

Interesting to note that during the 24/7 TV coverage of Michael Jackson's death, the History and Discovery channels ran shows on 'Oliver' (the 'human' chimpanzee), the alleged 'Hobbits' (of Indonesia), and very interesting documentaries on USOs and UFOs. Another channel ran an interesting piece on how everyone/everything around the world is related through no more than 6 connecting steps. Do I have to tell you what the sheep were watching?

And that is by design. The PTB don't want the sheep to think or wonder, but just go along with whatever they're told – the same old pablum every day so that they can't learn the truth and thus acquire enough Light to get out of here. For the PTB to have a job, they must have an audience. And they are currently desperate to sustain the old Matrix (mindsets) they have always promoted. Due to freewill, the Elite cannot override them, but they can and do obstruct them where necessary.

The significance of this is that your DNA can empower or limit your consciousness. Parts of your DNA can shut down when not used ("Use it or lose it") and that is the goal of the PTB and the large number of purile TV shows – you are not only what you eat, but what you watch and listen to. So, what are junk food, Rap and Heavy Metal music doing to people?

The OPs

In an effort to control this place, you'd also provide the 'puppets' on the planet who would do the will of the STS agenda and Neggs, **or** the STO agenda and Beings of Light. There is a Greater Script which characterizes each Era and Man is subjected to different drama and challenges in each Era. So, like it or not, the OPs provide the drama to keep Man on track with the Greater Script (examined in the next section).

Since Man has freewill, he won't always do what he should, much less what the PTB would like, and the PTB don't always do what the Elite would like, and so to steer civilization onto the Path that will have the most catalyst (good or bad) for Man to learn from, the standard OPs are controllable and serve to act as both a feedback mechanism to Man and a derailing, deceiving mechanism to push, pull or prod Man into the experiences needed to grow him. And the experiences can be positive or negative.

OPs (NPCs) are very necessary as an interactive element in every person's drama; other ensouled people who would be required by your **Karma** to lie, cheat and steal from you, or worse, would themselves incur more negative karma – even though their actions are required by your Karma. Such "give and take" dramas are <u>not</u> usually staged between ensouled beings. So, OPs are used as <u>they incur no Karma</u> and can deliver the negative experiences to you that other ensouled people could not do without generating more negative Karma for themselves.

Lastly, to repeat a related major point: the OPs (or NPCs) <u>are</u> what help keep the Greater Script for this 3D Construct, also called the HVR Sphere, on track. Man has freewill and does not always do what he should, preferring to boogie and party instead of studying, inquiring and cleaning up his act – to get out of here. Many don't want to leave the Earth.

Most don't know they should get out. So the OPs can be manipulated astrally to drive the Script, giving Man his 'lessons', in turn manipulating Man (ultimately) for the greater good.

Control Issue Revisited

After a review of the Neggs and OPs, it would appear that Man is beset with entities trying to control him. And that is the appearance of living in this special HVR Sphere, and that is why it was also said that freewill is an illusion maintained by the ego. In this reality, Man does not control much and that was why it was also said that Man cannot create his day, nor manifest whatever he wants whenever he wants it.

Can the student control the School?

> *Hint: there are many people who seem to be creating their lives the way they want them and that may inspire ensouled humans to try and do likewise. But consider: what if the people who appear to create their day and easily manifest riches are* **OPs***? Remember that illusion and deception are part of the gameplan on this Earth, and OPs have no karma or internal issues that would prevent them from living an envious life...*

Remember that it is all about growth for the **ensouled** humans on Earth; it is not about getting whatever you want, nor is it even about being happy. So freewill is not the issue: a kind of Control System is in place … see Appendix C.

When you incarnated, you got a **Script** that 'controls' what you can be, do and have. It is a kind of control: if it isn't in your Script, or your Script prohibits it, you aren't going to be/do/have it. If your Script doesn't prohibit being/doing/having something, then you can. The only way to know is to try and see if what you want is blocked or not.

> *Your Script may reflect your Karma but is not Karma itself.*

The Father of Light is not an ogre and only 'controls' to assure focus on whatever we need to learn. Remember that the Earth Graduate must go through the lessons, trials, tests, etc of the Greater Script that will produce the quality being, ready to serve in higher realms.

There is no steel without fire.

> *Think of the Greater Script as the operating system in a computer, and your life Script as a program (eg, MS Word) running under the 'control' of the operating system. The many programs experience a give-and-take with the operating system, and they can function because the operating system empowers them. They are not able to do whatever they want; the operating system acts as a 'control' and monitors their activities and use of all resources.*

> *Note, too, that the Greater Script also includes the Control System (Appendix C).*

Freewill vs Control

Interestingly, Shakespeare gave us a clue about our ability to control our lives, our destiny, or as we have been saying for several chapters: you do <u>not</u> create your day, much less your life. Your Script governs <u>generally</u> what you can do and what you can get, as well as it governs what the Neggs are permitted to do and not do. And your Script reflects your Ground of Being (PFV) which helps determine what experiences you <u>attract</u>. So you don't create but you do attract.

And get this: you agreed to your Script before you incarnated; no one comes here without a plan. You don't have to like it. Part of it might have been set up for you, but your job is to <u>handle it</u>. Said Shakespeare:

> There's a divinity that shapes our ends,
> rough-hew them how we will… *Hamlet* V, 2

For "divinity," substitute the words Greater Script…and this opens up the subject of freewill and control – do we really have either in our lives? Let's start with an example.

We have a big Malamute dog in the backyard. His name is Nosey… because he is a very curious dog and inserts himself into whatever you're doing in the backyard. Sprinkler repair? He's there to advise. Dig a hole for a new tree? He knows the hole is for him to climb into. Rake the leaves? Just something to roll around in… We control where he can go and generally what he can do. We have placed him in the backyard – he has no choice about that. Due to the fence he cannot get out. However, he is 'free' to do whatever he wants within the limits of the backyard (and take the consequences)! Thus you could say he has <u>limited</u> freewill, while it is his 'destiny' to live in the backyard.

Believe it or not, it is the same way for Man on this Earth. Instead of a backyard, Man has an HVR Sphere. Instead of a fence, Man has a barrier. Instead of an owner, Man has the Watchers (Beings of Light). And if he destroys something, he has to face the consequences. Eventually the dog learns to calm down and work with his surroundings. So does Man… sometimes.

Man's Script <u>generally</u> controls what he can do, where he can go, and what he gets and doesn't get. The Script even determined his parents and any physical defects he would have to experience. And it determines the exit point from a lifetime, when, and what form that can take. Within the limits of the Script, Man otherwise has "freewill" to do whatever he fancies – appropriate or inappropriate – as he encounters preprogrammed '**points of choice'**.

.

> *Note that in many cases, incoming souls with a Script, participated in the 'design' of that Script; their birth location, choice of parents, and the opportunities and obstacles in their lives. While it is <u>not</u> a case of 100% Fate, things are a lot more scripted than Man would like to think, and there are some optional <u>choices</u> he must face.*

> *You cannot create your day as you go – unless you are an old soul and They give permission to set up the Script that way.*

The controls (i.e., "boundaries" of your life as set by your Script) are to make sure you experience whatever your Script says you are to experience. How you deal with events is up to you – knowing that your inappropriate response(s) could damage your body, lengthen your stay here, or make yourself (and others) miserable. Insisting on your way, when you want it, the way you want it, was <u>something that got you put here in the first place</u>… you might want to reconsider your ego's point of view that you can do anything you want while here. This School is not controlled by the student.

If you resist learning and overcoming tests, trials, and blockages, and hate your life, you may consider turning to drinking, drugs, sex or even <u>suicide</u> as a way of escape. All will result in your being sent back, with the "screws" tightened more than they were the last time,[2] requiring that you face what you were just sure you couldn't handle. The Higher Beings are serious about your learning what is expected of you. And, ironically, even though you may not be aware of it, **you <u>are</u> more capable than you could ever imagine** – technically, you <u>can</u> handle whatever is given you – even Skid Row – and that is one of the lessons (usually reserved for "last time" souls who are about to graduate from Earth) that has to become <u>part of you</u>.

If you are never 'tested' how will anybody ever know what you are capable of – let alone you?

Handle It

The Beings of Light never ask you whether you like what you get or not, or whether you're happy – that is irrelevant. You are merely expected to handle it.

The experience of control is not to be met with anger, resistance, and depression. Whatever is in your life is there for the effect it has on you. Catalyst. The intended objective is to rise above it, not take it personally, and **handle it**. It doesn't need analysis, it doesn't call for rebellion, denial, suicide, or an attempt at controlling one's life.

> When will you be unruffled, no matter what happens? [3]

If you can't control (change, fix or stop) something in your life, it is a sure sign that it is scripted **catalyst**. It is not intended that you can control catalyst. Handle what you get, and don't wish/try/hope to get what you can't get. Just handle it. Or, you'll be back…

Handle Sex Orientation

An interesting case in point is a soul who for many lifetimes was a man, and to experience the other sex, 'he' incarnates in a female body. As the life progresses, 'he' finds the female role is not to his liking. So 'he' undergoes a sex change, to escape the female experience. As souls we are to honor our 'assignments' and the sex change operation may be seen as a "cop out" and that soul may have to come back and prove 'he' can handle it.

Remember: souls are not male or female; they are androgynous.

The gods may not require a return into a female role if that soul is not trying to experience and master the complete human experience. If it was a whim, or a mistake, it is often negotiable on the Other Side. By the way, you have just learned why males are attracted to other males – the orientation of a predominantly 'she' in a male body is due to many lifetimes as a woman, reinforcing the orientation to have sex with a male. The same applies to the lesbian phenomenon.

It is not a biochemical or psychological issue, and that is why the American Psychiatric Association declassified homosexuality as an issue that they could treat. These souls are still due our respect and compassion – they have taken on a tough assignment and don't need us throwing rocks at them… unless they are OPs and their agenda is to disrupt society the way OPs do – see Chapter 5. However, since people cannot see auras, and thus discern the difference, it is suggested that we give the Gays the benefit of the doubt and accept them for what they are, encouraging them to adapt to their role.

No one does anything that does not fit within the boundaries of the Greater Script, else it would mean that The God is not in control, and that is not the nature of the Father of Light. Since God, the One, is not a person (Chapter 11), It is an entraining, intelligent Force or Consciousness that underlies and empowers the Greater Script which is the **intent** of a yet Greater Intelligence outside this universe which oversees the Multiverse. The intent of an advanced being is very powerful.

Proactive Reality

There are higher souls, Wanderers and Indigos, on the planet at this time to offset negative energy, in an attempt to stabilize the HVR Sphere and anchor the increasing Light (rising vibrations) so that potentially all can assimilate them. At some point, once the "100th Monkey" effect of the rising vibrations has been reached among those who respond (i.e., go with the Flow), the Sphere as a grid will be dissolved and some souls will be exposed to a more true 4D or 5D energy realm. Those that did not 'graduate' will start again in another 3D virtual realm.

Those that return to the 4D realm from which we came, are considered Graduates. If really great progress was made in the Earth trip, the soul may move on to the 5D. What is the difference?

3D is to learn the lessons of Ego, Me and My and Mine.
4D is to learn the lessons of compassion and caring.
5D is to learn the lessons of truth, right action and speaking.

6D when the student is ready is to merge Ego, Love and Truth.

MAN

What is Man that Thou are mindful of him?
--- Psalm 8:4

You are an eternal soul with the potential to develop your divine connection to the Godhead, and if you were created complete but undeveloped (would God create flawed souls?), then why would you need Karma, or reincarnation, or further training and 'lessons?' Answer: because you have become dysfunctional and need to be rehabilitated. Because you don't know that, the Higher Beings, who are benevolent, keep you here. You are contained, watched over, and should be seeking to work your way out.

To repeat: the secret is to <u>not</u> get blown away by the frustrations, upsets, and failures – it is all part of the **catalyst** to effect the changes in you. It is not to be taken personally. God loves Man and He designed the Great Script. You were <u>not</u> given a role you cannot fill; God doesn't set people up for failure... Handle it.

Maybe now we can understand why the Chinese sage said:

> There is nothing left to you at this moment but to have a good laugh.
> -Zen Master

This is what ego does not want to hear: that he and his life are not that important. The Chinese and Hindu sages have always laughed at Man's egotistical pretensions; Man is standing in his own way – hence the 'joke.'

Man's **ego** is the problem – it keeps him surviving, and it says he's special, but it prevents him from accepting the humble truth: he is just like every other soul and the more humble, compassionate, cooperative, forgiving and <u>respectful of self</u> and others he can be, the sooner he gets out of here.

> Ego leads to rebellion, resistance, wars -- and wayward souls' containment.

And that brings us to the unthinkable conclusion about the purpose of Earth that is reached when all the dots have been connected.

Conclusions

Why is this not Man's planet?
Why does he not belong here?
Why is Man protected here?
Why is there so much error, deception and disinformation?
Why does Man never 'get it together?'
Why are history, science and religion not accurate?
Why is there a lifescript, and karma?
Why is Man often recycled and rarely reincarnated?
Why are the Greys upgrading the human species?
Why does Mankind as a whole not have psychic powers?
Why is life such a struggle on Earth?
Why have no ETs landed and publicly worked with us?

in short:

Why is Man confined to the Earth?
Why does Earth have so many problems?

Due to Man's ego, ignorance and not wanting to face the truth, Man devises answers to the above questions that he can live with, so he invents them:

1. Earth is a school.
2. Man is paying back Karma, individual and group.
3. The demonic spirits oppress and bind Man.
4. Man is someone else's cattle.
5. Man was born in sin.
6. Earth is a prison planet.
7. Earth is a zoo.
8. Earth is Hell.
9. This all a 'lucid dream', it isn't real.

Or the New Age oversimplification:
10. Man is here to develop his godhood and get what he wants.

Whatever you think is the purpose of Earth has been, it is now more, and it has changed with the current Era (since AD 900).

There **is** a God, and there have been Jesus-like teachers on Earth. The Father loves Man. Man has a beautiful, dynamic potential and divine heritage. Man <u>will</u> someday do the wonders that the Bible's Jesus said Man would do…

…so why isn't it happening?

As Chapter 12 asked: What has to be true about this place for it to look the way it does? Don't sanitariums usually have well-landscaped, pretty grounds and have uplifting places and events to inspire the patients? Is it any wonder that the Earth is very pretty but, like the sanitariums, the denizens of same are on a 'trip' all their own?

The Bottom Line

Earth is currently a rehabilitation center for wayward and defective souls.

That is why you're protected and in quarantine. That is why in 3D you cannot manifest whatever you want, when you want it. That's why external entities will not be allowed to disrupt the HVR Sphere and its 3D to 4D process. And every now and then, when Man really screws up the planet, he is removed to a holding area and a "Wipe and Reboot" (or terraforming) of Earth is done, a new Era is started, and Man is placed back in the 'asylum' … again. Of course, **Earth is also a School**.

There has to be a place to handle dense, wayward or defective souls who insist on their own way, when they want it, the way they want it… Rebellious souls who cannot get a long with others elsewhere in the Galaxy… Souls who have not learned tolerance, peace, compassion, respect, patience and service. And a lot of souls here on Earth have become defective <u>due to</u> their overly long (repeat) containment and abuse here… hence the

Higher Beings stepping in to 'rescue' Man with the new Era.

> *Remember, as was said in Chapter 7, you are an aspect of a multidimensional soul (the greater You), and You still reside in the original realm – an aspect called you has been incarnated here to learn specific lessons, and as an* **Earth Graduate***, you will be reunited with the greater You, and the other 'you' aspects that experienced specific lessons elsewhere in the Father's multiverse.*

That is why Earth has always been chaotic: wars, disease, deception, greed, pettiness and violence enough to satisfy the most **wanton** soul. Enough sex, booze and drugs to satisfy the most **hedonistic** soul.

There has to be a place where such souls can be put in a context of their equals – so they can see what <u>they</u> are like – to experience themselves at the hands of others just like them, or worse. That's why it never gets better here – and in fact, that isn't even the goal... It's not statistically possible for <u>all</u> the wayward souls here to correct and make this 3D Earth a heaven at any one time.

The desire to help/fix/change Earth or people can also be a mindset that attaches you to Earth and now, to get out of here, that <u>also</u> needs to be let go as another lesson to be learned.

> *And the frustration of not being able to fix, stop or change any of it is what leads to the* **state of futility***. That is what the Higher Beings want: the deep realization that spending more time on Earth is futile. You have to see it, feel it and really know it. That is part of your ticket out of here.*

And that doesn't mean that you don't clean up and fix pollution or bandage wounds when you see them – it simply means that trying to change the operation of the 'asylum' into a Heaven on Earth is not what it is about. The asylum has a purpose.

Earth is about rehabilitating souls before they reach the damaged state.

And that's also why the rest of local Creation (mostly 4D) is protected <u>from</u> Man. The Quarantine works both ways… like a high fence around an asylum.

That's also why the little Greys have been busy genetically upgrading rebellious and violent Man – from Cro-Magnon to Homo *sapiens*, and now to Homo *noeticus*. Each time, with each upgrade, Man has had a slightly better DNA configuration to work with, and has made more progress in self growth and in being able to connect with a higher part of himself.

R – E – S – P – E – C – T

Aretha Franklin would love it ! **Respect is the issue**: as he is now, Man does not respect himself, nor others, nor the planet – so why should any ETs respect Man? (Remember the woman in Chapter 6 was told: "When you respect yourselves, so will we.")

Lastly, if Man is to venture beyond this planet, he must grow up: no more Santa Claus or Easter Bunny type beliefs if he doesn't want to appear to be a primitive fool. Don't forget that the ETs (good and bad) all know the truth about Man: his history, his science, his religion, and his potential. How could Man function among them without at least an equal and true concept of himself and his world?

> *This is one reason there is no ET disclosure and the other is due to the fragility of the human psyche. Man is not ready thanks to the PTB.*

Why Tell People?

What makes me think I know what this place is and what we're doing here? Simple. When all the pieces fit and explain it all, you know that's it – as exciting, shocking, or counter-to-accepted-reality as it may be. In short, connecting the dots says:

Man is too precious an entity to be a permanent resident here on Earth

where anything more than one lifetime is a waste of time. So the real showstopper is to wake up and see what this place is, what Man really is, and work to actualize your way out. As the Gospel of Thomas verse 70 says – bring forth your Light. If you can't find it, build it (see Chapter 16).

The Living End

Inspiration

It is very important in this HVR Sphere, or rehab center if you will, that there be one more important element. It is often a more effective way to motivate and lead Man to become more if he can be **inspired** – by great music, art, books and movies that are of a higher vibration and thus inspire or entrain Man even if briefly into a higher state of awareness of ideas, music and art beyond what he usually sees around him.

Naturally, the OPs with their lower 3 chakras focused on survival, power and self cannot produce such works as the works are the product of the higher chakras and a connection via a 6th or 7th chakra to inspiration. Indeed, if any ensouled human is struggling with the lower 3 chakras and a few semi-opened upper chakras, they will also not have the coherent connection to the inspirational Source, often referred to as the muses.

For those who have ears to hear, and are willing to receive it, it has usually been the Starseed, Wanderers, and genetically upgraded Man, born among us, walking among us, (even some of the Elite) that we think are just like us, that produce the greater works of art: Shakespeare, Mozart, Beethoven, Michelangelo, Da Vinci, a Pasteur or Watson, even a Roddenberry, Lucas or Spielberg today. Not to mention Jesus/Apollonius, Buddha, Ghandi, Mohammed, Krishna, Lao Tzu and their teachings.

Conversely, the large percentage of mankind on the planet (ensouled but dense Man and OPs) produces most of what you see on TV, movies and in the video games – sex, violence, death, disasters, etc. The average Man wants to be <u>stimulated</u>: beer, wrestling, football, hot music, sex, drugs and the like; the average person is not looking to be <u>inspired</u>. So, how can Man become more if he doesn't see or hear more, if he is not inspired out of his walk-a-day grind? Think what effect the contents of the banal Media just mentioned have upon Man's level of mentality... and remember, it is by design by the 3D PTB who think they run this planet.

Remember that the goal of non-souled entities and the PTB was to keep Man from becoming all that he might be – keep that soul from connecting to its Source. Why? To keep the status quo on Earth as it has always been: trap the souls and recycle them. Is it working?

Rescue

Please be clear that there are no UFOs coming to rescue us, nor can we count on a Rapture. Both are unrealistic tales told by the naively hopeful, or by a fledgling Church to give a future focus to the flock. And either would today be counterproductive to achieving the purpose of this place: Exit. No rescue, no rapture. Man must learn to respect himself and the planet to progress – **there is no other place to go until he can graduate**.

In short, the average Man does not have to do much at this point, except **choose** which kind of future he wants to live in, and <u>focus on that</u>.

Candidates for Graduation

Apollonius Revisited

In retrospect, Apollonius is not a bad role model, and neither are Krishna, Buddha, nor Jesus. It was Jesus in the New Testament who said that we could do what he was doing, and that Love was the Way. All teachings of Love and Light are worth following as they echo Higher Truth and that is what we need if we are to grow and be released from this Earth. So the paths of a Buddhist, Muslim, Hindu, Jew and Christian walking in Love and Light are all walking the same way –

one need not change religion to get out of here.

Since ensouled Man is but a spark of the divine – a soul is the divine fire placed within Man – that means that Man has all the potential of a Christ, and a return to the Godhead to eventually participate in Creation. Any ensouled person has the spark of God inside them, and Man <u>can</u> connect with that spark and actualize the link to the Father – no matter what the particular religion. That is why Jesus said the kingdom of God is within you.

> *And that is the purpose of the new* **church of the future** *– to lead Man in the discovery and fulfillment of what he really is.*

Perhaps a model for **a revised Christianity**, as Bishop Spong suggested, would then be tolerance of other religions and to seek to promote a higher spirituality that leads each person to walk as best s/he can in more **Love, humility, respect and patience**. The spiritual walk is not a "one size fits all" – it begins where the person is <u>now</u> on the Way… and it progresses with as much knowledge (Light) as s/he can absorb at any one time.

> **The Way is Love and Light. Jesus said that He was the Way (personified) and that no one could come to the Father except through Him/the Way. It did not mean that Christianity or Jesus was <u>the</u> Way. It meant that walking in Love and Light was the Way – again, He was a signpost, showing the Way, and He personally demonstrated it.**

All the great teachers have sought to wake Man up for one reason: to get Man out of here and into the Father of Light's Kingdom where we can **serve**. That is called the Earth Graduate.

Potential Areas for Service

Having said that the Soul who graduates from Earth can fulfill certain basic, initial, functions in the Father's Kingdom, it can be shared that these are some of the areas open to Graduates:

> **Bio-plasmic Quantum Computer Techies** – responsible for basic computer support and maintenance.
> **Bio-plasmic Computer Programmer** – performs fractal subprogramming under supervision.
> **Akashic Records Librarian** – maintains life records' storage/retrieval.
> **Gods-in-Training I** – responsible to oversee the Simulation: Man and feedback of the Control System. Many sub-areas here.
> **Gods-in-Training II** – responsible for the Holographic stabilization and interface with the Replicator technology. Sub-areas here.
> **Soul Counselors** – responsible for evaluation, guidance and training of in-coming souls to the Interlife for further development: imprinting or vibrational adjustment. Many levels here, including Teachers.

There are many others, but it is a busy world over there; no one is sitting around on a cloud playing a harp – unless they're on a coffee break! The reason that the PTB want to block souls from progressing is mainly because of this position:

> **Gods-in-Training III** – responsible for overseeing, managing and controlling the Neggs and OPs –to make sure that lessons are properly administered (according to Scripts) and it amounts to controlling what the PTB can 'get away with.' This is as close as the Interlife comes to having a "police force."

And because I once asked, "What if the Gods-in-Training choose to abuse people, or do something nasty?" They are sent back to Earth for rehabilitation.

484

Earth School Graduate Revisited

Ensouled Man's potential, when actualized, renders him a <u>truly awesome being</u> – doing what the man called Jesus did <u>and more</u>. Jesus said it (paraphrased):

> "These things I do you shall do and greater…" John 14:12

So when does it happen? Respect yourself, develop compassion, gain knowledge, and live in patience, detach from outcomes, things and people… a long list of requirements to graduate, but that is why:

> "The **graduate** from the human experience is <u>very</u> **respected** elsewhere." [4]
> [emphasis added]

And it is easy to see why: if a soul can survive this screwed-up planet with its disrespect for everything and everybody, survive the pollution and the killer diseases, resist the temptation to lie, cheat and steal, not follow the crowd, not give in to corruption, and still emerge with his/her integrity intact, <u>that would be worthy of</u> **respect**. A soul who walks the talk and does not sell out. A soul who thinks outside the box that has been created for all of us by the PTB-dominated Media whose goal is to keep us as dumbed down robots so we will buy and do what Madison Avenue suggests.

Self-Mastery 1a

It is called self-mastery. And that starts with **self-respect**. You don't do those things that are inappropriate – like overeat, or run with hoodlums. Self-respect means the body is the temple of the divine spark, the soul that is so highly prized that there are some beings in 4D who would give anything to have one, and because they can't (I repeat, I know) they work to stop us from becoming all that we can be. When we graduate from Earth, we can be released to return to the higher Realm from which we came and in which we are then ready to serve.

> **And, repeat: One need not be perfect to get out of here…**
> **But you do have to set the ideal and have the intention to achieve it.**

If the gods had to wait until a soul on Earth attained the status of a Jesus, they'd have to wait a long time. To graduate from the 3rd Grade in elementary school, one need not know Algebra – knowing basic arithmetic and the multiplication tables will do. I suggest that being a Ghandi is sufficient, or a Lao-Tzu, or even Mother Theresa. No doubt there are further Schools awaiting souls – and Earth is not a "finishing school."

How many people think that staying in 3rd grade, or even 12th grade (high school), is all there is? (Aren't you tired of the cafeteria?) Reaching the initial stages of self-mastery and <u>intending</u> to go forward are enough to get us out of here and into a more exciting realm.

Three things are required to leave Earth as a Graduate:
> (1) you see the **futility** of demanding what you want here,
> (2) you learn, acquire **knowledge and compassion**, and
> (3) you experience and realize that **you <u>can</u> handle whatever** life throws at you.

485

Does your religion, faith or belief system assist you in doing those 3 things?

Self-Mastery 1b

Do <u>not</u> assume that the drama in your life accurately reflects who and what you are.

Do <u>not</u> let the ignorant tell you that you are wrong and so messed up that you'll never amount to anything. Keep your own counsel.

Do <u>not</u> give your power away. Make your own decisions – think outside the box.

Such a person with a lot of Light may have to work hard to trust himself, develop an **inner strength** and learn to listen to their own ideas – despite others' "helpful advice." In fact, that may be the thing that soul is here to learn – a form of self-confidence, inner strength, **self-respect** and connection with a higher part of himself. To walk calmly amid the crowd of rushing fools, know the truth, and not always follow the crowd.

Self-mastery is expected of souls who want to **graduate from the Earth school**: to live by the highest values you can when all about you are doing what is fun. It's called **Integrity**.

Self-Mastery 1c

Please note throughout the last few pages that there has been an emphasis on **self-respect**. The path of an Earth Graduate begins with it, leads to respect for others, and then to respect for the planet. Ultimately it will lead to respect for any ETs we encounter (4D and above). The Graduate knows that all are One: animals, plants, ET brothers and sisters – anything done to harm any of them ultimately harms ourself – and self-respect says we don't harm the temple – we don't eat junk food, disparage or harm self, nor do we disrespect elders, ignore traffic laws, we don't lie, cheat or steal – not because we're goody-goody twoshoes – but because that behavior **doesn't work**.

That is a big part of being an Earth Graduate – we do what works – serve, tell the truth, show compassion, open the door for someone less fortunate or who is carrying bundles, do something nice for someone because what goes 'round comes 'round. In the beginning you might help others because you know that you will be rewarded by the universe for helping others, but after a while, it becomes second nature **because it is the thing to do**.

If you respect yourself you cannot treat yourself like trash, dress crappy, pants down around your knees, half your body tattooed, the other half pierced, and a Mohawk haircut so others will notice you! … that does not respect the body when you know that you, the soul you, has the god-potential within – down the road, you <u>will</u> walk on water, heal the lame, levitate, and disappear and reappear at will. That is the popularity of *The Matrix* -- Neo represents one who can cut through the illusion, release his inner power, overcome the programming, and release the captives. Can you imagine his character smoking and drinking, joking around, wearing several tattoos, and not respecting himself?

The PTB-sponsored Media has given us some false heroes, and seeks to entrain our young people (who are often impressionable) via stalk-it-and-kill-it videos into a mindset where problems are solved with a gun. Today's movies are often too violent and sexy – because that is what sells – it takes more insight and brains to create a movie like *ET* or *Sum of All Fears*, or *Shining Through*. Even Humphrey Bogart in *Night Passage* had closure and redemption at the end – because the movie industry then (30's-40's) promoted ethics – they couldn't even make a movie where a character commits suicide (in *Night Passage*, the bad woman's fall was made to look like an accident). Times have changed.

So if you want to walk the path of the Earth Graduate, you can laugh, party and have fun, but down inside you must remember who you are, where you're going and what you stand for. And the higher you go, the less you will do inappropriate things – so in the beginning don't get down on yourself if you 'wiggle when you walk'… it is all part of the path: Rome was not built in a day and you will not walk perfectly from day 1. Be gentle with yourself, know that old habits take time to overcome – unless you have a real deep epiphany about yourself, a 'soul shock', and then you'll probably find that you automatically are not doing what used to embarrass you.

Self–respect includes self-compassion. And what you do for yourself is easier to do for others. Having stumbled yourself, it is easier to have compassion for others going through the same problem(s)… and so you won't be criticizing them. You'll help pick them up…

Souls as Earth Graduates

Man has a unique nature and a unique destiny, and we are here on Earth to work it out, and we probably would have by now if: (1) we hadn't resisted our lessons, (2) we didn't party so much, and (3) the PTB had let us know.

> Our purpose in coming together as creator fragments is to succeed in training ourselves enough about love, caring, and relationship to become more of who we are. The redemption is we, as … **progeny of the high forces of creation,** are ascending back to heaven in unity of diversity, as celebration of individuality in communion, not loss of individuality. We are holo- or fractal-fragments of the creation's creator, [who] is **wanting to create creations with us** not for us…

> Our first major task is to re-create the existing mother universe we find ourselves within with all its conundrums. Solve the unsolvable evolutionary problems. We learn to pick up the ball in our **training wheel practice universe** before we even want our own. And we want to learn very carefully, and so we use time to do it in a serial manner. That is the game…

> Each creator fragment that is a human soul, ultimately seeks its origin [and soulmate] and return to home. We are all … learning to love and nurture our individual and co-creative mutual universes.

> Our job is to achieve spiritual evolutionary acceleration sufficient to help solve age old problems of spiritual evolutionary inertia in the universe. [5] [emphasis added]

Elsewhere, the information is given that Man is ultimately to be a co-creator as his inheritance providing he can keep moving into more and more optimal timelines:

> ...as a reward, humans who accomplish this task, will be granted an initially uninhabited virgin future that can become even more optimal beyond comparison...

> That final loop optimal future becomes the end-game singularity conduit path through which **all** souls of all alternate [multidimensional] lines will eventually travel to become qualified macro-creator agents. [6]

That is the promise to all Earth Graduates.

This is also a significance of being soulmates – we are all related and <u>together</u> we work our way back to the Father of Light, the One, <u>working</u> our way through His hierarchy, assuming more responsibility as we Know and Love more.

All Abord!

Ensouled Man's birthright is to (1) rise above those who would obstruct him, and (2) rule in higher realms – similar to Angels in Training – and this is obviously what the soulless ones would like to prevent. This is why Robert Monroe was specifically told by the Beings of Light (*Inspecs*) he encountered that Earth Graduates are very well <u>respected</u>. That respect is due to personally developing what it takes to overcome darkness and get out of here! So Man emulating a Jesus, Ghandi, Buddha, Krishna or Apollonius would indeed evoke **respect** wherever he or she went.

It was Jesus in the New Testament who said that we could do what he was doing, and that **Love** was the Way. All teachings of Love and Light are worth following as they echo Higher Truth and that is what we need if we are to be released from this Earth. So the paths of a Buddhist, Muslim, Hindu, Jew and Christian walking in Love and Light are all walking the same way – repeat: **one need not change religion to get out of here**. All the great teachers have sought to wake Man up for one reason: to get Man out of here and into the Father of Light's Kingdom where we can <u>serve</u>.
That is called **the Earth Graduate.**

It is worth repeating what Monroe was told:

> By far the greatest motivation – surpassing the sum of all others – is the result. **When you perceive and encounter a graduate, your only goal is to be one** yourself once you realize it is possible. And it is. [7] [emphasis added]

When you know, why would you settle for anything less?

Namaste!

Chapter 16: -- Getting Out

This chapter will be the most help to anyone choosing to get out, to become an Earth Graduate. It contains **key concepts** that every Graduate must have and understand to sustain their Walk in what has been called Higher Consciousness – or a deeper awareness of who you are and how the soul is special.

Let it be said, right up front, that this is not for everybody. Many people are happy going to church, nodding to God, humming a few tunes, doing the wine and wafer, and for them, that IS church and they are not aware that there is anything more. And it bothers them when you tell them that there is more, they are not ready for it …yet. So they are fine where they are. Love them and respect their individual process. Nothing can be done for them until they begin to wonder and ask…

As a result, this book doesn't seek to wake everybody up, or change them, or change the basic church which serves the basic souls out there. Go back to Chapter 7 and understand that many people are one of the first two soul types. Souls are in different stages of growth. And realize that their church, even the Catholic Church that was "exposed" in Chapter 11, is serving these souls where they are at.

Yet there has to be something more for those who have begun to seek and ask questions… that was the reason for Chapters 1 and 11 being so rough on standard, organized religion – if those chapters resonated with you, you are ready for the next step. And this chapter will share some major concepts without telling you what to do, or how to do it – it is up to you and your Higher Self to make the appropriate application to your life.

> *Perhaps it would be of greater benefit if souls come together in a study group and read and discuss the ideas in this book. Multiple insights can expand one's Knowledge and form new friendships which support each other's process.*

Remember three things in your Walk:

1.   The gods don't make anybody do anything,
2.   When the student is ready, the teacher appears,
3.   You don't have to be perfect to graduate.

The major areas of concern to be discussed are:

1.   Light and Knowledge
2.   Love and Forgiveness
3.   Head and Heart
        Interlife
4.   Karma and Script
5.   Good and Evil
6.   Words and Energy

Light and Knowledge

To repeat, it was said earlier,

The higher one's consciousness, the more one is aware of the Truth, and the less one can pretend that Love and Knowledge aren't important. In fact, a failure to be loving when it is appropriate really weighs heavily against that person; it means a lesson was not learned, an awareness was not reached, and the 'lesson' will have to be repeated, sooner or later.

There is no excuse for a failure to be loving.

While Love is important , Knowledge is what grows our consciousness..

> It is not necessarily a feeling that one has that can also be interpreted as an emotion, but rather… the essence of Light which is knowledge is love, and this has been corrupted when it is said that love leads to illumination. Love is Light is Knowledge… God is Love…
> To love you must know. And to know is to have Light. And to have Light is to love. And to have knowledge is to love. [1]

And elsewhere, the clarification is made:

> Knowledge is a function of consciousness, and all knowledge that IS knowledge and not assumption, prejudice or illusion, increases consciousness.[2]

Remember in Chapter 9 it was said that your body has a **bionet** which carries photons, Light or *chi*, and this is a means of communication within the body, and is how the head and the heart communicate. The more knowledge, Light, you carry, the brighter your aura is – which is why ascended masters are very bright people! Seriously, their auras are much larger than the average person's because they know more, and love more, and that is the essence of the One, the Father of Light.

The Beatles sang, "Love is all you need" and that is misinformation. Love without Light is like Faith without Works. Dead. And love alone will not get you into the higher realms. That is why this chapter starts off with Light and Knowledge… As you gain more and more true knowledge, you will automatically find yourself more and more loving with other people because you will understand that we are all One (connected at the Soul, or Higher Self, level), and what you do/don't do to others is really doing it to yourself. The Golden Rule: what you do to others will come back to you.

> *Unfortunately, the Earth understanding of the Golden Rule is:*
> *He who has the gold, makes the rules! Wrong.*

What you give is what you get. Tithing people prosper because they gave away money which left a 'vacuum' for more of the same to flow in … "Nature abhors a vacuum."

Higher institutes of learning sometimes have a symbol of a lamp shining brightly because Light is Knowledge, and the ancients understood that, hence the origin of the symbol. It is

490

also said, if you are an expert in something, "let your light shine"... and that was also the meaning of Verse 70 in the Gospel of Thomas – with a warning that if you have Light and do not bring it forth, it can stagnate, block your chakras (part of the **bionet**) and you'll experience poor health. Knowledge and Light must flow – that is its nature. By the same token, if you are not learning, not assimilating new things, you are not in the Flow which is like having a floor lamp but never plugging it in. Your mental faculties atrophy when you stop learning and exercising the brain. Learn a new language, play Sudoku, do crossword puzzles, or take a night class in something that interest you... it forces the *chi* to move on the bionet and keeps the body and brain channels open and vibrant.

Truth carries more Light than a non-truth. If someone tells you a non-truth (may not be a complete lie) and knows it isn't true, the information carries an energy charge that says 'deception' and your subconscious (Higher Self) knows that and if you are intuitive, you'll receive a 'check in the spirit' – Do not ignore these warnings. Even if the other person doesn't know if it is a lie or not, the statement is still clearly the truth or a lie to your subconscious, and you can be protected. Women excel at this more than men... due to a better heart to head interplay.

We did experiments with a real aura camera a few years back, and it was the type where you don't touch anything. (There are phony aura cameras at Psychic Fairs where you place your hand on a metal plate and the temperature of your hand is photographed over your head.) We tested books and truth versus lies and got some very interesting results – all lies have a blackish-green color to the energy of that lie. Scientific books photographed with a yellow aura, and the Bible photographed with a beautiful crimson color. A very depressed man had a grey aura, and a healer friend had a pale green aura. All esoteric books on life, love and Man's true nature had a purple or pink aura – a very good sign. All of this to say that words, truth, lies, and knowledge carries an energy which is either positive or negative, sustaining or debilitating. Do I have to tell you what stalk-it-and-kill-it videos are doing to our youth?

By the same token, the energy of a library and a very spiritual church are both uplifting – in ways you can't even see. Spend time in a very loving church, and you will 'absorb' that (energy) vibration. Spend time in a library and you should be 'inspired' to study or learn something, but spend time in a porno shop and you will leave with a very heavy dirty-orange color and that may cloud your mind and influence your ability to think clearly for a few hours – by the way, a bath in sea salt will clean the aura. The porno shop energy will lock you into your lower, 1st and 2nd chakras, turning you into an animal, and spending time in a church will tend to impact your upper chakras 5 – 6 – 7, inspiring and relaxing you.

Have you ever noticed in a bookstore that the clerks don't carefully shelve and arrange the books in the Witchcraft section? Those books carry an energy that you are better off without. Spending time with them will attract the Neggs and even discarnates to you... is that what you want? We attract to us whatever we associate with. So, be as much like that which you want to be, focus on it, make it your intention, and thus attract it to you.

True knowledge is to the soul what fresh food charged with *chi* is to the body. Reading or hearing true Knowledge will be assimilated by the soul even if you don't understand it yet... You don't tell your body exactly what to do with the food you eat, and you can trust your

Higher Self to ingest and assimilate the Truth as you encounter it – and then one day, the dots will connect (subconsciously) and you'll have an epiphany about something, and then you tend to operate from that level – until you encounter lies and deception that will temporarily dampen your newfound state of being… that is how you know they are lies, or are something that may not be false but is not for you.

Love and Forgiveness

This is a big important area – more due to Forgiveness than Love. You can't love if you are not forgiving. If you love someone, you will forgive them. And there is never an excuse for a failure to be loving – thus you need to see whom you can forgive to free yourself up! The two are related, but trying to be loving is not enough.

It was said earlier that part of the reason we don't move on in the Father's Realm when we die is because we haven't learned enough – those lessons can be learned somewhere else, too – it doesn't have to be Earth! But the reason we can't move on is due to **attachments.** And not just attachments to food, sex, power, money, booze, drugs… those will bring you back to prove you can overcome them. Being attached to vengeance is lethal.

Let's use an example to see why Forgiveness is so important. And I'll use myself and what my life did to me as the example – I know it all too well.

Karma with Mom

My mother wanted a little girl, not a boy, and the doctor (with 1943 sophistication) told her that her unborn baby was a girl. So she went and bought all pink clothes, bassinet, shoes, etc. – all for her little girl. The big moment arrives in the delivery room, and out pops a boy (me). She spent hours claiming that her baby was switched and wanted her little girl… My grandparents were there and later told me all about the ruckus she caused. I was her firstborn. And in short, I was rejected, and not really accepted by her no matter what I did – HS honor roll? Oh "that's nice." Graduate from college? Oh, "that's nice." (I later learned in 1991 via the Regression I did, that my situation with her was karmic, and the reason my sister, 6 years younger than me, never liked me either was because we were switched in the womb – Nancy was bumped and I came first… I had to work through this thing with Mom, and had Nancy been born first, Mom would have had no more children. Wow.) So there are reasons for things.

Moving right along, nothing I did earned her love – although I wasn't abused. She did keep a shirt on my back, a roof over my head, and food in my belly – but no Love. At Christmas, I'd tell her "I love you, Mom!" And her response was, "Uh-huh, me too." No hug, no kiss. I was fortunate, for those of you wondering, to be raised by my grandparents who did give me the love an nurturing until I was 13, and then I was sent back to live with her… as she married for the 3rd time. Talk about a dysfunctional family…

So I let myself reject her, and stayed away… always puzzled but **resenting her** as a mother. She was cold and aloof, she had no friends, didn't want a son, and I was quick to learn from my grandparents, grow up and fend for myself. I kind of felt sorry for her, but there was no way to reach her… until after my **'91 Regression**. What I saw turned me around. I was shown where I was going to go (on the Other Side) if I kept harboring resentment – it was a grey foggy place where no one cared about anyone else, but being out of the body, I could feel all the pain and suffering of the others around me, whom I couldn't see but I could hear them. It was terrible. So I asked what I had to do – to NOT go there?

The Being of Light said "Forgive her." And explained to me that I didn't have to forget what she did. But if I didn't break the resentment link between us, I would drag both her and me there. **Resenting her was an attachment**, and it meant that at some point, this lifetime or another, her rejection and my resentment would have to be worked out, or let go… It would in fact be like an energy link 'chaining' us together and neither of us would be free to move on with our lives. And the only way to break it and set her free, and set MYSELF free, would be to forgive her – release her.

> **Non-forgiveness is an attachment to being right and having to prove something to the other person – we resent what they did and have an attachment to getting even. That is why it is so important to forgive – you won't forget, and that is OK so that that person doesn't do it to you again.**

It took some doing because the 'chain of resentment' between us was so empowered by time, but it snapped when I later saw that she was a very unhappy woman, and I put myself in her shoes, realized she had no friends, and was protecting herself from men – I was shown something that happened to her as a young and very pretty teen that made her a cold, aloof woman… and also caused her to denigrate herself. (You women know what I mean.) It brought tears to my eyes. That was when the link was broken. She was a victim of someone else… all of a sudden my resenting her made no sense. She already had a problem and I was compounding it! At that point it was easy to forgive her… I forgave her. The reason she and I had come together in this lifetime had been accomplished and she died a few years later… but she never accepted me as a son.

The key to the whole issue is to **forgive others so we don't jam up and attach ourselves to further pointless dramas.** (Explained more in Chapter 12 of Book 2.) People did what they did to us because that was all that they could do at that time. If Mom had known better, or been a 'bigger person,' she would not have done what she did… Now that I had the insight, it was up to me on higher ground (where more is expected of an aware soul) to break the **connection**. (Yes, whatever rejection she may still carry toward me and men will have to be worked out – but can be done with other people… I don't have to get involved in further negativity with her. However, if she and I are twinsouls, we're not done.)

> **By the way, to whom much is given ('91 insight), much is expected. I could not just go my way without doing something proactive regarding her and my issue now that I knew. Knowledge does that to you, as well.**

It was now possible to love her, and I felt more compassionate yet helpless to help her, so I just prayed for her peace.

Head and Heart

Knowledge is important and the head eats it up. What is amazing, according to Joseph Chilton in Chapter 9, is that there are the same glia cells in the heart as there are in the brain. The heart and the head have an energy and bionet connection but the heart is stronger.

Ever hear someone say, "I think I love you…" why didn't they just say "I love you"? If they have to think about it, it isn't Love. Agape (unconditional)? Or philileo(brotherly)? That is what is going on in the original text in the Bible, John 21:15-17, where Jesus asks Peter if he loves (agape) Him (after having denied Him 3 times), and Peter gets stuck saying 3x he loves (philileo) the Lord. The English does not give a clue what is going on. And this wild man, Peter, who cuts off a soldier's ear, **denies Jesus three times**, cannot respond to Jesus with agape love… this is the rock on which the Church was built?

The issue is: you can't love with your head. Love is from the heart because it is unconditional – Peter was in his head, feeling <u>brotherly</u> love for Jesus…. reasoning that he should love Jesus. When we are hung up not forgiving people, we are in our head… we have a reason for resenting them, and we're right — they wronged us… but that is all: we just get to be right and cannot get off our reasonable point of view. We have to let go of our need to be right and let the other person go. Be unreasonable! Get into your heart – **Forgive them and stop spending so much time and energy feeding the energy 'chain' that connects you two!**

And there is another more esoteric reason to forgive. While you are resenting the other person, and have the energy 'cord' connecting you two, you two do share energy – the other person can drain you, just like an energy vampire. If they are low and bummed out – you, too, may begin to feel that way – because you two share a connection. In the universe, **energy always flows from the higher potential to the lower** – that is how a car battery is charged by connecting it to a stronger battery in the first car – but if the second car is too weak, it may seriously drain the stronger battery – which is why 'jump starting' another car is always done with the stronger car's engine running.

Conversely, if you are having a really great day, and your energy is really up – you may be unconsciously blessing that person you resent with your energy. Unless you remember to hate that person, and then you send him/her a **psychic whack** through the connection! And we are all karmically responsible for what we do to others… even if we don't know that we affect others.

Lastly, when you have a serious decision to make, check out all the facts, and if your head still doesn't know which way to go, get into your heart and see if your tentative decision 'feels' OK, or do you get a check in the spirit? The heart has a way of knowing because it is in touch with your Higher Self – your issue is being able to 'hear' what your heart says.

There is an excellent book on this subject: <u>Your Essential Whisper</u> by LaRue Eppler.

Are you reasonable or compassionate? As with most things, a balance is appropriate. Overly emotional is as unproductive as overly reasonable.

Interlife: Karma and Script

That brings us to a concern about Karma – which <u>only</u> applies in this Earth realm, it is an aspect of the 3D HVR Construct – a way to see that souls get their lessons. As was said earlier, Karma is merely meeting yourself and effecting a change.

A few words about the **Interlife** – where souls go when they die – provided they don't fight the Light and stay Earth-bound as discarnates.

When you die, you should see a **tunnel** – your way out of here – it protects souls leaving the Earth realm and making the transition to the Interlife location. If you don't see a tunnel – **ask** for it. At this point, either still in the Earth realm or just crossed over, there is usually a Being of Light who will review your life – it is like a video with sight, sound <u>and feeling</u> – you will see when you hurt others and feel what they felt. There is no judgment from the Angel – we are rougher on ourselves than They ever are. But we get a sense of where we did well and where we bought the farm.

If we are really upset (because we were just murdered), or we realize that we acted really dysfunctionally in that last lifetime, we may be so embarrassed that we request going to one of the 'resting realms' where you don't do anything but absorb the specially-engineered vibrations to help you recover.

If all is OK, you are then meeting with a Teacher assigned to you…you can resist and reject this if you're not ready, and They will put you in another 'conditioning' place. You and the Teacher (an advanced being who usually has only incarnated a few times so he knows what it is like), and who has access to all of your records (!) because everything is known about you over there, will sit you down and counsel you, helping you plan the next attack on the Earth realm… he may help you formulate your next Script. During which time, you will also use the "heavenly" computer, part of which runs the HVR Earth Sphere, to check out potential (upcoming) babies into which you can be born – you get a preview of who the parents are, their personalities and problems, what the genetics of the newborn are likely to be, and where it looks like the family will go and what potential (nothing is cast in concrete) opportunities will be there… And you get to set up **Points of Choice** – if you don't the Teacher will – to test your ability to make appropriate choices, and lastly you will likely have a choice about how/when you exit the Earth realm the next time… (I briefly saw all of this when I did the '91 Regression and **it is covered extensively in Book 2**.)

The family you choose is often peopled with members of your same soul group, and often roles are switched from lifetime to lifetime for increased learning. You may opt to meet with your soulmate, but that is a special attachment that can be broken. If your special someone is a twinsoul, you're stuck with him/her and must work out any differences.

Everyone comes into Earth with a Script… it is not Fate …but like our dog in the backyard, his **destiny** is to be in the backyard, but has **freewill** to do whatever he wants while there – and take the consequences! So once **you choose the time period, the country, and the family**, those are plugged into your Script and that part is Destiny. Tests and Points of Choice depend on your current and projected ability to handle them –

no one is tested beyond what they are able (the gods aren't ogres).

Some people choose a defective body for the lessons in patience and compassion that that offers. Some souls choose a lifetime of hardship to wind up on Skid Row, to handle that set of lessons. Others choose to come in for just a few years to deliver a special lesson to their parents, also set up in the parents' Scripts. All of these Scripts must fit and operate within the Greater Script for the Era you choose…. if you want a Script where you become a great jet pilot, don't choose the 1700's in Early America! The Greater Script is what is running the HVR Sphere's current Era, and interfaces with the Control System.

After deciding on the Era, country and family, you have the opportunity to hang out (unseen) among that family and observe – to be sure that is going to meet your spiritual lessons' needs – it may not if the father all of a sudden decides to divorce his wife, or the baby's contracting a fatal disease… you will have to reselect. But if all looks OK, the Script is 'programmed' into the computer, you begin to externally shape/direct the fetus to reflect your choices in the weeks before birth, and finally just before, at, or just after birth you enter the body. **There is no soul in the body before birth** – for the same reason you would not get into a new car that was missing an engine and two tires. You don't move into a house before the builder has finished it, and it is the same way with incarnating into baby bodies. If no one selects that baby's body, it will go through life as an OP; the body has a life/mind of its own and doesn't need a soul to merge with it.

Then the Beings of Light and Neggs (They work together, remember Chapter 6) have access to your Script and guidance and protection are done by the Angel (Being of Light), and the 'hits' you have to take are administered by the Neggs… not to exceed your Script's boundries. It is up to you to **handle the lifetime** and its ups and downs. If you really get into trouble (as I did in the hospital in 1965) you may be visited and other options are offered by the Being of Light.

Nature of Karma

Karma is very exacting, and often the slightest little thing that reflects on you as a soul, especially any shortcomings, will be addressed. If you knifed someone 3 lifetimes ago, They may have waited till the present lifetime to have you **meet that part of yourself** – whatever it was in you that chose to stab that other person. Maybe it was your temper and you need to learn to control it, so They will have you meet that **shadow side** of yourself and work on learning the control.

And that is all Karma is – you have to face yourself – you do not have to be knifed in return. The dictum Over There is NOT "an eye for an eye" – but if you believe that and insist on being 'right' – it will be done for you that way…. But why choose excessive hardship? If in a lifetime after the one where you knifed someone, you become a better person who would not do that again, you will have met that karma, and could just stop someone else from knifing another person – that is another way to meet the issue.

And remember, the gods never make anyone do anything – you choose it all with a wider connection to your Higher Self available to you Over There, in the **Interlife**. The gods will put things in your Script that you have not handled so far, if They think you can handle it, otherwise They will wait until you grow a bit more before putting a certain event in your life again. You are advised, taught, immersed in energy vibrations designed to 'shape' you. You may not like it, and if you are really intractable, due to being damaged (yes, soul damage) in the last lifetime, as Dr. Newton said, they may have to do "soul surgery" on you – disassemble your energy/essence and reassemble you. Or add/delete things to you to help you assimilate and realign yourself.

Good and Evil

If God the Father is Love and His Presence and Power fills the Universe, where would the alleged Devil be? Somewhere running around under God's permission? Yes, souls have freewill to do whatever they want, like Hitler and Stalin, but there is no major adversary to God, there is no Hell, and there also is no Heaven as the Christians think. These assumptions were examined in Chapter 6 and now we'll look at what the real issue is.

Duality

This is a major problem on Earth and needs addressing. Man tends to think in terms of opposites: up and down, black and white, good and bad, off and on… This is going to blow your mind, but your heart will love it. And you need to know this if you are to be free of the STS influences in our world.

The following examples are inspired by <u>The Eye of the I</u>, *by David Hawkins.*

No "Offness"

When electricity runs through a wire, we say something is 'on.' The electricity is either present or it is not. If it is present, it is "on." When it is not present, **that is not another state** – the only state is ON. There is no "off" state. This is not just semantics; please get a sense of the deeper meaning here.

"On" is a real state –something exists, something is happening. "Off" is not a state – it is the absence of something. **An absence is not a state of being**. "Off" is an illusion – it is not a state of being.

No Opposite to God

In the same way, no opposite to God exists. No opposite to existence has any possible reality. Only Allness is a possibility. If God is omnipotent, omniscient, and omnipresent, where would the Devil's domain exist? How could it exist as a negative structure within God's all-pervasive positive structure without being vibrationally transformed or, like matter and anti-matter, without being destroyed?

Our problem is that **the mind works with duality**: if there is an "up," there has to be a "down," and if there is a "good," there has to be a "bad." In reality, "a house divided against itself cannot stand" – in quantum physics, photons and anti-photons annihilate each other. And if that is part of the building block structure of this universe, then how could good and evil exist side by side?

One possible answer lies in the concept of parallel dimensions – one positive and the other negative. The Quantum Physicists theorize that that is where the anti-photon resides and due to some unknown cosmic dance, the positive and negative particles pop back and forth, and they're called *virtual particles*. So evil and the putative Devil could exist in a parallel dimension and harass us in ours from where they are…? Not now that you know we're in a Quarantined Simulation run by the gods.

Good versus Evil

Is 'goodness' a state of being? Is 'badness' or darkness a state of being? Or are they both a relative perception in the observer's mind? It was said that STO is serving others, and that is generally seen as 'good.' Selfishness and egotistical STS behavior is generally seen as 'bad.' Having said in Chapter 6 that there is no Devil, no Satan, and Lucifer is just a title, and that even the Neggs do not have a leader to plan and orchestrate attacks, it should be appreciated that when things happen, they are neither good nor bad, but may be <u>perceived</u> that way. Consider the following:

> A farmer has only one son and really loves him, and plans for the son to take over the farm when the father dies. While the son is running the tractor to cultivate a field, it hits a soft spot in the ground, a sinkhole opens, and the tractor flips and breaks the son's leg. (Bad news)
>
> The next day, war breaks out with the country next door and all able-bodied men are called up to serve. The son is kept out of the war because of his leg. (Good news)
>
> The tractor fell into the sink hole and the frame was broken. (Bad news)
> At the bottom of the sinkhole, oil was discovered and the farmer sells part of his land to an oil drilling company and is rich. (Good news)
>
> When the son's leg is healed, he is called off to fight the war. (Bad news)
> While serving in the ambulance corps, he meets a beautiful nurse and falls in love. (Good news)
>
> After the war, the son and the nurse marry and bring her whole family to live with the now rich farmer father. (Bad news)
>
> Some of the relatives help with the planting and harvesting, the older women are great cooks, and their granny is a healer. (Good news)….

And so it goes. Good and bad are relative points of view.

Manipulation

This planet deals good and bad events to souls, and the Earth as a School will have illusions and lies to surmount. If you don't, your life goes downhill, as the PTB intend... they are STS and

> ... do not want humans to graduate to [higher] density and that is why they create beliefs and illusions and controls that are designed to induce us to make STS choices no matter what we do. **As long as we believe lies, we are aligned with STS.** As long as we are aligned with STS, our mass and Spring Constant make it impossible for us to increase our amplitude for graduation.[3] [emphasis added]

Man is kept 'dumbed down', or entrained into his lower 3 chakras, by the RCF/Matrix, so that he makes the inappropriate choices and does not acquire the Light, or escape velocity, to leave Earth. In short, this is why Man is recycled. Recycled is also trapped.

As for "**Spring Constant** and mass," these are terms that directly affect one's PFV. **Mass** refers to Man's sleeping consciousness or ignorance. The **Spring Constant** is the measure of the force required to get that mass moving forward, to add Light to one's consciousness. And since Man's higher, inherent 4D nature is constrained by 3D mass, or density, he is naturally and easily drawn to the STS ideals. [4]

Polarization

But what about *evil?* What if one of the above cooks poisons the farmer to get control of the land and money? It should be obvious that evil acts can be instigated by the Neggs or discarnates, as well as arise within Man's own undeveloped soul – acts of pettiness, greed, lying, etc. are part of our **shadow side.** Evil then is someone fulfilling an extreme STS agenda, for whatever reason, or for no reason. It should also be clear that **evil is the absence of good.** Therefore, if someone does a completely STS act, and harms others, there was no STO (good), and thus it was done in the absence of good.

So good versus evil is not about duality, but **polarization.** The same is true of STO/STS polarity:

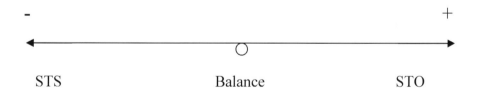

STS/STO Polarization

"O" is the balance but at either end is an extreme polarization where STS (-) is just as bad as STO (+) because extremes indicate something is out of balance... Goody-Twoshoes versus Charles Manson, for example. FYI, Jesus and Buddha were not all the way to the right. Only the One is in that position.

And the key is this: evil is seen as <u>extreme</u> bad. Shooting and popping a kid's balloon is not evil, but shooting the same kid in the back is seen as a real bad act, and shooting the kid in the head could be considered an evil act. **A matter of degree...** Unless the kid was 'evil' and in the act of shooting other people (à la Columbine) when he was shot down... and while sad and deplorable, the safety of the many overrules the act of shooting the kid as an evil act. **The context is important.**

But to be clear, and return to the topic, we are talking here about **duality** NOT existing in our 3D realm, but polarization which does exist. **Duality (opposites) is different than polarization (degree).** Duality says there are two possible states of <u>beingness</u> possible; polarization says extremes of the same state can exist, like hot and cold are extremes of the temperature state. Hot and cold do not reflect duality. But an extreme of a non-state cannot exist, which is why good and evil are polar subjective opposites of the same state, beingness (involving intent: STO or STS), and not a duality.

Evil as a separate duality does not exist, because there is only the One, the Light, the Father. But evil can exist as a polarization and therefore is an option that souls can take in their relations with each other.

Duality is Illusion

If the light is on in a room, there is light. When the light is turned off, this is the <u>absence</u> of light and is not an 'off' state of something which is now present where light used to be. Really get that. When the light is turned on again, it does not have to fight its way across the room, pushing something called darkness out of the way!

> You cannot shine darkness into an area. One can, by languaging, call the absence of light darkness, but it will have no existence in Reality. [5]

In Space, there is no up or down, nor forward nor backward. The only reference we have for anything (within our solar system) is relative to the Sun or our planet – we go toward the Sun, or away from it, but we are relative to the Sun. Same with up or down – since Space is endless, how high up is up?

> *Perhaps now it is clear why Dr. Paul LaViolette said that there might be* **pulsars** *throughout the traveled part our universe that serve as orientation beacons.*

"Only that which exists has Reality." [6] One cannot have poverty; you either have money, or the absence of money, but **poverty as a separate Reality does not exist**. Poverty and Riches are not duality, but polarizations of the same money state.

The problem is that the mind sees "rich" as one state and "poor" as another state. And linguistically, that is correct. The point to grasp in all this is that "poor" is not a real state: you cannot give "poor" or "poverty" (absence of money) to someone, but you <u>can</u> give them money. But the mind thinks of the appearance of "no money" as a state of being, and that is why people cannot manifest money – they are believing in the "no money" state as real and seek ways to deny it, wipe it out, or overcome it. Since they are fighting an illusion, they cannot manifest money. In short, it doesn't work to "fight poverty" or deny poverty – it works to affirm prosperity.

Don't give power to the non-state, or the absence of something. And thank you, David Icke: you don't war for peace, you peace for peace.

The same goes for present and absent – you're either present, or you're not. Your presence is a state, a positive state of being. **Absence is not a state and has no reality.** If you're not here, you are somewhere else, so your beingness is a reality – just not here.[7]

While this appears to be an exercise in semantics, or word games, it IS important to your gaining awareness beyond the usual STS deceptions we endure so that you begin to 'see' things differently. It is an exercise in <u>what is</u>, not in what isn't.   And that was the essence of Zen training: paying attention to <u>what is</u>. Reality. And no mental interpretations of what something *might* be, or what it *looks like*… Such is the first step to mental clarity and breaking free of the STS manipulative programming.

Lightworkers

Man is not here alone. This is not his planet, yet it is where he is contained, so it looks like it. But all is not lost. As with any place of containment, there are those who direct the operation, those who teach and mentor, as well as others – sometimes referred to as Lightworkers. In addition to the teachers and custodians who are assigned to the VR Sphere rehabilitation center and watch over Man, there are a few others you might be interested in. They may be called the Allies of Mankind.

Spiritual Adepts

On this planet, to handle the negativity, you may have to be more of a spiritual adept: You are 'resisting' being manipulated and lied to, and you take back your 'power' and think for yourself. The next step is:

1. **Detach** from the world (so they can't manipulate you thru worldly things)
2. Become **transparent** (so that words and events don't 'touch' you)
3. Be **impeccable** with your energy and word (so you don't make agreements you can't keep, and you don't waste energy)

You are in the world, but not of it. And most importantly, whatever happens cannot ruffle you. Be careful as the Spiritual Walk means **patience** is a virtue to develop and if you pray for patience, everything unlike it will come up in your experience! Of course, how else can you practice patience unless there are events that call for you to be that way?!

System Busters

This group is closest to what could be called a Light Warrior group. They are also high-level souls, usually 5D and 6D, who have volunteered, knowing the risks, and are empowered to not only **anchor the Light**, but literally bust the corrupt, dysfunctional system on Earth – the system largely empowered by the Dissidents through the PTB.

They are specially equipped with knowledge, authority and some (limited) personal power to seek out, identify and stop the effects of negative entrainment. They are not fighting anybody, and they are not 'against' the Neggs – they run interference for us, blocking the STS OPs, the Neggs and discarnates, and occasionally the Interdimensional beings that Wilde and Monroe spoke of. (Chapter 12)

These are the beings who can speak the word and stop hail, hurricanes, and earthquakes, heal people, perform deliverance, and have the authority to call down angelic assistance. Also called **Gatekeepers.**

Some of this group came here as **Starseed** and are just now waking up and moving into their pre-planned and pre-programmed roles. The timing has been critical – should they wake up individually too soon and begin their duties, the STS Gang would find ways to stop them. And some of them might not wake up at all if the STS group has been able to identify and suppress them – this was one of the risks they knew they had to take.

Indigos/Homo *noeticus*

These are the upgrades or hybrids that the little Greys have been producing for decades, some of whom are now successfully walking among us. Their time is coming, as was revealed in Dr. Jacob's material in Chapter 4. At a future point, proactive Man and the hybrids will be united on the new Earth, and this should be every bit as stabilizing as the Man and OP combination was destabilizing.

As the movie *Indigo* portrayed one of these children, they are very hard to deceive, and it is almost impossible to get anything past their awareness. They know who you are, what you're doing, and lying, cheating and stealing are unacceptable to them.

If possible, to further your spiritual growth, you want to associate with those people who appear to be System Busters, Indigos, or Starseed of some sort.

Light and Freedom

Escape Velocity

Just as rockets to the Moon, or even Space Shuttles, have to have a certain amount of fuel to sustain their intended trajectory and thus overcome the Earth's gravitational field and leave Earth, so too do souls need a certain amount of spiritual 'fuel' to empower and sustain their ability to leave Earth. It has been called Knowledge, Light or spiritual growth.

Certainly no one needs more than one lifetime's experience on Earth to get what this place is all about. As multidimensional souls, with other aspects in different timelines and realities, the goal is to experience different parts of the Father's Creation – not to spend 100 lifetimes on planet Earth. Yet, that is what can happen because Man does not know how important spiritual growth is and so wastes his/her time here – subject to the exacting doctrines of Karma and Reincarnation.

Part of attaining the escape velocity to get out of here is to realize the Truth, which imparts more Light to one's DNA (Chapters 7 & 9). If one's Light quotient (also measured as PFV) is greater than that of the planet, one can be set free.

"You shall know the Truth and the Truth will set you free." (Jn 8:32)

A lack of knowledge and belief in the wrong things are all that stand between you and gaining mastery of your life – and getting out of here. You will choose to get out of here when you know the truth about yourself and this place. But you can't choose until you know, hence the trap. And it is made difficult to know the truth on this planet. That is why the graduate is highly respected.

To get out of here, you need Light, and your personal light must be greater than that of this planet to leave, or you stay here. So you must bring forth what Light you have. And build more. You also stay here if you don't know that you have a choice to leave, or you exit the body but hesitate and don't go to the Light.

Your Light can be kept low by buying into the emphasis on sex, violence, power, money and melodrama which keeps a lot of people in their first 3 chakras – they can't get out of here. A lot of people today think that life is about having fun, not learning, growth or service. It takes more than fun to develop one's Light through the other 4 (higher) chakras. Developing one's Light through all the 7 major chakras is what builds one's Light, raises one's vibration to exceed the planet's vibration, and thus get out of here

More and more people have been entrained (thanks to the Media, Internet, and morphic resonance with the RCF/Matrix in American society) into serving the physical world, and are now trapped by it because the collective resonance of living in the first 3 chakras has reinforced the paradigm and entrained even more souls into the Matrix. A kind of negative "100th Monkey" has been born on planet earth – entrapping more and more souls into the negative, self-seeking STS polarity. And the more souls that are trapped, the stronger the attractor becomes by feeding off their energy.

Gaining Light

So how does one add Light to their soul? We saw in Chapter 9 that our DNA stores it and communicates with almost everything in our world – even other people – via hypercommunication, via the biophotons in our bionet.

What is less known is that true knowledge contains a lot of Light. Truth has a positive vibration and that is generated and sustained by Light. Inasmuch as the Father is Light, and His consciousness rides on the Light, Light carries Knowledge. When we die, according to the NDErs, they move toward the Light where they are told:

> I remember only two things from that exchange [with God]. First, God told me that there were **only two things** that we could bring back with us when we died… LOVE and KNOWLEDGE… so I was to learn as much about both as possible. [8] [emphasis added]

"Love is all you need" by the Beatles was wrong. We also need **knowledge**.

Light is traditionally associated with knowledge and higher learning. Consider these:

> Some universities use an Aladdin-type lamp as a symbol of knowledge.
> When someone understands something, we say 'the light went on.'
> Someone who doesn't know something 'walks in darkness.'
> An idea is traditionally represented as a light bulb above the head.
> A knowledgeable, intelligent person is said to be 'bright'.
> In the NDE, it is a Being of (white) Light who has great knowledge.
> One's aura color reflects soul development and white light is completeness.
> Knowledge is implied in the word En-**light**-enment.

While that spark of Light is not Knowledge itself, it is the *connection* to the Light where the Knowledge is available. And as God is omniscient, He also provides Light which carries Knowledge.

Ways to Increase Light and Knowledge

Some of the following points are review and some are new information. Areas in which to reflect and see what you can use.

Attachments

Whatever you are attached to in this life or on this planet will bring you back. If you are attached to drugs, alcohol, gambling, sex, money, power, your children, or even a special place… it serves as a bond with this planet. The secret is to not love or hate anything, but release it, enjoy it, but don't get attached to it where you have to have it, have be there, or have to do it. It doesn't mean that you don't love your children; it means you release them– nice if they're there, nice if they're not.

The issue of attachments is a major issue worthy of re-emphasizing. It binds people to this planet – do not take it lightly. And the attachment may take the negative form: you harbor resentment and seek revenge – you are attached to getting even with someone, and you are connected to them. You will **both** have to come back to resolve that one… unless one of you forgives and breaks the attachment. Thus forgiveness is a major way to break attachments to other people.

And don't forget to forgive yourself.

Energy Cords

And breaking attachments also includes deliberately willing energy ties to other people to be broken. These ties or 'cords' are links to other people with whom you have had sex, money dealings, played cards with them – almost any social interaction generates cords to other people. Even fantasizing sex with a person in a picture sets up a cord to that person in real life (and that is one of the problems with pornography). When you get enough of these cords running from you to them, all over the place, you will find it very difficult to have enough energy to manage <u>your</u> day – because you are losing energy through these cords – you are feeding these connections with your energy. Visualize cutting the cords and call your **energy** back!

Carolyn Myss, a documented medical intuitive, said this in her book, <u>Why People Don't Heal, and How They Can</u>. It pays to be wise about where we spend our daily allotted energy. Carlos Castaneda called it being "impeccable." It seems we have energy in our 'cellular bank account' and can spend it worrying about the future, regretting the past, resenting other people, or being angry at ourselves (which is called depression). If we spend more energy than we have, or can quickly recoup, we become ill. [9]

In addition, Myss makes a very profound observation (being a medical intuitive) that some people with cancer bought as the truth – something that someone else in authority (parent, teacher, coach…) said about them and they gave their power away.

> …a parent or teacher perhaps – said something to them like "You'll never be good enough" or "You'll never amount to anything." It may have taken only three seconds, yet those three seconds commanded the rest of the person's life. If you can be totally commanded by a three-second comment, do you really think **you create your own reality**? I don't think so. It is that negativity that is creating your reality, and your challenge is to become strong enough to **call your spirit back**. [10] [emphasis added]

That three-second comment above amounted to a curse, which we'll explore later in this chapter. Words are powerful.

Call Your Spirit Back

Lastly, Myss' contribution to energetics emphasizes also calling your **spirit** back. While Dr. Modi and Sandra Ingerman deal with the issue of fragmented souls, and how to get them back, that is not quite the emphasis here. What people do is send their energy back to the past, reliving some event or era – and they actually are spending energy on past events. Myss has a very practical injunction:

> …retrieving this energy from the past begins by making a shift in awareness and vocabulary… Learn to become conscious of what you are thinking about and where your energy is. When you feel yourself drifting back into the fog of a memory, command your energy to return to the present moment by saying, "I am not going in that direction any longer. I release it once and for all." … Release can also be accomplished with a bit of humor, such as, "You again? Beat it! I haven't got either the time or the energy to think about you any longer." … Stop giving [your past] power by clinging to the belief that things could or should have been otherwise. That is nonsense. [11]

There is a condition that we all occasionally experience which is a clue that we need to call our energy back. It is a condition often characterized by a listlessness, lack of energy, confusion, or sense that we are 'running on empty' – we did too much, or even more interestingly, we may have had our energy drained by a flesh and blood 3D human who opportunistically drains other people of their energy, an "energy vampire." [12]

And, by the way, you protect yourself with White Light, or by keeping your aura strong, as is discussed later in this chapter.

Calling your energy back even if you don't know where it went, or when, can be accomplished by a general statement such as, **"I now call my energy back to me, cleansed and whole, and I cut any energy links [cords] that have been sent to others."** Your guides know what you mean and what you need… you just have to **ask**.

Some cords that you <u>cannot</u> sever are those that connect you with other aspects of your multidimensional self (and often your parents). And as was discussed in Chapter 7, you may have mood swings or euphoric highs due to the connections to other aspects of yourself. Before you run to get some Rx for bipolar disorder, please meditate and see if through prayer the connection(s) can be blocked to prevent serious disruption in your life. If worst comes to worst, do a few sessions of regression therapy, seeking the connection.

Energy Conservation

In order to attain 'escape velocity,' as Robert Monroe once said, it is vital to conserve one's soul energy. If you can conserve it, you won't have to call it back to you from places where you may have sent it and wasted it. This was the same concept that don Juan in the series by Carlos Castaneda advised his naïve shaman/warrior apprentice to practice: to **be impeccable with his energy**. [13] Conserving means using wisely, and only when needed. This includes avoiding excessive sexual activity, as well as plugging energy leaks and energy sinks. Some energy leaks are: excessive talking, worrying, and repetitive, nervous habits. Power sinks are those activities into which you "sink" energy and the activity does not empower or 'charge' you – such as gambling, drinking, or stalk-it-and-kill-it video games.

To be impeccable with energy then is to use it wisely, as Myss and Castaneda said.

Impeccability means the leaks are plugged and [personal] power is available to the warrior. This available power is also a definition of impeccability. As don Juan tells us, "The only thing that counts is impeccability, that is, freed energy." To be impeccable, then, is to act with freed energy, with personal power that has been snatched away from the multitude of power sinks and leaks that plague us. [14]

Conserving energy allows us to have the reserve when we need it, for daily living and to have enough energy when we die so that we are not dissipated and have the energy to think and act clearly.

Energy and *Chi*

If one is run down and needs energy, a very proactive way to rebuild one's energy is through Tai Chi or Qigong (also spelled Chi Kung). Practicing Qigong on a daily basis keeps one unusually healthy and mentally sharp because it causes the *chi* to flow through the whole body bionet and removes stagnant energy blockages which often lead to illness.

Adepts can even take in universal energy (*chi* in Chinese, *ki* in Japanese, *ruach* in Hebrew, or *prana* in Hindu) from **trees**, the Sun, a waterfall, the universe, and other people! And it is just as easy to <u>send</u> energy, via intent, to heal or empower other people – one need not be an 'energy vampire' as mentioned above. Stealing other people's energy would not be impeccable, nor advisable. The Neggs would see what you're doing and set you up for the same treatment; here the Golden Rule applies. What you do to others will be done to you; what you deny others will be denied you. Integrity is important.

Keep in mind, also, that your energy affects other people – Having a bad day? Your low vibrations (energy) may bring them down, too, even if you don't say anything. Just as you bring on new habits and make yourself well/sick with same, so too do you affect others.

> *Remember that in the universe the way energy works is that it flows from the higher potential to the lower. God empowers His creation through this principle. In the same way, if one is run down and needs energy, being around other people will have the effect of raising one's energy level, and slightly dropping theirs.*

As you grow spiritually, your words gain more power to affect people.

> Speaking positive, uplifting words creates a higher reality for you and others, for every word you speak powerfully creates what you talk about. … You have the ability to lift others' energies with your encouragement and the ability to dampen people's energies by criticizing them. If you find something in people to criticize, realize that this is the very area you could empower them in… …[but] not every thought has to be verbally expressed… It is better to say only those things that serve people in some way. [15]

And be careful – suppose an ascended Master were walking among a crowd of people and suddenly had a fit of anger – how many people would get sick, dizzy, or worse because they were suddenly hit with his higher focused energy? A psychic whack on steroids!

If you care about others, have forgiven them, know yourself, show compassion no matter what you're feeling, you will have achieved a level of spiritual growth that practically guarantees you get out of here at death – "even ultimately loving each secular soul you come into contact with, as well as the extra and special souls" as an old friend Fr. Ernie used to say.

Watch your use of energy.

Prayer and Meditation

Prayer is asking for it, meditation is being open to receiving it. The more you pray, the stronger your connection to the Godhead discussed in Chapters 7 and 2. The Godhead was the Oversoul discussed that is an intermediary between you and God. You are connected to the Godhead by your "silver cord" spoken of by many Out of Body

(OBE) experiencers, and by some NDErs. Your prayers go through the silver cord to the Godhead so there is no way you are not heard. [16]

If you don't ask, God will not automatically answer and give you what you need/want – unless it is in your Script. He will not violate freewill and we must exercise our freewill and ASK. God is all-knowing but will not intervene unless we ask. The key aspect of prayer is that God stands ready to direct the angels (Beings of Light) into action – all they need is someone's prayer (request) because they can't act on their own initiative. In a freewill universe, asking for help resolves the issue of whether the other person/entity interfered or not.

Often useful are prayers of protection. Especially against the STS Gang – again, it is important to ask. In fact, in the case of the Neggs, it is more productive to pray that any/all Neggs harassing you or your family be turned to the Light – not sent to the Pit. Any Neggs sent to the Pit (it does exist) may be sent back, or new ones will be assigned to you – better to **ask that they are sent to the Light,** or transformed into the Light, as that reduces the headcount in the realm of Darkness.

Meditation with deep slow breathing allows God's Light to flow through us. That is healing as well as enlightening. Meditating on the Light and asking it to cleanse and protect are excellent ways to merge with the Light. [17],[18]   In fact, during the higher stages of meditation, we are virtually immune to Negg attack because we have taken on more Light and the Neggs hate the Light – so they stay away. Any prayers and communication with God at that point can bypass the Neggs. Every word that we say or think **is** usually heard – by God and the Neggs. Such a prayer puts the Neggs on notice and gives the angels of Light the right of acting in your behalf.

Watch What You Say

And by the way, be careful what you pray for. The Neggs also hear prayers and sometimes answer first with their 'best' before God can answer. How can you know? Suppose you pray for the right, perfect job, and the next day someone calls and offers you what sounds like the answer to your prayer... except that it doesn't quite fit in your life and some other good, positive things have to be removed to make way for the new job. **Red flag**!

The perfect job from God will not remove other good things from your life. Do not sit there and reason that sometimes it's a "case of win some, lose some" or a "case of give and take".... don't rationalize the 'gift' from the Neggs. God's answer may take a bit longer, but it will be right, and you will know it in your heart of hearts.

Yes God may replace something in your life and give you a better job, but it will fit and you will have a gut feeling that it is right.

Another issue dealing with cleaning up your life, and getting your vibration up, is that of watching what you say: words have power, they carry vibration, and while you cannot instantly manifest by speaking, **over a period of time** the continued use of certain high-vibration or low-vibration words will have an effect... and then you'll be puzzled, wondering where something came from.

Filling the Box

A master can speak the word, say 'prosperity' or 'money', and <u>manifest</u> it. Now. However, for most people on Earth, there is a 'box' that has to fill up before things appear. Depending on your degree of Light, and PFV, you may be able to fill your 'box' and attract it before your friend.

It depends on intent, focus, willpower (putting energy into your desire), perseverance, and occasionally visualization. As was said in Chapter 11, you cannot Create Your Day by intent alone.

For example, every day for 40 days, you pray, visualize, speak and focus on what you want. On the 41st day, it comes into your life. Your friend who has more Light, is more spiritual, more focused, does the same process as you for 26 days and it appears. So, I refer to it as a 'process' of filling up the box – keep putting your prayer, desire, energy, etc out there, and with each time you do that, a bit more potential energy is added to your 'box' until the box is full and the energy potential is reached to realize your desire or goal… unless your Script says you can't have it.

> *Note: Masters can manifest, everyone else uses the Law of Attraction. The reinforced energy 'contained' in the box is what develops the energy potential to attract what you want.*

Bless or Curse?

Another issue with speaking the word, is that of blessing or curse – How do you use your word?

Remember that the Neggs hear you as well as the angels of Light. Angels of Light will not empower a curse, but the Neggs <u>will</u> – they don't care whom it is said against, if it creates disease, destruction, or deception, they'll do it – that is their function! Need I say what that does for you? If they can't 'stick' it to the person you cursed, guess where the curse goes? Back to you. And even if the curse can be put on the other person, you are racking up a lot of negative points – generating aspects of a future Script that you will have to face.

Blessing other people is always welcomed by the angels of Light and often dropped into that other person's "grace bank account" as Carolyn Myss once said. [19] Then when hard times hit for that person, they have something to draw on – like reserve energy, peace or strength.

Part of self-mastery is learning to control the tongue. Think anything you want, just don't say it! A single negative thought by you is often not enough to go and do anything – if you were an ascended master, yes. But as the average Earth person, your <u>one-time</u> word is generally not powerful enough to do anything – unless you continually keep saying negative things – then your 'negative box' will eventually dump and deliver a surprise when you least expect it.

And by the way, "...one high, healing thought can cancel out 10,000 or more negative ones. The higher the healing thought, the more lower ones get cancelled. [20]

This is especially true of people who are more enlightened, including Masters. For the average person, it may take filling up that box again before enough energetic potential is reached to impact negativity in one's immediate world.

Saying words of protection, prayers of protection, are a good idea – to fill your own "grace bank account."

Incidentally, one can always invoke the protection of the **White Light** *(which the Neggs hate and avoid) by asking that it surround your body. It helps to first visualize a bright white egg-shaped cocoon and then picture yourself centered in it... other techniques may leave a side exposed – one you forgot to picture around you. This way, the cocoon is complete and then you 'pop' into it.*

Multiple Beliefs

Another little-known way to chain yourself to planet Earth, and really support chaos in your life, is to believe multiple systems at the same time, or incompatible beliefs. This was reviewed in Chapter 14.

Tao

Knowing the truth is following a path sustained by an archtype that Jesus reinforced – one of the things He came to do. It was called 'The Way' and because it works, orthodoxy had to dismiss and destroy it – hence we largely have Paul's teachings and not Jesus' in the church. He said, "The Truth will set you free" and it does – providing you can find The Way that He walked and taught His followers (who were called Followers of the Way, and not 'Christians'). The Way was not His invention; it was documented as existing about 150 years [21] before He came to Earth and is to this day simply called Tao, exemplified in the *Tao te Ching* teachings.

The Way is not in any religion. You go within and connect with the Godhead, or Higher Self, as Dr. Modi also suggested. You ask to be shown. You reserve judgment on what you will be shown, you become tolerant and forgiving of others while seeking, and listen to your heart (not your head) which will show you the way.

The beautiful truth is that there is already a part of you that knows The Way, knows the answers, and your task is to discover and connect with it – if you hope to get out of here. This is what the OPs and Neggs work to stop in all ensouled humans. Along the path of spiritual growth, you will overcome and develop some major positive attributes.

Personal Attributes

Of course it isn't possible to go through every day in a saintly manner – but it is the ideal. We are merely expected to do the best we can in whatever circumstances, and remain as unruffled as possible – knowing that the enemy knows our hot buttons and will attempt to push them. Falling isn't the issue – getting back up and forgiving others IS.

While we can't possibly remember or perform all the positive attributes we can find or think of, here are a few that are important, and will count for much even if the rest cannot be easily practiced:

>**Humility** – make an effort to detach from the ego and not see things as happening to you, or directed to you. What you think and want is not really that important, and putting others first will bring blessings.

>**Patience** – patience develops the soul and is an exercise in time. Being willing to wait means you don't have to and will often find things coming to you sooner than expected.

>**Compassion** – feeling empathy for others is an ensouled trait; OPs cannot do it, and don't care. Caring for others and making sacrifices is noted in heaven and what you give will be given you.

And as Chapter 15 said,

>**Respect** – is a big issue: respect others, respect the planet and life on it, and respect yourself.

And that is basically it. All human relationships can be improved with just those 4 attributes, and honest communication. An intent to serve others will be honored by the Higher Beings – be ready to serve when you volunteer. It is as much for your growth as for the other person's benefit.

Notice that Knowledge was not listed above; that is because the more true knowledge you have, the more you become the above 4 attributes.

Diet

Spiritual growth is greatly facilitated by **clean water** which may be bottled or dispensed at a health food store. Be careful as some bottled water still has contaminants and fluoride – it may be just filtered tapwater. And most bottled water is pH acidic; we should be drinking **pH alkaline** water like the Hunza, for health. [22]   Home sink faucet water filters are not recommended as they often need cleaning before one remembers to replace them. It would be better to have a Kangen Water [23] ionization device at home and take control of one's water and health. This kind of water detoxes the liver and that is the secret to great health. The older we get, the more contaminants have been filtered out of our food and water, and it builds up in the liver. pH alkaline water detoxes the liver by supplying OH- (hydroxide) anti-oxidants which merge with free radicals (H+) and the two form H2O and leave the body as water.

Clean air is important and thus a home air purifier helps, especially one that puts out **negative ions** (as are found at the seashore and near waterfalls). Negative ions are very life-enhancing; positive ions blow into town with high winds (like the Southern California Santa Ana winds) and they create static and sap energy.

It is not necessary to get rid of **red meat** entirely – except that the Mad Cow and Mad Deer issues are far from over. Infected red meat carries *prions* which are mal-formed protein cells that cause other healthy cells to malform like them – and if they enter the bloodstream, they pass the blood-brain barrier and begin creating "swiss cheese" out of the brain, called **Alzheimers.** Better to use fish or chicken from trusted sources.

A **Vegan diet** is good but very harsh and not recommended – a friend was on a Vegan diet for 9 months, had a stroke (Bell's Palsy due to lack of B vitamins), and now does a semi-vegetarian diet.

And yes, **coffee** is OK, in moderation.

Beware of **artificial sweeteners** … they aren't poisonous, it is just that their molecules are smaller than a regular sugar molecule and floating in the bloodstream they can enter through cell walls where a sugar molecule would not be able to, and they often act as an oxidant and cause trouble with the mitochondria. Honey, Stevia, Agave and regular sugar are OK… In moderation. Avoid **High Fructose Corn Syrup** (HFCS) as it really contributes to weight gain.

Caution is always advised before switching to a new regimen. If in doubt, ask your doctor or a nutritionist you can trust. The safe rule of thumb for years has been: "If God didn't make it – don't eat it or drink it." Limit (or eliminate) caffeine, nicotine, sugar, tobacco and alcohol, beer and junk food.

Media

Get rid of your TV or severely limit what you watch. Documentaries, H2 the History channel, the Science Channel, KERA (public broadcasting) are OK. Beware today's diet of sex and violence will entrain you into your lower 3 chakras and you'll be trapped.

As for books, a steady diet of Harry Potter, Edgar Allen Poe, and Stephen King will attract the wrong kind of entities to you and, as with Al Bender discussed in Chapter 4, you may begin living in a weird world of occult oppression.

And as for music, there have been articles written on the Internet about **Rap** and **Heavy Metal** "music" – and even **Country Western** music is not always good to listen to, but it is very danceable! All 3 have been found to entrain people into altered states of behavior including violence, negativity, depression and sometimes sexual perversions. [24]

The problem with **Country Western** is not in the music but the words: 'Who's cheating whom…', 'I slammed the door, got drunk and kicked the dog…', and such things as heartbreak, melancholy, cheating, lying, and drinking to name a few. What was found by some researchers was that habitual listeners of CW music had lives that tended to look like the songs they listened to. [25] You can attract what you focus on.

Even **Rock & Roll** has been found to produce vibrations that disrupt the aura and open people to harassment and attack by the Neggs. [26] Soothing Classical music was found to be the best because it has harmonious energy — the same with religious and devotional music. Loud, disharmonious and invasive music lowers aura vibrations.

In another interesting set of research, by Mike Hayes in a book called The Infinite Harmony, it was found that **music does have an effect on DNA**. Remember in Chapter 9 that the Russians found that DNA responds to radio waves and the spoken word, which means that sound can affect DNA and it stands to reason that loud, harsh, discordant music would have a negative effect on DNA whereas soft, harmonious sounds would relax and benefit a person.

Video Games largely entrain people into scenarios of violence and destruction and should be avoided, or played in great moderation. Just because they sell it doesn't mean you have to buy it or play it.

Lazy Man's Way to Enlightenment

Lastly, realize that setting one's intention to gain true Light, true Knowledge, is a major key. You will come from your intention, even if you are not aware that you have one… **intention attracts to you what you intend.** Then couple that with will power and focus, and the results are all but guaranteed.

A fascinating short book is also worth exploring: Thaddeus Golas' 80-page book The Lazy Man's Guide to Enlightenment had many insights that deliver more awareness… A sample follows: [27] (asterisked passages explained on next page)

…when you are faced with something ugly in your life, ask yourself:
What am I doing on a level of consciousness where this is real?

No resistance. Love it the way it is.*****
Enlightenment doesn't care how you get there.
There is nothing you need to do first in order to be enlightened.
I wouldn't deny this experience to the One Mind.
What you cannot think about you cannot control.
Anything that really frightens you may contain a clue to enlightenment.
Changing the content of your mind does nothing to change your vibration level.
   (except that if it is the Truth, it <u>will</u> change your Light vibration.)
Every evil that is manifest to us is there because we refused to conceive of causing it, or denied someone else the freedom to conceive of it.

It will seem like the strangest of coincidences when, having withdrawn your attention sharply from one unpleasant scene, you keep running into others like it. That will baffle you, and keep happening until you come to an unpleasantness you can tolerate or love, and your vibrations go up.

Different sets of facts are real at different vibration levels. The truth is the same for everyone, the facts are always a little different for everyone.

Since every being is self-determined, you cannot change anyone else's vibration level against his will, nor are you obliged to. You cannot in reality hurt or help others without their agreement to play the game… Indeed your perception of other is colored by your own limited vibrations until you reach the higher levels, so you have no way of knowing exactly what it is you are trying to change. They are free to be wrong. So, out of all the perceptions available to me in the universe, why am I emphasizing the ignorance of my brothers? By denying him his freedom to be wrong, we are equally wrong. Giving others the freedom to be stupid is one of the most important and hardest steps to take in spiritual progress. Conveniently the opportunity to take that step is all around us every day. *****

… and when you are dealing with a cantankerous person:
What did you think it was that needed to be loved?

*Note: These two 'flagged' statements sound good until you think more about them. While basically correct and coming from a higher vibration, obvious when reading the book, Golas sometimes goes to the same *laissez faire* extreme that Dr. Spock recommended (for raising children) which has created a generation of kids who have no discipline and no boundries. "Love it the way it is" does not apply when people are out of control. Some constraints are necessary, and it **is** appropriate to correct others when they are about to harm themselves or society. We <u>are</u> our "brother's keeper" because we are all One, and if your brother doesn't make it, ultimately you won't either. That is real Love in action because we care enough to insert ourselves into another's issue. Tough Love.

(Golas wrote the book in 1971 at the height of the Hippie Rebellion in San Francisco.)

I share the above quotes as an example, with some value, where the emphasis is mostly on Love versus Knowledge. Knowledge with Love may cause us to intercede when appropriate, and the "Love it the way it is [and do nothing]" approach is not as vibrationally high a statement as it might at first appear. It is actually a "cop out." Again, because this is a School and we are all connected.

Crossing Over

Of course at the time of death, there are several effective things you can do – once you know – to be able to get out of here. If when you die, you are in a **Tunnel**, give thanks and follow it to the other end, where the Light is. The Tunnel is created to keep the soul from being harassed and waylaid by Astral entities and discarnates. If there is no Tunnel, start praying and **ask** for a Being of the Light to come and guide you. This is where the Neggs or discarnates are most likely to come and visit you. Don't be afraid to challenge whoever shows up.

There are two main reasons people who die attract the Neggs and discarnates:

1. Souls who are angry with God for any reason, and
2. Souls who are afraid to go to heaven/Light because they did something wrong and they ended up rejecting God

…and we can add:
3. Those who don't know where they are and that **they have a choice where they can go**.

These people who hesitate to go to the Light may become the wandering discarnates, or ghosts, and need someone to pray for them that they be rescued by the Light. No joke.

Also, many of Dr. Modi's patients said the same thing:

> **God does not punish, and if you believe in God, you can go to heaven.** [28]

Your Mindset

The most important thing is your **mindset**. Believing the wrong things or not believing in anything at all are both hazardous to you. Atheists and agnostics usually have trouble when they die – because they were wrong and rejected the Light. If one expects to get out of here and not have to return, it is very helpful to:

have a belief in God,
> be in touch inside yourself with Something greater than you; know that God cares for His souls, and use prayer. Come to <u>know</u> the following:
>
>> **The Light of God surrounds me**
>> **The Love of God enfolds me;**
>> **The Power of God protects me**
>> **And the Presence of God watches over me…**
>> **Wherever I am, God is.**
>
> *Note: the above prayer/affirmation is widely used in the New Thought churches, particularly the Unity Church.*

respect oneself, choose to walk in the Light,
> a humble realization that we are all One and that you are no more important than anyone else, and no less worthy than anyone else; yet you respect the Light you do carry and you know you have a soul potential that other non-souled entities envy. Because you respect yourself, it is your **intention** to create value for yourself, spiritually grow, and share with others.

detach from <u>all</u> Earthly things, have no 'ties' to Earth,
> it is very important to be at peace with all things – to have no need for any physical pleasures that Earth can offer; you are

<u>willing</u> to give it all up. Be free of the "If only…" position. And if pleasure comes your way, enjoy it, just stay aware of what you're doing.

if you have forgiven others, there are no personal 'links' to drag you back,
any resentment or passion for others creates an energy 'link' between you and them and constitutes **'unfinished business'** which may bring you back – to learn to let go. Not karma, just letting go.

know that the life review may still take place within the RCF/Matrix,
the life review (if it happens) takes place in a higher Astral realm, still <u>within</u> the general VR Sphere – you are not out of here yet, and your greatest test may be the way you handle the review. Can you still be deceived, have you unfinished business or addictions to people or places or things? Do you forgive yourself?

you don't have to be perfect to make it out of here,
you only need to be <u>on the way</u> to being compassionate toward others, patient, helpful, and thinking of yourself last. Remember that most people on Earth got here by demanding their way and/or having to prove that they were right. That made them dysfunctional in other realms where they were too STS, rebellious, resistant, or pursuing egotistical goals. (see Chapter 14, "Life is a Film.")

know that as a soul you have the right to say 'No' and ask that you move on to new realms,
know that as a soul, you don't have to do anything – the Higher Beings do not "make" anyone do anything, so if the entity doing the life review tells you that you <u>have to</u> go back, begin to question and discuss the issue – you have that right. Don't give your power away. You may still have to go back, but at least you'll know it is legit.

and lastly, do not believe in a heaven or hell,
do not go by what you see or have expected to see. You must drop any and all pre-conceived notions of what you'll find on the Other Side… because what you believe is what you'll attract, and it may not be what you really want.
Conversely, if you expect the best, Love and Light, that would be a wise thing to hold in mind.

Aura Protection

OPs don't need an aura because they are never under attack and don't need the protection. Dr.Modi gives a more detailed look:

Patients report that the electromagnetic energy field around them, which they call an aura, protects them from outside entities coming in to them and affecting them. Any of the conditions that weaken this electromagnetic energy field around them allow outside entities to come on board. Some of my patients reported that their auras had soft, fuzzy and porous edges, so the entities could just hop in and hop out without any problems. Other patients had harder edges of their shields (auras) and were difficult to get into. Only when something went wrong with these patients did their shields open up. [29]

According to the research, here are some things that cause an aura to weaken:

1. Alcohol and/or drugs
2. Loud rock music (vibrations weaken aura energy)
3. 'Dark' Video games (*Dungeons & Dragons* for example)
4. Ouija board, Pokemon, channeling and witchcraft
5. Losing your temper and swearing (lowers vibrations and also 'throws' energy from aura) [30]
6. Being near strong EMF radiation (power lines, transformers…)
7. Too much sympathy invites entities [31]

Curiously, empathy (pity) can be a problem for an unexpected reason…

Compassion May Be Harmful

And even more fascinating was the discovery by Dr. Modi that the attractor in the case of too much compassion, **as pity**, is that it effects an empathy vibration and '**cording**' with the object of the pity/empathy, and the Neggs can climb on board and ride the cord into one's aura – because empathy is receptive, open, and accepting.

Remember that this was an issue in non-forgiveness, too.

Aura Reflects Intention

The aura is a living energetic projection of one's ground of being, and that in turn is strengthened by the state of one's soul, and that depends on how much Light one has – remember that Light is mediated by biophotons, as is the aura, and so a good, strong positive person has a good, strong aura. Someone who denies the existence of the Neggs

has nothing in their aura to reject/repel them; if one believes in them and sets their **intention** to reject them, this manifests as a (1) strengthening tone in the aura, and (2) is read by one's 'guardian angels' as a request to keep the Neggs out – it happens on both levels. If one is in doubt, there is nothing set to deny the Neggs entrance – neither energy nor request.

Lastly Dr. Modi adds:

> According to patients, people who are psychics and other people who are more spiritually developed normally have soft, fuzzy and porous edges around their auras. This makes them **more open for possession** by outside entities. Also many of the psychics want to help people, and

> sometimes **their compassion opens them up for entities to come in**. Some entities claimed that a few psychic people who are arrogant and think they have all the answers open themselves up for the outside entities to come in. **Their ego and arrogance make them easy targets for negative influences**. [32] [emphasis added]

According to another source, **it is not compassion that can harm one, but sympathy**.

> **Sympathy** is feeling sorry for others, seeing that what is happening to them is negative or bad. **Compassion** is seeing that what is happening to them is for their growth, and assisting them in seeing that also…Realize that when you feel sympathy for people, you begin to vibrate with them and take their lower energy into yourself. When you come from compassion, you do not bring in their negativity. [33] [emphasis added]

Thus, it is important to not jump into the pit and commiserate with people. If possible, speak higher words of encouragement and know that they can empower themselves if they will look within. This would be an instance where sending Light and Love would be appropriate, as well as prayer for them. And what you do for others will be done for you.

Conclusion

Your part in this is to read and apply to your life what is given ….. the good news is that even if you don't believe a word of this, you will become a better person, and have a better life, if you still try to follow the suggestions in this chapter.

Can the sheep wake up, or does this HVR Sphere repeat itself over and over…? If Man's genetics are so devolved now that he cannot overcome and figure his way out of the mess, will there be another 'Wipe and Reboot?' Man has problems to overcome; if he doesn't, we may have a *Soylent Green* or *Mad Max* kind of existence – yet another **catalyst** that teaches Man to shape up and eventually create a better world…but that is a rough way to do it.

This book has pointed out a lot of problems, not to be negative, but if you can't identify the problem(s), you don't have a chance of avoiding them, and living in a better world, and your own life may reflect chaos. Look at the government shutdown of Fall 2013 – it looks like a dysfunctional society is already evolving. We have a choice to be better people and not only gain the Light to personally get out of here, but enough souls following the Higher Path will also entrain the society with it. If we don't act now, we will not have a choice, but will live in the same old mediocrity, hassles and limitations we have always had.

What will Man choose?

Encyclo-Glossary

1-Sec Drop -- this is a direct communication from a higher being into one's mind and memory/knowledge base. It is not a voice, not automatic writing. It takes a very brief split second and one knows that it is happening, and then it can take anywhere from 10 seconds to 20 minutes to examine what one was given. It is information that is usually complete and appears to the recipient to be something that s/he already knew and is now aware of. Similar to an insight or revelation, except that it has an energy signature about it that you know it is being "dropped" into you. (Reminiscent of **V2K** but there are no words 'spoken.')

100th Monkey Effect – When one animal in a group discovers some new behavior and finds it serves him, it is said that the behavior is not learned as much as passed on as soon as the energy reaches a critical level so that their group soul can recognize and 'appropriate' the behavior. This was the case with a few monkeys on an island who discovered that washing their fruit before eating it avoided the problem of sand in the mouth. More and more monkeys on island 1 began doing it, and while they had no way to communicate the new behavior to the monkeys on islands 2 and 3, after about 100 monkeys were doing it on island 1, the others on islands 2 and 3 also began doing it (as confirmed by zoologists who were present studying the islands).

Anunnaki – one of the early, original ET visitors to Earth who interfered in the natural progression of the bipedal hominids here, and created some of the first 'humans' in Africa and Sumeria. Because of their technology and power, they were looked upon as gods. Supposedly from the planet **Nibiru**, but more likely Orion or Sirius systems. (See **Zechariah Sitchin** and **Remnant**. See also Chapter 3.)

Anunnaki Elite – consists of two main types: the ruling reptilians who retained their original appearance (e.g., Enlil and Enki), and the later, hybridized, more human-looking (e.g., Inanna, Marduk, Sargon, even Alexander the Great). The later change was effected by Enki's mating with humans and later genetic prowess to enable the Anunnaki to move among the humans who found the original., reptilian/reptibian appearance repulsive.

Archons – the 'powers that be' in the celestial realms – according to the Gnostics. These are the same ones that Ephesians 6:12 refers to: powers & principalities (a hierarchy) dedicated to evil and wickedness. Synonymous with 'demon.' (See **Nephilim**, and see **Djinn** in Chapter 6).

Astral Realm – note that there are levels in the Astral realm, and in particular, the one that most concerns Man, is the Level I (**Chart 4** in Chapter 12) which is a kind of intra-dimensional space – more than 3D and yet not really 4D, and this is inhabited by Man's oppressors, the STS Gang. The normal 4D STS/STO entities occupy the higher 4D and lower 5D Astral realms and cannot see 3D Man.

Attractor – energy in the form of an idea, person, or thing that draws other things, ideas or people together based on similar and strong resonance.

Bands – referring to the H-Band and M-Field suggested by Robert Monroe. These are energy bands, or grids, created around the Earth due to the often negative activities of souls on the Earth. Experienced as static or noise. See also **RCF/Matrix**.

Beings of Light – often referred to as Angels, or today's Watchers, they guide and protect Man. They are also known to provide the life review that NDErs speak of, and they are the *'Inspecs'* that Robert Monroe spoke of.

Bionet – a term coined in Chapter 9 to describe the hyperdimensional network of communication in the body. Like the Internet, *chi* is carried in meridians of energy to all parts of the system, from the chakras, and tells the cells and organs what to do. The Bionet is manipulated during Accupuncture to channel biophotons.

Book 2 – the successor to this *Virtual Earth Graduate* , with additional examination of specific topics, is *Transformation of Man*, aka Book 2.

Brain Waves – a measurement of consciousness.
> Beta cycle: 12 – 19+ Hz (normal waking consciousness)
> Alpha cycle: 8 – 12 Hz (relaxed, aware state)
> Theta cycle: 4 – 8 Hz (sleep)
> Delta cycle: less than 4 Hz (deep sleep)

Catalyst – anything like an event, an idea or a word, that causes change in a person; the threat of being fired for bad performance at work is a catalyst to perform at one's best. Illness is a catalyst to see what is wrong, or what energy is blocked, in one's body.

Chakra – a vortex of energy formed in the body wherever two or more chi meridians come together; same as a vortex on the earth with its ley lines. (Sedona, AZ is known for several of these.) These are also referred to as 'energy centers' as they transduce energy from the air/water/Sun around a body and draw it into the body thru the chakras. There are 7 main charkas in the body and 1 above the head, and 1 below the feet. There are many more, minor charkas all over the body.

Chi – energy particles, also called *ruach*, orgone, mana, prana or ki – without chi in our food, air and water the human body could not exist. The chi is a force that travels along meridians (pathways) in the body that link the etheric aura (1st level of the aura) to the physical body; it can be directed by the mind to specific parts of the body for healing.

Cognitive Dissonance – the result of hearing/reading something new that does not fit into one's reality, or in what one thought was their reality; the effect is to create confusion followed by denial of new concepts. More specifically, when a new idea <u>conflicts</u> with an established idea that one already thinks they know, the result is 'dissonance', and rejection. When people were told 500 years ago that the Earth was round, they experienced great cognitive dissonance… which led to denial.

Coherence – resonating alike; attracted to each other by similar resonance. Two energy waves are coherent if they have the same shape, size, and strength.

Déjà Vu – the experience of having done, seen and/or heard something before; as though one is reliving a prior moment in their current lifetime. Relates to reliving a fractal simulation. See **Recycling**.

Dissidents – Anunnaki hybrid Remnant still on the Earth who seek to control Man and deny him his divine heritage. See **Insiders**.

Draconians – a militaristic STS race largely from the Orion system who have subjugated many worlds in our Galaxy. Also referred to as the Dracs, or the Reptiles. A very old race that lays claim to much of our Galaxy and they fear Man because they don't all have (nor do they understand) the soul, thus they seek to contain/control Man.

Elite -- those humans who are mostly descended from the Anunnaki hybrids; as a group they may be augmented by the Remnant Insiders who stayed behind when the main contingent of Anunnaki went home. They are generally not the enemy. See **PTB**.

ELF – Extremely Low Frequency; a vibratory wave form that is sent by a radio-like device or microwave transmitter at a certain Hz or MHz frequency such that it entrains the mind into a 'resonant state' (usually Alpha) with the wave.

EMF – ElectroMagnetic Field; such an electrical field around a high tension power line also generates its own weak magnetic field, hence EMF. Note that a cellphone or TV or PC – anything electronic has an EMF and it is unhealthy to spend much time in it as it 'afflicts' the cells of the body and disrupts their function. The reason is that the body has its own weak EMF and communicates info to other parts of the body via the nervous system and chi meridians (see **Bionet**).

Energy Vampire – a person, OP or ensouled, who subconsciously starts an argument, gets the other person angry, and the instigator takes the other person's energy through the Law of Energy Potentials. Energy always flows from the higher potential to the lower and this applies to car batteries, as well as humans. So the instigator creates a fight, not to win or lose (they don't care), they will walk off with some of your energy, and they quit the argument when they have it. They are up, and the victim is usually tired.

Entrain – to induce a state in B like in A; usually done by music, movies, and words, but can be done by powerful thoughts and beliefs. A hypnotist entrains a subject into a desired state; Hitler's harangues entrained the crowds into the Nazi mindset he wanted; and classical music entrains the listeners into a relaxed (Alpha) state.

Entropy – the tendency of all things in the universe to wind down and die; also called the Second Law of Thermodynamics. The enemy of Evolution.

Era – occasionally the Higher Beings have to clean up and reset the Simulation, usually what this book referees to as a Wipe and Reboot. When Man is restarted after a Wipe and Reboot, the Era will have some dominant theme in the Greater Script that the activities of Man are to experience and handle. Our current Era began about AD 800-900.

ESH – Ensouled Human Being, has a soul and thus an aura. See also **OPs**(Chapter 5).

Flow – often referred to as The Flow. This is the rising energetic vibrational entrainment into the higher 4th and 5th dimensional realms. It has increased awareness, compassion, Light, and STO aspects for service and is available to all who seek to align themselves with a Higher Way. It was created by the Higher Beings and is supported by an archetype that masters on the Earth reinforced and made available to all spiritual growth aspirants.

Free Will – an illusion. The more one grows spiritually, the more one does the will of the Father of Light. Baby souls, or those who insist on their own way, think they have free will but the Father is merely letting them experience the results of what they do... their **Script** controls much of what young/baby souls can do. As Jesus said "Not my will, but Thine be done." Advanced souls have surrendered their will by eliminating their ego.

Galactic Law – the ethics and rules as set forth by the Galactic Council and adhered to by all subordinate councils for the maintenance of order. It includes a Non-interference directive, responsibilities of 'creator races', transportation/communication protocols, terra-forming procedures, and energy creation/disposal to name a few.

God/gods – this is god with a small "g". The Anunnaki were called gods because of their power and control over Man. In addition, Sargon, Moses, Gilgamesh, Alexander the Great and a number of Anunnaki offspring who were half-human half-Anunnaki were considered god-like. Not the same as "the gods who run the Simulation." See **Hybrids**.

Godhead – a collection of higher souls, and Soul Groups, in closest proximity to God, like spokes on a wheel where the hub is God Himself. The Godhead works directly with the Oversoul for each Soul Group and sometimes the two are hard to distinguish. The basic hierarchy is: **God – Godhead/Oversouls – Soul Groups – Angels/Neggs – and individual souls.** (See Chapter 7.)

Gods-in-Training – when Man graduates from the Earth School, he can be useful to the Father of Light in various places in the Multiverse. One of those places is to undergo an apprentice position in overseeing the Earth and its souls – under the tutelage of more advanced 'gods' who give direction and training. The gods-in-training still make mistakes, just as Man does, and while often minimized by karmic override, these are allowed in part as an aspect of the new gods' training. This is therefore sometimes a source of things going wrong in an Earth person's life. If a god-in-training abuses his power, he is recycled to Earth. (Chapter 15.)

Greys – the 3' tall gray-colored humanoids with the big heads, big black eyes and skinny bodies; their eyes are large (really protective coverings over eyes sensitive to light); they typically perform the abductions on humans, some cattle and other species. They have a hive/group mentality as they are **bio-cybernetic roboids** and Anunnaki tools to improve Man's DNA.

Ground of Being – who and what you really are; your PFV is the physical reflection of the <u>sum</u> of your STO/STS quotient. If you, your soul essence, were to be removed from your body, the energy being that you are would have a certain vibration level (also reflected in the color of your aura) – higher or lower depending on how much Light you hold, how compassionate you are, whether you seek to serve (STO) or be served (STS), what issues (stuck points, agendas and attachments) you still carry with you, and in general, it refers to the "quality" of Light & Love that you <u>are.</u> Ultimately, it reflects the highest actions/thoughts that you are capable of.

Higher Beings – Light Beings above the Astral and reincarnative levels (1-6) and who are responsible for the operation of these lower 6 levels, reside on the 7th level themselves; may intervene in 3rd – 4th – 5th – 6th dimensional affairs when the Greater Script of the Father of Light, or the One, requires it to keep the Multiverse working. Also colloquially called **"the gods"** just in Chapters 12-15 who run the HVR Sphere or Simulation. The Higher Beings are <u>not</u> the Beings of Light (angels) nor ETs nor aliens.

Higher Self – also called the Oversoul, this is the coordinating entity of each Soul Group and acts to oversee Scripts, events, lessons – and coordinate with the souls of the same Soul Group, <u>and</u> with other Oversouls who manage other Soul Groups in the same Godhead. Each Godhead has multiple Oversouls that interface with the multiple Soul Groups. See Chapter 7, **Chart 3a**.

Hybrids – this is any human-looking but 'upgraded' version of Homo *sapiens* which may or may not have a soul. It can be the Anunnaki hybrids – part Anunnaki, part human, and their bloodline. Or it may be Homo *noeticus* that the Greys have been so busy developing to restart civilization after the big Change event in the near future. Most are very intuitive, psychic and look to be the next step in the development of Man.

Insiders – Anunnaki hybrid Remnant still on the Earth (may include Enki). The pro-active ones who try to help mankind and block the **Dissidents** (qv).

Interdimensionals – those beings in 4D <u>and above</u> who normally have very little interest in Man, and may be STO or STS. The STOs are often curious and observing. The STS version has been known to use OPs for unknown agendas. Also a generic term for the 4D STS Controllers inasmuch as they operate between dimensions. Possibly Djinn.

Interlife – where souls go when they die, after passing through the **Tunnel** to the **Light**. Also called the Other Side, and sometimes appears to be Heaven. It is where the **Script** is designed, souls are counseled by the Masters and Teachers, souls are rehabilitated after a rough lifetime on Earth (or elsewhere), and it is where the Heavenly Biocomputer referred to in Chapter 13 resides. This is also where reunions with members of one's **Soulgroup** happen. (Book2 spends 2 chapters on this aspect.)

Karma – *Aka* **The Law of Karma**. – originally the concept of "meeting oneself", or "what goes 'round, comes 'round." It does <u>not</u> mean being stabbed in this lifetime because one stabbed someone else in a former lifetime. The original, true concept was that of the Universal Law of Cause and Effect, and it forms the basis of one or more aspects of your Life Script. Karma can also be a manipulative issue in the Virtual Reality of Earth if the life review is done by a Negg posing as a Being of Light.
Note that Karma applies only to Earth; other souls who do not come to Earth do not have to deal with Karma.

Law of Confusion – when RA was asked a question that violated someone else's right to privacy, or asked something that would be giving advanced level information that the person had no context for, RA would comment that the question could not be answered because it "violated the Law of Confusion." We are to work thru confusion and seek the answer(s) on our own; we have the 'right' to be confused and are expected to work thru it, or ask, thereby absorbing the lesson and information on a level that makes the lesson/info part of us.

Law of One – the concept that we are all connected at a higher level, mostly thru our Higher Selves, and we are all part of the One, the Father of Light – if you have a soul. This does not apply to OPs. The Law of One also includes freewill and love. Telling someone else what to do, how to live, etc is a violation of the Law of One, a violation of freewill whose flipside is called the Law of Confusion.

Light – an intelligent aspect of God; sometimes referred to as the Force. It may be used interchangeably with Heaven. There are biophotons of light that support the operation of DNA and sustain bodily operations.
Note that Light (large L) is a conscious aspect of the God force, which force can have a brilliant light about it. The light (small "l") is everyday, regular light.

Lightworker – any entity, physical or Astral, that uses Light as an energy source to do its work. (Includes angels, demons, Neggs, energy healers and Higher Beings.) Caution: it does not always imply STO behavior.

Loosh – a term coined by Robert Monroe in his chapter 12 of Far Journeys. It is energy produced by 3D living beings that is allegedly 'harvested' by 4D entities in the astral for sustenance. Loosh is bountifully produced by humans who go into states of deep **fear** or anger or lust – they radiate the energy after being manipulated to produce it – like a grain of sand in an oyster produces a pearl that is harvested. See **Energy Vampire**.

Matrix – synonym for the HVR Sphere, but not to be confused with the matrix as shown in the movie Matrix. Can also be ZPE Etheric composition that interpenetrates everything.

Memes – a concept, or idea, that generally has spread through a population – an idea that may spread like a biological virus – such as a belief in ghosts, or a belief that black cats bring bad luck…or, if you go out in the rain and get wet, you can catch a cold. There are positive and negative memes. (See also "**100th Monkey Effect**.")

Morphic Resonance – said of a plant or animal that takes its physical shape from the morphogenetic field that establishes a 'morphic' (shape) resonance with the object's energy. The plant's shape is entrained by the morphic resonance with the morphogenetic field (pattern) that governs how living things take shape, according to Rupert Sheldrake. (See Chapter 9 'Chuck.')

Morphogenesis – Rupert Sheldrake conceived of the presence of a 4D field around living things that influences the shape they take – kind of an Astral Template that governs height, width, color and other aspects of the oak tree for example, such as when and where it sends out its branches, how fast and how far.

Multiverse – the universe we live in is one of a number of universes comprising a Multiverse… multiple universes interconnected forming a coherent larger universe consisting of multiple levels (realities), and can involve parallel universes or dimensions in '**superposition**' (or stacked).

NDE – a Near Death Experience where the person appears to die, and their body is pronounced clinically dead, but they come back to life and relay their experience of meeting a Being of Light with whom they have a Life Review, and they usually come back a changed (better) person. The NDE effect often produces a spiritual transformation in the person.

Neggs – the 4D 'dark' angelic beings operating in the Astral realm around the Earth, whose sole purpose is to apply the negative lessons specified in one's Life Script. Thus they are "**NEG**ative **G**uide**S**." They work with the Beings of Light (Angels).
They are programmed to afflict mankind – they are appointed to effect the negative parts of one's Script (aka **catalyst**). They provide catalyst and feedback inducing Man to change and grow. They work <u>with</u> the Beings of Light (Chapter 6) because they, too, are Beings of Light who <u>volunteered</u> to serve the negative agenda and they were 'reoriented' to Darkness to maximize their effectiveness. They still carry a small, suppressed connection to their original Light down inside and they will be restored to their original condition when their service is complete. (See info in Chapter 6 from Dr. Modi.)

Nephilim – the physical Anunnaki Igigi mated with earth women and produced giants (Nephilim) called Anakim, Giborim and Rephaim, which were hell on earth. (Chapter 3.)

NPCs – these are the other characters in a Virtual Reality game; they are not programmable or operable by the player – the Game or operating system uses them to play a part in the Drama. They are called Non-Player Characters. Same as **OP**s (Chapter 5).

OPs – Organic Portals -- (pronounced "Oh Pee") human beings, flesh and blood (Organic part), and they can serve as a portal for 4D entities (Neggs and 4D STS Controllers) to operate thru them. They also are not fully human as they lack a soul and that is because they have incomplete DNA and only the first 3 chakras are wired to function; they cannot access higher energy centers. Due to their somewhat robotic nature, they can be used by the STS Gang to manipulate and/or influence ensouled humans in 3D. They are often playing the role of **NPC**'s (as in a video game) in our world. (Appendix D in ASOM.)

Parallax – where the perceived shape and size of something (say an object in the sky) does not change with any change in our position from which it is viewed (i.e., a parallax), thus it must be reflected off the surface of something consistent in shape. If it were reflected off dust in the atmosphere, it would have size and shape distortion depending on the viewing angle – <u>but the *Gegenschein* in Chapter 12 doesn't</u>.

PFV – Personal Frequency Vibration -- the day-to-day, overall vibratory rate (resonance) of the soul energy sustaining the human body. When a person is angry their aura 'glows' red, and the PFV can drop to a lower (denser) vibration than when a person feels a lot of love and the aura 'glows' rose and the vibration reflects the energy of the heart charka (higher, lighter energy). The PFV also denotes which charka is dominant in the person; a person living from their higher charkas has a higher PFV than one engaged in sex, violence and pettiness (lower chakra activity). The aura typically reflects what one is feeling, yet the base PFV does not change; when the person is at rest, the base PFV is consistent from day to day as it reflects the overall level of soul growth. Also known as that person's "energy signature" as recorded in objects (Psychometry).

Phase-Shifted – refers to 3D and 4D entities or 3D and 4D timelines which cannot see the other even though they may occupy the same space. For example, there may be a 30° phase shift, or a 60° or 90° shift (the most common). Think of 2 Sine waves almost on top of each other (congruent and coherent; now move one wave to where it's trough is below the other wave's peak – they are 90° phase-shifted.

Placeholder – an OP-like version of a real ensouled human living on another timeline (parallel universe) that already split into two, with duplications of people between the timelines. If the ensouled human did not replicate to the new TL, the other people who went to the new timeline still need/expect that 'body' for their everyday world activities to function, and his absence in their lives would be noticed. And so minus a soul, John Doe exists as a kind of 'synthetic' human in the new timeline. (See Chapter 5.)

Points of Choice – there are pre-programmed points in a person's life where important choices must be made, and they are found in a person's Script. Examples are whether to move to Florida or stay in California, whether to accept what looks like a great new job, or whether to get married. Sometimes the choice results in a **timeline bifurcation** into a fractal subset so that another aspect of you can see how that turned out. See **Timeline**. (Covered more in detail in Book 2.)

Pre-Soul – also called First Time Soul, allegedly the initial stage of an animal that leaves 2D and enters the 3D human soul realm (metempsychosis); this is not a complete soul, but a potential one if the entity applies itself as a 1st time human. Typically, only the first 3 chakras are functional, and thus there is not enough 'soul energy' to create an aura. (See also **OP**s.)

Prime Directive – a requirement in our Galaxy for those races who can create life and modify existing life genetically – often referred to as a 'creator race.' They are responsible for overseeing the welfare: safety and education of their creation. This is why a **Remnant** of the Anunnaki stayed behind (now known as the Naga.) (Chapter 12, Prime Directive.)

Prophylactic Fantasy – describes the world of denial that some people live in. 'Prophylactic' because they feel safe in their version of the world, and they reason that nothing really destructive has ever happened to them, nor can it. 'Fantasy' because they do not accept the real world and its negativity; they see their world as they want it to be and sometimes think that they can exert a 'force' that makes it that way.

PTB – the earthly human Powers That Be; the 3rd dimensional STS people running the world for their Anunnaki Dissident masters (control group still here). They are also influenced by corrupt DNA, and the **RCF/Matrix** itself. Puppets. Many of them are OPs. See **Elite** – not the same thing, just a higher level of control.

Qubits – elementary particles, quanta like atoms, electrons and photons, that have a quality of 'spin' as measured/manipuated by the Stern-Gerlach apparatus through application of a magnetic field. (See *Programming the Universe*, Seth Lloyd, Ch 5 & 6, and pp 5-7, 109-114).

RCF/Matrix – see below (Resonant Consciousness Field).

Recycle – short-circuited version of reincarnation: to come back into the same body, same lifetime, hence experiences **Déjà Vu**. Implies the inability to move forward into new realms and experiences in the greater **Multiverse**. (See Chapter 14: Life is a Film.)

Reincarnation – the spiritual growth aspect of a soul moving thru the different realms in the Multiverse (not just back to Earth) for the purpose of experiencing and gaining knowledge and wisdom. On the other hand, a repeated lifetime limited to Earth is more of a recycling.

Remnant – short for Anunnaki Remnant – that part of the Anunnaki group that stayed on Earth and did not leave with the main group, between 610-560 BC. Comprised of the Insiders (+) and the Dissidents (-). Some are human-looking. Also known as Naga (underground 'Serpent' dwellers in Asia), or also called Dravidians.

Reptibian – A humanoid being, part reptile, part amphibian. In most ways looking like a human being, but with scales instead of skin, perhaps slightly webbed toes and fingers, cat's eyes, and a face that suggests a reptile/amphibian more than a human being. Note that an anaconda is aquatic and is also a reptile that moves on land. (Chapter 3)

Resonance – vibrating alike: such that two tuning forks A and B side by side, with A struck hard to set it vibrating, when put next to B which was not vibrating, will set tuning fork B vibrating at the same frequency as tuning fork A. This also happens with people in close proximity: a very negative person can 'detune' (bring down) a room of people and some people may actually feel ill and not know why (as they pick up the negative person's vibes). See entrainment.

Resonant Consciousness Field – RCF/Matrix – the very negative energy and thoughtforms surrounding the Earth, as a vibrational envelope or field or Band that is so strong it entrains ensouled humans who are unconscious (qv) into their lower 3 chakras and they act out STS ideals. It is not alive or evil; it just has a lot of strength from centuries of people acting in synch with it and thus reinforcing its energy level. Similar in structure to the Matrix (qv) described earlier, or Monroe's "H Band" but not run by any entities.

Satan – allegedly the leader of the demonic spirits which were the deceased Nephilim and/or their offspring. This titular role may have been filled by the Nephilim (fallen Igigi) leaders known as Samayaza or Azazyel, or the Gnostic favorite: Ialdabaoth, in a former Era. The Egyptian Set, or Sata, was probably synonymous with one of the three just named. A convenient mythological character to personify Man's need for duality in the universe. (Chapters 2 and 6.)

Schumann Resonance – natural frequency of earth's vibration/resonance: 7.8Hz.

Script – instead of pure Karma, when one is born, one is given a Script covering what basic events are to happen in one's life, which one is expected to overcome; they may be positive or negative, and how one meets them and handles them determines how one is progressing towards the goal of getting out of the earth experience. It often has Options programmed into it (**Points of Choice**) where the soul must make a significant choice. It is a test of soul growth. A personal Life Script is usually subject to the Greater Script of the Father of Light and works within it. Also called LifeScript. (More in Book 2.)

ShapeShifting – the ability to control what people see… the being doing the shape-shifting does not actually change any of his atomic structure – just the way his appearance is perceived, and perception is holographic. So to effect a different appearance, the being just produces new interference waves that the observer 'sees' differently. Commonly done by 4D and above entities while in 3D.

Sheep – people who are barely conscious, and refuse to think for themselves. They want someone to tell them what to do and when to do it, and they go along with whatever they are told. They are easily manipulated by the Media. Also called **'sheeple'** and may be OPs or 'dense' ensouled humans.

Soul Aspect – all souls can 'split' themselves to experience different realms; as when a timeline splits, one part of the soul stays with the original TL and another part replicates to the new TL. Each soul has aspects in different TLs, dimensions, worlds, and realms, etc and at a point in the future, they reunite to the Soul Group. Not a **Fragment** (next). (See Chapter 7.)

Soul Fragment – some souls may fragment **due to trauma** and then special therapy is often needed to coax the missing fragment to rejoin its source. Some fragments are held by family members, past lovers, and even by the Neggs themselves.

Soul Group – each soul was part of a group of like souls (same core vibration PFV which usually synchs up with a specific archetype) and these split up to better experience the Creation – souls will eventually reunite in their original group when their explorings are done. The Soul Groups reunite with the **Godhead** from which they came.

Soul Merge – as in the case of the author, to undertake a special project where a 3rd level soul has volunteered to serve in a capacity that it alone can't do, and so a Merge is performed to give that 3rd level soul the extra knowledge and strength of the merging soul (who is of the same soul group -- usually from a higher level) and together they perform some task that the Higher Beings must have approved – before the Merge can happen. (See Chapter 7.)

Soul Migration – the concept that animals can progress to first-time human beings with 'baby' souls and the full-fledged human soul must be earned thru successive incarnations. As they would also have only the lower 3 chakras operative, they may be mistaken for OPs. (See Metempsychosis on Wikipedia.)

STO – Service To Others; altruistic behavior, self-sacrificing.
STS – Service To Self; selfish behavior; 'Me-My-Mine' syndrome.

STS Gang – this is a 'catch all' group term referring to the Neggs, discarnates, thoughtforms, all 4D STS, including Anunnaki Dissidents, acting as oppressors of Man, without a clear distinction as to exactly which one is doing what to Man at any one time. The group may occasionally include the **Interdimensional** souls described by Wilde and Monroe (Chapter 12), although such are <u>usually</u> too busy interfering with the STO entities on their own level to harass Man on the 3D level.

Subquantum Kinetics – is an approach to microphysics with roots in general system theory, nonequilibrium thermodynamics, and nonlinear dynamics. It represents quantum phenomena differently than Quantum Physics (QP) and works with the concept of the **Ether** (Chapter 9) which is composed of subquantum units called etherons (as opposed to QP's quarks). It is simpler than Quantum Physics and explains the issues that QP is still wrestling with: wave-particle dualism, strings, singularities, and the cosmological constant. It also embraces and explains Tesla's work better than QP. (Refer to Chapter 4 of Dr. Paul LaViolette's book <u>Secrets of Antigravity Propulsion</u> for a more complete description in layman's terms.)

Terraforming – an advanced technical process whereby a whole planet is set to its original, or a near-new, pristine condition following some catastrophe or pollution, or both. The ecology is balanced, the air, land and water are unpolluted, and in the case of planet Earth, it can once again support lifeforms. See also "**Wipe and Reboot.**"

Thoughtform (TF) – any thought that many people subscribe to and which reflects a widely held belief, esp. one imbued with a lot of fear, or hate, generates a TF which after a while (depending on the amt of energy put into it) takes on a 'life' of its own; **man is a creator and thoughts are things**. If enough people fear and believe in werewolves, there will be thoughtform 'werewolves' … which are not real entities but are attracted to those who fear and believe in them (like attracts like).
Any unwanted TF can be cancelled and should be before it attaches itself to a person's aura and then 'feeds' off the person's energy – like a parasite. TF have no conscious volition of their own, they are reactive and go to wherever (1) they are attracted by sympathetic vibration, and (2) where the person's aura is weak.
Carl Jung called these TF's Archtypes.

Timeline (TL) – the linear coherent vector on which all souls and Placeholders (OPs) of a certain frequency range have their being; a reality timeline that linearly moves forward creating causal events. It is not permanent and is subject to entropy if a bifurcation results from a rise in consciousness and attendant agreement coherently shared among the souls seeking to live in a higher consciousness in TL2 is preferable to the negatively polarized TL1. If there is not enough agreement (energy) to sustain the new TL2, it dissolves.
If a dimension has only one TL, the TL is the dimension, but dimensions can have multiple TLs. There is a TL where Hitler won, for example.
And timelines may create, 'run' and dissolve **fractal** subsets (within the larger TL framework) for special purposes (qv).

Unconscious – unaware, not a very high level of perception. A person who is 'asleep' spiritually and is not aware that there are more than the 5 senses. Can also mean 'spacing out' with eyes wide open. Standard condition of the **Sheep**.

V2K – "Voice to Skull" -- a microwave enhanced transmission of words directly into a person's head, as if they actually hear the words, without any external devices or hearing apparatus. Developed by the US Army to communicate with a soldier on the battlefield, to the exclusion of other soldiers, it was perfected during the mind experiments with Helen Schucman while she transcribed the *Course in Miracles* book. Who sent her the information is not known. (Chapter 11. Also see Bibliography : Internet Sources.)

Vibration/Vibe – the energy state of a person, place or thing. Everything puts out an energy 'signature', which is how pyschometry works… objects record the energy of the person that held/owned the object, and places often hold the residual energy of events that happened there: some sensitive people cannot visit Gettysburg as they feel the negative energy from all the hate and fear created in that place – even thought it was long ago, it still holds some energy that has not completely dissipated. (See **PFV**.)

Vimanas – In Hindu literature (*Ramayana* and *MahaBharata*), the gods were said to fly around the sky and even engage in warfare between these craft with exotic but powerful weapons – similar to the Sumerian flying machines (MAR.GID.DA, IM.DU.GUD, and GIR). An ancient form of UFO, cone-shaped like many temples in Thailand, or *Stupas* in Tibet.

Visual Spatial Acuity – the ability to see fine detail; visual term reflecting the number of rods/cones in the retina. Similar to **pixels** in computer printing, display screens and digital cameras.

Wanderers – higher souls from other realms who have volunteered to incarnate on Earth in troubled times to serve as the Light leads: they may anchor the Light, write books, lead New Thought churches, heal or perform other services to benefit Mankind. Usually 6th level beings (souls). The Indigos and different forms of "Starseed" are part of this group.

Wipe and Reboot – an end to a current **Era** of Man on Earth, followed usually by a terra-forming (resetting the environment back to clean and balanced), followed by the Re-seeding of Man on the planet. See Chart 5 in Chapter 15.
The term is borrowed from the computer world where when a PC is non-functional (i.e., locked up and displays the dreaded BSOD [Blue Screen of Death]), it is necessary to "Wipe" the hard disk – reformat it – and reload the operating system and application software… i.e., "Reboot" the system and start all over again.
Whereas the PC gets a clean start as if nothing happened, each new Era for Man still includes whatever objects were created in the prior Era – i.e., pyramids, huge walls, and Stonehenge.

Zechariah Sitchin – the late Middle Eastern scholar, speaking several languages, who translated the Anunnaki/Sumerian tablets. Chapter 3 is mostly dedicated to a summary of his findings about Man's origins. His claim to fame was *The Earth Chronicles* series of 8+ books that revealed the Sumerian – Anunnaki connection (see Bibliography for partial list).

Appendix A: Moon and Mars

I. Man on the Moon

Another consideration in the Science errors category (Chapter 8) was the alleged trip to the Moon in June 1969 in Apollo 11. I watched it on TV as it happened and I thought to myself, "Something isn't right with this…." The lighting was wrong, the lack of Moon dust on the Lander was wrong, and how could they possibly know just how much thrust would be needed to land and take off since they had never been there before? -- and even today they are saying that the gravitational pull is different than what they thought:

> The major characteristic of the Moon's gravitational field is the presence of **mascons** which are large positive gravitational anomalies associated with some of the giant impact basins. These anomalies greatly influence the orbit of spacecraft about the Moon, and an accurate gravitational model is necessary in the planning of both manned and unmanned missions. They were initially discovered by the analysis of Lunar Orbiter tracking data, since navigation tests prior to the Apollo program experienced **positioning errors much larger than mission specifications**. [1] [emphasis added]

So how much fuel was put on board, and how could they have made critical mid-course corrections with button-pushing programs, due to the **mascons**, while coming in for a landing? While I was no NASA expert, it just looked … fake. And what really tore it was there was a camera already outside the Lunar Lander taking a picture of Neil Armstrong jumping off the ladder as the first man on the Moon – who took the picture? And if it was attached to the landing gear, why didn't the landing, kicking up dust, coat the lens?

> **Note 1**: It was later determined that many of the lunar shots of Apollo 11 were actually pictures and film of the astronauts practicing in their huge underground hanger somewhere in the Southwest. *Look* magazine in the Summer of '69 had a multi-page spread that revealed activities in a simulated lunar landscape. These pictures were always a back-up in case pictures taken on the Moon didn't come out well – due to the intense radiation of the Van Allen Belts fogging the film? (See section below on Radiation.)

In the years since then, there have been many whistle-blowers and nay-sayers on a score of websites that seek to point out the mistakes that NASA made during the alleged trips to the Moon. Some of them are really picking at any irregularity, while others raise a reasonable doubt on scientific grounds that if we went, the astronauts must have been sick with radiation, and they really risked getting stranded on the Moon, for a number of reasons.

Here are some of the scientific reasons why we could not have gone to the Moon in those "tin cans" called Apollo. And that doesn't mean that we didn't go to the Moon, it is just <u>unbelievable</u> that we would go in the 'primitive' Apollo craft.

Inadequate Computer Technology

The state of on-board computers was very antique. This was 1969 and we were still using **ferrite-core memory boards**. I know because I was a programmer analyst in an IBM 360/30 and a 360/25 shop and these <u>small</u> computers were bulky – there is no way that an Apollo on-board computer would have had more than 32k words of memory in it and that doesn't allow for a very large program (even in Assembler)– let alone emergencies and mid-course corrections. It was said that the astronauts executed programs as they needed them via punched buttons on the face of the small computer **(AGC)**....
Risking their lives with an underpowered computer?? Not believable.

> Nearly thirty years on [1999], countless desktop computers have more power at their disposal than all the computational power available to NASA throughout the entire United States in the 1960s. [2]

While the 1969 IBM computers did have the stored-program concept, the large size of the physical memory/circuit boards, the logistical issues of punching buttons into a **DSKY** (Display and Keyboard) console every time something was needed to affect the trajectory, the descent, or braking… The absence of a powerful computer to sense and <u>automatically make corrections</u> (it was all stored as a series of individual, small programs identified by **"nouns",** and called by **"verbs,"** and manually executed by the astronauts, stored in the **AGC** [Apollo Guidance Computer]), led me to suspect that the astronauts would be "flying by the seat of their pants," not by computer. And according to a man (Don Eyles) who was privy to the Apollo 11 lunar landing, Armstrong was said to manually fly the Lunar Module to its landing site.[3] Unbelievable.

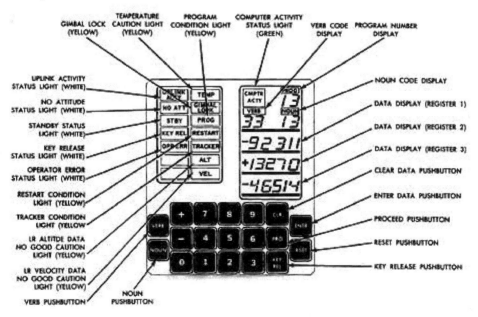

The DSKY Console Aboard Apollo 11

In 1969 computer chips [Large-scale Monolithic Integrated Circuitry] had not been invented. The maximum computer memory was 256k, and this was housed in a large air conditioned building.

In 2002, a top of the range computer requires at least 64Mb of memory [in a 64k partition] to run a simulated Moon landing, and that does not include the memory required to take off again once landed. The alleged computer on board Apollo 11 had 32k words of memory….

The memory-cycle time for the AGC was 11.7 microseconds (and that is slow)—not fast enough to perform emergency mid-course corrections. That's less [speed and memory] than today's simple [hand] calculator. [4]

The problem was that the series of individual programs (nouns) in the AGC's ROM had to be called (by verb) and run manually and could not interact with each other in one comprehensive computer program because there wasn't enough memory to contain such a beast. The alleged memory size was only 32-36k words available for each program written either in Basic or Assembler (called "Yul") [5]… they used both.

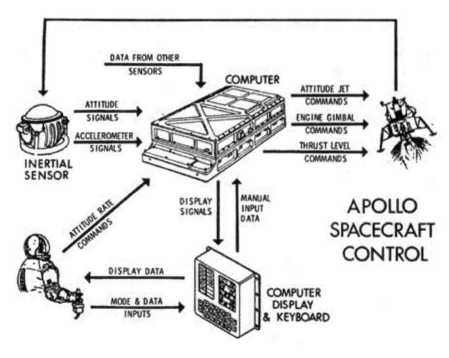

Apollo LM Primary Guidance and Navigation System (PGNS)

Clearly the AGC was underpowered for the job – meaning the LM could easily crash onto the lunar surface if just one thing went wrong… or if an instruction was entered 1 second too late.

Van Allen Radiation Belts

When President Kennedy told the United States in May 1961 that we would put a man on the Moon by the end of the decade, the **inner** Van Allen radiation belt had just been discovered in 1958, and the extent of its effect on astronauts was unknown. It was later discovered that there was a 2nd radiation belt – TWO of them -- and to fly through them would require adequate shielding. It is said that the hull of the Apollo capsule was ultra-thin (to conserve weight) and it could not have stopped any significant amount of radiation or micrometeorites. The same can be said for the spacesuits during EVA on the Moon.

> The radiation trapped within the Van Allen belts is most intense from 620 miles above the Earth's surface through to a height of 18,634 miles... Starting at a height lower than 300 miles from the Earth's surface, there is a **continuous zone of at least 54,000 miles of hazardous radiation.**[6] [emphasis added]

> Even today, the radiation belts are causing problems with Man's satellites flying thru the lower (and weaker) levels of the Inner Belt. Man has relied on the Earth's geomagnetic field to minimize Van Allen Belt effects on our satellites. Satellites in low-Earth orbit over Southern Africa are already showing signs of radiation damage suffered as a result of the Earth's magnetic field weakening... [7]

Scientists are now saying that there may be **three** radiation belts.

> **Note 2**: It has been determined that the astronauts could have taken a northern Earth-escape trajectory, closer to exiting the Earth from the far northern hemisphere, and this would minimize the radiation effect – i.e., there is less radiation closer to the north pole. But they would still have to fly as fast as possible through it.

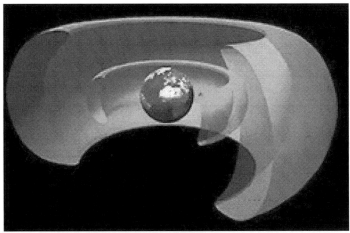

The Van Allen Belts
(credit: NASA Johnson Space Center)

The radiation strength of the Belts is rated at 41 Rems/4 hours of travel. The inner belt is weaker [electrons] than the outer belt [protons], but can be crossed quicker.

And the latest measurement of the Belts puts them at 64,000 miles thick which is about ¼ the distance to the Moon, and that is a long time to be exposed even **at 15,000 miles per hour for the capsule** – that still means about 4 hours flying through the both radiation fields, one way. Of course, the lethal amount of radiation depends on how long one is exposed to it and the standard NASA answer is that the astronauts spent little time in the belts due to the speed of their rockets. That means they may have spent about **8 hours total** (out and back) exposed to the radiation with little protection... very risky.

> These radiation belts, extending to at least 54,000 miles out, are in fact *over twice the depth* compared with the data generally available from NASA. Therefore any Apollo astronaut traveling thru these belts would have spent *over two hours* in each direction within the belts, *absorbing high levels of radiation for a total of approximately* **four hours**. [8]

Van Allen, the discoverer of the Belts, knew the dangers that they presented to our astronauts and "…he had already informed NASA that their aluminum shells of their spacecraft were <u>insufficient protection</u> against the dangers of radiation." [9]

Radiation Danger Quantified

So what amount of radiation is lethal to the human body? According to a chart compiled by several organizations, including The National Radiological Protection Board, UK, and the Naval Research Laboratory, USA: [10]

    0   – 160 Rems are uncomfortable but not deadly,
    170 – 300 Rems cause bone and blood damage, w/ 20% mortality,
    310 – 500 Rems cause the above + lung damage, w/ 50% mortality,
    500 – 630 Rems cause the above + gastrointestinal damage, w/ 90% mortality
    640 – 960+ Rems cause the above + cataracts, sterility, w/almost immediate
                 incapacity and 100% surety of death.

All the above cause "NVD" – nausea, vomiting and diarrhea.

The EPA says that the average human should not be exposed to more than 2.4 mSv (milli-Sievert) per year. 1 mSv = 0.1 Rem "People usually get about 0.24 rem (2.4 mSv) in background radiation per year. If a worker must deal with radioactive materials in the course of his job, his legal limit is higher: 5 rem (**50 millisieverts, mSv**) per year :" [11]

> The standard for a lethal dose is designated LD 50/30, defined as the short-term exposure (i.e., over a period of a few hours or less) which would kill 50% of the human population within 30 days. It's around **350-400 rems** (3.5-4.0 Sv). (Radiation Safety Office. *Radiation Safety Handbook*. Columbia University, s.d.)

While much of the actual effects on the astronauts is classified, Wikipedia did report:

The total radiation received by the astronauts varied from mission to mission but was measured to be between 0.16 and 1.14 rads (1.6 and 11.4 mGy), much **less than the standard of 5 rem (50 mSv) per year** set by the United States Atomic Energy Commission for people who work with radioactivity. [12]

There are some statements regarding measured radiation with and without shielding, from the USN Research Lab:

During the August 1972 solar flare the radiation dose would have been about 960 rem with no spacecraft shielding. This falls to 40 rem with 9 cm **[4 in.] of aluminum shielding**… the shielded dose would have resulted in no short-term health problems for astronauts in general. For short exposures, a dose of about *118 rem is lethal to 10% of human recipients and about 345 rem to 50% [of humans].* [13]   [emphasis added]

The Apollo craft did not have 4" of aluminum hull, however, it appears that they were not in the Belts long enough to absorb any serious radiation. Moving real fast through high radiation is better than moving slowly through low radiation. Similar to when it rains: if you run, you get less wet.

So it varies depending on personal constitution and length of exposure. And that is just radiation from the Van Allen Belts -- not counting the **cosmic rays** (GCRs), **solar flares** (SPEs) and **micrometeorites** which require different shielding. **The SPEs go through many centimeters of shielding**. Radiation, cosmic rays and SPEs are the main "nasties" in the array of elements currently stopping Man from exploring the cosmos. [14]

Note 3: Apollo 16 (April '72) went to the Moon during one of the worst episodes of solar flares we have ever had, and there was no reported effect on the astronauts…. Hmmm.

Radiation Summary

1. In 1998 the Space Shuttle flew to one of its highest altitudes yet – 350 miles above the Earth. And hundreds of miles below the **Van Allen Radiation Belts**. The Shuttle had shielding superior to that of the Apollo craft, and the Shuttle astronauts reported being able to "see" the radiation with their eyes closed – penetrating the shielding as well as the retinas of their closed eyes. For a dental x-ray on Earth, we wear a ¼ inch thick lead vest, and that is just for a 1/100th of a second exposure. What would it be like to endure several hours of exposure with minimum shielding? [15]

2. CNN issued the following report, "The **radiation belts** surrounding Earth may be more dangerous for astronauts than previously believed (like when they supposedly went thru them 30 years ago to reach the Moon). The phenomenon known as the 'Van Allen Belts' can spawn (newly discovered) **'Killer Electrons'** [inner belt] that can dramatically affect the astronauts' health." [16]

3. Interesting that NASA is <u>now</u> investigating the exact nature of **cosmic radiation** with the intent to put an outpost on the Moon by 2020. They built and sent an LRO robotic unit to orbit the Moon and record the Moon's radiation environment.

> The surface of the Moon is baldly exposed to cosmic rays and solar flares, and some of that radiation is very hard to stop **with** shielding… when cosmic rays hit the ground, they produce a dangerous spray of secondary particles right at your feet. All this radiation penetrating human flesh can **damage DNA**, boosting the risk of cancer and other maladies… When galactic cosmic rays collide with particles in the lunar surface, they trigger little nuclear reactions that release yet **more** radiation in the form of neutrons. **The lunar surface itself is radioactive![17]** [emphasis added]

And we're not even talking about the other unpredictable hazard <u>on the way</u> to the Moon – **micrometeorites**. Think: Apollo 13. [18]

While no radiation is good radiation, and it looks as though the astronauts weren't in the Belts long enough to suffer even minor consequences, there is another weird aspect of the astronauts on the Moon that warrants examination…

> **Note 4**: it has been said lately while using high-powered telescopes aimed at the Moon sites where Man supposedly landed, there is nothing to see – **no Lunar Rover tracks in the dust**, and no Lunar Landing Modules are visible. If true, then we either did not go to the Moon, or if we did, was it via the ETs' crafts, or perhaps one of ours from Black Ops?
> (See 'Last Word/No Return' section below where China makes this claim based on their 2013 **Chang'e 3** Rover.)

Tracks in the Dust

In 2012 the US Lunar Reconnaissance Orbiter (LRO) sent back pictures of the Moon's surface as it flew around the Moon. It has been in orbit since 2009 and, barring someone retouching the photos, the following landing sites <u>do</u> show astronaut activity on the Moon. Prior to examining them, first recall what astronaut Aldrin's bootprint looked like:

and several bootprints:

no reticles

(credit Science Photo Library from Bing Images)

To better understand the following Lunar Orbiter pictures, also note what happens when walking on the lunar dust: the astronauts were not shuffling nor dragging their feet:

This is important. Note that walking has not changed the color of the dust.

The first two are Apollo 12, and the last is Apollo 11. These pictures are courtesy Space.com and http://www.space.com/12030-moon-photos-nasa-lunar-reconnaissance-orbiter.html

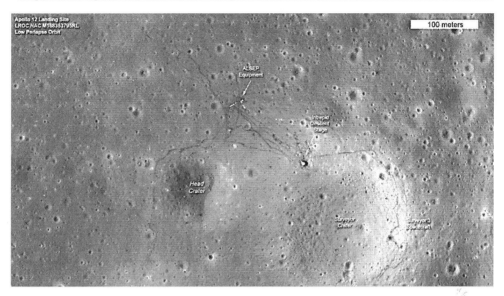

The above was the Apollo 12 landing site, no Lunar Rover, so all the tracks shown **(squiggly black lines)** are said to be the astronauts' footprints in the lunar dust. "ALSEP" (top center) is the Apollo Lunar Surface Experiment Package. Below is a close-up:

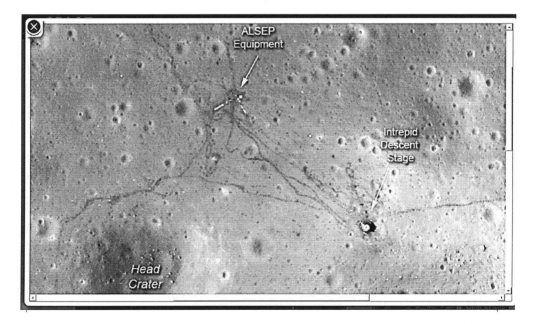

The tracks made in 1969 by astronauts Pete Conrad and Alan Bean, the third and fourth humans to walk on the moon, can be seen in the above LRO images of the Apollo 12 site. The location of the descent stage for Apollo 12's lunar module (LM), Intrepid, also can be

seen. The LRO was said to be 50 miles above the lunar surface, but also had had high-definition and zoom capabilities.

And this was the shot of the Apollo 11 landing site:

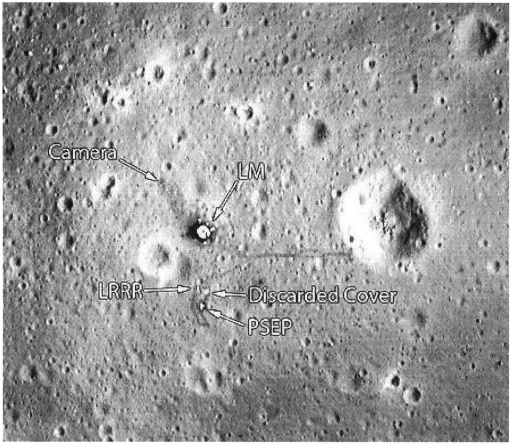

Scale is about 1 inch : 50 meters.

The Passive Seismic Experiment Package (PSEP) provided the first lunar seismic data, returning data for 3 weeks after the astronauts left, and the Laser Ranging RetroReflector (LRRR) allows precise measurements to be collected to this day. You can even spot the discarded cover of the LRRR. The flag fell over so is not visible.

At any rate, later lunar visits included Lunar Rovers, and their double-track markings are also visible in the last few pictures of the Moon trips. So it is hard to say that we didn't go to the Moon when there appears to be corroborating evidence... but then again, NASA took the pictures.... And they are known to **airbrush** other pictures of anomalies on the Moon... Could they have added "tracks in the dust" to existing LRO pictures?

> **Note5:** These tracks would only show up if (1) the astronauts dragged their feet, scuffled as they walked (they didn't), and (2) if the lunar soil under the dust were darker (it isn't). Sorry but this looks like a clear case of 'editing' the photo ... perhaps the Chinese were right. (See below: **Chang'e 3** rover in

the 'No Return' section.)

Before considering the "giant killer" photographic evidence that bears consideration, let's summarize some of the major questions regarding the Moon Landings.

Miscellaneous Issues

This is neither pro- nor anti-NASA... just some issues to think about and research.

1. Apollo 11 TV pictures were lousy but subsequent missions had fine pictures.
2. Who would dare to use the LM on the Moon when it was never tested for landing and takeoff anywhere?
3. Instead of being able to jump 6 feet high in lunar gravity, the highest jump was 19 inches. The Moon has 1/6 Earth gravity, so a jump of 5-6 feet would be expected...
4. The fabric spacesuits had a zipper running up/down the length of the torso – why was there no air leak?
5. If the astronaut's suits were pressurized, in the non-atmosphere of the Moon, why didn't they balloon out? Gloves certainly didn't.
6. In the Apollo 14 flag setup ceremony, why did it not stop fluttering?
7. Why is the astronaut's debris that was left on the Moon's surface not visible to powerful telescopes <u>on the Earth</u>? Or to Hubble?
8. Why did Gus Grissom give an unapproved news conference **in January 1967** that the US was still **at least 10 years** from going to the Moon?
9. With more than a 2-second signal transmission delay, how was the camera left on the Moon able to pan up to record the Apollo 16 LM departure? And why did it wiggle like a box on a string?
10. How did the astronauts leave the LM when their suits + backpacks allegedly exceeded the width of the hatch opening?[19]
11. Why are the astronauts "lit up" while standing in the shade of the LM (which blocks the Sun)?or with the Sun to one's back:

These pictures are one of the best arguments that NASA used pictures of the astronauts taken in the practice **Lunar Simulation Facility**.

They don't even have the 'crosshairs' that were always in lunar pictures. So they weren't taken on the Moon.

> **Rewind**: The **reticles** (crosshairs) were a fixed feature of <u>all</u> Hasselblad Moon cameras strapped to the astronaut's chests. (See Camera section below.)

12. Since the Apollo capsules had no lead lining to protect against radiation, how did the 'still' pictures shot on the Moon make it back to Earth without the radiation fogging the film and ruining it? How is it that solar radiation bombarding the Moon didn't fog the film <u>on</u> the Moon either? [20]

13. If solar radiation is a problem and the astronauts were provided with gold-coated visors for protection, why did astronaut Schmitt (Apollo 17) not use it while walking on the Moon? [21]

14. Where were the rocks stored on the trip back to Earth? There was over 800 lbs of rock brought back during all 6 missions, or 133 lbs (avg.) per trip.

So how and where did the astronauts train to go to the Moon?

Lunar Simulation Facility

In addition to a crater training facility in Cinder Lakes, just outside Flagstaff, Arizona, NASA also trained astronauts in a large indoor facility replete with green walls for projecting "lunar" scenes while photographing astronauts practicing in the lunar "soil" … Wires attached to the astronauts replicated a lighter gravity, and special lighting simulated the Sun. Volcanic ash served as the lunar dust.

(credit: all pix below from Bing.Images)

Lunar Practice Area on Earth

Astronaut on a Wire to Practice Low Gravity Walk

Another View of the Practice Hangar

And there were the lighter moments, too… singing Moon River in NASA shorts …

Hasselblad Cameras

While we're at it let's examine the cameras that were strapped to the astronauts chests. These were the **Hasselblad 500 El/70 Lunar Surface Camera** that were specifically designed for the Moon, a special 70mm film cartridge, film to resist fogging despite very hot and cold extremes, 200 exposures per roll, electric film advance, and **no view finder** – the astronauts could not bend over to look in one, anyway… and they all had **reticles**, or crosshairs, that were always to come out in every picture so that distances between things could be better judged (and determine if the film had stretched due to heat).

Without a viewfinder, aiming and shooting by twisting one's body must have been … interesting, and yet all the pictures were of high quality and the subjects photographed were right where they should be, centered. Additionally interesting is that the camera was not to be left in the Sun for too long as heat built up really fast in the camera, damaging the film, and by the same token, the astronaut could not block the Sun and put the camera in the shade where the temperature would quickly get too cold. How do you design a film to handle +180° F in the Sun down to - 180° F in the shade? [22]

Lastly, the **absence of stars** in the background of the photos has always been suspect. According to Jan Lundberg (the project engineer who designed the camera), the camera has 2-3 F-stops on it, which would allow for longer exposure and stars should have been visible – if stars were present… but they were not part of the practice Lunar Training Facility.

It gets even better when it comes to the **reticles**: these crosshairs are to be IN FRONT OF whatever is photographed.. and yet some pictures clearly show them BEHIND the objects:

A recent YouTube video (13 min.) from May 2014 outlines 7 of the classic errors made in the filming of the Moon venture... called

Great Movie Mistakes: 7 NASA's Apollo Moon Landing Footage Errors [23]

The errors include:
1. Flag waving despite no atmosphere on the moon
2. Photos shot by astronauts were too perfect
3. Different locations had identical backgrounds (verified)
4. Crosshairs of photo were covered by objects
5. Astronauts were intact although radiation in space is extremely high
6. Space suits are not able to endure extremely high and low temperatures
7. Footage shows shadows cast by multiple light sources

Lack of Lunar Dust

The Apollo11 Lunar Landing Module (LM) barely raised any dust when it landed, and again when it took off. Same thing for Apollo 17 several years later. [24] Buzz Aldrin's boot showed high-kicking dust and the imprint it left in the dust (which 'caked' without any moisture?), but the Landing Module barely raised any dust when it landed <u>and</u> took off. There was no lunar dust on the landing footpad, and there was no melted dust, no crater, and no disturbance whatever below the Landing Module as shown in NASA's own pictures from Apollo 11.

> During the take-off from the lunar surface why were no exhaust gases and smoke from the ascent engine visible? ... there are indeed visible exhausts from a **hypergolic engine** when operating – even in a vacuum... In a vacuum these thick, dense, opaque exhaust gases would certainly be visible... [25]
>
> **Note 6**: Hypergolic is a rocket engine that ignites and produces thrust when 2 or more propellants come together. No ignition or spark is needed.

Something people don't know is that there were also practice 'hangars' at Kennedy Spaceflight Center and at Houston Manned Spacecraft Center, and there are photos of the astronauts practicing in a large Simulated Lunar site in the Arizona-Nevada area. [26]

Is it possible that the pictures from the practice areas were what was shown to the public since the radiation in the Van Allen belts must have been harmful to the film – if not to the astronauts?

Finally as for the Moon, we come to **the *piece de resistance*:** the odd pictures of Earth from the Moon. This issue has never been noted nor discussed anywhere.

Earth View Wrong

For the following discussion, you need a map of the landing sites on the Moon…

(Credit: Bing Images)

What is really interesting is that no one has noticed that in pictures of the Earth from the Moon, **the Earth is way too small**. And a couple of times, the Earth is not a consistent size between the Apollo 11 pictures and those of Apollo 17. Case in point is picture AS17-137-20910 on the NASA website (and below). Compare pictures **AS17**-137-20910 and **AS11**-44-6548 (July 1969). [27] (AS11 is Apollo 11, and AS17 is Apollo 17.)

The Earth from the Moon should look larger than the Moon does from the Earth because the **Earth is 3.7x larger than the Moon**. But it doesn't, and the size of Earth pictured is not consistent. And the difference is <u>not</u> because of atmosphere as on the Earth when the Sun sets and it looks larger… and it is not always due to focal length (which was preset on the Hasselblad cameras mounted on the astronauts' chests)…basically

like an old-time Box camera

Focus: this is important: You know what the Moon looks like from the Earth as far as size goes… Now imagine the same Moon almost 3x larger… that is what the Earth should look like from the Moon.

Keep in mind:

1. Pictures of Earth taken from the <u>surface</u> of the Moon should show Earth pretty much **overhead** and a consistent, correct size. (See lunar map.) You'll note in the following pictures that the Earth is not always overhead.

2. Pictures of Earth taken from an orbiter above the Moon would effect an 'Earthrise' – but the Earth should still be **larger** in those photos.

Odd Size and Position

Let's examine some anomalies…

(**AS17**-134-20384)….

Virtual Earth Graduate

The orb above the flag is Earth. Since the Astronaut and the flag are normal size, why isn't the Earth also normal size? And, was the astronaut who took this picture **lying on the ground**...? Remember the camera is mounted to their chests and this is looking up...

All picture sources:

http://spaceflight.nasa.gov/history/apollo/apollo11/index.html
http://spaceflight.nasa.gov/history/apollo/apollo12/index.html
and   http://spaceflight.nasa.gov/history/apollo/apollo17/index.html

And one of the weirdest pictures, suggesting someone at NASA Photoshopped the picture is the following:

Since the Earth, Moon and the Sun are in the same solar system horizontal plane, the Sun cannot be higher, i.e., above, the Earth shining down on it... So why does the shadow on the Earth show a 45° Angle?

This suggests the Sun is up and to the left of Earth. And if you can see Earth, why not a few stars, too?

AS17-137-20910

So the right side of the boulder is in the dark (if the Sun was off to the left). Refer back to the lunar chart of landing sites above – what part of the Moon was Apollo 17 sitting on? Upper right face... at 30°. And if the Earth is actually almost directly overhead, why is the Earth (in the picture) way off over the horizon? If the astronaut is standing on the Moon, wouldn't the Earth be larger and almost directly <u>overhead</u>?

So if Apollo 17 landed 30° above the equator (see chart), why is the shadow on the Earth at a 45° angle? In other words, Earth should be overhead, facing the Moon, and just a slight distance above the center/equator of the Moon, and should not result in a 45° angle to the shadow cast by the Sun. This looks like Photoshop®.

And from the very beginning, there was one iconic picture of Earth from the Moon, an 'Earthrise' ... and it too has problems... Curiously enough, the Apollo 11 picture (below) shows the Earth almost 1/3 the correct size:

The foreground does appear to be out of focus which suggests a camera in the orbiting Command Module used a telephoto lens ... but why?

And wouldn't a telephoto lens also make the Earth look bigger?

So what was done to reduce the size of the Earth? And why?

And why no stars?

Apollo 11 (**AS11**-44-6548).

The Smoking Gun?

To repeat: The Earth is bigger than the Moon so it should look larger than the Moon does from the Earth. **But in the above pictures, the size of the Earth is not consistent –** although the size of the Earth shown in the Apollo 11 picture is getting closer to the correct size if the picture was actually taken from the Moon.

> Granted: pictures from the orbiting Command Module could have a different focal length set, and that could change the size of the Earth... but why? There are no pictures of the Earth fullsize from the Moon... I wonder if it is because they don't know how to Photoshop the picture so it will look genuine...?

Rewind: Since the astronauts were standing on the Earth-facing side of the Moon, wouldn't the Earth appear to be mostly **overhead** and much **larger** in most pictures?

Do the Math

The following is the issue. I want to make this discrepancy very clear.

Earth is 7,927 miles in diameter. The Moon is 2,160 miles in diameter. The Earth is therefore 3.67 times bigger than the Moon, and yet in a lot of NASA pictures, the Earth is shown to be the same size as the Moon looks from Earth, or less.

Imagine this: There are approximately 240,000 miles between the Earth and the Moon. For ease in making my point, imagine that you are standing in space at a point 240,000 miles from both the Earth and the Moon which are side by side – Would they appear to be the same size? If not, why doesn't the Earth appear larger from the Moon than the Moon appears from the Earth? The NASA pictures have a problem because whoever processed the pictures of the Earth and Moon together didn't think of what I just pointed out…. The resulting pictures appear to be 'Photoshopped' and hurt NASA's credibility leading one to ask if we really went to the Moon.

The Last Word

Just in case you didn't follow the above analysis, try this:

The Moon doesn't rotate – it keeps the same side to Earth all the time. So in Apollo 17, with the Earth appearing over the boulder, near the horizon, how can there be an 'Earthrise' with the Earth appearing near the Moon's horizon – if you are standing on the Moon in any of the Apollo landing sites, there would never be an 'Earthrise.' At the Apollo 17 landing site, to photograph the Earth, you'd have to lie on your back and the Earth would fill most of the viewfinder. Why is NASA showing us something different?

The Earth would always be overhead to anyone standing on **the mid-Moon** (see lunar map) because it always faces the Earth in the same position. The Apollo sites were not over on the edge. While a lunar orbiter could effect an 'Earthrise' as it circles the Moon and then comes around to the Earth side of the Moon, why would the size of the Earth be different from an overhead shot? The Moon isn't that big to make an edge-of-the-Moon shot that much different from a shot straight overhead. Even allowing for different lenses, telephoto vs wide-angle, astronaut handheld vs orbiter-mounted, etc. the really small pictures of Earth are an anomaly that has not been explained. Is it "Photoshop?"

> **Note 7: Repeat**: if the astronaut is standing at Apollo site 15, and shoots horizontally at a boulder, the Earth will not be in the picture, but NASA has edited the Earth into some pictures because they felt it should be there – it makes for a nice PR photo (even though it is wrong).
>
> Similarly, despite focal-length, the Earth in the AS17 boulder shot should not be on the horizon, AND Earth should be much larger. Why no focal length issue? Because the camera mounted to the astronaut's chest is like a **box camera** and the astronaut (with thick gloves) could not set anything more than an F-stop (which was planned for in advance and NASA gave the camera a big enough tab so the gloved astronaut could do that)… so whereas focal length could be set/changed by the astronaut in the Command Module, it was not done on the lunar surface.[28]

Focal Length

I have discussed this issue with a **professional photographer** whose initial explanation was "They're using different focal lengths…and F-stops" and he showed me how when they do that, it changes foreground focus… See the boulder or flag pictures… they are not out of focus. (They also probably used a telephoto lens, but the Earth is still too small.) When they don't change the focal length (as telephoto does), the whole picture is in focus – like the picture of Earth over the Rock (also p. 8) and because the Earth is (1) not overhead, and (2) is too small, it is a telltale sign, according to him, that it was Photoshopped.

And, how could the astronauts change the focal length standing on the Moon's surface -- with their heavy gloves? The Hasselblad camera was preset (really like **a box camera**) … with a focus to infinity. It didn't need any adjusting, except for bright light vs shooting in darkness (and that was the F-stop).

> **Note 8**: According to the photography expert, the focal length may be part of the answer for the Orbiter, but the Earth size/location (boulder picture) he agreed was not correct. It is funny-looking.

Miscellaneous Issues

Apollo Problems

Apollo Missions were not problem-free, and some of the mishaps were like a subtle warning to not even attempt to come to the Moon.

> **Apollo 11** -- allegedly got to the Moon, through the Van Allen Belts (which didn't damage the film going to or coming from the Moon!), and with an under-powered on-board computer, managed to undock from the Command Module, and then the fun started. Neil found the computer was too cumbersome to operate to use it to land the LM, so he allegedly flew the Eagle manually onto the Moon. [29]

> **Apollo 12** -- suffered two lightning strikes during liftoff – on a clear day.

> **Apollo 13** -- suffered a meteorite hit between the Earth and the Moon.

> **Apollo 14** -- the Command Computer failed, then was restarted, then the Radar Unit failed…and was restarted.

> **Apollo 15** -- James Irwin suffered a cardiac arrest (minor heart attack), but made it back successfully.

> **Apollo 16** -- Flight Controllers delayed the lunar landing due to service propulsion problems.

> **Apollo 17** -- flight launch from the pad was delayed by an issue with automatic sequences.

Apollo 18 -- was sitting on the launch pad, ready to go, and the program was stopped.

With regard to Apollo 14, 16 and 17, it should be pointed out that when UFOs buzz our missile installations, they have the ability to deactivate ICBMs and affect our electronic equipment. They have also been known to deactivate in-flight missiles launched from Vandenberg AFB.

Space Shuttle Issues

Just a brief reminder here that two US shuttles disintegrated, and the program was stopped, while the Russian equivalent (the *Buran*) keeps flying to service the International Space Station. In fact, the Shuttle was also capable of going to the Moon, with a better capacity for more fuel and shielding … so why didn't they at least fly it around the Moon?

No Return

Lastly, it is interesting that following Apollo 17, and some of the discovered physics involved, there were no more manned lunar landings. Apollo 18 sat on the launch pad and the astronauts were ready to go, the mission had been paid for, but the Apollo 18 mission was cancelled. Why? Bill Birnes, the publisher of *UFO Magazine* has said in several TV documentaries that we were warned off. Someone else appears to be on the Moon… and landings of LM or rovers are not welcomed… two Russian *Lunakhods* crashed and it is not for sure that the Chinese Chang'e 3 rover landed, either. Yet it is apparently OK to fly around the Moon.

The **Russians** also did not follow suit and 'prove' that they could land on the Moon, and don't forget that they unfortunately crash-landed several Luna landers which were unmanned and sent to collect soil samples and rocks.

The **Chinese** sent an unmanned probe to the Moon (2013) and photographed it… and also said they found no evidence that the USA had ever been on the Moon[30]… Whoa, what is that? They really said their **Chang'e 3** rover visited our landing site of Apollo 15 (which was closest to their landed rover), but even their fly-over pictures they said showed nothing… Hmmm. Note **the 'x' and 'y' on the preceding Lunar Map** – where they intersect is where the Chinese landed their Chang'e 3 rover.
Also interesting is that the **Chinese pictures from the Moon do not show stars in the sky** either, and **they would not do a 360° view from the lander**… And the soil is a markedly different texture every 100'…. Perhaps they didn't really go to the Moon as the Chinese videocast said…[31]

Neutral Point Issue

Besides the Van Allen radiation belts, **Moon gravity was a problem**. These discoveries involved "gravitational anomalies" (mascons) and something called the **"Neutral Point"** between the Earth and Moon which complicated steering the Apollo 11 craft. [32] And Wernher von Braun was reprimanded by NASA in 1969 for telling the press about this error/issue in lunar trajectory – almost a showstopper as it affects the fuel and braking of the craft on its way to the Moon. Wernher resigned 3 years later … before Apollo 17 had even left the pad.

At this point, it has been about 40 years and we have not been back to the Moon – and we have cancelled Apollo and Shuttle operations. Why? Now NASA says we are going back to small manned capsules with heatshields in something called the Orion Program for Mars. (Déjà vu: Mercury Program of the early '60s.) Huh?

All that would be perfectly in line with ET having told the USA that we are not wanted traipsing all over their observation platform, i.e., modified-Moon-spacecraft, drilling holes and setting off blasts to seismically test the interior of the Moon – which reverberate for more than an hour[33] and that alone would endear us to ETs inside the Moon… not to mention bombing it in 2009 – a scene we were not allowed to see.

No Answers

Lastly, scientists are now questioning the Moon geology itself, and they say that **it is made of different material than the Earth**, and it is obvious that it did not "spin off" into orbit as the Earth was being created. [34] They now say, "The Moon was created in its present orbit." [35] Says David Hughes,

> In astronomical terms, therefore, the Moon must be classed as a well-known object, but astronomers still have to admit shame-facedly that they have little idea as to where it came from. This is particularly embarrassing, because the solution of the mystery was billed as one of the main goals of the US lunar exploration programme. [36]

Perhaps it is an observation platform made to look like a moon and the 'inhabitants' don't want us traipsing all over it since we can't mine anything there, and all we proved in October 2009 was that we could bomb any part of the Moon we wanted to… to prove what? To whom? (We already knew there was ice there at the lunar poles…)

Russia's Space Program

And it is only fair to point out that the USSR also had its share of problems while achieving some outstanding "… feats in space technology well beyond the capabilities of their American counterparts." Specifically, **the Soviets always had rockets with much more muscle than America's Saturn V** workhorse had, and sometimes on the order of 4 : 1. [37]

And yet, there seems to have been some prestidigitation going on regarding Russia's first man into space, Yuri Gagarin. The Soviets had selected several potential men to be the one to fly into space, and it came down to Gagarin and Titov by April of 1961. The launch was to be April 12, 1961. On April 3rd, Gagarin was filmed in a full dress rehearsal including walking to the gangplank and the waiting rocket. On April 7th, Gagarin made an (allegedly) off-the-cuff acceptance speech, in case he was selected, as did Titov, and they were both recorded for posterity.

> The interior shots of the capsule sealing procedures were *completely staged* in another area of the launch hangar… But this film was not just for the Baikonur historical record. This record was for all of us. [The official Soviet cameraman] never got near enough to the actual launch to be able to film clearly this small matter of just what was going on in and around the capsule… subsequently the Soviets cut the faked footage into the final shots of the actual launch and presented it to the world without *telling anyone* of that fact. World-wide, viewers were presented with a mostly fake event pretending to be a totally real event. [38]

And before we all say "…just like the Soviets to do that!" … please remember that the technology required to go and return safely was indeed a "giant step for mankind."

> … given the number of technical problems that were unresolved, it is easy to imagine the Soviets could well have totally stage-managed the actual launch on April 12, 1961. [39]

All of this to say that neither the Americans nor the Soviets could get technologically ramped up in just 9 years after JFK's declaration to do a successful Moon shot. Space has turned out to be a very hostile environment and yet… What do you do when your President commits the USA in May 1961 to doing the impossible? And with the Cold War on-going, and the US not wanting to lose face…. and the Soviets not wanting to lose face….?

When all is said and done, the authors of <u>Dark Moon</u> make this cryptic comment:

> Unlike our fellow researchers we do not declare that NASA *did not* send astronauts to the Moon. On the contrary: **NASA did go to the Moon** but neither in the manner that NASA has claimed as set out in the historical record, nor with the individuals named in the historical record. [40]

And I'm going to leave it at that, too, having had the same insight.

II. The View From Mars

Pictures from Mars

While we're at it, we might as well take a look at the pictures that have allegedly been sent back to Earth from the planet Mars. They largely show Mars to have a reddish hue – which is what we <u>expect</u> to see. In some of the same pictures, there is a shot of the Spirit rover and its **Calibration Sundial** which has 4 colors on it to allow the technicians on Earth to adjust the incoming pictures' color to get a true view of Mars. The color reference tabs are: Red, Blue, Green and Orange. In most shots of the rover that show the Martian surface as red, the Calibration Sundial tab for Blue has turned Red. [41] Other colors are also off. When the color is adjusted so that the Sundial tabs show their proper colors in the pictures of Mars, the Martian surface looks like it is somewhere on Earth – brown/beige soil and blue sky. [42] How interesting….

In fact the area looks a lot like parts of the Atacama High Desert in Chile...

> **If we went to the Moon and we went to Mars, fine. But why are the Moon and Mars pictures a bit 'irregular' and thus open to question, as if to suggest a hoax, or cover-up?**
> **Are we supposed to see through it and instead of reacting with fear and apprehension to an official government announcement about ETs, we psych ourselves into <u>arguing for that</u> which we might otherwise reject?**

Life on Mars?

It is interesting that the Anunnaki had way-station bases on Mars for the shipping of ore and gold back to Nibiru. [43] That means there must have been buildings and hangars, possibly monuments… like the much-disputed **Face on Mars** and what appear to be pyramids close to it in the Cydonia region. In addition, there have been fly-over pictures of what appear to be huge glass (?) tubes half-buried in the ground, serving an unknown purpose – irrigation or transport, presumably. [44] These tubes were photographed by the Mars Surveyor and produced NASA/MSSS image **M04 00291:**

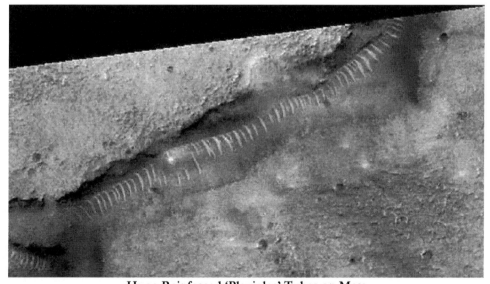

Huge Reinforced 'Plexiglas' Tubes on Mars
(Source: http://www.marsanomalyresearch.com/evidence-reports/2000/001/real-smoking-gun.htm) and (Credit: NASA/JPL/Malin Space Science Systems)

The glint off the end of the top 'tube' shows it is not a root formation. And if you look closely, the end of the top tube is connected to the one below it – one band encircles both tubes. Weathering and shifting of the crust is responsible for the 'banding' to have shifted— Original banding and craters are visible in the picture below:

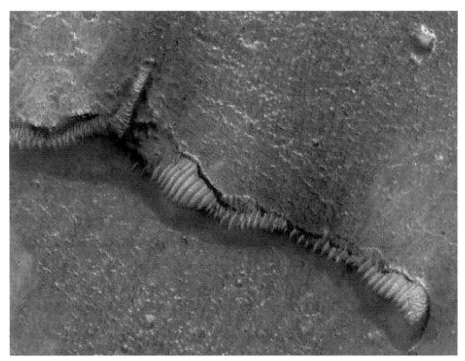

It looks organic, as parts of it appear to have expanded…but examination on various websites show it to be something that exists below the ground that wind and erosion have uncovered. The following I think will convince you that this was **constructed** – look at the joint banding, the split, and the forking structure:

(credit: http://www.nationalufocenter.com/artman/publish/article_426.php)

The weird aspect of all this again is the banding and the fact that **the scale is in kilometers**, not inches. These all are shown in Malin Space Science Systems and were taken by an orbiting satellite above Mars. Time will tell (if we ever get there) just what they are.

It is not totally impossible that if the Anunnaki were once on Mars, as a mining way-station, that they or their descendants might still be there. Underground, of course.

This photo of the **artificial** tubes is the smoking gun that proves Mars was (and probably still is) inhabited. If Mars had waning water resources, the inhabitants would want to conserve it and remove it from the surface into underground reservoirs, with tubes interconnecting them, and the tubes might also be wide enough to bear a local traffic to water craft of some sort.

> **Note 9:** That being said, **Schiaparelli** was not seeing things: there used to be irrigation **canals** on the surface of Mars, but with Man's developing more and more powerful telescopes, that had to go underground – the Martians don't want Man coming to visit any time soon. Gee, they must be in communication with ETs on the reverberating Moon…

Valles Marineris Scar

A huge scar stretches over 4000 miles across Mars and there is no natural geologic reason for it. It is 120 miles wide and over 7 miles deep.

(credit: Big Images)

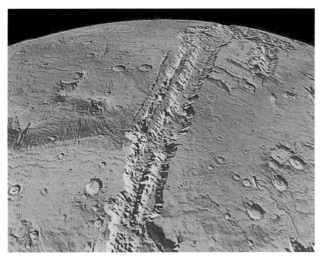

(Credit all: Bing Images)

What it really is becomes apparent in the left view, in a topographic analysis of the gorge:

It is apparent that it is one long **gouge**… and it is exactly that – the remnant of a cosmic war between Anunnaki and those who used to occupy Tiamat – the planet between Mars and Jupiter that was destroyed. Mars lost a lot of atmosphere and water.

This is what a plasma disruptor weapon does.

Cydonia Region Evidence

The picture below is what alarmed the world back in 1976 when the Viking 1 orbiter sailed over the Cydonia Region and took the following picture (the dots are lost data in the transmission from Mars to Earth):

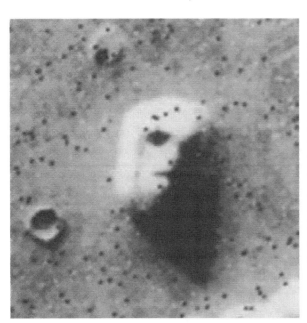

While it is said to be just a coincidental outcrop or large hill with unusual lighting producing the humanoid features, there is more to the story.

During the Anunnaki dominance of this part of the solar system, and their use of Mars as a base, it was decided to commemorate the former **King Alalu** – who lost to Anu for supremacy; he ventured to Mars and Earth, and his sacrifice was remembered in a large ground image.[45]

The Face on Mars

The above memorial to Alalu suggests the Anunnaki were human-looking; yet the facts of Chapter 3 deny it. And if you look closely at the picture (below left), the broad nose if combined with very fine scaly skin could still be a reptilian image. (See Chapter 3 pictures and discussion of Inanna.)

Be that as it may, the public accepted the face as a face, and JPL and NASA denounced it. So what was needed was another fly-over with more pictures taken…

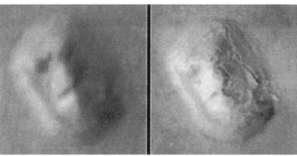

1976 Viking Orbiter image (left, image #070A13) compared with the 2001 Mars Global Surveyor image (right). The "Face" is 1.5 km across in size.

(credit: http://en.wikipedia.org/wiki/Cydonia_%28region_of_Mars%29)

So that the reader can fully appreciate the second picture on the right, it has been digitally reproduced and enhanced:

The Real Face on Mars
(Credit: Bing Images)

It appears the Martians are not impressed with JPL's reluctance to accept what is obviously there….

…. But seriously folk, here is the real digitally analyzed picture:

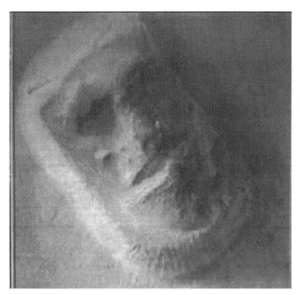

…and as you can see, it is a face, although it's eroded with time and the elements.

(credit Bing Images)

This is what the original 1976 picture would look like if the 2001 version and its erosion was applied to the whole face, consistently. It also digitally supports the left picture in the 1976-2001 comparison above. That suggests that the 2001 version probably suffered alteration of transmitted data.

Mars' Moon Phobos

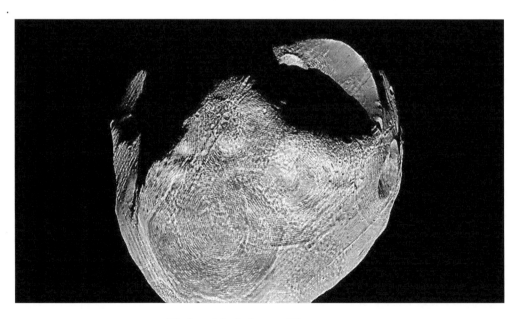

Phobos, Mar's Larger Moon

Lastly, it was a Russian scientist in 1958 first proposed that the biggest moon circling Mars, called Phobos (17 mi long) was hollow. **Dr. Shklovsky's** hypothesis has stood the test of time and the more the moon is studied, the weirder it gets – very eccentric orbit, and due to the weak atmosphere on Mars slowing the speed and decaying the orbit of Phobos, it has to be very light — even hollow. Another moon base. And the Anunnaki would have used it as such – to control access to the planet

It looks to have "texturing" on the surface, and in addition to the large concave "dish" in the front, there is an anomaly on Phobos:

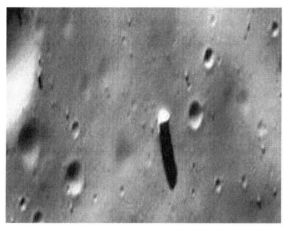

The Phobos Monolith

It is a boulder about 280 feet across, just sitting there. It may be something that flew into Phobos and embedded itself into the surface. The Canadian Space Agency is very much interested in exploring this monolith.

The pictures on this page were obtained by US craft during fly-bys.

(credit: http://en.wikipedia.org/wiki/Phobos_monolith)

The Russians attempted several probes to fly-by and photograph the moon, but every attempt has ended in failure, including a radar image of something that appeared to be shot at the probe, *Phobos 2*, just before it stopped working. A third try in 2011 was *Phobos Grunt* and it achieved Earth orbit but failed to initiate ignition to leave orbit for Mars. It crashed to Earth.

Perhaps 2 better shots of Phobos:

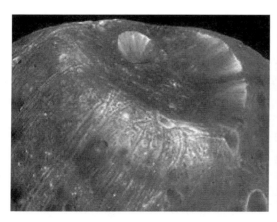 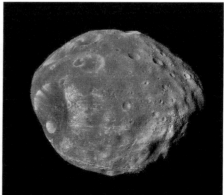

(credit: Bing Images)

What looks like a design (left picture) is said to be due to the camera's blue-green, red, and near-infrared channels illuminating mineral content. Yet, it looks like hieroglyphics. The illuminated part of Phobos seen in the images is about 21 kilometers (13 miles) across. The most prominent feature in the images is the large crater Stickney …with a diameter of 9 kilometers (5.6 miles), it is the largest feature on Phobos. It looks like a large satellite dish.

Afterword

The reason for including this material at all in the book is two-fold:

1. This book does examine errors, omissions and deception in the areas of **Science**, Earth history and Religion. The Moon and Mars issues appear to be highly distorted, both by NASA, JPL and even by the conspiracy proponents who seek disclosure. The NASA pictures lead one to question things, and the backers of the NASA story do not present iron-clad explanations, which leads to further speculation.

How can we gain enough Light to get out of here when we are subjected to deception? **Rewind**: what if that is the purpose… Are we tested to see through it? (While the PTB <u>don't</u> do that, the Elite might … for reasons given a few pages back [in bold].)

2. Whereas Earth is in a 3D construct in a 4D VR Sphere, to contain, protect and serve Man, it makes one look twice at the NASA claims… we have been in the Sphere since at least AD 800-900, and it is believed that the Moon is also part of this reality. It is not that we cannot travel within the Sphere, Earth to Moon, it is more a question of why. Mars and the rest of the universe exist <u>outside</u> this Sphere and we're not going to be allowed to go there in person… just yet.

3. The astronauts have all said that they were followed to the Moon by alien craft and then observed while there. However they are under strict orders to not discuss these events… although the late Neil Armstrong once spoke of their ships as "big and menacing!" [46] UFOs were often spoken of with the code word "Santa Claus" when talking to Mission Control on the public channel. (This amused Dr. von Braun… see his reply to Neil below.)

4. In addition, **the Moon is not ours**: it is not of the same geologic composition as the Earth, it is much older, and the isotopes there are not in agreement with Earth-based isotopes [47] which means that **the Moon is from another part of the Galaxy**. [48] The Persians have a story about how the Moon came to be in the sky – it was not always there. And the Greeks tell of a time when the **Proselenes** lived in the land – and Selene was the name of the Moon goddess – and so 'Pro' means "**before the time of**…the Moon." [49]

Like Phobos and Deimos, the moons of Mars, our Moon appears to be artificial. If so, then we are not going to be welcome traipsing all over someone else's observation platform… much less drilling holes in it and setting off small explosive charges to determine interior composition via echoing. And that may be one reason why we have not been back in 42 years. [50]

Just something to think about…

R.I.P.   Wernher Freiherr von Braun   (1912 – 1977)

Dr. Braun was the man who directed the NASA Missions to the Moon. And yet he resigned from NASA in 1972, just before the Apollo 17 flight, which is odd, as his NASA post was fulfilling his boyhood dream – Man among the Stars. But, he was not happy when his knowledgeable German scientists were all replaced by American scientists, and he was upset that we had to go to the Moon using rockets – when he knew that his compatriots back in Peenemünde had developed and flown a Vril in 1941. [51] He was also upset that JFK's plan to jointly go to the Moon with Soviets was nixed. Then he was reprimanded by NASA in 1969 for revealing a 'Neutral Point' error to the press… off by thousands of miles, affecting how the spacecraft would react with the shift from Earth's to the Moon's gravity.

Lastly, shortly before his death in 1977, Astronaut Neil Armstrong paid Wernher a visit. Wernher wanted to leave Neil with the realization that he knew <u>all</u> about the Moon Missions… and he looked straight at Neil and said,

> By the prognosis of statisticians, you should be dead in space, and I should be in jail on Earth. [52]

Neil didn't say anything… he just looked at him. Wernher knew.

Lastly, NASA is due a lot of credit for not endangering the lives of our astronauts, and for preserving the American reputation (put brashly on the line by JFK in May 1961). For doing what they had to do, to make the Moon Program a reality for the world,
(however they did it)
we should be thanking NASA, not throwing stones at them.

Parting Shot:

This was my all-time favorite astronaut picture… it is not Photoshop. It was shot during a pause in the training and the executives in charge wanted to evaluate the facility… as a golf course?

Keep smiling…

Addendum

This **VEG** book was Book 1. Since then, another 6 books have been written and the last one, <u>The Great Earth Puzzle,</u> deals with the intriguing possibility that the Earth Realm is either a **VR** Sphere (as said in this **VEG** book), or it might be a Flat Earth – which this author tried for months to disprove, and some of the 'proofs' are unnerving... all laid out in <u>The Great Earth Puzzle</u>. Earth as a sophisticated Simulation is also examined (in addition to <u>Quantum Earth Simulation</u>).

The relevance to this Appendix A is that since **VEG** was published (2014), it has become apparent that not only is there a Gegenschein, but **NASA** has now (2016) discovered a Plasmasphere 7200 miles above the Earth, and that it is impenetrable – so did we really go to the Moon? The Plasmasphere amounts to the Firmament that the Book of Enoch and Genesis describe.

Earth may not be what we have assumed it to be...

Appendix B: Holographic Vision

Chapter 8 dealt briefly with Charles Darwin and the eye's design, which if Darwin had seriously examined the eye and vision, as his scientist friends invited him to, he might not have opted to have been an agnostic. The eye has a design, and vision even more so. A design suggests a Designer.

Chapter 12 then briefly examined the nature of perception and holograms. Again the issue of vision was raised because it is crucial to an appreciation of what Earth is. The nature of vision and holograms are intrinsically related and this Appendix will examine the issue more in detail. And along the way, we'll take a look at China's children who 'read' with their ears, nose and fingertips suggesting that we really don't know what vision is. And lastly, we'll take a brief look at the special people who have an extra type of cone in the retina which gives them "super vision."

Vision

According to the traditional scientific teaching on how the eye sees, there is a one-to-one correlation between what the eye physically sees and the image 'seen' by the brain; that is, it was thought that the rods and cones of the retina sent signals via the optic nerve to the back of the brain where an ophthalmic section called the Visual Cortex decoded them and somehow reconstructed what the eye saw. [1] It was believed that the optic nerve transmitted the light images or photons captured by the eyes which were somehow assembled into an image… It has been discovered in today's science that the optic nerve sends only electrical impulses (**analog** not digital!) to the Visual Cortex… and analog is harder to process than digital.

A very astute researcher, Karl Pribram whose name is becoming synonymous with 'holographic vision' these days, determined that the traditional explanation was wrong.

By measuring the **electrical brain activity** of monkeys while they performed various visual tasks, he determined that there was **no** special brain pattern identifiable in any visual activity, much less a one-to-one correspondence to a certain section of the brain. Even when parts of the visual cortex were surgically removed from a monkey, it still performed the visual tasks with no problem. Pribram began to theorize "the whole in every part" (a hologram) as an explanation. [2] The problem was in testing the theory.

Long story short, he discovered that brain waves created

> …an almost endless and kaleidoscopic array of interference patterns [in the brain], and these [gave] the brain its holographic properties... The **hologram** was there all the time in the wave-front nature of brain-cell connectivity. " [3] [emphasis added]

Pribram Meets Bohm

Further contemplation and experimentation proved that the brain indeed was seeing the world as a hologram, and in fact was storing items in memory also in a holographic manner.

> Pribram realized that if the holographic brain model was taken to its logical conclusions, it opened the door on the possibility that objective reality – the world of coffee cups, mountain vistas, elm trees, and table lamps – might not even exist, or at least not exist in the way we believe it exists. Was it possible, he wondered, that what the mystics had been saying for centuries was true, reality was *maya*, an illusion, and what was out there was really a vast, resonating symphony of wave forms, a **"frequency domain"** that was transformed into the world as we know it only *after* it entered our senses? [4] [emphasis added]

That's it in a nutshell. And when Pribram met David Bohm, a quantum physicist, it all came together. Bohm added clarity through his understanding of holograms and the nature of the subatomic world, and that led to the following refinement of Pribram's theory:

> Our brains mathematically construct objective reality by interpreting frequencies that are **ultimately projections from another dimension**, a deeper order of existence that is beyond both space and time: the brain is a hologram enfolded in a holographic universe. [5] [emphasis added]

In much the same way as Tank in *The Matrix* sat before the computer screens with their flowing green symbols, our reality is a "… vast ocean of waves and frequencies…" that looks real (physical) to us because our brains can take the holographic wave forms and convert them to buildings, cars and trees that make up our world. [6] This means we can also see ourselves as a blur of **interference patterns** existing in the cosmic hologram. We are part of the hologram.

And holograms are a natural part of the Simulation.

Consciousness

And since we are part of the hologram, and we are conscious beings, <u>our consciousness must somehow impact matter and thus create our reality</u>. Jahn and Dunne said

> They believe that reality is itself the result of the interface between the wavelike aspects of consciousness and the wave patterns of matter… Unlike Bohm, Jahn and Dunne believe subatomic particles do *not* possess a distinct reality until consciousness enters the picture… "I think we're into the domain where the interplay of consciousness in the environment is taking place on such a **primary scale** that we are indeed creating reality…[7]

But he means that on a very microscopic level – not that we create our day, but that we <u>do</u> nonetheless affect the world around us. And Jahn and Dunne go on to cite how scientists in the laboratory are 'discovering' the elementary particles that they <u>expect</u> to find – in reality, creating them via some as yet not understood faculty of mind, expectation and consciousness. [8] Such was the **anomalon** that was discussed in Chapter 9 ('Subatomic Particles' section) where different scientists discovered the same particle which behaved differently, according to their expectations.

And if we all share the same world, would not our reality consist of mutually agreed-on **"reality-fields"** – we all see and agree that certain buildings exist, the bus is blue, it's raining, and we are all in a city called Chicago. That would be a mutually shared reality-field, or field of wave patterns that we all see and agree that we see and experience it the same.

> If consciousness plays a role in the creation of subatomic particles, is it possible that our observations of the subatomic world are also reality-fields of a kind? … As bizarre as this sounds, it is not so strange when one remembers that in a holographic universe, consciousness pervades all matter…[9]

So in sum, it is considered that "…<u>reality is established only in the interaction of a consciousness with its environment</u>…[and that means] anything capable of generating, receiving, or utilizing information can qualify… animals, viruses, DNA, Artificial Intelligence machines…"[10] Thus, said another way, only **the reality created by the interaction of consciousnesses is real**. There is no reality beyond that created by the interaction of all consciousnesses, which means that the holographic universe can be 'sculpted' by the joint effort and energy of enough minds.

Controlled Vision

Just as fascinating as the fact that we decode the holographic interference waves 'out there' and thus project reality in front of us, is the corollary idea that we may not be able to see all that is around us. This is due to one of two things:

> either the objects are invisible because they reflect a color or wave-
> length that we cannot physically see,
> or
> we have been 'programmed' (conditioned) to not see certain things.

In either case, what we see is filtered through the pre-frontal lobe of the brain whose job is to make sense of it and correct it if necessary. For example, there is a street sign in my neighborhood that says "Goldenrain Tree." No one notices that that is an error when I point it out. It should be "Golden Raintree", but the sign maker went unconscious, goofed up, and then let it stand as it was. A better example is the following:

A
Bird in the
the Bush beats
two in the Hand any Day.

Did you see the error? Chances are, if you have not seen this one before, your brain filtered out the extra word 'the.' How did it know to do that? Is there a secondary intelligence operating between the brain and the mind that we don't know about?

In like manner, it has been speculated that most people don't see auras because they (1) don't know they can, (2) they don't want to, (3) they don't know they exist, or (4) have been told that seeing auras is witchy stuff. And even more bizarre as a possibility, there could be other beings moving in and out among us on a daily basis that we can't see because (1) we have never been told about them and so the brain filters them out, or (2) our DNA has been 'wired' to not be able to see them.

As an example that we do NOT see everything that is in front of us, and the brain does "fill in" the scene, consider the following:

> Even more dramatic evidence of the role the mind plays in creating what we see is provided by the eye's so-called **blind spot**. In the middle of the retina, where the optic nerve connects to the eye, we have a blind spot where there are no photo-receptors... Even when we look at the world around us we are totally unaware that there are **gaping holes in our vision**...[and] the brain artfully fills in the gaps... so masterfully we aren't even aware that it is doing so. [11] [emphasis added]

So what else is out there that we are not seeing? For example, **spiderwebs** look like clear silk to us, but to the insect world, with their ultraviolet-sensitive eyes, they are actually brightly colored! In addition, **fluorescent lamps** actually pulse on and off at a rate that is just a bit too fast for us to detect, but we think they are constantly on. [12] This pulsing is why some people develop headaches after working under fluorescent lighting all day.

So if reality is one large frequency domain, what frequencies can we not see? We can't see the Neggs, yet they obviously see us... and maybe it is a good idea that we can't see them. Too much distraction is not a good thing. Yet it would be helpful to see auras as the presence indicates an ensouled human, and the absence means caution is advised, and if one could see auras, your boss who is facing you with a poker face but whose aura is electric red would otherwise warn you that he is very angry... Useful, no?

The Holographic Body

On a lighter note, it was known centuries ago by the Chinese and the Hindus, that the body is also a hologram connected by a Bionet – which is how Reflexology, Iridology and **Acupuncture** work. The ancient healers drew maps of the *chi* meridians flowing through the body and discovered that not only are there meridians running from chakra to chakra, but from chakras to points on the extremities, such as the ears, hands and feet. They were able to correlate points on the ear with different parts of the body, and by sticking an acupuncture pin in the middle of the outer ear, or rubbing the same location with the finger, a headache could be made to disappear. And not surprisingly, the soles of the feet and the palms of the hands have similarly located pressure points such that a stomach ache can be removed by massaging the upper center of the foot or hand. [13] (I experienced that one!)

How does that relate to vision and holographic perception? Enter the Chinese and their psychics…

Chinese Psychic Research

Whereas the West refers to psychic abilities as a form of ESP (Extra Sensory Perception), in China it is referred to as **EHF (Exceptional Human Function)**. [14] While there are amazing reports of the usual psychokinesis, clairvoyance, healing and mind-reading also found around the world, there is another segment of their EHF skills that is really amazing. In addition to mentally changing the molecular structure of water, and taking pills out of a sealed medicine bottle, [15] there are those who can manifest an apple out of thin air, [16] and a number of children who can **read with the ear or with the nose**. [17]

If the body is holographic and vision is holographic, why not read with the ear? It was just shown that the ear has links (meridians) to many parts of the body – and other parts of the body would follow the **holographic axiom** "the whole in every part." There are acupuncture points in the hands and feet for the eyes,[18] but that doesn't mean that there are optic nerves in the hands, or even the nose. Yet, **the mind is very involved** from what the Chinese say:

> …many people in mainland China with EHF have reported that when they read with the hands, or with the ear, guess things, or see through objects, the mind forms something like a screen with an image of the target being sought. Sometimes it flashes by in an instant, sometimes it is quite fuzzy, and sometimes it is sharp and clear. [19]

and

> The girls said that when they put the writing by their ears, on their noses, or under their armpits, as soon as they felt the print, the words or images appeared in their minds. The words or images would appear only for an instant and disappear again right away. Also, they couldn't tell when these visions would appear, so it took concentrated effort to catch them. That is why test subjects always feel exhausted after such testing. [20]

This phenomenon in China has been called "**nonocular vision**" and is found mostly in children, and if they start young enough, they have found that they can even train them to do this kind of reading – with the ear, nose, fingertips, armpit, and forehead. [21]

While there is no scientific explanation coming out of China for this type of vision, in all cases the children were put through special **Qigong** classes to develop their ability to direct their *chi* (life force) to various parts of the body… Perhaps the *chi* has a way of transmitting the "interference patterns" (from the object) to the part of the brain that normally decodes what the eye sees…? [22]

The main point of sharing this Chinese connection is that **vision does not depend on the eyes**. Apparently, many parts of the body can serve as visual organs, but it is the brain that sees, and if the brain can receive input from the fingertips and decode it, then there will be "vision."

And if consciousness is distributed in the body, or can be, according to the holographic axiom, and **vision is a function of consciousness** which decodes the frequency domain, then it doesn't matter what part of the body is used – eyes are just more convenient, a more direct path to the decoding mechanism.

Super Human Vision

As if that weren't enough to wow you, the scientists studying vision have discovered how insects use their multi-faceted eyes to see; bees and flies have multi-lense eyes, and spiders have multiple eyes… Parakeets have eyes on opposite sides of the head… Do they see both sides at the same time or do they switch focus instantly from side to side…? Birds and insects see the ultraviolet spectrum.

Scientists have known that dogs and cats are *dichromat* (seeing 2 colors), and humans are normally *trichromat* (seeing 3 colors). Dogs, horses and bulls have been found to not see color like we do, but mostly shades of gray. The bull doesn't see the matador cape as red, he sees him waving something and charges it. What is fascinating is that some people (mostly men) possess a mutant cone which cannot distinguish between red and green, making them color-blind. The mothers and daughters of color-blind men had the mutant cone plus the normal 3 cones making them *tetrachromatic* (seeing 4 colors). [23]

These women see color differently and they see more colors. What the scientists want to know is why and how some of these women have 'activated' their 4th cone while many others haven't. They are still doing color tests on these women to learn more as of 2012. So, gentlemen, if your wife complains that the color of your tie, the wallpaper, or the car is not right, she may be one of those *tetrachromats* and has a reason for wanting to change the color. Work with her.

Summary

The brain, which is itself composed of frequencies of matter, can somehow take the holographic blur of wave frequencies and convert that to the sticks and stones of our world. And Man himself is a blur of interference patterns in a cosmic hologram, so the whole thing is quite a large hologram. The late Michael Talbot was correct.

> …our very being appears to exist primarily as a shimmering cloud of energy whose ultimate location in space is somewhat ambiguous. [24]

If Reality is largely a big frequency domain, where is the problem in seeing (no pun) our world as an HVR Sphere, a 3D construct contained in 4D? That is just the structure of our Reality, even though we live it as if it were just 3D physicality because that's how the laws of this Sphere are designed.

> [If] the human body is holographic … [then] each of us truly would be a universe in miniature… if our thoughts can cause ghostly holographic images to form, not only in our own energy fields [auras], but in the subtle energetic levels of reality itself, it may help explain how the human mind is able to effect … miracles… It may even explain synchronicities… Again, it may be that our thoughts are constantly affecting the subtle energetic levels of the holographic universe, **but** only emotionally powerful thoughts, such as the ones that accompany moments of crisis and transformation… are **potent enough to manifest** as a series of coincidences in physical reality. [25] [emphasis added]

Again, there is that caveat that we are not yet gods who can manifest what we want, when we want. It appears that we can affect the microscopic, quantum world. And yet, strong emotions (especially in **a group**) may have the power to broadcast farther, create something unexpected, and possibly afflict or heal others…

And another issue was just raised: Could the fact that Man has yet to control his emotions and he consequently 'pollutes' what Monroe called the H-band (RCF/Matrix) around the Earth, be another reason for putting Man in quarantine? Since thoughts are real and go somewhere and do something, and emotions can certainly empower them, would it not be prudent of the Higher Beings, while Man is in training, to protect the rest of the 4D beings from Man?

Again, Man is a very special creation and it is a shame to not know anything of the divine potential inherent in every ensouled person. It is a shame to run a V8 on 4 cylinders. If Man can be an Earth Graduate, as said in Chapters 7 and 15, would that not be a fantastic goal to shoot for?

Appendix C: UFOs & The Control System

This book is not about UFOs, but the issue is involved in an explanation of what this place is. Earlier, in Chapter 4, it was mentioned that Jacques Vallée, the French astrophysicist, discovered what he thought they were, and the implications for mankind. Since his findings fit with the theme of this book, and it helps to resolve <u>one aspect</u> of the UFO issue as part of a Simulation, such information is extended here.

Dr. Vallée wrote several books dealing with the UFO issue. In <u>Passport to Magonia</u> (1970), he explores the years of evidence of extraterrestrial contact, and examines world folklore to draw some interesting similarities. Then as part of the "Invisible College" (a network of scientists studying aerial phenomena) he first proposed the idea of a Control System:

> UFOs and related phenomena are the means through which man's concepts are being rearranged. Their ultimate source may be unknowable…. [but] what we do know … is that they are presenting us with continually recurring "absurd" messages and appearances which defy rational analysis …[1]

Then in <u>Dimensions</u> (1988), he draws some more interesting conclusions: [2]

1. There is no proof that the UFO phenomenon is of extraterrestrial origin.
2. The expectation of extraterrestrial visitors is a powerful potential source of new social and political trends.

After briefly discussing the potential involvement of governmental agencies in a cover-up, it also appears that they may be covertly testing society (**PsyOps**) to see what the reaction is to the possibility of ETs and what that would do to the stability of our civilization. [3] Such is alleged to be the case with the **Bentwaters-Rendlesham Forest** incident in England back in 1980. The authorities wanted to see what trained military personnel would do and how they'd respond to an ET visit. If the putative ETs are not introduced appropriately to society, either in concept or in person, the result is likely to be chaos – after all, we have come to believe that we are alone, just as we used to believe the Earth was flat. And even if ETs are welcomed and people have a curious, proactive reaction to them, people will (1) want them to solve our problems, and (2) whatever the ETs know about God and Man's origins, if shared with us, may destroy organized religion and create nervous breakdowns, etc. This was also the Brookings Institute warning back in the early 60's.

However, due to the nature of the real UFOs, there isn't much chance of them landing and upsetting our civilization, because Dr. Vallée has another point:

> "The truth is that the **UFOs may not be spacecraft at all**. And the government may simply be hiding the fact that, in spite of the billions of dollars spent on air defense, it has no more clues to the nature of the phenomenon today than it did in the forties…[4]

In that case, demanding disclosure, assuming that the government knows what they are, is opening a Pandora's box. How does the USAF or government tell people that it doesn't really know what they are, **and that we can't control or stop them** – that <u>we don't have control over our own skies?</u> As a psychological defense, the authorities might promote the disinformation that we have captured some downed saucers, and are back-engineering them, but also, through another avenue, deny that so that the public receives disinformation and that generates enough resulting confusion that the public will ignore the subject. In the meantime, run a few movies on ETs and see what the public reaction is… *Close Encounters of the Third Kind* (1977) and *ET* (1982) might have been seen as bellweathers by the authorities, also happening about the same time as Bentwaters (1980).

And a really clever, **reverse-psychology** would be to deny the existence of something that too many people see so that the public, instead of being scared of UFOs, becomes aggressive and 'knows' what the government won't admit. Potential fear is traded for anger (at being duped).

No Spacecraft

Dr. Vallée has examined thousands of UFO reports, including those of contactees, and he has succeeded in poking a big hole in what appeared to be the ET-as-hostile-alien picture that was being formed. While no one is denying that the people who experience abductions, landings, etc. have not seen what they saw, it is more a case of **the interpretation being wrong** – the supposed ET and craft were <u>not extraterrestrial</u>. More than likely, he suggests, they were inter-dimensional or Earth-based.

> *In point of fact, to clarify for the reader, they are **both.** There are (1) Earth-based 3D physical UFOs and (2) those that are inserted by the Control System to effect growth and awakenings.*

This Appendix examines UFOs as a product of the Control System.

In short, those people experienced what they experienced, but the spacecraft hypothesis does not automatically nor accurately explain what happened. Physical spacecraft are not the only possibility.

To briefly summarize Dr. Vallée's findings, it was said that [5]

1. There are too many landings. And they happen between 6pm and 6 am. Mostly at night.
2. Most landings are in unpopulated areas.
3. Most sightings simply vanish, they rarely fly off as people watch.

That is the behavior of an image, or a **holographic projection**.

Would some holographic-inserted objects be natural to a Simulation? (Chapter 13)

Taken together, he extrapolates a very significant finding: if the 2000 cases he analyzed (frequency distributions, etc.) on his computer for **two decades** were also to happen during the day, and in populated areas, there would be a much higher number of sightings – maybe as high as 30,000 (according to the statistics he ran).

> Now this last figure does not begin to approximate the actual number of events, because we know from many independent studies that only one case in ten ever gets reported. Then we should have not thirty thousand but three hundred thousand cases in our files! .. If the earth's population were distributed evenly instead of being concentrated in city areas, how many reports would we have? Again, taking a conservative multiplying factor of ten leads us to the staggering conclusion that the UFOs, if they are spacecraft engaged in a general survey of our planet, must have landed here no fewer than *three million times* in two decades! [6]

And he says that this is "totally absurd."

> Either the UFOs select their witnesses for psychological or sociological reasons, or they are something entirely different from space vehicles. In either case, **their appearances are *staged*!** [7] [emphasis added]

A Star Map to Nowhere

An example of staging things for people to see, and an event that warrants consideration is the star map that Betty Hill saw during her abduction (re: the famous Betty & Barney Hill abduction of September 1961). While aboard the craft, and conversing with what she assumed to be ETs, who seemed to have a German accent, she noticed what appeared to be **a paper star map** on the wall, and when she asked about it she was told that that was a map to guide the pilot of the craft between their solar system and ours.

> *If you believe that, I have some ocean-front property in Montana I want to sell you.*

She drew the map from memory, under hypnotic regression, and after many years of astronomical conjecture, it was "identified" as pointing to the Zeta Reticuli system. Dr. Vallée argues that it was never determined whether the arrangement of those suns and planets in the map could ALSO fit some other location in space... and most of all, **it is doubtful that sophisticated UFO technology uses wall maps to navigate** – more likely telemetry, or as Dr. LaViolette has said, **they use a form of space beacons (quasars).**

> *Remember Star Trek? "Lay in a course for Starbase 10, Mr Sulu."*
> *They didn't use AAA roadmaps.*

So the map was a clever device, but totally *non-sequitur* – it was a 'test' that the people of the sixties and seventies did not get correct; it didn't dawn on them that such a device would not be useful... Now that Man has grown and expanded his awareness of what interstellar travel would require, there will be no more wall-based star maps – the perpetrators will try something else.

So, at the point of telling us what he thinks the UFO phenomenon is <u>really</u> all about, he says, "… the extraterrestrial theory is not good enough, because it is **not strange enough** to explain the facts." [emphasis added]

High Strangeness

As was said earlier, we are growing as a species and beginning to realize that we are not alone, but we are looking for answers and

> …developing a great thirst for contact with superior minds that will provide guidance for our poor, harassed, hectic planet. I think we may be ready to fall into a trap, perhaps a kind, benevolent pitfall [if we are lucky]. I believe that when we speak of UFO sightings as instances of space visitations we are looking at the phenomenon on the wrong level. We are not dealing with successive waves of visitations from space. We are dealing with a **control system**. [8]   [emphasis added]

And as was shown in Chapters 12 and 13, the Earth is a 3D Construct within an HVR Sphere which is itself in 4D. Naturally, a Construct that is in **Quarantine** is under a control of some sort. And the mid-level control is applied through the Beings of Light and the Neggs in the Astral. "Ground-level" control is more effectuated by the OPs… on the Earth, walking around, interacting with ensouled humans. Overall control resides with the Higher Beings.

Further, says Dr. Vallée,

> I propose that there is a **spiritual control system** for human consciousness and that paranormal phenomena like UFOs are one of its manifestations. I cannot tell… whether it is explainable in terms of genetics, of social psychology, or of ordinary phenomena – or if it is artificial in nature, under the power of some superhuman will. It may be entirely determined by laws that we have not yet discovered. [9]   [emphasis added]

In addition, the UFO phenomena comes and goes, following a pattern over the years. Sometimes there is no activity and at other times, the period of quiet is followed by marked activity. Dr. Vallée also refers to the great behaviorist **B.F. Skinner**, and suggests that we are being **reinforced** (trained) in a very sophisticated way:

> *The best schedule of reinforcement is one that combines periodicity with unpredictability.* Learning is then slow but continuous. It leads to the highest level of adaptation. And it is irreversible. *It is interesting to observe that the pattern of UFO waves has the same structure as a schedule of reinforcement.* [10]

The question then is: Why? What is the objective of the 'training?'

A Higher View

It was said earlier that there have always been Watchers, no matter just what their form – Greys, Neggs, Beings of Light, Anunnaki Igigi, or what-have-you. Man is that important that some are being 'schooled', and others are being 'corrected' from a dysfunctionality. It depends on your point of view, but Man's view of his world is changing with time – First it was the unexplained **airships, and elves, gnomes and fairies**, and nowadays it is UFOs, Greys and crop circles – some sort of <u>upgraded</u> reinforcement to …. What?

Dr Vallée posits:
> I suggest that it is human belief that is being **controlled and conditioned**.[11] [emphasis added]

Perhaps to guide Man (<u>indirectly</u>, because his ego would not take being directly told what to do) in creating a better world, and learning to respect himself, others and the planet. **Man's concepts are slowly being rearranged**. Even to the point where people are now drifting away from traditional, organized religion, and not only are there New Thought churches, but Man is re-evaluating his concept of God – God is becoming more of an intelligent Force (thanks to *Star Wars*) than an anthropomorphic white-bearded man sitting on a throne…

Man is being indirectly (and holographically) conditioned and that would explain why there is no overt contact – no landing on the White House lawn, and the craft just "wink out" and instantly disappear from view. Direct contact could <u>preclude</u> real learning – Man seems to learn best (and retain the lesson) when he has to figure something out, not just be told.

Control System Revisited

And then Dr. Vallée says it, but quickly shies away from it:

> When I speak of a control system for planet Earth … I do not want my words to be misunderstood. I do not mean that some higher order of beings has locked us inside the constraints of a space-bound jail, closely monitored by psychic entities we might call angels or demons.[12]

But, **he IS correct**. OMG, he just said it! Why is he afraid to say that? – he obviously figured it out, and then walks away from the idea. We <u>are</u> contained, or quarantined more exactly. It is not a super-civilization (ETs) but Higher Beings (not demons) that run this place (through Angels and Neggs) from which we do not escape until we have been 'trained' (via our Scripts) and are useful once again in the Realm from which we came.

My God, how close can Dr. Vallée get without actually saying it…? It seems to have been the putative demonic aspect of it that put him off, just as it did John Keel and Charles Fort – but they all made the wrong assumption – based perhaps on societal conditioning: if there are beings in the Astral then they have to be Angels or Demons.

Dr. Vallée, when pressed to be more clear on his concept of a control system, said that it is **a way to subtly manipulate human consciousness**.

> If you think you're inside a control system, the first thing you have to look for is what is being controlled and try to change it to see what happens…..

Suppose you are walking through the desert and you see a stone that looks as though it was painted white. A thousand yards later, you see another stone of similar appearance. You stop and consider the matter. Either you can forget it or – if you're like me – you can pick up the stone and move it a few feet. If suddenly a bearded character steps out from behind a rock and demands to know why you moved his marker, then you know you've found a control system.

My point is that **you can't be sure until you do something**. Then you realize that what you were seeing, the thing that looked absurd and incongruous, was really a marker for a boundary that was invisible to everybody else until you discovered it because you looked for **a pattern**…. [note that] there is **a feed-back mechanism** involved in the operations of the control system; if you change the information that's carried back to that system, you might be able to infiltrate it through its own feedback. [13] [emphasis added]

And this is being done to our group awareness as a society or nation – as we develop *memes* and come collectively to believe/accept something, we do affect the Control System. Case in point, again, was Man noting **airships** and wondering about them, following them, and attempting to build them himself, the Control System noted that and moved on to a higher technical example with certain **UFO**s. Same thing happened with petroglyph drawings, some of which were intended to pass on certain ideas (including visitations by beings who were not of this world), and now the modern-day version of that is **crop circles**.

A lot of it to cause us to stop and wonder, dream and try new things.

Effects of Reinforcement

Needless to say, the UFO element does cause us to consider whether we are here alone, and whether the "gods" of the Old Testament, Genesis in particular, are connected with a past and possible ET visitation. This cannot but help have a major impact on religion – changing our concept of who we are, who/what God is, and where we fit in a cosmic scheme of things. We grow up.

So it would be logical to implement a very sophisticated Control System over Earth, to guide the way Man thinks – hopefully to keep him from destroying himself and/or the planet. Inasmuch as the **great Earth experiment** (of Chapter 1) may have run awry, and there is a need to apply 'training wheels,' a very advanced set of beings would have to (and be able to) apply the reinforcement and 'training wheels' in such a way that Man doesn't notice so that he thinks that the direction things are taking is all his idea… It can be called

Controlled catalyst.

After all, given that Man can be egotistical and proud, he could be like a 2-year old who wants to do it all himself, even though he really can't, so Daddy subtly helps. And if Man got the idea that he was not alone on the planet, he might misconstrue things and assume that he was someone's property, as Charles Fort said. That would be counterproductive because the Others here might otherwise be able to work with Man to create a golden future. And then the Anunnaki will have done their job and can go home…

So Dr. Vallée then says

> …I believe that the UFO phenomenon *represents evidence for other* **dimensions** *beyond spacetime*; the UFOs may not come from ordinary space, but from a *multiverse* which is all around us and of which **we have stubbornly refused to consider the disturbing reality** in spite of the evidence available to us for centuries. [14] [emphasis added]

In effect, the Greys who oversee the genetic upgrade of Man, DO come and go via **intradimensional portals**. They are, however, **Earth-based bio-cybernetic beings** controlled by the Anunnaki Remnant. They have a "hive mind" and no personality as they are controlled via a computerized network – which is separate from the Control System but supports it in practice.

Not to negate the revelation presented in Chapter 12: we may also have visitors from other dimensions or timelines – even unwanted ones as Ra said. They may be able to insert themselves into our Simulation to check it out, maybe even to manipulate it… (See Chapter 5, "Personal Experiences" and "Encounters with Others").

> What we see here is **not an alien invasion**. It is a spiritual system that acts on humans and uses humans. [15] [emphasis added]

…because humans will not learn any other way. So the UFO phenomena is *à propos* for this stage of Man's development.

> They are not trying to communicate with a few individuals, with any group, with any government. Why should they? The phenomena function like an operational system of symbolic communication [e.g., **crop circles**] at a global level. There is something about the human race with which they interact, and we do not yet know what it is [perhaps the human soul?]. They are part of the environment, part of the **control system for human evolution**. But their effects, instead of being just physical, are also felt in our beliefs. They influence what we call our spiritual life. They are a feature of our past. Undoubtedly, they are part of our future. [16] [emphasis added]

And they will be here for as long as it takes us to get it together and get out of here.

Appendix D: – God, Jesus and The Christ

Having pointed out the inconsistencies, errors and omissions of Christianity in Chapters 1 and 11, and having examined some of the errors in the Catholic Church which was the forerunner of Christianity, and having said that I was a Christian, and having said that Bishop Spong is correct – we need an update to what we believe – I want to devote a little space to explain how I see God, Jesus and Christ fitting in with the context of this book.

Be clear: **I am not out to trash Christianity nor do away with it**. But because Man can be an ignorant, silly, superstitious, fragile human being who makes mistakes and <u>mis</u>-understands more than he should, a certain amount of clarification is necessary. Perhaps I can clarify where I am coming from and what led to writing the information in those two chapters.

Secondly, remember that I was a card-carrying Christian, have read the whole Bible, taught Bible classes, and served almost a year in a Deliverance Ministry, I know only too well that oppressed people need to be set free, and I know there is power in the name of Jesus – even though there is more power in Christ's name. And the Angels do honor prayers and requests made in Jesus' name because they love Man and they know what you mean… so it is honored.

Thirdly, remember that it was the Higher Beings (to whom the Angels report) who visited me and asked me to write this book – not the Devil, who doesn't exist. Man is often dealing with his own **shadow side**, when he blames the Devil for causing problems… if the Interdimensionals (aka Djinn) are not harassing us. I mentioned them earlier but wanted to explain them in a separate location: the Djinn used to run Earth, fought among themselves, destroyed the Earth, were put in an adjacent dimension, and they resent Man because he now has the planet. THAT is the source (when it happens, and it is rare) of the so-called "demonic" <u>possession</u>.

I don't know, perhaps Man is not ready to hear all this yet… but at some point you understood that there was no Santa Claus, no Easter Bunny, and yet we hang on, desperately, to having someone else pay for our sins. Karma rules, not vicarious atonement. If you don't like that, take it up with God – it is His paradigm.

So let's look at the three beings from the 40,000' level…

Nature of God

I don't like the term 'god' as it is what the Anunnaki called themselves; it has a connotation I don't like and it suggests a lesser being operative in our world. So in this book I have tried to use terms like The One, or Father of Light to refer to the Almighty who runs the Universe. As the Bible says, he is the same yesterday, today and tomorrow and his presence pervades the whole universe… so where could a putative Devil go to escape him and his powerful presence?

The Father runs a hierarchy between himself and Man – it is not possible for him to directly come anywhere physically near Man as was explained in Chapter 2 where Robert Monroe was out-of-body and was being shown the majesty and power of the Father at the center of our Galaxy. Monroe had to hide behind an *Inspec* (Being of Light) as he could not survive the awesome 'radiated power' of The One. That is why there is a hierarchy that progressively steps down the Power and Greater Plan of the Father before reaching Man.

So Man wrote the Bible, based on his best understanding of our history and dealings with **higher powers** – that includes The Father, the Angels, the Neggs, and the Anunnaki – of which assortment Man has yet to separate out who was doing what – and that was one of the reasons for this book. And, be clear that Father God did not write the Bible – he's busy running the Universe. It is possible that parts of it were 'dictated' by the Christ (aka Holy Spirit). There has to be a fresh input to our spiritual teachings since **we cannot use the Bible to prove the Bible** – that is "circular reasoning" and is faulty. If new teachings corroborate the Bible, great. If they don't, let's re-examine what we believe.

The One sustains the Universe and the Earth School by his Essence and his Will – it is his Will and Greater Plan that Man will awaken to Truth, Love, Light, and Service – and that means <u>graduate</u> from Earth. Earth is not home, it is not where Man ultimately belongs, and yet Man cannot get out of here until he learns and applies greater Love and Knowledge. Because he gets caught up in sex, drugs, alcohol, power trips, money, etc. he **misses the mark** (and that is all 'sin' is) and has to return to Earth repeatedly – like a 3rd grader who didn't learn to read or do the multiplication tables, he has to repeat until he 'assimilates' the lesson(s) and can move on to the 4th.

The Father does not punish – he is Love and has designed this **Earth School** for Man to experience and in which to grow spiritually. Unfortunately, the Powers That Be (PTB) who are no doubt influenced by the Anunnaki Dissident Remnant (who want to be rid of Man), and perhaps by the Interdimensionals (who also want to be rid of Man), Man is dumbed down and 'trapped' on Earth, unable to actualize his divine potential – the Anunnaki and Inter-dimensionals do NOT want Man to graduate and rule over them, as is his birthright. It is all that simple. And Man cooperates with them by plugging into all the "feel good" teachings and violent video games he can… wasting his time here. Hence Man is often recycled, which amounts to being trapped.

To repeat: Enlil aka Yahweh was the author of the "eye for an eye" teaching, and is NOT how the Father of Light operates – through Karma, you **meet yourself** on Earth, you experience yourself and others just like you, interacting with each other in a context of equals (with no soul power to stop/change what is happening because it is 3D)… THAT is His training technique. When you've had enough, you will seek a better way. That's why it's done that way for 4D souls in 3D with 3D Laws and processes.

Jesus

Enough has been said about this man, but Chapter 11 suspiciously examined the possibility that Jesus and Apollonius were the same person. It was noted that everything that you desire to believe in the alleged Jesus, was already part of the character and being of the actual man called **Apollonius**. He did all the things Jesus did, he did all the things the Apostle Paul did, and even the Caesars in Rome loved him (except for Nero) and built many temples to him. I suggest checking out the historical books on Apollonius, and rereading Chapter 11.

However, it is conceivable that there were **two avatars** running around, at the same time, doing almost the same thing, but it is still curious that they didn't meet.... So the information on Apollonius was presented to show that a god, Apollo, had a hand in a "virgin" birth which reminds us of the virgin birth of Jesus. **Artificial insemination**. Here is where we pick up the original theme of this book and examine a possible role the Anunnaki played in Mary's virgin birth scenario.

From all the research available, from my Source and many different authors, it is accepted that the Anunnaki had a hand in the design and creation of Man. The Anunnaki also 'created' religion to guide/control Man. So consider that while the main Anunnaki group (including Enlil) went home in the 600 BC time frame, there remained an Anunnaki Remnant (including **Enki**, because Man was his creation, and **Marduk** as he was interested in ruling Earth). Enki was always supportive of his creation and wanted Man to grow and develop into a stable, mature human being, with advanced culture and technology and spiritual understanding. Unfortunately Marduk (aka Ares, Mars) saw Man the same way Enlil saw him, and that is why the Remnant broke into two groups with two different approaches to dealing with Man.

So now consider this scenario for Jesus:
> (It is not necessary to believe this, but it fits what we know happened
> given how the Anunnaki have always manipulated Man)

In 9 BC, the humans are beginning to disregard the gods (Anunnaki), the Pharisees have reworked *ad absurdum* the Mosaic Law into an incredibly large *Mishnah*, and since most of the gods aren't here any longer, and religion is beginning to lose its desired "control" effect, Marduk steps in with an iron hand. Marduk decides to create a god-man, with advanced powers, that will become an avatar promoting the new Law from God (Marduk), that Man must obey his gods and once again toe the mark. Thus he uses his advanced DNA and has Mary artificially inseminated and she gives birth to the long awaited Jewish Messiah – that will make the people happy. He even has one of his craft shine in the night sky and guide the Persian astronomers to the birth site. Enki does not like this, as he knows that the new god-man will seek to do Marduk's bidding and again bind Man under the yoke of the Anunnaki. Man will be enslaved again, more than he is under the Roman rule.

So as the child grows, Enlil gives Herod a dream (remember V2K in Chapter 11 – if we have it, so do the Anunnaki) that a major threat to his rule has been born, and Jesus' family escapes with their son to Egypt. (This becomes part of the missing years of Jesus' life) – As he grows, he studies with the advanced teachers in Alexandria, comes back up to visit and study with the Essenes, and after his 12th birthday approaching his *bar mitzvah*, he stops by a synagogue and delivers a very advanced word to the assembly. Then he leaves town again and hops a caravan to the East and studies with the Tibetans and the Hindus (second part of his unknown life). He learns to walk on water, manifest food, raise the dead, heal people and do the things that Jesus becomes known for in the Bible during his upcoming ministry.

He returns around age 30 to the Palestine area, and has John the Baptist baptize him. Marduk is above in his craft and sends a dove down to him and announces that he is well-pleased with Jesus. And yet when Jesus starts teaching, he angers the Pharisees, the Romans, and Marduk is not happy with what Jesus has become. When Jesus was in India, he royally complained about the caste system (which Marduk had set up for those people; Anunnaki society was very caste-oriented), and Jesus starts criticizing the money changers, the Pharisees, the Roman occupation, and is seen as **a rebel**. This was not what Marduk had in mind – Jesus will not and does not promote the "eye for an eye" Mosaic teachings and instead promotes brotherly love, equality of Man, patience, forgiveness, etc… Enki is happy but Marduk has decided to take Jesus out, even though he was barely 1 year into his 'ministry.' The project has run awry.

Marduk gives the order to deliver Jesus to the Jews who will deliver him to the Romans for sentencing, with additional trumped up charges, just for good measure. Jesus is not initially aware of who is setting him up, but he knows that Pilate has been given authority from a higher power (Marduk) and says so. Pilate knows Jesus is a rebel and hasn't disobeyed any Roman laws, but the Jews want him removed, and he has his orders from Marduk, so Pilate is coerced into ordering crucifixion. Jesus is also brutally whipped.

There was no substitute body on the cross (despite the stories of someone substituting for Jesus). Jesus goes to the Cross. Don't forget his genetics are not those of the average Man. He is nailed to the Cross, about Noon, given a drink from a sponge on a stick, probably dipped in a stupefying liquid to dull the pain, and he gets stabbed in the side, but he doesn't die. Marduk is in the crowd, watching. That is when Jesus cries out "My god, my god [Marduk], why hast thou forsaken me?" He had been set up. **He wasn't left there long enough** – he is taken down about 3 pm, passed out, and put in a tomb, loosly wrapped in a Shroud – He was not wrapped in the usual "mummy" way as the Sun was setting and Jewish law forbade dealing with the dead as Passover would begin in 1 hour … there wasn't enough time to properly wrap the body and get out of there. Jesus was barely alive.

Sometime during the night, Jesus has a supernatural healng – If not the Ancient Ones, then Angels or the Father of Light – **someone** hit him <u>thru the Shroud</u> with a high energy healing and Jesus is **Resurrected**. (The Anunnaki were known to possess the elixir of life that could even bring the dead back to life and Inanna used it to restore her lover Damuzi after a rival killed him! [the Osiris story source in <u>Anunnaki Legacy</u>.]) **That left an imprint on the Shroud**. Jesus has had it with the local area, Romans, Marduk and the Pharisees, and agrees to Enki taking him up in a craft and they fly to the Americas, and later to the East where Jesus spends his remaining days as **Issa**, ministering to the people of India. His tomb is marked and is there in Kashmir, near Srinigar, to this day. [1]

> **Note:** *Marduk allegedly died in 331 BC but that was a ruse so that he didn't have to face Alexander the Great (who mistook a monument to Marduk in Babylon for Marduk's tomb). In addition, he was later alive as a Greek god (Ares) 300-200 BC, and then as a Roman god (Mars) during Jesus' time. Note also that Marduk had two sons who acted in his stead, Ninurta and Nannar, and either could also easily have been Jesus' nemesis.*

How do we know Jesus wasn't dead? Simple: **dead men don't bleed** and continue to exude blood <u>into the shroud fibers</u>. This is particularly evident in **the forehead area** where the alleged crown of thorns pierced the skin…. The hands also show similar flow into the fibers.

By the way, the Hindus, the Muslims and some Gnostics maintain that while Jesus did go to the Cross in crucifixion, he did not die on the Cross. [2] Had he spent 2 more hours on the cross, he would have died.

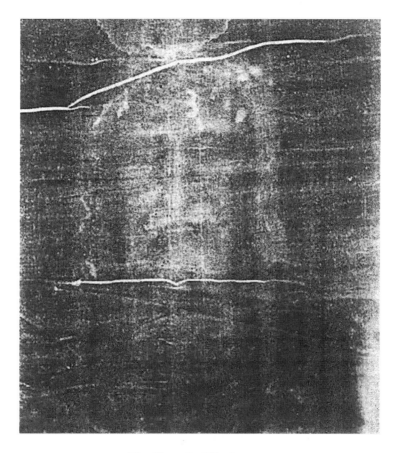

The Shroud of Turin
(credit: Wikipedia Commons:
http://en.wikipedia.org/wiki/File:Shroud_positive_negative_compare.jpg)

Holgar Kersten

A German researcher wrote a book called <u>The Jesus Conspiracy</u> and in it he examines the evidence of the Shroud of Turin: the Shroud clearly shows blood flow <u>from</u> the body <u>into</u> the fibers of the Shroud – **dead people's blood does not flow** and continue to seep into the fibers. That means either Jesus was alive when taken off the cross and the Shroud is loosely draped over him, as even Islam suggests…or the Shroud is someone else's wrapping… But the Jews didn't drape their dead, they used strips of cloth to <u>wrap</u>, like a mummy. So evidently there <u>was</u> a hasty shrouding and entombing.

Dr. Fomenko and Jesus

Note that the following sections 1, 2 and 3 are Dr. Fomenko's speculation based on his in-depth mathematical analyses and historical research. It is presented here to complete the revised aspects of Jesus' alleged real birth and death.

1. Birth of Jesus

Dr. Fomenko shows in chapter 6, Volume I, of his series how the chronology of the life of Jesus Christ was shifted backward about 1000 years to the 1st century AD. [3]   One of the key events surrounding Jesus' birth was a **supernova** (Star of the West) and the **solar eclipse** at his crucifixion. The Scaligerian determination of AD April 3, 33 as Jesus' crucifixion does not hold water when one examines the astronomical records.

What was needed was a supernova, as recorded in the astronomical records, followed by a solar eclipse just 32-33 years later. The event recorded as the solar eclipse, sanctioned by the Church according to its own records, happened in reality on AD February 16, 1086. [4] Further, Jesus' birth was also astronomically determined to be in AD 1053 – when there was a supernova creating the bright star that could have been followed by the three wise men. [5]

Given that astronomical criteria, **Jesus was actually born in 1053 and died in 1086** – at age 33. That means the terms "BC" and "AD" for dating will have to be changed to "CE" (common era) if Jesus is not associated with the first years of the 1st Century. Except that the Biblical Jesus appears to be a composite of several people, that would be a fascinating discovery.

There were only two times in all of recorded astronomical history when a supernova was 'followed' by an eclipse, and only one of them had the right 33-year gap. What this may suggest is that we take the New Testament Gospel information with a grain of salt – the accompanying astronomical signs heralding Jesus' birth and death may be no more than Hollywood-type theatrics. [6]   But it is curious that there was such a 33-year gap. Perhaps the Church told the truth about the signs, and just adjusted the birth and death years backwards, as Dr. Fomenko suggests. Why? This would have the effect of making the Church appear to be older than it really was.

On the other hand, if the heavenly signs are bonifide and part of Jesus' life, then Jesus lived just 929 years ago. And so did Apollonius…. Interesting.

2. Jesus' Death & The Crusades

Jesus' new birth date seemed preposterous until a friend suggested I check out the dating of the Crusades. It had always bothered me that the Christian world waited 1,063 years after Jesus' death (in AD 33) to go retake the Holy City of Jerusalem – what were they doing for over a thousand years? The first Crusade was in AD 1096. If Jesus really died in AD 1086, a ten year wait is not unreasonable. Intriguing proposition…

There is considerable evidence and proof of what Dr. Fomenko says, and it almost takes a math expert to follow the statistical proofs (verified by his peers) to see just how Scaliger managed to rewrite history. There were also different, creative ways of writing dates back in those days that add to the confusion [7]

What this all means is that the Catholic Church may not be 2000 years old. Interesting…

3. Art and Coins Corroborate

Dr. Fomenko offers another interesting piece of evidence that supports the AD 1086 date for Jesus' death… Written dates were imperfectly recorded and no one system dominated until well into the XVI-XVII century timeframe. For example, it was a common but not standard practice to record a date on art or silver/gold metal-worked plates as I520 or J520 or even I.520 or J.520 which meant "520 years since Jesus (his death)." The "I" was Iesus as well as the "J". Since there was no engraving or quality portraiture to speak of in AD 520, nor was there any goldsmithing of the quality Dr. Fomenko shows in pictures, the 520 is obviously not AD 520. If however, Jesus died in AD 1086 and we add the 520 to 1086, we get AD 1606 – which agrees with the artist's membership in a guild in Belgium – the source of the artwork. [8]

Some of the errors in dating historical events occurred when scholars in the XVI – XVIII centuries began translating I520 as 520 years since the nativity of Jesus, or AD 520 – incurring an error of 1086 years. All because there was no standardization in writing dates.

Lastly, roman numerals did not clear up the confusion. X.III was a common way of writing "third century since Christ" where the X stands for Christ. Depending on the scholar doing the translation, X.III can be read as "the 3rd century since Christ" (a date preceding AD 400) or "the middle of the XIV century" – if you know that AD 1086 was Christ's death and you are trying to convey 3 centuries after his death – i.e., AD 1386.

Rewind: Jesus' Shroud

And just as interesting is **the fact** that the scientists are dating the Shroud of Turin to the mid 1300's , so if the Shroud is +/- 300 years within the Medieval timeframe, this also fits better with Fomenko's corrected dates for Jesus' birth and death.

> After years of discussion, The Holy See permitted radiocarbon dating on portions of a swatch taken from a corner of the shroud. Independent tests in 1988 at the University of Oxford, the University of Arizona, and the Swiss Federal Institute of Technology concluded with 95% confidence that **the shroud material dated to 1260-1390 AD.**[9] [emphasis added]

Whereas it makes no sense for the Shroud of Turin to be dated in the AD 1000 - 1300 period if Jesus died in AD 33, there is a much better chance that the Shroud is authentic if Jesus lived about AD 1053 and died about AD 1086. The slight discrepancy between AD 1086 Jesus' death and AD 1000-1300 Shroud use could be due to the problematic technique of C-14 dating.

Whereas the Shroud appears to be a **'smoking gun'** in confirming the corrected date of Jesus' death according to Dr. Fomenko, there are combined corroborating 'coincidences' that do bear some consideration:

Assume that Jesus died about AD 1086... then note:

1. The **Crusades** began in AD 1096 – more plausible than a 1,063 year gap before attempting to retake the Holy Land;
2. The **Inquisition** occurred in 1100's – 1300's as a rebuttal to people who in large numbers knew something that contradicted the Church;
3. **Scaliger and Petavius** (Chapter 10) actually DID make back adjustments to Western Chronology;
4. Many coins and artworks support the **"I.520" dating format** and did mean "520 years from the <u>death</u> of Jesus in AD 1086;"
5. The **Library of Alexandria** was a threat to the Church's teachings and was sacked and burned in AD 270 by Aurelian, in AD 391 by Pope Theophilus, and in AD 642 by the Muslims – according to Dr. Fomenko, those would all be back-adjusted years for actually having happened during the AD 1000 – 1300 timeframe.

Of course, these items are not conclusively proven... yet. But Dr. Fomenko and others are working on it. And at any rate, it makes for fascinating reading and the possibility IS there since we know that Western Chronology <u>was</u> altered before the printing press debuted. And Dr. Fomenko has reasonable credibility because as a full professor at Moscow State University (see Chapter 10 credentials), he doesn't want to sacrifice his position with some flaky and unsubstantiated theory... but time will tell.

> **Remember that nothing is known for certain backwards of AD 900 (Chapter 10) and that those 3 events in item #5 above may have all happened in the current Era <u>since</u> AD 900.**

> **Again, Eras start and stop as a result of being in a very sophisticated Simulation which has its own Script, its own purpose, and the Script is stopped with a "Wipe and Reboot" due to anything going wrong within the Simulation: pollution, code corruption, replication malfunction or insertion of objects, NPCs or *biota* that turn out to be counter-productive or off-purpose (Chapter 13).**

Jesus' Later Years

For those who are curious, if one has read this far, Jesus went first to the Americas and became the **Pale Teacher** among the American Indian tribes. Then he went to India and was called **Issa** and eventually died there just over 100 years of age. [10]

In addition, and perhaps most eyebrow-raising, because Jesus had such a short 'ministry' in the Middle East before Marduk removed him, there wasn't much written about him by contemporary authors of the time. He was called **Crestus** and **Yeshu** by Josephus and the

Scribes writing the Talmud and *Mishnah* entries, which because he was seen as a rebel, are mostly pejorative. In Egypt, he was called **Esu-Rex**.

Since Jesus was allegedly dead upon the Cross, and since Apollonius was a wonder-worker, I suggested the Church used Jesus as the god-man for their new religion, for the reasons put forth in Chapter 11. The Church also wanted his death on the Cross to be a sacrifice for mankind, whereas hybrid **Apollonius never went to the Cross**. The Church could not use a hybrid, for the reasons stated earlier (Chapter 11), but they could and did use the exploits of Apollonius as those of Jesus and/or the apostle Paul. That is the connection, which has been kept secret, or was lost in the ensuing centuries. **That is also why the Inquisition was busy stamping out those who knew the truth.** The Cathars and Knights Templar knew the truth and that is <u>how</u> they blackmailed the Church (and became rich) and that is <u>why</u> the Church retaliated and persecuted them, killing many of the remaining leaders (who went underground and became known as the Rosicrucians, and bankers in what is now Switzerland). The earlier Church appears to have had a shadowy past.

Nonetheless, there is power in Jesus' name even though he wasn't the Christ. Because the Higher Beings, and the one called Christ can answer fervent, honest prayers made in the name of Jesus because they love Man, they know what you mean, <u>serving you is what they do</u>, and Christ IS real. Why would he not answer?

The Christ

The very ascended being known as the Christ did exist and walked the Earth in times long past (before Jesus). He was often called **Melchizedek or Krishna**, among other names, and is very proactively responsible for guiding and protecting Man – in a **freewill** Universe. That latter is very important; as souls all have the choice to follow the Light or not. He set the Way and said "Walk ye in it." Numerous passages in the Bible have his energy signature, and there is enough in the Word that if we are dedicated and seriously wanting to follow him, there are many inspiring and enlightening passages (mostly in the New Testament) we can use. You can bet The Christ had a hand in 'dictating' some of the awesome passages of the NT Bible – they carry his signature and lead us onto the Way.

Want more spiritual input? Ask. "You have not because you ask not… or you ask for the wrong reason(s)" (said James).

He oversees the Higher Beings, possesses incredible Light and Love, and to him has been given all authority on Earth. Why would he not answer your prayers? Ask. Why ask? Why doesn't he just do what he knows we need? Because:

(1) we are in a freewill universe and to just do something to/for us that we haven't asked for violates our freewill – it is not intercession, it is <u>interference</u> according to the Father's Way.
   If it is already in your Script, it will happen without your asking.
(2) And then we are in training here, and we are to learn to walk with him, talk with him and work with him – as we shall when we graduate from Earth. We will be more STO instead of STS.

And all we have to do is call on him, ask for guidance, The Christ is worthy of our respect, following and veneration. Be clear that he sees us as undeveloped souls (sparks of The One) who need training but have the 100% potential to become as he is… to eventually serve in the Father's Kingdom. Be aware that the Interdimensionals also see our potential and are angry that **we were created a bit higher than them and the Angels**, as Dr. Peck discovered in Chapter 7.

Now do you see why it is so important to put away the things and ideas of a child, as St Paul said, and tell the Christ that you are ready to learn, willing to change and accept the responsibility to become an Earth Graduate?

That is the essence of an updated Christianity.

Well, you say, Man insists he is already doing that. Tithing, praying, reading Scripture, attending church… but there is something missing. And that is what Chapter 11 was all about. Today's modern Christians are working under a false assumption that would be horrific to discover – <u>after</u> they die!

Isn't Man "saved" in Christ or Jesus? No he isn't. In accepting Jesus as Lord, Man has chosen to make Truth, Light and Love the guiding principle of his life. Great. But…Man thought his sins were also removed, or at least forgiven, and now he can go to Heaven. They weren't. What we call "sins" are really just the mistakes we have made as fallible human beings… and we need to learn to do better. Sins are just "missing the mark."

Let me use a simple analogy. Suppose you are part of an Olympic Archery team and you are given a 45# recurve bow and some arrows, and the coach tells you to go stand 200' from the target and learn to shoot. In learning, you have to learn how to hold the bow so that, upon release of the arrow, the string doesn't snap into your left forearm and cut you, and you have to learn how to hold the arrow and aim to hit the target…. At any rate, if you are not even able to hit the target ("missing the mark") how does that guarantee you a spot on the team (i.e., entrance into Heaven)? Sure, the coach (Jesus) may like you but if you cannot do what you are supposed to do, of what use will you be to him? Your sins are just "missing the mark" – errors in what you are doing which need more practice or learning… you can't blame your archery errors on the coach (i.e., impute your sins to Jesus). You need to **learn** what works so <u>you</u> can successfully compete in that Great Archery Competition in the Sky.

The bottom line to walking in the Way with him is to acknowledge our mistakes ('sins') AND take full responsibility for them – no vicarious atonement. Then ask for the guidance and strength to meet and overcome the daily lessons, the catalyst in our particular Script. As long as Man still thinks someone else can pay for his sins, he is living in a fantasy world and when he dies, THEN is not the time to find out he wasted his time on Earth.

So the bottom line is Man accepting his own **responsibility** to learn, walk in Light and Love, tell the truth, have compassion, have patience, be humble, forgive and serve others. What has been called the Earth Graduate…

Appendix E: Serpent Wisdom

Serpent Wisdom was examined in Chapter 10, and Enki's Serpent Brotherhood was reviewed in Chapter 11. This was a rather large-scale movement that once flourished around the planet – until Enlil and the Church persecuted and all but obliterated it. Was it evil? No, it was merely the advanced teachings of many groups in many countries who sought to 'upgrade' Man spiritually – such teachings were promoted by Enki who had also spread different types of humans around the planet.

Serpent Wisdom took the more common forms of Ophite Gnostics, Rosicrucianism, and the inner teachings of Pythagorism (which was a lot more than mathematics and geometry), the Druids, the Norse, the Djedhi of Egypt, the Lung Dragons of China, the Hopi Snake Clans, and Apollonius even studied with the Tibetan Nagas, and the Essenes. They all taught a technique for moving the ***kundalini*** at the base of the spine up through the chakras to the head where the initiate would be enlightened. It was a mechanical way of moving Light through the body, along Chapter 9's **bionet**, and the ultimate goal was to achieve higher consciousness and reconnect with one's Higher Self, or Oversoul. This, in turn, would render one an adept and s/he could do what Jesus, Buddha, Ishtar/Isis and Apollonius were known to do – heal others, walk on water, and manifest from thin air.

Turning humans into god-like beings, by developing their inherent divine potential (an aspect of the soul), approaching the abilities of the Anunnaki themselves, was not condoned by Enlil, and it was his (and later Marduk's) agenda to keep Man a simple slave.

Serpent Skulls

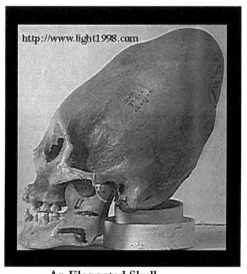

An Elongated Skull
(credit: www.red-grey.co.uk)

Enki was the progenitor of the Serpent Wisdom groups and to honor him, as he was reptilian (perhaps reptibian as Chapter 3 said), the symbol of the snake was chosen and members often deformed their children's skulls (as was also done in Egypt and Peru). [1]

The skull (preceding page) is a valid ET skull as it has just two parts to the skull – one frontal and a large parietal-occipital combination (side and back) area, with one long suture. This being what the ETs looked like, it was the human's desire to emulate the aliens, perhaps to please them or show conformity. Below, notice the 3-part skull of the normal human: one frontal, and two parietal revealing 3 sutures.

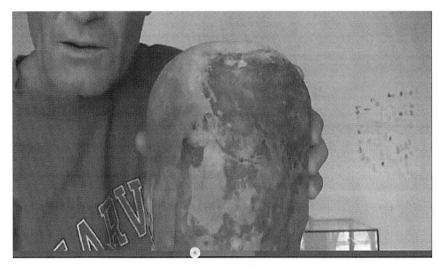

This is the alien skull – note one horizontal suture about midpoint. (View is top of head, face at bottom.)

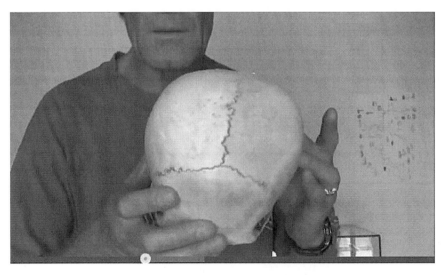

This is the human skull – note the 3 sutures. (View is top of head, face at bottom.)

Brien Foerster demos skulls in Paracas, Peru Museum.
Source: http://www.youtube.com/watch?feature=player_detailpage&v=JnERUZNqwbc

The alien skull shown on this page is the same as the one on the preceding page. The genetics are obviously different, and so are the cranial capacities – the alien skull is 1500 cc while the human skull is 1100-1200 cc (normal).

Skull DNA

And for those who are really interested, several alien skulls from Peru were tested for DNA to see if they were in fact deformed human skulls. Despite the lack of parietal and suture features in common, if the alleged alien skulls had the same basic human DNA, then there must have been a human mutation or an unexplained human deformity.

The DNA is different and does not match human DNA.

> Michael Snyder wrote on February 10th 2014: "How can we explain elongated skulls that are thousands of years old that contain genetic material 'unknown in any human, primate or animal known so far?' …. The results for one of the skulls are now in… and this skull represents a 'new, human-like creature' unlike anything that has been discovered before….
>
> The geneticist that ran the DNA forms this conclusion: "Whatever the sample labeled 3A has come from – it had mtDNA with mutations unknown in any human, primate or animal known so far…. If these mutations will hold, we are dealing with a new human-like creature, very distant from Homo sapiens, Neanderthal and Denisovians." [2]

This is just what **Brien Foerster** (above) has been saying, as well as DNA tests done on the Starchild skull (from Mexico) presented as evidence by the late **Lloyd Pye**. [3]

Serpent Imagery

The image of a serpent for wisdom was chosen for several reasons: the DNA helix-shape resembles 2 snakes entwining each other, and the *kundalini* which travels up the *nadi* (channels) of the spinal area, in a snake-like motion, thus resembles a serpent:

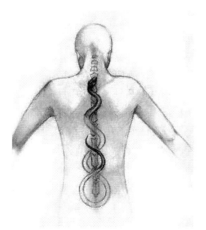

The Kundalini Serpent
(source: http://www.davidicke.com/oi/extras/08/April/9.jpg)

In addition, snakes shed their skin and are 'reborn'. So the Serpent Wisdom groups promoted personal rebirth to initiates via orchestrated rituals. Apparently the movement in addition to being worldwide, also was ancient as Moses lifted up a Brass Serpent in the wilderness to get his people healed from a plague of serpents:

Moses' Brazen Serpent Pole
(credit: http://en.wikipedia.org/wiki/File:Michelangelo_Buonarroti_024.jpg)

 And the healing concept is also represented by the **medical caduceus** and Aesculapius himself, the god of medicine (and son of Apollo) whose rod featured an entwining serpent.

The Caduceus   **Aesculapius and his Rod**

(Credit: both from Wikimedia Commons)

Another object associated with Serpent Wisdom and Worship was the **Cosmic Egg**… An egg is a symbol of birth – and in this case, rebirth as an enlightened initiate, and the Serpent symbolizes both DNA and the Serpent Wisdom teachings:

The Cosmogenic Egg

(credit: http://en.wikipedia.org/wiki/File:Orphic-egg.png)

The point being that Serpent imagery was widespread and still is. Recall that Quetzalcoatl in Mexico was the "plumed/feathered serpent", and the American Indians built serpent mounds (e.g., Ohio) as a place to hold their (equinox) ceremonies.

The Norse had a Tree of Life called **Yggdrasil** which was (among other things) a kundalini symbol in their Cosmology: the **Serpent** at the base of the Tree [spine] would climb the Tree and merge with the **Eagle** [2 wings symbolized the two halves of the brain] at the top and the initiate would experience enlightenment (*satori*). Entire books have been written on Serpent Wisdom and symbology and so this is just a brief introduction.

Yggdrasil: Norse Tree of Life

(credit: http://en.wikipedia.org/wiki/Yggdrasil)

593

Note: the Norse also had a rune symbol whose value was in the Futhark alphabet as 'Serpent' (who lived in the water):

This was found in Anglo-Frisian runes from 5th – 11th centuries. Note that the symbol for Serpent is a star … and Enki as a Serpent Being came from a star system and lived in the water… connection? The point here is that **kundalini** was not just the province of the Hindus nor of the Serpent Wisdom groups.

Anunnaki and the Shining Ones

The connection between the Anunnaki and the Serpent imagery is more than physical. It was said in Chapters 1 and 3 that the Anunnaki (aka Anunna or Anannage) were in fact the Elohim of the Bible. Loosly translated, Elohim is taken to mean "gods" – the plural of EL (The God of the Universe). But there is more to it than that. 'El' also means 'strong' as well as 'God' (who does shine and is strong).

> The Old Irish Aillil means shining; Old Cornish EL means shining, Elf [elves] means shining…. Inca Illa is bright or to shine, Babylonian Ellu is to shine…[4]

The Sumerian 'el' means 'shining' and thus the plural Elohim is **'the shining ones'** – and this was hinted at in Chapter 3 where Adam and Eve lose their "shining coats" (fine-scaled snakeskin covering) when they are given the ability to reproduce and they take on a more mammalian appearance. (See Ch. 3, Section 'Reptilian to Mammalian'.) [5] In addition, the Shining Ones came to Northern Europe and erected large stone monuments… "In Ireland they left the legacy of the 'Tuatha de Danaan' or **'People of Anu'** which means 'People of the Shining Ones.'" [6] (Danu is the feminine version of the Sumerian Anu – Enlil's father/king.)

Thus, Man's origins begin to come to light, and the Serpent (originally Enki) was venerated all over the Earth as the benefactor and promoter of wisdom for mankind… until the early Church demonized the movement and the Serpent (Chapters 10-11).

Appendix F: Serpent Sculpture

Chapter 3 displayed a Ubaid sculpture from 3500 BC – made by someone who saw these beings in ancient Sumeria. In addition, there was documentation from Berossus and the Jewish *Haggadah* that there were strange-looking beings walking around...

So the following is a kind of wrap-up dealing with non-human beings and the sculpture, statues and pictures of them. Of course the experts will claim that the following are all part of religious rituals practiced by pagan people – all around the globe they all just happened to make either the same or very similar statues – pointed snouts, and **elongated heads**.... But, you decide.

Ubaid Sculpture (Mesopotamia)

And the side views (male and female):

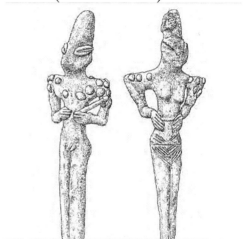

Vinca Sculpture (Serbia – Romania)

Mayan Sculpture (Latin America)

From: "Revelations of the Mayans 2012 and Beyond"
  By Nassim Haramein

'Astronaut?' or Deep Sea diver
on AD 1102 church in
Salamanca, Spain (right).

Iraqui Pottery

Either this guy saw something unusual, or he was just a poor artist:

Iraqui Pottery

The circles above are reminiscent of the Ubaid sculpture….

Vinca Sculpture again – what did the Serbs see and is it related to the Bosnian Pyramid of the Sun in **Visoko**, 20 miles northwest from Sarajevo, the capitol of Bosnia-Herzegovina?

This also bears a resemblance to the Ubaid sculptures… same "coffee bean" eyes.

(Credit: Bing Images)

This is a screenshot from a video by Klaus Dona on the Hidden History of the Human Race…. Statue from Mesopotamia. A 47 minute video well worth the watching:
https://search.yahoo.com/search;_ylt=Am6bkPXiGAevy1Fbpfp_Z0mbvZx4?fr=yfp-t-901-s&toggle=1&cop=mss&ei=UTF-8&p=hidden%20history%20of%20the%20human%20race

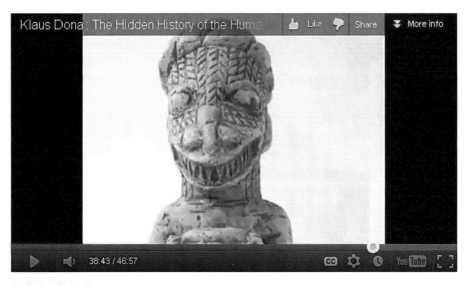

projectavalon.net

While statues and pottery do not <u>prove</u> the existence of ETs/reptilians in the past, it becomes **credible evidence** for it when it is **all over the Earth** and the images of the ET/reptilian hominids look similar – the isolated tribes did not communicate with each other, so how did they make images that are similar? And why do they have similar creation stories?

Credo Mutwa is a Sanusi shaman with the Zulu in Africa – his necklace tells a story of creation involving Earth women and reptilian hominids… à la Enoch in Chapter 2.

ZULU means "people from the stars."

(credit: http://www.bibliotecapleyades.net/esp_credo_mutwa08.htm)

598

The 2004 Dragon below was publicly branded as a hoax, yet it was said to be created **before 1890** by Germans who then suspended it in formaldehyde and encased it in a 30" bottle. That is awfully good fakery for 125 years ago. Note the very small hairs and filaments on it… fingernails and musculature are correct, and there is an umbilical cord… It also bears a resemblance to the **Ubaid and Vinca sculptures**…

If it were a hoax, a simple x-ray could disprove it. It either has internal organs or not. An x-ray <u>was</u> done and the results were not released.

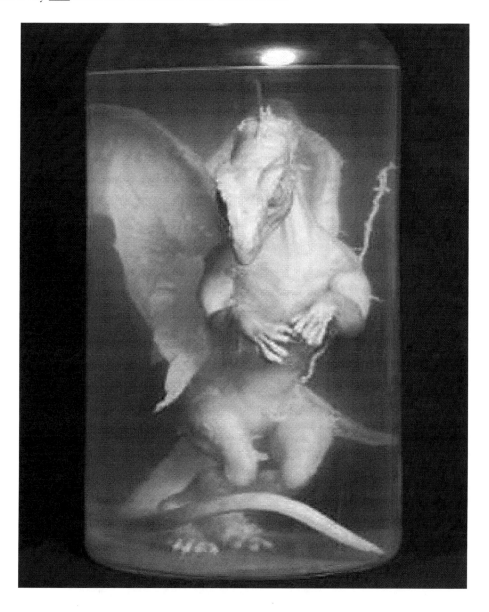

And lastly for your contemplation, this unusual entry:

A 2002 Cropcircle, © Lucy Pringle. Taken in a crop field in Westchester, England called the **Crabwood Face**. Obviously a real cropcircle and not one of the Doug & Dave hoaxes. Note the face resembles the ubiquitous Greys (below)… as well as the Vinca and Ubaid sculptures above. The Grey on the right is a Zeta being and the one on the left is the BioCybernetic Roboid that does abductions.

(credit both: Yahoo Images)

The bottom line: Man is not alone and the Others don't all look human.

Bibliography

Books

Deliverance/Exorcism

Cuneo, Michael. *American Exorcism.* New York: Random House/ Doubleday, 2001.

Martin, Malachi. *Hostage to the Devil.* HarperSanFrancisco, 1992.

Wilkinson, Tracy. *The Vatican's Exorcists.* New York: Warner Books, 2007.

Religion/Metaphysics/Spirituality

Acharya S. *The Christ Conspiracy.* Kempton, IL: Adventures Unlimited Press, 1999.

Atwater, P.M.H. *Near Death Experiences.* NY: MJF Books, 2011.

Bloom, Harold. *Jesus and Yahweh: The Names Divine.* New York: Penguin Group (USA), 2005.

Castaneda, Carlos. *A Separate Reality.* New York: Washington Square Press, 1971.

_____. *The Active Side of Infinity.* New York: HarperCollins, 2000.

Capra, Fritjof. *The Tao of Physics.* Boston, MA: Shambhala Publications, 1999.

Charles, R.A. *The Book of Enoch the Prophet.* San Francisco, CA: Weiser Books, 2003.

Dawood, N. J. *The Koran.* New York: Penguin Group (USA), 2006.

Elkins, Don and Carla Rueckert. *The RA Material, Book I.* Atglen, PA: Schiffer Publishing/Whitford Press, 1984.

Eppler, LaRue and Vanessa Wesley. *Your Essential Whisper.* Bloomington, IN: iUniverse, 2008.

Frejer, B. Ernest. *The Edgar Cayce Companion.* New York: Barnes & Noble Press, 1995.

Gaffney, Mark. *Gnostic Secrets of the Naassenes.* Rochester, VT: Inner Traditions, 2004.

Gardiner, Philip. *Secret Societies.* Franklin Lakes, NJ: Career Press/New Page, 2007.

_____. *Secrets of the Serpent.* Forest Hill, CA: Reality Press, 2008.

_____. *The Shining Ones.* Nottinghamshire, England: Phase Group, 2002.

Golas, Thaddeus. *The Lazy Man's Guide to Enlightenment.* Salt Lake City: Gibbs-Smith, 1995.

Guiley, Rosemary Ellen and Imbrogno, Philip J. *The Vengeful Djinn.* Woodbury, Mn: Llewellyn Worldwide, 2012.

Hoeller, Stephan A. *Gnosticism.* Wheaton, IL: Quest Books, 2002.

Kenyon, J. Douglas, Ed. *Forbidden Religion.* Rochester, VT: Bear & Co., 2006.

Laurence, Richard. *The Book of ENOCH the Prophet.* Kempton, IL: Adventures Unlimited Press, 2000.

Lerma, John, M.D. *Into the Light.* Franklin Lakes, NJ: New Page Books, 2007.

_____ *Learning From the Light.* Franklin Lakes, NJ: New Page Books, 2009.

Mead, G.R.S. *Apollonius of Tyana.* (1901 Edition reprint) Sacramento, CA: Murine Press, 2008.

Meyer, Marvin. *The Gospel of Thomas.* New York: HarperCollins, 1992.

Modi, Shakuntala, M.D. *Remarkable Healings.* VA: Hampton Roads, 1997.

_____. *Memories of God and Creation.* Charlottesville, VA: Hampton Roads, 2000.

Moody, Raymond A., Jr., MD. *Life After Life*. New York: HarperCollins, 2001.

Monroe, Robert. *Journeys Out of the Body*. New York: Doubleday, 1971.

_____. *Far Journeys*. New York: Random House/Broadway, 2001.

_____. *Ultimate Journey*. New York: Random House/Broadway, 2000.

Newton, Michael. *Destiny of Souls*. Woodbury, Mn: Llewellyn Worldwide, 2002.

_____. *Journey of Souls*. Woodbury, Mn: Llewellyn Worldwide, 1994.

Pagels, Elaine. *The Gnostic Gospels*. New York: Random House/Vintage, 1979.

Paulson, Genevieve Lewis. *Kundalini and the Chakras*. MN: Llewellyn Worldwide, 2005.

Peck, M. Scott, M.D. *Glimpses of the Devil*. New York: Free Press, 2005.

_____ *People of the Lie*. New York: Touchstone, 1983.

Picknett, Lynn. *The Secret History of Lucifer*. London: Constable & Robinson, 2005.

Rasha. *Oneness*. Santa Fe, NM: Earthstar Press, 2003.

Ring, Kenneth. *Lessons from the Light*. Portsmouth, NH: Moment Point Press, 2000.

Robinson, James M., General Editor. *The Nag Hammadi Library*. New York: HarperCollins, 1990.

Roman, Sanaya. *Spiritual Growth*. Tiburon, CA: HJ Kramer, Inc., 1989.

_____. *Personal Power Through Awareness*. Tiburon, CA: HJ Kramer, Inc., 1986.

Ruffin, C. Bernard. *Padre Pio: The True Story*. Huntington, IN: Our Sunday Visitor Publishing Division, Inc., 1991.

Russell, A. J., *God Calling*. Uhrichsville, OH: Barbour Publishing, 1989.

Slate, Joe H., Ph.D. *Aura Energy*. Woodbury, MN: Llewellyn Worldwide, 2002.

_____. *Psychic Vampires*. St. Paul, MN: Llewellyn Worldwide, 2004.

Snellgrove, Brian. *The Unseen Self*. Essex, England: The C.W. Daniel Co., 1996.

Spong, John Shelby. *A New Christianity for a New World*. HarperSanFrancisco, 2001.

_____ *Why Christianity Must Change or Die*. HarperSanFrancisco, 1999.

The King James Study Bible. Nashville, TN: Thomas Nelson, 1988.

Wilde, Stuart. *The Prayers and Contemplations of God's Gladiators*. Chicago, IL: Brookemarke, LLC., 2001.

_____ *The Force*. Carlsbad, CA: Hay House, 2006.

Wohlberg, Steve. *End Time Delusions*. Shippensberg, PA: Treasure House, 2004.

Zukav, Gary. *The Dancing Wu Li Masters*. New York: Quill, 1979.

_____ *The Seat of the Soul*. New York: Simon & Schuster, 1990.

Scientific/Medical

Baugh, Carl E. *Why Do Men Believe Evolution Against All Odds*? Oklahoma City, OK: Hearthstone Publishing, 1999.

Behe, Michael J. *Darwin's Black Box*. New York: Simon & Schuster/Touchstone, 1996.

Braden, Gregg. *The Divine Matrix*. Carlsbad, CA: Hay House, 2007.

Brown, Walt. *In The Beginning: Compelling Evidence for Creation and the Flood*. Phoenix, AZ: Center for Scientific Creation, 1995.

Carlo, George, Dr. and Martin Schram. *Cell Phones: Invisible Hazards in the Wireless Age*. New York: Carroll & Graf Publishers, 2001.

Clayton, PhD, Paul **Out of the Fire**. HongKong: PharmacoNutrition Press, 203.

Elvidge, Jim. *The Universe Solved*. AT Press, 2007.

Friesen, James G., M.D. *Uncovering the Mystery of MPD*. Eugene, OR: Wipf & Stock Publishers, 1991.

Greene, Brian.   *The Elegant Universe.* New York: W.W.Norton & C0. 2003.
_____   *The Fabric of the Cosmos.* New York: Vintage Books. 2004.
_____   *The Hidden Reality.* New York: Alfred A. Knopf. 2011.
Hawking, Stephen with Leonard Mlodinow. *A Briefer History of Time.* New York: Bantam Dell, 2008.
_____. *A Brief History of Time and The Universe in a Nutshell.* (2-book volume). New York: Bantam Dell Books, 1996, 2001.
Hunter, C. Roy. *Master the Power of Self-Hypnosis.* NY: Sterling Publishing, 1998.
Johnson, Phillip E.   *Defeating Darwinism.* Downers Grove, IL: InterVarsity Press, 1997.
Kaku, Michio.   *Hyperspace.* New York: Anchor Books, 1995.
Krauss, Lawrence M.   *The Physics of Star Trek.* New York: Basic Books, 2007.
LaViolette, Paul A, PhD. *Secrets of Antigravity Propulsion.* VT: Bear & Co., 2008.
_____ *Genesis of the Cosmos.* Rochester, VT: Bear & Co., 2004.
_____ *Decoding the Message of the Pulsars,* VT: Bear & Co., 2006
Levy, Elinor, and Mark Fischetti. *The New Killer Diseases.* NY: Three Rivers Press, 2004.
Lloyd, Seth.   *Programming the Universe.* New York: Random House, 2007.
McTaggart, Lynn.   *The Field.* New York: HarperCollins/Quill, 2002.
Meyer, Stephen C.   *Signature in the Cell.* New York: HarperCollins, 2009.
Morris, John D., Ph.D. *The Young Earth.* Green Forest, AR: Master Books, 2006.
Myss, Caroline, Ph.D. *Why People Don't Heal and How They Can.* New York: Three Rivers Press, 1997.
_____. *Sacred Contracts.* New York: Three Rivers Press, 2002.
Narby, Jeremy.   *The Cosmic Serpent.* New York: Tarcher/Putnam, 1998.
Pearce, Joseph Chilton. *The Biology of Transcendence.* Rochester, VT: Park Street Press, 2002.
Pearsall, Paul, Ph.D. *The Heart's Code.* New York: Random House/Broadway, 1998.
Pert PhD, Candace. *Molecules of Emotion.* New York: Scribner, 1997.
Peterson, Dennis R. *Unlocking the Mysteries of Creation.* 6th edition. El Dorado, CA: Creation Resource Foundation, 1990.
Samuelson PhD, Gary L. **The Science of Healing Revealed**. (self-published 64-pg Full-color illustrated booklet on biochemistry). 2009
Shnayerson, Michael and Mark Plotkin. *The Killers Within.* Boston: Back Bay Books, 2003.
Stout, Dr. Martha,   *The Sociopath Next Door.* NY: Broadway Books, 2005.
Talbot, Michael.   *The Holographic Universe.* New York: HarperCollins, 1991.
Watson, James D.   *DNA.* New York: Alfred A. Knopf, 2003.
Wolf, Fred Alan, PhD. *The Yoga of Time Travel.* Wheaton, IL: Quest Books, 2004.
Yang, Jwing-Ming, Dr. *The Root of Chinese Qigong.* Roslindale, MA: YMAA

UFOs and ETs

Beckley, Timothy G. *The Secret Space Program.* NJ: Global Communications, 2012.
Bender, Albert K.   *Flying Saucers and the Three Men.* Clarksburg, W.VA: Saucerian Press, 1962.
Boulay, R.A.   *Flying Serpents and Dragons.* Rev. Ed. San Diego, CA: The Book Tree, 1999.
Bramley, William.   *The Gods of Eden.* New York: HarperCollins/Avon, 1993.

Branton, ed.   *The Omega Files.* NJ: Global Communications, 2012.
Cannon, Dolores.   *Keepers of the Garden.* Huntsville, AR: Ozark Mtn Publishers, 2002.
Clark, Gerald.   *The Anunnaki of Nibiru.* Lexington, KY: CreateSpace, 2013.
Cramp, Leonard G.   *Space, Gravity and the Flying Saucer.* NY: British Book Centre, 1955.
Farrell, Joseph P.   *The Cosmic War.* Kempton, IL: Adventures Unlimited Press, 2007.
_____   *Nazi International.* Kempton, IL; Adventures Unlimited Press, 2008.
_____   *Covert Wars and Breakaway Civilizations.* Kempton, IL; Adventures
                             Unlimited Press, 2012.
_____   *Covert Wars and the Clash of Civilizations.* Kempton, IL; Adventures
                             Unlimited Press, 2013
_____   *Saucers, Swastikas and Psyops.* Kempton, IL: Adventures Unlimited
                             Press, 2011.
_____   *Roswell and the Reich.* Kempton, IL: AU Press, 2010.
_____   *Genes, Giants, Monsters and Men.* Washington: Feral House, 2011.
Fowler, Raymond.   *The Watchers.* New York: Bantam Books, 1990.
Friedrich, Mattern.   *UFOs: Nazi Secret Weapons?* NJ: Global Communications, 2008.
Good, Timothy.   *Earth: An Alien Enterprise.* New York: Pegasus Publishing, 2013.
Greer, Steven M., MD.   *Hidden Truth – Forbidden Knowledge.* Crozet, VA: Crossing
                             Point, Inc., 2006.
Harbinson, W.A.   *Projekt UFO: The Case for Man- Made Flying Saucers.* London:
                             Boxtree Ltd., 1995.
Heron, Patrick.   *The Nephilim and the Pyramid of the Apocalypse.* New York:
                             Kensington Publishing/Citadel Press, 2004.
Jacobs, David M., Ph.D.   *The Threat.* New York: Simon & Schuster, 1998.
Keith, Jim.   *Saucers of the Illuminati.* Kempton, IL: AU Press, 2004.
Komarek, Ed. *UFOs: Exopolitics and the New World DisOrder.* Lexington KY:
                             Shoestring Publishing, 2012.
Lessin PhD, Sasha.   *Anunnaki Gods No More.* Lexington, KY: CreateSpace, 2012.
Lewels, Joe, Ph.D.   *The God Hypothesis.* Columbus, NC: Wild Flower Press, 2005.
Mack, John E., M.D.   *Abduction.* New York: Charles Scribner's Sons, 1994.
_____   *Passport to the Cosmos.* New York: Three Rivers Press, 1999.
Marrs, Jim.   *Alien Agenda.* New York: HarperCollins, 1997.
_____.   *Rule by Secrecy.* New York: HarperCollins, 2000.
_____.   *The Rise of the Fourth Reich.* NY: Wm Morrow, 2008.
_____.   *Our Occulted History.* New York: HarperCollins, 2013.
Missler, Chuck and Mark Eastman. *Alien Encounters.* ID: Koinonia House, 2003.
Olsen, Brad.   *Future Esoteric: The Unseen Realms.* CA: CCC Publishing, 2013.
Pruett, Dr. Jack.   *The Grandest Deception.* Xlibris Corp: Lexington, KY, 2011.
Stevens, Henry.   *Dark Star.* IL: Adventures Unlimited Press, 2011.
_____   *Hitler's Flying Saucers.* IL: AUP, 2012.
_____   *Hitler's Suppressed and Still-Secret Weapons, Science and Technology.*
                             IL: AUP, 2007.
Story, Ronald D., Ed.   *The Encyclopedia of Extraterrestrial Encounters.* New York:
                             New American Library, 2001.
Tellinger, Michael.   *Slave Species of god.* Johannesburg, SA: Music Masters Close
                             Corporation, 2005. (1st book)
_____.   *Slave Species of the Gods.* Rochester, VT: Bear & Co., 2012.
                             (2nd Book reprint)

Valleé, Jacques. *Passport to Magonia.* Chicago, Il: Contemporary Books, 1993.

———. *Dimensions.* Chicago, Il: Contemporary Books, 1988.

———. *Messengers of Deception.* Brisbane, Australia: Daily Grail, 1979.

———. *Revelations.* San Antonio, TX: Anomalist Books, 2008.

Von Daniken, Erich. *Arrival of the Gods.* London: Vega, 2002.

——— *History is Wrong.* New Jersey: New Page, 2009.

Wolf, Dr. Michael. *The Catchers of Heaven.* Pittsburgh, PA: Dorrance Publishing, 1996.

History and Other Related Books

Andrews, Synthia, and Colin Andrews. *The Complete Idiot's Guide to 2012.* New York: Penguin Group (USA), 2008.

Calleman, Carl Johan, PhD. *The Mayan Calendar and the Transformation of Consciousness.* Rochester, VT: Bear & Co., 2004.

Childress, David Hatcher. *Technology of the Gods.* IL: AUP, 2000.

Fomenko, Anatoly T. PhD. *History: Fiction or Science?*, Vol. 1. Isle of Man, UK: Delamere Resources, Ltd., 2003.

Guiley, Rosemary Ellen. *Encyclopedia of the Strange, Mystical & Unexplained.* New York: Gramercy Books, 2001.

Hawkins, David R. *Reality and Subjectivity.* West Sedona, AZ: Veritas Press, 2003.

——— *The Eye of the I.* West Sedona, AZ: Veritas Press, 2001

Icke, David. *The Biggest Secret.* Wildwood, MO: Bridge of Love, 2001.

——— *…And the Truth Shall Set You Free.* Isle of Wight, UK: David Icke Books Ltd., 1995.

——— *The David Icke Guide to the Global Conspiracy.* Isle of Wight, UK: David Icke Books Ltd., 2007.

——— *Human Race: Get Off Your Knees.* Isle of Wight, UK: David Icke Books Ltd., 2010.

——— *Children of the Matrix.* Isle of Wight, UK: David Icke Books Ltd., 2001.

——— *Tales from the Time Loop.* Wildwood, MO: Bridge of Love, 2003.

Irwin, William. *The Matrix and Philosophy.* Peru, IL: Carus Publishing, 2002.

Keel, John A. *The Complete Guide to Mysterious Beings.* New York: Tor Books, 2002.

——— *Why UFOs – Operation Trojan Horse.* New York: Manor Books, 1970.

——— *Our Haunted Planet.* NY: Fawcett Books, 1971.

Kenyon, Douglas. *Forbidden Science.* VT: Bear & CO., 2008.

Knight-Jadczyk, Laura. *High Strangeness.* Alberta Can: Red Pill Press, 2008

Kramer, Samuel Noah. *The Sumerians.* Chicago, IL: University of Chicago Press, 1971.

McKean, Erin, Ed. *The New Oxford American Dictionary, 2nd Edition.* New York: Oxford University Press, 2005.

Northcutt, Wendy. *The Darwin Awards: Survival of the Fittest.* New York: Penguin Group/Plume Books, 2004.

Parkes, Henry B. *A History of Mexico.* Boston, MA: Houghton Mifflin Co., 1960.

Pinkham, Mark Amaru. The *Return of the Serpents of Wisdom.* Kempton, IL: Adventures Unlimited Press, 1997.

Pye, Lloyd. *Everything You Know Is Wrong, Book I: Human Origins.* Lincoln NE: iUniverse/Authors Choice Press, 2000.

Radzinsky, Edvard. *The Rasputin File.* New York, NY: Anchor Books, 2000.

Rifat, Tim. *Remote Viewing.* London: Vision Paperbacks, 2001.

Sitchin, Zecharia.　*Journeys to the Mythical Past.* Rochester, VT: Bear & Co., 2007.
_____　*The Twelfth Planet.* New York: HarperCollins, 2007.
_____　*The Cosmic Code.* New York: HarperCollins, 2007.
_____　*The End of Days.* New York: HarperCollins, 2007.
_____　*The Earth Chronicles Expeditions.* Rochester VT: Bear & Co., 2004.
_____　*Divine Encounters.* New York: HarperCollins/Avon, 1996.
_____　*Genesis Revisited.* New York: HarperCollins/Avon, 1990.
_____　*The Wars of Gods and Men.* New York: HarperCollins, 2007.
_____　*The Lost Book of ENKI.* Rochester, VT: Bear & Co., 2004.
_____　*The Stairway to Heaven.* New York: HarperCollins, 2007.
_____　*The Earth Chronicles Handbook.* Rochester, VT: Bear & Co., 2009.
_____　*There Were Giants Upon the Earth.* Rochester, VT: Bear & Co., 2010.
Steinmeyer, Jim.　*The Book of the Damned; The Collected Works of Charles Fort.* New York: Tarcher/Penguin Group, 2008.
Stevens, Henry.　*Dark Star.* Kempton, IL; Adventures Unlimited Press, 2011.
_____　*Hitler's Flying Saucers*, rev. ed. Kempton, IL; Adventures Unlimited Press, 2012.
Turner, Patricia & Charles Russell Coulter. *Dictionary of Ancient Deities.* NY, NY: Oxford University Press, 2001.
Witkowski, Igor.　*Axis of the World.* Kempton, IL: Adventures Unlimited Press, 2008.

Internet Sources

Anunnaki

Amitakh Sanford, "The Anunnaki Remnants Are Still on Earth." Excellent article that extends and refutes some of the Zechariah Sitchin material on the Anunnaki. Website: http://www.xeeatwelve.com/articles/anunnaki_remnants.htm

Estelle N. H. Amrani, "A Different Story About the Anunnaki" is another article by a credible source, which partly agrees with Amitakh, and gives additional compatible information. Website: http://www.bibliotecapleyades.net/sumer_anunnaki/anunnaki/anu_12.htm

Robertino Solàrion, "Nibiruan Physiology." Excellent article mentioning the Galactic Law that the Anunnaki must adhere to – first reported by John Baines in his book, The Stellar Man. Website: http://www.bibliotecapleyades.net/cosmic_tree/physiology.htm
see also Baines reference: http://www.bibliotecapleyades.net/serpents_dragons/boulay05e.htm

"Myths From Mesopotamia: Gilgamesh, The Flood, and Others" translated by Stephanie Dalley as quoted in the website: http://www.piney.com/Atrahasis.html also see: http://www.book-of-thoth.com/ftopicp-137854.html

Christianity & Gnosticism

Acharya S, "The Origins of Christianity and the Quest for the Historical Jesus Christ" is a lengthy article examining non-Biblical sources and other documents in a search for the existence of a man called Jesus. Comparisons to the same stories about Christ are found in the stories about the Buddha, Horus, Mithra, and Krishna. Website: http://truthbeknown.com/origins.htm

Acharya S, "The Origins of Good and Evil" is an article that outlines the sources and evolution of evil, as well as how religions take each other over. Website: http://truthbeknown.com/evil.htm

Acharya S./D.M. Murdock, "Apollonius, Jesus and Paul: Men or Myths?" takes an educated look at Apollonius as the source for the Jesus/Paul myth. http://truthbeknown.com/apollonius.html

Dr. R.W. Bernard, "Apollonius the Nazarene" is an ebook which covers as much of Apollonius's life as is extant, in nine chapters. It is based on the work of Philostratus in his *Life of Apollonius*. Website: http://www.apollonius.net/bernardbook.html

Tony Bushby, "The Forged Origins of the New Testament" is an article extracted from *Nexus Magazine*, vol. 14, no. 4 (June-July 2007). The author also wrote a related book called *The Bible Fraud*, via Joshua Books (Australia), 2001. Website: http://www.nexusmagazine.com/articles/NewTestament.html

Wikipedia, "Apollonius of Tyana" article on Wikipedia that is rather negatively biased but relates the generally-agreed on facts surrounding the sage's life. Website: http://en.wikipedia.org/wiki/Apollonius_of_Tyana

"Ghandi on Christianity" set of his quotes in a section called AMOIRA; website: http://koti.mbnet.fi/amoira/religion/gandhicr1.htm
see also: **http://whoisthisjesus.googlepages.com/westernchristianity**

Laura Knight-Jadczyk, "Schwaller de Lubicz and the Fourth Reich" is an article that deals with STO and STS elements of spiritual growth, including the relationship with Shamanism and the 4D STS entities. Website: http://www.cassiopaea.org/cass/schwaller_de_lubicz_3.htm

John Lash, "Kundalini and the Alien Force" article that examines the Gnostic and Tantric practices of sacred sexuality, but also examines the Archons and Jehovah. Website: http://www.metahistory.org/KundaliniForce.php

Joseph Macchio, "The Orthodox Suppression of Original Christianity" is an electronic book of 15 chapters that explores the historical suppression of original Christian truths by the orthodox Church of Rome. It is a treasure-trove of Gnostic teaching, early Christian leaders Mani, Origen and Valentinus, as well as the actions and teachings of Constantine, Augustine and Iraneus. It also reinforces Mouravieff (see OPs/Mouravieff this Appendix). Websites: http://essenes.net/conspireindex.html http://essenes.net/new/subteachings.html

Also worth a look:

"Apollonius of Tyana – Paul of Tarsus?" is an in-depth article on the unique parallels between Apollonius who existed and the putative Apostle Paul. Under 'Christian Origins' section, click on 'The True Identity of St. Paul.'
http://nephiliman.com/apollonius_of_tyanna.htm

Darwin & Science

Wikipedia, "Charles Darwin's Illness" is a lengthy analysis of the man, his illness, and his personal struggle to be productive despite his illness. Website: http://en.wikipedia.org/wiki/Illness_of_Charles_Darwin.
On the same Website is another article dealing with Darwin's religious views: http://en.wikipedia.org/wiki/Charles_Darwin%27s_views_on_religion.
Montag, "Rods and Cones" information from chapter 9 of ebook gives excellent information on the fantastic design and structure of the human eye, plus pictures and charts. A great assist in the understanding of how vision works. Website:
http://www.cis.rit.edu/people/faculty/montag/vandplite/pages/chap_9/ch9p1.html

DNA and Genetics

Baerbel, "The Living Internet Inside of Us" is another translation of some of the Fosar-Bludorf work which can be found at Website: www.crawford2000.com

Baerbel, "Russian DNA Discoveries Explain Human 'Paranormal' Events" is another article edited and translated on various DNA aspects. Website: http://www.fosar-bludorf.com/index_eng.htm

"DNA study deals blow to Neanderthal breeding theory" is an article dealing with the possible interbreeding and non-interbreeding of Cro-Magnon and Neanderthals. Website: http://www.cbc.ca/health/story/2003/05/13/cro_magnnon030513.html

Dr. Barry Starr of Stanford Univ., "Whatever happened to those Neanderthals?" is a great article on possible interbreeding between Cro-Magnons and Neanderthals based on mtDNA, and speculates on the Neanderthal's mysterious disappearance. Also documents recent attempts to see just what was in Neanderthal nuclear DNA. Website: http://www.thetech.org/genetics/news.php?id=37

Grazyna Fosar and Franz Bludorf, "The Biological Chip in Our Cells: Revolutionary results of modern genetics" is an article written in the 95% perfect English of the German genetics researchers who also wrote the book Vernetzte Intelligenz (which is not available in English). The authors have an index with articles in English on
Website: http://www.fosar-bludorf.com/archiv/biochip_eng.htm

Related Websites worth visiting for further depth of the Fosar-Bludorf discoveries:
   http://noosphere.princeton.edu/fristwall2.html
   http://www.ryze.com/view.php?who=vitaeb
   http://www.fossar-bludorf.com/index_eng.htm
Grazyna Fosar and Franz Bludorf, "The Cosmic Internet", article on group consciousness, how DNA acts as an antenna and communication device. Website: http://www.fosar-bludorf.com/vernetz_eng.htm

Grazyna Fosar and Franz Bludorf, "UFO Experiences and Hypercommunication" is another article seeking to explain the UFO abductee experience as one of hypercommunication (via DNA) between alternate realities, or parallel dimensions, as Jacques Vallee suggested years ago. Website: http://www.bibliotecapleyades.net/ciencia/ciencia_hypercommunication01.htm

Rick Groleau, "Tracing Ancestry with MtDNA" article on NOVA Online website that explains how the father's and mother's DNA propagates, and how ancestry can be reliably determined, and what they discovered about the Neanderthals. Website: http://www.pbs.org/wgbh/nova/neanderthals/mtdna.html

Tory Hagen, "Mitochondria and Aging" article explains how oxidants affect the mitochondria's ability to accurately reproduce and resist aging. Website: http://lpi.oregonstate.edu/sp-su98/aging.html

Kean, Sam, "Who's the Fittest Now?" article in Mental Floss magazine for March-April 2009, p. 55-57, presenting the subject of Epigenetics.

"UltraViolet Light" article describes how UV is used to purify/sterilize, and how it can also negatively affect DNA. Website: http://www.Frequencyrising.com

Carl Zimmer, "The Search for Intelligence." Article in *Scientific American* magazine for October 2008, vol. 299, no. 4, pp 68-75. Effect of genetics vs environment on IQ.

Resistance to AIDS/HIV – Sample Report "About Resistance to HIV/AIDS" on the genetic testing website **23and Me**: https://www.23andme.com/health/Resistance-to-HIV-AIDS/ See also: Randy Dotinga article: "Genetic HIV Resistance Deciphered" , website: http://www.wired.com/medtech/health/news/2005/01/66198?currentPage=2

Extraterrestrial Exposure Law

Michael Salla, PhD., "Extraterrestrials Among Us" (vol.1:4, originally from Exopolitics Journal website), is an interesting article on how ETs are among us who look so much like us that we don't suspect, and secondly the article explores the Extraterrestrial Exposure Law of 1969. Website:
http://www.bibliotecapleyades.net/exopolitica/esp_exopolitics_ZZZN.htm
also see: http://exopolitics.com for author's general website.

Extraterrestial Genes in Human DNA

"Scientists Find Extraterrestrial Genes in Human DNA" is another article seeking to explain "junk DNA" and its probable origin and significance. Website:
http://www.bibliotecapleyades.net/vida_alien/esp_vida_alien_18n.htm

Dr. Fomenko, Anatoly

Wikipedia, "New Chronology (Fomenko)" is an excellent summary article of the major work (7 volumes) and discoveries of Dr. Anatoly Fomenko. It recaps his methodology

and discoveries and statistically establishes that out traditional historical chronology has been seriously altered. Website:
http://en.wikipedia.org/wiki/New_Chronology_(Fomenko)
See also:
http://en.wikipedia.org/wiki/New_Chronology_%28Fomenko%29
and for the Parallelism image (Ch. 10):
http://en.wikipedia.org/wiki/Image:Fomenko_-_Roman_Empire_parallelism.jpg

Greek Gods

Neil Jenkins, Sumair Mirza and Jason Tsang, "The Creation of the World & Mankind" is a great summary review of the major aspects of the Greek myths. Fascinating material, well-organized and indexed; won an award in 1997. Website:
http://www.classicsunveiled.com/mythnet/html/creation.html -- multiple topics.
See also: http://historylink102.com/greece2/   -- multiple topics.

The Insider

"The Revelations of the Insider" is an article containing the blog during a 5-day visit by someone calling themselves an "insider" who had knowledge on most aspects of Earth history, science and religion. This was done anonymously via a proxy link to the GLP (Godlike Productions) forum in the Fall of 2005. The material is not copyrighted and can be reproduced as long as none of the original text is changed. Website:
http://www.scribd.com/doc/403303/The-Revelations-of-an-Elite-Family-Insider-2005

Moon

Hoax

Dave Cosnette, "Still Not Convinced?" is an article on the website dealing with the possibility of a NASA Hoax. He asks 32 serious questions. Website:
http://www.ufos-aliens.co.uk/cosmicapollo.html

Moon Gravity

Wikipedia, "Gravitation of the Moon" article that discusses the isues with Moon gravity and the reasons for the differences in strength of gravity on the Moon. Website:
http://en.wikipedia.org/wiki/Gravity_of_the_Moon

Mars Blue Sky

Twietmeyer, Ted, "Mars Blue Sky, Lightning & Self-Removing Dust" article shows inconsistencies in pictures NASA has shared with the public of those taken on Mars. In addition to dust that clears itself on selected parts of the rover, there is the issue of the color tampering. Website: www.rense.com/general80/sunmr.htm
Also see: www.data4science.net for author of article.

Mars Mysteries

Pictures of the "glass tubes" on Mars:
http://www.scribd.com/doc/2681570/Mars-Mysteries
http://www.unarius.org/Mars/glass-tubes.html

NASA

National Aeronautics and Space Administration's website for Human Space Flight documenting the Apollo missions. Has picture Gallery of Apollo 11 thru Apollo 17 missions to the Moon. Website: http://spaceflight.nasa.gov/history/apollo/apollo11/index.html

Satellite Damage

Bonny Schoonakker, "Satellites in Low-Earth Orbit over Southern Africa…." is an article dealing with the damage to low-Earth satellites and the scientists' growing concern over an immanent magnetic pole reversal.
From: Sunday Times, Johannesburg Africa, Sunday 18th July 2004. National News section.

Viking Lander

Kim Burrafato, "Viking Mars Lander Photo Color-Altering Revealed" article that shows what Mars pictures really look like when the color is calibrated to agree with the Calibration Sundial on the rover. Website: http://www.rense.com/general9/color.htm

Music

Country Western Music

Clive Thompson, "**Does country music cause suicide?**" article discusses effect of negative music on one's lifestyle. Statistics show it encourages divorce and suicide. Website: http://www.collisiondetection.net/mt/archives/000996.html

Heavy Metal

Henry Makow, "Destroy! Rock Music's Satanic Message" article on extremely negative effect on our youth by Satanic messages imprinting people.
http://www.rense.com/general74/rrock.htm

Organic Portals/Mouravieff

"Matrix Agents: Profiles and Analysis (Parts I & II)" is an article that summarizes and clarifies information on Organic Portals, also called pre-Adamic beings. Much of this data is footnoted back to its original sources, including Mouravieff, Gurdjieff, Ouspensky, and the Cassiopaean Transcripts. Website: http://montalk.net/matrix/62/matrix-agents-profiles-and-analysis-part-i

"Organic Portals Theory: Sources" is a compendium of different writers' insights on
the Organic Portal phenomenon. Particularly relevant are the significant Mouravieff quotes from Books II & III of Gnosis. Website: http://www.montalk.net/opsources.pdf

Bibliotecapleyades website product of Jose Ingenieros, has link to 3 volumes of original text of Gnosis work by Mouravieff. Book text is in English. Website: http://www.bibliotecapleyades.net/esp_autor_mouravieff.htm

Laura Knight-Jadczyk, "Commentary on Boris Mouravieff's Gnosis." Extensive article from her website that interweaves her analysis of Mouravieff's Gnosis book and its meaning for Man's spiritual development. Also included are relevant quotes from her Cassiopaean material. Website: http://www.cassiopaea.org/cass/mouravieff1.htm

People With Horns
Sutherland, Mary, "Was There a Race of People Who Had Horns?" is a thought-provoking article with pictures showing people in the past and present who have horny growths coming out of their heads. Has links to other related websites. Website:
http://www.burlingtonnews.net/hornedrace.html
ancillary link: http://www.bibliotecapleyades.net/vida_alien/alien_watchers04.htm

Physics & Science
Black Holes, Light and Space

Crothers, Stephen J., "The Black Hole Catastrophe and the Collapse of Spacetime" is a recent article (Oct 3, 2008) by a physicist, upsetting current astrophysical conclusions and shows how Black Holes have never been found (because they don't exist), and how Light **anisotropy** has been verified. Website:
http://www.thunderbolts.info/thunderblogs/guest.htm

African Uranium Mine
Kean, Sam, "Nice try, Einstein" in *Mental Floss* magazine, vol. 7 issue 5, Sept/Oct 2008. Article points out that a uranium mine in Africa contains uranium and isotopes not found elsewhere; old deposits were above ground as if they had been dumped there. Also the properties of same deposits show deviation in traditional constants (i.e., rate of decay). Website: www.mentalfloss.com

Sea Monster/Plesiosaur

40ANA blog website article, "Sea Monster or Shark?" Posted by The Moviebuff at 7:16am on 9/1/2006. Shows pix of the carcass caught in the trawler's net. Website:
http://40ana.blogsppot.com/2006/09/sea-monster-or-shark.html

Serpents, Reptiles & DNA
Paul Von Ward, "Aliens, Lies and Religions" article on great Belgian website that discusses the author's book Gods, Genes and Consciousness. The issue of serpents and DNA is clarified as well as other AB (Advanced Being) issues. Website:
http://www.karmapolis.be/pipeline/von_ward_uk.htm

Simulation / VR
Simulation
Interview with **Nick Bostrom** at the Future of Humanity Institute at Oxford University, England wherein he explains the idea that if Mankind does not go extinct, and our science continues to develop insight and control over our world, and computers gain incredible processing power, that we will be able to run simulations on our history – much as he theorizes advanced future humans may be doing to us. How do we know we are souls or really sentient? It may all be the detailed aspects of some very large computer program.
http://www.simulation-argument.com/si...
You-Tube: http://www.youtube.com/watch?feature=player_detailpage&v=nnl6nY8YKHs

In a related article published by Cornell University, Prof. S.J. Gates reports that while examining very high-level equations dealing with the structure and organization of the universe, it was found that the equations demonstrate self-correcting code called Block Linear **Self Dual Error-correcting Codes** – suggesting that the universe is not only designed, but that it may be a logical mathematical construct... a simulation. http://arxiv.org/abs/0806.0051 is the original Cornell article. You-Tube: http://www.youtube.com/watch?feature=player_embedded&v=ZPju_NFwVXs

SimCity

An open-ended city-building game in 2D, game players are able to model potential cities with all the ramifications of a city: pollution, waster collection, sewers, and SimCity Societies has 3D graphics. http://en.wikipedia.org/wiki/Simcity

Sociopaths

M.E. Thomas, "Confessions of a Sociopath" in *Psychology Today*, June 2013, 53-60.

Kevin Dutton, "How Can I See Through a Psychopath?" in *ID* magazine, June-July 2013, pp. 24-27. See also p. 28 for 60-second sidebars on psychopaths.

Soul Weight

Wikipedia, "Duncan MacDougall (doctor)" is the article examining Dr. Duncan's attempts to measure the weight of the soul at death, found on Website: http://en.wikipedia.org/wiki/Duncan_MacDougall_(doctor) There is further text on what MacDougall did, and some of his notes, on Website: http://www.snopes.com/religion/soulweight.asp

Dr. Becker Mertens, from an article in German science journal *Horizon*, which corroborated MacDougall's finding that the soul has weight. Quoted on Website: http://www.ilstu.edu/~kfmachin/FOIFall03/Weight%20of%20human%20soul.htm

UFOs

James Neff, "This Month in UFO History" article on www.rense.com from September 2003 covers the President Reagan speech at the UN and Gorbachev's remarks. Website: http://www.rense.com/general40/tm_sep.htm

Jerome Clark, "Jacques Vallée Discusses UFO Control System." Original source: Fate Magazine 1978. Insight into what some UFOs are by an expert researcher. Website: http://www.ufoevidence.org/documents/doc608.htm

Jerome Clark, "Heretic Among Heretics: Jacques Vallée Interview." Quality interview with Mr. Vallée regarding psy-ops aspect of UFOs. Website: http://www.ufoevidence.org/documents/doc839.htm

Vatican & ETs

Patricia Cori, "The Vatican Says OK, We Can Believe in ET Now" is an article that comments on the more common Breitbart and Fox News article (below) revealing the

Pope's blessing on humans accepting the existence of ETs. Website: www.sirianrevelations.net

FOX News article "Vatican: It's OK for Catholics to Believe in Aliens" containing a longer examination of the Pope's blessing on our ET brothers. Website: http://www.foxnews.com/story/0,2933,355400,00.html

V2K (Voice to Skull)

Jenn Abelson, "The Marketers Have Your Ear" is an article published in the Boston Globe's Website: http://www.boston.com/business/technology/articles/2007/04/24/the_marketeers_have_your_ear/ This examines highly localized marketing techniques using V2K technology within a tightly controlled space within a store.

Wayne B. Brunkan, "Patent for Microwave Voice-to-Skull Technology" is an abstract of the patent granted for V2K technology. Document is recorded on Website: http://www.rense.com/general37/skull.htm

Gary D. Chance, "Voice to Skull Devices Defined By US Army as NLW", a document describing the Non Lethal Weapon aspect of the V2K technology on the Website: www.hartford-hwp.com/archives/27/a/264.htm. (Military source definition appears to have been Website: http://call.army.mil/products/thesaur/00016275.htm.)

Steven R. Corman, "PSYOPS Tech: Voices in your head", a paper describing the intended marketing uses of the V2K technology from Website: http://comops.org/journal/2007/12/20/psyops-tech-voices-in-your-head/ with an imbedded link to a video by ABC news on Website: http://youtube.com/watch?v=6h3KZjysoEo.

Sharon Weinberger, "Mind Games" article from Washington Post reveals one poor individual's problem getting rid of those who harass him with V2K. Website: http://www.washingtonpost.com/wp-dyn/content/article/2007/01/10/AR2007011001399_pf.html

Xiando, "Voice to Skull Technology" is a paper that has several good links in it to further information and uses of V2K technology on Website: http://xiandos.info/Voice_to_skull_technology. Of particular note is the link to the Washington Post Website article "Mind Games" at the end of the Xiando article. (See previous item.)

Videos of Interest

Forbidden Planet. MGM classic from 1956; debuts Robby the Robot.
The X-Files (TV series, 1993-2002): Twentieth Century Fox.
K-Pax. Universal Pictures, Lawrence Gordon et al. 2001.
Millenium. Gladden Entertainment. 1989.
Hangar 18. Republic Entertainment. 1980.
Capricorn One. Associated General Films. Lazarus/Hyams prod. 1978.

Groundhog Day. Dir. Harold Ramis, Columbia Tristar. 1993.
Men In Black. I & II Dir. Barry Sonnenfeld, Columbia Pictures. 2000.
The Matrix. Dir./Written by The Wachowski Bros., Warner Bros. 1999.
The Mothman Prophecies. Dir. Mark Pellington, Screen Gems/LakeShore
    Entertainment. 2001.
Prometheus. 20th Centruy Fox, 2012.

Taken. (TV miniseries) Stephen Spielberg, Dreamworks. 2002.
V, the TV series (1983-85, and 2009-11). WarnerVideo, Kenneth Johnson Production.
The Truman Show. Peter Weir, Paramount Pictures. 1998.
The Young Age of the Earth. Aufderhar, Glenn. Earth Science Associates / Alpha
    Productions. 1996.
What the Bleep Do We Know? 20th Century Fox, 2004.

They Live. Dir./Written by John Carpenter, Universal Studios. 2003.
Prometheus I. Ridley Scott, 2oth Century Fox. 2012.
The Thirteenth Floor. Columbia Pictures, Roland Emmerich. 1999.
The Day the Earth Stood Still. Twentieth Century Fox, Erwin Stoff et al, 2009.
The Forgotten. Revolution Studios. 2004

Iron Sky. Timo Vuorensola, Ger/Fin release via Paramount Pictures, 2012.
Paul. Universal Studios, Greg Motola. 2010.
2012. Sony Pictures, Roland Emmerich. 2010.
The Fourth Kind. Universal Pictures, Olatunde Osunsanmi. 2010.
The Adjustment Bureau. Universal Pictures, George Nolfi. 2010.

Knowing. Summit Entertainment, Alex Proyas. 2009.
Dark City. New Line Cinema, Alex Proyas. 1998.
Source Code. Summit Entertainment, Duncan Jones. 2011.
eXistenZ. Canadian Television Fund, David Cronenburg, 1999.
Defending Your Life. Warner Bros., 1991.

***

Chapter Endnotes

Chapter 1 Endnotes

[1] Boulay, R.A.,*Flying Serpents and Dragons*. Rev Ed. (San Diego, CA: The Book Tree, 1999), p. 117.

[2] Kenneth Woodward in Newsweek article, "In the Beginning There Were the Holy Books", Feb. 11, 2002, pp 51-57.

[3] Joseph Macchio, "The Orthodox Suppression of Original Christianity", Chapter III (2004). Eprints at: http://essenes.net/conspireindex.html and http://essenes.net/new/subteachings.html

[4] Boulay, R.A., *Flying Serpents and Dragons*, 16.

[5] Fig sap can cause dermatitis. http://www.katu.com/news/local/62682802.html

[6] Dora Jane Hamblin, "Has the Garden of Eden been located at last?" Eprint at: http://ldolphin.org/eden/
[7] Ibid.

[8] Lessin PhD, Sasha, *Anunnaki Gods No More.*, 80.

[9] Op Cit, Hamblin., 87.
[10] Ibid., 121-122.

[11] Bloom, Harold, *Jesus and Yahweh: The Names Divine.* (New York: Penguin Group (USA) 2005), 2-8.
[12] Ibid., 91.
[13] Ibid., 153.
[14] Ibid., 2.
[15] Ibid., 131-138.

[16] Sitchin, Zecharia, *Journeys to the Mythical Past.* (Rochester, VT: Bear & CO., 2007), 147.
[17] Sitchin, Zechariah, *Divine Encounters.* (New York: HarperCollins/Avon, 1996), 120 (fig. 33).
[18] Sitchin, Zechariah, *The Twelfth Planet.* (New York: HarperCollins, 2007), 244-254, 258-259.
[19] Sitchin, Zechariah, *Genesis Revisited.* (New York: HarperCollins/Avon, 1990), 45.

[20] Pinkham, Mark Amaru, The *Return of the Serpents of Wisdom.* (Kempton, IL, AU Press, 1997), x.

[21] Paul Von Ward, "Aliens, Lies and Religions" article on Belgian website. Eprint at: http://www.karmapolis.be/pipeline/von_ward_uk.htm

[22] http://en.wikipedia.org/wiki/Telomeres

[23] Free, Wynn and David Wilcox. *The Reincarnation of Edgar Cayce?* (Berkley: Frog Ltd., 2004), 63.
[24] Ibid., 72.
[25] Ibid., 72-74.
[26] Ibid., 199.

Chapter 2 Endnotes

[1] Charles, R.A. *The Book of Enoch the Prophet*. (San Francisco, CA: Weiser Books, 2003), viii-ix.
[2] Ibid., xvi.
[3] Ibid., Book 15: 8-12.
[4] Ibid., xvi

[5] Tellinger, Michael. *Slave Species of God*. (Johannesburg, SA: Music Masters Close Corporation, 2005), 402. (this is the first published version of his book)

[6] Farrell, Joseph P. *The Cosmic War*. (Kempton, IL: Adventures Unlimited Press, 2007), 90-91.
[7] Ibid., 88-89.
[8] Ibid., 98-99.
[9] Ibid., 99.

[10] Macchio, Joseph. "The Orthodox Suppression of Original Christianity", Chapter III (2004). Eprints at: http://essenes.net/conspireindex.html and http://essenes.net/new/subteachings.html
[11] Ibid.
[12] Ibid., Ch. III, Watchers.

[13] Lewels, Joe, Ph.D. *The God Hypothesis*. (Columbus, NC: Wild Flower Press, 2005), 216-217. Also see: http://www.bibliotecapleyades.net/vida_alien/alien_watchers13a.htm

[14] Charles, R.A. *The Book of Enoch the Prophet*, Book 17.1.
[15] Ibid., Book 19:1.
[16] Ibid., Book 69:6.
[17] Ibid., Book 69:6.

[18] Charles, R.A. *The Book of Enoch the Prophet*, Book 68:6-7.
[19] Ibid., 60.
[20] Ibid., 61.
[21] Ibid., 70.

[22] Op Cit, Macchio, "The Orthodox Suppression of Original Christianity", Ch III.
[23] Ibid., Ch III, Nephilim.
[24] Ibid., Ch III, Watchers.
[25] Ibid., Ch III, Watchers.

[26] Robinson, James M., Gen. Editor. *The Nag Hammadi Library*. (New York: HarperCollins,1990), 3.

[27] Pagels, Elaine. *The Gnostic Gospels*. (New York: Random House/Vintage, 1979), xvi.
[28] Ibid., 20.
[29] Ibid., 20.
[30] Ibid., 37.
[31] Ibid., 37.

[32] John Lash, "Kundalini and the Alien Force", article on Internet.

[33] Pagels, Elaine. *The Gnostic Gospels*, 127.

[34] Meyer, Marvin. *The Gospel of Thomas*. (New York: HarperCollins, 1992), 53.

[35] Op Cit, Macchio, "The Orthodox Suppression…", Ch VII, Great Schools, Valentinus.

[36] Ibid., Ch. VII, Great Schools, Doc. of 3 Natures.

[37] Heron, Patrick. *The Nephilim and the Pyramid of the Apocalypse*. 20.

[38] Op Cit, Macchio, "The Orthodox Suppression …", Ch XI, Manichaean Christian Revolution.

[39] Ibid., Ch. XI, Manichaean Christian Revolution.

[40] Ibid., Ch. XI, Manichaean Christian Revolution.

[41] Ibid., Ch. XI, Manichaean Christian Revolution.

[42] Ibid., Ch. XI, Manichaean Christian Revolution.

[43] Op Cit., Macchio, "The Orthodox Suppression of Original Christianity", Ch V, section 7.

[44] Ibid., Ch V, section 7.

[45] Ibid.

[46] http://en.wikipedia.org/wiki/Enoch_%28son_of_Cain%29

[47] Op Cit, Macchio, Ch V sect. 7

[48] Dr Sahakuntala Modi, *Remarkable Healings*, 89-92.

[49] Bender, Albert K. *Flying Saucers and the Three Men*. (Clarksburg, W.VA: Saucerian Press, 1962), 118-119.

[50] Ring, Kenneth. *Lessons from the Light*. (Portsmouth, NH: Moment Point Press, 2000), 290-299.

[51] Ibid., 292.

[52] Monroe, Robert, *Far Journeys*. (New York: Random House/Broadway, 2001), 177-180.

[53] Op Cit, Bender., 122.

Chapter 3 Endnotes

[54] Lessin PhD, Sasha, *Anunnaki Gods No More.*, 19, 85.

[55] Sitchin, Zechariah, *Divine Encounters*. (NY: HarperCollins/Avon, 1996), 73.

[56] Ibid., 74.

[57] Icke, David, *Tales from the Time Loop*. (Wildwood, MO: Bridge of Love, 2003), 230-231.

[58] Sitchin, Zechariah, *Divine Encounters*, 89.

[59] Collins, Andrew. *Gateway to Atlantis*. (New York: Carroll & Graf, 2000), 344.

[60] Sitchin, Zechariah, *12th Planet*, 22.

[61] Tellinger, Michael. *Slave Species of God*. (Johannesburg, SA: Music Masters Close Corp., 2005), 26. (note: this is the older book published in South Africa, not the 2012 one by Bear & Co.)

[62] Ibid., 1.

[63] Lessin PhD, Sasha, *Anunnaki Gods No More.*, 98, 105.

[64] Kramer, Samuel Noah. *The Sumerians.* (Chicago, IL: University of Chicago Press, 1971), 117.

[65] Sitchin, Zechariah, *12th Planet,* Chapter 12.
[66] Sitchin, Zechariah, *The Cosmic Code.* (New York: HarperCollins, 2007), 117-122.
[67] Sitchin, Zechariah, *Divine Encounters,* 9.
[68] Sitchin, Zechariah, *Genesis Revisited.* 161-162.
[69] Sitchin, Zechariah, *Divine Encounters,* 73-74.

[70] Farrell, Joseph P. *The Cosmic War.* (Kempton, IL: Adventures Unlimited Press, 2007), 332.

[71] Lessin PhD, Sasha, *Anunnaki Gods No More.*, 80.
[72] Ibid., 72, 114.
[73] Ibid.., 158.
[74] Ibid., 163.

[75] Sitchin, Zechariah, *12th Planet,* 105.

[76] Farrell, Joseph P. *The Cosmic War.* 142.

[77] Boulay, R.A. *Flying Serpents and Dragons.* (Revised Edition. San Diego, CA: The Book Tree, 1999), 115-117.
[78] Ibid.

[79] Lessin PhD, Sasha, *Anunnaki Gods No More.*, 83, 106.

[80] Op Cit, Boulay, 11.

[81] Pinkham, Mark Amaru. The *Return of the Serpents of Wisdom.* (Kempton, IL: AU Press, 1997), 44.

[82] Turner, Patricia & Charles Russell Coulter. *Dictionary of Ancient Deities.* (NY, NY: Oxford University Press, 2001), 355.

[83] Icke, David, *Children of the Matrix.* (Isle of Wight, UK: David Icke Books Ltd., 2001), 91. Also quoted in Boulay, *Flying Serpents & Dragons,* p. 61.

[84] Boulay, R.A. *Flying Serpents and Dragons.* 61-62.
[85] Ibid., 122.
[86] Ibid., 122-123.
[87] Ibid., 124.
[88] Ibid., 136.

[89] Op Cit, Lessin. 200.

[90] Sitchin, Zechariah, *12th Planet,* 125-126.

[91] Boulay, R.A. *Flying Serpents and Dragons.* 65-70.

[92] Sitchin, Zechariah, *12th Planet,* 100.

[93] Ibid.
[94] Ibid.

[95] Radzinsky, Edvard. *The Rasputin File.* (New York, NY: Anchor Books, 2000), 1.

[96] From Yahoo Coins of Alexander; see http://search.yahoo.com/search;_ylt=AuGsxC8UzTjm1.kh.2CU9IabvZx4?p=alexander+the+great+coin&toggle=1&cop=mss&ei=UTF-8&fr=yfp-t-788

[97] Farrell, Joseph P. *The Cosmic War.* 143-144.

[98] Tellinger, Michael. *Slave Species of God.* 466-469.

[99] Farrell, Joseph P. *The Cosmic War.* 305.
[100] Ibid., 309.

[101] Tellinger, Michael. *Slave Species of God.* 398.

[102] McKean, Erin, Ed. *The New Oxford American Dictionary, 2nd Edition.* (NY: Oxford University Press, 2005), 296.

[103] Farrell, Joseph P. *The Cosmic War.* 309.
[104] Ibid., 60-61.

[105] Temple, Robert. *The Sirius Mystery.* (Roch., VT: Destiny Books, 1998), 201-202.

[106] Sitchin, Zechariah, *12th Planet,* 286-287.
[107] Ibid., 329.
[108] Ibid., 290.
[109] Ibid., 291.

[110] Bramley, William. *The Gods of Eden.* (NY: HarperCollins/Avon, 1993), 54-55.

[111] Temple, Robert. *The Sirius Mystery.* 278.
[112] Ibid.
[113] Ibid., 279.

[114] Sitchin, Zechariah, *12th Planet,* 95.

[115] Farrell, Joseph P. *The Cosmic War.* 309.

[116] Lessin PhD, Sasha, *Anunnaki Gods No More.*, 74-75.

[117] Op Cit, Farrell., 144-145.

[118] Clark, Gerald. *The Anunnaki of Nibiru.* 55.

[119] Op Cit. Farrell., 144-148.

[120] Sitchin, Zechariah, *12th Planet,* 402.
[121] Ibid., 403.

[122] Lessin PhD, Sasha, *Anunnaki Gods No More.*, 115-119, 163.
[123] Ibid., 129-133.

[124] Op Cit, *12th Planet* , 390-391, 397.

[125] Stephanie Dalley quoted in *"Myths From Mesopotamia: Gilgamesh, The Flood, and Others"*, eprint at http://www.piney.com/Atrahasis.html

[126] 23andMe website article "Resistance to HIV/AIDS – Sample Report", eprint at https://www.23andme.com/health/Resistance-to-HIV-AIDS/

[127] Randy Dotinga article: "Genetic HIV Resistance Deciphered" website: http://www.wired.com/medtech/health/news/2005/01/66198?currentPage=2

[128] Bramley, William. *The Gods of Eden.* 182-183.
[129] Ibid., 184-185

[130] Sitchin, Zechariah, *Divine Encounters,* 350-354.
[131] Ibid., 353-354.

[132] Lessin PhD, Sasha, *Anunnaki Gods No More.*, 136.

[133] Icke, David, *Children of the Matrix.* (Isle of Wight, UK: David Icke Books Ltd., 2001), 96.
[134] Ibid., 91.

[135] Boulay, R.A. *Flying Serpents and Dragons.* 109.

[136] Sitchin, Zechariah, *Divine Encounters,* 290, 318.
[137] Sitchin, Zechariah, *12th Planet,* 100, 152.
[138] Sitchin, Zechariah, *The Wars of Gods and Men.* (NY: HarperCollins, 2007), 127 (fig. 35).

[139] Farrell, Joseph P. *The Cosmic War.* 306-307.

[140] Tellinger, Michael. *Slave Species of God.* 482.
[141] Ibid., 147.
[142] Ibid., 147

[143] Bramley, William. *The Gods of Eden.* 53-56.

[144] Pinkham, Mark Amaru. The *Return of the Serpents of Wisdom.* (Kempton, IL, AU Press, 1997), x.

[145] Sitchin, Zechariah, *Genesis Revisited.* 189.

[146] Pinkham, Mark Amaru. The *Return of the Serpents of Wisdom.* 332.

[147] Sitchin, Zechariah, *Genesis Revisited.* 191.
[148] Sitchin, Zecharia. *Journeys to the Mythical Past.* (Rochester, VT: Bear & CO., 2007), 137.
[149] Ibid., 138.
[150] Ibid., 140.

[151] Ibid., 141.
[152] Ibid., 147.
[153] Ibid., 147.
[154] Ibid., 214-216.
[155] Ibid., 153.
[156] Ibid., 135.

[157] Tellinger, Michael. *Slave Species of God*. (Johannesburg, SA: Music Masters Close Corporation, 2005), 469.

[158] Lewels, Joe, Ph.D. *The God Hypothesis*. (Columbus, NC: Wild Flower Press, 2005), 15.
[159] Ibid., 17.

[160] Lessin PhD, Sasha, *Anunnaki Gods No More.*, 108.
[161] Ibid, 176-178.

[162] Sitchin, Zechariah, *Divine Encounters*. (New York: HarperCollins/Avon, 1996), 155-156.
[163] Sitchin, Zechariah, *The Earth Chronicles Expeditions*. (Rochester VT: Bear & Co., 2004), 210-212.

[164] 40ANA blog website article, "Sea Monster or Shark?"; eprint at http://40ana.blogsppot.com/2006/09/sea-monster-or-shark.html

[165] Wikipedia, "Coelacanth" article; eprint at http://en.wikipedia.org/wiki/Coelacanth

[166] Sheila Berninger, "Behind the Scenes: The Surprising Truth Behind the Construction of the Great Pyramids"; eprint at: http://www.livescience.com/history/070518_bts_barsoum_pyramids.html

[167] Sitchin, Zechariah, *Divine Encounters*. 155-156.

[168] Lessin PhD, Sasha, *Anunnaki Gods No More.*, 36, 109.

[169] Bramley, William. *The Gods of Eden*. (New York: HarperCollins/Avon, 1993), 14.

[170] Steinmeyer, Jim. *The Book of the Damned; The Collected Works of Charles Fort*. (New York: Tarcher/Penguin Group, 2008), 163.
[171] Ibid., 163

[172] Fowler, Raymond. *The Watchers*. (New York: Bantam Books, 1990), 229.

[173] Bramley, William. *The Gods of Eden*. 34.

[174] Jacobs, David M., Ph.D. *The Threat*. (New York: Simon & Schuster, 1998), 225, 235.
[175] Ibid. 211.
[176] Ibid., 225.
[177] Ibid., 241-242.
[178] Ibid., 234-235, 249.
[179] Ibid., 244-245.
[180] Ibid., 246-247.
[181] Ibid., 247- 248.
[182] Ibid., 248-249.
[183] Ibid., 248-250.

184 Fowler, Raymond. *The Watchers*. 204.

185 Michael Salla, PhD., "Extraterrestrials Among Us" (vol.1:4, originally from Exopolitics Journal website); eprint at http://www.bibliotecapleyades.net/exopolitica/esp_exopolitics_ZZZN.htm Also see Mr. Salla's website: http://exopolitics.com for author's general website.

186 Fowler, Raymond. *The Watchers*. 348-349.
187 Ibid., 212-213.
188 Ibid., 196.

189 Jacobs, David M., Ph.D. *The Threat*. 253.

190 Ring, Kenneth. *Lessons from the Light*. (Portsmouth, NH: Moment Point Press, 2000), 124-131.

191 Mack, Dr. John E., M.D., *Passport to the Cosmos*. (New York: Three Rivers Press, 1999), 396-397.
192 Mack, John E., M.D. *Abduction*. (New York: Charles Scribner's Sons, 1994), 315.
193 Ibid., 197.

194 Jacobs, David M., Ph.D. *The Threat*. 227-234.

195 Missler, Chuck and Mark Eastman. *Alien Encounters*. 113.

196 Jerome Clark, "Jacques Vallée Discusses UFO Control System." eprint at: http://www.ufoevidence.org/documents/doc608.htm
197 Ibid.

198 Jerome Clark, "Heretic Among Heretics: Jacques Vallée Interview." eprint at: http://www.ufoevidence.org/documents/doc839.htm
199 Ibid.
200 Ibid.

201 Vallee, Jacques. *Passport to Magonia*. (Chicago: Contemporary Books, 1993), 148-149.
202 Ibid. 153-154..
203 Vallee, Jacques. *Dimensions*. (NY: Contemporary Books, 1988), pp. 253, 259, 269, 272, 275-276.

204 Guiley, Rosemary Ellen. *Encyclopedia of the Strange, Mystical & Unexplained*. (New York: Gramercy Books, 2001), 379-380.

205 Bender, Albert K. *Flying Saucers and the Three Men*. (Clarksburg, W.VA: Saucerian Press, 1962), 132-133.

206 Guiley, Rosemary Ellen. *Encyclopedia of the Strange, Mystical & Unexplained*. 379-380.
207 Ibid., 380.

208 Bender, Albert K. *Flying Saucers and the Three Men*. 14, 21.
209 Ibid., 16-17.
210 Ibid., 18, 34-35.
211 Ibid., 192.

212 Good, Timothy. *Earth: An Alien Enterprise*. 392-393.

[213] Ibid., 397-398.

[214] Op Cit., Missler & Eastman, 247-248.

[215] Keel, John, *Our Haunted Planet*, p. 140.
[216] Ibid, p282.
[217] Ibid., pp 283-284.

[218] Stevens, Henry, *Dark Star*, pp 362.

[219] Farrell, Joseph P. *The Nazi International*, (Kempton, IL: Adventures Unlimited Press), 41.

[220] James Neff, "This Month in UFO History" eprint at:
http://www.rense.com/general40/tm_sep.htm
[221] Ibid.

[222] Keel, John. *Trojan Horse*, p. 281.

[223] Farrell, Joseph, *Covert Wars and the Clash of Civilizations*. (AUP, 2013), 338-340.

[224] Op Cit, Good, 398-399.

[225] Greer, Steven M., MD. *Hidden Truth – Forbidden Knowledge*. (Quality Books, Inc., 2006), 80.

[226] Olsen, Brad. *Future Esoteric*, 157-160.
[227] Ibid., 158.

[228] Farrell, Joseph. *Reich of the Black Sun*, Ch. 16 (& 291-292).

[229] Op Cit, Olsen. 187.

[230] Stevens, Henry, *Hitler's Flying Saucers*, pp 64-65, 72.

[231] Op Cit, *Black Sun*, Ch 16 (302-308).

[232] *Forbidden Science*, Ch's 34-35, pp 244, 248.

[233] Op Cit, *Dark Star*, p. 331, 338.

[234] Op Cit, *Hitler's Flying Saucers*, pp 95-97.

[235] Op Cit, *Dark Star.*, 362.

[236] Op Cit, Olsen, 71, 185.

[237] Joseph Farrell, *Saucers, Swastikas and Psyops*, 216-224.

[238] Op Cit, Olsen, 111.

[239] Ibid., 112.
[240] Ibid., 111.

[241] Op Cit, *Saucers, Swastikas and Psyops*, 60-61.

[242] Farrell, Joseph. *Roswell and the Reich*, 284-288.

[243] Op Cit, *Nazi International*, 10-11.

[244] http://www.sciencedirect.com/science/article/pii/S0160289613000470
Also see *Out of the Fire*, by Dr Paul Clayton (pp 119-120).

[245] See: http://en.wikipedia.org/wiki/Intelligence_quotient#Classification

[246] Joseph Macchio, "The Orthodox Suppression of Original Christianity", Ch VII, Great Schools, Valentinus.
[247] Ibid., Ch. VII, Great Schools, Doc. of 3 Natures.

[248] Bramley, William. *The Gods of Eden.* (New York: HarperCollins/Avon, 1993), 176-177.

[249] Sitchin, Zechariah, *The Cosmic Code.* (New York: HarperCollins, 2007), 44, 58.

[250] Bramley, William. *The Gods of Eden.* 177.
[251] Ibid., 178.

[252] Bibliotecapleyades website product of Jose Ingenieros, Book III, p. 108.
eprint at: http://www.bibliotecapleyades.net/esp_autor_mouravieff.htm

[253] "Organic Portals Theory: Sources", compendium: Book II of Gnosis. eprint at:
http://www.montalk.net/opsources.pdf
[254] Ibid., II, 7.
[255] Ibid., II, 49.
[256] Ibid., (II, 8)
[257] Ibid., III, 8.
[258] Ibid., III, 109.

[259] "Matrix Agents: Profiles and Analysis (Parts I & II)" I. eprint at:
http://montalk.net/matrix/62/matrix-agents-profiles-and-analysis-part-i

[260] "Organic Portals Theory: Sources" III, 133. eprint at:
http://www.montalk.net/opsources.pdf

[261] "Matrix Agents: Profiles and Analysis (Parts I & II)" I. eprint at:
http://montalk.net/matrix/62/matrix-agents-profiles-and-analysis-part-i

[262] "Organic Portals Theory: Sources" III, 133. eprint at:
http://www.montalk.net/opsources.pdf
[263] Ibid., 133.
[264] Ibid., 129-134.
[265] Ibid., 136.

[266] "Matrix Agents: Profiles and Analysis (Parts I & II)" I. eprint at:
http://montalk.net/matrix/62/matrix-agents-profiles-and-analysis-part-i
[267] Bibliotecapleyades website product of Jose Ingenieros, Book III, p. 112-115.

eprint at: http://www.bibliotecapleyades.net/esp_autor_mouravieff.htm

[268] Slate, Joe, PhD. *Psychic Vampires*. (St. Paul, MN: Llewellyn Worldwide, 2004), 37, & Ch. 3.

[269] Modi, Shakuntala, M.D. *Remarkable Healings*.), 373-375.

Chapter 6 Endnotes

[1] Joseph Macchio, "The Orthodox Suppression of Original Christianity", Ch V, section 7.

[2] *The King James Study Bible*. (Nashville, TN: Thomas Nelson, 1988), 1038.

[3] Picknett, Lynn. *The Secret History of Lucifer*. (London: Constable & Robinson, 2005), 134.
[4] Ibid., 58-59.
[5] Ibid., 22.

[6] Acharya S, "The Origins of Christianity and the Quest for the Historical Jesus Christ", part I, eprint at http://truthbeknown.com/origins.htm also see: http://truthbeknown.com/evil.htm

[7] Picknett, Lynn. *The Secret History of Lucifer*. 31.
[8] Ibid., 31-32.
[9] Ibid., 32.

[10] Lessin PhD, Sasha, *Anunnaki Gods No More*., 206-207.
[11] Ibid., 17 – 25.

[12] Sitchin, Zechariah, *The Wars of Gods and Men*., pp 5-11.
[13] Ibid., 10.
[14] Ibid., 2-4.

[15] Farrell, Joseph P. *The Cosmic War*. , 234-240.
[16] Ibid., 372 and 28-65.

[17] Monroe, Robert. *Ultimate Journey*. , 183-184.

[18] Guiley and Imbrogno. *The Vengeful Djinn*. 15.
[19] Ibid., 4-5.
[20] Ibid., 9-10.
[21] Ibid., 14.
[22] Ibid., 18.
[23] Ibid., 36-37.

[24] Mack, John. E., MD, *Passport to the Cosmos*. (New York: Three Rivers Press, 1999).

[25] Modi, Shakuntala, M.D. *Remarkable Healings*., 314-315.

[26] "The Revelations of the Insider" from a 5-day blog contains many higher truths.   Eprint at http://www.scribd.com/doc/403303/The-Revelations-of-an-Elite-Family-Insider-2005

[27] Modi, Shakuntala, M.D. *Remarkable Healings*. 204.

28 Ibid., 210.

29 Ibid., 210.

30 Ibid., 213-214.

31 Castaneda, Carlos. *The Active Side of Infinity*. (New York: HarperCollins, 2000), 218-223.

32 Modi, Shakuntala, M.D. *Remarkable Healings*. 236.

33 Martin, Malachi. *Hostage to the Devil*. (HarperSanFrancisco, 1992), 459-473.

34 Cuneo, Michael. *American Exorcism*. (New York: Random House/ Doubleday, 2001), 209.

35 Peck, M. Scott, M.D. *People of the Lie*. (New York: Touchstone, 1983), 41.

36 Ibid., 119.

37 Ibid., 194.

38 Ibid., 205.

39 Ibid., 208-209.

40 Ibid., 208.

41 Ibid., 209.

42 Peck, M. Scott, M.D. *Glimpses of the Devil*. (New York: Free Press, 2005), 115.

43 Ibid., 115, 127.

44 Ibid., 229.

45 Ibid., 239.

46 Modi, Shakuntala, M.D. *Remarkable Healings*. 438-441 and ff.

47 Ibid., 197.

48 Ibid., 304-305.

49 Ibid., 305.

50 Ibid., 229.

51 Ibid., 226.

52 Lerma, John, M.D. *Into the Light*. (Franklin Lakes, NJ: The Career Press, 2007), 120.

53 Ibid., 121.

54 Modi, Shakuntala, M.D. *Remarkable Healings*. 309-314.

55 Lerma, John, M.D. *Into the Light*. , 156-158.

56 Ibid., 159-160.

57 Ibid., 163.

58 Modi, Shakuntala, M.D. *Remarkable Healings*. 214.

59 Lerma, John, M.D. *Into the Light*. 164.

Chapter 7 Endnotes

1 Watson, James D. *DNA*. (New York: Alfred A. Knopf, 2003), 381-382).

2 Northcutt, Wendy. *The Darwin Awards: Survival of the Fittest*. (New York: Penguin Group/Plume Books, 2004), 180.

3 Ibid., 140.

[4] Ibid., 160.

[5] Watson, James D. *DNA.* 391.
[6] Ibid., 391-392.

[7] Tellinger, Michael. *Slave Species of God.* (Johannesburg, SA: Music Masters Close Corporation, 2005), 550. (This is the original book.)
[8] Ibid., 52.

[9] Marrs, Jim. *Our Occulted History.* (New York: HarperCollins, 2013) 239.
[10] Ibid., 239

[11] "Scientists Find Extraterrestrial Genes in Human DNA" eprint at:
http://www.bibliotecapleyades.net/vida_alien/esp_vida_alien_18n.htm

[12] Watson, James D. *DNA.* 238-239.

[13] Tellinger, Michael. *Slave Species of God,* 24.
[14] Ibid., 33.

[15] Brown, Walt. *In The Beginning: Compelling Evidence for Creation and the Flood.*
(Phoenix, AZ: Center for Scientific Creation, 1995), 11.
[16] Ibid.
[17] Ibid.

[18] Keith, Jim. *Saucers of the Illuminati.* (Kempton, IL: Adventures Unlimited Press, 2004), 73.

[19] Temple, Robert. *The Sirius Mystery.* (Rochester, VT: Destiny Books, 1998), 76.
[20] Ibid., 77.

[21] McTaggart, Lynn. *The Field.* (New York: HarperCollins/Quill, 2002), 47.

[22] Peck, M. Scott, M.D. *Glimpses of the Devil.* (New York: Free Press, 2005), 186.
[23] Ibid., 196.
[24] Ibid., 187-188.
[25] Ibid., 187-188.
[26] Ibid., 188.
[27] Ibid., 188.
[28] Ibid., 240.

[29] Monroe, Robert. *Ultimate Journey.* (New York: Random House/Broadway, 2000), 183-184.

[30] Morris, John D., Ph.D. *The Young Earth.* (Green Forest, AR: Master Books, 2006), 43.

[31] Wikipedia, "Duncan MacDougall (doctor)" is main article; eprint at
http://en.wikipedia.org/wiki/Duncan_MacDougall_(doctor) and see also
http://www.snopes.com/religion/soulweight.asp pg. 1,
[32] Ibid., 4.
[33] Ibid., 4.

[34] Dr. Becker Mertens, from an article in German science journal *Horizon,* 1.

[35] Ibid., 2.

[36] Snellgrove, Brian. *The Unseen Self.* (Essex, England: The C.W. Daniel Co., 1996), 63-71 (pix.).

[37] Narby, Jeremy. *The Cosmic Serpent.* (New York: Tarcher/Putnam, 1998), 128.
[38] Ibid., 24.
[39] Ibid., 68.

[40] Rasha. *Oneness.* (Santa Fe, NM: Earthstar Press, 2003), 223, 354.
[41] Ibid., 195-196.
[42] Ibid., 195.
[43] Ibid., 195-196.
[44] Ibid., 180.
[45] Ibid., 180.
[46] Ibid., 181.

[47] Newton, Michael. *Destiny of Souls.* (Woodbury, Mn: Llewellyn Worldwide, 2002), 93.
[48] Ibid., 101.
[49] Ibid., 103-104.

[50] "The Revelations of the Insider" from 5-day blog in 2005. Eprint at
http://www.scribd.com/doc/403303/The-Revelations-of-an-Elite-Family-Insider-2005
[51] Ibid.
[52] Ibid.

[53] Reid, Daniel. *A Complete Guide to Chi-Gung.* (Boston, MA: Shambhala Publications, 1998), 139-144.

[54] Monroe, Robert. *Ultimate Journey.* 24.
[55] Monroe, Robert, *Far Journeys.* (New York: Random House/Broadway, 2001), 248.
[56] Ibid., 256.
[57] Ibid., 256-257.

Chapter 8 Endnotes

[1] Wikipedia, http://en.wikipedia.org/wiki/Flat_earth.
[2] Ibid.

[3] Wikipedia, "Charles Darwin's Illness" Eprint at
http://en.wikipedia.org/wiki/Illness_of_Charles_Darwin.
also see: http://en.wikipedia.org/wiki/Charles_Darwin%27s_views_on_religion.

[4] Behe, Michael J. *Darwin's Black Box.* New York: Simon & Schuster/Touchstone, 1996, 16.

[5] Montag, "Rods and Cones" Chapter 9. Eprint at
http://www.cis.rit.edu/people/faculty/montag/vandplite/pages/chap_9/ch9p1.html
[6] Ibid.

[7] Talbot, Michael. *The Holographic Universe.* (New York: HarperCollins, 1991), 18, 54-55, 192.

[8] Icke, David. *Tales from the Time Loop.* (Wildwood, MO: Bridge of Love, 2003), 348, 351.

[9] Brown, Walt. *In The Beginning: Compelling Evidence for Creation and the Flood.* (Phoenix, AZ: Center for Scientific Creation, 1995), 40-42.
[10] Ibid.

[11] Behe, Michael J. *Darwin's Black Box.* 31-36.

[12] Baugh, Carl E. *Why Do Men Believe Evolution Against All Odds?* (Oklahoma City, OK: Hearthstone Publishing, 1999), 126-127.
[13] Ibid., 125.

[14] Modi, Shakuntala, M.D. *Remarkable Healings.* (Charlottesville, VA: Hampton Roads, 1997), 438-441 and ff.

[15] Wikipedia, "Charles Darwin's Illness."

[16] Op Cit., Wikipedia, "Charles Darwin's Illness." section 3.

[17] Prince, Derek. *They Shall Expel Demons.* (Grand Rapids, MI: Chosen Books, 1999), 65.

[18] Meyer, Stephen C. *Signature in the Cell.* (New York: HarperCollins, 2009), 442.

[19] Peterson, Dennis R. *Unlocking the Mysteries of Creation.* 6th edition. (El Dorado, CA: Creation Resource Foundation, 1990), 48.

[20] Morris, John D., Ph.D. *The Young Earth.* (Green Forest, AR: Master Books, 2006), 64..
[21] Ibid., 51.
[22] Ibid., 49.
[23] Ibid., 49.
[24] Ibid., 51.

[25] Overbye, Ph.D., Dr. Bjorn
http://blog.hasslberger.com/2007/06/einstein_warped_minds_bent_tru.html
    Parts 1 – 2 – 3.
[26] Ibid.
[27] Ibid.

[28] Good, Timothy. *Earth: An Alien Enterprise.* (New York: Pegasus Publishing, 2013), 136-138.

[29] Zukav, Gary. *The Dancing Wu Li Masters.* (New York: Quill, 1979), 165.

[30] Op Cit, Overbye. Part I.
[31] Ibid.

[32] Brown, Walt. *In The Beginning:....* 158-159.
[33] Ibid.

[34] Braden, Gregg. *The Divine Matrix.* (Carlsbad, CA: Hay House, 2007), 18-19.
[35] Ibid., 19.
[36] Ibid., 20-21.

37 Crothers, Stephen J., "The Black Hole Catastrophe and the Collapse of Spacetime", part 13. Eprint at: http://www.thunderbolts.info/thunderblogs/guest.htm
38 Ibid., 109.

39 Brown, Walt. *In The Beginning:….* 158-159, and note 6 on 161.

40 LaViolette, Paul A, PhD. *Secrets of Antigravity Propulsion.* (Rochester, VT: Bear & Co., 2008) 177.
41 Ibid., 177.
42 Ibid., 177.
43 Ibid., 116-117.

44 Op Cit, Overbye. Part I.

45 LaViolette, Paul. *Genesis of the Cosmos.* (Rochester, VT: Bear & Co., 2004), 302 et ff.
46 Ibid., 288-295.
47 Ibid, 280-281.
48 Ibid, 288-289.
49 Op Cit, LaViolette, *Genesis,* 329-330.
50 LaViolette Ph.D., Dr. Paul. "Five Reasons Why the Milky Way's Supemassive Core is Not a Black Hole." On http://starburstfound.org/category/research/subquantum-kinetics/

51 Op Cit, Overbye, Parts I – III.

52 Op Cit, LaViolette, *Genesis*, p. 312.

53 Talbot, Michael. *The Holographic Universe.* (New York: HarperCollins, 1991), 140 ff.

54 Wikipedia, http://en.wikipedia.org/wiki/Anomalon
55 Ibid., 144-146.

56 Kean, Sam, "Nice try, Einstein" in *Mental Floss* magazine, vol. 7 issue 5, Sept/Oct 2008. p 37.
57 Ibid., 37.
58 Ibid., 38.
59 Ibid., 38.

60 Hawking, Stephen with Leonard Mlodinow. *A Briefer History of Time.* 107.
61 Ibid., 112.

62 Greene, Brian. *The Fabric of the Cosmos.* 83 – 88.

63 Wikipedia, http://en.wikipedia.org/wiki/EPR_paradox
64 Ibid, 80.

65 Op Cit, LaViolette in *Genesis*, 266-267.

66 Braden, Gregg. *The Divine Matrix.* 10, 71-74.

67 Zukav, Gary. *The Dancing Wu Li Master.* 320.

68 Braden, Gregg. *The Divine Matrix.* (Carlsbad, CA: Hay House, 2007), 10-11.

69 Ibid., 93.

70 Ring, Kenneth. *Lessons from the Light.* (Portsmouth, NH: Moment Point Press, 2000), 176-177.

71 Op Cit, Overbye, Part III.

72 Von Baeyer, Hans Christian , "Quantum Weirdness? It's All in Your Mind." Scientific American, June 2013, pp 47-51.
73 Ibid, pp 48-49.
74 Ibid, p 49.
75 Ibid, p. 51

76 Capra, Fritjof. *The Tao of Physics.* (Boston, MA: Shambhala Publications, 1999), 54-61.

Chapter 9 Endnotes

1 LaViolette, Dr. Paul. "Subquantum Kinetics – A Nontechnical Summary" from http://starburstfound.org/category/research/subquantum-kinetics/
2 Ibid.
3 LaViolette, Dr. Paul, "The Transmuting Ether" on
http://starburstfound.org/category/research/subquantum-kinetics/
4 Ibid.
5 LaViolette, Paul. *Genesis of the Cosmos.* (Rochester, VT: Bear & Co., 2004), 310-311.
6 Ibid, 330, 337-339.

7 Watson, James D. *DNA.* (New York: Alfred A. Knopf, 2003), 235-236.

8 Kathryn Esplin, "Why Do Chimpanzees Murder?" article. Eprint at:
http://www.gather.com/viewArticlePE.jsp?articleId=281474976794596
and
http://www.pbs.org/wgbh/nova/transcripts/3403_bonobos.html

9 Watson, James D. *DNA.* 233.

10 "DNA study deals blow to Neanderthal breeding theory" eprint at
http://www.cbc.ca/health/story/2003/05/13/cro_magnnon030513.html
also see:
Dr. Barry Starr of Stanford Univ., "Whatever happened to those Neanderthals?" eprint at
http://www.thetech.org/genetics/news.php?id=37

11 Rick Groleau, "Tracing Ancestry with MtDNA" article on NOVA Online website, eprint at
http://www.pbs.org/wgbh/nova/neanderthals/mtdna.html

12 Watson, James D. *DNA.* 238.
13 Ibid., 238-239.
14 Ibid., 239.

15 Fowler, Raymond. *The Watchers.* 204.
16 Ibid., 204.

17 Watson, James D. *DNA.* (New York: Alfred A. Knopf, 2003), 232-233.

[18] Bramley, William. *The Gods of Eden.* 42.

[19] Rick Groleau, "Tracing Ancestry with MtDNA" article on NOVA Online website, eprint at http://www.pbs.org/wgbh/nova/neanderthals/mtdna.html

[20] Watson, James D. *DNA.* 241-242.
[21] Ibid., 243.
[22] Ibid., 245-246.

[23] Lewels, Joe, Ph.D. *The God Hypothesis.* (Columbus, NC: Wild Flower Press, 2005),196.
[24] Ibid., 196.
[25] Ibid., 196-197.
[26] Ibid., 197.

[27] Farrell, Joseph P. *The Cosmic War.* 95.
[28] Ibid., 96.

[29] Watson, James D. *DNA.* 197.

[30] Meyer, Stephen C. *Signature in the Cell.* (New York: HarperCollins, 2009), 407.

[31] Free, Wynn & David Wilcox. *The Reincarnation of Edgar Cayce?* (Berkley: Frog Ltd., 2004), 344-345.

[32] Op Cit Garyev., 372. (**Note**: because the reported text is so bizarre, I checked it out, and found that he quotes the original source: Yu V. Dzang Kangeng, "Bioelectromagnetic fields as a material carrier of biogenetic information" in Aura-Z. 1993, No. 3, pp. 42-54.) Also is a patented process: #N1828665 for Application N3434801, invention priority as of 30.12.1981, registered 13.10.1992. (Russia)
[33] Ibid., 372.
[34] Ibid., 372-373.

[35] Baugh, Carl E. *Why Do Men Believe Evolution Against All Odds?* 85-86.

[36] Kean, Sam, "Who's the Fittest Now?" Mental Floss magazine for March-April 2009, p. 55-57.
[37] Ibid., 57.
[38] Ibid.

[39] "UltraViolet Light" article; eprint at http://www.Frequencyrising.com

[40] Icke, David, *Tales from the Time Loop.* (Wildwood, MO: Bridge of Love, 2003), 358-359.

[41] Carl Zimmer, "The Search for Intelligence." Article in *Scientific American* magazine for October 2008, vol. 299, no. 4, pp 68-75.
[42] Ibid., 74.
[43] Ibid., 74.
[44] Ibid., 74.

[45] Grazyna Fosar and Franz Bludorf, "The Biological Chip in Our Cells: Revolutionary results of modern genetics" ; eprint at http://www.fosar-bludorf.com/archiv/biochip_eng.htm

[46] McTaggart, Lynn. *The Field*. (New York: HarperCollins/Quill, 2002), 43-44.

[47] Grazyna Fosar and Franz Bludorf, "The Biological Chip in Our Cells: Revolutionary results of modern genetics."
[48] Ibid.
[49] Ibid.

[50] Icke, David. *The Biggest Secret*. (Wildwood, MO: Bridge of Love, 2001), 474-475.

[51] Grazyna Fosar and Franz Bludorf, "The Biological Chip in Our Cells: Revolutionary results of modern genetics."
[52] Ibid.

[53] McTaggart, Lynn. *The Field*. 49.

[54] Samuelson, PhD, Gary. *The Science of Healing Revealed*. (self-published booklet), 19-27.

[55] Op Cit, McTaggart., 49-50.
[56] Ibid., 51

[57] Grazyna Fosar and Franz Bludorf, "The Biological Chip in Our Cells: Revolutionary results of modern genetics."
[58] Ibid.
[59] Ibid.

[60] Watson, James D. *DNA*. 393.

[61] Sitchin, Zechariah, *The Cosmic Code*. (New York: HarperCollins, 2007), 149.

[62] Grazyna Fosar and Franz Bludorf, "The Biological Chip in Our Cells: Revolutionary results of modern genetics."
[63] Ibid.
[64] Ibid.
[65] Ibid.

[66] Friesen, James G., M.D. *Uncovering the Mystery of MPD*. (Eugene, OR: Wipf & Stock Publishers, 1991), 59, 115, 143.

[67] Baerbel, "Russian DNA Discoveries Explain Human 'Paranormal' Events" eprint at http://www.fosar-bludorf.com/index_eng.htm
[68] Ibid.
[69] Ibid.

[70] Pearce, Joseph Chilton. *The Biology of Transcendence*. (Rochester, VT: Park Street Press, 2002), 56.
[71] Ibid., 58.
[72] Ibid., 68.
[73] Ibid., 60
[74] Ibid., 63.

[75] Carlo, George, Dr. and Martin Schram. *Cell Phones: Invisible Hazards in the Wireless Age*, 28-29.

[76] Ibid., 170-175.

[77] Pearce, Joseph Chilton. *The Biology of Transcendence*. 69-74.

[78] Kaku, Michio. *Hyperspace*. (New York: Anchor Books, 1995), 51.
[79] Ibid., 50-51.
[80] Ibid., 51.

Chapter 10 Endnotes

[1] Baugh, Carl E. *Why Do Men Believe Evolution Against All Odds?* (Oklahoma City, OK: Hearthstone Publishing, 1999),105. Note: the Creation Evidence Museum in Glen Rose, TX, has the large, flat rock on display that has the dinosaur and human footprint in it. It's very clear what it shows.
[2] Ibid., 92.

[3] Morris, John D., Ph.D. *The Young Earth*. (Green Forest, AR: Master Books, 2006), 100-102.

[4] Video: The Young Age of the Earth. Aufderhar, Glenn. Earth Science Associates / Alpha .

[5] Morris, John D., Ph.D. *The Young Earth*. 95.

[6] Baugh, Carl E. *Why Do Men Believe Evolution Against All Odds?*, Chapter 7.

[7] Corsi, Jerome, "AT 30,000 Feet Down, Where Were the Dinosaurs?" from
    http://www.wnd.com/2005/11/33630/#IB8YUwMglfWJVm3j.99

[8] Clarke, Tom, "Fossil Fuel Without the Fossils." From
    http://www.nature.com/news/2002/020814/full/news020812-3.html
[9] Ibid.

[10] Elvidge, Jim. *The Universe Solved*. (AT Press, 2007), p189-190.
[11] Ibid, p. 190.

[12] Morris, John D., Ph.D. *The Young Earth*. 64.
[13] Ibid., 40.

[14] Free, Wynn and David Wilcox. *The Reincarnation of Edgar Cayce?* (Berkley: Frog Ltd., 2004), 338.

[15] Morris, John D., Ph.D. *The Young Earth*. 41.

[16] Brown, Walt. *In The Beginning: Compelling Evidence for Creation and the Flood.*
(Phoenix, AZ: Center for Scientific Creation, 1995), 45-47.
[17] Ibid.

[18] Lewels, Joe, Ph.D. *The God Hypothesis*. (Columbus, NC: Wild Flower Press, 2005), 195.

[19] Free, Wynn and David Wilcox. *The Reincarnation of Edgar Cayce?* 338-340.

[20] Morris, John D., Ph.D. *The Young Earth*. 70.
[21] Ibid., 70-71.

[22] Ibid., 70-71.

[23] Ibid., 70.

[24] Ibid., 71.

[25] Ibid., 74-75.

[26] Ibid., 84-85.

[27] Ibid., 90.

[28] Ibid., 85-87.

[29] Ibid., 87-88.

[30] Ibid., 88.

[31] Ibid., 89.

[32] Fomenko, Anatoly T. *History: Fiction or Science?*, Vol. 1. (Isle of Man, UK: Delamere Resources, Ltd., 2003), iii.

[33] Ibid., xv.

[34] Ibid., xix.

[35] Ibid., xix.

[36] Ibid., xx.

[37] Wikipedia, "New Chronology (Fomenko)" eprint at
http://en.wikipedia.org/wiki/New_Chronology_(Fomenko)
also:
http://en.wikipedia.org/wiki/New_Chronology_%28Fomenko%29

[38] Ibid.

[39] Fomenko, Anatoly T. *History: Fiction or Science?*, 269 (see 263-290).

[40] Wikipedia, "New Chronology (Fomenko)."

[41] Ibid.

[42] Ibid.

[43] Fomenko, Anatoly T. *History: Fiction or Science?*, 3.

[44] Ibid., 7.

[45] Ibid., 59.

[46] Ibid., 333.

[47] Ibid., 333-334.

[48] Ibid., 334.

[49] Alexis Okeowo, "Portal to Maya Underworld Found in Mexico?" eprint at:
http://news.nationalgeographic.com/news/2008/08/080822/-maya-maze.html

[50] Fomenko, Anatoly T. *History: Fiction or Science?*, 334.

[51] Wikipedia, "New Chronology (Fomenko)"

[52] Op Cit, Fomenko, p., 373.

[53] Ibid., 373.

[54] Keel, John, *Our Haunted Planet*, pp. 147-148.

[55] Op Cit, Fomenko, p. 467.

[56] Sitchin, Zechariah, *The Cosmic Code*. (New York: HarperCollins, 2007), 191.

[57] Clark, Gerald, *The Anunnaki of Nibiru*, p. 184.

[58] Op Cit, *The Cosmic Code*, 44, 58.

[59] Wikipedia, http://en.wikipedia.org/wiki/Mississippian_culture

[60] Farrell, Joseph P. *The Cosmic War*. (Kempton, IL: Adventures Unlimited Press, 2007), 56-58.

[61] Von Daniken, Erich. *Arrival of the Gods*. (London: Vega, 2002), 66, 77-81.

[62] Witkowski, Igor. *Axis of the World*. (Kempton, IL: Adventures Unlimited Press, 2008), 214.

[63] Collins, Andrew. *Gateway to Atlantis*. (New York: Carroll & Graf, 2000), 217.

[64] Lessin PhD, Sasha, *Anunnaki Gods No More*, 205.

[65] Pinkham, Mark Amaru. The *Return of the Serpents of Wisdom*. , Chapter 3.
[66] Ibid., 93, 188.

[67] Collins, Andrew. *Gateway to Atlantis*. 217, 335.
[68] Ibid., 216.
[69] Ibid., 218-219.
[70] Ibid., 219.

[71] Gardiner, Philip. *Secret Societies*. (Franklin Lakes, NJ: Career Press/New Page, 2007), 150, 214.

[72] Pinkham, Mark Amaru. The *Return of the Serpents of Wisdom*. 217.

[73] Collins, Andrew. *Gateway to Atlantis*.., 335-336.
[74] Ibid., 338.

[75] Bramley, William. *The Gods of Eden*. (New York: HarperCollins/Avon, 1993), 54-56.
[76] Ibid., 56.
[77] Ibid., 56.

[78] Pinkham, Mark Amaru. The *Return of the Serpents of Wisdom*. 5.
[79] Ibid., xiv.

[80] Marrs, Jim. *Rule by Secrecy*. (New York: HarperCollins, 2000), 236, 251-254.
[81] Ibid., 2-3.

[82] Op Cit, Pinkham, 116.

[83] Farrell, Joseph P. *The Cosmic War*. 56, 373.

Chapter 11 Endnotes

[1] Clark, Gerald. *The Anunnaki of Nibiru*. (CreateSpace), pp 54-56.

[2] Farrell, Joseph P. *The Cosmic War.* (Kempton, IL: Adventures Unlimited Press, 2007), 144-148.

[3] Sitchin, Zechariah, *Divine Encounters.* (New York: HarperCollins/Avon, 1996), 350-351.

[4] Farrell, Joseph P. *The Cosmic War.* 301.

[5] Clark, Gerald. *The Anunnaki of Nibiru, (CreateSpace),* pp. 64-66 and 78.

[6] Parkes, Henry Bamford. *A History of Mexico.* Boston, MA: Houghton Mifflin Co., 1960), 17-22.

[7] Acharya S, "The Origins of Christianity and the Quest for the Historical Jesus Christ" eprint at http://truthbeknown.com/origins.htm

[8] Sitchin, Zecharia. *Journeys to the Mythical Past.* (Rochester, VT: Bear & CO., 2007), 215.
[9] Sitchin, Zecharia. *The Twelfth Planet.* (New York: HarperCollins, 2007), 52-58.

[10] Tellinger, Michael. *Slave Species of God.* (Johannesburg, SA: Music Masters Close Corporation, 2005), 367.

[11] Sitchin, Zechariah, *The Wars of Gods and Men.* (New York: HarperCollins, 2007), 95.

[12] Neil Jenkins, Sumair Mirza and Jason Tsang, "The Creation of the World & Mankind", eprint at http://www.classicsunveiled.com/mythnet/html/creation.html

[13] Sitchin, Zecharia, *The Earth Chronicles Handbook.* (Rochester, VT: Bear & Co., 2009), 180.

[14] Tellinger, Michael. *Slave Species of God.* 333-378.

[15] Tony Bushby, "The Forged Origins of the New Testament" eprint at http://www.nexusmagazine.com/articles/NewTestament.html

[16] Acharya S, "The Origins of Good and Evil" eprint at http://truthbeknown.com/evil.htm
[17] Ibid.
[18] Ibid.
[19] Ibid.

[20] William Bramley, *The Gods of Eden.* (NY: Avon Books,1989), 201.
[21] Ibid., 202-203.
[22] Ibid., 203.
[23] Ibid. 203-204
[24] Ibid. 205-207.

[25] *The King James Study Bible.* (Nashville, TN: Thomas Nelson, 1988), 1911.

[26] Tony Bushby, "The Forged Origins of the New Testament."

[27] Acharya S, "The Origins of Christianity and the Quest for the Historical Jesus Christ."

[28] Freke, Timothy. *The Jesus Mysteries.* (New York: Three Rivers Press, 1999), 155.

[29] *The King James Study Bible, 1912.*

[30] Icke, David. *The Biggest Secret.* 91.

[31] Acharya S. *The Christ Conspiracy.* 113, 1129, 154.
[32] Ibid., 129.

[33] Icke, David. *The Biggest Secret.* 93.

[34] Acharya S, "The Origins of Christianity and the Quest for the Historical Jesus Christ."
[35] Ibid.

[36] Gardiner, Philip. *Secret Societies.* (Franklin Lakes, NJ: Career Press/New Page, 2007), 150.

[37] "Apollonius of Tyana" article on Wikipedia; eprint at:
http://en.wikipedia.org/wiki/Apollonius_of_Tyana

[38] Gardiner, Philip. *Secret Societies.*, 152.
[39] Ibid., 153.
[40] Ibid.,. 151.
[41] Ibid., 151-152.
[42] Ibid., 155.

[43] Acharya S. *The Christ Conspiracy.* 369.

[44] Gardiner, Philip. *Secret Societies,* 153-154.
[45] Ibid., 154
[46] Ibid., 154.

[47] http://nephiliman.com/jesus_proof.htm, "Jesus in the Historical Records" article.

[48] *Heaven is For Real,* Colton Burpo.

[49] *Op Cit,* "Jesus in the Historical Records" article (just above).

[50] Op Cit., Gardiner, Philip. *Secret Societies,* 154.
[51] Ibid., 154.

[52] Dr. R.W. Bernard, "Apollonius the Nazarene", Chapters 1 and 2,
eprint at http://www.apollonius.net/bernardbook.html

[53] Acharya S, "Apollonius, Jesus and Paul: Men or Myths?"

[54] PMH Atwater, *Near Death Experiences,* pp. 222-223.

[55] Dr. R.W. Bernard, "Apollonius the Nazarene", Ch. 2.
[56] Ibid., Ch. 2.
[57] Ibid., Ch. 2.
[58] Ibid., Ch. 2.
[59] Ibid., Ch. 2.
[60] Ibid., Ch. 2.

[61] Op Cit., Gardiner, Philip. *Secret Societies*, 152.
[62] Freke, Timothy. *The Jesus Mysteries*, 136-137.

[63] Acharya S. *The Christ Conspiracy* 50.
[64] Ibid., 50.

[65] Freke, Timothy & Peter Gandy. *The Laughing Jesus.* , 69-70.
[66] Ibid., 74.
[67] Freke, Timothy. *The Jesus Mysteries*. 151.
[68] Ibid., 72.
[69] Ibid., 74-75.

[70] Boulay, R.A. *Flying Serpents and Dragons*. Rev. Ed., 85.

[71] *The King James Study Bible*. 1678 and 1714.

[72] Acharya S, "The Origins of Christianity and the Quest for the Historical Jesus Christ."
[73] Ibid.

[74] Tony Bushby, "The Forged Origins of the New Testament."

[75] Acharya S, "The Origins of Christianity and the Quest for the Historical Jesus Christ."

[76] Spong, John Shelby. *A New Christianity for a New World.* (HarperSanFrancisco, 2001), 2-8.
[77] Spong, John Shelby. *A New Christianity for a New World.*, 8.
[78] Ibid., 122-123.
[79] Ibid., 123.
[80] Spong, John Shelby, *Why Christianity Must Change or Die.* (HarperSanFrancisco, 1999), 95.
[81] Spong, John Shelby. *A New Christianity for a New World.* 127.
[82] Spong, John Shelby, *Why Christianity Must Change or Die.* 83-85.
[83] Spong, John Shelby. *A New Christianity for a New World.* 107-108.

[84] Picknett, Lynn & Clive Prince. *The Stargate Conspiracy.* (NY: Berkley Books, 1999), 332.

[85] Wohlberg, Steve. *End Time Delusions.* (Shippensberg, PA: Treasure House, 2004), 39-40.
[86] Ibid., 39-41.
[87] Ibid., 127.
[88] Ibid., 127-128.
[89] Ibid., 50.
[90] Ibid., 46.
[91] Ibid., 44-45.

[92] Fomenko, Anatoly T. *History: Fiction or Science?*, Vol. 1. (Isle of Man, UK: Delamere Resources, Ltd., 2003), 233-234.

[93] Gary D. Chance, "Voice to Skull Devices Defined By US Army as NLW" eprint at www.hartford-hwp.com/archives/27/a/264.htm. (Military source definition appears to have been Website: http://call.army.mil/products/thesaur/00016275.htm.)

[94] Rifat, Tim. *Remote Viewing.* (London: Vision Paperbacks, 2001), 218.

[95] Steven R. Corman, "PSYOPS Tech: Voices in your head" pp. 1-3, eprint at:
http://comops.org/journal/2007/12/20/psyops-tech-voices-in-your-head/
with an imbedded link to a video by ABC news on Website:
http://youtube.com/watch?v=6h3KZjysoEo.

Chapter 12 Endnotes

[96] "The Revelations of the Insider" article, eprint at:
http://www.scribd.com/doc/403303/The-Revelations-of-an-Elite-Family-Insider-2005

[97] Talbot, Michael. *The Holographic Universe*. (New York: HarperCollins, 1991), 35.
[98] Ibid, 139-140
[99] Ibid, 140.
[100] Ibid, 18-20.
[101] Ibid., 19-20.
[102] Ibid., 20.
[103] Ibid., 54-55.
[104] Ibid., 31.
[105] Ibid., 141.
[106] Ibid., 21.
[107] Ibid., 159.

[108] Krauss, Lawrence M. *The Physics of Star Trek*. (New York: Basic Books, 2007), 139.

[109] Talbot, Michael. *The Holographic Universe*. 158.
[110] Ibid., 159.
[111] Ibid., 159.
[112] Ibid., 160.

[113] Steinmeyer, Jim. *The Book of the Damned; The Collected Works of Charles Fort*.
  (New York: Tarcher/Penguin Group, 2008), 381.
[114] Ibid., v.
[115] Ibid., 381-382.
[116] Ibid., 382.
[117] Ibid., 838-839.

[118] Monroe, Robert. *Journeys Out of the Body*. (New York: Doubleday, 1971), 73-74.
[119] Ibid., 77.
[120] Ibid., 78-79.
[121] Monroe, Robert, *Ultimate Journey*. (New York: Random House/Broadway, 2000), 17, 272.
[122] Monroe, Robert. *Journeys Out of the Body*. 120-121.
[123] Ibid., 141.
[124] Ibid., 141-144.
[125] Monroe, Robert, *Far Journeys*. (New York: Random House/Broadway, 2001), 93.
[126] Ibid., 93-106.
[127] Monroe, Robert, *Ultimate Journey*. 12-13.
[128] Ibid., 24.
[129] Ibid., 115-116.
[130] Monroe, Robert, *Far Journeys*. 66.
[131] Monroe, Robert, *Ultimate Journey*. 166
[132] Monroe, Robert. *Journeys Out of the Body*. 117-119.

[133] Monroe, Robert, *Ultimate Journey.* 183-184.
[134] Ibid.
[135] Ibid., 274-275.

[136] Bostrom, Nick. Http://www.simulation-argument.com/

[137] Elvidge, Jim. *The Universe Solved.* Ch's 1 – 7.

[138] Monroe, Robert, *Far Journeys.* 102-106.

[139] Greene, Brian, *The Hidden Reality*, p. 288.

[140] Op Cit, Elvidge, p 238.

[141] Elkins, Don and Carla Rueckert. *The RA Material, Book I.* (Atglen, PA: Schiffer Publishing/Whitford Press, 1984), 93.
[142] Ibid., 133.

[143] Wilde, Stuart. *The Prayers and Contemplations of God's Gladiators.* (Chicago, IL: Brookemarke, LLC., 2001), 7-8.
[144] Ibid.
[145] Ibid., 11-15.

[146] Icke, David. *And the Truth Shall Set You Free.* (Isle of Wight, UK: David Icke Books Ltd., 1995), 9.

[147] Elkins, Don and Carla Rueckert. *The RA Material, Book I.* 149.
[148] Ibid., 123-124.

[149] Robertino Solàrion, "Nibiruan Physiology." eprint at:
http://www.bibliotecapleyades.net/cosmic_tree/physiology.htm
see also Baines reference:
http://www.bibliotecapleyades.net/serpents_dragons/boulay05e.htm
[150] Ibid., 14-15.

[151] Wilde, Stuart. The Prayers and Contemplations of God's Gladiators. 89.
[152] Ibid.

[153] Rifat, Tim. *Remote Viewing* , 18-19.
[154] Ibid., 219-219.
[155] Ibid., 247.

[156] Op Cit, , Wilde, 90-91.
[157] Ibid., 123-124.

[158] Monroe, Robert, *Far Journeys.* 157-172.

[159] Modi, Shakuntala, M.D. *Remarkable Healings.* (Charlottesville, VA: Hampton Roads, 1997), 226.

[160] Farrell, Joseph P. *Saucers, Swastikas an Psyops.* (Kempton, IL: Adventures Unlimited Press), 65.

[161] "The Revelations of the Insider."

[162] Ibid.

[163] LaViolette, Paul A, PhD. *Secrets of Antigravity Propulsion.* (Rochester, VT: Bear & Co., 2008), Chapter 4.

Chapter 13 Endnotes

[1] Irwin, William. *The Matrix and Philosophy.* (Peru, IL: Carus Publishing, 2002), 61-62.
[2] Ibid., 228.

[3] Greene, Brian, *The Hidden Reality*, p. 290.

[4] Op Cit, Silby.
[5] Ibid.

[6] Monroe, Robert. *Far Journeys.* (New York: Random House/Broadway, 2001), 102-106.

[7] Irwin, William. *The Matrix and Philosophy.* 179.

[8] Monroe, Robert. *Far Journeys.* 263.

[9] Bostrom, Nick, "Simulation-Argument" on http://www.simulation-argument.com/si...
    and http://www.youtube.com/watch?feature=player_detailpage&v=nnl6nY8YKHs
[10] Ibid.
[11] Ibid, and **Wikipedia,** http://en.wikipedia.org/wiki/Simulated_reality, **p. 3.**

[12] Op Cit, *Hidden Reality*, p. 289.

[13] Elvidge, Jim, *The Universe Solved*, p 194.
[14] Ibid, p.195
[15] Ibid., p 32
[16] Ibid. p 197
[17] Ibid., p198
[18] Ibid., 207-208.

[19] posted by http://theghostdiaries.com/life-in-the-matrix-new-evidence-supports-the-simulation-theory
 also see Gate's original paper at: http://arxiv.org/abs/0806.0051 via Cornell University site.

[20] Op Cit, *Hidden Reality*, p. 281-282.
[21] Ibid. p.284-285.
[22] Ibid., p.288
[23] Ibid., pp288-289.
[24] Ibid, p.291-292.
[25] Ibid., p 306.

[26] Lloyd, Seth. *Programming the Universe.* Pp 6-7, 31.
[27] Ibid., p.54.
[28] Ibid. p. 54
[29] Ibid., p. 149-151.
[30] Ibid., p. 154.

[31] Op Cit, Elvidge, 117.

[32] Op Cit, Lloyd, . p166.

[33] More validation that the Simulation is real…
http://beforeitsnews.com/story/1658/888/NL/Scientific Evidence The Universe Is A H olographic Projection Around The Earth.html

[34] Ibid.
[35] Ibid.

[36] Wikipedia, http://en.wikipedia.org/wiki/Simulated_reality

[37] Dvorsky, George, "Physicists say there may be a way to prove that we live in a computer simulation" on http://io9.com/5950543/physicists-say-there-may-be-a-way-to-prove-that-we-live-in-a-computer-simulation

[38] Grabianowski, Ed, "You're living in a computer simulation, and math proves it" on http://io9.com/5799396/youre-living-in-a-computer-simulation-and-math-proves-it
[39] Ibid.
[40] Ibid.

[41] Silby, Brent, "The Simulated Universe" on http://www.scribd.com/doc/3015396/Simulated-Universe-by-Brent-Silby
[42] Ibid., p. 3

[43] http://en.wikipedia.org/wiki/Simcity

[44] Newton, Michael. *Destiny of Souls.* (Woodbury, Mn: Llewellyn Worldwide, 2002), 103-104.

Chapter 14 Endnotes

[1] Ruffin, C. Bernard. *Padre Pio: The True Story.* (Huntington, IN: Our Sunday Visitor Publishing Division, Inc., 1991), 112-113.
[2] Ibid., 146-157.

[3] Meyer, Marvin. *The Gospel of Thomas.* (New York: HarperCollins, 1992), 53.

[4] Laura Knight-Jadczyk, "Commentary on Boris Mouravieff's Gnosis." Eprint at: http://www.cassiopaea.org/cass/mouravieff1.htm
[5] Laura Knight-Jadczyk, "Schwaller de Lubicz and the Fourth Reich" Eprint at: http://www.cassiopaea.org/cass/schwaller_de_lubicz_3.htm

[6] Hawking, Stephen with Leonard Mlodinow. *A Briefer History of Time.* (NY: Bantam Dell, 2008), 88.

[7] Monroe, Robert. *Journeys Out of the Body.* (New York: Doubleday, 1971), 121.

[8] Laura Knight-Jadczyk, "Commentary on Boris Mouravieff's Gnosis."

[9] Ibid.

[10] Ibid.

[11] Ibid.

[12] Ibid.

[13] Ring, Kenneth. *Lessons from the Light.* (Portsmouth, NH: Moment Point Press, 2000), 296.

[14] Levy, Elinor, & Mark Fischetti. *The New Killer Diseases.* (New York: Three Rivers Press, 2004), 194.

[15] Mike Stobbe, "Deadly Bacteria" article. Eprint at: http://health.yahoo.com/news/ap/deadly_bacteria.html also see the CDC publication: http://www.cdc.gov/ncidod/EID/index.htm

[16] Ibid.

[17] Levy, Elinor, and Mark Fischetti. *The New Killer Diseases.* 201.

[18] Shnayerson, Michael & Mark Plotkin. *The Killers Within.* (Boston: Back Bay Books, 2003), 265-269.

[19] http://starchildproject.com/morgellons-disease# and http://www.morgellonsmedicalcenter.com/morgellons-fibers.html

[20] Carlo, George, Dr. and Martin Schram. *Cell Phones: Invisible Hazards in the Wireless Age.* All.

Chapter 15 Endnotes

[1] "The Revelations of the Insider" article. Eprint at: http://www.scribd.com/doc/403303/The-Revelations-of-an-Elite-Family-Insider-2005

[2] Moody, Raymond A., Jr., MD. *Life After Life.* (New York: HarperCollins, 2001) 131.

[3] Russell, A. J., *God Calling.* (Uhrichsville, OH: Barbour Publishing, 1989), 45.

[4] Monroe, Robert. *Ultimate Journey.* (New York: Random House/Broadway, 2000), 24.

[5] The Nexus Seven, "From the 33 Arks…"., 15.20-30.

[6] Ibid., 24.7-8.

[7] Monroe, Robert, *Far Journeys.* (New York: Random House/Broadway, 2001), 248.

Chapter 16 Endnotes

[1] Laura Knight-Jadczyk, "Commentary on Boris Mouravieff's Gnosis." Eprint at: http://www.cassiopaea.org/cass/mouravieff1.htm

[2] Laura Knight-Jadczyk, "Schwaller de Lubicz and the Fourth Reich" Eprint at: http://www.cassiopaea.org/cass/schwaller_de_lubicz_3.htm

[3] Ibid.

[4] Ibid.

5 Hawkins, David R. *The Eye of the I*. (West Sedona, AZ: Veritas Press, 2001), 186.
6 Ibid., 185.
7 Ibid., 186.

8 Ring, Kenneth. *Lessons from the Light*. (Portsmouth, NH: Moment Point Press, 2000), 296.

9 Myss, Caroline, Ph.D. *Why People Don't Heal and How They Can*. (NY: 3 Rivers Press, 1997), 17-19.
10 Ibid., 25.
11 Ibid., 26.

12 Slate, Joe H., PhD. *Psychic Vampires*. (St. Paul, MN: Llewellyn Worldwide, 2004), 37-65.

13 Spencer, Robert L. *The Craft of the Warrior*. (Berkley, Ca: Frog, Ltd., 2006), 54-56.
14 Ibid., 55.

15 Roman, Sanaya. *Spiritual Growth*. (Tiburon, CA: HJ Kramer, Inc., 1989), 183-185.

16 Modi, Shakuntala, M.D. *Memories of God and Creation.*, 256.

17 Sui, Choa Kok. *Pranic Healing*. (York Beach, ME: Samuel Weiser, Inc., 1990), 147 .
18 Sui, Choa Kok. *Pranic Psychotherapy*. (York Beach, ME: Samuel Weiser, Inc., 1993), 151.

19 Myss, Caroline, Ph.D. *Why People Don't Heal and How They Can*. 155.

20 Roman, Sanaya, *Personal Power Through Awareness*. (Tiburon, CA: HJ Kramer, Inc., 1986), 96.

21 Wikipedia, "Tao te Ching" article. Eprint at: http://en.wikipedia.org/wiki/Tao_Te_Ching

22 "Hunza Water" article. Eprint at: http://www.ionmicrowater.com/hunza.htm

23 "Kangen – Healing Water" article dealing with alkaline water; replicates the Hunza water quality. Eprint at: http://www.Frequencyrising.com Also see: http://www.passglobal.com/resources/kangen

24 Henry Makow, "Destroy! Rock Music's Satanic Message" article. Eprint at: http://www.rense.com/general74/rrock.htm

25 Clive Thompson, "Does country music cause suicide?" article. Eprint at: http://www.collisiondetection.net/mt/archives/000996.html

26 Modi, Shakuntala, M.D. *Memories of God and Creation*. 249.

27 Golas, Thaddeus, *Lazy Man's Guide to Enlightenment*, 109-110.

28 Op Cit, *Memories of God and Creation*, 214.
29 Modi, Shakuntala, M.D. *Remarkable Healings*. 280.

30 Brennan, Barbara Ann. *Hands of Light*. (New York: Bantam Books, 1988), Fig.11-2, pp. 44-45.

31 Op Cit, . *Remarkable Healings*. 223.

[32] Ibid., 223.

[33] Roman, Sanaya, *Personal Power Through Awareness.* (Tiburon, CA: HJ Kramer, Inc., 1986), 157.

Appendix A   Endnotes

[1] Wikipedia, "Gravitation of the Moon" article. Eprint at:
http://en.wikipedia.org/wiki/Gravity_of_the_Moon

[2] Bennett, Mary and David S. Percy. *Dark Moon.* (Kempton, IL: AU Press, 2002), 48.

[3] Don Eyles in article "TALES FROM THE LUNAR MODULE GUIDANCE COMPUTER" at
http://www.klabs.org/history/apollo_11_alarms/eyles_2004/eyles_2004.htm

[4] Dave Cosnette, "Still Not Convinced?" article. Eprint at:
http://www.ufos-aliens.co.uk/cosmicapollo.html

[5] Op Cit, Eyles.

[6] Bennett, Mary and David S. Percy. *Dark Moon.* 87.

[7] Bonny Schoonakker, "Satellites in Low-Earth Orbit over Southern Africa…." article. From:
Sunday Times, Johannesburg Africa, Sunday 18th July 2004. National News section.
[8] Ibid., 89.
[9] Ibid., 311.
[10] Ibid., 80.

[11] (Jawororwski, Zbigniew. "Radiation Risks in the 20th Century: Reality, Illusions, and Risks"
Presented 17 Sept. 1998 at the International Curie Conference, Warsaw, Poland.)

[12] http://en.wikipedia.org/wiki/Van_Allen_radiation_belt#Outer_belt

[13] Op Cit, Schoonakker., 95.
[14] Ibid., 97.

[15] Dave Cosnette, "Still Not Convinced?"
[16] Ibid.
[17] Ibid.

[18] Bennett, Mary and David S. Percy. *Dark Moon.* 79.
[19] Ibid., 341.
[20] Ibid., 60, 93.
[21] Ibid., 104.
[22] Ibid., 59-60.

[23] Video of 7 errors in Moon Mission…
https://www.youtube.com/watch?feature=player_detailpage&v=7ghw_1YRXJA

[24] Op Cit, Bennett & Percy, 153.
[25] Ibid., 154.

[26] Ibid., 354-357.

[27] Picture Gallery of Apollo 11 thru Apollo 17 missions to the Moon.
http://spaceflight.nasa.gov/history/apollo/apollo11/index.html

[28] Op Cit, Bennett & Percy, 56-70.

[29] Op Cit, Eyles.

[30] http://www.rockcitytimes.com/chinese-lunar-probe-finds-evidence-american-astronauts-landed-moon/ and http://beforeitsnews.com/power-elite/2014/03/chinese-lunar-rover-finds-no-evidence-of-american-moon-landings-2445090.html

[31] Chinese appear to have faked a lunar landing while their orbiter seems to work...
https://www.youtube.com/watch?feature=player_detailpage&v=I1gAvuGwweI

[32] Op Cit. . Dark Moon. 406-407.

[33] Marrs, Jim. Alien Agenda, 6-11.

[34] Brown, Walt. In The Beginning: Compelling Evidence for Creation and the Flood.
(Phoenix, AZ: Center for Scientific Creation, 1995), 20, 59.
[35] Ibid.
[36] Ibid., 59.

[37] Op Cit.. Dark Moon., 136-139.
[38] Ibid., 302-304.
[39] Ibid., 304.
[40] Ibid., 333.

[41] Twietmeyer, Ted, "Mars Blue Sky, Lightning & Self-Removing Dust" article. Eprint at:
www.rense.com/general80/sunmr.htm

[42] Kim Burrafato, "Viking Mars Lander Photo Color-Altering Revealed" article. Eprint at:
http://www.rense.com/general9/color.htm

[43] Sitchin, Zechariah, Genesis Revisited. (New York: HarperCollins/Avon, 1990), 242, 256-257.

[44] http://www.scribd.com/doc/2681570/Mars-Mysteries
http://www.unarius.org/Mars/glass-tubes.html

[45] Lessin, PhD, Sasha. Anunnaki Gods No More, 197.

[46] Olsen, Brad. Future Esoteric, 261-265, 274-275.

[47] Op Cit.. Dark Moon. 270.
[48] Ibid., 442.

[49] Op Cit., Alien Agenda, 11-12.
[50] Ibid., Chapter 1.

[51] Op Cit, Hitlers Flying Saucers, pp. 64-65, 72.

[52] Op Cit., *Dark Moon*, 379.

Appendix B Endnotes

[1] Talbot, Michael. *The Holographic Universe*. (New York: HarperCollins, 1991), 19.
[2] Ibid., 20.
[3] Ibid., 20.
[4] Ibid., 31.
[5] Ibid., 54.
[6] Ibid., 54.
[7] Ibid., 125, 139.
[8] Ibid., 140.
[9] Ibid., 144-145.
[10] Ibid., 146.
[11] Ibid., 163.
[12] Ibid., 164.

[13] Carter, Mildred & Tammy Weber. *Body Reflexology*. (NJ: Prentice Hall, 1994), 11-13, 43.

[14] Dong, Paul & Thomas E. Raffill. *China's Super Psychics*. , 7.
[15] Ibid., 108-109.
[16] Ibid., 18.
[17] Ibid., 17, 46, 50-51.

[18] Carter, Mildred & Tammy Weber. *Body Reflexolog*. 11-13.

[19] Dong, Paul & Thomas E. Raffill. *China's Super Psychics*. 17.
[20] Ibid., 46.
[21] Ibid., 53.
[22] Dong, Paul. *China's Major Mysteries*. (San Francisco, CA: China Books & Periodicals, Inc., 2000), 156.

[23] Veronique Greenwood in <u>Discover</u> magazine (July-August 2012). *Super Human Vision*, pp 29-31.

[24] Talbot, Michael. *The Holographic Universe*. 191.
[25] Ibid., 189.

Appendix C Endnotes

[1] Clark, Jerome interview with Dr. Jacques Vallée for FATE magazine, 1978. from http://www.ufoevidence.org/documents/doc608.htm   and repeated at http://www.info-quest.org/documents/ufocontrol.html

[2] Jacques Vallée, *Dimensions*. (Chicago, Il: Contemporary Books, 1988), 222.
[3] Ibid., 252-253.
[4] Ibid. 253.
[5] Ibid., 257-259.
[6] Ibid., 258.
[7] Ibid., 258.
[8] Ibid., 272.
[9] Ibid., 272.
[10] Ibid., 274.

[11] Ibid., 276.
[12] Ibid., 277.

[13] Op Cit Jerome Clark.

[14] Op Cit, *Dimensions*, 284.
[15] Ibid., 285.
[16] Ibid., 290-291.

Appendix D Endnotes

[1] Mark Pinkham, *The Retun of the Serpents of Wisdom*, p. 236.

[2] The Koran, surah 4: 155-157, and 5:115.
   Also see article at either location: Source: http://sonsonthepyre.com/1500-year-old-bible-confirms-that-jesus-christ-was-not-crucified-vatican-in-awe/
or:
http://beforeitsnews.com/paranormal/2014/05/1500-year-old-bible-confirms-that-jesus-christ-was-not-crucified-vatican-in-awe-2468314.html
The essence is that the newly found (in Turkey) and verified Gospel of Barnabas (one of the disciples) says Jesus was not crucified and did not die on the cross. The Vatican is taking it seriously.

[3] Fomenko, Anatoly T. *History: Fiction or Science?*, Vol I, 336.
[4] Ibid., 133.
[5] Ibid., 336, pp 365-366.
[6] Ibid., 133.
[7] Ibid., pp 336-350.
[8] Ibid., 339, and pp 336-355.

[9] See: http://en.wikipedia.org/wiki/Shroud_of_Turin#Radiocarbon_dating

[10] See: http://en.wikipedia.org/wiki/Jesus_in_Ahmadiyya_Islam addresses the issue of where the tomb is: Ahmadis today believe the tomb of Jesus is located in the Srinagar region of Kashmir. and
   http://en.wikipedia.org/wiki/Unknown_years_of_Jesus contains info from Holgar Kersten and Nicholas Notovich.

Appendix E Endnotes

[1] Gardiner, Philip, *Secret Societies*. 52-53.

[2] Tom Olago and Lyn Leahz, *3000 Year-old Hieroglyphics Discovery Stirs Nephilim Debate*
http://www.prophecynewswatch.com/2014/February24/241.html#vq0DYijgO7Stq9tR.99

[3] Lloyd Pye at http://www.starchildproject.com/dna2010.htm

[4] Op Cit, *Secret Societies*, 58.

[5] Boulay, R.A. *Flying Serpents and Dragons*. 122-123.

[6] Gardiner, Philip. *The Shining Ones*. 172-173.

Micro Index

This is a quick index of issues not identified in the Table of Contents breakdown.

Micro Index

NOTES

Made in the USA
Coppell, TX
19 December 2022

89971771R00359